Lecture Notes in Computer Science 14335

The series Lecture Notes in Computer Science (LNCS), including its subseries Lecture Notes in Artificial Intelligence (LNAI) and Lecture Notes in Bioinformatics (LNBI), has established itself as a medium for the publication of new developments in computer science and information technology research, teaching, and education.

LNCS enjoys close cooperation with the computer science R & D community, the series counts many renowned academics among its volume editors and paper authors, and collaborates with prestigious societies. Its mission is to serve this international community by providing an invaluable service, mainly focused on the publication of conference and workshop proceedings and postproceedings. LNCS commenced publication in 1973.

Yanio Hernández Heredia ·
Vladimir Milián Núñez · José Ruiz Shulcloper
Editors

Progress in Artificial Intelligence and Pattern Recognition

8th International Congress
on Artificial Intelligence and Pattern Recognition, IWAIPR 2023
Varadero, Cuba, September 27–29, 2023
Proceedings

Springer

Editors
Yanio Hernández Heredia
Universidad de las Ciencias Informáticas
Havana, Cuba

Vladimir Milián Núñez
Universidad de las Ciencias Informáticas
Havana, Cuba

José Ruiz Shulcloper
Universidad de las Ciencias Informáticas
Havana, Cuba

ISSN 0302-9743 ISSN 1611-3349 (electronic)
Lecture Notes in Computer Science
ISBN 978-3-031-49551-9 ISBN 978-3-031-49552-6 (eBook)
https://doi.org/10.1007/978-3-031-49552-6

This Springer imprint is published by the registered company Springer Nature Switzerland AG
The registered company address is: Gewerbestrasse 11, 6330 Cham, Switzerland

Paper in this product is recyclable.

Preface

The 8th International Congress on Artificial Intelligence and Pattern Recognition (IWAIPR 2023) was the latest edition in a series of biennial conferences on artificial intelligence and pattern recognition aimed at serving the scientific community active in these fields in Cuba and other countries.

As has been the case for previous editions of the conference, IWAIPR 2023 hosted worldwide participants with the aim of promoting and disseminating ongoing research on mathematical methods and computing techniques for Artificial Intelligence and Pattern Recognition, and in particular in bioinformatics, cognitive and humanoid vision, computer vision, image analysis and intelligent data analysis, as well as their application in a number of diverse areas such as industry, health, robotics, data mining, opinion mining and sentiment analysis, telecommunications, document analysis, and natural language processing and recognition. Moreover, IWAIPR 2023 was a forum for the scientific community to exchange research experience, to share new knowledge, and to increase the cooperation among research groups working in artificial intelligence, pattern recognition, and related areas.

IWAIPR 2023 received 68 contributions from authors in 15 countries. After a rigorous double-blind reviewing process, where three highly qualified reviewers reviewed each submission, 38 papers authored by 117 authors from 15 countries were accepted. The scientific quality of the accepted papers was above the overall mean rating.

Like the most recent editions of the conference, IWAIPR 2023 was a single-track conference in which all papers where presented in oral sessions. IWAIPR 2023 presentations were grouped into three sessions: Artificial Intelligence, Data Mining and Applications; Pattern Recognition and Applications; and Biometrics, Image, and Video and Signals Analysis and Processing.

We would like to point out that the reputation of the IWAIPR conferences is growing and therefore the proceedings are published, as in the case of previous editions, in the series Lecture Notes in Computer Science by Springer.

Besides the 38 accepted submissions, the scientific program of IWAIPR 2023 also included the keynote talk "The role of Artificial Intelligence in Industry 4.0" by an outstanding invited speaker, Juan Humberto Sossa Azuela, Head of the Robotics and Mechatronics Laboratory at the Computer Science Research Center of the National Polytechnic Institute, Mexico.

Also we included three other invited plenary talks: "Computation at the edge of chaos: natural systems as computation paradigms" by Ernesto Estevez Rams (Member of the IUCr Commission in Mathematics and Theoretical Crystallography, and Vice-President of the Cuban Physics Society, Cuba), "Quantum Soft Computing: Applied SW & HW of Robust Intelligent Robotic Controllers" Sergey V. Ulyanov (Professor of Moscow State University of Geodesy and Cartography, Russia) and "Artificial intelligence applications towards digital transformation" by Rafael Esteban Bello Pérez (Director of the Informatics Research Center of the Central University of Las Villas, Cuba). The abstracts of these presentations appear in these proceedings.

IWAIPR 2023 was endorsed by the International Association for Pattern Recognition (IAPR) and therefore the conference conferred the IAPR-IWAIPR Best Paper Award. The aim of this award is to acknowledge and encourage excellence, originality, and innovation in new models, methods, and techniques with an outstanding theoretical contribution and practical application to the field of artificial intelligence, pattern recognition, and/or data mining.

The selection of the winners was based on the wish of the author to be considered for the prize, the evaluation and recommendations from members of the Program Committee, and the evaluation of the Award Committee. This committee, carefully chosen to avoid conflicts of interest, evaluated each nominated paper for the Best Paper. In this edition, after an arduous process of selection by the jury, the award for the best work was awarded jointly to the works

- Weighted t-Distributed Stochastic Neighbor Embedding for Projection-based Clustering; authored by Leonardo Concepción Pérez, Gonzalo Nápoles, Büşra Özgöde Yigin, Görkem Saygili, Koen Vanhoof, Rafael Bello
- Polarity Prediction in Tourism Cuban Reviews using Transformer with Estimation of Distribution Algorithms; authored by Orlando Grabiel Toledano López, Miguel Ángel Álvarez Carmona, Alfredo Simón Cuevas, Hector R. Gonzalez Diez, Yoan Antonio López Rodríguez, Julio Madera

We would like to express our most sincere thanks to the members of the Best Paper Award Committee: Heydi Mendez-Vazquez (CENATAV, Cuba), Juan Humberto Sossa Azuela (National Polytechnic Institute, Mexico) and Maria Matilde García Lorenzo (Universidad Central Marta Abreu de Las Villas, Cuba).

IWAIPR 2023 was organized by Universidad de las Ciencias Informáticas, Cuba (UCI) and the Cuban Association for Pattern Recognition (ACRP) with the sponsorship of the Cuban Society for Mathematics and Computer Sciences (SCMC). We acknowledge and appreciate their valuable contribution to the success of IWAIPR 2023.

We gratefully acknowledge the help of all members of the Organizing Committee and of the Program Committee for their support and for their rigorous work in the reviewing process.

We also wish to thank the members of the local committee for their unflagging work in the organization of IWAIPR 2023 that helped create an excellent conference and proceedings.

We are especially grateful to Ronan Nugent (Editorial Director, Computer Science Proceedings, Springer Nature) and the staff of Springer for their support and advice during the preparation of this LNCS volume.

Special thanks are due to all authors who submitted their work to IWAIPR 2023, including those of papers that could not be accepted.

Finally, we invite the artificial intelligence and pattern recognition communities to attend IWAIPR 2025 in Havana, Cuba.

September 2023

Yanio Hernández Heredia
Vladimir Milián Núñez
José Ruiz Shulcloper

Organization

Program Chairs

Yanio Hernández Heredia	Universidad de Las Ciencias Informáticas, Cuba
Vladimir Milián Núñez	Universidad de Las Ciencias Informáticas, Cuba
Héctor Raúl González Diez	Universidad de Las Ciencias Informáticas, Cuba

Local Committee

Yunia Reyes González	Universidad de las Ciencias Informáticas, Cuba
José Eladio Medina Pagola	Universidad de las Ciencias Informáticas, Cuba
José Ruiz Shulcloper	Universidad de las Ciencias Informáticas, Cuba
Orlando Grabiel Toledano López	Universidad de las Ciencias Informáticas, Cuba

IAPR-IWAIPR Best Paper Award Committee

Heydi Mendez-Vazquez	CENATAV, Cuba
Juan Humberto Sossa Azuela	National Polytechnic Institute, Mexico
Maria Matilde García Lorenzo	Universidad Central Marta Abreu de Las Villas, Cuba

Program Committee

Sergey Ablameyko	Belarusian State University, Belarus
Yudivián Almeida	Universidad de La Habana, Cuba
Leticia Arco García	Vrije Universiteit Brussel, Belgium
Fernando Alonso-Fernandez	Halmstad University, Sweden
Leopoldo Altamirano	INAOE, Mexico
Rafael E. Bello Pérez	Central University of Las Villas, Cuba
César Beltran Castañon	Pontificia Universidad Católica del Perú, Peru
Rafael Berlanga	Universitat Jaume I, Spain
Ana María Bernardos	Universidad Politécnica de Madrid, Spain
Gunilla Borgefors	Uppsala University, Sweden
Ramon Brena	Tecnológico de Monterrey, Mexico
Lázaro Bustio-Martínez	Universidad Iberoamericana, Mexico

Jesús Ariel Carrasco-Ochoa	INAOE, Mexico
César Castellanos	Universidad Nacional de Colombia, Colombia
Shridhar Devamane	KLE Institute of Technology, India
Abel Díaz Berenguer	Vrije Universiteit Brussel, Belgium
Hugo Jair Escalante	INAOE, Mexico
Alfonso Estudillo-Romero	Université de Rennes 1, France
Jacques Facon	Universidade Federal do Espírito Santo, Brazil
Alicia Fernandez	Nova Southeastern University, USA
Francesc J. Ferri	Universidad de Valencia, Spain
Yaima Filiberto	Universidad de Camagüey, Cuba
Marcelo Fiori	Universidad de la República, Uruguay
Giorgio Fumera	University of Cagliari, Italy
Maria Matilde García Lorenzo	Universidad Central Marta Abreu de Las Villas, Cuba
Edel Garcia Reyes	GeoCuba, Cuba
Milton García-Borroto	Universidad de La Habana, Cuba
Jose Garcia-Rodriguez	University of Alicante, Spain
Eduardo Garea Llano	Centro de Neurociencias de Cuba, Cuba
Herman Gomes	Universidade Federal de Campina Grande, Brazil
Luis Gomez Deniz	CTIM, Spain
Héctor Raúl González Diez	Universidad de las Ciencias Informáticas, Cuba
Antoni Grau	Technical University of Catalonia, Spain
Bilge Günsel	Istanbul Technical University, Turkey
Michal Haindl	Institute of Information Theory and Automation of the Czech Academy of Sciences, Czech Republic
Yanio Hernández Heredia	Universidad de las Ciencias Informáticas, Cuba
Ruber Hernández García	Universidad Católica del Maule, Chile
Laurent Heutte	Université de Rouen, France
Maria-Jose Jimenez	Universidad de Sevilla, Spain
Xiaoyi Jiang	University of Münster, Germany
Gerdys Ernesto Jiménez Moya	Universidad de las Ciencias Informáticas, Cuba
Martin Kampel	Vienna University of Technology, Austria
Vitaly Kober	CICESE, Mexico
Manuel S. Lazo-Cortés	TecNM/Instituto Tecnológico de Tlalnepantla, Mexico
Marcos Antonio Levano	Catholic University of Temuco, Chile
Xaviera López	Universidad Católica del Maule, Chile
Aurelio Lopez-Lopez	INAOE, Mexico
Daniela López De Luise	CI2S Labs, Argentina
Julio Madera	University of Camagüey, Cuba

Jose Francisco Martinez-Trinidad	Instituto Nacional de Astrofísica Óptica y Electrónica, Mexico
Rosana Matuk	Universidad Nacional de Luján, Argentina
José Eladio Medina Pagola	Universidad de las Ciencias Informáticas, Cuba
Ana Maria Mendonça	University of Porto, Portugal
Marcelo Mendoza	Universidad Técnica Federico Santa María, Chile
Vladimir Milián Núñez	Universidad de las Ciencias Informáticas, Cuba
Miguel Moctezuma-Flores	UNAM, Mexico
Eduardo Morales	INAOE, Mexico
Aythami Morales	Universidad Autónoma de Madrid, Spain
Annette Morales-González	Advanced Technologies Application Center, Cuba
Sebastian Moreno	Universidad Adolfo Ibañez, Chile
Heydi Mendez-Vazquez	CENATAV, Cuba
João Neves	IT - Instituto de Telecomunicações, Portugal
Lawrence O'Gorman	Bell Labs, USA
Roman Osorio	Universidad Nacional Autónoma de México, Mexico
Martha R. Ortiz-Posadas	Universidad Autónoma Metropolitana Iztapalapa, Mexico
Volodymyr Ponomaryov	Instituto Politécnico Nacional, Mexico
Kalman Palagyi	University of Szeged, Hungary
Joao Papa	São Paulo State University, Brazil
Billy Peralta	Universidad Andres Bello, Chile
Talita Perciano	Lawrence Berkeley National Laboratory, USA
Marieta Peña Abreu	Universidad de las Ciencias Informáticas, Cuba
Adrián Pérez-Suay	Universitat de València, Spain
Alejandra Quiros	University of Konstanz, Germany
Pedro Real	University of Seville, Spain
Yunia Reyes González	Universidad de las Ciencias Informáticas, Cuba
Bernardete Ribeiro	University of Coimbra, Portugal
Edgar Roman-Rangel	ITAM, Mexico
José Ruiz Shulcloper	Universidad de las Ciencias Informáticas, Cuba
Guillermo Sanchez-Diaz	Universidad Autónoma de San Luis Potosí, Mexico
Antonio-José Sánchez-Salmerón	Universitat Politècnica de València, Spain
Carlo Sansone	University of Naples Federico II, Italy
Alfredo Simón-Cuevas	Universidad Tecnológica de La Habana José Antonio Echeverría, Cuba
Rafael Sotelo	Universidad de Montevideo, Uruguay
José Salvador Sánchez Garreta	Universitat Jaume I, Spain
Orlando Grabiel Toledano López	Universidad de las Ciencias Informáticas, Cuba
Ruben Tolosana	Universidad Autónoma de Madrid, Spain

Sergio A. Velastin	Queen Mary University of London, UK
Vera Yashina	Federal Research Center "Computer Science and Control" of the Russian Academy of Sciences, Russia

Sponsoring Institutions

IAPR International Association for Pattern Recognition
ACRP Cuban Association for Pattern Recognition
UCI Universidad de las Ciencias Informáticas

Keynote Lecture

The Role of Artificial Intelligence in Industry 4.0

Juan Humberto Sossa Azuela

Head of the Robotics and Mechatronics Laboratory at the Computer Science Research Center of the National Polytechnic Institute, Mexico

Abstract: Artificial Intelligence is the ability of machines to imitate intelligent human behavior and perform human-like tasks. It combines algorithms that allow computers to: 1) Perceive their environment, 2) Learn from the perceived data, 3) Solve problems, and 4) Make appropriate decisions, with the aim of carrying out functions that until now were only achievable by human beings. In this talk, after defining what Artificial Intelligence is, several of its current applications worldwide are briefly described in areas as diverse as the environment, energy management, safety, mobility and health, all within the framework of Industry 4.0. Next, several of the technological developments that we are currently carrying out in our laboratory in the field of health are described, with an emphasis on COVID. Afterwards, it is briefly discussed why basic research and technological development in artificial intelligence should be supported. Later on, a series of recommendations and personal actions in this direction are presented. Finally, the conclusions are presented.

Plenary Talks

Computation at the Edge of Chaos: Natural Systems as Computation Paradigms

Ernesto Estevez Rams[1] and Danays Kunka[2]

[1] Member of the IUCr Commission in Mathematics and Theoretical Crystallography, and Vice-President of the Cuban Physics Society, Cuba
[2] KIT, Karlsruhe Institute of Technology, Germany

Disorder in solids is a form of encoding information within a crystal structure, with the potential for computational capabilities. This concept applies to non-linear coupled oscillators as well, which exhibit long spatial and temporal correlations. To explore these possibilities, tools are necessary to identify enhanced computational capabilities and develop a systematic approach. This talk presents the strategies employed to address this task. Computation can be interpreted in various ways. Traditionally, it refers to a system's ability to perform meaningful tasks by transforming input into output. Alternatively, computation can be viewed as the capacity to function as a universal Turing machine or to produce, store, transmit, and manipulate information. Consequently, any system possesses intrinsic computational abilities, which can be quantified using measures that assess resource efficiency and the balance between randomness and pattern production. The talk focuses on several studied cases that examine pattern recognition and its evolution in space and time. Initially, the quantification of correlation levels in human language is demonstrated, revealing their connection to information production, transmission, and storage. Another example investigates pattern production evaluation in layered solids with disorder, revealing a Finite State Machine description that exhibits computational power. Furthermore, two more complex models are discussed: continuously deformed cellular automata and coupled non-linear oscillators. In both cases, enhanced computation emerges at the edge of chaos, evidenced by significant changes in the system dynamics' entropic markers. Finally, the implications of this approach are considered, along with the potential to harness the computational capabilities of natural systems.

Quantum Soft Computing: Applied SW & HW of Robust Intelligent Robotic Controllers

Sergey V. Ulyanov[1] and Viktor Ulyanov[2]

[1] Laboratory of Information Technologies, Joint Institute for Nuclear Research (JINR), Dubna, Russia
[2] Department of Information Technologies, Moscow State University of Geodesy and Cartography (MIIGAiK), Moscow, Russia

A generalized design strategy of intelligent robust control systems based on quantum/soft computing technologies that enhance robustness of hybrid intelligent controllers by supplying a self-organizing capability is described. We stress our attention to the robustness features of intelligent control systems in unpredicted control situations with the simulation of Benchmark. For complex and ill-defined dynamic control objects that are not easily controlled by conventional control systems (such as P-[I]-D-controllers) — especially in the presence of fuzzy model parameters and different stochastic noises — the System of Systems Engineering methodology provides fuzzy controllers (FC) as an alternative way of control systems design. Soft computing methodologies, such as genetic algorithms (GA) and fuzzy neural networks (FNN) expand the application areas of FC by adding optimization, learning and adaptation features. But it is still difficult to design an optimal and robust intelligent control system, when its operational conditions have to evolve dramatically (aging, sensor failure and so on). Such conditions can be predicted, but it is difficult to cover such situations with a single FC. Using an unconventional computational intelligence toolkit, in this talk we propose a solution of this kind of generalization problems by introducing a self-organizing design process of robust KB - FC supported by a Quantum Fuzzy Inference (QFI) based on quantum soft computing ideas.

Quantum Soft Computing: Applied SW & HW of Robust Intelligent Robotic Controllers

[illegible]

[illegible]

Artificial Intelligence Applications Towards Digital Transformation

Rafael Esteban Bello Pérez

Director of the Informatics Research Center of the Central University of Las Villas, Cuba

The recent results of Artificial Intelligence (AI) have had an impact that may establish a parallel with the revolution that the emergence of electricity meant for the socio-economic development of humanity in the past. This occurs in a context characterized by the transversal development of information and communication technologies. This talk addresses the relationship between AI and the digital transformation of society, dealing with aspects such as the factors that have made this boom possible; as well as possible applications in different fields such as health, precision agriculture, Industry 4.0, energy, smart cities and cybersecurity. This development of AI is closely linked to the results achieved in the discovery of knowledge, which in turn is based on the enormous amount of information in digital format that is generated and stored. The development of intelligent systems resulting from learning processes based on data, and the ability of these systems to self-develop, generates new challenges, since it means that the existing control over the systems can be questioned, sowing doubts and fears about possible developments and their effects on man. So the issue of the ethical use of AI and the need for responsible AI are also considered.

Contents

Pattern Recognition and Applications

Fuzzy Employees Shuttle Bus Routing Problem. A Practical Application

Eduardo Sánchez-Ansola(✉), Alejandro Rosete, and Isis Torres-Pérez

Universidad Tecnológica de La Habana "José Antonio Echeverría", La Habana, Cuba
{esancheza,rosete,itorres}@ceis.cujae.edu.cu

Abstract. The study of transport optimization problems is significant in modern societies. One of these is the Employee Shuttle Bus Routing Problem. This problem is very similar to the School Bus Routing Problem in the context of school transportation. This paper presents a fuzzy mathematical model, developed for the School Bus Routing Problem, which is used to solve a practical case of the Employee Shuttle Bus Routing Problem for CUJAE University executives. The results confirm that fuzzy optimization can be successfully used in the Employee Shuttle Bus Routing Problem. The results allow the decision-makers to evaluate a set of solutions with different trade-offs in terms of the total cost of the routes and the degree of fulfillment of the constraint of the problem.

Keywords: Employees Shuttle Bus Routing Problem · fuzzy optimization · parametric approach · School Bus Routing Problem

1 Introduction

The School Bus Routing Problem (SBRP) is a variant of the Vehicle Routing Problem (VRP). The objective of this problem is to carry out efficient planning of the routes necessary to transport a group of students from specific stops to their corresponding schools [1]. In general, the main difference between the SBRP and other variants of the VRP is that all the stops must not be visited, since these are not the students' residences, but other locations to which the students must go.

The SBRP can be applied in other contexts besides school transportation. Such is the case of employee transportation. In this context, it's called the Employees Shuttle Bus Routing Problem (ESBRP) [2]. In the ESBRP, the conveyance of the employees to their workplace is the main goal to achieve. Recently, this problem has been extensively studied by multiple researchers [3–8].

In [9], a model was defined for the SBRP with a homogeneous fleet and bus stop selection that can be used in the context of the ESBRP. On the other hand, in [10, 11], a fuzzy model is proposed for the SBRP that allows decision-makers to have alternative solutions, based on the relaxation of the distance that students can walk. The results presented in [11] show that, with these alternatives, a decision maker has different solutions to make the most appropriate decision depending on the situation that expects to

Y. Hernández Heredia et al. (Eds.): IWAIPR 2023, LNCS 14335, pp. 3–15, 2024.
https://doi.org/10.1007/978-3-031-49552-6_1

resolve. As far as it has been possible to investigate, only in [10–12] fuzzy optimization has been used to model certain levels of uncertainty in the SBRP or the ESBRP.

This research's objective is to use the fuzzy model proposed in [11] to solve a practical situation of ESBRP. This situation focuses on the transportation of executives from the Universidad Tecnológica de La Habana José Antonio Echeverría (CUJAE). By using the parametric approach proposed by Verdegay in [13] to find the solution to the model presented in [11], CUJAE decision-makers will be able to have multiple compromise solutions between the distance that executives can walk and the total distance traveled by the bus fleet.

The rest of the paper's organization is as follows. A brief literature review on the SBRP and the ESBRP is conducted. Next, we present the model used, and how to apply the parametric approach to this model. Subsequently, the study characteristics of the instances to solve the ESBRP in CUJAE are shown. Finally, the results achieved and the corresponding analysis are exhibited.

2 School Bus Routing Problem

The School Bus Routing Problem (SBRP) was first defined in [1]. The SBRP is a type of Vehicle Routing Problem (VRP) where the goal is to design a set of school bus routes to transport students to/from their respective schools [14]. In particular, the uniqueness of this problem concerning the VRP is that each student it's not to be transported to/from his home location, but to/from a bus stop to which they have previously been assigned.

The SBRP is a combinatorial optimization problem [15] and, due to its complexity, is classified as an NP-Hard problem [16]. Based on this criterion, to solve this type of problem, it's common to use approximate methods like metaheuristics. They allow getting reasonable solutions in adequate times [17].

Although the SBRP is currently widely discussed in the literature, before 2010 there had been few studies on the subject. These works are collected and analyzed in [18]. However, in [19], it can be seen how only in the decade of 2009–2019 occurred a significant increase in the publication of studies and results on the SBRP, with more than 60 publications. This fact allows us to affirm that SBRP is a problem that presently has the interest of scientists and researchers around the world.

2.1 Employees Shuttle Bus Routing Problem

Several authors utilize the SBRP to model and solve the ESBRP [2–5, 7]. Authors of [2] drive a literature review about the ESBRP and its variants concluding that it has been an increasing movement in the use of shuttle bus routing models through recent years. In [7], the author extends the formulation of the SBRP and proposes a solution for the ESBRP based on an Area-Based method. This study uses real data that is about a shuttle bus company located in Gebze, Turkey.

On another hand, in [5], the ESBRP it's also defined as a variant of the SBRP but named as Office Bus Routing Problem (OBRP). The proposed solution is based on a Mixed Integer Programming (MIP) model and uses a GRASP + VND metaheuristic to solve it. The solution focuses on selecting the bus stops, assigning the employees to the specified bus stop, and finding the optimal routes. Other research, like [4], considers a real-world application of the ESBRP. This proposal presents a mathematical model that enables the study company with mixed loads allowance and dis-allowance choices, based on COVID-19 situations.

The focus of attention of [3] investigation is on a real-life application of a personnel service shuttle routing problem. They conceive a mathematical model to minimize the total travel time of employees, a conjunction of the walking times, the time spent by the shuttles at each stop, and the route times. The outcomes showed that the savings in total travel time were quite significant concerning the current practice.

Finally, other authors like [6, 8], model the ESBRP like different variants of VRP. In the case of [8], they present a Split Delivery Vehicle Routing Problem with Time Windows (VRPSDTW). They propose a Tabu Search to minimize the costs. In the case of [6], they present three alternatives for Capacitated Vehicle Routing Problem (CVRP). Two of these scenarios use clustering techniques to minimize the walking distance of employees to the meeting point (bus stop). These two final research focuses on finding the optimal routes, that's why other kinds of VRP than SBRP are modeled.

3 Mathematical Model

The model presented below was developed for the first time in [11]. Its objective is to minimize the total distance traveled by buses in the fleet, posing the constraint of the student's maximum walking distance as fuzzy. It focuses on an SBRP with a homogeneous fleet, bus stops selection, and route generation and it includes the constraint that each selected stop is visited only once by a single bus.

Parameters

c: Capacity of each bus.
B, b: Set and index of buses, $b = 1...|B|$.
P, p: Set and index of possible bus stops, $p = 0...|P|$, where $p = 0$ indicates the school.
E, e: Set and index of students, $e = 1...|E|$.
d: Maximum walking distance for student e.
V^p: A set of vectors with coordinate pairs representing the possible bus stops.
V^e: A set of vectors with pairs of coordinates representing the house of each student.
H: Maximum admissible tolerance for the distance that the student e could walk.

Auxiliary Parameters

D: A distance function that indicates the cost between a pair of stops or between a student and a bus stop.
C^P_{pq}: A distance matrix between each pair of stops (p, q).
C^E_{ep}: A distance matrix between each pair of student-stop (e, p).
c^P_i: Coordinates of the stop located on the i index of V^p.

c^e_j: Coordinates of the student located on the j index of V^e.

$$C^P_{pq} = \begin{cases} D(c^P_p, c^P_q), p \neq q \\ 0, p = q \end{cases} \quad \forall p, \forall q \in P \tag{1}$$

$$C^E_{ep} = D(c^e_e, c^P_p) \quad e \in E, p \in P - \{0\} \tag{2}$$

Decision Variables

R_{bm}: Indicates the stop that is visited by bus b in the order m. $|R_{bm}|$, indicates the number of bus stops visited by the bus b.
Z_e: Indicates the stop where the student e is picked up

Objective Function

$$\text{Min} \sum_{b=1}^{|B|} \left(C^P_{0[1]} + \sum_{m=1}^{|P|-1} C^P_{[R_{bm}][R_{bm+1}]} + C^P_{[|R_{bm}|]0} \right) \tag{3}$$

Constraints
$\leq^f$: A fuzzy comparison operator indicating the fuzzy imprecision of the constraint (5).

$$\{R_{bm}|R_{bm} = p\}| \leq 1 \quad \forall p \in P - \{0\}, \forall b \in B, \forall m \in \{1, \ldots, |P|\} \tag{4}$$

$$\{(e, p)|Z_e = p\} \subseteq \left\{(e, p)|C^E_{ep} \leq^f d\right\} \quad \forall e \in E, \ \forall p \in P \tag{5}$$

$$|\{e|\exists m\ R_{bm} = Z_e\}| \leq c \quad m \in \{0, \ldots, |P|\}, \ \forall b \in B, \forall e \in E \tag{6}$$

$$|\{R_{bm}|R_{bm} = Z_e\}| = 1 \quad \forall e \in E \tag{7}$$

The objective function, Eq. (3), minimizes the total distance traveled by the complete bus fleet. Equations (4), (5), (6), and (7) represent the constraints that must be met for the solution to be feasible. Equation (4) guarantees that each bus stop is visited at most once, except for the stop that represents the school, the final destination of all buses. Equation (5) ensures that all students can reach their assigned bus stop. Equation (6) assured that the capacity of each bus doesn't be exceeded on a route. And finally, Eq. (7) ensured that each bus stop to which at least one student is assigned is visited by a bus. Equation (8), shown below, is used to replace Eq. (5), following what was stated in Verdegay's parametric approach [13].

$$\{(e, p)|Z_e = p\} \subseteq \left\{(e, p)|C^E_{ep} \leq d + H(1 - \alpha_w)\right\} \tag{8}$$

Figure 1 represents the constraint of the maximum walking distance with different α and the same H for each student. In this representation, the points correspond to the students (employees), the triangles to the bus stops, and the rhombus to the school (work center). The circles with various shades of green represent the distinct relaxation degrees of the maximum walking distance. The darker shade symbolizes the problem without relaxation, while the lighter shade refers to the problem with the maximum allowed relaxation. In the image, can be appreciated how the relaxation's increase (by decreasing the value of α) causes some stops (yellow triangles), that were necessary to give access to a student, to be no longer required and, therefore, these stops do not have to be visited by any bus.

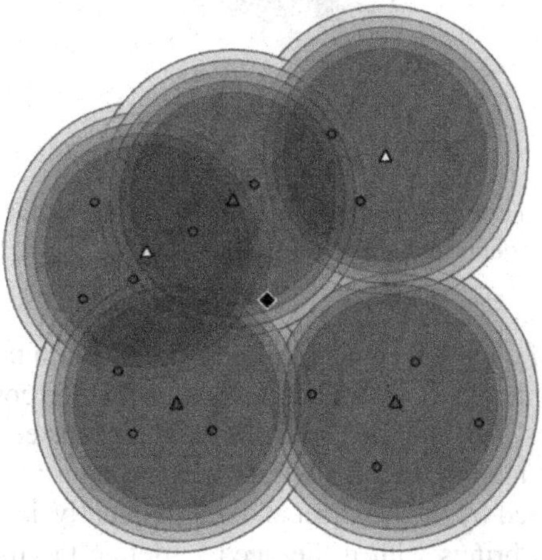

Fig. 1. Representation of an example that reflects the levels of allowed relaxation in the model for the students' maximum walking distance.

3.1 Parametric Approach

The constraint presented in Eq. (5) is the core of the proposed fuzzy model. This way of modeling this constraint implies that the feasibility that a student can reach a stop is fuzzy. Consequently, it is possible to satisfy this constraint with different degrees of membership.

Considering this fact, if the original students' maximum walking distance is 200 m, then a student who has to walk 190 m satisfies the constraint with a degree of membership equal to 1. On the other hand, if a student must walk 210 m, then the degree of membership (which represents the degree of satisfaction of the constraint) is less than 1, but at the same time, it's greater than the membership if he had to walk 250 m. Conversely, a bus stop placed 500 m away from all the students should be considered unreachable. Therefore, the membership degree of the availability of that stop for that student is 0. Figure 2 shows a representative graph of this example, where the triangle represents a bus stop, and the small circles represent students. The intensity of the color of the small circles determines the satisfaction degree of each student to reach the bus stop.

All these values (i.e., 200 and 250 m for the walking distance) depend on the permissible conditions and the acceptable tolerances. These values imply that the solutions

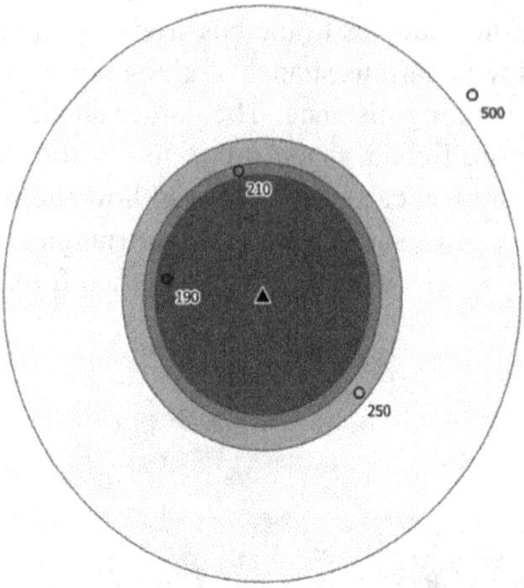

Fig. 2. Representation of the membership degree of the constraint for the maximum walking distance between several students and a bus stop.

have different degrees of compliance with this constraint. From the point of view of the decision-makers, by using these constraint's relaxations, at the cost of allowing modest increases in the students' walking distance, they obtain relaxed solutions with better values of the objective function. In this particular case, better values imply a reduction in the total lengths covered by the bus fleet and, consequently, in its associated costs.

Using this approach brings with it the need to define the list of α-values for the α_w parameter in Eq. (8). In this case, we employed a Conscious strategy that considers previous knowledge of the specific problem instance [12]. In the case of SBRP with fuzzy walking distance, the main feature to be taken into account is the distance that relates the students to the bus stops. This distance is calculated with the locations of each student and each bus stop which are part of the model's parameters. Then a matrix that contains all the pair student-bus stop distances is calculated and becomes part of the auxiliary parameters on the model (Eq. (2)).

To obtain the alpha-cuts, the mentioned distances values are split into three groups: (a) the distances that are less or equal to d, (b) the distances between d and d + H, and finally, (c) the distances that are greater than d + H. Knowing that distance in group (a) will always satisfy the constraint and distances in group (c) will always be beyond the allowed limits, then only the distances in group (b) have a certain value for the analysis. In this way, in an instance where all the distances are in groups (a) or (c), the relaxation that is given by H does not contribute any improvement to the solution of the crisp instance. Thus, there is no need to explore any alpha-cuts, and the fuzzy solution will always be the same as the initial crisp solution. Authors of [12] present a full explanation of this strategy.

4 Case of Study for the Transportation of Executives in the CUJAE

The case in question is in the context of planning the transportation of CUJAE executives. The purpose of this plan is to guarantee that the University executives can arrive at the center on time to fulfill their duties, reducing transportation costs. This plan can be done in a way that includes all the executives or only the subset of these that must be in the CUJAE on a given day. This implies that planning can change daily.

The application of the proposed fuzzy model for planning the transport of employees has an objective: minimize the cost (distance traveled) of the routes planned for the transportation of the executives of the CUJAE. In this sense, the model's parameters can be interpreted from the proposed situation. The location of the students corresponds to the location of the executives and the school with the workplace (CUJAE). The remaining parameters, such as bus stops, distances, buses, and capacity, correspond to similar elements in the context of student transportation.

For this case of the study, we take the addresses of the 114 executives of the CUJAE. Using these addresses, we obtain the geographic coordinates using a geocoding service [20]. It must be taken into account that after this process, the four executives located outside the Havana province were eliminated, leaving 110 executives to be transported. Figure 3 shows the locations of the executives (points) and CUJAE (diamond) from where the buses depart and return.

To define the executives' maximum walking distance, we assumed what was expressed in the Sustainable Development Goal (SDG) 11: Sustainable Cities and Communities. This SDG establishes that convenient access to public transport implies that people have a public transport stop less than 500 m from their homes [21]. Therefore, we assume 500 m as the maximum walking distance. Likewise, taking into account the characteristics of the city and the distances that people usually tend to walk, the maximum tolerance allowed is set at 200%, which is up to 1500 m. Figure 3 shows a representation in a map of these distances as green circles, dark green (500 m), and light green (1500 m).

The set of available bus stops used, represented as red triangles in Fig. 3, are selected from the 3097 public transport stops in the city. Based on these bus stops, the locations of the executives, and to use the minimum number of bus stops, a subset of these is selected so that as few as possible remain to cover all the executives within a 500-m radius. As a consequence of this filter, 86 bus stops were obtained.

We decided to investigate two instances of the study case, where the number of executives varied. The first assumes a fleet of four vehicles with a capacity for 30 seated passengers. With this number of buses, it is possible to transport up to 120 passengers, so all the executives can be transported on the routes. The second instance only contemplates the transport of 50 executives in two vehicles with a capacity of 30 seated passengers. These 50 executives are arbitrarily selected from the 110 executives available for the case. This last instance is more suitable for the daily planning of routes in the CUJAE since not all executives use transportation day-to-day.

The current transportation of CUJAE executives is performed using buses with a capacity of only 30 seated passengers. To select the α-values needed in the parametric approach the Conscious strategy, proposed in [12], is used. This strategy chooses three α-values in addition to the original problem without relaxation, with a walking distance

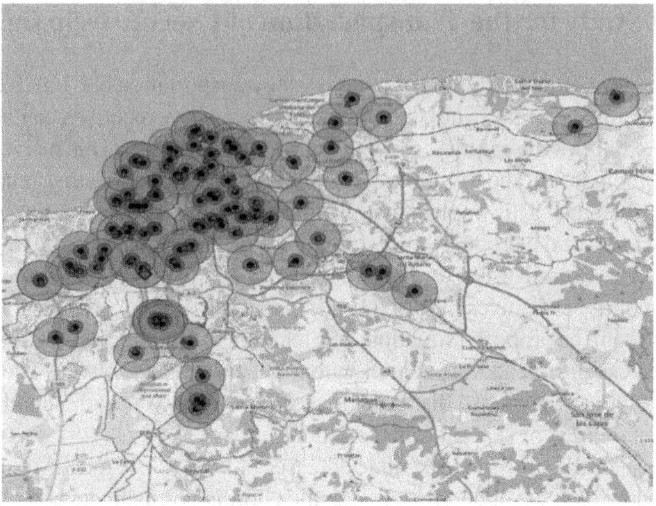

Fig. 3. Map with the locations of the executives, the possible bus stops, and the CUJAE.

of 500 m ($\alpha = 1$), and the problem with the maximum allowed relaxation of 1500 m ($\alpha = 0$). For each α-value in each instance, a Best Ascent Local Search (BALS) metaheuristic is executed with ten executions and 10,000 iterations, taking the best solution value of the 100,000 evaluations of the objective function.

To develop this case, we build an application in Java programming language, which includes the modeling and solution of the SBRP and the parametric treatment of the fuzzy model using the Conscious strategy [12]. Likewise, to represent each instance's spatial information, we employ QGIS [22], a Geographic Information System.

5 Results and Discussion

To evaluate the quality of the routes, it is necessary to consider two elements: the total distance traveled by buses and the number of different values in the solutions of the fuzzy model. In Table 1, these two elements can be seen in the Total distance traveled columns. Likewise, Table 1 also shows the α-values obtained by the Conscious strategy (**Alpha** column), the executives' maximum walking distance, and average traversed distances to reach the assigned bus stop (because the optimal solution for each case does not imply identical distances to be walked by all executives).

Figure 4 shows the trade-off values for the average walked distance and the total fleet traveled distance for both instances, 110 executives (right) and 50 executives (left).

When analyzing the values obtained from the instance of 110 executives, it can be verified that, by applying the relaxation in the executives' walking distance, it is possible to significatively reduce the value of the total distance traveled by the bus fleet. At the same time, decision-makers can choose between four relaxation levels of interest (with $\alpha = 0.24$, better results can't be obtained) to make a more appropriate decision regarding how much executives should walk and how much savings can be achieved in the total traveled distance.

Table 1. Solution's values of each instance fuzzy problem.

Instance	Alpha	Maximum Walking Distance (meters)	Average Walked Distances (meters)	Total traveled distance (kilometers)	Saving from α = 1
110 executives and four buses	1	500	308.69	**197.31**	0%
	0.69	810	370.06	**185.64**	6%
	0.43	1070	474.11	**182.11**	8%
	0.24	1260	626.99	182.11	8%
	0	1500	735.99	**176.18**	11%
50 executives and two buses	1	500	281.18	**106.13**	0%
	0.63	870	352.20	**93.79**	12%
	0.35	1150	550.91	**89.92**	15%
	0.17	1330	625.94	**86.32**	19%
	0	1500	761.80	**85.09**	20%

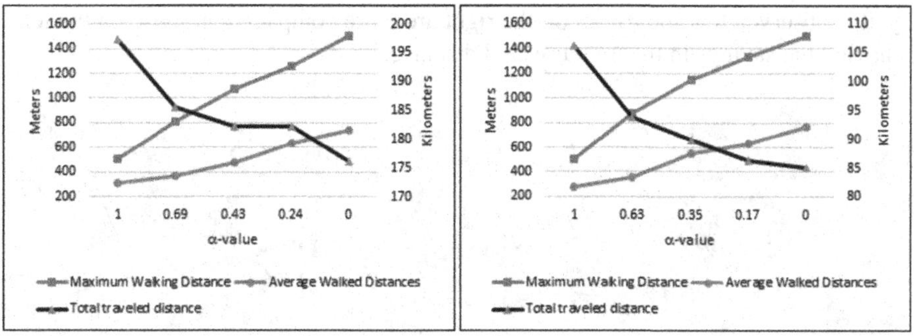

Fig. 4. Trade-off values between executives' walking distance and total fleet traveled distance.

In the same way, it can be observed that by applying the maximum allowed relaxation, an approximate saving of 11% is obtained, which in this instance is equivalent to 21 km. Figure 5 shows a representation on a map of the planned routes and the assignment of the executives to the bus stops, for the instance of 110 executives, without relaxation (left) and fully relaxed (right). These maps show how, as relaxation increases, executives walk more to reach the corresponding stop (little red lines). Likewise, it can be noticed how the routes generated in each relaxation have different paths. On the other hand, it can be seen in the **Average Walked Distance** column of Table 1 that, on average, executives never walk the maximum allowed distance.

A similar analysis can be performed with the results obtained for the instance with 50 executives. In these results, it can be seen how, for each level of relaxation, different values of the total distance to be traveled by vehicles are obtained, with which the

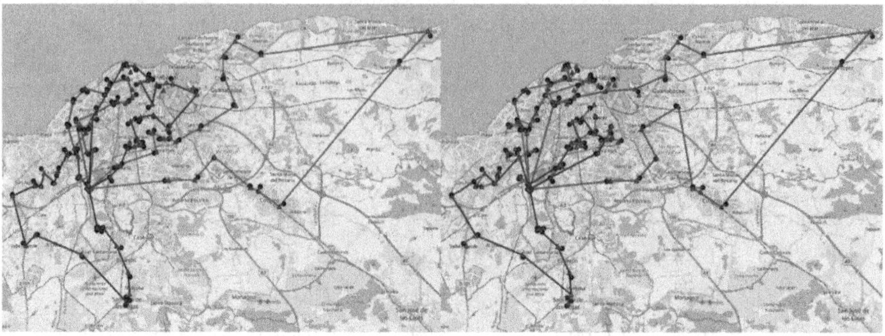

Fig. 5. Maps with the representation of the solutions to the 110 executives' instance: without relaxation ($\alpha = 1$) (left) and fully relaxed ($\alpha = 0$) (right).

decision-maker has five options to decide how much executives should walk and how much can be saved in the traveled distance, and therefore, in fuel use. The savings with the maximum allowed relaxation amounts to 20%, which implies about 21 km. Figure 6 shows two maps that represent the routes obtained for this instance without relaxation (left) and fully relaxed (right). It can be seen, on the right map, how executives must travel to a bus stop further from their place of residence (little red lines). In the same way, it is observed that the routes on the right are more compact than those on the left, displaying the savings in the total traveled distance.

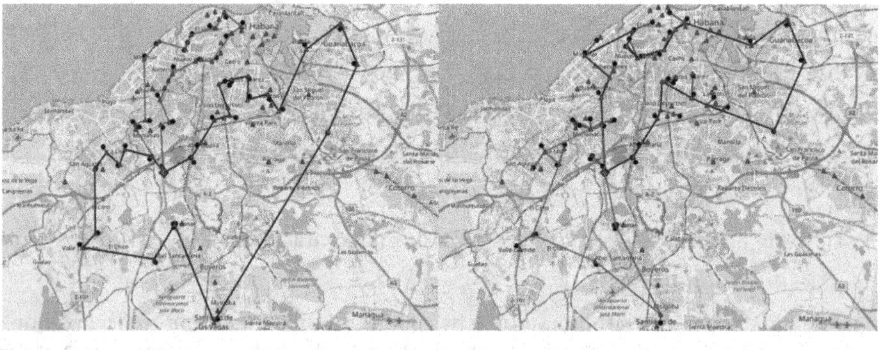

Fig. 6. Maps with the representation of the solutions to the 50 executives' instance: without relaxation ($\alpha = 1$) (left) and fully relaxed ($\alpha = 0$) (right).

Figure 7 shows the relationship between an executive and his assigned bus stop according to the value of α associated with relaxation. It can be seen while relaxation increases, the executive must walk a little more and, in this way, collaborate in reducing the total distance traveled by the bus fleet.

Based on the above results, we can confirm that the SBRP model with fuzzy walking distance applies in the context of the ESBRP and, in particular, to the route planning scenario for CUJAE executives. Applying this model, by relaxing the walking distance, better transportation costs are obtained. Likewise, decision-makers can choose

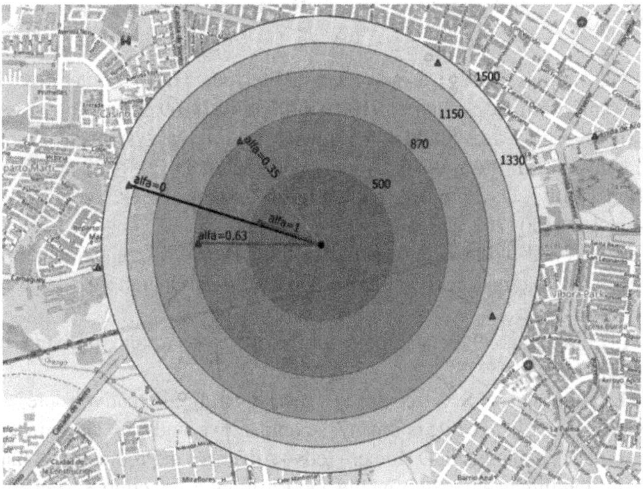

Fig. 7. Change of assignment of an executive according to the allowed degree of relaxation.

between several compromise values between the executives' walking distance and the total distance that the buses in the fleet must travel.

In the case of transporting all the executives, achieve a saving of 11% in the total distance traveled by the fleet of vehicles and, in the case of the daily transportation of 50 executives, this saving increases up to 20%. Both cases achieve these savings by applying the maximum allowable relaxation of twice the original distance of 500 m, with which the executives can walk a maximum of 1,500 m. However, on average, they walk less than 800 m in both cases. Thus, when all the executives walk approximately 2.7 times more, the routes' cost is reduced by 20%. Meanwhile, when the 50 executives walk about 2.4 times more, the routes' cost is reduced by 11%.

6 Conclusions

The achieved results allow us to demonstrate the practical applicability of the fuzzy model for the SBRP in the context of the ESBRP. The obtained solutions show that by allowing a greater walking distance by the CUJAE executives (twice the original distance), between 11% and 20% of the total distance traveled by the vehicles fleet can be saved and, therefore, the necessary fuel. This saving depends on the number of executives to be transported and their locations. At the same time, decision-makers have several solutions that establish a compromise between cost-savings and walking distance. Hence, they can make better decisions.

This practical investigation opens the way for future applications of fuzzy models in the ESBRP. In such a way the future scope of this work resides in the opportunity to explore other fuzziest elements, such as the capacity of the buses. Likewise, variations in the models (heterogeneous fleet, time windows, and others) can be used for situations in which were necessary.

References

1. Newton, R.M., Thomas, W.H.: Design of school bus routes by computer. Soc.-Econ. Plann. Sci. **3**(1), 75–85 (1969). https://doi.org/10.1016/0038-0121(69)90051-2
2. Gaye, P., Türsel Eliiyi, D.: Shuttle bus service routing: a systematic literature review. Pamukkale Üniversitesi Mühendislik Bilimleri Dergisi **28**(1), 160–172 (2022)
3. Gaye, P., Türsel Eliiyi, D.: Employee shuttle bus routing problem: a case study. Eur. J. Sci. Technol. (46), 151–160 (2023)
4. Bideq, H., et al.: A real-world Employee Bus Routing Problem application with mixed loads. In: 2022 IEEE 6th International Conference on Logistics Operations Management (GOL) (2022)
5. Goswami, A., et al.: A novel metaheuristic for the office bus routing problem. In: 2021 IISE Annual Conference (2021)
6. Eligüzel, İM., Yağbasan, N.S., Özceylan, E.: Investigating alternative routes for employee shuttle services arising in a textile company: a comparative study. In: Dolgui, A., Al Bernard, D., von Lemoine, G., Cieminski, D Romero (eds.) Advances in Production Management Systems. Artificial Intelligence for Sustainable and Resilient Production Systems: IFIP WG 5.7 International Conference, APMS 2021, Nantes, France, September 5–9, 2021, Proceedings, Part V, pp. 68–76. Springer International Publishing, Cham (2021). https://doi.org/10.1007/978-3-030-85914-5_8
7. Yalçindağ, S.: Employee shuttle bus routing problem. Mugla J. Sci. Technol. **6**(1), 105–111 (2020)
8. Purba, A.P., Siswanto, N., Rusdiansyah, A.: Routing and scheduling employee transportation using Tabu search. AIP Conf. Proc. **2217**(1), 030143 (2020)
9. Pérez Pérez, A.C., Sánchez-Ansola, E., Rosete, A.: A metaheuristic solution for the school bus routing problem with homogeneous fleet and bus stop selection. Ingeniería **26**(2), 233–253 (2021). https://doi.org/10.14483/23448393.15835
10. Sánchez-Ansola, E., Pérez-Pérez, A.C., Rosete, A.: A fuzzy approach for organizational transportation aligned with the sustainable development goals: health promotion, inequality reduction, and responsible consumption. In: Verdegay, J.L., Brito, J., Cruz, C. (eds.) Computational Intelligence Methodologies Applied to Sustainable Development Goals, pp. 205–219. Springer International Publishing, Cham (2022)
11. Sánchez-Ansola, E., Pérez-Pérez, A.C., Rosete, A.: School Bus Routing Problem with fuzzy walking distance. Polytechnic Open Library International Bulletin of Information Technology and Science (POLIBITS). Special Issue: Emerging Challenges and Trends in Business Intelligence (62), 69–75 (2020)
12. Sánchez-Ansola, E., et al.: Conscious exploration of alpha-cuts in the parametric solution of the school bus routing problem with fuzzy walking distance. Comput. Intell. Neurosci. **2022**, 4821927 (2022)
13. Ebrahimnejad, A., Verdegay, J.L.: Fuzzy sets-based methods and techniques for modern analytics. In: Kacprzyk, J. (ed.) Studies in Fuzziness and Soft Computing, 1st edn. Springer Cham., vol. XIII, p. 361 (2018)
14. Li, L.Y.O., Fu, Z.: The school bus routing problem: a case study. J. Operat. Res. Soc. **53**(5), 552–558 (2002)
15. Miranda, D.M., et al.: A multi-loading school bus routing problem. Expert Syst. Appl. **101**, 228–242 (2018)
16. Bock, A., et al.: The school bus problem on trees. Algorithmica **67**(1), 49–64 (2013)
17. Talbi, E.G.: Metaheuristics: From Design to Implementation. Wiley (2009). https://doi.org/10.1002/9780470496916

18. Park, J., Kim, B.-I.: The school bus routing problem: a review. Eur. J. Oper. Res. **202**(2), 311–319 (2010)
19. Ellegood, W.A., et al.: School bus routing problem: contemporary trends and research directions. Omega **95**, 102056 (2020)
20. Alfonso Cantillo, O., Sánchez Ansola, E.: Computación paralela para la geocodificación de direcciones postales cubanas. Ingeniería Investigación y Tecnología **21**(4), 1–12 (2020)
21. Nations, U.: The Sustainable Development Agenda. Sustainable Development Goals 2021. https://www.un.org/sustainabledevelopment/development-agenda/ (2021)
22. QGIS.org: QGIS Geographic Information System. QGIS Association (2023)

Oversampling Method Based Covariance Matrix Estimation in High-Dimensional Imbalanced Classification

Ireimis Leguen-de-Varona[1(✉)], Julio Madera[1], Hector Gonzalez[2], Lise Tubex[3], and Tim Verdonck[3]

[1] Universidad de Camagüey "Ignacio Agramonte Loynaz", Camaguey, Cuba
{ireimis.leguen,julio.madera}@reduc.edu.cu

[2] Universidad de las Ciencias Informaticas (UCI), Havana, La Habana, Cuba
hglez@uci.cu

[3] University of Antwerp, Antwerp, Belgium
{lise.tubex,tim.verdonck}@uantwerpen.be

Abstract. Class imbalance is a common problem in (binary) classification problems. It appears in many application domains, such as text classification, fraud detection, churn prediction and medical diagnosis. A widely used approach to cope with this problem at the data level is the Synthetic Minority Oversampling Technique (SMOTE) which uses the K-Nearest Neighbors (KNN) algorithm to generate new, artificial instances in the minority class. It is however known that SMOTE is not ideal for high-dimensional data. Therefore, we propose an alternative oversampling strategy for imbalanced classification problems in high dimensions. Our approach is based on the sparse inverse covariance matrix estimated trough the Ledoit-Wolf method for high-dimensional data. The results show that our proposal has a competitive performance with respect to popular competitors.

Keywords: Imbalanced classes · Oversampling · High-dimensional data · Sparse Covariance Matrix Estimation · Ledoit-Wolf estimator

1 Introduction

Oversampling is a popular solution to the problem of imbalanced data, where the number of instances in one class, i.e. the minority class, is significantly lower than the number of instances in the other class. In oversampling strategies, the minority class is artificially increased by creating new synthetic data based on the existing sample [21,23].

A very popular and widely used oversampling method is SMOTE (Synthetic Minority Oversampling Technique) [2,5]. Various alternatives have been proposed in literature to achieve a good balance such as: SMOTE-Borderline [6], SMOTE-RSB* [18], ADASYN [7], ROS [22] and SMOTE-COV [13].

Y. Hernndez Heredia et al. (Eds.): IWAIPR 2023, LNCS 14335, pp. 16–23, 2024.
https://doi.org/10.1007/978-3-031-49552-6_2

The sample covariance matrix is a commonly used estimator of the true covariance matrix, and is calculated directly from the data by taking the average of the outer product of the centered data matrix. However, the sample covariance matrix can be unreliable when the number of variables is large compared to the number of observations, as it can be noisy and have unstable eigenvalues.

Covariance matrix estimation methods with sparsity and shrinkage estimation like the Ledoit-Wolf estimator improved the accuracy and stability of the estimated covariance matrix [10–12]. These methods typically involve some form of regularization or shrinkage, which involves adding a bias to the estimator to reduce its variance [3,14]. In addition to the Ledoit-Wolf shrinkage estimator, there are several other methods that have been proposed for estimating the covariance matrix in high-dimensional settings. Some of these methods include Graphical Lasso with ℓ_1 regularization, Sparse PCA, Random matrix theory and Bayesian methods [12].

In high-dimensional imbalanced data, oversampling can be particularly challenging to generate meaningful synthetic samples. One approach to overcome this challenge is to simulate synthetic data by using the sparse covariance matrix while oversampling and improve the classifiers. It is known that the behavior of SMOTE in high-dimensional data is not always ideal. (i) Oversampling can lead to an increase in the number of redundant or irrelevant features, which can reduce the performance of the classifier. This is because synthetic samples generated by SMOTE are based on existing features, and can therefore inherit the same irrelevant or noisy features [9]. (ii) SMOTE can lead to overfitting. This is because SMOTE generates synthetic samples by interpolating between existing samples, which can lead to over-representation of certain regions of the feature space. In high-dimensional data this can be biased, since the number of combinations of features grows exponentially [9]. (iii) SMOTE can be computationally expensive in high-dimensional data, as the number of possible combinations of features grows exponentially. This can make it difficult to generate a sufficient number of synthetic samples to balance the class distribution in the minority class [9]. (iv) SMOTE uses the classical Euclidean distance metric to compute the neighbors. In the high-dimensional case, it may follow that a lot of instances or all of them have the same distances. This can lead to an ineffective interpolation [1]. (v) SMOTE can experience over-generalization. Class overlap can be increased because the method ignores the majority class, allowing the creation of synthetic samples over the majority class [8,15,16].

Some modifications of SMOTE to balance data sets by applying feature selection or reduction before or after generating synthetic instances to obtain good results in high-dimensional classification problems have been proposed recently, see for example SDDSMOTE [17], FW-SMOTE [19] and SMOTE-SF [20].

The main contributions of this paper are: (i) We introduce a novel strategy of the resampling based on the Ledoit-Wolf covariance matrix and shrinkage selection in high-dimensional imbalanced classification. (ii) We propose an empirical evaluation of the SMOTE algorithms for imbalanced classification in small and high dimensions synthetics data sets.

2 Covariance Matrix Estimation in High-Dimensional Imbalanced Classification

Let a set of data, independent and identically distributed (i.i.d.) $X = \{X_1, \dots X_N\}$ with $X_i \in \mathbb{R}^p$, be N samples drawn from a p-dimensional Gaussian distribution $\mathcal{N}(\mu, \Sigma)$. The task to estimate the inverse covariance matrix $\Theta = \Sigma^{-1}$ (also known as the covariance precision), solves the following loglikelihood regularized optimization problem

$$\Theta^* = \underset{\Theta \succeq 0}{\text{argmin}}\{-\text{logdet}(\Theta) + \text{tr}(S\Theta) + g(\Theta)\}. \tag{1}$$

where $g(\Theta)$ is the convex and normally non-differentiable regularization function and $S, \Theta \in \mathbb{R}^{p \times p}$ are the estimated sample covariance matrix and inverse covariance matrix. The expression to compute the sample mean μ and the sample covariance matrix S are:

$$\mu = \frac{1}{N}\sum_{i=1}^{N} X_i, \qquad S = \frac{1}{N}\sum_{i=1}^{N}(X_i - \mu)(X_i - \mu)^T. \tag{2}$$

In high-dimensional conditions ($p \approx N$ or $p \gg N$) the sample covariance matrix S will be singular [4], and the likelihood estimator of the covariance matrix has many weaknesses such as inaccuracy. Several studies [2,3,8–11], research the problem of the high dimensions using sparsity and shrinkage methods for estimating Θ considering that the number of the parameters increase quadratically with respect to the number of variables p.

In the Ledoit-Wolf class of estimators a linear combinations of the identity matrix $\mathbb{I}_p$ and the sample covariance matrix S is considered, so that the optimization problem of the shrinkage estimation and selection became

$$\begin{aligned} &\min_{\rho_1, \rho_2} \mathbb{E}\left[\|\hat{\Theta} - \Theta\|_F^2\right] \\ &s.t. \;\; \hat{\Theta} = \rho_1 \mathbb{I}_p + \rho_2 S. \end{aligned} \tag{3}$$

The solution to Eq. 3 can also be written as a convex linear combination

$$\hat{\Theta}^* = \lambda^* \mu_p \mathbb{I}_p + (1 - \lambda^*)S, \;\; \lambda^* = \frac{\beta^2}{\gamma^2}, \tag{4}$$

where $\beta^2 = \mathbb{E}\left[\|S - \Theta_T\|_F^2\right]$ and $\gamma^2 = \|S - \mu\mathbb{I}_p\|_F^2$. With the asymptotic analysis we have special interest in the problem with a large number of attributes $p/N \to c \in (0, \infty]$, that is p and N have similar behaviour in infinity. The case of $p \gg N$ was not considered in this study. Finally, the covariance matrix estimator $\hat{\Theta}^*$ and the optimal shrinkage parameter λ^* can be computed in the following steps described in Algorithm 1. The synthetic data that must be generated for the minority class can be simulated using the multivariate normal distribution with $\mathcal{N}(\mu, \Sigma^*)$ in the proportion established in the configuration.

Algorithm 1. Ledoit-Wolf covariance matrix estimation

Input: X
Output: Θ^*, λ^*
Compute μ and S (eq. 2)
$\hat{\gamma}^2 = \|S - \mu\mathbb{I}_p\|_F^2$
$\hat{\beta}^2 = \min\{\hat{\gamma}^2, \frac{1}{N}\sum_{i=1}^{N}\|S - X_i^T X_i\|_F^2\}$
Compute λ^* and Θ^* with eq. 3

3 Numerical Data Simulation and Empirical Study

In this empirical evaluation, we compare several classifiers (MLP, SVM, KNN) in different conditions of imbalance and number of features (Twelves synthetics datasets with $p = \{50, 200, 500, 1000, 3000, 5000\}$ and $IR = \{0.03, 0.05\}$). Also, some variants of the SMOTE oversampling strategy were combined with the classifiers to improve the accuracy. Table 1 shows in details the main characteristics of the classifiers and the resampling methods. In case of the oversampling methods studied, two resampling strategies were evaluated while the classifiers tuned several parameters to choose the best model parameter. Each pipeline was executed over five splits and three iterations of the classifier. In this primary research, it was decided to conduct an empirical study with data sets generated using the multivariate normal distribution $\mathcal{N}(0, \Sigma)$ for the binary classification problem. Two levels of the imbalance were considered, namely 3% and 5%. Also, six different feature sizes ($p = 50, 200, 500, 1000, 3000, 5000$) were used to build the numerical simulation of the moderate (first three p values) and high-dimensional (the last three) case. In all of the databases, the number of samples was $N = 1000$ ($p/N \to c = 5$ for the more high-dimensional cases) and 60% of the features were considered informative. Figure 1 shows the two principal component of a simulated database.

Table 1. The parameters considered for fine tuning of the classifiers.

	Method	Fine Tunning
Oversampling strategies	SMOTE	Resampling 50:50
	ADASYM	Resampling 50:50
	ROS	Resampling 50:50
	Cov_HD	
Classifiers	KNN	n_neighbors
	Random Forest	max_depth, n_ estimators, min_ samples_ split, min_ samples_ leaf
	MLP	hidden_ layer_ sizes, activation, solver, learning rate, alpha, learning_rate
	SVM	kernel, gamma, C

In our future work, five highly imbalanced and high-dimensional data sets from the GEMLeR collection with continuous attributes and a binary class will be considered for the empirical evaluation.

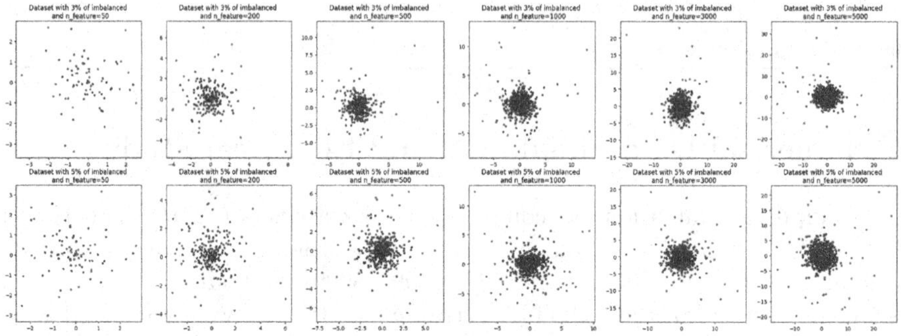

Fig. 1. A simulated database in high-dimensional imbalanced classification.

3.1 Empirical Evaluation

The AUC (Area Under the Curve) is commonly used in machine learning for evaluating the performance of binary classification models. The AUC represents the area under the Receiver Operating Characteristic (ROC) curve, which is a plot of the true positive rate (TPR) against the false positive rate (FPR) at various classification thresholds. The TPR is the fraction of positive samples that are correctly classified as positive, while the FPR is the fraction of negative samples that are incorrectly classified as positive. Similar to precedent works, the AUC is also useful for imbalanced classification problems. The AUC metric is attractive because it is insensitive to the threshold used to classify instances, and provides a single number that summarizes the overall performance of the model.

In Table 2, we show the AUC metric for each classifier and oversampling strategy with all possible combinations of data sets that we propose. The best values are indicated in bold.

The AUC metric in the combination of KNN + COV_HD shows the most difference with respect to the rest of the combinations. The Friedman test with Holm correction posthoc, for each classifier in combination with the oversampling strategies, shows only significant differences in the combination KNN + COV_HD with respect to the rest of the strategies.

Another encouraging result in the empirical evaluation is that, although there are no significant differences, in the case of SVM and MLP the Friedman rankings give the proposed approach the first place. A differentiated analysis of the Friedman test where we focus on the three bases we considered high-dimensional for our study, is shown in Table 3.

Table 2. The AUC metric in the empirical evaluation. The best values are indicated in bold.

Classifiers	Algorithms	50 features	100 features	500 features	1000 features	3000 features	5000 features
KNN 3% imbalance	COV_HD	**0.895201**	**0.914929**	**0.873684**	**0.93615**	**0.936687**	**0.933655**
	ADASYN	0.810062	0.871649	0.565015	0.60443	0.5	0.501577
	ROS	0.639319	0.743857	0.723529	0.7742	0.539938	0.752563
	SMOTE	0.873375	0.844378	0.585139	0.587025	0.501548	0.506309
KNN 5% imbalance	COV_HD	**0.847678**	**0.962677**	**0.89195**	**0.908879**	**0.943653**	**0.932986**
	ADASYN	0.5	0.5	0.5	0.5	0.5	0.5
	ROS	0.734211	0.673678	0.868885	0.766381	0.587616	0.780436
	SMOTE	0.5	0.5	0.5	0.5	0.5	0.5
Classifiers	Algorithms	50 features	100 features	500 features	1000 features	3000 features	5000 features
MLP 3% imbalance	COV_HD	0.866873	0.89315	**0.868421**	**0.887193**	**0.822291**	0.730087
	ADASYN	0.765325	**0.921258**	0.855418	0.8414	0.809288	**0.761632**
	ROS	0.754489	0.916977	0.829721	0.880305	0.669969	0.669558
	SMOTE	**0.871207**	0.88347	0.729412	0.800819	0.780186	0.707216
MLP 5% imbalance	COV_HD	0.574303	**0.69099**	0.627245	0.634773	0.612384	0.604617
	ADASYN	0.66161	0.670514	0.60031	0.526806	0.604334	0.495532
	ROS	0.544892	0.622673	0.65356	**0.694713**	0.375851	**0.632725**
	SMOTE	**0.673375**	0.587118	**0.721053**	0.601452	**0.613003**	0.520104
Classifiers	Algorithms	50 features	100 features	500 features	1000 features	3000 features	5000 features
SVM 3% imbalance	COV_HD	**0.873976**	**0.946667**	0.80901	**0.925051**	0.787658	0.83101
	ADASYN	0.796351	0.918283	**0.872673**	0.886465	**0.801065**	0.844747
	ROS	0.866158	0.508333	0.852197	0.89707	0.5	0.5
	SMOTE	0.863179	0.912727	0.803611	0.882525	0.785489	**0.853636**
SVM 5% imbalance	COV_HD	0.600521	**0.758586**	0.621742	**0.645657**	0.642219	0.5
	ADASYN	0.630119	0.661717	0.503351	0.5	**0.649106**	**0.671818**
	ROS	**0.766754**	0.5	**0.633842**	0.53626	0.5	0.514747
	SMOTE	0.627513	0.657778	0.5	0.526061	**0.649106**	0.671717

Table 3. The Friedman test analysis in high-dimensional data sets.

	Classifier	Ranking	Statistic	P-value
high-dimensional	KNN	COV_HD, ADASYN, SMOTE, ROS	11.45	**0.009**
	SVM	COV_HD, ADASYN, ROS, SMOTE	3.6	0.308
	MLP	COV_HD, ADASYN, SMOTE, ROS	1.4	0.706

4 Concluding Remarks and Further Work

In this paper we have introduced a new classification approach for high-dimensional imbalanced problems based on sparse inverse covariance estimation using the Ledoit-Wolf method. The empirical evaluation demonstrated the effectiveness of oversampling data trough sparser covariance estimation compared to others state-of-the-art methods. COV_HD showed similar or comparable results considering the results of the AUC metric and the Friedman test. In addition, we found significant differences for specific classifiers. In general, we can conclude that the strategy of resampling based on sparser covariance matrix is a competitive method for high-dimensional imbalanced classification problems.

Future work is planned in several directions to expand this contribution. On the one hand, the most exhaustive evaluation of the sparser covariance matrix for high dimensions should be considered while introducing the new block-wise covariance learning with very high efficiency. On the other hand, a real problem in high and ultra-high dimensions with imbalanced classes from several domains can be consider.

Acknowledgments. We would like to thanks VLIR (Vlaamse Inter Universitaire Raad, Flemish Interuniversity Council, Belgium) for supporting this work under the project Cuban ICT NETWORK programe: "Strengthening the ICT role in Cuban Universities for the development of the society"; specifically to Project 1: "Strengthening the research on ICT and its knowledge transference to the Cuban society (RESICT)" and also to the Cuban national project "Plataforma para el análisis de grandes volúmenes de datos y su aplicación a sectores estratégicos".

References

1. Blagus, R., Lusa, L.: SMOTE for high-dimensional class-imbalanced data. BMC Bioinform. **14**, 106 (2013). https://doi.org/10.1186/1471-2105-14-106
2. Chawla, N.V., Bowyer, K.W., Hall, L.O., Kegelmeyer, W.P.: SMOTE: synthetic minority over-sampling technique. J. Artif. Intell. Res. **16**, 321–357 (2002)
3. Chen, Y., Wiesel, A., Hero, A.O.: Shrinkage estimation of high dimensional covariance matrices. In: 2009 IEEE International Conference on Acoustics, Speech and Signal Processing, pp. 2937–2940. IEEE (2009)
4. Clemmensen, L., Hastie, T., Witten, D., Ersbøll, B.: Sparse discriminant analysis. Technometrics **53**(4), 406–413 (2011)
5. Fernández, A., Garcia, S., Herrera, F., Chawla, N.V.: SMOTE for learning from imbalanced data: progress and challenges, marking the 15-year anniversary. J. Artif. Intell. Res. **61**, 863–905 (2018)
6. Han, H., Wang, W.-Y., Mao, B.-H.: Borderline-SMOTE: a new over-sampling method in imbalanced data sets learning. In: Huang, D.-S., Zhang, X.-P., Huang, G.-B. (eds.) ICIC 2005. LNCS, vol. 3644, pp. 878–887. Springer, Heidelberg (2005). https://doi.org/10.1007/11538059_91
7. He, H., Bai, Y., Garcia, E.A., Li, S.: ADASYN: adaptive synthetic sampling approach for imbalanced learning. In: 2008 IEEE International Joint Conference on Neural Networks (IEEE World Congress on Computational Intelligence), pp. 1322–1328. IEEE (2008)
8. He, H., Garcia, E.A.: Learning from imbalanced data. IEEE Trans. Knowl. Data Eng. **21**(9), 1263–1284 (2009)
9. Hsieh, C.-J., Sustik, M.A., Dhillon, I.S., Ravikumar, P.K., Poldrack, R.: BIG & QUIC: sparse inverse covariance estimation for a million variables. In: Advances in Neural Information Processing Systems, vol. 26 (2013)
10. Ledoit, O., Wolf, M.: Honey, i shrunk the sample covariance matrix. UPF Economics and Business Working Paper (691) (2003)
11. Ledoit, O., Wolf, M.: A well-conditioned estimator for large-dimensional covariance matrices. J. Multivar. Anal. **88**(2), 365–411 (2004)
12. Ledoit, O., Wolf, M.: The power of (non-) linear shrinking: a review and guide to covariance matrix estimation. J. Financ. Economet. **20**(1), 187–218 (2022)
13. Leguen-deVarona, I., Madera, J., Martínez-López, Y., Hernández-Nieto, J.C.: SMOTE-Cov: a new oversampling method based on the covariance matrix. In: Vasant, P., Litvinchev, I., Marmolejo-Saucedo, J.A., Rodriguez-Aguilar, R., Martinez-Rios, F. (eds.) Data Analysis and Optimization for Engineering and Computing

Problems. EICC, pp. 207–215. Springer, Cham (2020). https://doi.org/10.1007/978-3-030-48149-0_15
14. Lotfi, R., Shahsavani, D., Arashi, M.: Classification in high dimension using the Ledoit-Wolf shrinkage method. Mathematics **10**(21), 4069 (2022)
15. López, V., Fernández, A., García, S., Palade, V., Herrera, F.: An insight into classification with imbalanced data: empirical results and current trends on using data intrinsic characteristics. Inf. Sci. **250**, 113–141 (2013)
16. Nekooeimehr, I., Lai-Yuen, S.K.: Adaptive semi-unsupervised weighted oversampling (A-SUWO) for imbalanced datasets. Expert Syst. Appl. **46**, 405–416 (2016)
17. Li, M., Wan, Q., Deng, X., Yang, H.: Synthetic minority oversampling technique based on sample density distribution for enhanced classification on imbalanced microarray data. In: ICCDA (2022)
18. Ramentol, E., Caballero, Y., Bello, R., Herrera, F.: SMOTE-RSB*: a hybrid preprocessing approach based on oversampling and undersampling for high imbalanced data-sets using SMOTE and rough sets theory. Knowl. Inf. Syst. **33**, 245–265 (2012). https://doi.org/10.1007/s10115-011-0465-6
19. Fernandez, A., Maldonado, S., Vairetti, C., Herrera, F.: FW-SMOTE: a feature-weighted oversampling approach for imbalanced classification. Pattern Recogn. **124**, 108511 (2022)
20. López, J., Maldonado, S., Vairetti, C.: An alternative SMOTE oversampling strategy for high-dimensional datasets. Appl. Soft Comput. J. **76**, 380–389 (2019)
21. Sharma, S., Gosain, A., Jain, S.: A review of the oversampling techniques in class imbalance problem. In: Khanna, A., Gupta, D., Bhattacharyya, S., Hassanien, A.E., Anand, S., Jaiswal, A. (eds.) International Conference on Innovative Computing and Communications. AISC, vol. 1387, pp. 459–472. Springer, Singapore (2022). https://doi.org/10.1007/978-981-16-2594-7_38
22. Saadatfar, H., Mayabadi, S.: Two density-based sampling approaches for imbalanced and overlapping data. Knowl.-Based Syst. **241**, 108217 (2022)
23. Wei, G., Weimeng, M., Song, Y., Dou, J.: An improved and random synthetic minority oversampling technique for imbalanced data. Knowl.-Based Syst. **248**, 108839 (2022)

Multivariate Cuban Consumer Price Index Database, Statistic Analysis and Forecast Baseline Based on Vector Autoregressive

Reynaldo Rosado, Héctor González Diéz(✉), Orlando Grabiel Toledano-López, and Yanio Hernández Heredia

Universidad de las Ciencias Informaticas (UCI), La Habana, Cuba
{rrosado,hglez,ogtoledano,yhernandezh}@uci.cu

Abstract. The global Consumer Price Index (CPI) is a monthly multivariate time series, which allows measuring the variation of the final consumer prices of a given set of goods and services of households living in a given geographic region, city or country. The present work addresses the problem of the multivariate time series database of Cuba's CPI and a respective forecasting model based on Vector Autoregressive to establish a baseline for this dataset. An statistical analysis of the data will allow characterizing each variable of the series in terms of relevance to the multivariate problem, its causal relationships and the respective stationary analysis to evaluate the best lag to be considered in the forecasting model. The main statistics evidences of each test were reported in the paper as starting point for futures researches in the field of deep learning.

Keywords: Consumer Price Index · Multivariate Time Series Forecasting · Vector Autoregression

1 Introduction

The Consumer Price Index (CPI) is a measure of the average change over time in the prices paid by urban consumers for a market basket of consumer goods and services. The CPI is a widely indicator of inflation, and is managed, in Cuba, by the Government of the National office of the Statistic and Information (ONEI) and by similar organizations and institutes in other countries. The CPI is systematically way taken as a reference for decision-making regarding monetary policies by governments and financial entities. It is also used for various aspects of social finance, such as retirement, unemployment and government financing [25]. The CPI is typically calculated using a Laspeyres index formula [5], which holds the basket of goods and services constant over time. However, the ONEI also calculates a multivariate CPI, which accounts for changes in the quality of goods and services over time. This is done using a hedonic regression model, which estimates the value of different product characteristics (such as Food and Drinks, Health, Houses, Transportation, among others) and adjusts prices accordingly [18,24].

Y. Hernndez Heredia et al. (Eds.): IWAIPR 2023, LNCS 14335, pp. 24–34, 2024.
https://doi.org/10.1007/978-3-031-49552-6_3

The multivariate CPI is generally considered to be a more accurate measure of inflation than the traditional CPI, as it better accounts for changes in quality. However, it is also more complex to model by the relevance of the goods and service (normally need to define the weight manually by experts). The multivariate CPI accounts for changes in the quality of goods and services over time, whereas the univariate CPI assumes that the quality of the basket of goods and services remains constant. This means that the multivariate CPI provides a more accurate measure of inflation, since it adjusts for changes in quality and captures the true cost of living. The work [15] provides an overview of identification problems in macroeconomics, including those related to constructing price indexes and the main advantage of the multivariate approach.

In the case of Cuba, the weighting reflects the data obtained in the National Survey of Household Income and Expenditures (ENIGH), which was conducted between August 2009 and February 2010. The weights of goods and services are therefore based on the consumption expenditures that households have access to at that time. The goods and services that affect Cuba's CPI are: 01 Food and non-alcoholic beverages; 02 Alcoholic beverages and tobacco; 03 Clothing; 04 Housing services; 05 Furniture and household items; 06 Health; 07 Transportation; 08 Communications; 09 Recreation and culture; 10 Education; 11 Restaurants and hotels; 12 Miscellaneous personal care goods and services [6].

The Monthly Publication of the CPI from the National Office of Statistics and Information (ONEI), allows to know the average variation experienced by the prices of a basket of goods and services, representative of the consumption of the population in a given period. Approximately 33 596 prices are collected monthly, in 8 607 establishments, located in 18 municipalities throughout Cuba, the urban area of the head municipalities of 14 provinces and 4 municipalities of Havana province, obtaining national coverage. This means that the index to be shown is only representative of the country; it does not exist at the level of regions or municipalities. The basket of goods and services includes 298 items that represent more than 90.0% of household expenditure. The data are published in the form of reports in pdf format, which makes it difficult to process and analyse them because there is no integrated view of the database [18].

Both the prices of the products and services that give origin to the CPI estimate, as well as the CPI itself, are calculated systematically, so they are time series data type. As CPI forecast helps to estimate future trends, it is key for decision making. Moreover, it allows the application of price stabilization policies to reduce the economic impact on the prices of products and services demanded by consumers. In those economies that present instability, CPI data fluctuate over time, which translates into a non-linear and non-stationary behaviour [19].

In general, several approaches in the CPI forecasting field, modelling the problem as a univariate time series, concentrating only on the study of the global indicator. Approaching it as a multivariate problem, taking into account the variation of the prices of each goods or service included in the basket, is not very well treated since the global index is composed of the weighted aggregation of the prices to each products. The most widely used statistical method for forecasting the CPI as a univariate time series problem has been the family of the Autoregressive models [2,7,9,14,16,17]. Recently, deep learning techniques for time series forecasting have improved the performance of CPI prediction. Recurrent Neural Networks (RNN) or Long Short-Term Memory (LSTM) architectures have the ability to capture time dependence in data, while handling more than one output variable to estimate more than one time instant. Three examples that show good performance with simple LSTM [25] model and temporal data at different time intervals are from Mexico [11], Ecuador [20,21] and Indonesia [13]. In spite of the prominent performance of RNN models for time series forecasting, particularly for financial series, they have been studied on the basis of autoregressive models such as VAR. This is due to the limited availability of data in this scenario which is also reflected in the CPI as described in the previously works.

The aim of this paper are to propose a new multivariate time series database of Cuba's monthly CPI and a respective forecasting model based on Vector Autoregressive model as a baseline follow the statistics methodologies of analysis. A statistical analysis of the data will allow characterizing each variable of the series in terms of relevance to the multivariate problem, its causal relationships and the respective stationary analysis to evaluate the best lag to be considered in the forecasting model.

2 Multivariate Analysis

2.1 Definitions and Notation

A multivariate time series is defined as a collection of the multiples variables spatially related and individually shows a temporal relationship. Classical statistical or machine learning models need to consider the univariate or multivariate problem differently, however deep learning models can handle both indistinctly with high accuracy. Time series are usually characterized by three components: trend, seasonality and residuals [23]. In real-world time series and, in particular the CPI problem, seasonality can be affected by external agents such as the economic and financial crisis, prices of the main products in the world market, and emerging situations such as the COVID-19 pandemic.

In a more formal definition of the Multivariate Time Series we have m variables or observations, each of which has a time series. These variables are correlated in a way that the value of them at time t is related to the temporal window of size p previous values of all other variables including its own past values. We can represent each forecast in the set of variables at time t as a linear combination:

$$\begin{aligned} \hat{y}_t^1 &= w_0^1 + w_{11}^1 y_{t-1}^1 + \dots w_{m1}^1 y_{t-1}^m \\ &+ \dots w_{1p}^1 y_{t-p}^1 + \dots w_{mp}^1 y_{t-p}^m + \epsilon_t^1 \\ &\vdots \\ \hat{y}_t^m &= w_0^m + w_{11}^m y_{t-1}^1 + \dots w_{m1}^m y_{t-1}^m \\ &+ \dots w_{1p}^m y_{t-p}^m + \dots w_{mp}^m y_{t-p}^m + \epsilon_t^m \end{aligned} \tag{1}$$

Finally, the corresponding time series forecasting problem consists of the estimating a predictor $F : \mathbb{R}^{(m+1)} \times \mathbb{R}^m \times \mathbb{R}^p \to \mathbb{R}$ in such a way that the expected deviation between true and predicted outputs is minimized for all possible inputs. The model associated with the Eq. (1) is to known as Vector of Auto-Regression (VAR). In the context of the CPI, this scenario makes it possible to forecast the price of goods and services that contribute to the overall or general CPI.

2.2 Statistical Analysis in Multivariate CPI.

Granger's Causality Test
The Granger causality test [8] is a statistical hypothesis test used to determine whether one time series is useful in forecasting another time series. The test is based on the idea that if a time series x "Granger-causes" another time series y, then past values of x should contain information that helps predict future values of y, beyond what can be predicted using past values of y alone.

The Granger causality test is commonly used in econometrics, finance, and other fields to investigate causal relationships between time series. Several applications in the multivariate CPI can be found in recently researches [1,10,12,22].

It is also worth noting that the Granger causality test assumes that the time series are stationary, so it is often preceded by a test for stationarity such as the Augmented Dickey-Fuller (ADF) test. Additionally, the test is sensitive to the choice of lag length and model specification, so it is important to carefully choose these parameters based on the data and the research question at hand.

Augmented Dickey-Fuller Test
The multivariate Augmented Dickey-Fuller (ADF) test is an extension of the standard ADF test that allows for multiple time series to be analysed simultaneously, taking into account possible relationships between them.The multivariate ADF test involves estimating a vector autoregressive (VAR) model for the set of time series and testing for the presence of unit roots in the model. Test examines whether the residuals of VAR model are stationary, which is equivalent to testing for stationarity of each individual time series after controlling for the other time series in the model [4].

The multivariate ADF test is useful in identifying whether a set of time series are stationary in a joint sense, which can be important for modelling and forecasting purposes. For example, if a set of economic variables are jointly non-stationary, it may be difficult to develop accurate forecasting models that account for the interrelationships between variables. It is important to note that the multivariate ADF test has some limitations and assumptions. For example, it assumes that the VAR model is correctly specified and that the residuals are normally distributed and free from serial correlation. Additionally, the test can be sensitive to the lag length of the VAR model and the number of variables included in the model [3]. Therefore, it is important to carefully select the appropriate model specification based on the data and the research question at hand.

3 Results and Discussion

3.1 Exploratory Analysis and Dataset

The Cuban Consumer Price Index database was collected from the official website National Office of the Statistic and Information ONEI [18]. This is a monthly time series from January 2010 to December 2020 with very low variability in the data as we can show in Table 1.

Table 1. Characteristic of the Cuban Consumer Price Index dataset.

	Overall	ABNA	BAT	PBC	SV	MAH	S	T	C	RC	E	RH	BSD
count	120.00	120.00	120.00	120.00	120.00	120.00	120.00	120.00	120.00	120.00	120.00	120.00	120.00
mean	103.35	109.74	101.02	91.88	101.65	102.90	107.92	105.41	81.66	99.91	100.69	104.15	105.36
std	1.37	4.35	1.33	4.07	0.96	0.87	1.47	2.35	5.08	0.86	0.95	1.95	1.20
min	100.12	99.66	92.32	77.32	99.57	100.79	100.04	100.93	72.40	95.64	99.46	100.09	99.93
25%	102.66	107.28	100.18	88.58	101.12	102.12	108.41	103.74	78.93	99.26	99.96	102.49	105.52
50%	103.15	109.58	100.32	91.52	101.70	102.79	108.41	104.49	80.03	99.59	100.53	104.80	105.68
75%	103.88	111.66	101.94	95.17	101.94	103.67	108.46	107.85	80.46	100.67	100.93	105.22	105.80
max	109.50	126.54	104.76	100.59	106.07	104.34	108.48	109.92	100.00	101.72	104.51	111.32	107.63

LEGEND

ABNA: Food and non-alcoholic beverages
BAT: Alcoholic beverages and tobacco
PBC: Clothing
SV: Housing services
MAH: Furniture and household items
S: Health
T: Transportation
C: Communications
RC: Recreation and cultur
E: Education
RH: Restaurants and hotels
BSD: Miscellaneous personal care goods and services

The values are the overall averages of the Cuban CPI for 11 category groupings and almost 298 goods and services. It is necessary to clarify that the data sets in the context of the CPI are very short series where learning models that require a lot of data are not effective in this context. Under these conditions we have modelling an appropriated problem as a time series forecasting. The Fig. 1 show the trends of the series and seasonality for each category (dashed line) respect to the overall.

3.2 Statistics Analysis

Overall, Granger's causality test is a useful tool for analysing causality between two time series, but it should be used in conjunction with other methods and careful interpretation of the results. The results of the Granger causality test involves assessing the statistical evidence for causality, determining the direction of causality, assessing the strength of causality, and considering the context and theoretical implications of the result. It is important to be cautious in interpreting Granger causality results and to consider other evidence and methods when assessing causality in time series data.

The null hypothesis is that the past values of x do not help in predicting y, while the alternative hypothesis is that the past values of x do help in predicting y. In Fig. 2 we can show that series like Transportation and Food and Non Alcohol Drinks have very low predictive power respect to another series. Also, this two series have similar causality relation respect to General CPI.

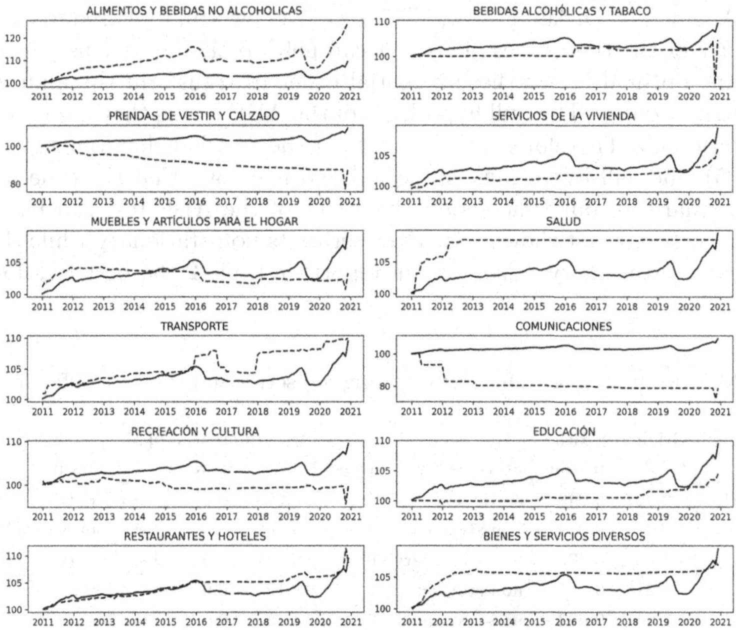

Fig. 1. Cuba CPI 2010–2021 by categories.

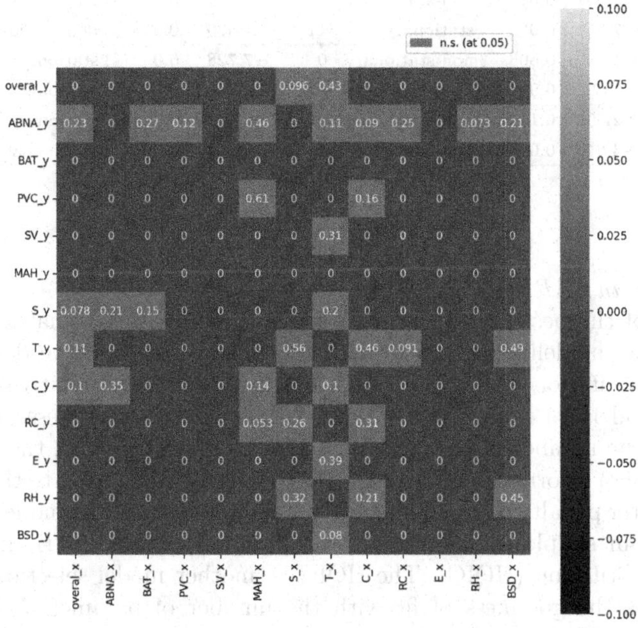

Fig. 2. Test the Granger to causality analysis in the Multivariate CPI.

The Augmented Dickey-Fuller (ADF) test is a powerful tool used to check the stationarity of the time series. This test can help to choose various parameters such as the optimal lag or the differential order to transform the multivariate series into stationary. The null hypothesis of the ADF test is that the time series is non-stationary. Therefore, if the p-value of the test is below the significance level (0.05), the null hypothesis is rejected and it follows that the time series is truly stationary. In our time series, the result of the ADF test can be find in Table 2. The test result showing that the series its non-stationary while the first differential its stationary. Also, we can report in Table 2 the best lags for each series.

Table 2. Multivariate ADF Test over original series and the first differential.

Series	Original Series				First differential of the Series			
	F-fuller	p-value	Stationarity	Lags	F-fuller	p-value	Stationarity	Lags
OVERALL	−2.867	0.049	stationary	1	−6.594	0.0	stationary	0
ABNA	−2.67	0.079	non-stationary	1	−5.402	0.0	stationary	0
BAT	−1.614	0.476	non-stationary	0	−8.457	0.0	stationary	1
PVC	−1.316	0.622	non-stationary	2	−8.123	0.0	stationary	1
SV	−2.841	0.053	non-stationary	3	−4.482	0.0	stationary	2
MAH	−1.533	0.517	non-stationary	2	−7.046	0.0	stationary	1
S	−3.631	0.005	stationary	5	−3.787	0.003	stationary	12
T	−1.531	0.518	non-stationary	0	−8.801	0.0	stationary	0
C	−7.551	0.0	stationary	11	−1.539	0.514	non-stationary	11
RC	−1.56	0.503	non-stationary	0	−7.728	0.0	stationary	1
E	1.047	0.995	non-stationary	1	−11.694	0.0	stationary	0
RH	−2.506	0.114	non-stationary	2	−8.607	0.0	stationary	1
BSD	−4.643	0.0	stationary	11	−3.783	0.003	stationary	12

Lag Selection in VAR

The choice of the best metric for lag selection in time series analysis depends on the specific modelling approach and the characteristics of the data. Akaike Information Criterion (AIC): The AIC is a measure of the relative quality of statistical models for a given set of data. It balances the goodness of fit of the model with the number of parameters used. The lower the AIC, the better the model. Bayesian Information Criterion (BIC): The BIC is similar to the AIC but places a greater penalty on the number of parameters used in the model. The BIC tends to favour simpler models with fewer parameters. Finally, Hannan-Quinn Information Criterion (HQIC): The HQIC is another model selection criterion that balances the goodness of fit with the number of parameters used. It is similar to the AIC, but it places a greater penalty on the number of parameters than the AIC [4].

In Table 3 the AIC metric drops to lowest at lag 5, then continue with instability at lag 6 and then continuously drops further.

Table 3. Lags selection in vector autoregressive.

Lag	Original Series			First differential of the Series		
	AIC	BIC	HQIC	AIC	BIC	HQIC
Lag Order = 1	−41.0	−36.11	−39.02	−40.55	−35.63	−38.56
Lag Order = 2	−44.76	−35.27	−40.93	−43.24	−33.68	−39.38
Lag Order = 3	−46.21	−32.05	−40.5	−43.78	−29.52	−38.02
Lag Order = 4	−48.29	−29.41	−40.67	−44.92	−25.91	−37.25
Lag Order = 5	−54.73	−31.05	−45.18	−51.95	−28.12	−42.34
Lag Order = 7	−726.14	−692.7	−712.66	−843.13	−809.46	−829.56
Lag Order = 8	−740.28	−701.85	−724.8	−864.16	−825.47	−848.58
Lag Order = 9	−737.67	−694.19	−720.17	−866.59	−822.81	−848.97

Forecasting Measures
As in other similar papers, we use the most common metrics for CPI time series forecasting. The Root Mean Squared Error (RMSE), Mean absolute Error(MAE), Mean absolute Percentage Error(MAPE) among others metrics were report in Table 4. It's important to note that no single metric is universally better than the others, and the choice of metric depends on the specific problem being solved and the context in which the forecasting is being applied. For example, in some cases, minimizing the overall error (as measured by MSE) may be more important than accurately predicting individual values (as measured

Table 4. Report of the forecasting metrics applied to the performance of the VAR method.

	MAPE	ME	MAE	MPE	RMSE	CORR	MinMax
Overall	0.014	−0.718	1.493	−0.007	1.922	0.655	0.014
ABNA	0.037	−1.588	4.343	−0.012	5.476	0.646	0.037
BAT	0.008	0.407	0.783	0.004	2.175	−0.092	0.008
PVC	0.012	−0.281	0.979	−0.003	1.895	0.452	0.011
SV	0.007	−0.707	0.707	−0.007	1.074	0.878	0.007
MAH	0.002	0.043	0.174	0.0	0.368	0.123	0.002
S	0.005	0.562	0.568	0.005	0.695	NAN	0.005
T	0.003	−0.114	0.371	−0.001	0.432	0.924	0.003
C	0.028	−2.046	2.223	−0.026	2.568	0.319	0.028
RC	0.004	−0.041	0.39	−0.0	0.788	0.264	0.004
E	0.005	−0.498	0.524	−0.005	0.823	0.883	0.005
RH	0.006	−0.694	0.694	−0.006	1.207	0.576	0.006
BSD	0.002	0.132	0.229	0.001	0.311	0.752	0.002

by MAE or RMSE). Conversely, in other cases, accurately predicting individual values may be more important than minimizing overall error, such as in financial forecasting.

In general the overall performance of the multivariate Cuba CPI show very good adjust in the test set (the last two years) with the mean MAPE in the very low order of the 1.4% in the general CPI. The Fig. 3 we have the forecast results over test set considered in this analysis as a baseline for futures research.

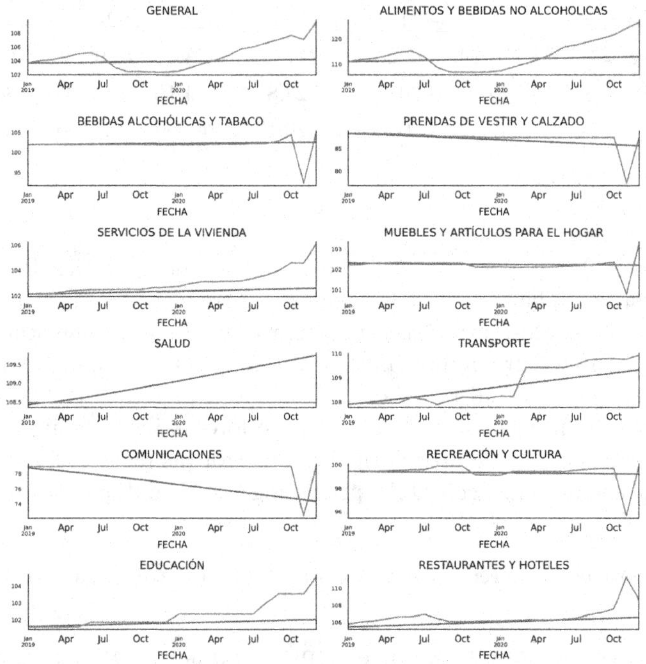

Fig. 3. Forecast over last two years of the Multivariate Cuba CPI.

4 Concluding Remarks and Further Work

A new dataset has been proposed for the CPI study in Cuba with a multivariate approach of which there are no references of previous researches in the field of forecasting. In this sense, this work has followed a standard statistical analysis methodology that has allowed establishing a baseline in terms of the VAR models, being these methods, reported in the literature as the starting point in the Multivariate CPI problem. Additionally, statistical tests for the study of the causality have been performed, showing in general strong relationships between the main components of the dataset. Likewise, the ADF test to study stationarity showed that the first differential of the series avoided stationarity with an 95% of the significance.

Future work is being planned in several directions with a view to extending this contribution. On the one hand, work is being done on an in-depth study of deep learning methods based on RNN and auto-encoder models to improve forecasting metrics and take advantage of the capabilities of the DL to handle non-linearity in the feature engineering. In another direction, variable selection should be exploited to achieve learning schemes with greater generalization.

Acknowledgement. This work has been partially funded by FONCI through project: Plataforma para el anélisis de grandes volúmenes de datos y su aplicación a sectores estratégicos.

References

1. Akin, A.C., Cevrimli, M.B., Arikan, M.S., Tekindal, M.A.: Determination of the causal relationship between beef prices and the consumer price index in turkey. Turk. J. Vet. Anim. Sci. **43**(3), 353–358 (2019)
2. Banerjee, A.: Forecasting price levels in India-an Arima framework. Acad. Mark. Stud. J. **25**(1), 1–15 (2021)
3. Cheung, Y.-W., Lai, K.S.: Lag order and critical values of the augmented dickey-fuller test. J. Bus. Econ. Stat. **13**(3), 277–280 (1995)
4. Cromwell, J.B.: Multivariate Tests for Time Series Models. Number 100. Sage (1994)
5. Diewert, W.E.: Index number issues in the consumer price index. J. Econ. Perspect. **12**(1), 47–58 (1998)
6. García Molina, J.M.: La economía cubana a inicios del siglo XXI: desafíos y oportunidades de la globalización. CEPAL (2005)
7. Ghazo, A., et al.: Applying the ARIMA model to the process of forecasting GDP and CPI in the Jordanian economy. Int. J. Financ. Res. **12**(3), 70 (2021)
8. Granger, C.W.J.: Investigating causal relations by econometric models and cross-spectral methods. Econom.: J. Econom. Soc. 424–438 (1969)
9. Jere, S., Banda, A., Chilyabanyama, R., Moyo, E., et al.: Modeling consumer price index in Zambia: a comparative study between multicointegration and ARIMA approach. Open J. Stat. **9**(02), 245 (2019)
10. Korkmaz, S., Abdullazade, M.: The causal relationship between unemployment and inflation in g6 countries. Adv. Econ. Bus. **8**(5), 303–309 (2020)
11. Anaya, L.M.L., Moreno, V.M.L., Aguirre, H.R.O., López, M.Q.: Predicción del ipc mexicano combinando modelos econométricos e inteligencia artificial. Rev. Mexicana Econ. Finanzas **13**(4), 603–629 (2018)
12. Mallick, L., Behera, S.R., Dash, D.P.: Does CPI granger cause WPI? Empirical evidence from threshold cointegration and spectral granger causality approach in India. J. Dev. Areas **54**(2) (2020)
13. Manik, D.P., et al.: A strategy to create daily consumer price index by using big data in statistics Indonesia. In: 2015 International Conference on Information Technology Systems and Innovation (ICITSI), pp. 1–5. IEEE (2015)
14. Mohamed, J.: Time series modeling and forecasting of Somaliland consumer price index: a comparison of ARIMA and regression with ARIMA errors. Am. J. Theor. Appl. Stat. **9**(4), 143–53 (2020)
15. Nakamura, E., Steinsson, J.: Identification in macroeconomics. J. Econ. Perspect. **32**(3), 59–86 (2018)

16. Nyoni, T.: Modeling and forecasting inflation in Kenya: Recent insights from ARIMA and GARCH analysis. Dimorian Rev. **5**(6), 16–40 (2018)
17. Nyoni, T.: ARIMA modeling and forecasting of consumer price index (CPI) in Germany (2019)
18. ONEI. Índice de precios al consumidor base diciembre 2010 (2022)
19. Qin, X., Sun, M., Dong, X., Zhang, Y.: Forecasting of china consumer price index based on EEMD and SVR method. In: 2018 2nd International Conference on Data Science and Business Analytics (ICDSBA), pp. 329–333. IEEE (2018)
20. Riofrío, J., Chang, O., Revelo-Fuelagán, E.J., Peluffo-Ordóñez, D.H.: Forecasting the consumer price index (CPI) of Ecuador: a comparative study of predictive models. Int. J. Adv. Sci. Eng. Inf. Technol. **10**(3), 1078–1084 (2020)
21. Rosado, R., Abreu, A.J., Arencibia, J.C., Gonzalez, H., Hernandez, Y.: Consumer price index forecasting based on univariate time series and a deep neural network. In: Hernández Heredia, Y., Milián Núñez, V., Ruiz Shulcloper, J. (eds.) IWAIPR 2021. LNCS, vol. 13055, pp. 33–42. Springer, Cham (2021). https://doi.org/10.1007/978-3-030-89691-1_4
22. Sünbül, E.: Linear and nonlinear relationship between real exchange rate, real interest rate and consumer price index: an empirical application for countries with different levels of development. Sci. Ann. Econ. Bus. **70**(1), 57–70 (2023)
23. Torres, J.F., Hadjout, D., Sebaa, A., Martinez-Alvarez, F., Troncoso, A.: Deep learning for time series forecasting: a survey. Big Data **9**(1), 3–21 (2021)
24. Triplett, J.: Handbook on Hedonic Indexes and Quality Adjustments in Price Indexes: Special Application to Information Technology Products (2004)
25. Zahara, S., Ilmiddaviq, M.B., et al.: Consumer price index prediction using long short term memory (LSTM) based cloud computing. J. Phys.: Conf. Ser. **1456**, 012022 (2020)

Climatic Factors that Impact the Consumption Patterns Tame of Water. A Case of Study

Mario Ramos Joseph[1(✉)], Alcides J. León Méndez[2], Raisa Socorro Llanes[2], Reniel Carvajal Alfonso[1], and Carlos M. González Ramírez[3]

[1] Aguas de La Habana, La Habana, Cuba
mramos@ahabana.co.cu
[2] Cujae, La Habana, Cuba
[3] INSMET, La Habana, Cuba

Abstract. In our days, climatic change is a **novel** factor that impels the appearance of extreme events associated with such changes. Among the various undesirable effects, droughts impose conditions of hydric stress more and more frequently to numerous supply systems. This scenario has created favorable conditions for the application of data mining techniques as a powerful tool that allows us to interpret and accurately forecasting the current and future scenarios. This study aims at recognizing the main climatic and bioclimatic factors that play a role in the domestic demand for water and its relative weight through the application of data mining techniques. Starting from a sample of clients within a sector of Aguas de la Habana the domestic consumptions were contrasted based on climatic and bioclimatic variables. The analysis spans a period from 1 January 2008 through 31 December 2020. Applying techniques for selection of variables satisfactory results are obtained that allow defining those variables having a higher impact on consumption.

Keywords: consumption domestic · bioclimatic variable · mining of data

1 Introduction

At present, numerous studies and research lines are conducted targeting the conservation of natural resources, among these the ones related to water, which have great influence, being this, the most important resource for the survival and human wellbeing, as well as for many sectors of the economy. Due to the world population's increase, the appearance of continuous extreme events associated with climatic change has raised the consumption of this valuable liquid to significant levels as stated by Lizcano et al. (2022).

Today it is self-evident that water demand is increasing and its sources are diminishing, accordingly, evidence shows that there is a shortage and although 70% of the planet is covered with water, only 2.5% of it is drinking water, and out of this figure access for human use accounts for less than 1% according to Morote (2017); Adamowski et al. (2012).

Y. Hernández Heredia et al. (Eds.): IWAIPR 2023, LNCS 14335, pp. 35–47, 2024.
https://doi.org/10.1007/978-3-031-49552-6_4

Many countries face the problem of the increased demand for water, accompanied by a shortage of water resources. Specifically, developing countries operate inefficient distribution systems with losses of water and significant billing. Factors that impact on this situation as: deteriorated infrastructure, high pressures, intermittent service, measuring errors, illegal use, operations and inefficient management practices according to Ramos Joseph and León Méndez (2016); Haque et al. (2015).

The key to developing a strategy for the reduction of losses of water is to obtain a better understanding of the reasons for these losses and the factors that have an incidence on them. Each technique and procedure that may be delivered should be adapted to the specific characteristics of the network and factors of local influence, to tackle with each of the causes on a priority order. Among the losses of water, it is important the management or knowledge of consumption patterns because they are fundamental tools for the operation, planning, design and forecast and conformation of future demand.

The patterns of water consumption are distributed irregularly in space and in time. They are affected by diverse variables that can be socioeconomic, climatic, geographic location, and technologic.

Waters of Havana is the company that manages water supply for the 15 municipalities of the capital, and it also deals with a large volume of water losses. According to their estimates, this volume reaches levels of 333.2 annual cubic hectometers.

This study focuses on determining the main climatic and bioclimatic factors that play a role in the domestic water demand and its relative weight employing the application of data mining techniques.

2 Background

The consumption of water can be affected by several causes, most of the previous studies on the topic were mainly conducted in developed countries such. In these studies different classifications are used, among which sociodemographic, economic or political-economic, climatic, technological, town planning, and psychological causes prevailed.

Another new analysis approach recently stated highlights the existence of consumption levels based on social status, as underscored by (Morales and Gori, 2021).

Among the topics of consumption patterns and as part of the multiple variables that intervene actively in domestic consumption according to Soto-Montes and Herrera-Pantoja (2016), climatic variability becomes more and more important, entailing the monitoring of scholars and scientists given the current link with climatic change. A brief analysis of some of the main studies conducted on the topic shows the following outputs.

House-Peters et al. (2010) based on a study conducted in the city of Hillsboro, Oregon, in the Portland metropolitan area. The study concluded that the characteristics of the physical properties and socioeconomic variables have an impact on water demand and this relationship varies depending on the season of the year and the average precipitation.

Sarker et al. (2013) conducted a study in Greater Melbourne (Australia) on the threshold values of temperature and rainfall at which there is an effect on water consumption. Using a series of daily data on water consumption, temperature, and rainfall for 30 years (1980 to 2009), it can be concluded from their analysis that the limiting value of temperature for which there was an effect on water consumption was 15.53 °C, showing that water use increases with increasing temperature and for temperature values below the limiting value there was no influence. For rainfall, the limit value was 4.08 mm, and it was observed that for precipitation values below the above-mentioned, water use increases as precipitation decreases.

Haque et al. 2015 present a study conducted in New South Wales, Australia, a region characterized by average maximum temperatures of 12 °C and 22 °C during the winter and summer seasons respectively, based on a 15-year data series (1997 to 2011), through Principal Component Analysis. From this study it was found that monthly average maximum temperature and rainfall have a low correlation with monthly water consumption per dwelling, being positive for temperature and negative for rainfall. Temperature was the variable with the greatest effect compared to rainfall, indicating an increase in demand with an increase in rainfall.

A study was conducted in Sweden (Brandner, 2016) to determine, among several factors, the influence of climatic factors on water consumption in different regions of that country. In this work, a simple linear regression analysis model was used for the three municipal areas studied. The results indicate that water consumption tends to increase with increasing temperature. For each of the three areas, the increase in water demand is, respectively, 5.5%, 1 to 2%, and 2 to 12% for each 2 °C rise in temperature for a 12 °C limit. It is observed that for the last municipality, the area studied is characterized by temperatures ranging from a minimum of −25 °C to a maximum of 25.9 °C and by the existence of houses for summer activities.

The study conducted by Soto-Montes and Herrera-Pantoja (2016) in Mexico City based on a regression analysis of a sample of 58 456 domestic consumers for the period from 2007 to 2013, it was found that the effects on water consumption are positively influenced by temperature and negatively influenced by precipitation. A 10% increase in temperature is associated with a 5% increase in domestic water consumption and a 10% increase in precipitation is associated with a 1.2% decrease in the amount demanded. The average annual temperature is 16.7 °C for the northern region and 11 °C in the south.

Another reading of the phenomenon is provided by Bich-Ngoc and Teller (2018) who in a literature review concluded that indoor water end uses do not vary regardless of climate and that most of the studies analyzed focus on arid and semi-arid climates leaving a knowledge gap in geographies, that the occurrence of rainfall causes an immediate decrease in average water consumptions. Meanwhile in Cuba, Guilherme et al. (2017) conducted a study that for the first time determines the relationship between domestic per capita consumption and climatic and bioclimatic variables. The study concluded that maximum relative humidity and maximum temperature alone affect per capita consumption with an increasing ratio in the order of 15.9% and 16.7% respectively. Per capita consumption increases with the increase of ET (Effective Temperature), in the order of 10.7%, Meanwhile, the EET (Equivalent effective temperature) affects per capita consumption positively in the order of 13.1%; in a simultaneous scenario with precipitation it causes an increase in consumption with the increase in EET and the decrease in precipitation with a variation ratio of consumption of 14.6%. This study concludes that the EET is the bioclimatic variable with the greatest impact on consumption.

According to experts from the Institute of Meteorology (INSMET), the Cuban archipelago has a seasonally humid tropical climate with maritime influence and semi-continental features, and high solar radiation throughout the year, in addition to the seasonal influence of tropical and extra tropical weather phenomena. It has two well defined climatic seasons, a rainy season (May-October) that coincides with the summer and another one with little rain (November-April) that coincides with the winter stage. With this behavior, the EET analysis goes much further, since the human being has a great capacity to adapt to heterogeneous climates and environments, but is vulnerable to major changes in atmospheric conditions such as warmer or colder conditions.

Somewhat more recently, Pomares et al. (2022) in Aguas de La Habana, Cuba managed to apply data mining techniques to obtain a correlation coefficient of 29% to explain the relationship between domestic consumption and a group of climatic and bioclimatic variables.

For this purpose, the KNIME (Konstanz Information Miner) tool was used, a data mining environment that allows the development of models (Klenzi et al., (2018).

Applying this tool, Pomares et al. (2022) define consumption as the dependent variable and use 15 independent variables. The novelty here is the inclusion of ET, EET, and TA (Thermal Amplitude) as independent variables, in this case, 1 more than Guilherme et al. (2017).

Of the variants analyzed, the best result reported an adjusted R2 of 0.295. Of these variables analyzed, 4 of the 15 were determined to be the best fit to the model; these are TA, Maximum Relative Humidity (RH max.), ET, and the Rain Sheet (Rain) and they were predictor variables.

All these works and criteria constitute the necessary basis to be able to establish a more precise knowledge of the multilateral factors that determine domestic consumption. This knowledge can become an extraordinary tool for the characterization and forecasting of consumption in each supply system.

3 Materials and Methods

The work is framed within the study of the hydraulic sector called AB among the sectors managed by the company Aguas de La Habana.

This sector is located in one of the most populated municipalities of Havana. It presents metered connections with a consumption history since 2000; it is characterized by a very similar socioeconomic level; it is made up of houses of similar average typology; the existence of at least one bathroom and with the presence of a perimeter fence, with a low presence of single-family houses or predominance of multi-family houses.

It has a continuous service network, and all connections are metered, with a total of 159 customers. Of the total number of customers, there are 46 metered in single-family homes and 113 in multifamily homes, (Guilherme et al., 2017).

For the study of metered customers, we eliminated all those who for various reasons did not maintain the same conditions throughout the period in terms of quality of measurements, changes of use and ownership, replaced or broken meters during periods that made it very difficult to accurately determine their monthly record, after this purification we selected 34 customers who are those who make up the sample of the study using their monthly data and obtaining the average consumption of the 34 customers to reach a single average monthly value expressed in (lppm) liters per person per month.

The monthly consumption data of the 34 customers were provided by the company's Commercial Department, based on the consumption analysis carried out by the company to guarantee to bill based on metered records.

In the case of meteorological variables, the data were obtained from the daily records of the Casablanca Meteorological Station, which is part of the climatological network of the Institute of Meteorology (INSMET), and were transformed from their daily frequency to mean values for subsequent comparison with the average monthly consumption.

The Knime tool was used to process and analyze the information collected, as well as to obtain associations between the variables, based on mathematical and statistical criteria.

The study covers a period from January 1, 2008, to December 31, 2020, based on the objective set, consumption in (lppm) was defined as the dependent variable. Consumption was provided in cubic meters per month for each client or dwelling in the sample, and was transformed into liters per person per month (lppm) for each client, obtaining a monthly average for better analysis and comparison with similar studies in other latitudes; this monthly average during the 13 years covered by the study provides a total of 156 rows in the minable view. This consumption represents the volume of water consumed by a person in a month. The rest of the variables analyzed are described below as independent variables:

- Precipitation sheet (Rainfall): represents the amount of rainfall in a given area and is measured in mm with the help of a rain gauge at the weather station. It is obtained in the form of daily records and its monthly average was calculated.
- Occurrence of Rainfall (OcLl): this variable is obtained from the precipitation sheet records. It was transformed into a binary value. The 0 represents the absence of rain and 1 means that it rained, it is dimensionless. This variable was included as quantitative variable because, although it doesn't gather the actual values of rainfall, if it has a value and relative weight inside the pattern because it defines if it rained or it didn't rain, classifying as fictitious or dichotomic variable.
- Precipitation intensity (r 24h): represents the amount of water that pours or rains per unit of time and is expressed in millimeters per hour. It is obtained from daily records, which are transformed to obtain its average according to the time unit.
- Minimum (T min.), average (T med.), and maximum (T max.) temperatures: represents the historical records of atmospheric temperature measured with a thermometer at the meteorological station in °C. It is obtained in the form of daily records and is transformed by obtaining its average according to the time unit.
- Minimum relative humidity (RH min), average relative humidity (RH med), and maximum relative humidity (RH max): it is the ratio between the amount of water vapor contained in the air and the maximum amount that the air would be able to contain at that given temperature in percentage, expressed in %. It is obtained in the form of daily records and is transformed by obtaining its average as a function of the time unit.
- Average wind speed (FF med.) and maximum wind speed (FF max.): measures the horizontal component of wind displacement at a given point and time and is closely

related to wind chill. It is obtained in the form of daily records and is transformed by obtaining its average according to the proposed time unit kilometers per hour.

- Wind direction (DD max.): measures the horizontal component of wind speed expressed in sexagesimal degrees counted clockwise from geographic north using the Wind Rose headings. They were obtained in the form of daily records and were transformed by obtaining their average according to the proposed time unit.
- Relative Humidity Amplitude (HrA): it is the numerical difference between the maximum and minimum humidity values recorded at a given point during a period of time. The inclusion of this variable was conceived thanks to the contribution of INSMET experts; it is expressed in %.
- Effective Temperature (ET): is defined as the sensation experienced at a given temperature and humidity, with saturated and still air. It is valid for a young, healthy subject, acclimatized to the site, lightly dressed, and subjected to light activity. This variable is given in °C and is classified as a bioclimatic variable and is a novel contribution to the relationship between domestic consumption and climatological variables.
- Equivalent effective temperature (EET): is defined as the air temperature at which the human energy balance, for assumed indoor conditions, is balanced with the same skin temperatures and sweating rates as those calculated in open-air conditions. This variable is expressed in °C and, like the previous one; it is a bioclimatic variable as it incorporates the thermal sensations of human beings into the study.
- Thermal Amplitude (TA): represents the temperature differential present in the atmosphere, providing greater weight to its variability and highlighting anomalous behaviors of drastic fluctuations, it is expressed in °C. It is the numerical difference between the maximum and minimum temperature values observed at a given point during a period of time. The inclusion of this variable was conceived thanks to the contribution of INSMET experts, therefore, like the two previous ones, it is a bioclimatic variable.

Finally, a set of data is obtained that makes up the mineable view composed of 156 rows or records and 19 columns, disaggregated into 16 independent meteorological variables, 2 temporal variables, and 1 dependent variable.

It is important to recognize that the effective temperature, the equivalent temperature, and the thermal amplitude classify as bioclimatic variables obtained by the transformation of other variables. No references using this analysis have been found in the literature consulted, and this is a relevant aspect to be taken into account because of its impact on domestic consumption.

This section presents a proposal to determine the influence of climatic and bioclimatic variables on the prediction (forecast) or estimation of domestic consumption.

This is achieved by using variable selection techniques such as the progressive introduction of variables (forward) and the progressive elimination of variables (backward) during the process of estimating consumption, by comparing both methods, the variables having higher impact on consumption estimates are determined.

The consumption prediction model was performed using different regression techniques, of those described in Witten (2016) among which are, **RBF Regressor, Isotonic Regression, Linear Regression, Pace Regression, Additive Regression, Regression by discretization, Ensemble regressor and M5P**.

Figure 1 shows an example of the Knime flow used to perform forward variable selection using the RBF Regressor technique.

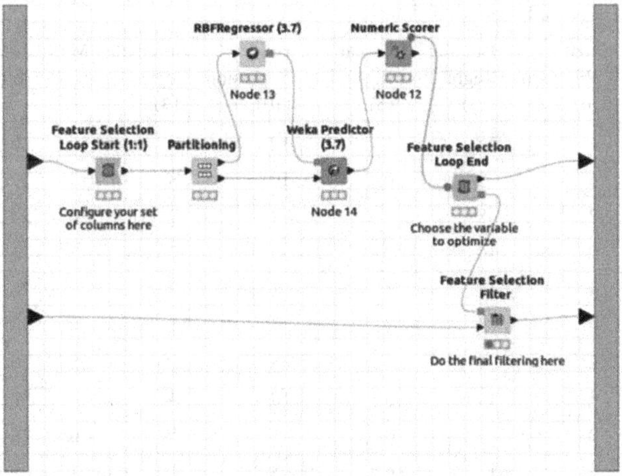

Fig. 1. Example of Knime flow for the forward with RBF regressor algorithm. Source: Own elaboration

Once the variable selection method has been executed, those scenarios with an adjusted r^2 value above 54.7% for the forward and 50% for the backward are selected. The frequencies of occurrence of the variables in each of the regression techniques analyzed are shown in Tables 1 and 3 respectively. In both tables, the number of scenarios in which each variable appears according to the technique applied is presented in columns. The total column quantifies the number of scenarios in which each variable appears and the percentage represents the total frequency of appearance of each variable concerning the total number of scenarios.

4 Results and Discussion

The models proposed in the previous section were applied to the data set described in the Study Area section. The models are built using 80% of the available data selected randomly and the remaining 20% is used to evaluate the quality of the model in each case. In these experiments, the adjusted r^2 was used to evaluate the quality of the estimate obtained by each of the models. In this case, only those combinations of variables (scenarios) are analyzed in which the prediction model built from them manages to predict with a value of r^2 equal to or greater than 54.7% for the forward and 50% for the backward, which guarantees that at least 50% of the values of the dependent variable respond to this model.

Table 1 shows the number of scenarios that meet the requirements explained above, as well as the frequency of occurrence of the variables used in each scenario, which will allow us to recognize those that predominate.

Table 1. Frequency of occurrence of variables in the scenarios obtained with the Forward variable selection method for different algorithms. For each algorithm, the number of scenarios with an r^2 greater than 54.7% is presented between parentheses. Source. Own elaboration

Variable/Scenarios	Forward Algorithms							
	RBF Regressor (6)	Isotonic Regresión (15)	Linear Regresión (6)	Pace Regresión (10)	Ensemble Regresor (13)	M5P (10)	Total (60)	% Appearance
LPPM	6	15	6	10	13	10	60	100.00
T mín	5	2	0	10	3	7	27	45.00
T med	2	8	1	4	9	0	24	40.00
T máx	0	10	2	9	7	3	31	51.67
TA	4	13	5	1	3	0	26	43.33
RHmín	0	5	4	3	11	10	33	**55.00**
RHmed	2	4	1	8	3	8	26	43.33
RHmáx	6	14	5	10	4	0	39	**65.00**
HrA	2	11	0	5	5	6	29	48.33
OcLl	3	12	6	8	1	1	31	51.67
ET	2	1	3	10	9	0	25	41.67
EET	2	0	6	6	12	0	26	43.33
r 24h	3	9	4	10	4	5	35	**58.33**
Rain	1	0	6	2	10	9	28	46.67
FFmed	3	6	5	8	6	0	28	46.67
FFmáx	0	15	4	10	5	0	34	**56.67**
DDmáx	0	7	6	7	3	4	27	45.00

From the analysis of Table 1, it can be summarized that all the selected variables influence residential consumption with a frequency of occurrence ranging from 40% to 65%, the most important of which are RHmax, r24h, FFmax, and RHmin.

In the case of bioclimatic variables, those with higher frequency are TA and EET, both with the same value, followed by ET in a range from 43.33% to 41.67%.

Table 3 shows the number of scenarios that meet the requirements. In addition, the frequency of occurrence of the variables used in each scenario is presented, which will make it possible to recognize all those that predominate.

The techniques that justify the scenarios used to predict the necessary variables of that universe are below shown (Table 2).

Of these, as can be seen in the forward table above, the best performance was obtained by isotonic regression using the r-squared as a metric. In this scenario, the variables have the following distribution that shows the relative weight that each one of them has in the forward prediction process.

Table 3 shows that the selected variables influence residential consumption with a frequency of occurrence ranging from 38.2% to 80%, the most important of which are TA, r24h, and FFmax. The analysis of the bioclimatic variables shows that the one with

Table 2. Main techniques used in the selection of variables

Techniques used	Forward Model		MSE	MAE
	RMSE	R-Squared		
Isotonic Regresion	909.577	0.612	827329.971	741.794
Pace Regresion	1179.373	0.405	1390921.441	843.374
Ensemble Regresor	738.663	0.535	545623.727	601.746
RBF Regresor	1139.657	0.257	1298817.513	917.707
Linear Regresion	1112.163	0.27	1236905.809	925.586
M5P	871.273	0.541	759117.408	702.587

Table 3. Frequency of occurrence of variables in the scenarios obtained with the Backward variable selection method for different algorithms. For each algorithm, the number of scenarios with an r^2 equal or greater than 50% is presented between parentheses. Source. Own elaboration

Variables/Scenarios	Backward Algorithms							
	RBF Regressor (6)	Isotonic Regresión (13)	Linear Regresión (7)	Pace Regresión (10)	Ensemble Regresor (11)	M5P (8)	Total (55)	% Appearance
LPPM	6	13	7	10	11	8	55	100.00
T mín	3	13	0	1	5	0	22	40.00
T med	0	8	2	9	3	8	30	54.55
T máx	0	12	2	6	11	8	39	70.91
TA	5	11	2	10	8	8	44	**80.00**
RHmín	6	0	1	7	6	1	21	38.18
RHmed	4	2	2	8	4	6	26	47.27
RHmáx	4	6	0	10	11	2	33	60.00
HrA	1	13	0	5	11	5	35	63.64
OcLl	3	5	4	9	9	8	38	69.09
ET	1	4	0	10	10	8	33	60.00
EET	0	10	4	5	0	8	27	49.09
r 24h	6	9	4	10	11	4	44	**80.00**
Rain	5	13	0	3	5	8	34	61.82
FFmed	6	1	3	2	11	3	26	47.27
FFmáx	5	11	0	9	11	8	44	**80.00**
DDmáx	1	7	4	4	1	8	25	45.45

the highest frequency of occurrence is TA followed by ET and EET in values ranging from 49.1% to 80%; this algorithm shows a greater impact of these variables on domestic consumption.

The comprehensive analysis of the results of the tables indicates that in both selection methods, r24h and FFmax stand out thanks to their higher frequencies. They are the variables with the highest frequency of occurrence, followed by RHmax, RHmin, and TA, which allows us to recognize them as those that should be taken into account for the preparation of a predictive model of domestic consumption, in other words, they are recognized as predictor variables for the existing database of the case study analyzed. The FFmax is a variable that is closely related to thermal sensation, which feeds the criterion of the significance of those variables that incorporate the bioclimatic behavior of people to explain domestic consumption.

An analysis of the bioclimatic variables selected by both forward and backward methods shows that TA presents the highest frequency of occurrence, in one case followed by EET and ET or by ET and EET according to the case. This result indicates that they can be used as predictor variables in the preparation of a domestic consumption prediction model, either combined with those of higher frequency or as a single block of elements with sensory effects in their relationship with residential consumption.

According to this result, there are studies in Cuba that have demonstrated changes in the behavior of extreme temperature values, such as those conducted by Rodríguez (2022). These studies show an increase in the minimum temperature, at the same time that there are meteorological conditions that reveal continental characteristics, especially in those regions that are far from the coasts. At the same time, there are conditions similar to "heat islands" that occur in large cities. All of the above contributes to the increase in the difference between the maximum daytime temperature and The minimum values of this variable, which leads to an increase in TA.

The results obtained are in agreement with previous studies such as those submitted by HousePeters et al. (2010); and Brandner, (2016) among others, which take into account the effects of temperature on consumption present in TA as a transformed bioclimatic variable, while r24 is similar to the studies of Sarker et al. (2013); Haque et al. (2015), which is also consistent with previous results obtained in Cuba by Guilherme et al. (2017) and Pomares et al. (2022).

The techniques for the backward scenarios that justify this performance are shown in the table below.

Table 4. Main techniques used in the selection of variables

Techniques used	Backward Model		MSE	MAE
	RMSE	R-Squared		
Isotonic Regresion	897.542	0.484	805581.861	693.815
Pace Regresion	1017.907	0.305	1036134.27	717.14
Ensemble Regresor	1044.45	0.387	1090875.703	813.569
RBF Regresor	790.929	0.442	625569.104	653.92
Linear Regresion	1195.058	0.311	1428162.54	917.851
M5P	1026.63	0.408	1052806.138	826.275

As can be seen for the backward, the technique showing the best performance based on the r-squared as a metric is the isotonic regression, while the behavior of the variables associated with this technique and the relative weight of the associated variables can be seen in the Table 4.

For a company like Aguas de La Habana, which manages the water supply service in an island environment increasingly affected by climate variability, it is essential to know which are the main meteorological variables that define the behavior of domestic consumption in terms of activities such as planning and operation of distribution systems. If, in addition to this fact, the analysis encompasses the novel aspect of including the bioclimatic behavior of people, essential tools would be provided to forecast the behavior of future demand based on climatic variability. This knowledge, together with the availability of the resource that conditions supply, allows for a holistic approach that is important for decision making in all types of management scenarios.

5 Conclusions

This work shows that the studies carried out in Cuba so far in this line of research are quite discrete and located mainly in Aguas de La Habana.

It is also noted that most of the studies carried out on a global scale are aimed at characterizing domestic consumption and its application as a powerful predictive tool. The multifactorial nature of domestic consumption and the need for a holistic approach to obtain the greatest benefits from the knowledge acquired in its correct characterization is recognized.

The use of data mining techniques in the selection of variables made it possible to determine those climatic and bioclimatic variables that have an impact on consumption, highlighting those that most affect it and stand out as predictors in a sample of the sector of Aguas de La Habana.

The experiments were carried out for 6 regression techniques, and it was possible to identify that the variables that appear most frequently in the model are: r24, FFmax, TA, RHmax, and RHmin, and according to the model they are predictor variables.

The case of the bioclimatic variables is relevant, of which the one that appears most frequently is TA, so it is the variable that prevails in this section, followed by ET and EET, so they are the ones that are proposed to be included in a consumption prediction model that is being built and that should provide answers in a short period.

It should be noted that FFmax takes into account sensory behavior, which demonstrates the importance of bioclimatic variables in the prediction of consumption.

Acknowledgement. The research that gave rise to the results submitted in this contribution received funding from the National Institute of Hydraulic (Water) Resources (INRH) of the Republic of Cuba.

References

Adamowski, J., Adamowski, K., Prokoph, A.: A spectral analysis based methodology to detect climatological influences on daily urban water demand. Int. Assoc. Math. Geosci. (2012). https://doi.org/10.1007/s11004-012-9427-0, https://www.mcgill.ca/bioeng/files/bioeng/a_spectral_analysis_based_methodology_to_detect_climatological_influences_on_daily_urban_water_demand.pdf

Brandner, H.: Identifying the influential factors of the temporal variation of water consumption: a case study using multiple linear regression analysis. In: KTH Architecture and the Built Environment, Environmental Engineering and Sustainable Infrastructure Program (EESI), SE-100 44 Stockholm, Sweden (2016). https://kth.diva-portal.org/smash/get/diva2:971606/Fulltext01.pdf

Bich-Ngoc, N., Teller, J.: A review of residential water consumption determinant (2018). https://orbi.uliege.be/handle/2268/226248

Guilherme Foquiço, E., Ramos Joseph, M., León Mendez, A.: Determination of domestic consumption patterns and their relationship with climatic factors, in a sector of Aguas de La Habana. Master's thesis, Instituto Superior Politécnico José Antonio Echeverría, Havana. Cuba (2017)

Haque, Md.M., Egodawatta, P., Rahman, A., Goonetilleke, A.: Assessing the significance of climate and community factors on urban water demand. Int. J. Sustain. Built Environ. (2015). https://doi.org/10.1016/j.ijsbe.2015.11.001

House-Peters, L., Pratt, B., Chang, H.: Effects of urban spatial structure, sociodemographics, and climate on residential water consumption in Hillsboro, Oregon. J. Am. Water Resour. Assoc. (JAWRA) **46**(3), 461–472 (2010). https://doi.org/10.1111/j.1752-1688.2009.00415.x. https://www.scinapse.io/papers/2031027751#fullText

Klenzi, Raúl O., Malberti, M., Beguerí, G.E.: Visualization in a data mining environment from a human-computer interaction perspective. Comput. Syst. **22**(1), 279–290 (2018). http://www.scielo.org.mx/scielo.php?script=sci_arttext&pid=S1405554620180001000279

Lizcano Chapeta, C.J., Chamorro Valencia, D.J., Patricio Vega. E., Cachimuel Colta, G.:. Legal provisions of community water management and indigenous peoples in Ecuador. Rev. Univ. Soc. **14**(4), 514–522. (2022)

Morales Martínez, D., Gori Maia, A.: The effect of social behavior on residential water consumption. Water **13**, 1184 (2021). https://doi.org/10.3390/w13091184.(2021)

Morote Seguido, Á.F.: Factores que inciden en el consumo de agua doméstico. Estudio a partir de un análisis bibliométrico. In: Estudios Geográficos, LXXVIII/282, pp. 257–281 (2017). https://doi.org/10.3989/estgeogr.201709, https://estudiosgeograficos.revistas.csic.es/index.php/estudiosgeograficos/article/view/511. ISSN 0014-1496 and ISSN 1988-8546

Pomares, P.J., Ramos, J.M., León, M.A.: Main climatic factors affecting domestic demand. Diploma thesis, Instituto Superior Politécnico José Antonio Echeverría, Havana. Cuba (2022)

Ramos, J.M., Leon, Mendez, A.J.: Integrated water loss management. A case study. Hydraul. Environ. Eng. **37**(3) (2016). ISSN 1680-0338

Rodríguez Díaz, Y., R. V.: Efecto de las sensaciones térmicas en la enfermedad cerebrovascular en la región Occidental de Cuba. 2001-2012. Revista Cubana De Meteorología 28(3) (2022). Recuperado a partir de http://rcm.insmet.cu/index.php/rcm/article/view/643

Sarker, R.C., Gato-Trinidad, S., Imteaz, M.: Temperature and rainfall thresholds corresponding to water consumption in greater Melbourne, Australia. In: 20th International Congress on Modelling and Simulation, Adelaide, Australia (2013). https://www.researchgate.net/publication/281042716_Temperature_and_Rainfall_Thresholds_corresponding_to_water_consumption_in_Greater_Melbourne_Australia

Schleich, J., Hillenbrand, T.: Determinants of residential water demand in Germany. Working Paper Sustainability and Innovation No. S 3/2007 Fraunhofer, Institute Systems and Innovation Research. Germany (2007). https://www.econstor.eu/bit-stream/10419/28515/1/538778458.pdf

Soto-Montes, G., Herrera-Pantoja, M.: Implications of climate change on water resource management in megacities in developing countries: Mexico City case study. Environ. Manage. Sustain. Dev. **5**(1) (2016). https://doi.org/10.5296/emsd.v5i1.8807. ISSN 2164-7682

Witten, H.I.: Data Mining Practical Machine Learning Tools and Techniques, 4th edn. Elsevier, Amsterdam (2016)

An M-SALD_AHP and GIS-Based Approach to Watershed Analysis During the Development of Small and Large-Scale Hydraulic Structure Construction Projects

Solangel Rodríguez Vázquez[1](✉) and Nataliya V. Mokrova[2]

[1] University of Informatics Sciences, 10800, Havana, Cuba
solrusita85@gmail.com
[2] Russian Biotechnological University, 125080, Moscow, Russia

Abstract. Multi-criteria analysis techniques provide a useful tool to support decision making. To date, different methods have been developed using different approaches. However, in the literature and in particular for the analysis of areas for the location of hydraulic structures it is well known that one of the most widely used methods is the Analytic Hierarchy Process (AHP). This paper presents a modified AHP that allows expanding the number of criteria and alternatives evaluated, as well as eliminating the subjective evaluation of the experts towards the alternatives and reducing the inconsistencies that are obtained during the construction of paired matrices. The modifications made focus on the automatic construction of paired comparison matrices and the proposal of a new normalization method for the evaluation and weighting of the alternatives through the use of real parameter data extracted from raster and/or vector layers in the GIS tool. The new M-SALD_AHP method was applied in the analysis of hydrographic sub-basins corresponding to the municipality of Manicaragua, in the province of Villa Clara, Cuba. For the analysis, a total of 25 sub-criteria distributed in 4 criteria and 29 alternatives (hydrographic sub-basins) were taken into account. The results show that the proposed method is effective and reliable for the analysis of watersheds during the feasibility analysis of construction projects and locations of hydraulic structures.

Keywords: AHP · Multicriteria Analysis · Hydraulic Structures · Decision Making · GIS · Watersheds

1 Introduction

The search for greater efficiency and productivity in industrial sectors and regions contributes to the implementation of supportive decision-making methodologies in general and to greater competitiveness, in particular in scenarios with multiple variables or selection criteria. The current conditions of hydraulic research differ in the rapidity and intensity of the changes that occur, which means that economic, social and environmental

Y. Hernández Heredia et al. (Eds.): IWAIPR 2023, LNCS 14335, pp. 48–59, 2024.
https://doi.org/10.1007/978-3-031-49552-6_5

agents are obliged to continuously make decisions (and assume their consequences) that depend on a variety of criteria or characteristics of a quantitative, qualitative or mixed type. The above highlights the growing need to use analysis methods with a multi-criteria approach to reduce or mitigate the risks associated with the assumptions that may arise in the search for a higher level of development.

The approach of multiple criteria techniques (MCDM) applied in a GIS context have turned out to be one of the most widely used techniques and with the potential to provide a rational, objective and unbiased approach to making decisions in the identification of potential sites. Decision-making in the context of territorial structure is usually a rather complex process due to the large number of experts who tend to have opposing and often contradictory points of view. In this context, the multicriteria evaluation is necessary, since it allows the integration of the opinions of different experts and different decision makers, in the decision-making process about what should be done in the territory.

The multicriteria evaluation takes into account a series of steps that first involve identifying the problem to be solved or determining the objective to be achieved. On the basis of this, the mechanisms by which the final goal is achieved are opened, which, depending on the decision-makers, or the experts involved, usually one or the other goal is achieved. In the multicriteria evaluation there are a number of elements such as: who participates in the decision process, the criteria that the experts consider necessary for the analysis, the alternatives that are available, and the goal to which you want to reach.

The hierarchical analysis method known as (AHP) determines the objective $O_{a_i} = f(a_i, c_j, w)$ based on the subjective evaluation of the weights (w) by the experts when ordering the alternatives (a_i) and in relation to the criteria $\left(c_j\right)$. In doing so, the evaluation is performed manually, which limits the possibility of using a large number of sub-criteria (P), criteria (C) and alternatives (A). The uncertainty of the evaluation reinforces the mismatch of the matrix of pairwise comparisons and, consequently, increases the information processing time and increases the probability of error. The authors of this article propose the M-SALD_AHP method as a way of solving some of the limitations raised by Socarras [1] regarding Saaty's original AHP method [2].

2 Methodology and Methods

According to Saaty [3], the AHP method is a decision model that interprets data and information directly by making judgments and measurements on a ratio scale within an established hierarchical structure. It is a method of selecting alternatives (strategies, investments, selection of areas, etc.) based on a series of criteria or variables, which are usually in conflict.

The M-SALD_AHP method, like Saaty's AHP [2], is composed of a series of steps:

Step 1. The decision problem is modeled by a hierarchy whose top vertex is the main objective $\left(O_{a_i}\right)$ of the problem, goal to be achieved, and at the base are the possible alternatives (A) (hydrological basins) to be evaluated. In the intermediate levels the criteria (C) are represented (which in turn can also be structured in hierarchies i.e. sub-criteria (P)) on the basis of which the decision is made.
Step 2. Establishment of the priorities between the criteria and sub-criteria. The objective of this step is to construct a vector of priorities or weights that evaluates the relative

importance that the decision-making unit attaches to each criterion. The essential problem that arises at this point is to answer how a numerical value can be assigned to each criterion that represents, as closely as possible, the preference of the decision-maker of one criterion over another.

Table 1. Scale proposal for the direct assignment made by the expert [2].

Qualitative assessment	Quantitative valuation
Very Low Importance	1
Low Importance	3
Moderately important	5
Strong importance	7
Highest importance	9

The M-SALD_AHP method proposes that it is the expert who assigns to each element of type $\left(c_j; p_u\right)$ a qualitative value $\left(k_j; k_u\right)$ taking into account the evaluations offered in the Table 1, in such a way that they should only evaluate according to their opinion the importance of each of the elements with respect to the element of the immediately higher level in the hierarchy of the problem.

In order to establish the priorities between the elements at each level, a measurement methodology proposal is made that allows the proposed scale to be merged into the Table 1 (expert ratings) and the scale proposed by Saaty [4] in the Table 2 for performing the paired comparison. For this, the methodology is assisted by two fundamental steps:

Step 2.1. The expert determines the importance of each criterion with respect to the objective and the sub-criteria with respect to each criterion. This is done by making use of the Table 1. For cases in which the evaluation of C and P are performed by more than one expert it will be necessary to obtain a consensus of the preferences $\overline{\left(k_j; k_u\right)}$ regarding each c_j and p_u. Therefore, $j\left(k_j\right)$ and $u(k_u)$ is obtained through $\overline{k_j} = \overline{x}_{геом\_j}$ and $\overline{k_u} = \overline{x}_{геом\_u}$. Where $\overline{x}_{геом\_j}$ and $\overline{x}_{геом\_u}$ are obtained from Eq. (1).

Geometric Mean:

$$\overline{x}_{геом} = \sqrt[l]{x_1 x_2 \ldots x_l} = \sqrt[l]{\prod_{i=1}^{l} x_i} \tag{1}$$

where: $\prod$ – multiplication operator; l – number of options.

Step 2.2. With the aim of decreasing human error in the construction of the paired comparison matrix and to increase the consistency of the matrices, the proposed scale was created in the Table 3 from the Tables 1 and 2 of Saaty. From this scale, each of the values of the comparison of k_L with respect to k_Y are obtained (Eqs. 2, 3 and 4). This means that for each pair $k_{L,Y} \in C, P$, one of the three relations take place:

Table 2. Fundamental paired comparison scale [2].

FUNDAMENTAL PAIRED COMPARISON SCALE		
Numerical scale	Verbal comparison scale	Explaining
1	Equal importance	Two activities contribute equally to the objective
3	Moderate importance of one element over another	Experience and judgment are in favor of one element over another
5	Strong importance of one element over another	One element is strongly favored
7	Very strong importance of one element over another	One element is very dominant
9	Extreme importance of one element over another	An element is favored by at least an order of magnitude difference

$k_L \succ k_Y -$ k_L is preferable to k_Y;
$k_L \prec k_Y -$ k_L is less preferable than k_Y;
$k_L \sim k_Y -$ for decision makers, both sets have the same degree of preference;

Preference relations possess at least the following properties:

1) If $k_1 \succ k_2, k_2 \succ k_3$, then $k_1 \succ k_3$;
2) If $k_1 > k_2$, then $k_1 \succ k_2$.

Table 3. Comparison scale of values making use of Tables 1 and 2.

Scales of comparison of the values assigned by the expert	Values obtained by comparison	Scales of comparison of the values assigned by the expert	Values obtained by comparison
$1 \prec\sim k$	$1/k$; $(k = 1, 3, 5, 7, 9)$	$k \sim\succ 1$	k; $(k = 1, 3, 5, 7, 9)$
$3 \prec 5$	$1/3$	$5 \succ 3$	3
$5 \prec 7$		$7 \succ 5$	
$7 \prec 9$		$9 \succ 7$	
$3 \prec 7$	$1/5$	$7 \succ 3$	5
$5 \prec 9$		$9 \succ 5$	
$3 \prec 9$	$1/7$	$9 \succ 3$	7

$$(k,q)_L > (k,q)_Y \rightarrow \left[\left((c_i,p_i)^{k_L}, a_i^{q_L}\right) \succ \left((c_j,p_j)^{k_Y}, a_j^{q_Y}\right)\right] \therefore ((c_{ij},p_{ij},a_{ij}) = w_i) \wedge \left((c_{ji},p_{ji},a_{ji}) = 1/w_i\right) \quad (2)$$

$$(k,q)_L < (k,q)_Y \rightarrow \left[\left((c_i,p_i)^{k_L}, a_i^{q_L}\right) \prec \left((c_j,p_j)^{k_Y}, a_j^{q_Y}\right)\right] \therefore ((c_{ji},p_{ji},a_{ji}) = w_i) \wedge \left((c_{ij},p_{ij},a_{ij}) = {}^1/_{w_i}\right) \quad (3)$$

$$(k,q)_L = (k,q)_Y \rightarrow \left[\left((c_i,p_i)^{k_L}, a_i^{q_L}\right) \sim \left((c_j,p_j)^{k_Y}, a_j^{q_Y}\right)\right] \therefore (c_{ij},p_{ij},a_{ij}), (c_{ji},p_{ji},a_{ji}) = w_i = 1 \quad (4)$$

Step 3. Establishment of the paired comparison matrices of criteria, sub-criteria and alternatives with respect to each sub-criterion, criterion respectively. Based on the information collected using the above measurement methodology, a matrix R of dimensions $n \times n$ is constructed, where r_{ij} represents the priority between factor i and factor j and the values of the lower half with respect to the diagonal (reciprocal values) correspond to the inverse values of the upper half $\left(r_{ji} = {}^1/_{r_{ij}}\right)$, being $r_{ij} = 1, (i, j = 1, 2, ..., n; i = j)$.
Step 3.1. Calculation of priority vectors $\overrightarrow{w}$. In the comparison matrix R the columns represent the relative weights of each factor with respect to the others. To determine the most preferred factor, for a given criterion, the values are normalized by dividing each element of column j by the sum of all the elements of said column (Eq. 5), and then, estimating a vector of weights $\overrightarrow{w} = [w_1, w_2, ..., w_n]$, where n is the number of criteria. The weight w_i reflects the relative importance of the criterion c_i in the decision and is assumed to be positive. The weight vector $\overrightarrow{w}$ is obtained by averaging each row of the normalized matrix (Eq. 6), and its value indicates the relative importance of each factor in a range between 0 and 1.

$$x_{ij} = \frac{r_{ij}}{\sum_{i=1}^{n} r_{ij}} \quad (5)$$

$$w_i = \sum_{j=1}^{n} \frac{x_{ij}}{n} \quad (6)$$

Step 3.2. Calculation and verification of the consistency ratio (CR). As the evaluations are subjective, there may be inconsistencies. Because of this it becomes necessary to measure the consistency of the paired comparison matrix. If a matrix is consistent it must be verified that where R is the paired comparison matrix for which the priorities or weights are known, $\overrightarrow{w}$ is the priority vector and λ is a scalar, if the judgments are consistent, then the matrix R would have a single eigenvalue $\lambda = n$, that is equal to the number of elements compared, but since it is not possible for a person to be perfectly consistent then there will always be inconsistency. The important thing is that a certain permissible limit is not exceeded. This is one of the limitations that are eliminated in M-SALD_AHP, because, this type of analysis is prone to the number of parameters to be used is large and therefore if the comparison between elements is performed manually by the expert, there could be errors. The fact that it is the method itself through an algorithm that performs the comparison of priorities makes the margin of error decrease or at best it is eradicated. However, the consistency evaluation process is carried out with the aim of verifying that the analysis carried out has been correct. The above implies that the paired comparison matrix will have more than one eigenvalue λ_i. The maximum eigenvalue (λ_{max}) allows to estimate the degree of consistency of the paired comparison matrix using the consistency index (CI) (Eq. 9).

To obtain the value of λ_{max} it is first necessary to multiply the paired comparison matrix R by the priority vector $\overrightarrow{w}$ obtaining a consistency vector $\overrightarrow{\lambda w} = [\lambda w_1, \lambda w_2, ..., \lambda w_n]$ (Eq. 7). If the matrix R were perfectly consistent the sum of the elements of the obtained vector should be equal to n. The above situation does not usually happen, so, to determine the degree of inconsistency it is necessary to divide each element of the consistency vector $\overrightarrow{\lambda w}$ by its corresponding one in the priority vector $\overrightarrow{w}$, and in this way all the possible values λ_i are obtained, then to finally obtain λ_{max}, we proceed to perform the equation (Eq. 8):

$$\begin{bmatrix} r_{11} & r_{12} & r_{13} \\ r_{21} & r_{22} & r_{23} \\ r_{31} & r_{32} & r_{33} \end{bmatrix} \times \begin{bmatrix} w_1 \\ w_2 \\ w_3 \end{bmatrix} = \begin{bmatrix} \lambda w_1 \\ \lambda w_2 \\ \lambda w_3 \end{bmatrix} \tag{7}$$

$$\lambda_{max} = \sum_{i=1}^{n} \frac{\lambda_i}{n} \tag{8}$$

$$CI = \frac{\lambda_{max} - n}{n - 1} \tag{9}$$

Then, to verify if the degree of consistency is acceptable, a random consistency index (*RI*) is used as a reference [5, 6] (Table 4).

Table 4. Random consistency index (*RI*) based on matrix dimension (*n*).

n	1	2	3	4	5	6	7	8
RI	0	0	0,525	0,882	1,115	1,252	1,341	1,404
n	9	10	11	12	13	14	15	16≤
RI	1,452	1,484	1,513	1,535	1,555	1,570	1,583	1,595

The consistency ratio (*CR*) (Eq. 11) measures the degree of inconsistency of the paired comparison matrix and is calculated as follows:

$$CR = \frac{CI}{RI} \tag{10}$$

If $CR = 0$, then the matrix is consistent, if $CR \leq 0{,}10$ the matrix has an admissible inconsistency, which means that it is considered consistent and therefore the weight vector $\overrightarrow{w}$ is also admitted as valid. But if $CR > 0{,}10$ the inconsistency is inadmissible and it is advisable to review the assessments made.

Step 4. Establishment of local and global priorities among the alternatives. Once the weighting of the criteria and sub-criteria has been obtained in the previous steps, the alternatives are evaluated in order to calculate the corresponding local priorities. For the comparison of priorities between the alternatives with respect to each sub-criterion, an evaluation strategy is proposed to obtain a final weighting of each of the alternatives based on each of the sub-criteria. This strategy is based on the comparison of the values of each of the parameters that directly influence each of the alternatives individually.

Strategy of evaluation of the alternatives with respect to the values of the parameters:

1. The values of the parameter are analyzed with respect to each of the alternatives, $\underset{u}{Max}(g_{ui})$ is selected, and then $\frac{\underset{u}{Max}(g_{ui})}{5}$ is divided (5 – dimension of the scale used by experts to evaluate (Table 1)).
2. A scale is created at 5 levels with respect to the number obtained in the previous point:

$$\begin{cases} 1, \textit{if}\,(0 \le g_{ui} \le g) \\ 2, \textit{if}\,(g \le g_{ui} \le 2g) \\ 3, \textit{if}\,(2g \le g_{ui} \le 3g) \\ 4, \textit{if}\,(3g \le g_{ui} \le 4g) \\ 5, \textit{if}\,(4g \le g_{ui} \le 5g) \end{cases}; \quad \text{where:} \quad g = \frac{\underset{u}{Max}(g_{ui})}{5}$$

3. It is analyzed according to the criterion, which of the parameter values gives the criterion the best feasibility. Sometimes $\underset{u}{Max}(g_{ui})$ turns out to be the best variant for the objective, however, there are parameters for which $\underset{u}{Min}(g_{ui})$ turns out to be the best variant.
4. According to the analysis carried out in point 3, Table 1 is used to assign the values to each of the levels obtained in point 2.
5. Subsequently, the value of the parameter corresponding to each alternative is taken, it is evaluated to which level of the scale obtained in point 2 it belongs, and the value established in point 4, corresponding to that level of the scale, is assigned.
6. The steps performed from point 1 to point 5 are performed iteratively for each parameter and internally it is performed for each of the values obtained with respect to that parameter corresponding to each of the alternatives. A matrix $M = (q_{ui})_{p\times a}$ is created; where (p)– parameter (sub-criterion), (a)– alternatives, and q_{ui}– value obtained in point 5, corresponding to each of the parameters for each of the alternatives.
7. After completing point 6, we proceed to perform the procedure of step 3 but in this case for the creation of the paired comparison matrix between alternatives with respect to each sub-criterion.

The resulting weight vectors of each alternative with respect to each sub-criterion are joined into a weight vector matrix. This matrix is multiplied by the vector of weights of the sub-criterion of the corresponding criterion, and this action is repeated for each criterion, obtaining the vector of local weights of each alternative with respect to the criterion that encompasses the respective sub-criteria. Finally, the evaluation matrix of the alternatives is obtained with respect to the criteria according to the Table 5.

where:

- $\vec{w} = [w_1, w_2, ..., w_n]$ – vector of relative weights or priorities associated with the criteria;

Table 5. Valuation *Matrix*

	w_1	w_2	...	w_j	...	w_n
	C_1	C_2	...	C_j	...	C_n
A_1	x_{11}	x_{12}	...	x_{1j}	...	x_{1n}
A_2	x_{21}	x_{22}	...	x_{2j}	...	x_{2n}
...	...	...	...	...	...	...
A_i	x_{i1}	x_{i2}	...	x_{ij}	...	x_{in}
...	...	...	...	...	...	...
A_m	x_{m1}	x_{m2}	...	x_{mj}	...	x_{mn}

- $\overrightarrow{x_j} = \begin{bmatrix} x_{1j} \\ x_{2j} \\ \vdots \\ x_{mj} \end{bmatrix}$ – vector of local priorities of the alternatives established based on C_j;
- $\overrightarrow{x_i} = [x_{i1}, x_{i2}, ..., x_{in}]$ – a vector of local priorities associated with a_i, whose components are the local priorities associated with this alternative according to each of the criteria.

The objective of the weighted sum method procedure is to find the global vector $\overrightarrow{s}$ of priorities that aggregates the priorities obtained in the two hierarchies considered: criteria and alternatives. The components s_i of this vector are the total priorities associated with each alternative a_i, which reflect the total value that each alternative has for the decider. Each component of this vector is calculated according to the expression:

$$s_i = \sum_{j=1}^{n} \left(w_j \times r_{ij}\right) \quad i = 1, 2, ..., m \tag{11}$$

where w_j are the weights associated with each of the criteria that are considered and r_{ij} are the components of the evaluation matrix after the normalization process. Finally, by ordering the alternatives based on the values $s_1, s_2, ..., s_m$ it is possible to solve the decision problem and determine the best alternative among the possible ones, which will be the one with the highest weighted sum.

3 Results and Discussion

With the purpose to validate the M-SALD_AHP method, an evaluation analysis was applied to the hydrological sub-basins through vector layers that were created from a raster file extracted from the SRTM "Earth Explorer" file download center, in relation to the municipality of Manicaragua, Villa Clara province, Cuba.

Following each of the steps of the M-SALD_AHP method, the objective of the study was determined: Analysis of the sub-basins corresponding to the municipality of Manicaragua for the feasibility analysis of dam construction for the development of agriculture and industry, the drinking water supply system and electricity generation in the region. The M-SALD_AHP method *is independent of the data* and *allows to eliminate the limitation of the order inversion problem.* This is because the alternatives to be analyzed are fixed areas belonging to a vector layer.

For the analysis, 4 general criteria were used (Hydrology, Geology, Topography, Socio-economic) divided into 25 sub-criteria or parameters and 24 alternatives (sub-basins hydrologies). An expert group consisting of 4 specialists was selected, 3 of them members of the INRH and one of them member of the chair of Hydraulic Resources of the MGSU, University of Moscow, Russia, which selected and weighted the c_j from the set C and $c_{j.u}$ of the set P (see Fig. 1), which will be used for the evaluation of the a_i. The information of the layers is collected (*.shp*) main for the work on the GIS, and an analysis of the hydrological information is carried out.

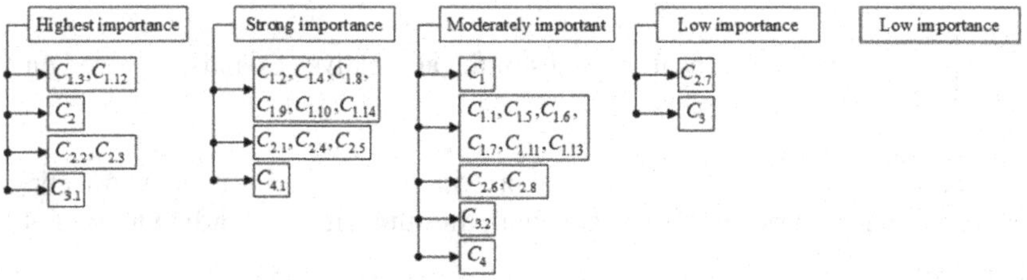

Fig. 1. Preferences of the criteria and sub-criteria

The inter-criteria pair comparison matrices are used to obtain a priority vector (see Table 6). Pairwise comparison matrices between sub-criteria are obtained according to the criterion (see Table 7).

Table 6. Priority vector derived from criterion and evaluation of inconsistency.

Criteria	C_1	C_2	C_3	C_4
$\vec{w}$	0,52	0,20	0,20	0,08
CR	0,012			

In the case of the pairwise comparison matrices between alternatives, the comparison is performed first with respect to the sub-criteria, as described in the measurement methodology developed for M-SALD_AHP in the case of the creation of the paired comparison matrix with respect to the comparison between the alternatives with respect to each sub-criterion and subsequently with respect to the criteria obtaining one $\vec{w}$ of the alternatives with respect to each of the defined criteria. In the Fig. 2 the results of the prioritization of weights of the alternatives according to the criteria are shown in the normalized matrix. The results obtained for C_4, coincide for the case of all the evaluated alternatives, with $\vec{w} = 0{,}0163$.

Table 7. Priority vector resulting from the sub-criteria in relation to the C_1 and evaluation of the inconsistency

C_1	$C_{1.1}$	$C_{1.2}$	$C_{1.3}$	$C_{1.4}$	$C_{1.5}$	$C_{1.6}$	$C_{1.7}$
$\vec{w}$	0,05	0,13	0,05	0,13	0,05	0,13	0,02
	$C_{1.8}$	$C_{1.9}$	$C_{1.10}$	$C_{1.11}$	$C_{1.12}$	$C_{1.13}$	$C_{1.14}$
$\vec{w}$	0,13	0,05	0,05	0,02	0,02	0,02	0,13
CR	0,007						

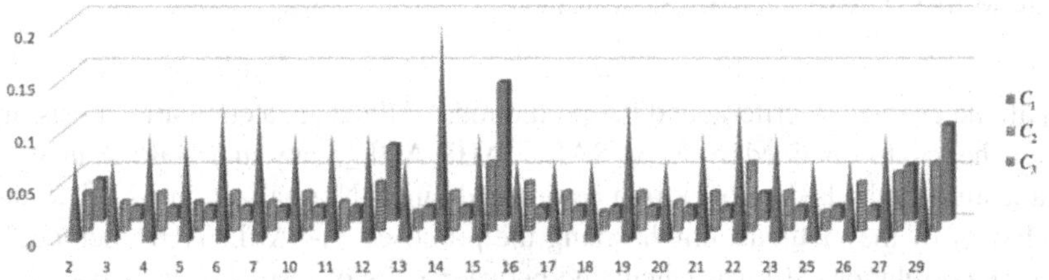

Fig. 2. Prioritization of the weights of the alternatives.

Finally, as a result of Eq. (12) are obtained the prioritization results shown in the Fig. 3.

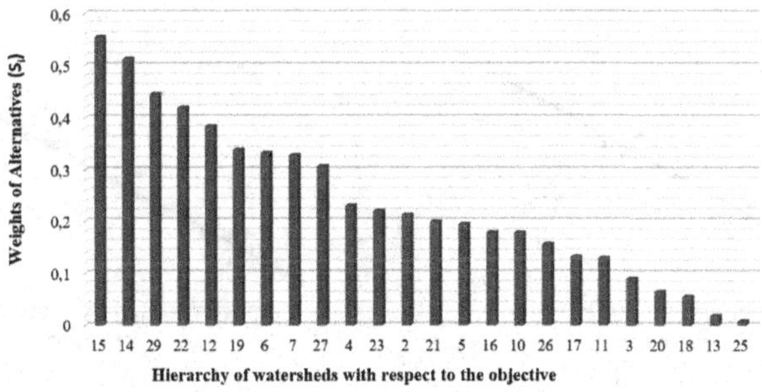

Fig. 3. Hierarchical order of the evaluated alternatives.

For the validation of the M-SALD_AHP method, a comparative study was carried out between the three largest percent of inconsistencies (Fig. 4) obtained during application of the proposed method and by the application of the AHP_Saaty method in its original form (both methods applied to the same case study). The result shows that the proposed method, despite the increase in the number of variables (criteria, sub-criteria, alternatives) used, allows to reduce the inconsistency obtained and keep the value below 0.02.

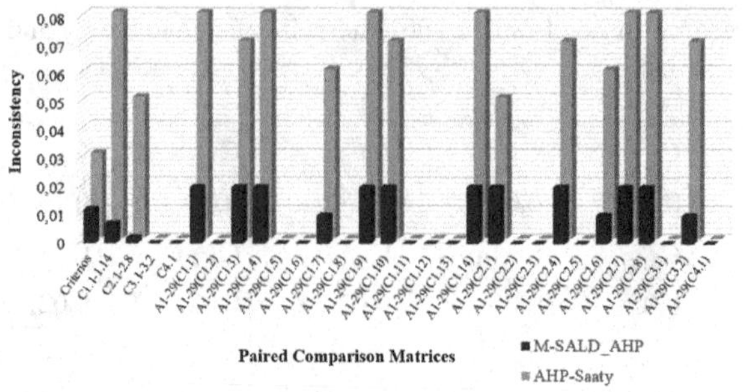

Fig. 4. Comparison of inconsistencies obtained during the process of creating paired matrices using the M-SALD_AHP and AHP_Saaty method.

With the evaluation criteria and the predictions of the data, a comparison was made between the results obtained by the M-SALD_AHP, AHP_Saaty, and TOPSIS using two normalization methods (Vector Normalization and Linear Normalization) [7–9], to check the behavior of the methods, emphasizing the proposed M-SALD_AHP method. The Spearman correlation [10] was calculated between pairs of results presented due to its ability to detect non-parametric correlations, when the data are not normally distributed (Fig. 5). From the results obtained based on the correlation by ranks, it can be said that there is a very high relationship between all the methods used, however, it is noteworthy that the proposed model has a higher correlation for both evaluations with respect to AHP compared to the other two methods used.

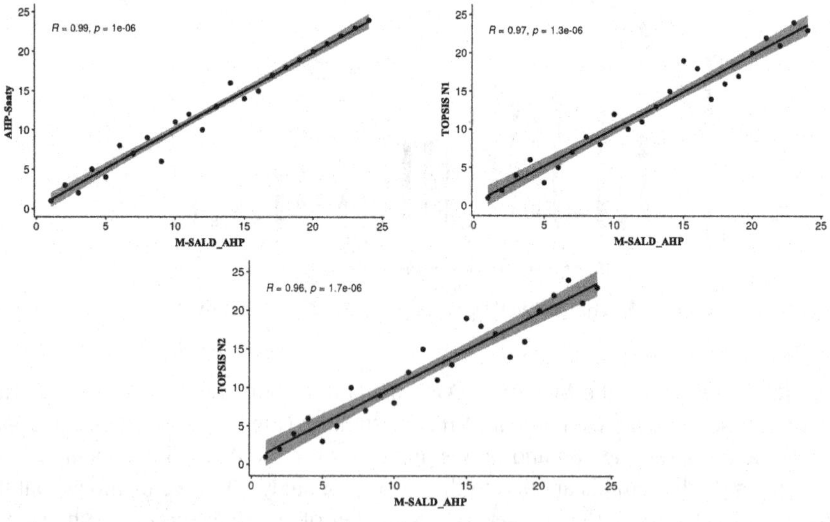

Fig. 5. Comparison of results of M-SALD_AHP, AHP_Saaty, TOPSIS method using two normalization methods.

4 Conclusions

Based on the observed and taking into account the number of sub-criteria and alternatives considered in this paper, the application of the M-SALD_AHP is valid because it allows to eliminate the subjectivity of the evaluation of alternatives by experts by selecting candidate points with the evaluation of the proximity of the alternatives to the ideal solution and the prioritization of environmental aspects. In addition, it has reduced the inconsistency by up to 2% in the paired comparison matrices in the multicriteria selection problem. It allows to expand the list of parameters, criteria and estimated alternatives to be evaluated, taking into account the requirements of the water conservation zones and the possible scenarios of hydrological development.

References

1. del Socorro García Cascales, M.: Métodos para la comparación de alternativas mediante un Sistema de Ayuda a la Decisión (S.A.D.) y 'Soft Computing. Universidad Politécnica de Cartagena (2009)
2. Saaty, T. L.: The Analytic Hierarchy Process (1980). https://doi.org/10.3414/ME10-01-0028
3. Saaty, T.L.: Fundamentals of decision making and priority theory. RWS Publications, Pittsburgh (1994)
4. Saaty, T.L.: Decision making with the analytic hierarchy process. Int. J. Serv. Sci. **1**(1), 83–98 (2008). https://doi.org/10.1504/IJSSci.2008.01759
5. Clemen, R.T.: *M*aking Hard Decisions: An Introduction to Decision Analysis. Brooks/Cole Publishing Company (1996)
6. Aguarón, J., Moreno-Jiménez, J.M.: The geometric consistency index: approximated thresholds. Eur. J. Oper. Res. **147**(1), 37–145 (2003). https://doi.org/10.1016/S0377-2217(02)00255-2
7. Pomerol, J.-C., Barba-Romero, S.: Multicriterion Decision in Management: Principles and Practice. Kluwer Academic Publishers, Boston/Dordrecht/London (2000)
8. Jaradat, R.M., Hossain, N.U.I., Kerr, C.S.: Application of method for non-linear scaling of multi-criteria decision making attribute values. In: SYSCON 2020 – 14th Annual IEEE International System Conference Proceedings (2020). https://doi.org/10.1109/SYSCON47679.2020.9275918
9. Shih, H.-S., Shyur, H.-J., Stanley Lee, E.: An extension of TOPSIS for group decision making. Math. Compu. Model. **45**(7–8), 801–813 (2007). https://doi.org/10.1016/j.mcm.2006.03.023
10. Schober, P., Boer, C., Schwarte, L.A.: Correlation coefficients: appropriate use and interpretation. Anesth. Analg. **126**(5), 1763–1768 (2018). https://doi.org/10.1213/ANE.0000000000002864

Fuzzy Granulation for Feature Extraction in EEG-Based Stress Pattern Recognition

Sandra Eugenia Barajas-Montiel(✉), Carlos Alberto Reyes-García, and Luis Villaseñor-Pineda

Computer Science Department, Instituto Nacional de Astrofísica, Óptica y Electrónica, Luis Enrique Erro No. 1, Sta. María Tonantzintla, Puebla, Mexico
{sandybarajas,kargaxxi,villasen}@inaoep.mx

Abstract. The study of different techniques for the characterization of biosignals tends to facilitate and promote improvement in the results of their analysis and classification. We propose electroencephalogram (EEG) characterization through fuzzy methodologies based on fuzzy partitions. The present work explores four different fuzzy granulation techniques to extract characteristics from EEG signals to perform multi-class stress recognition. Our experiments show that feature extraction through fuzzy granulation allows to achieve results that exceed the accuracy percentage in the classification of three different stress patterns previously reached in other works focused on the same classification problem with the same database.

Keywords: Biosignals · Fuzzy granulation · EEG · Feature extraction · Classification · Stress patterns

1 Introduction

Fuzzy granulation provides a new approach to data analysis, granulation allows to set different levels of detail in the description of an object and human reasoning purposes this type of description through concepts such as small, medium, far, which are fuzzy concepts. Fuzzy granulation is based on how human reasoning describes and manipulates information [1]. It has been used for example to build information granules that describe data structures [2], to reduce redundant attributes [3], also to model time series [4]. Hence, we propose to experiment granulation of electroencephalogram (EEG) signals to extract features and recognize different stress patterns.

The reviewed literature, e.g. [5–11], demonstrates that when working with biosignals as EEG, a significant number of processing steps are required to extract features. Most related works are based on frequency domain features. This work aims to take advantage of fuzzy logic descriptive nature to characterize signals and then recognize patterns of more than two stress scenarios. No

This work is funded by CONACyT under grant 49245.

Y. Hernndez Heredia et al. (Eds.): IWAIPR 2023, LNCS 14335, pp. 60–71, 2024.
https://doi.org/10.1007/978-3-031-49552-6_6

work has been found in which EEG are characterized through fuzzy granulation and then processed by a classifier for the distinction of multiple classes in EEG stress signals.

We have explored four fuzzy granulation methods based on [12] and [13], to extract features from EEG signals. To show the advantage on how fuzzy granulation is useful to represent changes in time series, we propose to adapt this approach as a feature extraction method for EEG signals. The aim was to observe the EEG signal classification results obtained after applying four fuzzy granulation techniques and determine which of them yielded the best results in multi-class stress recognition. The rest of this paper is organized as follows: Basic concepts about fuzzy granulation and the applied algorithms are explained in Sect. 2. Then, in Sect. 3 we describe experiments and results. Finally in Sect. 4 we present our conclusions.

2 Fuzzy Granulation

In general, when we break down an object, problem, or concept into simpler parts, it is easier to represent the object, to solve the problem, or to understand the concept. Fuzzy granulation techniques could be applied in order to discover a family of information granules to characterize the input space [14] of a classification task, as they allow the decomposition of a whole into parts. Fuzzy granulation represents an analogy to how human reasoning tends to describe entities with terms that do not have precise limits: close, far, almost, enough, etc., this type of decomposition is useful to represent changes in time series. Other applications of fuzzy granulation include the reduction of attributes as fuzzy granulation consists of extracting data from information abstraction in such a way that redundant information is eliminated, breaking down a complex problem into simpler parts/granules. The approaches followed in this work for the extraction of features in EEG signals through fuzzy granulation are presented below.

2.1 Fuzzy Information Granulation for Time Series

According to [4] time series granulation can be seen as a process composed by four layers: discretization, granulation, linguistic description and prediction. We base our feature extraction strategy in the first three layers of the mentioned framework. For granulation and linguistic description we adapted the methodology presented in [12]:

1. Discretization. This layer is responsible for dividing the time series into windows of the same size. Having a time series $T = \{t_1, t_2, ..., t_{n-1}, t_n\}$ and $1 <= l <= n$ the size of the window, if $l = n$ then the time series is represented by one window, if $l = 1$ then T is discretized in n windows. Once l has been set, time series T can be split into windows $W_1 = \{t_1, t_2, ..., t_l\}, W_2 = \{t_{l+1}, t_{l+2}, ...t_{2l}\}, ..., W_l = \{t_{n-l+1}, ..., t_{n-1}, t_n\}$.

2. Granulation. This process consists in extracting granules of the segmented windows from the previous layer they are distributed throughout the time window. Granules are a representation of the data in windows using intervals, rough sets, or other type of sets. The interest of this proposal is in using fuzzy sets for extracting granules since they provide information with different level of detail of problems with imprecise information. Fuzzy membership functions (Mf) are applied to granulate the values in each window.
3. Linguistic description. In this layer, each granule is associated with a linguistic term that describes it. In fuzzy logic, linguistic descriptors are used to represent concepts to be manipulated. When selecting a linguistic descriptor, it must be taken into account that the objective is to represent the concept to be treated in the most appropriate way. For this, different strategies can be followed such as the definition of linguistic descriptors using adjectives that describe physical characteristics. For example, to represent temperature you can use language descriptors such as cold, warm, hot. A time series could be granulated using linguistic terms as high amplitude, medium amplitude and small amplitude, each of them calculated for each window W_i.

To granulate the values in each subset, four different approaches were tested: Fuzzy Clustering, Triangular, Trapezoidal and Minmax-based granulation.

Fuzzy Clustering. Clustering is a grouping technique, generally applied to unsupervised learning, where given a set of objects, each object is assigned to a subset (cluster/class) of these objects, represented by a centroid. In Fuzzy Clustering, objects belong to more than one cluster with different degrees of membership in the interval [0,1]. A simple version of the Fuzzy Clustering algorithm used for granulation is presented in Table 1.

Table 1. Fuzzy C Means Basic Algorithm.

Choose a number of clusters k and set m the fuzzyness coefficient
Randomly assign to each object x a membership degree to clusters, W_0
While change in W_i is less than a set threshold e:
Calculate the centroid for each group
$c_k = \frac{\sum_x w_k(x)^m x}{\sum_x w_k(x)^m}$
Calculate new W_i
For each object, calculate its belonging to the clusters and
its coefficients of being in the groups
$w_{ij} = \frac{1}{\sum_{k=1}^{c}(\frac{\lVert x_i - c_j \rVert}{\lVert x_i - c_k \rVert})^{\frac{2}{m-1}}}$
End while
Return c and M

The centroid of a cluster represents the relevant information of the granules of the segmented windows with the highest degree of membership in that cluster. Keeping only the centroid of a cluster eliminates redundant information. Clustering allows us to describe a data set in a two-level structure, first by calculating several information granules at the same time, and then describing each cluster with the resulting information granules [15]. After applying the Fuzzy C Means clustering algorithm, the centroids of each cluster are ordered. The smallest cluster is labeled as *low*, the middle one as *mid*, and the largest as *high* as shown in Fig. 1.

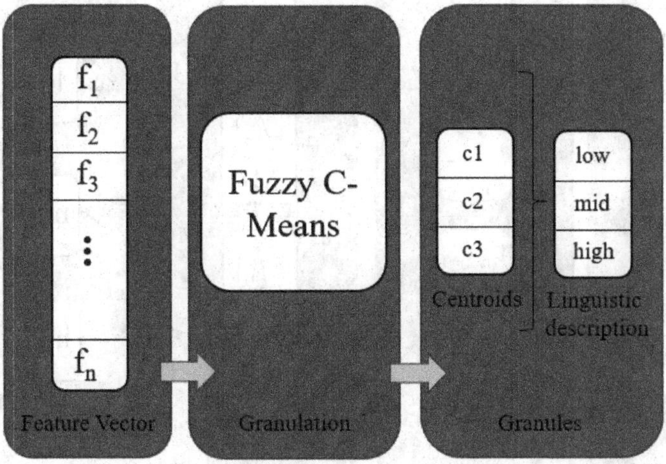

Fig. 1. Fuzzy granulation applying fuzzy clustering.

Triangular, Trapezoidal and Minmax Granulation. To extract features from the EEG signals each sample is sorted resulting in the time series $T = \{t_1, t_2, ..., t_{n-1}, t_n\}$ then they are divided in two subseries $T_l = \{t_1, t_2, ..., t_{n/2}\}$ and $T_h = \{t_{(n/2)+1}, ..., t_{n-1}, t_n\}$.

Granules *low* and *high* are extracted form T_l and T_h respectively. The median of ordered time series T is computed to represent *mid* granule. This process is ilustrated in Fig. 2. The functions used to extract granules were: Triangular-granulation (TG), Trapezoidal-granulation (TZG) and Minmax-granulation (mMG).

$$TG = \begin{cases} low = \frac{2\sum_{j=1}^{n/2} t_j}{n/2} - median\{t_1, ..., t_n\} \\ mid = median\{t_1, t_2, ..., t_n\} \\ high = \frac{2\sum_{j=n/2+1}^{n} t_j}{n/2} - median\{t_1, ..., t_n\} \end{cases} \tag{1}$$

$$TZG = \begin{cases} low = \frac{2\sum_{j=1}^{n/2} t_j}{n/2} - t_{n/2} \\ mid = median\{t_1, t_2, ..., t_n\} \\ high = \frac{2\sum_{j=n/2+1}^{n} t_j}{n/2} - t_{n/2+1} \end{cases} \tag{2}$$

$$mMG = \begin{cases} low = t_1 \\ mid = median\{t_1, t_2, ..., t_n\} \\ high = t_n \end{cases} \tag{3}$$

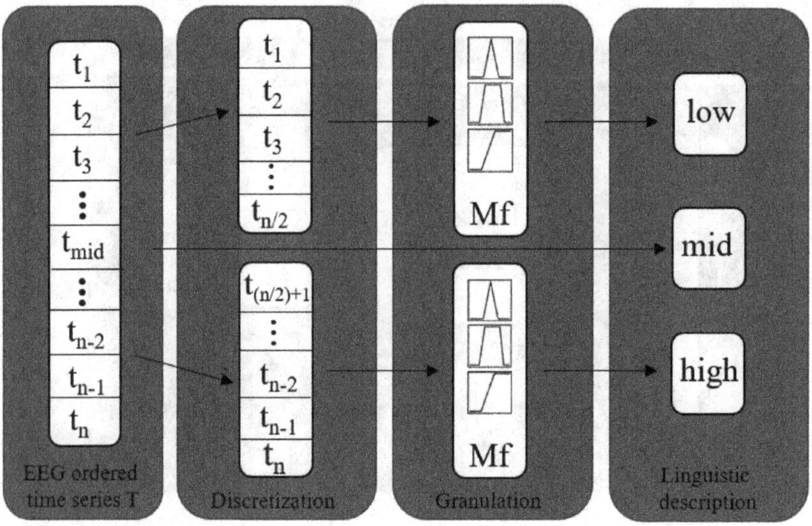

Fig. 2. Fuzzy granulation for time series.

3 Experiments and Results

For the development of this work, fuzzy information granulation for time series was applied, taking each channel of the EEG signal and computing granules using Fuzzy Clustering, Triangular, Trapezoidal and Minmax-based granulation.

We worked with a corpus of electroencephalographic signals from 12 participants under different sound stimuli recorded with a commercial EEG headband (Epoc+ from EMOTIV). The signals were acquired with a sampling frequency of 128 Hz. The channels that record the biosignal in the device used are based on the international 10–20 system; AF3, F7, F3, FC5, T7, P7, O1, O2, P8, T8, FC6, F4, F8 and AF4.

The sampling of this database was carried out in a controlled environment and each subject participated in three sessions: one in total silence (silent), another with relaxing music (relaxing), and another with pleasant music chosen by the subject participating in the session (pleasant). In each session, participants are asked to keep their eyes closed for 40 s, then open them and do basic multiplication exercises for 5 min. To induce a state of emotional stress, each exercise must be solved within a time limit of less than 5 s and if the answer is wrong, the participants get negative feedback. At the end of the mathematical test, the participants close their eyes for another 30 s to finish taking the sample.

This protocol for inducing stress is motivated by the interest of observing whether listening to music generates an effect on the perception of stress, such that it can be identified in brain waves, which can result in identifying stimuli that can be used in the management of stress and thus prevent its unwanted health effects. For details of this database, consult [7].

The signals were preprocessed for noise removal, to eliminate visible artifacts in the signal, such as thermal noise, electromagnetic interference, flickering and other muscular movements that influence the signal, following the steps described in Fig. 3.

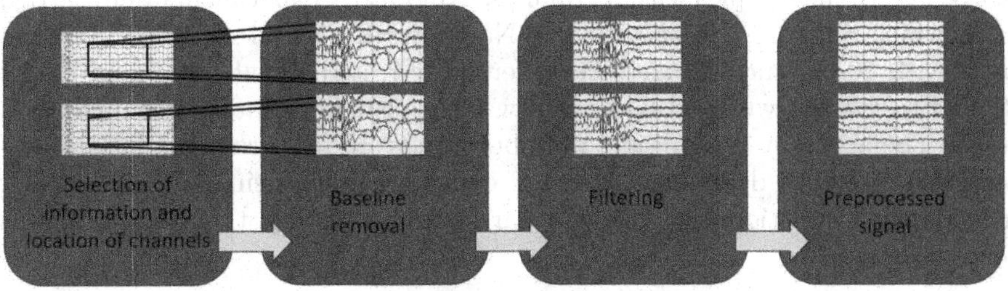

Fig. 3. General steps for signal preprocessing.

The whole signal has a duration of almost 7 min, but the interest is focused in only one minute of the signal, from second 240 to second 300 as this is the segment when the participants are more concentrated on the mathematical task, the 14 channels recorded were selected for signal analysis. After useful information segment selection, the signal was subjected to the elimination of the average of the signal per channel, called baseline removal. Baseline removal eliminates electrical activity that is not related to the event being analyzed, can improve signal quality and reduce noise.

Then, the resulting signal was filtered with the intention of obtaining only the data within a range of 4–32 Hz, since the Theta, Alpha and Beta frequency bands are found in this interval. The patterns of electrical activity recorded in the brain are classified into five main frequency band types: Delta, Theta, Alpha, Beta and Gamma. Each type of brain wave has a characteristic frequency and amplitude and is associated with different mental and emotional states. In the study of stress, Alpha, Beta and Theta waves can be useful because they are associated with relaxation and meditation.

This filtering was followed by visual inspection and manual removal of certain types of noise by cutting out useless fragments of the signal. Independent component analysis was applied to remove artifacts and channel interpolation was calculated to counter information removal. This process was carried out with the help of the EEGLAB MATLAB toolbox [16]. Although the removal of the baseline and the application of filters is done automatically, the cutting of useless segments of the signal is performed manually to prevent the cutting of relevant information. This process is secondary to the main objective of our work which is to propose the extraction of characteristics of the EEG signal by fuzzy granulation.

A common way to analyze EEG data is to decompose the signal into functionally distinct frequency bands, we propose fuzzy information granulation for feature extraction. First the signal was divided into granulation windows, each of these windows where used to extract granules $low, mid, high$ as described above. The extracted granules are used as characteristics to represent samples of EEG signals used to classify three stress scenarios.

A classification model was generated for each participant, since stress is perceived by each person differently, and EEG signals present inter-subject variability. To classify the samples with 3 granules, exploratory experiments were carried out in which Support Vector Machine, Naive Bayes, Neural Network, Random Forest with 20, 50 and 100 trees classifiers were tested. Finally Random Forest (RF) with 50 trees was used because it was the classifier that achieved the best results. The accuracy percentages are obtained by 10-fold cross-validation, randomly partition the data into 10 sets of equal size, then using 90% of samples for training (9 partitions) and 10% (1 partition) for testing, then repeating this process 10 times.

3.1 Fuzzy Clustering

When using fuzzy clustering, 10 s windows were segmented from the preprocessed unordered signal. 3 sets of samples were constructed: low granules, mid granules, high granules. Each sample has 14 features corresponding to the 14 original channels of EEG signal. Each set is composed of samples of the three classes: silent, pleasant and relaxing. Experiments were made classifying the three described stress scenarios generating separate models for each granule. Classification results are showed in Table 2.

Considering the model presented in [12] a model for each low, mid and high granule was constructed, and then the classification results were combined to emit a final classification for each sample. We trained different models for each set of granules with the same data. When we have new data, we will get a prediction of each model. Each model will have an associated vote. In this way, we will propose as a final prediction what most models vote. For Fuzzy Clustering granulation the results do not reach higher accuracy than when the granules are classified separately, as shown in Table 3.

To take advantage of the information from all the granules at the same time, a set of samples was created where each instance is characterized by 42 attributes, corresponding to the concatenation of 3 granules from each of the 14 channels

Table 2. Fuzzy C Means Granulation. Accuracy percentage achieved.

Subject	low	mid	high
1	98.11%	98.33%	93.33%
2	90.44%	93.33%	93.33%
3	97.66%	9766.00%	83.33%
4	93.33%	73.33%	96.67%
5	76.67%	60.00%	83.33%
6	97.33%	93.33%	96.67%
7	86.67%	98.67%	96.67%
8	97.66%	73.33%	76.67%
9	90.33%	73.33%	96.67%
10	80.00%	94.44%	86.67%
11	96.67%	88.89%	94.44%
12	86.67%	83.33%	86.67%
Average	90.96%	85.67%	90.37%

Table 3. Fuzzy C Means Granulation. Combination of classification results of the 3 granules. Classification accuracy percentage.

Subject	low/mid/high	Subject	low/mid/high
1	96.67%	7	93.33%
2	93.33%	8	73.33%
3	96.67%	9	96.67%
4	90.00%	10	83.33%
5	77.78%	11	94.44%
6	96.67%	12	88.89%
	Average	90.09%	

Table 4. Fuzzy C Means granulation. Granule concatenation. Accuracy percentage achieved.

Subject	low_mid_high	Subject	low_mid_high
1	98.66%	7	94.44%
2	93.33%	8	98.66%
3	93.33%	9	94.44%
4	96.67%	10	88.89%
5	93.33%	11	93.33%
6	98.66%	12	88.88%
	Average	94.39%	

of the EEG signal. With this group of samples the results shown in Table 4 were obtained.

The average classification accuracy obtained by concatenating granules is the highest for granulation with Fuzzy Clustering, reaching 94.39% compared to 90.09% achieved by combining the results of the models obtained for each granule set and 90.96% obtained with the low granule model.

3.2 Triangular, Trapezoidal and Minmax Granulation

To granulate the EEG signal based on MF, first the signal was segmented in 10 s granulation windows, then each granulation window was ordered in ascending order. Each of this windows where used to extract granules *low*, *mid*, *high* applying the MF described above. We worked with tree different data sets to model classifiers for each granule separately: the data set with granules low, the data set with granules mid and the data set with granules high. Each sample has 14 features corresponding to the 14 original channels of EEG signal. Classification results are showed in Table 5.

Table 5. Triangular, Trapezoidal and Minmax Granulation. Classification Accuracy Percentage.

	TG	TZG	mMG
low	91.66	86.67	89.89
mid	90.00	91.01	91.01
high	93.34	88.76	89.89

Subsequently, the classification results of each separate granule were taken and combined to give way to the results of the Table 6. In this case the classifications assigned by each classifier were taken as votes to assign the final classification of each sample. For instance, a sample is classified as silent class when using the model obtained with the low granules, while the same sample is classified as relaxing by the model obtained with the mid granules and as silence by the model generated by the high granules, therefore the assigned class is silent because this classification had two votes.

Also concatenated granules were used to classify three stress scenarios, each sample is described with 42 characteristics, corresponding to 3 granules of each of the 14 channels of the EEG signal, the classification accuracy results are shown in Table 7.

In [7] characteristics were extracted by calculating statistical measures (maximum, average, standard deviation, variance, statistical asymmetry and kurtosis) of the absolute power of the Alpha, Beta and Theta bands. Each of the bands was used separately, representing distinct sets of characteristic modeling three independent classifiers using Random Forest. Afterwards, the characteristics of

Table 6. Triangular, Trapezoidal and Minmax Granulation. Combination of Classification Results from low, mid and high Granules. Classification accuracy percentage.

	TG	TZG	mMG
low/mid/high	95.45	93.33	91.66

Table 7. Triangular, Trapezoidal and Minmax Granulation. Concatenation of low, mid and high Granules. Classification accuracy percentage.

	TG	TZG	mMG
low_mid_high	95.55	96.59	92.13

Table 8. The results reported in [7] focused on the same classification problem with the same database. Average percentage of classification accuracy.

	Alpha	Beta	Theta	Concatenated
Average Accuracy	79.5	92.2	78.9	93

the 3 bands were concatenated to model a single classifier also with random forest. The results obtained in the work of Reyes [7] are shown in Table 8:

As can be seen in Tables 7 and 8 the average accuracy classification obtained by concatenating the low, mid and high (low_mid_high) fuzzy granules reaches 96.59% while the concatenation of characteristics extracted from the Alpha, Beta and Theta bands have an average accuracy of 93%.

4 Conclusions

The present work proposes fuzzy granulation as a way to characterize EEG signals for the classification of different stress conditions. In total, we tested four different techniques of fuzzy granulation time series to extract features from EEG signals: Fuzzy C-Means, Triangular Mf, Trapezoidal Mf and Minmax granulation. Granulation of time series to extract features from EEG signal is an approach that allows finding relevant information in electroencephalographic signals recorded in different stress scenarios. These feature extraction proposal leads to encouraging results in multi-class stress classification. Accuracy percentage classification of 96.59% has been achieved by extracting three granules from the EEG signal using TZG, generating a data set where each EEG sample is characterized by the concatenation of the extracted granules, as shown in Table 7.

The study of the effects of music on stress has long been of great interest, for example in [17] it was found that preoperative music can help normalize hypertensive responses during outpatient surgical stress, in [18] data show that in the presence of music, the level of salivary cortisol stopped increasing after psychological stress, in [19] is presented a mobile application that used yoga therapy and music to help users relax. However none of these works have the focus of using machine learning or fuzzy granulation for automatic classification of different stress patterns.

By being able to clearly differentiate the three scenarios in which the EEG signal sampling was done, total silence, relaxing music and pleasant music; it is possible to assure that listening to music has effects on the body's reaction to a cognitive challenge. This allows us to consider music as a tool with the potential to reduce the negative effects of stress in its early stages and thus mitigate its negative effects on health. More research is needed in this regard in order to effectively identify stimuli that reduce stress.

Regarding the results obtained with Fuzzy Clustering, with an average classification accuracy that is within the range of 85.67% to 94.39%, it can be said that they are below the results achieved with the MF granulation approach. Changing multi-class approach to a binary classification could improve the results. This is because binary classification algorithms are simpler and easier to implement than multi-class classification algorithms. In addition, binary classification algorithms may be more accurate than multi-class classification algorithms when classes are not well separated, there is less chance of error and less complexity in the model. Furthermore testing the fuzzy granulation on the preprocessed signal, in smaller time windows could also increase accuracy classification results. All these experiments are proposed as future work.

References

1. Zadeh, L.A.: Toward a theory of fuzzy information granulation and its centrality in human reasoning and Fuzzy Logic. Fuzzy Sets Syst. **90**(2), 111–127 (1997)
2. Ouyang, T., Pedrycz, W., Reyes-Galaviz, O.F., Pizzi, N.J.: Granular description of data structures: a two-phase design. IEEE Trans. Cybern. **51**(4), 1902–1912 (2021)
3. Huang, Z., Li, J.: Feature subset selection with multi-scale fuzzy granulation. IEEE Trans. Artif. Intell. 1 (2022)
4. Lu, W., Pedrycz, W., Liu, X., Yang, J., Li, P.: The modeling of time series based on fuzzy information granules. Expert Syst. Appl. **41**(8), 3799–3808 (2014)
5. Subhani, A.R., Mumtaz, W., Saad, B.M., Kamel, N., Malik, A.S.: Machine learning framework for the detection of mental stress at multiple levels. IEEE Access **5**, 13545–13556 (2017)
6. Zanetti, M., et al.: Multilevel assessment of mental stress via network physiology paradigm using consumer wearable devices. J. Ambient. Intell. Humaniz. Comput. **12**(4), 4409–4418 (2019)
7. Reyes Galaviz, R.S.: Análisis con electroencefalografía (EEG) de la escucha de música para el estudio de estrés académico. Item 1009/2048: Repositorio INAOE (2021)
8. Gu, X., et al.: EEG-based brain-computer interfaces (BCIs): a survey of recent studies on signal sensing technologies and computational intelligence approaches and their applications. IEEE/ACM Trans. Comput. Biol. Bioinf. **18**(5), 1645–1666 (2021)
9. AlShorman, O., et al.: Frontal lobe real-time EEG analysis using machine learning techniques for mental stress detection. J. Integr. Neurosci. **21**(1), 020 (2022)

10. Tsai, Y.-H., Wu, S.-K., Yu, S.-S., Tsai, M.-H.: Analyzing brain waves of table tennis players with machine learning for stress classification. Appl. Sci. **12**(16), 8052 (2022)
11. Liu, L., Ji, Y., Gao, Y., Li, T., Xu, W.: A novel stress state assessment method for college students based on EEG. Comput. Intell. Neurosci. **2022**, 1–11 (2022)
12. Zhang, R., Shen, F., Zhao, J.: A model with fuzzy granulation and deep belief networks for exchange rate forecasting. In: 2014 International Joint Conference on Neural Networks (IJCNN), pp. 366–373 (2014)
13. Ruan, J., Wang, X., Shi, Y.: Developing fast predictors for large-scale time series using fuzzy granular support vector machines. Appl. Soft Comput. **13**(9), 3981–4000 (2013)
14. Reyes-Galaviz, O.F., Pedrycz, W.: Granular fuzzy models: analysis, design, and evaluation. Int. J. Approximate Reasoning **64**, 1–19 (2015)
15. Pedrycz, W., Homenda, W.: Building the fundamentals of granular computing: a principle of justifiable granularity. Appl. Soft Comput. **13**, 4209–4218 (2013)
16. Delorme, A., Makeig, S.: EEGLAB: an open source toolbox for analysis of single-trial EEG dynamics including independent component analysis. J. Neurosci. Methods **134**(1), 9–21 (2004)
17. Allen, K.J., et al.: Normalization of hypertensive responses during ambulatory surgical stress by perioperative music. Am. J. Hypertens. **11**(4), 19A (1998)
18. Khalfa, S., Bella, S.D., Roy, M., Peretz, I., Lupien, S.J.: Effects of relaxing music on salivary cortisol level after psychological stress. Ann. N. Y. Acad. Sci. **999**(1), 374–376 (2003)
19. Vijayaragavan, G.R., Raghav, R.L., Phani, K.P., Vaidyanathan, V.: EEG monitored mind de-stressing smart phone application using yoga and music therapy. In: 2015 International Conference on Green Computing and Internet of Things (ICGCIoT), Greater Noida, India, pp. 412–415 (2015)

A Parallel Approach for RegularSearch Algorithm

Jairo A. Lefebre-Lobaina(✉) and José Ruiz-Shulcloper

Universidad de Ciencias Informáticas, La Habana, Cuba
jairo.lefebre@gmail.com, jshulcloper@uci.cu

Abstract. The process of finding minimal subsets of features that can differentiate objects belonging to different classes, known as typical testors, is an exponential complexity problem. Several algorithms have been proposed to improve the search process efficiency by utilizing different properties and techniques, including parallelism. In this paper, we propose a parallel version of the RegularSearch algorithm to find all typical testors related to a supervised classification problem. The proposed algorithm is compared with the most recent algorithm in the literature, and the comparative analysis shows the advantages of our proposal over the compared methods, using both synthetic and real problem datasets.

Keywords: Feature selection · Typical testors · Reducts · Parallelization

1 Introduction

Supervised classification problems often involve structured data represented as features that describe a set of objects. However, as the number of features increases, it becomes more challenging to estimate the relevance of each feature and can impact the efficiency and accuracy of classification algorithms. Feature selection methods (*FS*) can help reduce the time required to train classification algorithms while maintaining accuracy [13]. One such approach to FS is the Test Theory, which was proposed by Zhuravlev [3].

Initially used for classification problems with two classes and objects described by Boolean features in the Pattern Recognition context, the concept of a *testor* was later extended to allow for its application in more complex situations [8]. Testors Theory has been successfully used to solve various problems, including text categorization [16], document clustering [11], fault diagnosis in steam turbines [5], and breast cancer diagnosis in medicine [4]. Moreover, it has been applied to estimate the relevance of each feature classification problems and for the *FS* process with mixed and incomplete data [20]. This is done by searching for *typical testors*, a concept related to *reducts* from Rough Sets Theory [9] and *minimal transversal* from Hyper Graph Theory [1].

The process of finding all *typical testors* (TT) has an exponential time complexity of 2^n, where n is the number of features describing the objects [8]. Also,

Y. Hernndez Heredia et al. (Eds.): IWAIPR 2023, LNCS 14335, pp. 72–83, 2024.
https://doi.org/10.1007/978-3-031-49552-6_7

several algorithms have been developed to improve the efficiency of this search process in different scenarios [19]. The algorithms for searching all *typical testors* can be divided into two main groups based on their search strategy: *external type* algorithms and *internal type* algorithms. The *external type* algorithms induce an order on the power set of features and use logical properties to minimize the number of comparisons carried out with most efficient approaches published in [6,12,15,17]. However, none of the recent approaches of mentioned algorithms have a proposed parallel version to find all typical testors.

On the other hand, the *internal type* algorithms focus their strategy on selecting comparisons between objects that fulfill certain properties and use these elements to build the *typical testor* set [2]. The updated version of YYC algorithm proposed by Piza et al. [14] is the latest and fastest approach for finding all typical testors in a parallel way.

In this paper, we propose a parallel approach for the internal type algorithm *RegularSearch* [10] to search for all typical testors related to a supervised classification problem. The rest of the paper is structured as follows: Sect. 2 presents the concepts used in this work, Sect. 3 describes the proposed algorithm in detail, Sect. 4 shows the results of the experimental study carried out, and finally, Sect. 5 presents our conclusions and proposals for future work.

2 Concepts Definition

Testor theory current research is based on three main concepts: the training matrix (*TM*), the difference matrix (*DM*), and the basic matrix (*BM*). The *TM* contains m objects, $\{O_1, O_2, ..., O_m\}$, each of which is described by n features, $R = \{x_1, x_2, \ldots, x_n\}$. We denote the value of feature x_i in object O_j as $x_i(O_j)$. The MD is a matrix that represents the difference or not (value 0) between each feature related to objects that belong to different classes.

Given a row $f_i \in MD$ and a feature $x_q \in R$, we denote the value of f_i in the feature x_q as $f_i[x_q]$. A row $f_i \in MD$ is considered a *sub-row* of $f_s \in MD$ if and only if for each $x_q \in R$, $f_i[x_q] \leq f_s[x_q]$ and there exists a feature x_p such that $f_i[x_q] < f_s[x_q]$. The matrix formed by all *sub-rows* in *DM* is called *basic matrix* (*BM*) and the rows in *BM* are a subset of the set of rows in *DM* [7].

Table 1. Transformations from *TM* to *DM* to *BM*.

TM		x_1	x_2	x_3	x_4
C_1	O_1	0	a	1	7
	O_2	1	b	0	4
	O_3	?	b	1	4
C_2	O_4	1	a	0	4
	O_5	1	b	1	7

DM	x_1	x_2	x_3	x_4
O_{14}	1	0	1	1
O_{15}	1	1	0	0
O_{24}	0	1	0	0
O_{25}	0	0	1	1
O_{34}	1	1	1	0
O_{35}	1	0	0	1

BM	x_1	x_2	x_3	x_4
O_{24}	0	1	0	0
O_{25}	0	0	1	1
O_{35}	1	0	0	1

In Table 1, we provide an example of an ME and the corresponding MD and MB. In this example, several data types are used in the presented features, including missing values (represented as ?), and all comparisons are made using a strict equality function with Boolean output. However, the testor theory has evolved to allow for more than two disjoint classes, different kinds of features, and comparison output values [8].

The density of value 1 is defined as $D(1) = U/(m_b * n)$, where m_b is the number of rows in *BM* and U is the number of 1 values contained in *BM*. $D(1)$ represents the minimum difference degree between objects that belong to different classes. If there are not many differences between objects that belong to different classes, the $D(1)$ value is low. For the *BM* presented in Table 1, we have $D(1) = 0.416$.

A subset of features T is a *testor*, if and only if when all features except those on T are removed from *TM*, the resulting sub matrix ME_t, contains no descriptions of equal objects that belong to different classes. This means that there are no zero rows in the sub matrix from the *BM* and *DM* formed by the features in T. T is a *typical testor* if and only if $\nexists T', T' \subset T$ and T' is a testor [7]. For the *TM* presented in Table 1, and corresponding *BM* (and *DM*), the *typical testor* set is $T = \{\{x_1, x_2, x_3\}, \{x_2, x_4\}\}$.

2.1 Compatible and Regular Sets

Given two elements $a_{ij} = a_{pq} = 1$ from *BM* (or *DM*) in different rows and columns, the element a_{ij} is said to be *compatible* with a_{pq} if and only if $a_{pj} = a_{iq} = 0$. We will denote the compatibility relation between a_{ij} and a_{pq} as $a_{ij} \sim a_{pq}$. The set of elements $D = \{e_1, e_2, ..., e_r\}, D \in BM$ is a *compatible set* if and only if $r = 1$ or $e_t \sim e_p$ for $t \neq p$ and $t, p = 1, 2, ..., r$ [7]. Let *MC* be a sub-matrix of *BM* formed by the columns associated with the elements in D. For each feature $x_a \in MC$, there exists at least one row with value 0 in all features except in x_a.

From the previous definition, it can be deduced that any non-empty subset $Q \subset D$ is also a *compatible set*. Moreover, if Z is not a compatible set, any superset W that holds $Z \subset W$ will also not be a compatible set.

Let D be a *compatible set* and *MC* be the sub-matrix of *BM* formed by the columns associated with the elements in D. D is a *regular set* if and only if the corresponding features in *MC* satisfy the testor property, which is equivalent to saying that *MC* does not have any row with 0 values. Moreover, if D is a *regular set*, then the set of features $T \in MC$ is also a *typical testor* [7].

3 Parallel RegularSearch

In this work, is proposed a parallel version of the *RegularSearch* algorithm to identify all *typical testors* related to a supervised classification problem. The original *RegularSearch* algorithm was presented in [10] with the aim of finding all *regular sets* in the power sets of features from *BM*. The algorithm starts by selecting the first feature in *BM* as an initial candidate and then incrementally adds new features during the search process.

In [10] is also proposed an arrangement process for *BM* to avoid comparisons with elements that will never be a testor. However, in order to provide a simpler description and better understanding of the parallel approach, we have simplified the sorting method.

The first step in the sorting process is to arrange the rows in *BM* in such a way that the first row in the matrix has the lowest number of elements with value 1. If there is more than one row that meets this criteria, any of them can be selected. The order of the remaining rows is not relevant. In the second step, the columns are sorted so that all elements with value 1 in the first row are grouped on the left side of *BM*. An example of this process is presented in Table 2, where BM^s is the sorting output.

Table 2. Sorting process example.

BM	x_1	x_2	x_3	x_4	x_5
O_1	0	0	1	1	1
O_2	1	0	0	0	1
O_3	0	1	0	1	0
O_4	1	1	1	0	0

BM^s	x_1	x_5	x_2	x_3	x_4
O_2	1	1	0	0	0
O_1	0	1	0	1	1
O_3	0	0	1	0	1
O_4	1	0	1	1	0

The search process begins with a *candidate set* of features denoted by C, where $|C| = 1$ and contains a single feature that, by definition, is a *compatible set*. Let MC be the submatrix from *BM* formed by the features in C. The algorithm continues to add new features to C incrementally, also checking that MC contains at least one subset of elements that holds the compatible set property and involves all the features in C. If MC contains a regular set (i.e., it has no zero rows), then C is added to the typical testor set (TT), and the search process for that candidate stops, because any superset will be a testor but will not hold the typicity property. If a feature $x_a \in BM$ is added to C, and the corresponding MC does not contain a *compatible set*, the search process stops because any superset from C will not be a *compatible set* either. In that situation, x_a is replaced with the feature x_{a+1} in C to continue the search process. If x_a is the last feature, the process stops.

All the steps mentioned above are described in the algorithm *GetRegularities* used by *RegularSearch* [10], and updated in Algorithm 1. This process is carried out in a recursive way. In every recursive call, the compatible set description contained in MC is generated. The behavior of the algorithm can be topologically represented as a depth-first tree search with a pre-order traversal strategy and a pruning process based on the compatible and regular sets properties. The main difference with [10] is that in the current proposal, *GetRegularitiesT* initializes the sets TT, ZR, and OD to run independently in a parallel process call (*thread*), and returns a subset of the typical testor set.

To ensure proper data structuring between iterations, hashing-based dictionaries are utilized as a data structure to store tuples in the form of (x_i, r_i). A dictionary is denoted as $OD[x_i] = r_i$, where OD is the dictionary, x_i is a feature from *BM*, r_i is a set of row positions in *BM*, and $|OD|$ represents the number of stored tuples in OD. Additionally, the set of row positions in *BM* related to the feature x_i that only contains zeros is denoted as $z(x_i)$, while the remaining rows are denoted as $o(x_i)$.

Algorithm 1. *GetRegularitiesT*

```
input: BM, F, C, TT, ZR, OD
output: TT

define c_n as last element in C
if |C| = 1 then
    define TT = ∅
    ZR = z(c_n)
    OD[c_n] = o(c_n)
end if
for all f_j ∈ F, where c_n ∈ F and j > n do
    define Inf as ZR ∩ o(f_j)
    if |Inf| > 0 then
        define row_unitary as True
        define nOD as an empty dictionary
        for all x_i, r_i ∈ OD do
            nOD[x_i] = r_i − o(f_j)
            if |nOD[x_i]| = 0 then
                define row_unitary as False
                break loop
            end if
        end for
        if row_unitary then
            if |ZR| = 0 then
                add C to TT
            else
                nOD[f_j] = Inf
                define nC = C ∪ {f_j}
                define nZR = ZR − o(f_j)
                GetRegularitiesT(BM, F, nC, TT, nZR, nOD)
            end if
        end if
    end if
end for
return TT
```

Let TT be a typical testor set from BM, F the sorted set of features in BM, a sorted candidate set $C \neq \emptyset, C \subset F$, MC the submatrix from BM formed by the features in C, ZR the set of zero row positions in MC, and OD a dictionary to store the relation associated with feature $x_i \in C$ with the row position set from BM with zero value in all features except in x_i. Algorithm 1 describes the search for regular sets.

Let BM a basic matrix related to a supervised classification problem, and let TT the typical testor set in BM. The process to find all TT in a parallel way is described in Algorithm 2. It's important to highlight that, after the sorting process, the number of threads required will be the same as the number of non-zero values in the first row of BM.

Algorithm 2. *ParallelRegularSearch*

input: BM **output:** TT

sort BM according to 1 values contained in rows
define F **as** sorted set of features in BM
define $TList$ **as** a list of threads
define $TT = \emptyset$
for all $x_i \in F$ **do**
    define r_1 **as** first row position in BM
    if $r_1 \in z(x_i)$ **then**
        break loop
    end if
    define $C = \{x_i\}$ **as** a sorted set of features
    if $|z(x_i) = 0|$ **then**
        add C to TT
    else
        add *GetRegularitiesT*(BM, F, C, ZR, OD) as a thread call to $TList$
    end if
end for
for all $tc_i \in TList$ **do**
    define tt_i **as** the output of tc_i thread
    $TT = TT \cup tt_i$
end for
return TT

The *ParallelRegularSearch* algorithm uses the *GetRegularitiesT* subroutine as the search strategy over the feature set in BM. Avoiding unnecessary comparisons is the core reason behind the efficiency of the *GetRegularitiesT* subroutine. Additionally, the tree-like search process ensures that every possible candidate is evaluated only once, which is the main characteristic that allows the parallelization of the searching process, increasing the efficiency without losing effectiveness. Since *GetRegularitiesT* does not compare $x_i \in F$ with previous features in F during the search process, *ParallelRegularSearch* provides each feature x_i as a new candidate for each thread. Each thread will return the typical testor subset, where x_i is the first feature, and the remaining features x_j hold $j > i$. Finally, the set union of the different outputs will be the typical testor set associated with the input BM.

3.1 Execution Example

To show how the *ParallelRegularSearch* algorithm works, Table 3 describes each step executed using BM^s presented in Table 2 for a single thread call. Since the presented example is only for a single thread call the output will contain all typical testors that contains x_1.

Table 3. Execution steps description.

Step	C	Description
1	$\{x_1\}$	Take x_1 as candidate, due is not a typical testor and (by definition) is a compatible set
2	$\{x_1, x_5\}$	Add x_5 to C, due MC contains a compatible set, but C is not a testor
3	$\{x_1, x_5\}$	Ignore x_2, due MC corresponding to $\{x_2\} \cup C$ not contains a compatible set that include all features
4	$\{x_1, x_5\}$	Ignore x_3, due MC corresponding to $\{x_3\} \cup C$ not contains a compatible set that include all features
5	$\{x_1, x_5\}$	Ignore x_4, due MC corresponding to $\{x_4\} \cup C$ not contains a compatible set that include all features. Since there is no other combination the search process for $\{x_1, x_5\}$ stop (β)
6	$\{x_1, x_2\}$	Add x_2 to C, due MC contains a compatible set, but C is not a testor
7	$\boldsymbol{\{x_1, x_2, x_3\}}$	Add x_2 to C, due MC contains a compatible set and also a regular set, the current C is a typical testor and is added to TT set; since any super set of features form C will be not a typical testor (β)
8	$\{x_1, x_2\}$	Ignore x_4, due MC corresponding to $\{x_4\} \cup C$ not contains a compatible set that include all features. Since there is no other combination the search process for $\{x_1, x_2\}$ stop (β)
9	$\{x_1, x_3\}$	Add x_3 to C, due MC contains a compatible set, but C is not a testor
10	$\{x_1, x_3\}$	Ignore x_4, due MC corresponding to $\{x_4\} \cup C$ not contains a compatible set that include all features. Since there is no other combination the search process for $\{x_1, x_3\}$ stop (β)
11	$\boldsymbol{\{x_1, x_4\}}$	Add x_4 to C, due MC contains a compatible set and also a regular set, the current C is a typical testor and is added to TT set; since any super set of features form C will be not a typical testor (β)
12	–	Return the typical testors found since there is no possible feature to compare with after x_4. $TT = \{\{x_1, x_2, x_3\}, \{x_1, x_4\}\}$

In each step of the algorithm, a different candidate is tested, and the algorithm will not proceed to the next step if MC does not contain a compatible set with at least one element in each column. This is why the values in C in Table 3 can change without an explicit insertion or elimination; the algorithm backtracks (represented as β) to a previous state. When C satisfies the typical testor definition, the values are highlighted in bold.

In the sorted matrix, if the search process takes the feature x_2 as a new candidate in C, to find the possible typical testors with the remaining features (x_3 and x_4), any combination will not generate a testor because it will contain a row with zero values in MC. For this reason, only two threads are required to process that dataset.

The remaining steps using BM^s are carried out in parallel. Theoretically, if an infinite number of threads were available, the searching time would be the time required for the first thread to finish, because the search space is reduced by half in each following thread. Also, the amount of threads required is the same as the amount of ones in the first row of BM^s. The output of the second thread for searching the typical testors associated with x_5 in BM^s is $\{x_5, x_2\}, \{x_5, x_3, x_4\}\}$. The final TT set is the set union of each thread result:

$TT = \{\{x_1, x_2, x_3\}, \{x_1, x_4\}, \{x_5, x_2\}, \{x_5, x_3, x_4\}\}$.

4 Experimental Results

To demonstrate the advantages of the parallel approach for the *RegularSearch* algorithm (P-RS), several experiments were conducted using synthetic and real-world problem datasets. For the comparison process, the proposal was compared with the parallel version of the *YYC* algorithm (P-YYC).

Recent research has shown that modern algorithms exhibit variations in efficiency based on the $D(1)$ value [18]. To focus on the efficiency of the compared algorithms, the primary comparison criteria selected were the $D(1)$ value and the total time required to find all typical testors.

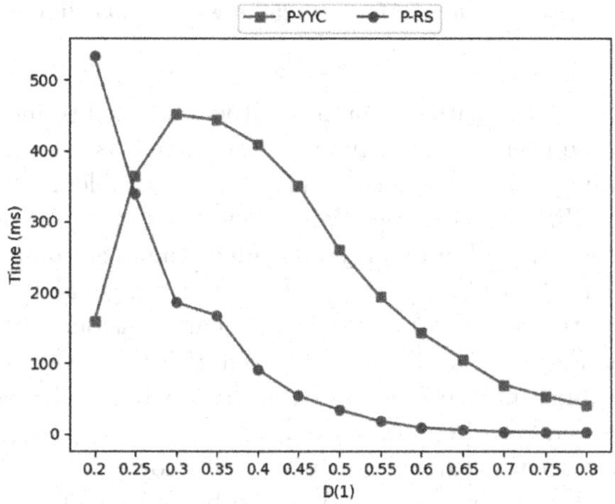

Fig. 1. Results for BMs with 250 rows and 20 columns.

To conduct experiments with synthetic matrices, several BMs of fixed dimensions were randomly generated. To match the expected $D(1)$ value, the synthetic matrices were generated with a similar distribution of ones in each row. For each $D(1)$ value 50 matrices were generated, and then calculated the mean execution time, for a total of 650 BMs. All experiments were conducted on an Asus ROG Zephyrus G14 computer equipped with an AMD Ryzen™ 7 4800HS processor and 16 GB of RAM.

As shown in Fig. 1, the *P-RS* algorithm has better results for higher $D(1)$ values, while *P-YYC* performs better for lower values. However, to show how the obtained values may change when using more complex datasets, two more test sets were conducted following the same comparison criteria.

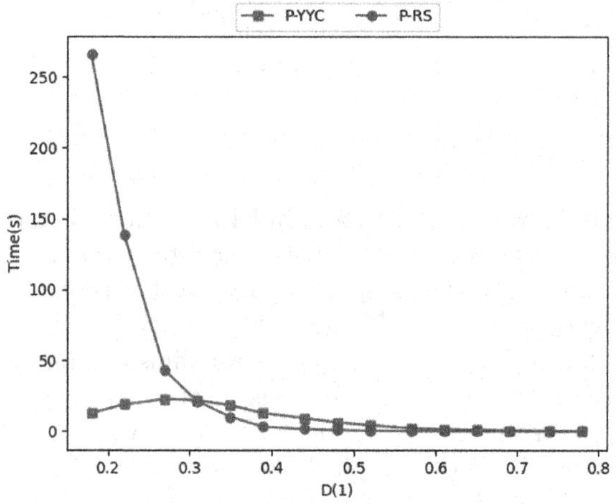

Fig. 2. Results for BMs with 250 rows and 30 columns.

For the next test with synthetic datasets, it was decided to increase the number of features while keeping the number of rows fixed. Is a know fact that the search space will increase and the complexity of the problem as the number of features increases. However, the Fig. 2 also shows that the relationship between the number of rows and columns may also affect the performance of the algorithms. Although *P-RS* still outperforms *P-YYC* for high $D(1)$ values with up to 9 s of difference, the results for lower densities are considerably worse. On the other hand, in the Fig. 3, it can be observed that *P-YYC* always performs worse than *P-RS*, with differences up to 13 s, when the number of rows is increased while keeping the number of columns fixed.

The second test set was carried out using well-known datasets from the UCI Machine Learning Repository[1] to evaluate the behavior of the compared algorithms on real-life problems. The only dataset that is not from UCI is the *Higher Education Students Performance Evaluation* (K-higher edu) dataset, which was

[1] UCI Machine Learning Repository https://archive.ics.uci.edu/.

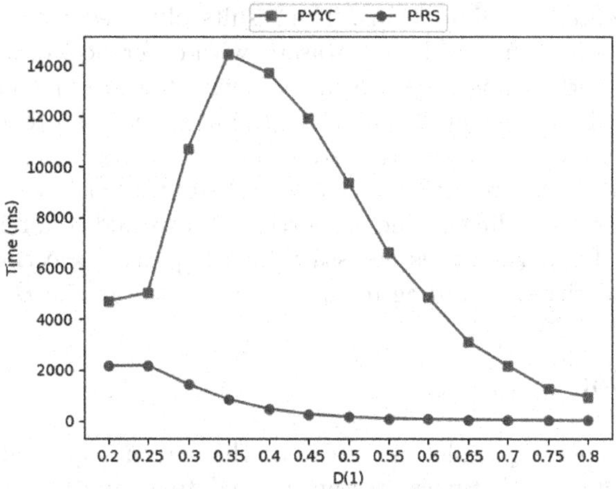

Fig. 3. Results for BMs with 1000 rows and 20 columns.

taken from Kaggle[2]. Since the previous experiments were conducted according to the $D(1)$ value, several datasets with different $D(1)$ values associated with BM were selected. The algorithms were implemented in Java using the *Runnable* interface and published on GitHub.[3].

Table 4. Dataset experimets.

Dateset	Rows	Cols	*D(1)*	P-YYC	P-RS
kr.vs.kp	29	36	0.02	**<1**	2
anneal	93	38	0.13	**30**	177
soybean	30	35	0.2	13	**6**
dermatology	1124	34	0.34	311791	**51969**
K-higher edu	2367	32	0.46	4272242	**172153**
cardiotocography	9751	35	0.54	23455339	**125839**
HCV-Egyptian	1442	28	0.67	15412	**159**
promoter	2761	57	0.75	26751971	**28994**
waveform5000	908	40	0.92	6	**<1**
DARWIN	1681	451	0.98	650407	**198**

The table presented in Table 4 provides a description of the BM associated with each dataset, sorted in ascending order according to the $D(1)$ value. Additionally, the table includes the execution time required for the algorithms *P-YYC*

[2] Kaggle dataset https://www.kaggle.com/datasets/mariazhokhova/higher-education-students-performance-evaluation.

[3] GitHub shared repository https://github.com/J41R0/RegularSearch.

and *P-RS*, presented in milliseconds. The results obtained are consistent with the experimentation using synthetic datasets, with differences of up to 7 h showing the superior performance of *P-RS* in *BM*s with high $D(1)$ value. Also, in all experiments can be appreciated that *P-YYC* for $D(1) > 0.5$ tends to improve the performance, but in any experiment get better results that *P-RS*.

The experimentation results clearly demonstrate that the algorithms exhibit different behavior depending on the proportion of rows and columns in the input BM. Therefore, further study is necessary for the precise selection of a typical testor finding algorithm according to the characteristics of the BM.

5 Conclusions

This paper presents a parallel approach to the internal type algorithm *RegularSearch* for finding all typical testors related to a supervised classification problem. The proposed algorithm parallelizes the search process of all typical testors associated with a feature with others on the left of the basic matrix, and the complete typical testor set is obtained by taking the union of all the subsets found.

The experiments conducted show that the proposed algorithm is more efficient than the parallel version of the YYC algorithm when $D(1)$ values are high. The results obtained with synthetic and real-life datasets confirm the behavior of the algorithm and its ability to handle real problems that generate a *BM* with high $D(1)$ value.

For future work, we suggest developing a methodology for comparing typical testor finding algorithms that considers the input matrix dimensions and $D(1)$ value. It would be interesting to investigate the relationship between the proposed approach and parallelization paradigms for BigData and HPC. Additionally, we propose developing a version of the algorithm that can take advantage of the computing capabilities of GPUs.

References

1. Alba-Cabrera, E., Godoy-Calderon, S., Lazo-Cortés, M.S., Martínez-Trinidad, J.F., Carrasco-Ochoa, J.A.: On the relation between the concepts of irreducible testor and minimal transversal. IEEE Access **7**, 82809–82816 (2019)
2. Alba-Cabrera, E., Ibarra-Fiallo, J., Godoy-Calderon, S., Cervantes-Alonso, F.: YYC: a fast performance incremental algorithm for finding typical testors. In: Bayro-Corrochano, E., Hancock, E. (eds.) CIARP 2014. LNCS, vol. 8827, pp. 416–423. Springer, Cham (2014). https://doi.org/10.1007/978-3-319-12568-8_51
3. Dmitriev, A., Zhuravlev, Y.I., Krendeliev, F.: About mathematical principles of objects and phenomena classification. Diskretni Analiz **7**, 3–15 (1966)
4. Gallegos, A., Torres, D., Álvarez, F., Soto, A.T.: Feature subset selection and typical testors applied to breast cancer cells. Res. Comput. Sci. **121**(1), 151–163 (2016)

5. Gómez, J.P., Hernández Montero, F.E., Gómez Mancilla, J.C.: Variable selection for journal bearing faults diagnostic through logical combinatorial pattern recognition. In: Hernández Heredia, Y., Milián Núñez, V., Ruiz Shulcloper, J. (eds.) IWAIPR 2018. LNCS, vol. 11047, pp. 299–306. Springer, Cham (2018). https://doi.org/10.1007/978-3-030-01132-1_34
6. Gómez, J.P., Montero, F.E.H., Sotelo, J.C., Mancilla, J.C.G., Rey, Y.V.: RoPM: an algorithm for computing typical testors based on recursive reductions of the basic matrix. IEEE Access **9**, 128220–128232 (2021)
7. Lazo-Cortés, M., Ruiz-Shulcloper, J.: Determining the feature relevance for non-classically described objects and a new algorithm to compute typical fuzzy testors. Pattern Recogn. Lett. **16**(12), 1259–1265 (1995)
8. Lazo-Cortes, M., Ruiz-Shulcloper, J., Alba-Cabrera, E.: An overview of the evolution of the concept of testor. Pattern Recogn. **34**(4), 753–762 (2001)
9. Lazo-Cortés, M.S., Martínez-Trinidad, J.F., Carrasco-Ochoa, J.A., Sanchez-Diaz, G.: Are reducts and typical testors the same? In: Bayro-Corrochano, E., Hancock, E. (eds.) CIARP 2014. LNCS, vol. 8827, pp. 294–301. Springer, Cham (2014). https://doi.org/10.1007/978-3-319-12568-8_36
10. Lefebre-Lobaina, J.A., Ruiz-Shulcloper, J.: Regularsearch, a fast performance algorithm for typical testors computation (ND) (Under review)
11. Li, F., Zhu, Q.: Document clustering in research literature based on NMF and testor theory. JSW **6**(1), 78–82 (2011)
12. Lias-Rodriguez, A., Sanchez-Diaz, G.: An algorithm for computing typical testors based on elimination of gaps and reduction of columns. Int. J. Pattern Recognit. Artif. Intell. **27**(08), 1350022 (2013)
13. Mafarja, M., Qasem, A., Heidari, A.A., Aljarah, I., Faris, H., Mirjalili, S.: Efficient hybrid nature-inspired binary optimizers for feature selection. Cogn. Comput. 1–26 (2019)
14. Piza-Davila, I., Sanchez-Diaz, G., Lazo-Cortes, M.S., Noyola-Medrano, C.: Enhancing the performance of YYC algorithm useful to generate irreducible testors. Int. J. Pattern Recognit. Artif. Intell. **32**(01), 1860001 (2018)
15. Piza-Dávila, I., Sánchez-Díaz, G., Lazo-Cortés, M.S., Villalón-Turrubiates, I.: An algorithm for computing minimum-length irreducible testors. IEEE Access **8**, 56312–56320 (2020)
16. Pons-Porrata, A., Gil-García, R., Berlanga-Llavori, R.: Using typical testors for feature selection in text categorization. In: Rueda, L., Mery, D., Kittler, J. (eds.) CIARP 2007. LNCS, vol. 4756, pp. 643–652. Springer, Heidelberg (2007). https://doi.org/10.1007/978-3-540-76725-1_67
17. Rodríguez-Diez, V., Martínez-Trinidad, J.F., Carrasco-Ochoa, J.A., Lazo-Cortés, M.S.: A new algorithm for reduct computation based on gap elimination and attribute contribution. Inf. Sci. **435**, 111–123 (2018)
18. Rodríguez-Diez, V., Martínez-Trinidad, J.F., Carrasco-Ochoa, J.A., Lazo-Cortés, M.S.: The impact of basic matrix dimension on the performance of algorithms for computing typical testors. In: Martínez-Trinidad, J.F., Carrasco-Ochoa, J.A., Olvera-López, J.A., Sarkar, S. (eds.) MCPR 2018. LNCS, vol. 10880, pp. 41–50. Springer, Cham (2018). https://doi.org/10.1007/978-3-319-92198-3_5
19. Sánchez-Díaz, G., Lazo-Cortés, M.S., Aguirre-Salado, C.A., Piza-Davila, I., Garcia-Contreras, J.P.: A review of algorithms to computing irreducible testors applied to feature selection. Artif. Intell. Rev. 1–22 (2022)
20. Solorio-Fernández, S., Carrasco-Ochoa, J.A., Martínez-Trinidad, J.F.: A survey on feature selection methods for mixed data. Artif. Intell. Rev. **55**(4), 2821–2846 (2022)

An Improved Fault Diagnosis Scheme Based on a Type-2 Fuzzy Classification Algorithms

Adrián Rodríguez-Ramos[1], Antônio J. da Silva Neto[2], and Orestes Llanes-Santiago[1](✉)

[1] Universidad Tecnológica de la Habana José Antonio Echeverría, CUJAE, La Habana, Cuba
adrian.rr@automatica.cujae.edu.cu, orestes@tesla.cujae.edu.cu
[2] Instituto-Politécnico - Universidade do Estado do Rio de Janeiro, Nova Friburgo, RJ, Brazil
ajsneto@iprj.uerj.br

Abstract. The Industry 4.0 paradigm aims to obtain high levels of productivity and efficiency, more competitive final products and compliance with the demanding regulations related to industrial safety. To achieve these objectives, the industrial systems must be equipped with condition monitoring systems for the detection and isolation of faults. The paper presents the design of a fault diagnosis system with robust behavior for industrial plants by using Type-2 Fuzzy algorithm. In order to improve the classification, a kernel variant is implemented in the proposed algorithms to accomplish a better differentiation between classes. Several experiments were conducted (without noise, 2%, and 5% of noise level) by using the T2FCM, IT2FCM, KT2FCM, and KIT2FCM algorithms for the DAMADCIS benchmark, obtaining excellent results.

Keywords: Industry 4.0 · Fault diagnosis · Industrial Plants · Type-2 Fuzzy sets

1 Introduction

A main premise in the Industry 4.0 paradigm is to obtain high production levels with low operating expenses to improve the relation benefits-costs [6,10]. An important cause of the increase in operating expenses and the descending productivity in industrial plants is the occurrence of faults [3,17].

Many research results on the fault diagnosis topic in industrial systems have been published in the scientific literature in the last two decades under two main approaches: model based, and data based fault diagnosis [14,15]. However, the advances in the Internet of Things (IoT) and Big Data technologies have currently allowed a major attention and results in the last approach [2,11].

Several computational tools have been displayed in scientific papers and books to improve the performance of industrial fault diagnosis systems [7,8].

Y. Hernndez Heredia et al. (Eds.): IWAIPR 2023, LNCS 14335, pp. 84–95, 2024.
https://doi.org/10.1007/978-3-031-49552-6_8

However, the need to develop new strategies remains open because the results depend on the type of industrial plant analyzed.

The training stage of a data-based supervised fault diagnosis system is decisive for achieving the best online performance. To accomplish better results in training, the different classes that represent the operation of the industrial plant have to be very well identified [16]. However, this is a very complex task due to the uncertainties that characterize the industrial measurements by the effect of external disturbances and noise [18].

To overcome some difficulties of type-1 fuzzy sets to deal with the uncertain that characterize the industrial process due to noise and external disturbances type-2 fuzzy sets are used. In type-1 fuzzy sets, the memberships degree is a crisp number, but in type-2 fuzzy sets, the memberships degree is a type-1 fuzzy number. The goal is that higher membership values should contribute more than memberships that are smaller when the cluster centers are updated [19,20]. In this paper, a fault diagnosis methodology based on type-2 fuzzy classification algorithms is presented.

The main contribution of this paper is to present a robust condition monitoring scheme versus external disturbances and noise. For this, a scheme based on the use of Type-2 Fuzzy sets is displayed. For misclassification reduction, a kernel variant is implemented of the proposed algorithms to accomplish a better differentiation between classes. The proposal exhibits high performance in the presence of noisy observations

2 Materials and Methods

2.1 Type-2 Fuzzy C-Means Algorithm (T2FCM) and Kernelized T2FCM (KT2FCM)

For updating the cluster centers in T2FCM, the weighted mean of all observations is used [19]. The membership values for the Type 2 membership are obtained as follow:

$$a_{ik} = u_{ik} - \frac{1 - u_{ik}}{2} \tag{1}$$

where a_{ik} and u_{ik} are the type-2 and type-1 memberships respectively. The cluster centers are updated according to the traditional FCM but taking into account the new type-2 fuzzy membership . Although T2FCM has proven effective for spherical data, it fails when the data structure of input patterns is non-spherical. A way of increasing the accuracy of the T2FCM is using a kernel function for calculating the distance of data point from the cluster centers, i.e., mapping the data points from the input space to a high dimensional space. This algorithm is used to obtain a better separability among classes improving the classification results. In the KT2FCM algorithm is minimized the following objective function:

$$J_{KT2FCM} = \sum_{i=1}^{l}\sum_{k=1}^{N} a_{ik}^{*m} \left\|\boldsymbol{\Psi}(\mathbf{z_k}) - \boldsymbol{\Psi}(\mathbf{v_i})\right\|^2 \tag{2}$$

where, $\left\|\boldsymbol{\Psi}(\mathbf{z_k}) - \boldsymbol{\Psi}(\mathbf{v_i})\right\|^2$ is the square of the distance between $\boldsymbol{\Psi}(\mathbf{z_k})$ and $\boldsymbol{\Psi}(\mathbf{v_i})$. In the feature space, the distance is computed through the kernel in the input space as:

$$\begin{aligned}\left\|\boldsymbol{\Psi}(\mathbf{z_k}) - \boldsymbol{\Psi}(\mathbf{v_i})\right\|^2 &= \mathbf{K}(\mathbf{z_k}, \mathbf{z_k}) - \mathbf{2K}(\mathbf{z_k}, \mathbf{v_i}) \\ &+\mathbf{K}(\mathbf{v_i}, \mathbf{v_i})\end{aligned} \tag{3}$$

In the scientific bibliography, many kernel functions are found, and the most appropriate depends on the applications [13]. Nonetheless, the most used is the Gaussian Kernel Function (GKF).

If the GKF is used, then $\mathbf{K}(\mathbf{z}, \mathbf{z}) = \mathbf{1}$ and $\left\|\boldsymbol{\Psi}(\mathbf{z_k}) - \boldsymbol{\Psi}(\mathbf{v_i})\right\|^2 = \mathbf{2}\left(\mathbf{1} - \mathbf{K}(\mathbf{z_k}, \mathbf{v_i})\right)$. So, Eq. (2) can be expressed as:

$$J_{KT2FCM} = 2\sum_{i=1}^{l}\sum_{k=1}^{N} a_{ik}^{*m} \left\|1 - \mathbf{K}(\mathbf{z_k}, \mathbf{v_i})\right\|^2 \tag{4}$$

where,

$$\mathbf{K}(\mathbf{z_k}, \mathbf{v_i}) = e^{-\|\mathbf{z}_k - \mathbf{v}_i\|^2/\delta^2} \tag{5}$$

where δ is the bandwidth which illustrates the smoothness degree of the GKF. Minimizing Eq. (4), yields:

$$a_{ik}^{*} = \frac{1}{\sum_{j=1}^{l}\left(\frac{1-\mathbf{K}(\mathbf{z_k},\mathbf{v_i})}{1-\mathbf{K}(\mathbf{z_k},\mathbf{v_j})}\right)^{1/(m-1)}} \tag{6}$$

$$\mathbf{q}_i = \frac{\sum_{k=1}^{N}\left(a_{ik}^{*m}\mathbf{K}(\mathbf{z_k}, \mathbf{v_i})\mathbf{z_k}\right)}{\sum_{k=1}^{N} a_{ik}^{*m}\mathbf{K}(\mathbf{z_k}, \mathbf{v_i})} \tag{7}$$

2.2 Interval Type-2 Fuzzy C-Means Algorithm (IT2FCM) and Kernelized IT2FCM (KIT2FCM)

The parameter m is crucial in fuzzy clustering algorithms to determine the partition matrix uncertainty. Nevertheless, it is not an easy task to decide the value of m in advance. IT2FCM regards the fuzzification coefficient as an interval $[m_1,m_2]$ and minimizes the objective function as [20]:

$$J_{IT2FCM} = \sum_{i=1}^{l}\sum_{k=1}^{N} u_{ik}^{*m} d_{ik}^2 \tag{8}$$

where the parameter m is substituted by m_1 and m_2 that represent different fuzzy degrees and provide different objective functions compared with FCM. To minimize the objective function [20]:

$$\overline{u_i}(k) = max\left(1/\sum_{j=1}^{l}(d_{ik}/d_{jk})^{2/(m_1-1)}, 1/\sum_{j=1}^{l}(d_{ik}/d_{jk})^{2/(m_2-1)}\right) \tag{9}$$

$$\underline{u_i}(k) = min\left(1/\sum_{j=1}^{l}(d_{ik}/d_{jk})^{2/(m_1-1)}, 1/\sum_{j=1}^{l}(d_{ik}/d_{jk})^{2/(m_2-1)}\right) \tag{10}$$

where $d_{ik}^2 = \|z_k - q_i\|$ is the distance between input patterns z_k and cluster centers q_i. $\overline{u_i}(k)$ ($\underline{u_i}(k)$) is the upper (lower) membership function of z_k to q_i.

Distinct from FCM, the output of IT2FCM algorithm is an interval type-2 fuzzy set, that it is not possible to convert to a crisp set directly by a defuzzication operation. To calculate the centroid of a type-2 fuzzy set and reduce the type-2 fuzzy set to the type-1 fuzzy set is executed the type reduction just as the first step of output processing [9]. The interval-valued cluster centers are calculated as:

$$\widetilde{\mathbf{q}}_i = [\widetilde{q}_{i,1}, \widetilde{q}_{i,2}] = \sum_{u_{i1}} \cdots \sum_{u_{i1}} \frac{1}{\frac{\sum_{k=1}^{N} u_{ik}^{m^*} z_k}{\sum_{k=1}^{N} u_{ik}^{m^*}}} \tag{11}$$

supported on such type-2 memberships. m^* switches from m_1 to m_2, and $\widetilde{q}_{i,1}$ and $\widetilde{q}_{i,2}$ are usually obtained by Karnik-Mendel algorithm [5]. The procedure to obtain the kernel version of the IT2FCM algorithm (KIT2FCM) is similar to the one used in the case of T2FCM algorithm. The distance is calculated through the kernel function using the Gaussian Kernel Function (GKF).

2.3 Proposed Methodology

The proposed classification scheme for Fault Detection and Isolation (FDI) is displayed in Fig. 1. It exhibits an offline training phase and a recognition phase executed online. In the first phase, the fuzzy classifier is trained using a training database builds with historical data of the process. In the online phase, the classifier analyzes each observation collected from the process. The result offers information to the operator about the state of the system in real time. Training is the most important stage, since the center of each of the classes that represent the operation of the process will be determined, either in normal operation or in the presence of faults.

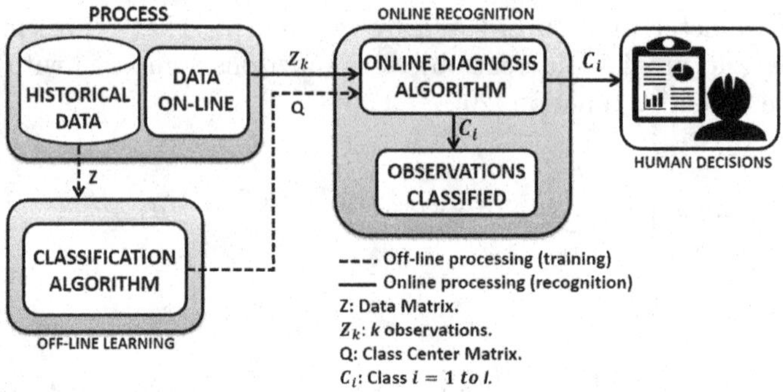

Fig. 1. Classification scheme for detection and isolation of faults.

Offline Training Phase. In this phase, the FDI system is trained with a set of historical data which contain the necessary information of each known operating state or class of the industrial plant (normal operation condition (NOC) and states of fault). The main aim of the training process is to determine the center of the known classes $\mathbf{Q} = \mathbf{q}_1, \mathbf{q}_2, \ldots, \mathbf{q}_c$ is determined to be used in the on-line recognition stage.

On-Line Recognition Phase. In this phase, it is determined to which class each observation k belongs at each time instant. First, the distance between the observation and the centers of the classes that were determined in the offline stage is computed. Subsequently, the degree of membership of the observation k is obtained for each class. It will be assigned to the class with the highest degree of membership (See Algorithm 1).

Algorithm 1: Recognition stage

Data: observation z_k, class centers $\mathbf{Q}$, m, c

Result: Current State

1. Calculate the distances among the observation z_k and the class centers;
2. Calculate the membership degree of the observation z_k to the c classes;
3. Determine the class to which observation z_k belongs;

2.4 Case Study: DAMADICS

To verify that, the proposed methodology was used in the DAMADICS test problem. It represents an intelligent electro-pneumatic actuator widely used in industries [1]. The diagram of this actuator is shown in Fig. 2. Table 1 and Fig. 3 (with 300 observations per class) shows the operation modes evaluated in the actuator and the measured variables used. Selected faults occur in different parts of the actuator and were selected in order to test the robustness of the diagnostic system.

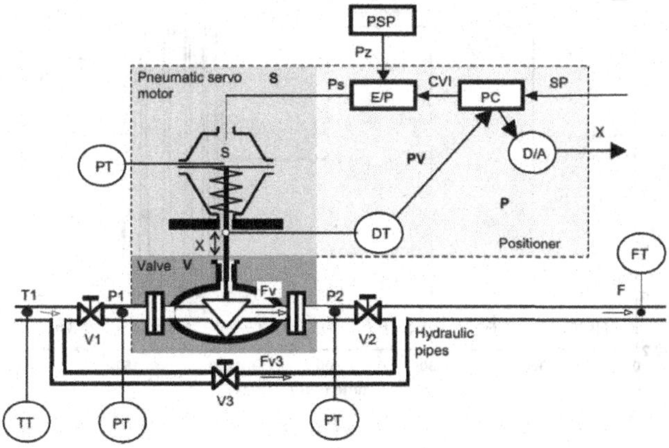

Fig. 2. Diagram of benchmark actuator system [1].

Table 1. Operation modes and measured variables in DAMADICS.

Operation Mode	Description	Variable	Description
NO	Normal Operation	CV	Process control external signal
F1	Valve clogging	P1	Pressure on inlet valve
F7	Critical flow	P2	Pressure on outlet valve
F12	Electro-pneumatic transducer fault	X	Valve plug displacement
F15	Positioner spring fault	F	Main pipeline flow rat
F19	Flow rate sensor fault	PV	Process value

2.5 Design of Experiments

Table 2 shows the characteristics of the training database used, which is free of outliers, noise, and missing variables. The values of the parameters used for the applied algorithms were: $\epsilon = 10^{-5}$, $m = 2$, $\sigma = 50$. The parameters were taken from [12].

K-cross-validation method with $K = 5$ was chosen for training (800 observations) and validation (200 observations). In the experiments of the online phase 2400 observations were used (400 new observations of each operation mode not used in the training). Each experiment was replicated 100 times to ensure repeatability of results. The average of the 100 results was considered as final result. To evaluate the robustness of the proposal, three experiments were developed:

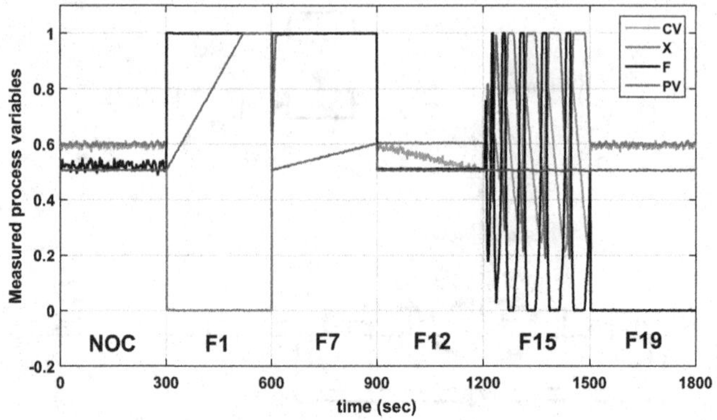

Fig. 3. Operation modes.

Table 2. Characteristics of the training database.

Parameter	Description	Quantity
l	Operation Modes (Classes)	6
p	Measured Variables	6
k	Number of Observations per class	1000
n	Number of Observation in the training database	6000

1. Observations without noise.
2. Observations with 2% of noise level
3. Observations with 5% of noise level.

3 Discussion of Results

4 Online Recognition Stage

The confusion matrix (CM) tool was used to evaluate the performance of the FDI system proposed. The values CM_{rs} for $r \neq s$ in the CM show the number of observations of the operation mode r that the classifier algorithm misclassifies in the operation modes.

Table 3 shows the confusion matrix (without noise in the measurements) where the results for the operation states Normal Operation Condition (NOC), Fault 1 (F1), Fault 7 (F7), Fault 12 F12), Fault 15 (F15) and Fault 19 (F19) are presented. In the main diagonal are presented the number of observations well classified. The accuracy of the classification process is obtained as TA=correctly classified observations/total observations. The average (AVE) of TA is displayed in the last row.

Figure 4 show the classification results for the different operation modes (NOC and faults 1, 7, 12, 15, 19) by using the T2FCM, IT2FCM, KT2FCM and KIT2FCM algorithms for DAMADICS process. They show a classification percentage obtained for each data set. Figure 5 displays a global classification percentage obtained for each algorithm (without noise, 2% and 5% of noise level).

Table 3. Confusion matrix for the DAMADICS process (NOC: 400, F1: 400, F7: 400, F12: 400, F15: 400, F19: 400)

T2FCM							
	NOC	F1	F7	F12	F15	F19	TA (%)
NOC	**398**	0	0	0	2	0	99.50
F1	10	**282**	25	8	7	68	70.50
F7	3	40	**277**	15	65	0	69.25
F12	0	0	10	**390**	0	0	97.50
F15	55	0	45	22	**260**	18	65.00
F19	0	0	10	0	0	**390**	97.50
AVE							**83.21**

KT2FCM							
	NOC	F1	F7	F12	F15	F19	TA (%)
NOC	**400**	0	0	0	0	0	100
F1	0	**373**	0	0	0	27	93.25
F7	0	0	**400**	0	5	0	100
F12	0	0	0	**400**	0	0	100
F15	15	0	12	6	**357**	10	89.25
F19	0	0	2	0	0	**398**	99.50
AVE							**97.00**

IT2FCM							
	NOC	F1	F7	F12	F15	F19	TA (%)
NOC	**399**	0	0	0	1	0	99.75
F1	10	**285**	24	8	7	66	71.25
F7	3	40	**280**	14	63	0	70.00
F12	0	0	6	**394**	0	0	98.50
F15	55	0	45	20	**262**	18	65.50
F19	0	0	10	0	0	**390**	97.50
AVE							**83.75**

KIT2FCM							
	NOC	F1	F7	F12	F15	F19	TA (%)
NOC	**400**	0	0	0	0	0	100
F1	0	375	0	0	0	25	93.75
F7	0	0	**400**	0	0	0	100
F12	0	0	0	**400**	0	0	100
F15	12	0	10	8	**360**	10	90.00
F19	0	0	1	0	0	**399**	99.75
AVE							**97.25**

4.1 Statistical Tests

Since several algorithms are used, statistical tests should be applied to compare their performance [4]. The statistical Friedman test can be used in order to establish if the differences among the obtained performances are significant. If significant differences are found, a comparison in pairs should be developed to find the best classifier. In this case, the statistical Wilcoxon test was used.

Friedman Test. Applying the test for $k = 4$ algorithms and $N = 10$ datasets, the value obtained for the statistical Friedman $F_F = 241$. F_F is distributed according to the F distribution with $k-1 = 3$ and $(k-1)\times(N-1) = 27$ degrees of freedom. From the distribution F table, $F(3{,}27)$ for $\alpha = 0.05$ is 2.9604, so the null-hypothesis ($F(3{,}27) < F_F$) is rejected. This means that there are significant differences among the obtained performances.

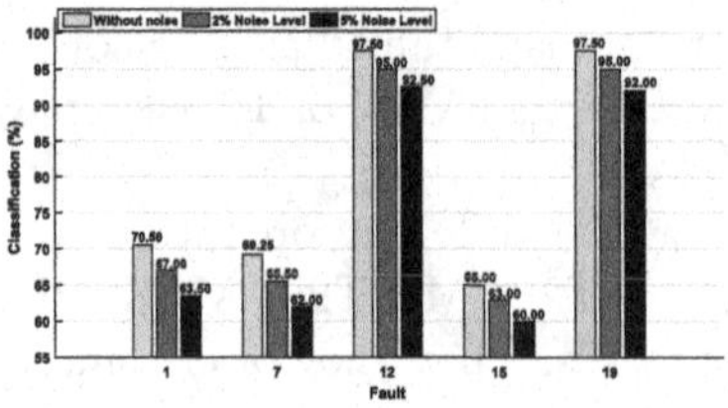

(a) T2FCM algorithm

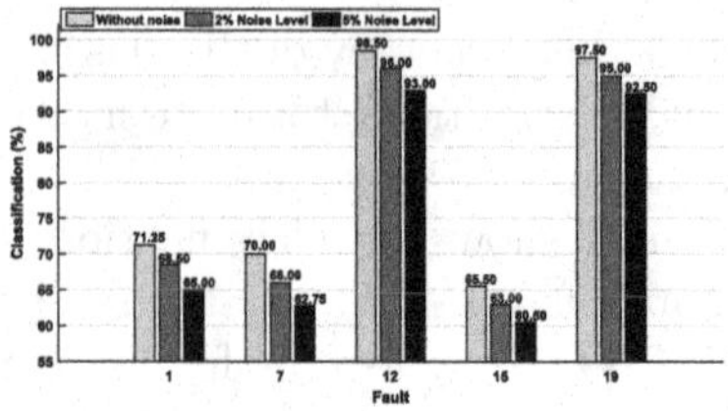

(b) IT2FCM algorithm

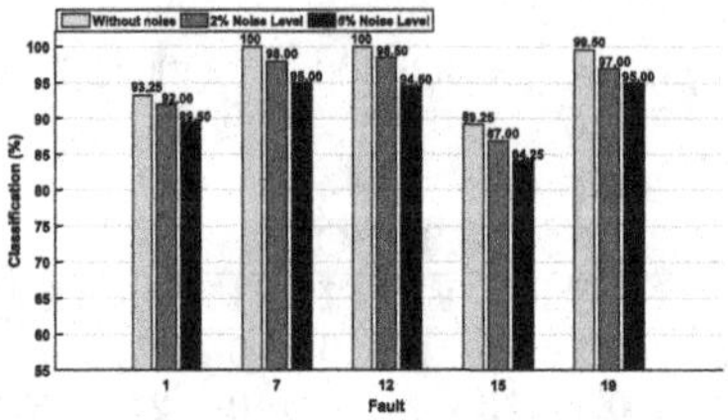

(c) KT2FCM algorithm

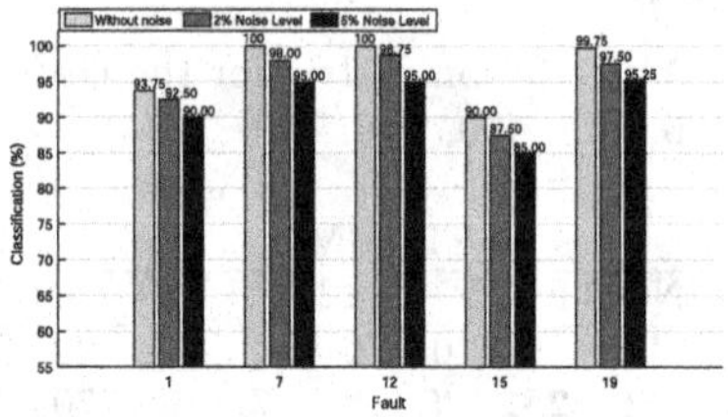

(d) KIT2FCM algorithm

Fig. 4. Classification (%) for DAMADICS process.

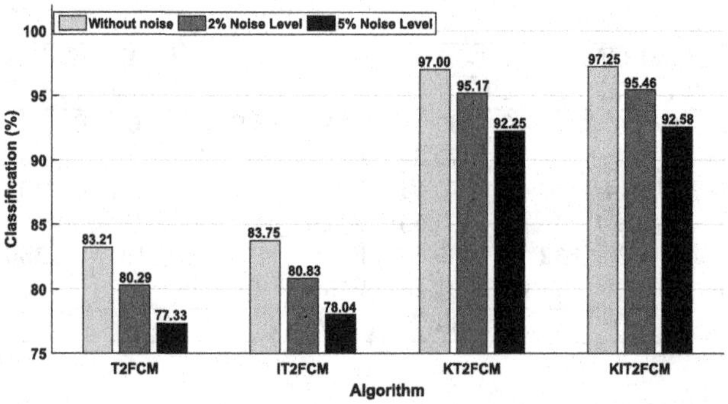

Fig. 5. Global classification (%) obtained for each algorithm.

Wilcoxon Test. Table 4 exhibits the results of applying the Wilcoxon test (A1: T2FCM, A2: IT2FCM, A3: KT2FCM, A4: KIT2FCM). First row displays the sum of positive ranks R^+, and the second rows displays the sum of the negative ranks R^- obtained from the comparison developed. The values of the T statistic and its critical values for a significance level $\alpha = 0.05$ are shown below. Finally, the winning algorithm are shown in each comparison. Table 5 shows that KT2FCM and KIT2FCM obtain the best results.

Table 4. Results of the Wilcoxon test

	A1 vs A2	A1 vs A3	A1 vs A4	A2 vs A3	A2 vs A4	3 vs 4
$\sum R^+$	10	0	0	0	0	15
$\sum R^-$	45	55	55	55	55	40
T	10	0	0	0	0	15
$T_{\alpha=0.05}$	8	8	8	8	8	8
Winner	–	3	4	3	4	–

Table 5. Algorithm comparison summary

Algorithm	No.Wins	Ranking
T2FCM	0	2
IT2FCM	0	2
KT2FCM	2	1
KIT2FCM	2	1

5 Conclusions

This paper presented the design of a fault diagnosis system with robust behavior by using type-2 fuzzy classification algorithm. The main contribution of the proposal was the application of the theory of Type-2 Fuzzy Sets to overcome the effect of uncertainties that characterize the industrial process due to noisy observations and external disturbances.

The capacity of the function kernels to discriminate better among the operation modes reducing misclassification was demonstrated in the developed experiments. The proposed FDI scheme was successfully validated using the DAMADICS process benchmark.

Acknowledgements. The authors acknowledge the financial support provided by FAPERJ, Fundacão Carlos Chagas Filho de Amparo à Pesquisa do Estado do Rio de Janeiro; CNPq, Consehlo Nacional de Desenvolvimento Científico e Tecnológico; CAPES, Coordenação de Aperfeiçoamento de Pessoal de Nível Superior, research supporting agencies from Brazil and the project PN223LH004-23 from the Science and Technology National Program in Automation, Robotic and Artificial Intelligence (ARIA) of the Ministry of Science, Technology and Environment (CITMA) of Cuba.

References

1. Bartys, M., Patton, R., Syfert, M., de las Heras, S., Quevedo. J.: Introduction to the DAMADICS actuator FDI benchmark study. Control Eng. Pract. **14**, 577–596 (2006)

2. Chi, Y., Dong, Y., Wang, Z., Yu, F., Leung, V.: Knowledge-based fault diagnosis in industrial internet of things: a survey. IEEE Internet Things J. **9**(15), 12886–12900 (2022). https://doi.org/10.1109/JIOT.2022.3163606
3. Fernandes, M., Corchado, J., Marreiros, G.: Machine learning techniques applied to mechanical fault diagnosis and fault prognosis in the context of real industrial manufacturing use-cases: a systematic literature review. Appl. Intell. **52**, 14246–14280 (2022). https://doi.org/10.1007/s10489-022-03344-3
4. García, S., Molina, D., Lozano, M., Herrera, F.: A study on the use of non-parametric tests for analyzing the evolutionary algorithms behavior: a case study on the CEC'2005 special session on real parameter optimization. J. Heuristic **15**, 617–644 (2009)
5. Karnik, N., Mendel, J.M.: Centroid of a type-2 fuzzy set. Inf. Sci. **132**, 195–220 (2001)
6. Lasi, H., Fettke, P., Kemper, H.: Industry 4.0. Bus. Inf. Syst. Eng. **6**, 239–242 (2014). https://doi.org/10.1007/s12599-014-0334-4
7. Li, W., et al.: A perspective survey on deep transfer learning for fault diagnosis in industrial scenarios: theories, applications and challenges. Mech. Syst. Signal Process. **167**, 108487 (2022). https://doi.org/10.1016/j.ymssp.2021.108487
8. Lv, H., Chen, J., Pan, T., Zhang, T., Feng, Y., Liu, S.: Attention mechanism in intelligent fault diagnosis of machinery: a review of technique and application. Measurement **199**, 111594 (2022). https://doi.org/10.1016/j.measurement.2022.111594
9. Mendel, J.M., Liu, F.: Super-exponential convergence of the karnikmendel algorithms for computing the centroid of an interval type-2 fuzzy set. IEEE Trans. Fuzzy Syst. **15**(2), 309–320 (2007)
10. Popkova, E.G., Ragulina, Y.V., Bogoviz, A.V. (eds.): Industry 4.0: Industrial Revolution of the 21st Century. SSDC, vol. 169. Springer, Cham (2019). https://doi.org/10.1007/978-3-319-94310-7
11. Quiñones-Grueiro, M., Verde, C., Prieto-Moreno, A., Llanes-Santiago, O.: An unsupervised approach to leak detection and location in water distribution networks. Int. J. Appl. Math. Comput. Sci. **28**(2), 283–295 (2018). https://doi.org/10.2478/amcs-2018-0020
12. Rodríguez-Ramos, A., Javier-Ortiz, F., Llanes-Santiago, O.: A proposal of robust condition monitoring scheme for industrial systems. Computación y Sistemas **27**(1), 223–235 (2023)
13. Rodríguez-Ramos, A., de Lázaro, J.B., Cruz-Corona, C., Neto, A.S., Llanes-Santiago, O.: An approach to robust condition momitoring in industrial processes using pythagorean memberships grades. Ann. Braz. Acad. Sci. **94**(4), 1–22 (2022)
14. Rodríguez-Ramos, A., de Lázaro, J.B., Prieto-Moreno, A., Neto, A.S., Llanes-Santiago, O.: An approach to robust fault diagnosis in mechanical systems using computational intelligence. J. Intell. Manuf. **30**(4), 1601–1615 (2019). https://doi.org/10.1007/s10845-017-1343-1
15. Torres, P.R., Mercado, E.S., Llanes-Santiago, O., Rifón, L.A.: Modeling preventive maintenance of manufacturing processes with probabilistic boolean networks with interventions. J. Intell. Manuf. **29**, 1941–1952 (2018). https://doi.org/10.1007/s10845-016-1226-x
16. Verron, S., Tiplica, T., Kobi, A.: New features for fault diagnosis by supervised classication. In: 18th Mediterranean Conference on Control and Automation (MED'10) (2010)
17. Webert, H., Döß, T.D., Kaupp, L., Simons, S.: Fault handling in industry 4.0: definition, process and applications. Sensors (Basel) **22**(6), 2205 (2022). https://doi.org/10.3390/s22062205

18. Wolpert, D., Macready, W.: No free lunch theorems for optimization. IEEE Trans. Evol. Comput. **1**(1), 67–82 (1997). https://doi.org/10.1109/4235.585893
19. Yang, X., Yu, F., Pedrycz, W.: Typical characteristic-based type-2 fuzzy c-means algorithm. IEEE Trans. Fuzzy Syst. **29**, 1173–1187 (2021)
20. Yin, Y., Sheng, Y., Qin, J.: Interval type-2 fuzzy c-means forecasting model for fuzzy time series. Appl. Soft Comput. **129**, 1–7 (2022)

A New Proposal for Detection and Location of Cyberattacks in Industrial Processes

Adrián Rodríguez-Ramos[1], Eloy Irigoyen[2], Antônio J. da Silva Neto[3], and Orestes Llanes-Santiago[1](✉)

[1] Universidad Tecnológica de la Habana José Antonio Echeverría, CUJAE, La Habana, Cuba
adrian.rr@automatica.cujae.edu.cu, orestes@tesla.cujae.edu.cu
[2] Universidad del País Vasco, Bilbao, Spain
eloy.irigoyen@ehu.eus
[3] Instituto-Politécnico - Universidade do Estado do Rio de Janeiro, Nova Friburgo, RJ, Brazil
ajs_neto@uol.com.br

Abstract. In the Industry 4.0 paradigm, the cybersecurity is a key aim to obtain high levels of performance of the industries based on the use of the IoT technology and the Big Data analysis. To achieve this objective, the cyberphysical industrial plants must be equipped with cybersecurity systems for early detection and location of cyberattacks. This paper presents a robust approach of an industrial cybersecurity system by using non-standard Pythagorean membership grades. The proposed scheme was validated using the Two-Tanks benchmark with excellent results. The proposal was compared with other computational intelligence tools recently presented in the scientific literature, and the results showed the best performance of the proposed scheme.

Keywords: Industry 4.0 · Cybersecurity · Industrial Plants · Fuzzy algorithms · Pythagorean fuzzy sets

1 Introduction

At present, terms such as Smart Factory and Industry 4.0 are closely related to the automation of industrial plants characterized by increasingly connected physical systems and a stronger integration of digital technologies [4,8]. This higher level of integration allows higher levels of productivity, more competitive final products, and excellent compliance of the industrial safety standards. However, despite these significant commercial benefits, the safety risk of these cyberindustrial environments is also increased. Therefore, there is an urgent need for increasing the cybersecurity in industrial processes [1,2].

A major quality of the use of fuzzy sets is the insertion of membership degrees. With the aim of improving the ability of fuzzy sets to capture and model membership information, several researchers have begun to use non-standard fuzzy

Y. Hernndez Heredia et al. (Eds.): IWAIPR 2023, LNCS 14335, pp. 96–107, 2024.
https://doi.org/10.1007/978-3-031-49552-6_9

sets such as the intuitionistic [3], that allow to insert imprecision and uncertainty in the specification of the membership degrees.

The Pythagorean Fuzzy Sets (PFS) were presented in [10], where it is demonstrated that the space of Pythagorean membership degrees is larger than the space of intuitionistic membership degrees. This represents an important advantage in condition monitoring because it allows the insertion of uncertainty in the specification of membership degrees as result of noisy measurements.

The aim of this paper and its main contribution is to propose a cybersecurity scheme with a high performance in the detection and location of cyberattacks and with a robust behaviour versus noisy observations obtained from an industrial plant. The proposal is based on the modification of the Kernel Fuzzy C-Means algorithm by using the non standard Pythagorean membership grades. The modified algorithm, called Kernel Pythagorean Fuzzy C-Mean algorithm (KPyFCM), significantly reduces classification errors in the attack detection and location even in the presence of noisy observations. On the other hand, a performance comparison is developed with successful algorithms used in different applications [6,12].

2 Materials and Methods

2.1 Main Characteristics of Pythagorean Fuzzy Sets

In [10], the PFS were introduced. The Pythagorean Membership Grades (PMG) associated with them are expressed as follow:

- Two values, $r(z)$ and $d(z)$, are assigned for each $z \in Z$.
- If $r(z) \in [0, 1]$, it is labeled *strength of commitment* at z
- If $d(z) \in [0, 1]$, it is labeled *direction of commitment* at z.
- $\mathcal{H}_Y(z)$ is a membership grade which indicates the support for membership of z in $\mathcal{H}$.
- $\mathcal{H}_N(z)$ is a membership grade which indicates the support against membership of z in $\mathcal{H}$.
- $\mathcal{H}_Y(z)$ and $\mathcal{H}_N(z)$ are defined as

$$\mathcal{H}_Y(z) = r(z)cos(\varphi(z)) \tag{1}$$

$$\mathcal{H}_N(z) = r(z)sin(\varphi(z)) \tag{2}$$

where

$$\varphi(z) = (1 - d(z))\frac{\pi}{2} \tag{3}$$

and $\varphi(z) \in [0, \frac{\pi}{2}]$ is expressed in radians.

Lemma: *$\mathcal{H}_Y(z)$ and $\mathcal{H}_N(z)$ are Pythagorean complements with respect to $r(z)$*

Proof: See [11]

In general, a PMG is formalized by using a pair of values (e, f) such that $e, f \in [0, 1]$ and $e^2 + f^2 \leq 1$.

Intuitionistic membership grades are also represented by a pair (e, f) which satisfies $e, f \in [0, 1]$ and $e + f \leq 1$ [3].

Theorem: *The set of Pythagorean Membership Grades is greater than the set of intuitionistics membership grades*

Proof: See [11]

This result indicates the possibility of using PFS in more situations than intuitionistics fuzzy sets. For cybersecurity systems this characteristic of the PFS is very important for improving their performance.

2.2 Kernel Pythagorean Fuzzy C-Means Algorithm

Using the PFS theory, the objective function of the Pythagorean FCM (PyFCM) algorithm can be obtained in the similar form to the Intuitionistic Fuzzy C-Means algorithm (IFCM) [3] according to the equation

$$J_{PyFCM} = \sum_{i=1}^{l} \sum_{k=1}^{N} u_{ik}^{*m} d_{ik}^{2} + \sum_{i=1}^{l} \pi_i^* e^{1-\pi^*} \tag{4}$$

where $m > 1$ is the fuzziness regulation factor of the partition [9], l is the quantity of classes, N is the quantity of observations.

$u_{ik}^* = u_{ik}^m + \pi_{ik}$. u_{ik}^* represents the pythagorean fuzzy membership, u_{ik} denotes the typical fuzzy membership of the kth observation in the ith class, and π_{ik} is the hesitation degree, formalized as:

$$\pi_{ik} = 1 - u_{ik}^2 - (1 - u_{ik}^{\alpha})^{2/\alpha}, \alpha > 0 \tag{5}$$

and

$$\pi_i^* = \frac{1}{N} \sum_{k=1}^{N} \pi_{ik}, k \in [1, N] \tag{6}$$

Kernel functions permit to map non-linear observation of the input space into a higher-dimensional space. This is very useful in classification tasks because allow for greater separability among classes. With this aim, the Kernel Pythagorean Fuzzy C Mean algorithm (KPyFCM) is designed. In this algorithm, the following objective function is minimized:

$$J_{KPyFCM} = \sum_{i=1}^{l} \sum_{k=1}^{N} u_{ik}^{*m} \left\| \mathbf{\Psi}(\mathbf{z_k}) - \mathbf{\Psi}(\mathbf{q_i}) \right\|^2 + \sum_{i=1}^{l} \pi_i^* e^{1-\pi^*} \tag{7}$$

where, $\left\| \mathbf{\Psi}(\mathbf{z_k}) - \mathbf{\Psi}(\mathbf{q_i}) \right\|^2$ denotes the square of the distance between $\mathbf{\Psi}(\mathbf{z_k})$ and $\mathbf{\Psi}(\mathbf{q_i})$. In the feature space, the distance is computed by using the kernel function as follows:

$$\left\| \mathbf{\Psi}(\mathbf{z_k}) - \mathbf{\Psi}(\mathbf{q_i}) \right\|^2 = \mathbf{K}(\mathbf{z_k}, \mathbf{z_k}) - \mathbf{2K}(\mathbf{z_k}, \mathbf{q_i}) + \mathbf{K}(\mathbf{q_i}, \mathbf{q_i}) \tag{8}$$

There exist many kernel functions and the choice of the most appropriate depends on the application [5]. Nonetheless, the most used is the Gaussian Kernel function (GKF).

If the GKF is used, then $\mathbf{K}(\mathbf{z},\mathbf{z}) = \mathbf{1}$ and $\|\boldsymbol{\Psi}(\mathbf{z_k}) - \boldsymbol{\Psi}(\mathbf{q_i})\|^2 = \mathbf{2}\,(\mathbf{1} - \mathbf{K}(\mathbf{z_k},\mathbf{q_i}))$. So, Eq. (7) can be expressed as:

$$J_{KPyFCM} = 2\sum_{i=1}^{l}\sum_{k=1}^{N} u_{ik}^{*m} \|1 - \mathbf{K}(\mathbf{z_k},\mathbf{q_i})\|^2 + \sum_{i=1}^{l} \pi_i^* e^{1-\pi^*} \tag{9}$$

where,

$$\mathbf{K}(\mathbf{z_k},\mathbf{q_i}) = e^{-\|\mathbf{z}_k - \mathbf{q}_i\|^2/\delta^2} \tag{10}$$

where δ is the bandwidth which indicates the smoothness degree of the GKF [9]. Minimizing Eq. (9), yields:

$$u_{ik}^* = \frac{1}{\sum_{j=1}^{l}\left(\frac{1-\mathbf{K}(\mathbf{z_k},\mathbf{q_i})}{1-\mathbf{K}(\mathbf{z_k},\mathbf{q_j})}\right)^{1/(m-1)}} \tag{11}$$

$$\mathbf{q}_i = \frac{\sum_{k=1}^{N}(u_{ik}^{*m}\mathbf{K}(\mathbf{z_k},\mathbf{q_i})\mathbf{z_k})}{\sum_{k=1}^{N} u_{ik}^{*m}\mathbf{K}(\mathbf{z_k},\mathbf{q_i})} \tag{12}$$

KPyFCM algorithm is displayed in Algorithm 1.

Algorithm 1: KPyFCM algorithm

Data: l, $\gamma > 0$, $m > 1$, δ, Itr_{max} (maximum number of iterations)
Result: fuzzy partition **U**, class centers **Q**

```
Initialize U to random fuzzy partition;
Itr ← 1 ;
repeat
    Update the class centers Q according to (12);
    Calculate the distances according to (8);
    Update U according to (11).;
    Itr ← Itr + 1;
until ||U_t − U_{t−1}|| < γ ∧ Itr ≥ Itr_max;
```

2.3 Proposal of Scheme for Detection and Localization of Cyberattacks

The proposal of scheme for Detection and Location of Cyberattacks is shown in Fig. 1. It is formed for two phases: a training phase executed offline and a recognition phase developed online. In the first phase, the data obtained from the process allow to train offline the Cyberattack Detection and Location (CADL) algorithm. After training, the CADL algorithm is used online to analyze each new observation taken from the process. Training is the most important stage, since the center of the different classes that represent the process operation states are determined (normal operation class and the classes that represent the different cyberattacks).

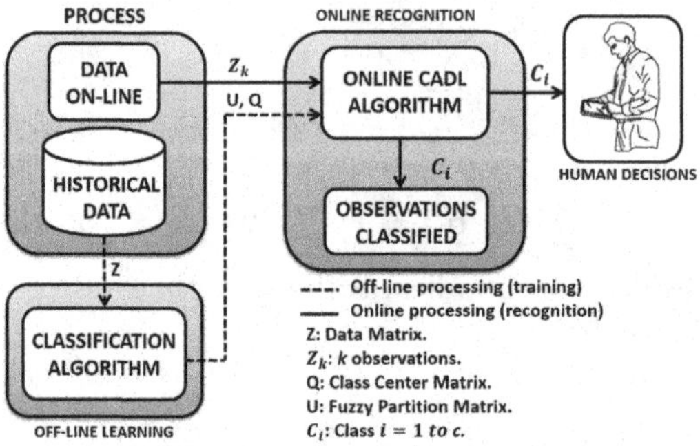

Fig. 1. Proposal of scheme for cyberattack detection and location.

Offline Training Stage. In this stage, the CADL system is trained with a set of historical data which contain the necessary information of each known operating state or class of the industrial plant (normal operation condition (NOC) and states of attack). The main aim of the training process is to determine the center of the known classes $\mathbf{Q} = \{\mathbf{q}_1, \mathbf{q}_2, ..., \mathbf{q}_c\}$ to be used in the on-line recognition stage.

On-Line Recognition Stage. In this stage, each observation (O_k) obtained from the process is assigned to a known class based on the distance between the observation and the centers of the different classes. Subsequently, the membership degree of the observation k for each class is obtained. The observation is assigned to the class with the highest membership degree such as is showed in Eq. (13). (See Algorithm 2).

$$C_i = \{i : max\,\{u^*_{ik}\}\,, \forall i, k\} \tag{13}$$

2.4 Case Study: Two-Tanks

The test system consists of two tanks (T_1, T_2) interconnected through a pipe with a valve V_b which is actuated by an ON-OFF controller (see Fig. 2) [7]. Tank T_1

Algorithm 2: Recognition stage

Data: observation z_k, class centers $\mathbf{Q}$, m, c
Result: Current State
1 Calculate the distances among the observation z_k and the class centers using Eq. (8);
2 Calculate the membership degree of the observation z_k to the c classes according to Eq. (11);
3 Determine using Eq. (13) the class to which observation z_k belongs;

is fed by the pump P_1 controlled by a proportional integral (PI) controller. Tank T_2, is equipped with the manual outlet valve V_0. The variables of the process are: Inflow to T_1 (Q_p), Water level in T_1 (h_1), Water level in T_2 (h_2), Pump control signal on T_1 (U_p, Outflow to consumers (Q_0), Outflow at T_1 (Q_{f1}) and Outflow at T_2 (Q_{f2}).

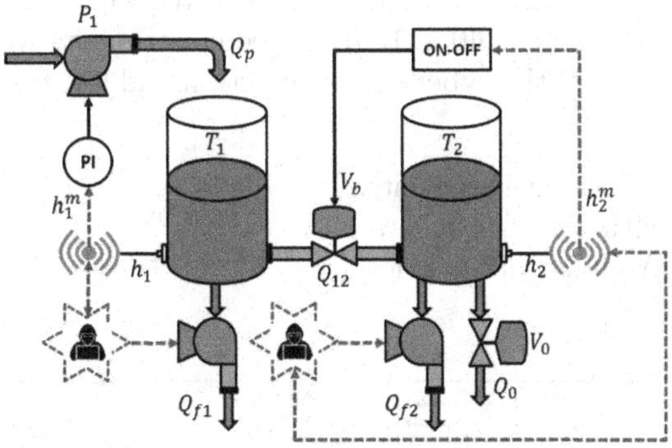

Fig. 2. Schematic diagram of the Two-Tank test system.

In dependence of the type of cyberattack, different scenarios can be obtained. In this paper, the following five scenarios were simulated:

- **Scenario 1 (NOC):** Normal Operation Condition.
- **Scenario 2 (A1):** Scenario corresponding to Attack 1 due to a water leak in Tank 1 (T_1) at a constant flow $Q_{f1} = 10^{-4}\ m^3/\text{s}$ in the period of time from $t = 40$ s to $t = 80$ s.
- **Scenario 3 (A2):** Short-term water theft from T_1 with hidden signal added to the h_1^m level measurement (Deception attack). The attacker extracts a constant flow $Q_{f1} = 10^{-4}\ m^3/\text{s}$ through the pump between $t = 40$ s and 80 s. In this period of time a signal is added to the level sensor output at T_1 to hide the theft. For the PI controller the level at T_1 seems to remain constant and its output does not change.
- **Scenario 4 (A3):** This scenario corresponds to Attack 3 due to a water leak in Tank 2 (T_2) at a constant flow $Q_{f2} = 10^{-4}\ m^3/\text{s}$ in the time period $t = 40\,\text{s} - t = 80\,\text{s}$.

– **Scenario 5 (A4):** The attacker steals water when the system has reached the steady state. Before doing so, the attacker saves several measurements of the level sensors before the water is stolen from the tanks. In the attack phase, the attacker steals water and replacing the real data with the saved ones (Replay attack). Specifically, water is stolen in the period of time between $t = 100$ s and $t = 200$ s and the controller is fooled by using the measurements saved in the 50 s prior to the attack.

2.5 Design of Experiments

For building the training database, simulations were carried out to obtain 160 observations of each class (NOC and Attacks). For validating the behavior of the CADL system in the online stage were used another set of 40 observations of each class. Figures 3 and 4 shows a comparison between the water levels in the tanks with scenario 1 (NOC) and the different attacks scenarios (2, 3, 4 and 5). The values of the parameters used in the KPyFCM algorithm were: $\epsilon = 10^{-5}$, $m = 2$, $\sigma = 10$. The value of σ was selected after the development of 10 experiments (σ = 10,20,30,40,...,100). Three experiments were developed to evaluate the robustness of the cyberattack detection and location system against noise:

1. Without noise in the measurements.
2. Measurements with 2% of noise level.
3. Measurements With 5% of noise level.

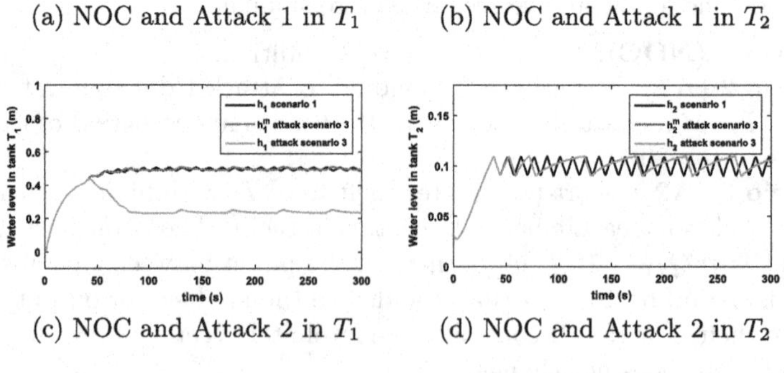

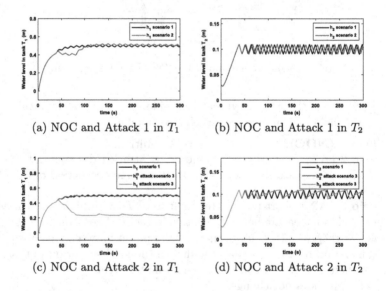

(a) NOC and Attack 1 in T_1 (b) NOC and Attack 1 in T_2

(c) NOC and Attack 2 in T_1 (d) NOC and Attack 2 in T_2

Fig. 3. Comparison between scenarios 1 (NOC), 2 (Attack 1) and 3 (Attack 2).

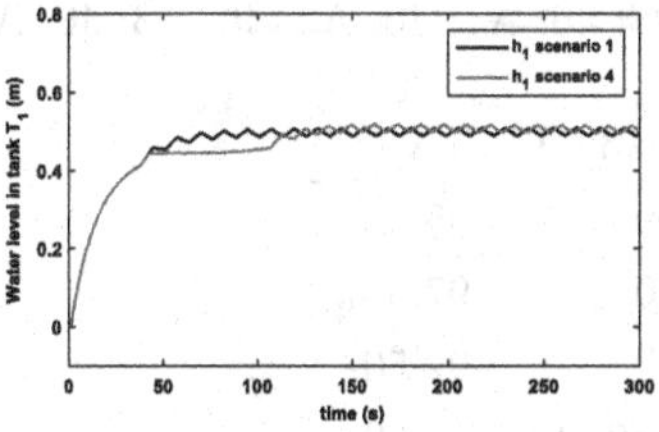

(a) NOC and Attack 3 in T_1

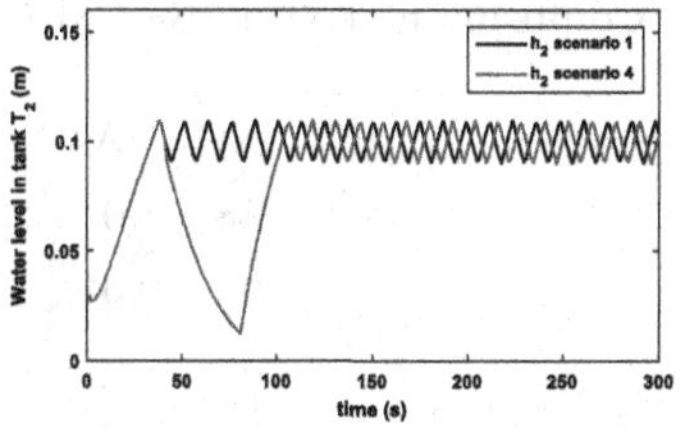

(b) NOC and Attack 3 in T_2

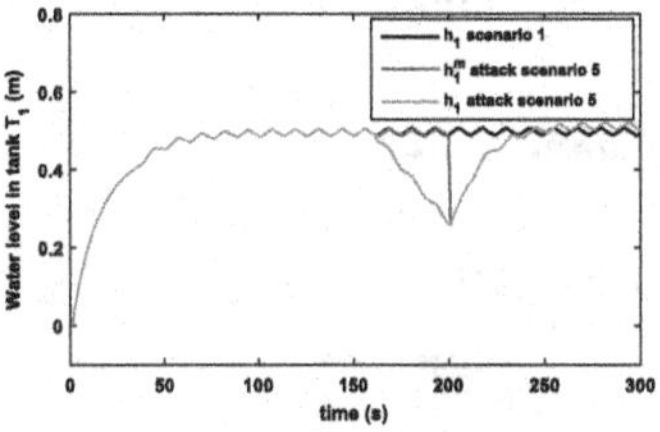

(c) NOC and Attack 4 in T_1

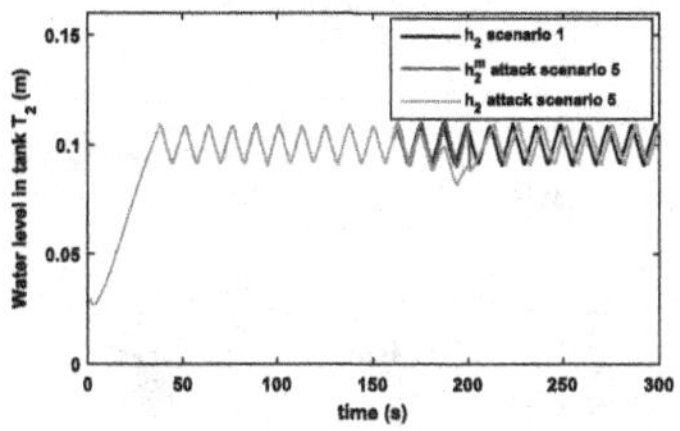

(d) NOC and Attack 4 in T_2

Fig. 4. Comparison between scenarios 1 (NOC), 4 (Attack 3) and 5 (Attack 4).

3 Analysis and Discussion of Results

For the performance analysis of the proposed CADL system the Confusion Matrix (CM) was used. The values CM_{rs} for $r \neq s$ in the CM show the number of observations of the operation mode r that the CADL system misclassifies in the operation modes.

Table 1 shows the CM (without noise in the measurements) where NOC: Normal Operation Condition, A1: Attack 1, A2: Attack 2, A3: Attack 3 and A4: Attack 4. The main diagonal presents the number of observations successfully classified. The accuracy TA for each class was computed as TA = correctly classified observations of the class/total observations of the class. The last row shows the average (AVE) of TA. Figure 5 show the classification results for the different scenarios by using the proposed CADL system for Two-Tank benchmark.

3.1 Comparison with Other Algorithms

For improving the classification process, the Density-Based Weighted FCM (DBFCM) algorithm [6], the Maximum-Entropy-Regularized Weighted FCM (EWFCM) algorithm [12], and the Kernel based EWFCM (KEWFCM) algorithm [12], all of them with excellent performance in different applications, have been presented in the scientific literature. Follow a comparison with these algorithms.

Density-Based Weighted Fuzzy C-Means Algorithm. In this algorithm, the weight of an object is decided by the density of the objects around this

Table 1. Confusion matrix: KPyFCM (NOC: 40, A1: 40, A2: 40, A3: 40, A4: 40)

	NOC	A1	A2	A3	A4	TA (%)
NOC	**38**	0	2	0	0	95.00
A1	0	**39**	1	0	0	97.50
A2	3	0	**37**	0	0	92.50
A3	0	0	0	**40**	0	100.0
A4	2	0	0	0	**38**	95.00
AVE						**96.00**

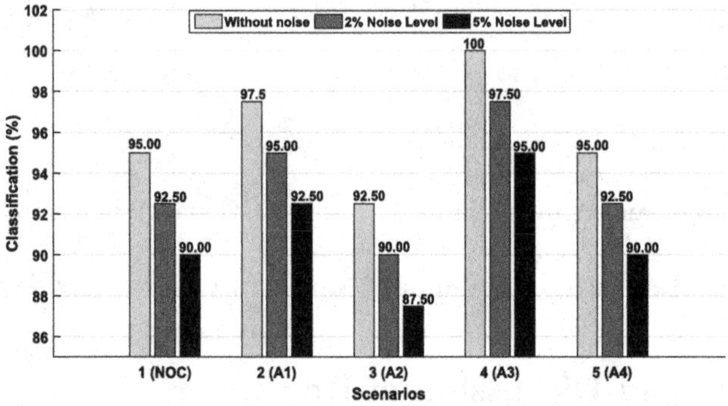

Fig. 5. Classification (%) for Two-Tank process.

object. There are two stages of the density-based weighted FCM. The first stage is designed to calculate the weights of every object, the second stage is the clustering stage.

Maximum-Entropy-Regularized Weighted Fuzzy C-Means and Kernel Maximum-Entropy-Regularized Weighted Fuzzy C-Means Algorithms. A maximum-entropy-regularized weighted fuzzy c-means (EWFCM) algorithm is proposed to extract the important features and improve the clustering. In EWFCM algorithm, the attribute-weight entropy regularization is defined in the new objective function to achieve the optimal distribution of the attribute weights. The kernel based EWFCM (KEWFCM) clustering algorithm is developed for clustering the data with non-spherical shaped clusters.

Table 2 show the results of the CM (without noise) corresponding to the algorithms used in the comparison.

Figure 6 shows the classification results by using the mentioned algorithms and the KPyFCM algorithm for the observations without noise, with 2% and 5% of noise level.

All experiments were performed on a computer with the following characteristics: Intel Core i7-6600U 2.6–2.81 GHz, memory RAM: 16 GB. The average computational time of each algorithm to perform an execution was: DBFCM

Table 2. Confusion matrix: DBWFCM, EWFCM, KEWFCM (NOC: 40, A1: 40, A2: 40, A3: 40, A4: 40)

	NOC	A1	A2	A3	A4	TA (%)
NOC	**34**	1	5	0	0	85.00
A1	0	**36**	3	1	0	90.00
A2	4	2	**34**	0	0	85.00
A3	0	4	1	**35**	0	87.50
A4	5	0	0	1	**34**	85.00
AVE						**86.50**

(a) DBWFCM

	NOC	A1	A2	A3	A4	TA (%)
NOC	**35**	1	4	0	0	87.50
A1	0	**36**	3	1	0	90.00
A2	4	2	**34**	0	0	85.00
A3	0	4	0	**36**	0	90.00
A4	5	0	0	1	**34**	85.00
AVE						**87.50**

(b) EWFCM

	NOC	A1	A2	A3	A4	TA (%)
NOC	**36**	0	4	0	0	90.00
A1	0	**38**	1	1	0	95.00
A2	4	1	**35**	0	0	87.50
A3	0	3	0	**37**	0	92.50
A4	4	0	0	0	**36**	90.00
AVE						**91.00**

(c) KEWFCM

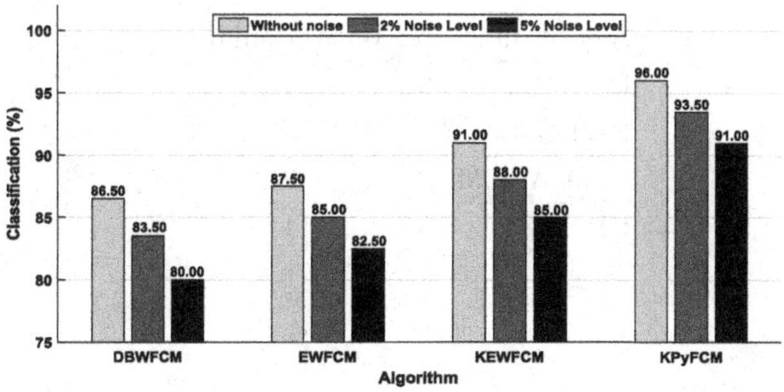

Fig. 6. Global classification (%) obtained for each algorithm.

(0.5520 s), EWFCM (0.4962 s), KEWFCM (0.6315 s), and KPyFCM (0.6035 s). When comparing these times with the time constant of the process, it can be seen that they are very small and, therefore, show the feasibility of their application to the proposed scheme.

The Friedman was applied, and its results confirmed that at least, the performance of one algorithm is significantly different to the performances of the other algorithms.

The Wilcoxon test was applied to compare the algorithms in pairs where 1: DBWFCM, 2: EWFCM, 3: KEWFCM, 4: KPyFCM. Table 3 displays the results. The first row contains the values of the sum of the positive rank (R^+) and the second row presents the sum of the negative rank (R^-) for each comparison. The third row shows the statistical values T, and the fourth row, the critical value of T for a significance level $\alpha = 0.05$. The last row displays number the winner algorithm in each comparison. Table 4 shows the times that each algorithm was the winner. This results demonstrate the proper performance of the CADL scheme proposed.

Table 3. Results of the Wilcoxon test

	1 vs 2	1 vs 3	1 vs 4	2 vs 3	2 vs 4	3 vs 4
$\sum R^{+}$	5	0	0	0	0	0
$\sum R^{-}$	50	55	55	55	55	55
T	5	0	0	0	0	0
$T_{\alpha=0.05}$	8	8	8	8	8	8
Winner	2	3	4	3	4	4

Table 4. Final result of the comparison between algorithms

Algorithm	No.Wins	Ranking
DBWFCM	0	4
EWFCM	1	3
KEWWFCM	2	2
KPyFCM	3	1

4 Conclusions

To achieve the successful implementation of the Industry 4.0 paradigm in industrial plants, cybersecurity must be guaranteed. In this paper, an attack detection and location system with a high performance and robustness versus noisy measurements was presented. The CADL system was implemented by using a KPyFCM algorithm which significantly improves the performance in the detection and location process based on two key characteristics of the elements that make it up. The first is related with the fact that the Pythagorean membership grades permit to use a larger set of numeric values for assigning the membership degree to an observation than the standard and intuitionistic membership grades. The second is related with use of kernel functions which allow to achieve greater separability among the classes. The high performance of the proposal of CADL scheme was confirmed using the Two-Tank process benchmark. The results obtained by the proposed CADL system were compared with the results of three algorithms of high performance recently presented in the scientific literature demonstrating the superiority of the proposal for detection and location of cyberattacks. For future research, an interesting idea will be designing a monitoring scheme that integrally addresses fault diagnosis and cyberattacks in industrial plants.

Acknowledgements. The authors acknowledge the financial support provided by FAPERJ, Fundacão Carlos Chagas Filho de Amparo à Pesquisa do Estado do Rio de Janeiro; CNPq, Consehlo Nacional de Desenvolvimento Científico e Tecnológico; CAPES, Coordenação de Aperfeiçoamento de Pessoal de Nível Superior, research supporting agencies from Brazil and the project PN223LH004-23 from the Science and Technology National Program in Automation, Robotic and Artificial Intelligence (ARIA) of the Ministry of Science, Technology and Environment (CITMA) of Cuba.

References

1. Alanazi, M., Mahmood, A., Morshed, M.: Scada vulnerabilities and attacks: a review of the state of the art and open issues. Comput. Secur. **125**, 1–29 (2023)
2. Alladi, T., Chamola, V., Zeadally, S.: Industrial control systems: cyberattack trends and countermeasures. Comput. Commun. **155**, 1–8 (2020)
3. Atanassov, K.: On Intuitionistic Fuzzy Sets Theory. Springer, Heidelberg (2012). https://doi.org/10.1007/978-3-642-29127-2
4. Bashendy, M., Tantawy, A., Erradi, A.: Intrusion response systems for cyber-physical systems: a comprehensive survey. Comput. Secur. **124**, 1–27 (2023)
5. Bernal de Lázaro, J., Cruz Corona, C., Silva Neto, A., Llanes-Santiago, O.: Criteria for optimizing kernel methods in fault monitoring process: a survey. ISA Trans. **127**, 259–272 (2022)
6. Li, Y., Yang, G., He, H., Jiao, L., Shang, R.: A study of large-scale data clustering based on fuzzy clustering. Soft Comput. **20**, 3231–3242 (2016)
7. Quevedo, J., Sánchez, H., Rotondo, D., Escobet, T., Puig, V.: A two-tank benchmark for detection and isolation of cyber-attacks. IFAC Paper OnLIne **51**, 770–775 (2018)
8. Rodríguez-Ramos, A., Bernal-de Lázaro, J., Prieto-Moreno, A., Silva Neto, A., Llanes-Santiago, O.: An approach to robust fault diagnosis in mechanical systems using computational intelligence. J. Intell. Manuf. **30**, 1601–1615 (2019)
9. Rodríguez-Ramos, A., Silva-Neto, A.J., Llanes-Santiago, O.: An approach to fault diagnosis with online detection of novel faults using fuzzy clustering tools. Expert Syst. Appl. **113**, 200–212 (2018)
10. Yager, R.R.: Pythagorean membership grades in multicriteria decision making. IEEE Trans. Fuzzy Syst. **22**, 958–965 (2014)
11. Yager, R.R.: Properties and applications of Pythagorean fuzzy sets. In: Angelov, P., Sotirov, S. (eds.) Imprecision and Uncertainty in Information Representation and Processing. SFSC, vol. 332, pp. 119–136. Springer, Cham (2016). https://doi.org/10.1007/978-3-319-26302-1_9
12. Zhou, J., Chen, L., Chen, C.P., Zhang, Y., Li, H.: Fuzzy clustering with the entropy of attribute weights. Neurocomputing **198**, 125–134 (2016)

Computational Capabilities of Adler Oscillators Under Weak Local Kuramoto-Like Coupling

K. García Medina[1], J. L. Beltrán[2(✉)], E. Estevez-Rams[1], and D. Kunka[2]

[1] Facultad de Física, Universidad de La Habana, San Lazaro y L, 10400 La Habana, Cuba

[2] Institute of Microstructure Technology, Karlsruhe Institute of Technology, Karlsruhe, Germany

jorge.beltran@partner.kit.edu

Abstract. The computational capabilities of coupled nonlinear oscillators in implementing computational systems are discussed. A Kuramoto-type, locally coupled Adler oscillator is analyzed in terms of its emergent behaviours. Despite the local nature of the interactions, the model exhibits a wide range of long-time dynamics, spanning from stationary global phase synchronization (coherence) to more sophisticated long-range long-lived structures. Regions of non-trivial complex behaviour are identified through entropic analysis of space-time diagrams. Computational complexity is discussed regarding entropic measures, and its behaviour in parameter space is studied. Evidence of an enhancement in computational capabilities in the vicinity of highly sensitive regimes points to critical behaviour, which could be further exploited in implementing dedicated computational electronic systems.

Keywords: EOC · non-linear oscillators · complexity

1 Introduction

Coupled non-linear oscillators are among the most representative models when approaching complex systems since they can sustain the range of long-term dynamics characteristic of complex systems. Their rich dynamical spectrum makes them an ideal candidate to model all sorts of processes [13,21]. Even though they are one of the most visited models in the context of the complex system, there are still open questions regarding the internal mechanisms ruling emergent behaviours and the transmission of information throughout the system. Wiener [16,17] took a first step towards understanding complex emergent behaviour in terms of coupled oscillators when studying alpha rhythms in the brain. Winfree later introduced significant simplifications [18] with the weak coupling approximation, under which the units in the system are regarded as phase oscillators.

Supported by The Alexander von Humboldt Foundation.

Y. Hernndez Heredia et al. (Eds.): IWAIPR 2023, LNCS 14335, pp. 108–118, 2024.
https://doi.org/10.1007/978-3-031-49552-6_10

Building from previous ideas, Kuramoto [11,12] proposed one of the most representative examples of modelling complex behaviour through coupled non-linear oscillators. Kuramoto obtained a universal phase equation that explains the large-time limit dynamics of any system of almost identical limit cycle oscillators under the weak coupling approximation [15]. Even after this approximation, the general problem approached is still highly dependent on the specific topology, initial research focused on the simplest case possible, where all units are directly connected to the rest of the system, and a mean-field approximation is possible. A straightforward variant is to consider coupling in the local scale [11], where the oscillators of the system occupy the vertices of an n-dimensional cubic network, and interaction is only possible with their nearest neighbours.

Both in globally and locally interacting topologies, the fact that systems of coupled non-linear oscillators can exhibit a rich set of long-term dynamics suggests the existence of some inherent capacity to sustain the emergence of correlated behaviour and the propagation of information along different portions of the system, even in the simplest cases. A simple model was recently proposed in [8] to shed light on the mechanisms behind global coherence in locally interacting systems. The model consisted of N identical phase oscillators with time evolution given by Adler law [1]. The units interact locally with their immediate neighbours through their phase differences, and periodic boundary conditions were imposed. Hereafter, this model will be named the Local Adler-Kuramoto model or LAK.

Positive feedback between coherence and effective coupling was found at a local scale, and competition between different local coherence centres was proposed as the main mechanism behind the propagation of order from a local to a global scale. Global coherence was proven possible and stable for only a specific portion of parameter space, which poizes the possibility for more sophisticated emergent behaviour.

Despite their simple nature, this contribution aims to probe whether a case can be made for computational capabilities in the context of LAK. Their evolution is studied throughout the corresponding space-time matrices. The first steps towards an entropic characterization of their computational complexity are presented, and comparisons are made to the evolution of specific elementary cellular automata (ECA) rules as a benchmark of computational complexity.

The paper is structured as follows: Sect. 2 gives a short description of the model, along with some known results. Section 4 deals with the discussions regarding the computational complexity of coupled oscillators. Comparisons with ECA, systems with known computational capabilities, are done in Sect. 3. Finally, conclusions are drawn in Sect. 5.

2 The LAK Model

The model consists of N weakly coupled identical excitable oscillatory units arranged in a ring with nearest neighbour coupling. The dynamics of the individual units, in isolation, obey an Adler-type law [1]. The state of each unit is

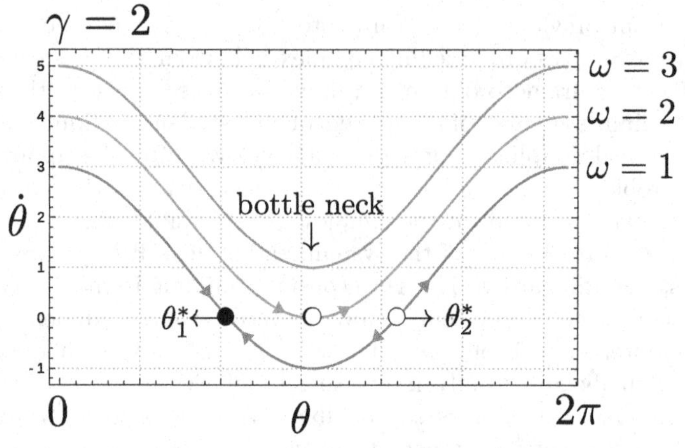

Fig. 1. The oscillator phase speed as a function of the phase value θ. For $\omega > \gamma$, no critical point is present. A bottleneck with a minimum speed value happens. A critical saddle point appears for $\omega = \gamma$, which decomposes into two critical points, one stable and one unstable for $\omega < \gamma$.

determined by its phase, so the equation of motion for each unit in isolation takes the form

$$\dot{\theta} = \omega + \gamma \cos(\theta), \tag{1}$$

$\omega \geq 0$ represents the natural oscillation frequency in the absence of the excitation term, while $\gamma \geq 0$ is the intensity of that excitation. Observable in these systems is taken to be $\sin(\theta)$, commonly referred to as the activity (for a thorough discussion of the isolated unit, see, for example, [5,6]). For each unit, there will be a certain critical phase value θ^*, such that $\dot{\theta}|_{\theta^*} = 0$, given by

$$\theta^* = \pm \arccos\left(-\frac{\omega}{\gamma}\right) \tag{2}$$

with the existence condition $\omega \leq \gamma$. When $\omega > \gamma$, the function $\dot{\theta}$ does not intersect the θ-axis at any point, so there will be no critical point, and the units will oscillate continuously with a period that depends on ω and γ. A bottleneck region will be present where units move at a slower speed. This minimum approaches zero as the value of ω approaches that of γ. In the case of equality, $\omega = \gamma$, a critical point arises at $\theta^* = \pm \arccos(-1) = \pm\pi$, corresponding to a single point on the phase circle. This critical point attracts all units whose evolution starts from lower phase values and repels those that start from higher values, allowing for a saddle point. For further decrease of ω below the ω value, two critical points emerge, one stable and one unstable (Fig. 1).

N Adler units are coupled locally using a weak Kuramoto-like coupling [8]. Each unit interacts only with its nearest neighbours, excitation and inhibition are balanced locally. The corresponding dynamical equations are

$$\dot{\theta}_i = \omega + \gamma \cos(\theta_i) + (-1)^i k \left[\sin(\theta_{i-1} - \theta_i) + \sin(\theta_{i+1} - \theta_i)\right], \tag{3}$$

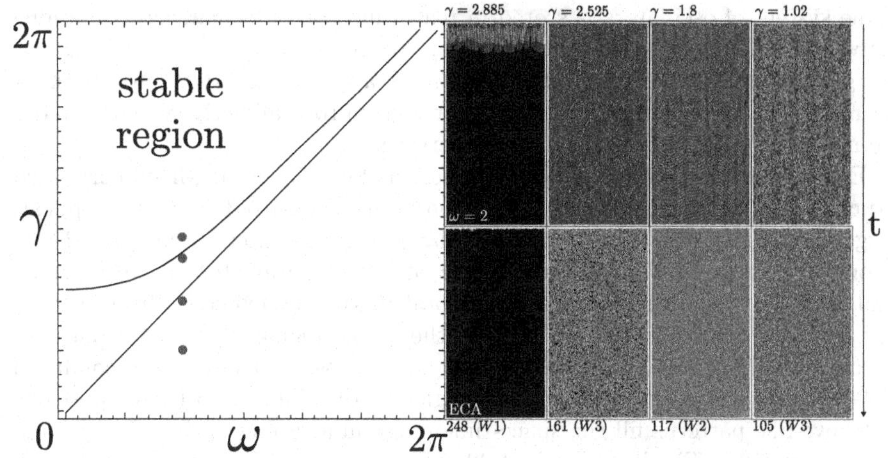

Fig. 2. left Stability region in parameter space for the globally coherent solution of Eqs. (3) with $N = 500$ units. **top right** Space-time diagrams of representative points in parameter space. **bottom right** Space-time diagrams for representative ECA rules. Visual similarities are visible between ECA rules and coupled non-linear oscillators.

with k being the coupling strength between the units, $i \in [1, N]$. Equations (3) describes the LAK model. The further the units in the phase circle (up to $\pi/2$), the stronger they interact. In the following, all parameters in the model are taken in units of k [8]. An even number of units is taken.

In the simplest case possible ($N = 2$), stationary points in configuration space appear in the form

$$\theta_1^* = \theta_2^* = \pm \arccos\left(-\frac{\omega}{\gamma}\right), \tag{4}$$

and

$$\theta_1^* = -\theta_2^* = \pm \arccos\left(x\right), \tag{5}$$

with x given by the quadratic form

$$x\left(\gamma \pm 4\sqrt{1 - x^2}\right) + \omega = 0. \tag{6}$$

Up to six different stationary points can exist simultaneously for some parameter space regions, only one being an attractor [8], which speaks of the wide dynamical range displayed by the model, even in its simplest formulation.

In the more general case ($N \geq 4$), globally coherent configuration given by $\theta_i = \arccos[-\omega/\gamma]$, $\forall i \in [1, N]$ was numerically found to be stable on a specific region of parameter space, as shown in Fig. 2 (left). This poses the possibility for richer, more sophisticated, long-term behaviours.

Such behaviours can be observed by inspecting the space-time diagrams shown in Fig. 2 (top right) for $\omega = 2$. To build these diagrams time evolution of the system of oscillators is stored in real-valued activity matrices containing the values of $\sin[\theta_i(t)]$. Each row in the matrix represents the system's state at any given time, while each column represents a given unit's time evolution. A discretization procedure is performed. For a given row, all activity values above the mean value are taken as 1 and 0 otherwise.

Emergent collective behaviours manifest as long-range long-lived correlated structures on the diagrams. Triangular long-range long-lived structures appear, suggesting highly space and time-correlated configurations. For $\gamma = 2.885$, belonging to the stable-global-coherence region of parameter space, a trivial final state is reached in the spatiotemporal matrix, as expected from a globally coherent configuration. As we exit the stable region, less trivial matrices are obtained. For $\gamma = 2.525$ global coherence is possible, as existence condition $\omega \leq \gamma$ is met, yet unstable. At $\gamma = 1.8$ global coherence is no longer possible, and wave-like patterns fill the space-time diagram as a fingerprint of space and time correlations. Finally, for $\gamma = 1.02$, no apparent patterns or structures are visible.

Thus, an overall inspection of spatiotemporal diagrams reveals the wide dynamical range accessible to a fundamentally simple model. Furthermore, the main features of its space-time diagrams resemble those of well-known dynamically complex systems, namely cellular automata (CA) [20].

3 Comparison to Cellular Automata

The kind of cellular automata of interest for our comparison is a N length array organized in a ring, the sites of which evolve according to an updating rule of local nature. In the case of boolean CA, the sites of the array can be in one of two states at each time, namely 0 and 1. The system evolves in discrete time steps, simultaneously applying the rule throughout the entire array. Under the updating rule, each site's future state is defined by its current state and that of its neighbours, only immediate neighbours in the elementary cellular automata (ECA) case. A tag is assigned to each local ECA rule [19], given by the decimal equivalent of the binary vector resulting in the way the rule acts upon each possible binary 3-tuple

Thus, 256 possible ECA rules are distributed along 88 equivalency classes due to symmetries in their defining binary vectors [20]. One of the most cited classification schemes classifies CA rules, starting from random initial conditions, in [20]

- **W1**: The system evolves towards homogeneous states.
- **W2**: The system evolves to time-periodic behavior.
- **W3**: The system evolves to states with aperiodic chaotic patterns.
- **W4**: The system evolves to states with complex correlated long-lived structures.

Despite its ambiguity [3], the scheme is a practical qualitative guide.

A binary matrix can be obtained from the time evolution of ECA, with each row representing the state of the N-length array at some given time and each column the time evolution of some given site in the array. That means that spatial-temporal maps can also be built for ECA. Such diagrams are shown in Fig. 2 (bottom right).

Fractal, long-range long-lived structures directly indicate the presence of time and space correlations at different scales in the system. Out of all four classes, the more interesting structures and patterns tend to appear in ECA rules of classes $W4$. One could argue that rules in $W4$ classes are best in sustaining long correlation distances in the system's evolution and a sense of memory of the system's recent history, both key features when speaking of computational capabilities. On the other hand, rules in $W3$ are asymptotically chaotic, and any long-range memory or spatial correlation is lost.

In the next section, an analysis based on the entropic measure will be used to compare the spatiotemporal map of the oscillator system Eq. (3) with ECA; we only advance a qualitative idea here upon visual inspection. ECA rule 248, belonging to class $W1$, resembling that of $\gamma = 2.885$ as both dynamical systems evolve to trivial homogeneous configurations. In the case of $\gamma = 2.525$, triangular long-range long-lived fractal structures emerge in the diagram similar to ECA rule 162, belonging to class $W3$. For $\gamma = 1.02$, the corresponding ECA rule closest to the observed behaviour is rule 162, belonging to $W3$. No good visual match was found in the context of ECA for $\gamma = 1.8$, which could be pointing to a different nature of computation taking place in coupled oscillators or even a broader dynamical spectrum than ECA. Rule 117, belonging to class $W2$, is one of the closest visual matches found for the wave-like patterns observed in the coupled oscillators system.

4 Computational Complexity

The more general idea of computation could be defined in terms of three fundamental tasks: storing, transmitting and modifying incoming information [4]. In order to store some information over time, it is relatively simple to notice that some level of time correlations is needed, so the system's trajectory in configuration space is effectively and meaningfully determined by its initial state, which can be seen as the incoming information under this computational approach. Transmission, however, can be related to space correlations so that signals or perturbations emerging in some system regions can travel throughout it. Finally, a trivial rule would be incapable of any meaningful modification in incoming information. No destructive rule, either evolving to trivially homogeneous or uncorrelated random states, can be considered a computational system. These are incapable of any of the three fundamental computational tasks. Rules in $W3$ can be equivalent to a Universal Turing Machine (UTM) like the now famous rule 110 [20].

For our task, the fact that patterns in space-time diagrams of coupled oscillators resemble those observed in similar diagrams of computationally capable systems, like some ECA rules, could be a direct indicator of computational capabilities in coupled oscillators. One could quantify the computational complexity similarity between ECA and coupled Adler oscillators by defining some quantitative markers of computational complexity. Important steps in that direction have been taken by [6,7] when studying the time evolution of non-linear systems. To do so, information theory quantities are exploited.

When discussing complexity, a fine balance between correlations and unpredictability is usually present [5]. A natural measure of unpredictability could be the entropy density (h) as defined by Shannon [14]. Entropy density h can be interpreted as the remaining uncertainty about an information source once every possible outcome has been observed [2]. Absolutely unpredictable sequences will have a maximum entropy density, while completely determined sequences will have a minimum entropy density.

On the other hand, a natural measure of spatial correlation at all scales is the effective complexity measure or excess entropy E as defined by Grassberger [10]. E is an exhaustive recollection of how much we overestimate the randomness of an information source at each scale because of ignoring correlations at bigger scales. At all scales, the more spatially correlated the sequence, the highest the value of E.

Both entropic markers' extreme values are incompatible with the capacity to perform the three basic computational tasks discussed above [4,9]. Final sequences with minimum values of h or E would be totally predictable (trivial). Those with maximum values of h would be unpredictable, which implies that all correlations present in the initial sequence are lost at some point. There is no maximum possible value for E, yet, highly high values could indicate redundancies to the level of trivial repetitive sequences. In general, large values of E and low h indicate the prevalence of patterns in the sequence. Thus, sufficiently long observations of portions of the sequence lead to a good prediction of the entire sequence, a high sense of memory and low information production are in place. When high h and low E are observed, predictability is harder; the system has a poor sense of memory yet a high rate of information production [9].

Random sequences do not correlate at any scale whatsoever. Excess entropy is zero, and the system has no intrinsic memory. Entropy density is maximum; no site can be predicted from observing other sites. Systems with meaningful computational capabilities must balance information storage and production. Thus, intermediate values of both entropic markers can be taken as an indication of such balance.

Comparations were drawn between coupled oscillators and ECA rules, shown in Fig. 2, through the computation of the mentioned entropic measures. Besides the entropic measure, symbol density ρ was also calculated as the total fraction of 1's. Coupled oscillators simulations were performed, using Runge-Kutta (4,5) method (**RKF45**)[1], for $N = 5 \times 10^2$ oscillators starting from random initial

[1] As implemented in GNU Scientific Library (GSL).

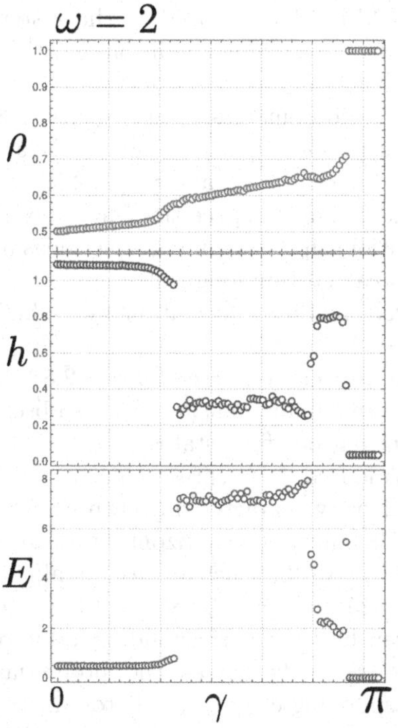

Fig. 3. Behaviour of entropic measures (h and E) and symbolic density (ρ) as a function of γ for $\omega = 2$. Representative γ values appear highlighted, and corresponding ECA rules are signalled with coloured dots. The closer the dots are to the curve, the more similar the corresponding ECA rule and the coupled oscillators instance.

configurations uniformly distributed in $[0, 2\pi]$ and evolving for $T = 2 \times 10^3$ time steps, with $\omega = 2$. Parameter γ was varied within $[0, \pi]$ with a $\pi/100$ step, binarizations were performed as explained above and entropic measures were determined for the last hundred states. Average values were taken at each instance. Similarly, ECA rules shown in Fig. 2 (248, 161, 117, 105) were simulated for random initial binary sequences of length $N = 5 \times 10^2$ evolving for $T = 2^3$ time steps. Entropic measures were determined for the last hundred states, and average values were taken. Both coupled oscillators and ECA rules simulations were repeated over ten different initial settings so that values shown in Fig. 3 result from averaging over $100 \times 10 = 10^3$ different instances.

Three dynamically distinctive regions appear in the γ axis in Fig. 3. For $0 \leq \gamma < 1.1$, the system barely modifies the density of 1's in the initial binarized random sequence ($\rho = 0.5$). This means that information modification in this region is mainly based on the reshuffling of symbols rather than substitution [4]. Furthermore, final states in this region are essentially random and uncorrelated since no substantial changes are observed in h and E when compared to their initial values, corresponding to random sequences. Thus, this first regime ($0 \leq \gamma < 1.1$) could be characterized by the system's inability to reduce the randomness present in the starting condition and the lack of computational capabilities.

A second distinctive region emerges for $1.1 \leq \gamma < 2.88$ where intermediate values of entropic measures and slightly higher final values of ρ are observed. This region includes the values $\gamma = 1.8$ and $\gamma = 2.525$, for which the more interesting patterns were observed in the space-time diagrams in Fig. 2. This confirms our ideas about the relationship between entropic measures and computational capabilities. The system can sustain long-range, long-lived pattern formation in this region and effectively modify information by reshuffling and substituting symbols [4].

Finally, a third trivial region is observed for $\gamma > 2.88$, where all entropic measures drop to zero, and a maximum density of 1's is observed as an unequivocal indication of trivial homogeneous final states.

Figure 3 also shows coloured dots representing the final values of all entropic measures and symbolic density characterizing each ECA rule in Fig. 2 (105 blue, 117 red, 161 green and 248 black). The horizontal position of each dot is given by the corresponding γ value in Fig. 2, which are also highlighted in the same colours (γ=1.02 blue, 1.8 red, 2.525 green and 2.885 black). Their vertical positions, on the other hand, are given by their corresponding value of each measure (ρ, h, E). The closer the dots are to the curves, the more quantitatively similar the ECA rule and the corresponding coupled oscillators instance.

The worst quantitative agreement appears between ECA rule 117 and $\gamma = 1.8$ inside the computationally capable regime, as one could expect from the absence of wave-like patterns in ECA space-time diagrams. The similarity is the highest in the random ($0 \leq \gamma < 1.1$) and trivial ($\gamma > 2.88$) region, which confirms the visual inspection of the corresponding space-time diagrams on Fig. 2. Very good agreement is also found between ECA rule 161 and $\gamma = 2.525$ inside the computationally capable regime ($1.1 \leq \gamma < 2.88$), as quantitative confirmation of the high resemblance between the patterns observed in the corresponding space-time diagrams in Fig. 2.

5 Conclusions

The main contribution of this study is to argue about the presence of general computational capabilities in systems of coupled non-linear oscillators, even in simple formulations and topology. A set of identical locally coupled Alder oscillators was studied regarding their binarized space-time diagrams, and similarities with other computationally capable systems were discussed. Comparations were made both visually and quantitatively using entropic complexity measures.

Three dynamically distinctive regions were identified with γ as the control parameter regarding the behaviours displayed by entropic measures and symbolic density. Very good visual and quantitative agreement with ECA rules was found in the random and trivial regions of the γ axis, both computationally incapable. Only partial agreement was found for γ values inside the computationally capable region, as no good match was found visually or quantitatively for the wave-like patterns present inside this region. The reported result can be used as an argument that coupled LAK non-linear oscillators can have high computational capabilities.

Acknowledgments. The authors thank Alexander von Humboldt Stiftung for financial support and the KIT for a great working environment.

References

1. Adler, R.: A study of locking phenomena in oscillators. Proc. IEEE **61**, 1380–1385 (1973)
2. Crutchfield, J.P., Feldman, D.P.: Regularities unseen, randomness observed: levels of entropy convergence regularities unseen, randomness observed: levels of entropy convergence, vol. 25 (2013)
3. Culik, K., Yu, S.: Undecidability of ca classification schemes. Complex Syst. **2**, 177–190 (1988)
4. Estevez, E., Estevez, D., Garcia, K., Lora, R.: Computational capabilities at the edge of chaos for one dimensional systems undergoing continuous transitions. Chaos **29**, 043105 (2019)
5. Estevez-Moya, E., Estevez-Rams, E., Kantz, H.: Complexity and transition to chaos in coupled adler-type oscillators. Phys. Rev. E **107**, 004212 (2023)
6. Estevez-Rams, E., Estevez-Moya, D., Aragón-Fernández, B.: Phenomenology of coupled nonlinear oscillators. Chaos **28**, 023110–023121 (2018)
7. Estevez-Rams, E., Lora-Serrano, R., Nunes, C.A.J., Aragón-Fernández, B.A.: Lempel-Ziv complexity analysis of one dimensional cellular automata. Chaos **25**, 123106–123116 (2015)
8. García-Medina, K., Estevez-Rams, E.: Behavior of circular chains of nonlinear oscillators with kuramoto-like local coupling. AIP Adv. **13**, 035222 (2023)
9. García-Medina, K., Estevez-Moya, D., Estevez-Rams, E.: Stability and transition in continuously deformed cellular automata. Revista Cubana de Física **37** (2020)
10. Grassberger, P.: Towards a quantitative theory of self-generated complexity. Int. J. Theor. Phys. **25**, 907–938 (1986)
11. Kuramoto, Y.K.: Self-entrainment of a population of coupled non-linear oscillators. In: Araki, H. (eds.) International Symposium on Mathematical Problems in Theoretical Physics. LNP, vol. 39, pp. 420–422. Springer, Berlin, Heidelberg (1975). https://doi.org/10.1007/BFb0013365
12. Kuramoto, Y.K.: Chemical Oscillations, Waves, and Turbulence. Springer Series in Synergetics, vol. 19, pp. 110–140. Springer, Berlin, Heidelberg (1984). https://doi.org/10.1007/978-3-642-69689-3_7
13. Mosekilde, E., Maistrenko, Y., Postnov, D.: Chaotic Synchronization: Application to Living Systems, pp. 15–42. World Scientific, Singapore (2006)
14. Shannon, C., Weaver, W.: The Mathematical Theory of Communication. The Mathematical Theory of Communication, University of Illinois Press (1962)
15. Strogatz, S.H.: From Kuramoto to Crawford: exploring the onset of synchronization in populations of coupled oscillators. Phys. D **143**, 1–20 (2000)
16. Wiener, N.: Nonlinear Problems in Random Theory, p. 509. MIT Press, MA (1958)
17. Wiener, N.: Cybernetics, p. 509, 2nd edn. MIT Press, Cambridge, MA (1961)

18. Winfree, A.T.: Biological rhythms and the behavior of populations of coupled oscillators. J. Theor. Biol. **16**, 15–42 (1967)
19. Wolfram, S.: Universality and complexity in cellular automata. Phys. D **10**, 1–35 (1984)
20. Wolfram, S.: A New Kind of Science. Wolfram Media Inc., Champaign, Illinois (2002)
21. Zillmer, R., Livi, R., Politi, A., Torcini, A.: Desynchronization in diluted neural networks. Phys. Rev. E **74** (2006)

Echo State Networks for the Prediction of Chaotic Systems

Daniel Estévez-Moya[1,2], Ernesto Estévez-Rams[1(✉)], and Hölger Kantz[2]

[1] University of Havana, Havana, Cuba
destevez@mpg.pks.de, estevez@fisica.uh.cu
[2] Max Planck Institute for the Physics of Complex Systems, Nöthnitzer Str. 38, 01187 Dresden, Germany

Abstract. Chaotic systems are complex and challenging to predict due to their sensitive dependence on initial conditions and the complexity of their dynamics. This paper improves the prediction accuracy of chaotic systems using Echo State Networks (ESNs) by considering a complex graph adjacency matrix as the recurrent layer. This helps ESNs better capture the nonlinear dynamics of chaotic systems. ESNs are a type of recurrent neural network with a fixed, randomly generated hidden layer, making them computationally efficient and able to handle large, high-dimensional datasets. This study applies ESNs to the Lorenz, Mackey-Glass, and Kuramoto-Sivashinsky models, which are well-studied examples of chaotic systems. Our results demonstrate that ESNs can effectively capture the dynamics of these systems and outperform existing prediction methods made with ESNs.

Keywords: Chaotic systems · Reservoir Computing · Echo State Networks · ESN · Recurrent neural networks · Nonlinear dynamics · Prediction · Lorenz model · Mackey-Glass model · Kuramoto-Sivashinsky model · Graph adjacency matrix · High-dimensional datasets

1 Introduction

Chaotic systems are ubiquitous in various fields, such as physics, biology, and economics. Understanding and predicting the behaviour of these systems is crucial for many applications, including weather forecasting, speech recognition and stock market prediction [4,8,17]. However, chaotic systems are notoriously difficult to predict due to their sensitive dependence on initial conditions and the complexity of their dynamics.

Recent advances in machine learning have shown promise in predicting chaotic systems, with Echo State Networks (ESNs) being one of the most successful approaches. ESNs are a type of recurrent neural network with a fixed, randomly generated internal state, making them computationally efficient and

Supported by Max Planck Institute for the Physics of Complex Systems.

Y. Hernndez Heredia et al. (Eds.): IWAIPR 2023, LNCS 14335, pp. 119–128, 2024.
https://doi.org/10.1007/978-3-031-49552-6_11

able to handle large, high-dimensional datasets. This study applies ESNs to the Lorenz, Mackey-Glass, and Kuramoto-Sivashinsky models, which are well-studied examples of chaotic systems [7,10,13].

In this paper, we present an improvement in the prediction accuracy of chaotic attractors on these models using ESNs, considering its internal hidden layer as the adjacency matrix of a Watts-Strogatz graph. Our results demonstrate that with this consideration ESNs can effectively capture the dynamics of these systems and outperform existing reported prediction accuracy [14,15].

2 Echo State Networks

Reservoir computing is a neurocomputing paradigm that employs a reservoir of dynamical nodes to compute temporal features internally, requiring only a linear readout layer to map the reservoir state to the desired output. There are two main paradigms: liquid state machines (LSM) [12] and echo state networks (ESN) [6].

Echo State Networks (ESNs) are recurrent neural networks successfully applied to various applications, including time-series prediction, speech recognition, and control problems [16]. Herbert Jaeger introduced them in 2001 to simplify the training of recurrent neural networks [6].

Mathematically, an ESN can be defined as follows: Let $\mathbf{h}(t)$ denote the state vector of the network at time t, $\mathbf{x}(t)$ be the input vector, and $\mathbf{y}(t)$ be the output vector. The dynamics of the ESN can be written as follows:

$$\mathbf{h}(t+1) = f(\mathbf{W}_{in}\mathbf{x}(t) + \mathbf{W}_r\mathbf{h}(t) + \mathbf{W}_{fback}\mathbf{y}(t)) \tag{1}$$

where $\mathbf{W}_{in}$ is the input weight matrix, $\mathbf{W}_r$ is the randomly initialized recurrent weight matrix, $\mathbf{W}_{fback}$ is a feedback weight matrix from the outputs $\mathbf{y}(t)$ to the internal state $\mathbf{h}(t)$, and $f(\cdot)$ is a non-linear activation function, tipically tanh or some other sigmoid function. The output of the ESN is then given by:

$$\mathbf{y}(t+1) = \mathbf{W}_{out}\mathbf{h}(t+1) \tag{2}$$

where $\mathbf{W}_{out}$ is the output weight matrix learned during training.

The critical feature of ESNs is the echo state property (ESP) [5], which allows the network to store and process information in its recurrent connections without complex training algorithms. The ESP refers to the ability of a recurrent neural network with a dynamic recurrent layer to process input information effectively and stably. ESP is achieved by randomly initializing the recurrent connections of the network and fixing them during training. The recurrent connections then act as a "reservoir" of information that can be used to process input data. Jaeger argues that a neural network complies with ESP if its recurrent layer can gradually forget irrelevant information and retain only the crucial features from the input signal.

To ensure the echo state property in an ESN, it is important for the spectral radius of the recurrent weight matrix $\mathbf{W}_r$ to be less than 1. The spectral radius can be controlled by scaling the weights of the recurrent matrix. This guarantees that the dynamics of the network converge over time and that the network does not amplify small perturbations in the input. Although this condition is very restrictive, other criteria that may also be applied to ensure the achievement of the ESP [19] have been developed.

Owing to the dynamics of a reservoir exhibiting the Echo State Property, the network can operate as a filter solely for the input signal, irrespective of the internal state's original conditions. Accordingly, the denomination "Echo State Network" alludes to the reservoir's echoing of the input history.

Another way to achieve the echo state property is to use a sparsely connected recurrent weight matrix, where only a tiny fraction of the connections are non-zero. It is then natural to consider this sparse matrix to be the adjacency matrix of a complex graph, as this allows the network to exploit the complex information propagation dynamics of the graph in its recurrent activity. The connectivity pattern encoded in the adjacency matrix captures the higher-order structure of the complex graph, which can influence the emergent computational properties of the reservoir. For this reason we then used the adjacency matrix of a Watts-Strogatz model as the recurrent layer of the ESN. This choice of Watts-Strogatz topology for the reservoir is motivated by the capacity of its small-world networks to facilitate complex information flow dynamics that we seek to leverage for computational purposes within the ESN framework.

Another advantage of ESNs is that they can be trained using simple linear regression techniques, which makes them computationally efficient and easy to implement. During training, the output weight matrix is learned by minimizing the mean squared error between the network and target output using ridge regression [3]. The input and feedback weight matrices can also be optimized during training to improve further the network's performance [11].

2.1 Training an ESN

The training process for an ESN has two main stages: internal state harvesting stage and regression stage.

After initializing the ESN with random weights and achieving ESP, input data is fed into the network during the *harvesting stage*. The network processes this input data, generating an internal state $h(t)$ for each time step t. These sequence of internal states at each time step are then collected and used to train the output layer.

During the output *regression stage*, the collected internal states are used to train the output matrix W_{out}. This is done by solving a linear regression problem of the form $W_{out}h(t) = y(t+1)$ for W_{out}, where W_{out} represents the weights that map the internal states to the desired output, and $y(t)$ is the target output at time step t, in our case the next time step of the time series, i. e. $x(t+1)$. The weights W_{out} are typically learned using a regularized least-squares regression method such as Ridge regression. Ridge regression is a version of linear regression that adds a penalty term to the least squares objective function to prevent overfitting. The objective function for this regression is given by:

$$\mathbf{y}_{target} - \mathbf{W}_{out}\mathbf{h} + \beta|\mathbf{W}_{out}|^2 \tag{3}$$

where $\mathbf{y}_{target}$ is the target output, $\mathbf{h}$ is the state vector of the ESN, and β is a regularization parameter that controls the strength of the penalty term. The output weight matrix is learned by minimizing this objective function. Other methods, such as gradient descent or the Moore-Penrose pseudoinverse [1], can also achieve similar results.

One important consideration in training ESNs is the choice of hyperparameters, such as the spectral radius, input scaling factor, the regularization parameter for ridge regression, and the reservoir size (i.e., the number of neurons in the ESN). These hyperparameters can significantly impact the performance of the ESN and are often chosen through trial and error or using more sophisticated methods such as grid search or Bayesian optimization [2,9,18].

In this work, we will be using a free-running ESN with no input vector $x(t)$; only the feedback from the network output will be combined with the internal state, i. e.:

$$\mathbf{h}(t+1) = f(\mathbf{W}_r\mathbf{h}(t) + \mathbf{W}_{fback}\mathbf{y}(t)) \tag{4}$$

The training will consist of feeding the network with the actual signal data to make the internal state harvesting. Afterwards, $\mathbf{W}_{out}$ is computed by a Ridge regression and the network loop is closed to make the predictions, Fig. 1.

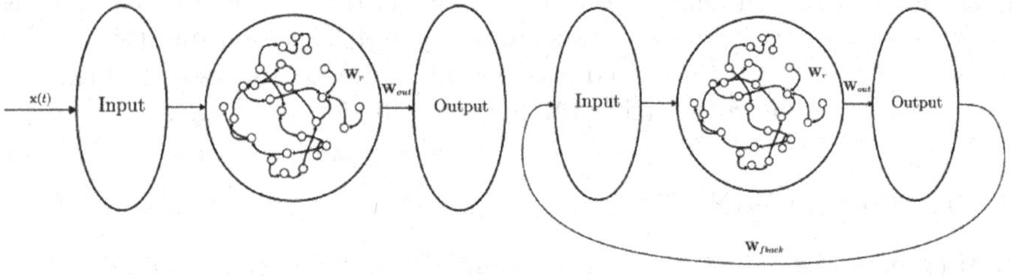

Fig. 1. Diagram of an Echo State Network. Left: the open loop phase with correct signal input. Right: prediction phase with network feedback.

In the training phase (open loop), the network will be fed with the actual data from the time series as if it were the network's output. Then in a prediction phase (closed loop), once the output matrix W_{out} is obtained, the feedback will be the one provided by the network, Fig. 1.

3 Results

We applied our ESN model to predict the trajectories of the Lorenz, Mackey-Glass, and Kuramoto-Sivashinsky systems. We used an adjacency matrix generated from a Watts Strogatz small-world graph with a rewiring probability of

0.5 and an average degree of 6 for the recurrent weight matrix. Ridge regression was used to train the output weights. The reservoir size and spectral radius of the recurrent matrix for the Lorenz system and the Kuramoto-Sivashinsky, were the same as reported in [14,15].

3.1 Lorenz System

The Lorenz system describes the dynamics of convective fluid motion [10]. This system is described by the equations:

$$\dot{x} = \sigma(y - x) \tag{5}$$

$$\dot{y} = x(\rho - z) - y \tag{6}$$

$$\dot{z} = xy - \beta z \tag{7}$$

For the simulations, we will use the classic parameter choice of $\sigma = 10$, $\rho = 28$, $\beta = \frac{8}{3}$, where the system exhibits chaotic behaviour; hence it makes it a good benchmark for the network to compare.

Figure 2 shows a plot of our prediction horizon compared to previous work. Our model achieved significantly more prolonged and more accurate predictions of the Lorenz attractor, clearly capturing the folding and stretching dynamics of the system. We could predict the Lorenz trajectory up to 10 time units in the future before diverging from the correct trajectory, compared to 5 time units reported by Ott et al. in [15].

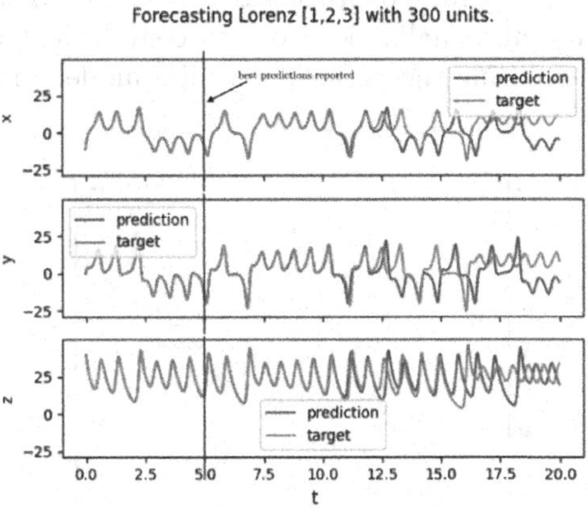

Fig. 2. Prediction horizon of the Lorenz system

Although the predictions eventually diverged from the actual trajectory after some time steps due to the chaotic nature of the system, it is worth noting that the ESN was still able to capture the complex internal dynamics of the system. This is evident from Fig. 3, which shows the Lorenz attractor obtained from the

ESN predictions. The fact that the ESN produced a similar attractor to the actual Lorenz attractor indicates that it captured the essential features of the Lorenz system's dynamics.

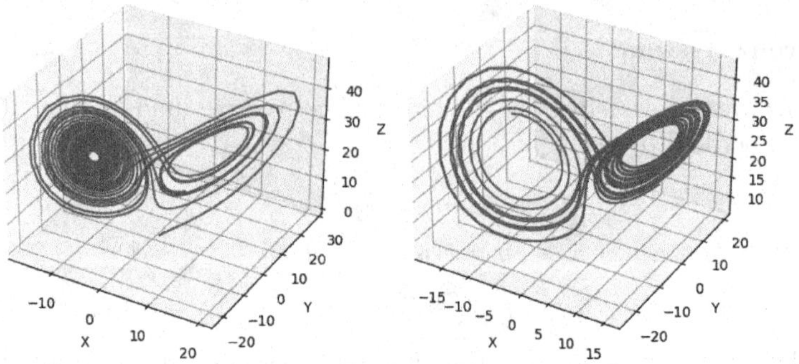

Fig. 3. Lorenz 3d plot. Left: the attractor of the original Lorenz model. Right: the ESN is running free after training. Both exhibit the same nature of internal dynamics.

Another way to confirm the system dynamics are being captured by the ESN is by examining the return plot of the system compared to that of the network, Fig. 4. This shows that the ESN can reproduce the characteristic folding structure and spread of points in the Lorenz attractor, indicating it has successfully learned the system's nonlinear dynamics. Any deviations in the return plot would suggest that the ESN is not fully capturing the dynamics of the chaotic system. Return plots are a useful visualization tool to complement other metrics like prediction error in evaluating the performance of a model on a chaotic system.

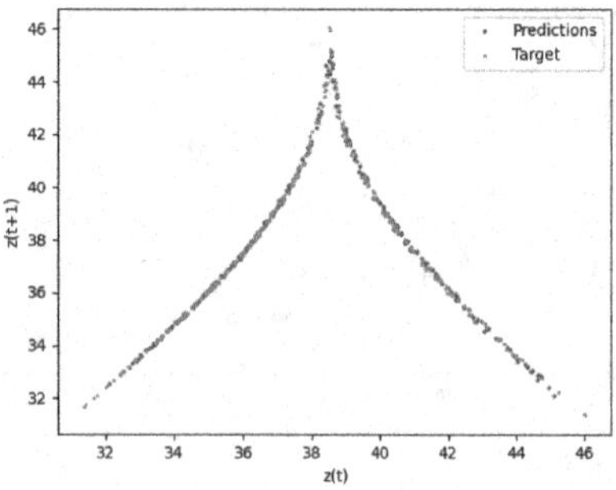

Fig. 4. Lorenz return map for the Z dimension, a comparison between the system and the ESN predictions.

3.2 Mackey-Glass System

The Mackey-Glass equation models physiological control systems with long delay times [13]. Physiological systems like blood cell production control involve feedback loops where the measurement and regulation happen at different time scales. This time delay can introduce inestability and chaotic behaviour in the system dynamics. The Mackey-Glass equation captures this behaviour through a time-delayed differential equation. The system equations are:

$$\dot{x} = \frac{\alpha x(t-\tau)}{1 + x(t-\tau)^{\beta}} - \gamma x(t) \tag{8}$$

Here, $x(t)$ represents the state variable, like blood cell concentration. The first term on the right-hand side represents the production rate, where $x(t-\tau)$ is the delayed state. The second term represents the decay or loss rate. The parameters α, β, τ, and γ determine the behavior of the system. For certain parameter ranges, the delayed feedback through $x(t-\tau)$ can give rise to chaotic oscillations in $x(t)$. This simple equation exhibits phenomena like period doubling and route to chaos, making it useful for studying chaos in dynamic systems. It is typically used to benchmark the performance of recurrent neural networks due to the time-delay nature of its dynamics.

The parameter τ represents the **delay time**, which governs the "memory" of the system. When τ is small, the system behaves linearly. As τ increases, the system becomes increasingly chaotic due to the long delay.

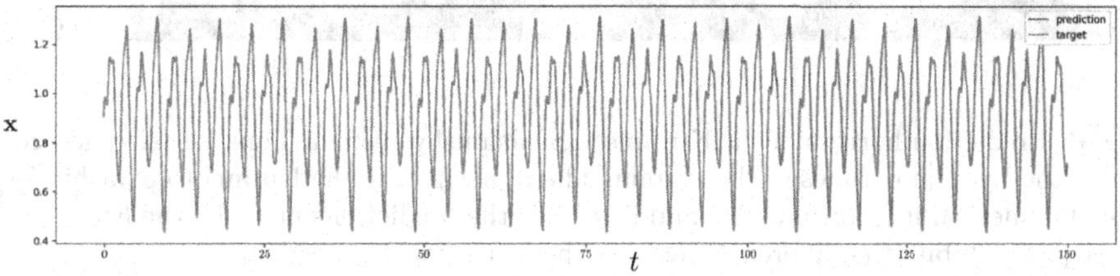

Fig. 5. Prediction horizon of the Mackey-Glass system. Comparison between the numerically calculated simulation and the predictions of the ESN.

For the Mackey-Glass system with $\alpha = 0.2$, $\beta = 10$, $\gamma = 0.1$, $\tau = 17$, where it exhibits chaotic behaviour, our ESN model was able to accurately predict the behaviour of the system entirely, an undoubted improvement compared with what has been done in previous ESN studies. Figure 5 shows the longer prediction horizon achieved by our model.

The performance likely reflects how well our model captured the Mackey-Glass system's dynamics. The results demonstrate how important is the topology of the recurrent layer in ESN for modelling and predicting chaotic time series with long delay times.

3.3 Kuramoto Sivashinsky System

The Kuramoto-Sivashinsky model describes the propagation of a flame front in a premixed gas. The Laplacian and bi-Laplacian terms model heat diffusion and finite flame thickness, while the nonlinear term models convection due to gas expansion behind the flame front [7]. The system is described by the equation:

$$\frac{\partial u}{\partial t} + u\frac{\partial u}{\partial x} + \frac{\partial^2 u}{\partial x^2} + \frac{\partial^4 u}{\partial x^4} = 0 \tag{9}$$

For this system, our ESN achieved predictions up to 12 Lyapunov times, as shown in Fig. 6, whereas, in previous studies, this was up to 6 Lyapunov times [14]. This indicates that our model can capture the complex spatiotemporal dynamics of the Kuramoto-Sivashinsky system for a more extended period.

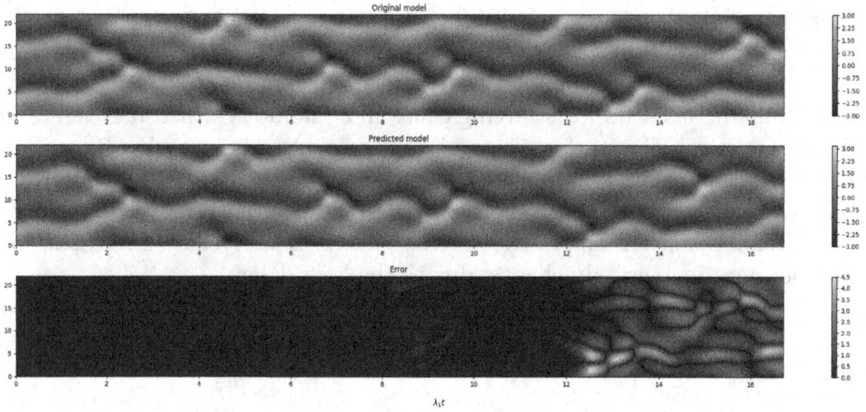

Fig. 6. Prediction horizon of the Kuramoto Sivashinsky system. Time is scaled according to the Lyapunov times of the system. The upper plot is the Kuramoto-Sivashinsky model numerical integration. The middle plot is the predictions made by the ESN. The lower plot exhibits the difference between the other two.

The fact that our model can better learn the system's underlying patterns and long-term dependencies coule be explained by a few possible reasons:

1. Complex dynamical systems like Kuramoto Sivashinsky exhibit complex information propagation, with interactions spanning both short and long timescales. Using a complex graph as the recurrent layer in our echo state network allows us to model this complex information flow better, as complex networks have been shown to capture real-world connectivity patterns more accurately.
2. The additional long-range connections in complex networks can help propagate information over longer timescales. This is crucial for predicting long-term behaviour in dynamic systems, which often depends on integrating information from both recent and distant history.

3. The non-locality and small-world properties of complex networks give them advantages in memory capacity and efficiency compared to an Erdos-Renyi network. Using the same computational resources, they can learn and store information from more inputs.

4 Discussion and Conclusions

Our ESN model achieved significantly more prolonged and accurate predictions for each chaotic system studied: the Lorenz, Mackey-Glass, and Kuramoto-Sivashinsky models.

For the Lorenz system, our model could predict the trajectory of up to 10 time units in the future compared to 5 time units reported in previous studies. The Lorenz attractor produced by the ESN closely resembled the actual Lorenz attractor, indicating that the ESN captured the underlying dynamics well.

Our ESN achieved complete predictions for the Mackey-Glass system. This suggests that our model captured the Mackey-Glass system dynamics more accurately, likely due to using a small-world network as the recurrent layer.

For the Kuramoto-Sivashinsky system, our model achieved predictions up to 12 Lyapunov times compared to 6 Lyapunov times in previous studies. Again, this better performance can be attributed to using a small-world network in the ESN.

The longer prediction horizons achieved by our model can be attributed to the small-world network structure of the recurrent weights. The short path lengths and high clustering of the Watts-Strogatz graph allow information to propagate more efficiently through the reservoir, enabling it to extract and store relevant temporal patterns from the input data for longer. This shows that the topology of the recurrent connections can profoundly impact an ESN's computational abilities, with small-world graphs conferring significant advantages for chaotic systems prediction.

In summary, the improved performance of our model demonstrates the benefits of utilizing complex graph structures as recurrent layers for capturing complex spatiotemporal dynamics. The non-trivial topology of complex networks helps model the non-trivial information propagation in real-world dynamical systems. This highlights the importance of network structure in designing recurrent layers that can better learn long-term dependencies and predict long-horizon behaviours.

Acknowledgements. One of the author EER would like to akwnowledge support from the Alexander von Humboldt Stiftung. This research was partially financed by the Cuban Ministry of Science under the Basic Science Program. Karel García is gratefully aknowledge for rewarding discussions.

References

1. Dresden, A.: The fourteenth western meeting of the American mathematical society. Bull. Am. Math. Soc. **26**(9), 385–396 (1920)

2. Feurer, M., Hutter, F.: Hyperparameter optimization. Autom. Mach. Learn. Methods Syst. Challenges 3–33 (2019). ISBN 978-3-030-05318-5
3. Hoerl, A.E., Kennard, R.W.: Ridge regression: biased estimation for nonorthogonal problems. Technometrics **12**(1), 55–67 (1970)
4. Hsieh, D.A.: Chaos and nonlinear dynamics: application to financial markets. J. Financ. **46**(5), 1839–1877 (1991)
5. Jaeger, H.: The echo state: approach to analysing and training recurrent neural networks. GMD-Report, GMD - Forschungszentrum Informationstechnik (2001)
6. Jaeger, H., Haas, H.: Harnessing nonlinearity: predicting chaotic systems and saving energy in wireless communication. Science **304**(5667), 78–80 (2004)
7. Kuramoto, Y., Tsuzuki, T.: Persistent propagation of concentration waves in dissipative media far from thermal equilibrium. Progress Theor. Phys. **55**(2), 356–369 (1976)
8. Langi, A., Kinsner, W.: Consonant characterization using correlation fractal dimension for speech recognition. In: IEEE WESCANEX 95. Communications, Power, and Computing. Conference Proceedings, vol. 1, pp. 208–213. IEEE (1995)
9. Li, D., Han, M., Wang, J.: Chaotic time series prediction based on a novel robust echo state network. IEEE Trans. Neural Netw. Learn. Syst. **23**(5), 787–799 (2012)
10. Lorenz, E.N.: Deterministic nonperiodic flow. J. Atmos. Sci. **20**(2), 130–141 (1963)
11. Lukosevicius, M.: Echo state networks with trained feedbacks (2007)
12. Maass, W., Markram, H.: On the computational power of circuits of spiking neurons. J. Comput. Syst. Sci. **69**(4), 593–616 (2004)
13. Mackey, M.C., Glass, L.: Oscillation and chaos in physiological control systems. Science **197**(4300), 287–289 (1977)
14. Pathak, J., Hunt, B., Girvan, M., Lu, Z., Ott, E.: Model-free prediction of large spatiotemporally chaotic systems from data: a reservoir computing approach. Phys. Rev. Lett. **120**, 3 (2018)
15. Pathak, J., Lu, Z., Hunt, B.R., Girvan, M., Ott, E.: Using machine learning to replicate chaotic attractors and calculate Lyapunov exponents from data, October 2017
16. Salmen, M., Ploger, P.G.: Echo state networks used for motor control. In: Proceedings of the 2005 IEEE International Conference on Robotics and Automation, pp. 1953–1958. IEEE (2005)
17. Vaidyanathan, S., Volos, C.: Advances and Applications in Chaotic Systems, vol. 636. Springer, Cham (2016). https://doi.org/10.1007/978-3-319-30279-9
18. Yang, L., Shami, A.: On hyperparameter optimization of machine learning algorithms: theory and practice. Neurocomputing **415**, 295–316 (2020)
19. Yildiz, I.B., Jaeger, H., Kiebel, S.J.: Re-visiting the echo state property. Neural Netw. Off. J. Int. Neural Netw. Soc. **35**, 1–9 (2012)

Artificial Intelligence, Data Mining and Applications

Weighted t-Distributed Stochastic Neighbor Embedding for Projection-Based Clustering

Gonzalo Nápoles[1], Leonardo Concepción[2,3](✉), Büşra Özgöde Yigin[1], Görkem Saygili[1], Koen Vanhoof[3], and Rafael Bello[2]

[1] Department of Cognitive Science and Artificial Intelligence, Tilburg University, Tilburg, The Netherlands
g.r.napoles@uvt.nl, {b.ozgodeyigin,g.saygili}@tilburguniversity.edu
[2] Department of Computer Science, Universidad Central de Las Villas, Santa Clara, Cuba
lcperez@uclv.cu, rbellop@uclv.edu.cu
[3] Business Intelligence Group, Hasselt University, Hasselt, Belgium
koen.vanhoof@uhasselt.be

Abstract. This paper presents a projection-based clustering method for visualizing high-dimensional data points in lower-dimensional spaces while preserving the data's structural properties. The proposed method modifies the t-Distributed Stochastic Neighbor Embedding (t-SNE) algorithm by adding a weight function that adjusts the dissimilarity between high-dimensional data points to obtain more realistic lower-dimensional representations. In our algorithm, the centroids obtained with a prototype-based clustering algorithm attract high-dimensional data points allocated to their respective clusters, while repelling those points assigned to other clusters. The simulations using real-world datasets show that the Weighted t-SNE produces better projections than similar algorithms without the need for any previous dimensionality reduction step.

Keywords: Projection-based clustering · dimensionality reduction · t-SNE

1 Introduction

Data have been growing exponentially in recent years in parallel with technological breakthroughs. The growth trend does not occur only in the number of samples but also in dimensionality, bringing several high dimensional data challenges in data science applications. Single-cell RNA sequencing (scRNA-seq) data is an example of high dimensional data with dimensions up to several thousands and sample size up to millions [6]. As the dimensionality increases, visualization of the data becomes problematic [5] together with other challenges such as the curse of dimensionality for machine learning applications and clustering [10].

Y. Hernndez Heredia et al. (Eds.): IWAIPR 2023, LNCS 14335, pp. 131–142, 2024.
https://doi.org/10.1007/978-3-031-49552-6_12

Dimensionality reduction (DR) algorithms reduce the dimension of the data while preserving its information content as much as possible. Many different DR algorithms have tackled the challenges introduced by high dimensional data throughout the decades [19]. These algorithms can be classified into two groups depending on their ability to preserve data structures. The first group aims to preserve global structures. Some examples for this group of algorithms are Principal Component Analysis (PCA) [9], Multi-Dimensional Scaling (MDS) [4], Isometric Feature Mapping (ISOMAP) [18], Autoencoders [8], and Maximum Variance Unfolding (MVU) [21]. In contrast to global structure-preserving algorithms, local structure-preserving ones aim to preserve local neighborhoods. The set of such algorithms includes Locally Linear Embedding (LLE) [16], Sammon mapping [17], Stochastic Neighbor Embedding (SNE) [7], and t-Distributed Stochastic Neighbor Embedding (t-SNE) [13]. These algorithms have proven their performances in various tasks however recent comparative research has shown the impressive performance of t-SNE which explains its wide usage in many different tasks [22]. t-SNE relies on the student's t distribution in the lower dimensional space in contrast to the Gaussian distribution approximation of SNE to alleviate the crowding problem. Although prone to errors [15], it produces visually pleasing embeddings of high dimensional data.

The t-SNE algorithm is an unsupervised machine learning method that does not require target labels to create the embeddings. However, it has been evaluated using target labels starting from its original paper [13]. The aim of t-SNE and many other DR algorithms is to create faithful representations of high-dimensional data in the latent space. From the unsupervised point of view, we argue that the main expectation from these algorithms should be the preservation of the clusters of the high dimensional data in the embeddings rather than the original class labels of the samples, which might not even exist for many unsupervised machine learning tasks.

In this paper, we propose a weighted t-SNE algorithm designed for projection-based clustering. In other words, in our adaptive t-SNE algorithm, we use the centroid information of clusters discovered in the high-dimensional space to adjust the similarities between data points. Computed weights scale the attractive and repulsive interaction between the samples in the embedding based on their positions with respect to high dimensional centroid, eventually leading to much better representations of discovered clusters. Both perceptual and quantitative results have shown that our weighted t-SNE improved the results of the original t-SNE and other DR algorithms substantially.

2 Related Works

Various techniques have been proposed to project high-dimensional representations into low-dimensional space according to either linear or nonlinear relationships underneath the high-dimensional data. Methods based on linear projections, such as PCA [9] and linear discriminant analysis (LDA) [2], are often used in many fields to simplify the presentation of high-dimensional data points.

However, since these techniques do not take into account nonlinear patterns in the data, they are not applicable for large, complex data such as biological data that can contain tens of thousands of cells. Numerous nonlinear manifold learning techniques, such as Laplacian eigenmaps (LE) [3], Locally Linear Embedding (LLE) [16], Sammon mapping [17], ISOMAP [18], MDS [4], MVU [21], t-SNE [13], and uniform manifold approximation and projection (UMAP) [14] have been proposed to address this issue.

The techniques mentioned above generally involve identifying the neighbors of samples and computing the pairwise distances between them. The nonlinear transformation between high-dimensional space and low-dimensional embeddings is then accomplished using various optimizations and the eigenvectors of a suitably defined matrix. Nonlinear dimensionality reduction methods are generally designed to preserve either global or local structures. The development of techniques like LE, Sammon mapping, and t-SNE has allowed the preservation of distances within small neighborhoods of points, in contrast to general approaches like ISOMAP, MDS, MVU, and PCA, which concentrate on retaining general spatial relationships in data. Although preserving local structure by considering neighborhood distances makes nonlinear methods effective for identifying local clusters in the data, they often fail to maintain the global intercluster structure that can shed light on many biological systems [23]. In this study, we weighted the attractive and repulsive forces between the samples in the latent space in such a way that the cluster structures in the high dimensional space are also preserved in the latent space.

3 The Proposed Method

In this section, we first introduce the fundamentals of the t-SNE algorithm and then present the modified algorithm for projection-based clustering.

3.1 The Traditional t-SNE Algorithm

Let $\{x_1, \ldots, x_n\}$ denote a set of n high-dimensional data points to be represented in a lower-dimensional space. To do that, the t-SNE algorithm first computes probabilities p_{ij} that are proportional to the similarity of data points x_i and x_j such that $i \neq j$. Such probabilities can be computed using the following equation:

$$p_{j|i} = \frac{\exp(-||x_i - x_j||^2/2\sigma_i^2)}{\sum_{k\neq i} \exp(-||x_i - x_k||^2/2\sigma_i^2)} \tag{1}$$

where $p_{i|i} = 0$ and $\sum_j p_{j|i} = 1$ for all i.

The similarity between data points x_i and x_j can be seen as the conditional probability $p_{j|i}$ of x_j being the neighbor of x_i if neighbors were obtained in proportion to their probability density under a Gaussian distribution centered at x_i. Therefore, we can define p_{ij} as follows:

$$p_{ij} = \frac{p_{j|i} + p_{i|j}}{2n} \tag{2}$$

such that $p_{ii} = 0$ and $\sum_{i,j} p_{ij} = 1$.

Overall, the t-SNE algorithm aims to learn a d-dimensional map $\{y_1, \ldots, y_n\}$ capturing the similarities between the points as well as possible. To this end, it measures similarities q_{ij} between data points y_i and y_j in the map using an approach similar to Eq. (1). Being more explicit, for $i \neq j$, we can define q_{ij} as follows:

$$q_{ij} = \frac{(1 + ||y_i - y_j||^2)^{-1}}{\sum_k \sum_{l \neq k} (1 + ||y_k - y_l||^2)^{-1}} \tag{3}$$

where $q_{ii} = 0$. This equation defines a heavy-tailed Student t-distribution (with one-degree of freedom) that is used to measure similarities between low-dimensional data points. The intuition of this formalism is that dissimilar data points are allocated far apart in the map.

More explicitly, the locations of the points y_i in the map are determined by minimizing the (non-symmetric) Kullback-Leibler divergence of the distribution P from the distribution Q. This is done as follows:

$$min \rightarrow \mathbf{KL}(P||Q) = \sum_{i \neq j} p_{ij} \log \frac{p_{ij}}{q_{ij}}. \tag{4}$$

The minimization of the Kullback-Leibler divergence with respect to the low-dimensional points y_i is performed using gradient descent. Moreover, the algorithm performs a binary search aimed at estimating the value of σ_i in Eq. (1). This procedure leads to probability distributions with a fixed perplexity as defined by the user.

3.2 The Weighted t-SNE Algorithm

Although the map generated by t-SNE is expected to reflect the similarities between the high-dimensional inputs, it might deliver poor knowledge representations when used for projection-based clustering. This happens because the latent representations do not include explicit information about the location of data points with respect to the cluster centers. In other words, preserving the structure of clusters would require that the projection is made based on the distance between the individual data points and the distance between each data point and the cluster centers.

Let $C = \{C_1, \ldots, C_k, \ldots, C_h\}$ be the clusters obtained with a prototype-based clustering method (such as k-means) such that c_k is the center of the k-th cluster. These clusters are assumed to generate a partition of the data points in the high-dimensional space to be projected to the lower-dimensional space. Equation (5) shows our modification to t-SNE for projection-based clustering,

$$p_{j|i} = \frac{\exp(-\omega(x_i, x_j)||x_i - x_j||^2/2\sigma_i^2)}{\sum_{k \neq i} \exp(-\omega(x_i, x_k)||x_i - x_k||^2/2\sigma_i^2)} \tag{5}$$

such that

$$\omega(x_i, x_j) = \begin{cases} 1 & \theta(x_i) \neq \theta(x_j) \\ \phi^2 & \theta(x_i) = \theta(x_j) \end{cases} \tag{6}$$

where $\theta(x_i)$ denotes a function that gives the index of the cluster containing the high-dimensional point x_i. Notice that, since C is a hard partition, $\theta(x_i) = \theta(x_j)$ means that x_i and x_j belong to the same cluster. Finally, the re-scaling factor ϕ is defined as follows:

$$\phi = max\left\{ \frac{||x_i - c_{\theta(x_i)}||}{\sum\limits_{1 \leq l \leq h} ||x_i - c_l||}, \frac{||x_j - c_{\theta(x_j)}||}{\sum\limits_{1 \leq l \leq h} ||x_j - c_l||} \right\}. \tag{7}$$

The intuition of this modification is that each cluster center will attract those data points allocated to that cluster since it holds that $\phi < 1$. In other words, two points that belong to the same cluster will always be more similar than two points that belong to different clusters. Moreover, the farthest data point within a cluster will define the radius of a hyper-sphere in which all points allocated to that cluster lie. Both features help produce well-separated projection-based clusters that are easy to visualize and inspect.

It is worth mentioning that the Wt-SNE method narrows down to replacing Eq. (1) with Eq. (5), (6) and (7) while retaining the remaining formulae.

Finally, it is known that both the temporal and spatial complexity of t-SNE is $\mathcal{O}(n^2)$ [13]. The proposed Wt-SNE algorithm brings two main additions when compared to t-SNE: (i) the estimation of cluster centers, and (ii) the estimation of the weights (see Eq. (6) and (7)). The extra computations maintain the overall complexity of Wt-SNE as $\mathcal{O}(n^2)$.

4 Experimental Methodology

This section presents the datasets and algorithms used during the numerical simulations. Moreover, we visualize the low-dimensional embeddings produced by selected algorithms and compare their performance using quantitative metrics. Overall, these measures quantify the extent to which the low-dimensional embeddings preserve the cluster structure and local properties of the data.

4.1 Datasets

A total of three datasets were used to evaluate our method, of which two are real scRNA-seq datasets and one is a handwritten digit image dataset. We used a small subset of the MNIST dataset [11] of 10-class handwritten digits with 2500 samples and 784 features. Similarly, we obtained all the scRNA-seq datasets used in this study from https://doi.org/10.5281/zenodo.3357167, already curated and preprocessed as described in a benchmark study [1]. These datasets include pancreatic cells (Muraro and Baron Mouse). There are 18915 genes, 2122 cells, and 9 different cell types in the Muraro dataset. The Baron Mouse dataset consists of 13 different cell types, 1886 cells, and 14861 genes. During preprocessing, raw scRNA-seq count datasets were log-transformed.

4.2 Plotting the Embeddings

The numerical simulations presented next will focus on contrasting the performance of our method against other popular approaches used for projection-based clustering. The algorithms used in our experiments are the classic t-SNE, PCA, ISOMAP, LE, LLE, MDS, MVU and SM. Finally, the clustering algorithm used in this proposal is k-means and the number of clusters is the same as the number of decision classes in each problem.

For each dataset, we produce a two-dimensional embedding using the algorithms described above, which are deemed state-of-the-art dimensionality reduction methods. Figures 1, 2 and 3 visualize the obtained two-dimensional embeddings for MNIST, Muraro and Baron Mouse datasets, respectively. In all the plots, the colors represent high-dimensional clusters.

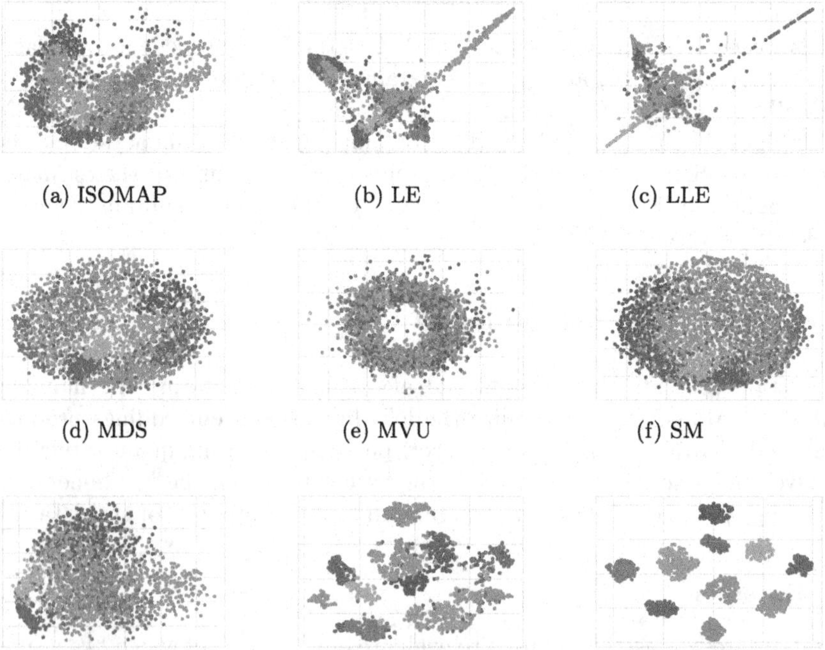

Fig. 1. Low-dimensional cluster visualization for MNIST (10 classes).

When it comes to visualizing the generated low-dimensional embeddings, it is desirable to obtain clusters with data points of the same color. It would mean that clusters in the high-dimensional space are faithfully mapped to clusters in the two-dimensional space. This happens because k-means is a hard clustering algorithm where each data point belongs to a single cluster. This perfect mapping can only be seen for our Wt-SNE method in Figs. 1 and 3.

A closer inspection of the embedding shown in Fig. 1 reveals that the proposed Wt-SNE method separates the data points better than the remaining algorithms, with t-SNE being the closest competitor.

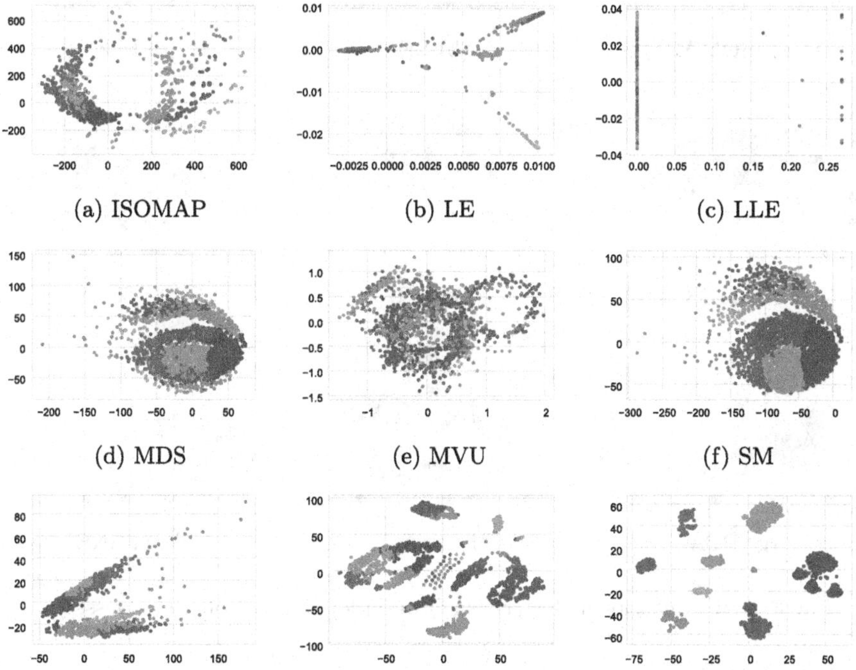

(a) ISOMAP (b) LE (c) LLE

(d) MDS (e) MVU (f) SM

(g) PCA (h) t-SNE (i) Wt-SNE

Fig. 2. Low-dimensional cluster visualization for Muraro (9 classes).

Figures 2 and 3 show that producing two-dimensional embeddings clearly separating the clusters is a difficult task. In these datasets, we can notice that some clusters are not pure, meaning that there are clusters in the embedded space with points that do not belong to the same high-dimensional cluster. However, Wt-SNE separates the clusters better than the other algorithms in both cases. Figure 2 shows that ISOMAP, MDS, SM, PCA and t-SNE yield fair visualizations. Finally, the plots in Fig. 3 indicate that Wt-SNE separates the clusters better than the other algorithms, with t-SNE and PCA being its closest competitors.

Although it was not observed during simulations for the selected datasets, we might obtain more clusters in the low-dimensional space than those in the high-dimensional space. This outcome is naturally undesirable even when we can obtain purer low-dimensional clusters.

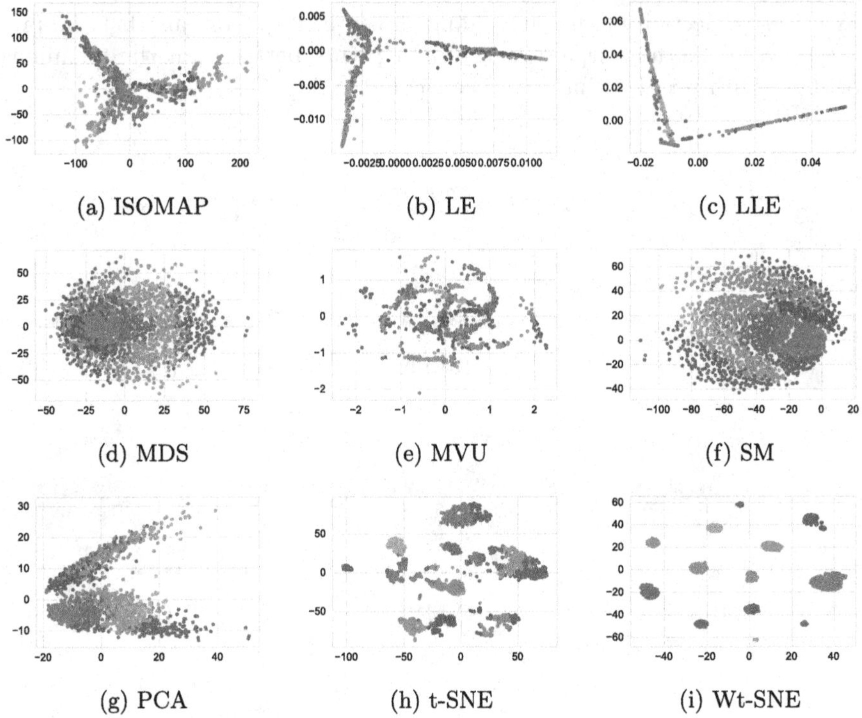

(a) ISOMAP (b) LE (c) LLE

(d) MDS (e) MVU (f) SM

(g) PCA (h) t-SNE (i) Wt-SNE

Fig. 3. Low-dimensional cluster visualization for Baron Mouse (13 classes).

4.3 Quantitative Comparison

While the human-eye perspective is relevant when generating low-dimensional cluster visualizations, it might not be enough to draw formal conclusions about the superiority of the proposed method. In the following subsections, we will conduct an empirical analysis using three quantitative performance metrics for such a purpose.

Performance Measures. In the second part of our experiments, we will use the *precision*, *recall* and *trustworthiness* measures to evaluate the quality of the generated projections. While precision and recall allow assessing how well the projection retains the cluster structure, the latter measures the extent to which the local properties of the data are preserved.

To compare the clusters' structure, the k-means clustering algorithm is applied to both the data in the high and low-dimensional spaces. Let C and C^* be the set of clusters for the high and low-dimensional spaces, respectively. The goal of Wt-SNE is to produce a visualization of C through C^*. Therefore, a desirable outcome is that data points sharing a cluster in C will also share a cluster in C^*. The precision and recall will be calculated considering C as the ground truth, so the clusters in the high-dimensional space will be deemed the true clusters of data points.

The trustworthiness measure quantifies the extent to which the local structure of the data is retained after a dimensionality reduction [12,20]. This performance measure produces values in the [0, 1] interval and can defined as follows:

$$T(k) = 1 - \frac{2\sum_{i=1}^{n}\sum_{j\in\mathcal{N}_i^k} max(0, r(i,j) - k)}{nk(2n - 3k - 1)} \tag{8}$$

where $\mathcal{N}_i^k$ are the k nearest neighbors of the i-th sample in the output space, and $r(i, j)$ denotes the j-th nearest neighbor of the i-th sample in the input space. In this performance measure, any unexpected nearest neighbors in the output space are penalized in proportion to their rank in the input space. The authors in [20] claim that trustworthiness quantifies how far from the original neighborhood (in the input space) the new points entering the (output-space) neighborhood come. Therefore, values close to 1 mean that the data's local structure is retained, while values close to 0 mean the opposite.

Numerical Results. Tables 1, 2 and 3 report the performance measures for MNIST, Muraro and Baron Mouse datasets, respectively. The best-performing algorithm according to each measure appears in boldface. Also, it must be noticed that in these tables, the trustworthiness measure is represented by TW.

It is worth mentioning that perfect precision and recall values mean that clusters in the high-dimensional space are mapped to clusters in two dimensions without any mistakes. In contrast, precision and recall values different from one indicate that some points in the low-dimensional clusters do not belong to the same clusters in the high-dimensional space. In our experiments, the Wt-SNE method produces a perfect mapping for MNIST (see Table 1) and Baron Mouse (see Table 3). For Muraro (see Table 2), the Wt-SNE method produces the largest precision values, whereas LE and LLE report the largest recall values, respectively, followed by our algorithm. It is also noticeable the relatively low recall and precision values produced by the t-SNE algorithm for these datasets.

Concerning the trustworthiness measure, t-SNE and Wt-SNE stand as the best-performing algorithms. While t-SNE slightly outperforms Wt-SNE for Baron Mouse, in the case of MNIST and Muraro the differences between both algorithms can be considered marginal.

In contrast, the algorithms reporting the lowest trustworthiness values are as follows: MVU for MNIST, LLE for Muraro, and MDS for Baron Mouse. Hence, these algorithms are not well-suited for preserving the local properties of these datasets, even when some of them fairly preserve the cluster structure.

Overall, the experiments allow us to conclude that Wt-SNE is much better than the state-of-the-art algorithms for projection-based clustering. Such a conclusion is supported by the large precision and recall values, which indicate that Wt-SNE fairly preserves the cluster structure when mapping the high-dimensional data points to the low-dimensional space. Equally important is the

Table 1. Quality measurements for MNIST.

Algorithms	Precision	Recall	TW
ISOMAP	0.3743	0.3718	0.7852
LE	0.4025	0.4818	0.8432
LLE	0.4235	0.5256	0.8748
MDS	0.3629	0.3449	0.8151
MVU	0.1172	0.1138	0.5612
SM	0.3301	0.3147	0.8074
PCA	0.3268	0.3195	0.7647
t-SNE	0.5686	0.5513	**0.9916**
Wt-SNE	**1.0000**	**1.0000**	0.9896

Table 2. Quality measurements for Muraro.

Algorithms	Precision	Recall	TW
ISOMAP	0.4834	0.4497	0.9041
LE	0.2887	**0.9438**	0.9252
LLE	0.1669	0.1407	0.505
MDS	0.5083	0.3773	0.8717
MVU	0.2804	0.2212	0.6972
SM	0.6115	0.4522	0.9064
PCA	0.5322	0.5365	0.8803
t-SNE	0.5331	0.4072	**0.9676**
Wt-SNE	**0.9875**	0.7941	0.9647

Table 3. Quality measurements for Baron Mouse.

Algorithms	Precision	Recall	Trustworthiness
ISOMAP	0.5231	0.4518	0.8163
LE	0.4858	0.5269	0.8046
LLE	0.3439	0.6692	0.7696
MDS	0.3389	0.2628	0.7346
MVU	0.3664	0.3236	0.759
SM	0.516	0.3923	0.7956
PCA	0.6624	0.5977	0.7766
t-SNE	0.6398	0.5081	**0.8949**
Wt-SNE	**1.000**	**1.000**	0.8785

fact that Wt-SNE retains the local property of the data since the generated embeddings report large trustworthiness values. Finally, it should be noticed that the increase of the computational complexity attached to Wt-SNE narrows down to computing the cluster centers and the weights of data points.

5 Concluding Remarks

In this paper, we have proposed a dimensionality reduction method called weighted t-SNE for projection-based clustering. It modifies the classic t-SNE algorithm by adding a weight function to adjust the dissimilarity between high-dimensional data points to obtain more realistic embeddings. More specifically, the centroids obtained with a prototype-based clustering algorithm attract high-dimensional data points allocated to their respective clusters, while repealing those points assigned to other clusters.

The numerical simulations using three real-world datasets showed that the proposed Wt-SNE algorithm is the preferred approach when considering all performance metrics. It ranks first in precision, first or second in recall while reporting trustworthiness values comparable to those produced by the classic t-SNE method. Consequently, Wt-SNE produces better projections than the state-of-the-art methods as it fairly retains the cluster structure while also preserving the local structure of the data.

The Wt-SNE algorithm has some relevant limitations, such as the assumption that the clusters form hyper-spheres with a clear cluster center. As widely known, such an assumption is likely to be violated in real-world problems. Therefore, exploring different strategies to define the weight function regardless of the data organization seems to be a relevant research avenue. Adapting the algorithm for supervised settings is another interesting research direction. In practice, this can be accomplished by replacing the concept of *cluster* with the concept of *decision class*. In that way, we could obtain embeddings with fairly separated decision classes while retaining the local properties of the data. However, equipping the algorithm with generalization capabilities is key towards using the generated embedding in more general pattern classification applications.

References

1. Abdelaal, T., et al.: A comparison of automatic cell identification methods for single-cell RNA sequencing data. Genome Biol. **20**(1), 1–19 (2019)
2. Belhumeur, P.N., Hespanha, J.P., Kriegman, D.J.: Eigenfaces vs. fisherfaces: recognition using class specific linear projection. IEEE Trans. Pattern Anal. Mach. Intell. **19**(7), 711–720 (1997)
3. Belkin, M., Niyogi, P.: Laplacian eigenmaps for dimensionality reduction and data representation. Neural Comput. **15**(6), 1373–1396 (2003)
4. Borg, I., Groenen, P.J.: Modern Multidimensional Scaling: Theory and Applications. Springer, New York (2005). https://doi.org/10.1007/0-387-28981-X
5. Cakir, B., Prete, M., Huang, N., Van Dongen, S., Pir, P., Kiselev, V.Y.: Comparison of visualization tools for single-cell RNAseq data. NAR Genomics Bioinform. **2**(3), lqaa052 (2020)
6. Cao, J., et al.: The single-cell transcriptional landscape of mammalian organogenesis. Nature **566**(7745), 496–502 (2019)
7. Hinton, G.E., Roweis, S.: Stochastic neighbor embedding. In: Advances in Neural Information Processing Systems, vol. 15 (2002)
8. Hinton, G.E., Salakhutdinov, R.R.: Reducing the dimensionality of data with neural networks. Science **313**(5786), 504–507 (2006)
9. Hotelling, H.: Analysis of a complex of statistical variables into principal components. J. Educ. Psychol. **24**(6), 417 (1933)
10. Kiselev, V.Y., Andrews, T.S., Hemberg, M.: Challenges in unsupervised clustering of single-cell RNA-seq data. Nat. Rev. Genet. **20**(5), 273–282 (2019)
11. LeCun, Y., Bottou, L., Bengio, Y., Haffner, P.: Gradient-based learning applied to document recognition. Proc. IEEE **86**(11), 2278–2324 (1998)
12. Van der Maaten, L.: Proceedings of the Twelth International Conference on Artificial Intelligence and Statistics. Proceedings of Machine Learning Research, vol. 5, pp. 384–391. PMLR, 16–18 April 2009
13. Van der Maaten, L., Hinton, G.: Visualizing data using t-SNE. J. Mach. Learn. Res. **9**(11), 2579–2605 (2008)

14. McInnes, L., Healy, J., Melville, J.: UMAP: uniform manifold approximation and projection for dimension reduction. arXiv preprint arXiv:1802.03426 (2018)
15. Ozgode Yigin, B., Saygili, G.: Confidence estimation for t-SNE embeddings using random forest. Int. J. Mach. Learn. Cybern. **13**(12), 3981–3992 (2022). https://doi.org/10.1007/s13042-022-01635-2
16. Roweis, S.T., Saul, L.K.: Nonlinear dimensionality reduction by locally linear embedding. Science **290**(5500), 2323–2326 (2000)
17. Sammon, J.W.: A nonlinear mapping for data structure analysis. IEEE Trans. Comput. **100**(5), 401–409 (1969)
18. Tenenbaum, J.: Mapping a manifold of perceptual observations. In: Advances in Neural Information Processing Systems, vol. 10 (1997)
19. Van Der Maaten, L., Postma, E., Van den Herik, J., et al.: Dimensionality reduction: a comparative. J. Mach. Learn. Res. **10**(66–71), 13 (2009)
20. Venna, J., Kaski, S.: Neighborhood preservation in nonlinear projection methods: an experimental study. In: Dorffner, G., Bischof, H., Hornik, K. (eds.) ICANN 2001. LNCS, vol. 2130, pp. 485–491. Springer, Heidelberg (2001). https://doi.org/10.1007/3-540-44668-0_68
21. Weinberger, K., Packer, B., Saul, L.: Nonlinear dimensionality reduction by semidefinite programming and kernel matrix factorization. In: International Workshop on Artificial Intelligence and Statistics, pp. 381–388. PMLR (2005)
22. Xiang, R., Wang, W., Yang, L., Wang, S., Xu, C., Chen, X.: A comparison for dimensionality reduction methods of single-cell RNA-seq data. Front. Genet. **12**, 646936 (2021)
23. Zhou, Y., Sharpee, T.O.: Using global t-SNE to preserve intercluster data structure. Neural Comput. **34**(8), 1637–1651 (2022)

Evaluation of XAI Methods in a FinTech Context

Falko Gawantka[1(✉)], Franz Just[2], Markus Ullrich[1], Marina Savelyeva[1], and Jörg Lässig[1,3]

[1] University of Applied Sciences Zittau/Görlitz, 02826 Görlitz, Germany
{Falko.Gawantka,M.Ullrich,Marina.Savelyeva}@hszg.de
[2] Universidad de Granada, 18012 Granada, Spain
Franz.Just@hszg.de
[3] Fraunhofer IOSB-AST, 02826 Görlitz, Germany
joerg.laessig@iosb-ast.fraunhofer.de

Abstract. As humans, we automate more and more critical areas of our lives while using machine learning algorithms to make autonomous decisions. For example, these algorithms may approve or reject job applications/loans. To ensure the fairness and reliability of the decision-making process, a validation is required. The solution for explaining the decision process of ML models is Explainable Artificial Intelligence (XAI). In this paper, we evaluate four different XAI approaches - LIME, SHAP, CIU, and Integrated Gradients (IG) - based on the similarity of their explanations. We compare their feature importance values (FIV) and rank the approaches from the most trustworthy to the least trustworthy. This ranking can serve as a specific fidelity measure of the explanations provided by the XAI methods.

Keywords: ML · XAI · Local Interpretable Model-Agnostic Explanations (LIME) · SHapley Additive exPlanations (SHAP) · Contextual Importance and Utility (CIU) · Integrated Gradients (IG)

1 Introduction and Motivation

Automated systems are increasingly present in various aspects of our lives. Current research shows that it is even possible to use AI to automate the processing of job applications so that positions can be filled as quickly as possible and suitable candidates can be found more efficiently [1]. In the field of medical imaging, AI is being used as a decision support system to more effectively evaluate the large amounts of data generated by procedures such as MRI [13,19]. AI also has a significant impact on the financial sector, with the growing field of financial technology (FinTech) using AI in decision-making processes, including lending and insurance [3,12]. However, there is a gap in providing meaningful information to human decision makers. Given the vast amounts of data, these decision-makers rely on AI evaluations, but these evaluations should also be justified.

This work is supported with tax funds on the basis of the budget passed by the Saxon State Parliament.

Y. Hernndez Heredia et al. (Eds.): IWAIPR 2023, LNCS 14335, pp. 143–154, 2024.
https://doi.org/10.1007/978-3-031-49552-6_13

2 Problem Description and Motivation

In the financial context, automated decisions can have a critical impact on individuals. Credit approval serves as a representative use case to illustrate the limitations and issues of using AI predictions in this domain. To address the lack of transparency, Fig. 1 illustrates the AI-assisted part of the credit approval process, which relies on a predictive model built using deep learning. The model uses various features to determine an individual's ability to repay the loan.

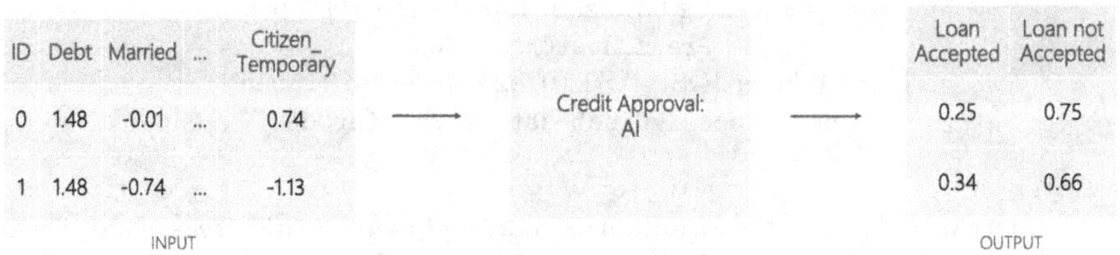

Fig. 1. An example for the lack of transparency in the credit approval use case. The input and output behavior of a black box predictor is shown. For the clarity of the *standardised* input data, there are two test instances presented and the resulting probabilities by the AI model.

The input to the *Credit Approval: AI* model is a set of features presented in tabular form on the left side of Fig. 1. Each row represents a person as vector, consisting of 34 features. The model's outcome is a probability of accepting or rejecting the credit, visualized on the right side of the figure. The problem with this approach is the lack of transparency in the decision-making process. The model makes predictions based on specific features without revealing the underlying decision process for the individual case. Providing an explanation of the decision-making process can increase the transparency of the prediction model. For instance, an individual denied credit could ask, "Why was the credit rejected?". Additionally, there may be laws and regulations that require accountability for automated decisions. XAI algorithms can help bridge the transparency gap by providing optimal support for people in decision-making positions, such as credit approval. The research questions (RQx) as well as the hypothesis (Hx) of this paper are as follows.

- RQ1: How similar are the explanations provided by XAI approaches for inputs that differ by no more than 1% in one feature?
- H1: If the inputs are almost identical, then it is expected that only minor changes appear in the explanation. This can be used as a scoring metric for the stability of a XAI algorithm.
- RQ2: Is there a correlation between scaling a selected feature by a factor of a and the resulting feature importance value?
- H2: Scaling a feature by a certain degree, results in a correlation with the feature importance movement.

3 Background and Related Work

Minh *et al.* [17, p. 3511] define XAI in their survey paper as "the study of explainability and transparency for socio-technical systems, including AI." There are several taxonomies according to [4,7,15,21] to classify XAI methods. The focus of this work lies on the evaluation of model-agnostic and model-specific XAI approaches.

3.1 LIME by Ribeiro et al. 2016 [20]

The idea behind LIME is to consider the local model as a black box model. The mode of operation of LIME is based on perturbing an original data point as input into the black box model and using the resulting predictions to train an interpretable surrogate model, which locally approximates the predictions of the black box model. The explanation provided by LIME is defined by:

$$\xi(x) = \underset{g \in G}{\operatorname{argmin}}\ \mathcal{L}(f, g, \pi_x) + \Omega(g) \tag{1}$$

In Eq. 1, ξ is the explanation of instance x, which is obtained through an optimization task. Function g is an interpretable local model and G is a class of potentially interpretable models. The function f is the original predictor, and π_x defines the radius of the neighborhood around instance x. $\mathcal{L}$ is the loss function that measures the accuracy of the prediction from instance x with respect to the interpretable model g and the original prediction by f in the area of π_x around the original prediction. Ω is a complexity measure of g and serves as a penalty function. LIME calculates feature importance values that show the contribution of each feature for and against a prediction in a certain classification category.

3.2 SHAP by Lundberg and Lee 2017 [16]

The idea of the SHAP has its origins in the game theory. It calculates the extent to which a coalition (set of features) contributes or does not contribute to a particular classification based on the so-called Shapley values. The used implementation was the framework by Lundberg and Lee [16], known as SHap Additive exPlanations. The following definition describes the generation of explanations by the algorithm [16,18]:

$$g(z') = \phi_0 + \sum_{i=1}^{M} \phi_i z'_i \tag{2}$$

The function g describes the explanatory model and z' describes the data instance to be interpreted. Here, z' may have only a subset of all features. The explanation is generated by a linear model where $\phi_i \in \mathbb{R}$ and z'_i is either zero or one for representing the presence or absence of a value from the feature set

z' [16]. Lundberg and Lee provide in their framework (implementation) different explainer models. The computational model approximates Shapley values with perturbations of z'. By that, the complexity problem of computing Shapley values could be solved. SHAP also generates feature importance values like LIME and the expressive power are the same.

3.3 CIU by Främling Initially 1996 [9]

The third model-agnostic algorithm is based on Decision Theory, more specifically on the sub-domain of Multiple Criteria Decision Making (MCDM). In contrast to LIME and SHAP, this approach distinguishes between the measured importance and the utility of an attribute. On the premise of the feature relevance, the focus lies on the contextual importance. This is described in [9,11]:

$$CI_j(\vec{C}, \{i\}) = \frac{C_{max_j}(\vec{C}, \{i\}) - C_{min_j}(\vec{C}, \{i\})}{absmax_j - absmin_j} \tag{3}$$

The explanation model CIU calculates with the function CI_j the importance of feature i in the feature vector $\vec{C}$ for an output label (value) j. The function C_{max_j} determines the maximum output of the prediction j for a certain feature i. The C_{min_j} calculation follows a similar approach. The functions $absmax_j$ and $absmin_j$ determine the highest and lowest prediction from the given data set. More details are provided in the paper by Kary Främling [9–11].

3.4 IG by Sundararajan et al. 2017 [22]

Integrated Gradients is a model-specific approach that differs from the other XAI methods and serves as a verification method. Basic axioms are defined that the XAI approach must fulfil. The most important of these are "Sensitivity", "Implementation Invariance" and "Completeness". The details can be found in the paper, the following describes the parts of the function [22]:

$$\text{IntegradGrads}_i(x) = (x_i - x_i') \times \int_{\alpha=0}^{1} \frac{\partial F(x' + \alpha \times (x - x'))}{\partial x_i} d\alpha \tag{4}$$

In Eq. 4, F represents the predictor model, x is the input instance, and x' is the baseline input instance, which stands for a neutral prediction, such as a black image. The feature of the input instance is selected by choosing the dimension (feature) of i. $\frac{\partial F(x)}{\partial x_i}$ is the gradient along the predictor of the i-th dimension. Integrated Gradients takes into account the difference between a feature of the input instance and the baseline instance, which is then multiplied by the integrated gradients value of that particular feature.

4 Methodology

According to Bruckert et al. [5], the combination of global and local XAI algorithms is key to ensure the confidence and performance of future ML models.

Building upon this idea, a framework is proposed that utilizes a combination of model-agnostic methods, contrasting and comparing it with a model-specific approach. The main goal is hereby to further analyse the quality of certain XAI explanations by conducting tests with very similar data samples.

Considering the complexity in evaluating a unsupervised model, an approach was developed to get quality insights by conducting changes in the test dataset. The underlying assumption is hereby that minimal changes in the test data, should result in similar explanations. That means, several data sample pairs are generated, which differ in one feature by around 1%. The XAI algorithm is then measured based on the similarity of the resulting explanations. A high variation leads to poor results and less trust. On the other hand, the smaller the variation of the feature importance value (FIV) among the data sample pairs are, the better and more trustworthy is the XAI algorithm.

$$\text{Similarity} = \frac{\text{FIV}_{\text{original}} \cdot 100\%}{\text{FIV}_{\text{perturbated}}} \tag{5}$$

The Eq. 5 shows the formula used to compute the degree of similarity among the data sample pairs. A 100% similarity means hereby that the explanations are identical and that the feature change had no impact on the explanation. In contrast, a value bigger or smaller 100% means that the importance value for a certain feature changed. Besides the similarity computation, the Spearman rank correlation coefficient was applied for the results in RQ2 due to the sake of illustration. The value ranges hereby from -1 to 1 and represents the monotonic relationship of the data. A value of 1 means that by increasing the first part of the data, the second part increases too. In contrast, -1 indicates that while increasing the first part of the data, the second one decreases.

The credit approval task was chosen in the context of AI for critical domains. The "Credit Approval Data Set" from [8] was used for training and testing, but the original dataset only contained acronyms in the column headers for privacy reasons, making it difficult to interpret. To address this, we obtained a cleaned version of the data from Kaggle [6] and used the column headers provided there. For the predictor, a simple neural network was implemented using TensorFlow with two layers, each consisting of 32 neurons, and trained using the Adam optimizer. The output of the model was generated using a softmax function. To interpret the prediction using IG, the same network architecture was used and trained with a sigmoid function in the output layer.

For the use case of the credit approval system that requires explainable AI, a suitable XAI approach must be selected. The approach should be easy to integrate into the existing system (Req. 1), provide explanations of the predictor's behavior (Req. 2), and allow examination of individual features (Req. 3). Post-Hoc models fulfill the first requirement since they do not require changes to the predictor or data. They produce Feature Importance Values for explaining the impact of single features or interdependence between features, meeting the Req. 2.

Table 1. Comparison of the requirements for XAI methods.

Method	LIME	SHAP	CIU	IG
Requirement 1–3	Fulfills	Fulfills	Fulfills	Fulfills
Model Access	No	No	No	Yes
Scope	Local	Local/Global	Local	Local
Approach	Functional	Game Theory	Decision Theory	Functional

As shown in Table 1, each introduced algorithm could be used for evaluating the FIV. The only distinction among the algorithms is whether the predictor is accessible or not. In most cases where a service is used, the predictor may not be accessible, and so LIME, SHAP, and CIU could be chosen. If access to the ML model is granted, then IG is also an option.

The reference implementations of LIME and SHAP from [20] and [16] were used respectively. The CIU implementation presented in [2] and the implementation from the Alibi collection [14] were used as the reference implementations of CIU and Integrated Gradients. For the experiments, the standard arguments of the XAI algorithms, which are listed in Table 2, were used. The library versions used in the experiments are also listed.

Table 2. Overview of parameters for XAI approaches.

Used explainer (data specific)	Input data (type of data)	Model (required)	Optional parameters	Lib. version
LimeTabular Explainer (Yes)	data point, (tabular)	Yes	Top labels: 1 Samples: 5000 Features: 34	0.2.0.1
SHAP Explainer (No)	data point, (tabular)	Yes	–	0.41.0
determine_ciu (No)	data point, (tabular)	Yes	List of min. and max. values	0.0.3
IntegratedGradients (No)	data point, (tabular)	Yes	n_steps: 50 method: gausslegendre baselines: None	0.9.1

Since the credit approval dataset contains nominal variables (such as "Industry" and "Ethnicity"), a one-hot encoding was applied, resulting in a dataset with 690 samples and 34 features each. To train and test the deep neural network, the data was splitted (80/20) and transformed along the columns using the StandardScaler from scikit-learn, resulting in an average of 0 and a standard deviation of 1. The same preprocessing was applied to the test data used for the XAI algorithms. RQ1: To analyze the similarity of explanations for almost identical data sample pairs, 100 data samples were selected and further processed. Four copies of each sample were created, with each copy having one column changed by +1%. The columns "Age", "Debt", "YearsEmployed", and "Income" were chosen for this purpose, as they contain continuous numerical data. The data of these features is in decimal form and therefore possible to change by around 1%. After the feature changes, the data was merged into a dataset with a total of 500 rows and 34 columns. RQ2: In contrast to RQ1, RQ2 conducts changes on just one column and 10 data samples. These have six copies each, representing a feature change of +1%, +5%, +10%, −1%, −5%, and −10%. The objective is to analyze the relationship between the feature change and the similarity changes of the explanations. The merged dataset has 70 rows, where rows 10–70 represent the changed data samples. As only one feature-column is changed, the other 33 remain the same throughout the copies. The "Age" and "Income" columns are changed, resulting in two datasets, each with a shape of (70,34). After obtaining the explanations from the XAI models, the data was shifted on a positive scale. To avoid any problems for the following similarity calculation of the data pairs, a minimum value of $1 \cdot 10^{-12}$ was chosen. A data pair refers to a data sample that was created through minimal changes in one column. For RQ1, we have 100 original data samples, each of which has four pairs (total 400 pairs). In contrast, the dataset in RQ2 originated based on 10 data samples, each of which has six pairs (total 60 pairs/dataset).

5 Results

As mentioned in Sect. 4, the explanation similarity analysis for RQ1 is based on the feature changes in the column "Age", "Debt", "YearsEmployed" as well as "Income". The result is hereby a similarity matrix of 400×34, which represents the degree of similarity for all data pairs and their feature values.

Due to the size of the result set (for each algorithm 400×34), the explanation similarities of the "Income" column are presented in Fig. 2. The figure illustrates the distribution of the similarities for each XAI algorithm, where it can be clearly seen that most of the explanation pairs have a similarity of 99 to 101%. That means, a feature change of around 1% resulted in a explanation similarity of mostly 99 to 101% for the "Income" column. By comparing the results of the algorithms which each other, it can be said that especially SHAP has great results.

The same applies for CIU, which performs slightly worse then SHAP. Most of the samples lie in a similarity range of 99–101%, while the amount of samples lower or higher then that is very small. Even though Integrated Gradients achieved comparable results, a higher data dispersion as well as a few outliers could be observed. In contrast to the results of CIU, SHAP as well as Integrated Gradients, the results of LIME are highly distributed and less centered. As illustrated in Fig. 2, small changes in the features can lead to big differences in terms of the explanations. According to the quality approach mentioned in Sect. 4, this makes it unreliable and less trustworthy. On the other side, CIU, Integrated Gradients and especially SHAP deliver good results.

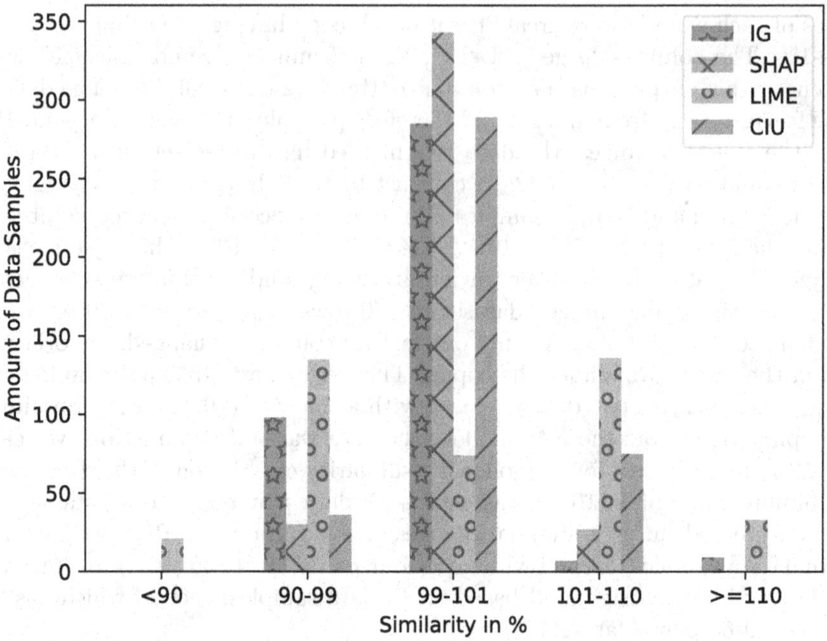

Fig. 2. Algorithm Comparison about the similarity of the explanations for the feature "Income" - representation of the feature importance similarities for the data pairs. The similarity measures the percentage match between the explanation of the original data sample as well as the one with a feature change of around 1%. The results of "Integrated Gradients", "SHAP", "LIME" and "CIU" are compared.

However, these conclusions relate to the column "Income" and can change among the different features. For instance in Fig. 3, it can be seen that the explanation similarity analysis for the column "Age" leads to slightly different results. The dispersion of the data got larger, especially for the results of LIME and IG.

In contrast to RQ1, RQ2 focuses on a relation between an increasing feature change as well as the similarity in the explanations. That means, if increasing or decreasing the value of a feature, has the same impact on the feature importance values. Table 3 compares hereby the similarity of the explanations. If the similarity is above 100%, it means the feature importance shrinked and vice versa. Except for the results of CIU, no clear relation of the changes in the feature values and their resulting feature importance values could be observed. For the values of CIU however, a monotonic relationship could be analysed. That means for instance, the change of the "Income" feature values caused a similar feature importance movement in "Age" for the CIU algorithm. By considering that every decision is based on 34 features, the change of the feature importance value can be considered as big. This is crucial by comparing the results with each other,

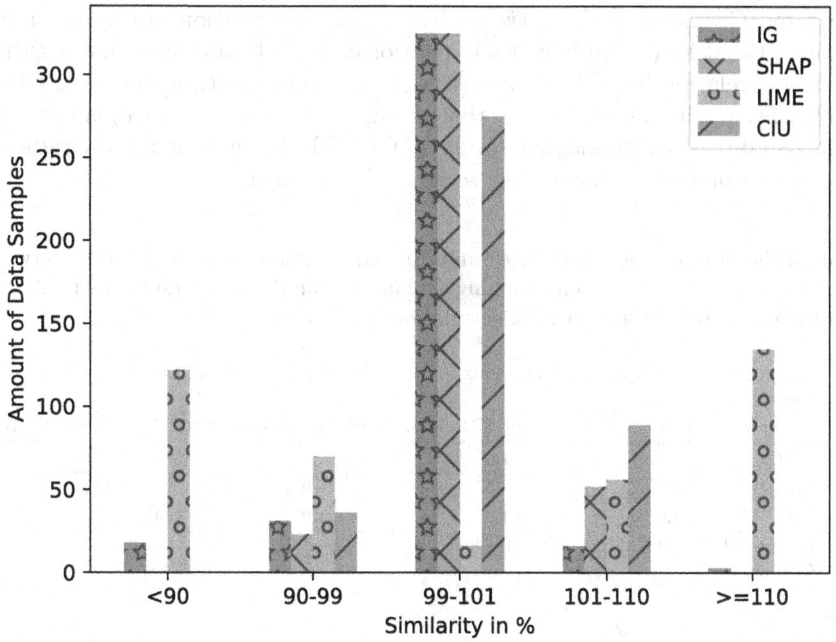

Fig. 3. Algorithm Comparison about the similarity of the explanations for the feature "Age" - representation of the feature importance similarities for the data pairs. The similarity measures the percentage match between the explanation of the original data sample as well as the one with a feature change of around 1%. The results of "Integrated Gradients", "SHAP", "LIME" and "CIU" are compared.

Table 3. Feature Changes for "Income" - Analysis of the relation between the varying values of feature "Income" and the changing explanation similarities of the feature "Age".

	Feature Change	Changes in Income Column					
		+1%	+5%	+10%	−1%	−5%	−10%
Age	LIME	81,87	93,60	95,25	193,12	157,12	105,29
	SHAP	99,98	100,05	100,02	99,96	99,82	99,87
	CIU	100,70	102,23	105,38	99,64	97,79	95,83
	Integrated Gradients	94,93	93,74	92,50	102,56	99,04	99,06

since a lot of times when similar movements occur, the similarity changes are not significant.

This can be seen in Table 4, which further processes the data by computing the Spearman rank correlation coefficient. Details about the exact feature importance changes are missing in Table 4 and therefore make it hard to distinguish similar values. As mentioned in Sect. 4, the values range from -1 to 1 and represent the monotonic relationship. In comparison to LIME, SHAP and

Integrated Gradients, CIU shows a clear monotonic relationship in all of the columns. Besides positive monotonic relationships, CIU also has some negative monotonic relationships. That means, a change in the feature value can either result in feature importance values that change in the same (positive) or opposite (negative) direction. Besides the results of CIU, LIME and Integrated Gradients had a monotonic relationship with some of the features.

Table 4. Feature Changes for "Age" and "Income" - analysis of the relation between varying feature values and their changing explanation similarities. Results are presented with the computed Spearman rank correlation coefficient.

	Feature Change	Changes in Income Col.		Changes in Age Col.	
		+1%, +5%, + 10	−1%, −5%, −10%	+1%, +5%, +10%	−1%, −5%, −10%
Age	LIME	1.0	1.0	−0.5	−1.0
	SHAP	0.5	0.5	−0.5	−1.0
	CIU	1.0	1.0	1.0	1.0
	Integrated Gradients	−1.0	0.5	−1.0	−0.5

6 Conclusion

The first aspect of the research was to analyse the similarity of explanations for slightly different test instances (RQ1), which can be understood as an metric approach to evaluate the trustworthiness of certain XAI algorithms. For the investigated algorithms (CIU, Integrated Gradients, LIME, and SHAP), it was hypothesized that minimal feature deviations would only lead to very small changes in the feature importance values. SHAP performed consistently well due to its theoretically well-founded calculation model, which tries many coalitions to calculate an objective interpretation. Molnar et al. also considers SHAP to be highly robust in terms of legal traceability [18]. Due to it's model-specific procedure, which uses both the I/O behavior of the predictor and the internal gradients to generate explanations, Integrated Gradients could achieve great results. However, in contrast to SHAP and CIU, a larger dispersion of the data as well as more outliers could be observed. The results of LIME were highly distributed and therefore the least trustworthy model. One possible reason for this is the local fidelity of LIME and the random generation of neighbor instances used to train the interpretable proxy model. Based on the similarity metric, CIU, IG, and SHAP consistently rank high, but also show some noticeable deviations. Focusing solely on the "High Accuracy Similarity Range" (i.e., 99% to 101%) is not enough to provide a definitive answer. It is crucial to take into account the outliers and the quantity of non-centered data. This could potentially form the foundation for future research. The range and number of outliers with respect to similarity give a more objective overview. This approach could also be utilized as a starting point for creating an enhanced metric that objectively assesses the efficacy of XAI algorithms.

In RQ2, the aim was to examine the correlation between changing feature importances and the changed feature values. CIU showed hereby a clear correlation. On the other hand, there was only a partial correlation found for LIME, IG, and SHAP. Therefore, the initial hypothesis can not be confirmed. One possible explanation for this could be the interdependencies between the features, which were not investigated.

Finally, the evaluation of the ML model is beneficial in critical areas such as finance. The evaluation of these black box predictive models can reveal the internal processes by explaining the decision path. It has been shown that explanatory approaches such as CIU, Integrated Gradients and SHAP produce more precise explanations, according to the presented metric, than LIME.

References

1. Amro, B., Najjar, A., Macido, M.: An intelligent decision support system for recruitment: resumes screening and applicants ranking (2022)
2. Anjomshoae, S., Kampik, T., Främling, K.: Py-CIU: a python library for explaining machine learning predictions using contextual importance and utility. In: IJCAI-PRICAI 2020 Workshop on Explainable Artificial Intelligence (XAI) (2020)
3. Anshari, M., Almunawar, M.N., Masri, M., Hrdy, M.: Financial technology with AI-enabled and ethical challenges. Society **58**(3), 189–195 (2021). https://doi.org/10.1007/s12115-021-00592-w
4. Arya, V., et al.: One explanation does not fit all: a toolkit and taxonomy of AI explainability techniques. CoRR abs/1909.03012 (2019). http://arxiv.org/abs/1909.03012
5. Bruckert, S., Finzel, B., Schmid, U.: The next generation of medical decision support: a roadmap toward transparent expert companions. Front. Artif. Intell. **3**, 507973 (2020)
6. Cortinhas, S.: Credit card approvals (clean data) from kaggle (2022). https://www.kaggle.com/datasets/samuelcortinhas/credit-card-approval-clean-data. Accessed 16 Apr 2023
7. Das, A., Rad, P.: Opportunities and challenges in explainable artificial intelligence (XAI): a survey (2020). https://doi.org/10.48550/ARXIV.2006.11371. https://arxiv.org/abs/2006.11371
8. Dua, D., Graff, C.: UCI machine learning repository (2017). http://archive.ics.uci.edu/ml. Accessed 16 Apr 2023
9. Främling, K.: Decision theory meets explainable AI. In: Calvaresi, D., Najjar, A., Winikoff, M., Främling, K. (eds.) EXTRAAMAS 2020. LNCS (LNAI), vol. 12175, pp. 57–74. Springer, Cham (2020). https://doi.org/10.1007/978-3-030-51924-7_4
10. Främling, K.: Explainable AI without interpretable model. CoRR abs/2009.13996 (2020). https://arxiv.org/abs/2009.13996
11. Främling, K.: Contextual importance and utility: a theoretical foundation. In: Long, G., Yu, X., Wang, S. (eds.) AI 2022. LNCS (LNAI), vol. 13151, pp. 117–128. Springer, Cham (2022). https://doi.org/10.1007/978-3-030-97546-3_10

12. Guo, H., Polak, P.: Artificial intelligence and financial technology FinTech: how AI is being used under the pandemic in 2020. In: Hamdan, A., Hassanien, A.E., Razzaque, A., Alareeni, B. (eds.) The Fourth Industrial Revolution: Implementation of Artificial Intelligence for Growing Business Success. SCI, vol. 935, pp. 169–186. Springer, Cham (2021). https://doi.org/10.1007/978-3-030-62796-6_9
13. Kaur, C., Garg, U.: Artificial intelligence techniques for cancer detection in medical image processing: a review. Mater. Today Proc. **81**, 806–809 (2021)
14. Klaise, J., Looveren, A.V., Vacanti, G., Coca, A.: Alibi explain: algorithms for explaining machine learning models. J. Mach. Learn. Res. **22**(181), 1–7 (2021). http://jmlr.org/papers/v22/21-0017.html
15. Liao, Q.V., Singh, M., Zhang, Y., Bellamy, R.: Introduction to explainable AI. In: Extended Abstracts of the 2021 CHI Conference on Human Factors in Computing Systems, pp. 1–3 (2021)
16. Lundberg, S.M., Lee, S.I.: A unified approach to interpreting model predictions. In: Proceedings of the 31st International Conference on Neural Information Processing Systems, NIPS 2017, pp. 4768–4777. Curran Associates Inc., Red Hook (2017)
17. Minh, D., Wang, H.X., Li, Y.F., Nguyen, T.N.: Explainable artificial intelligence: a comprehensive review. Artif. Intell. Rev. **55**, 3503–3568 (2021)
18. Molnar, C.: Interpretable machine learning (2022). https://christophm.github.io/interpretable-ml-book/. Accessed 16 Apr 2023
19. Reddy, S., Allan, S., Coghlan, S., Cooper, P.: A governance model for the application of AI in health care. J. Am. Med. Inform. Assoc. **27**(3), 491–497 (2020)
20. Ribeiro, M.T., Singh, S., Guestrin, C.: "Why should i trust you?": explaining the predictions of any classifier. In: Proceedings of the 22nd ACM SIGKDD International Conference on Knowledge Discovery and Data Mining, KDD 2016, pp. 1135–1144. Association for Computing Machinery, New York (2016). https://doi.org/10.1145/2939672.2939778
21. Speith, T.: A review of taxonomies of explainable artificial intelligence (XAI) methods. In: 2022 ACM Conference on Fairness, Accountability, and Transparency, pp. 2239–2250 (2022)
22. Sundararajan, M., Taly, A., Yan, Q.: Axiomatic attribution for deep networks. In: Proceedings of the 34th International Conference on Machine Learning, ICML 2017, vol. 70, pp. 3319–3328. JMLR.org (2017)

Towards Automatic Principles of Persuasion Detection Using Machine Learning Approach

Lázaro Bustio-Martínez[1(✉)], Vitali Herrera-Semenets[2], Juan-Luis García-Mendoza[3], Jorge Ángel González-Ordiano[1], Luis Zúñiga-Morales[1], Rubén Sánchez Rivero[2], José Emilio Quiróz-Ibarra[1], Pedro Antonio Santander-Molina[5], Jan van den Berg[4], and Davide Buscaldi[3]

[1] Universidad Iberoamericana, Ciudad de México, Prolongación Paseo de Reforma 880, 01219 Mexico City, Mexico
{lazaro.bustio,jorge.gonzalez,jose.quiroz}@ibero.mx, luis.zuniga@correo.uia.mx

[2] Centro de Aplicaciones de Tecnologías de Avanzada (CENATAV), 7a # 21406, Playa, 12200 Havana, La Habana, Cuba
{vherrera,rsanchez}@cenatav.co.cu

[3] Université Sorbonne Paris Nord, LIPN, Villetaneuse, France
{garciamendoza,davide.buscaldi}@lipn.univ-paris13.fr

[4] Intelligent Systems Department, Delft University of Technology, Mekelweg 4, 2628CD Delft, The Netherlands
j.vandenberg@tudelft.nl

[5] Pontificia Universidad Católica de Valparaíso, Valparaíso, Chile
pedro.santander@pucv.cl

Abstract. Persuasion is a human activity of influence. In marketing, persuasion can help customers find solutions to their problems, make informed choices, or convince someone to buy a useful (or useless) product or service. In computer crimes, persuasion can trick users into revealing sensitive information, or even performing actions that benefit attackers. Phishing is one of the most common and dangerous forms of persuasion-based attacks, as it exploits human vulnerabilities rather than technical ones. Therefore, an intelligent system capable of detecting and classifying persuasion attempts might be useful in protecting users. In this work, an approach that uses Machine Learning to analyze messages based on principles of persuasion and different data representations is presented. The aim of this research is to detect which data representation and which classification algorithm obtain the best results in detecting each principle of persuasion as a prior step to detecting phishing attacks. The results obtained indicate that among the combinations tested, there is one combination of data representation and classification algorithm that performs best. The related classification models obtained can detect the principles of persuasion at a rate that varies between 0.78 and 0.86 of AUC-ROC.

Keywords: Principles of Persuasion · Machine Learning · Artificial Intelligence · Data representation · Phishing detection

Y. Hernndez Heredia et al. (Eds.): IWAIPR 2023, LNCS 14335, pp. 155–166, 2024.
https://doi.org/10.1007/978-3-031-49552-6_14

1 Introduction

There is a branch of psychology where the persuasion is studied. This concerns studying the reasons that cause a person to change his/her behavior due to an external influence [6]. In marketing, persuasion aims to create a positive image of a product or service to influence the customer's decision making process. In computer crimes such as phishing, persuasion is used to deceive and to seduce people into revealing sensitive information or performing harmful actions. Phishing is a serious threat that exploits the human factor, which is often the most vulnerable element in a security system. Detecting phishing emails is not an easy task, as they vary greatly in sophistication and appearance. Therefore, a tool that can assist human users in identifying and avoiding phishing emails is needed and would be highly valued [8]. Although phishing has been used for a long time, there are still no completely effective ways to prevent it or to make people aware that they are exposed to it. There is always a risk of falling victim to some type of phishing attack. In this sense, identifying persuasion attempts would be valuable in identifying and preventing a phishing attack. Persuasion can be grouped into some patterns called the "principles of persuasion". So, the principles of persuasion are patterns that can be used to influence the reasoning process by promoting certain opinions, beliefs, and moods. Robert Cialdini was the first to study these principles of persuasion in his book "Influence: The Psychology of Persuasion" [1].

The prevailing view in literature is that phishing messages use principles of persuasion to increase their effectiveness. Thus, the identification of such principles might improve the phishing detection tools. A tool based on Machine Learning (ML) techniques can be an effective solution to support human judgment about phishing attacks. Based on this assumption, this work aims to evaluate the performance of ML techniques in detecting persuasion attempts in emails using an optimized set of principles of persuasion and applying different data representations. Based on Cialdini's work, Ana Ferreria et al. proposed an optimized set of principles of persuasion specially focused on phishing attacks [4], which are used in this research. The data representations investigated in this research are based on different ways of encoding the textual information of messages into numerical vectors that can be processed by ML algorithms. These include bag-of-words, term frequency-inverse document frequency (TF-IDF), and sentence embeddings. Furthermore, this work evaluates the performance of different ML classification algorithms such as Support Vector Machines (SVM), Random Forests (RF), k-Nearest Neighbors (KNN), Naïve Bayes (NB) and pretrained language models.

The main contribution of this research is to identify both effective data representation and data classification algorithms for detecting persuasion principles in messages using an optimized set of persuasion principles. The knowledge obtained will be used to propose an approach to phishing detection based on principles of persuasion.

The remainder of this paper is structured as follows. First, the related work about persuasion detection using ML is analyzed in Sect. 2. Second, the proposed methodology for persuasion detection, and the data used, are presented in Sect. 3. Third, in Sect. 4, the experimental results using different settings are presented and discussed. Finally, the conclusions and future work are outlined in Sect. 5.

2 Related Work

Since 2015, Ana Ferreira et al. [3,4] have focused on comprehending and identifying how the principles of persuasion can be employed in phishing attacks. Their work searched for a comprehensive and unified list of principles by integrating three different perspectives (i.e., those found in [1,5] and [12]). The principles of persuasion identified by Ferreira et al. when looking at phishing attacks are: i)- "authority": people are trained to follow authority without questioning; ii)- "social proof": people mimic majority to share responsibility; iii)- "liking, similarity and deception": people follow familiar individuals but can be manipulated; iv)- "distraction": emotions can cloud decision-making; and v)- "commitment, integrity and reciprocation": reciprocation and trust can influence behavior.

According to [4], there is a close relationship between these principles of persuasion and the content of phishing messages. In 2019, Van der Heijden et al. [13] identified cognitive vulnerabilities in email content. The authors use a supervised method based on labeled Latent Dirichlet Allocation (LDA). Their solution treats each incoming email as a mixture of topics derived from the labeled input data and estimates email-label distributions, where labels correspond to principles of persuasion.

Only three principles of persuasion proposed by Cialdini ("authority", "reciprocation" and "scarcity", which are equivalent to Ferreira's "distraction" principle), were used by Li et al. in [9] to label a dataset. However, the reason why they only use these three principles is not substantiated in their report. Applying the TF-IDF data representation, the authors associated a set of words with each of these principles: if one of those words appears in an email content, it is labeled with the corresponding principle of persuasion. To detect phishing emails, they trained and evaluated several ML classifiers on the labeled data set, being the Nearest Neighbor the one that achieved the best results. This approach may be inadequate since several principles of persuasion can be associated with the same words, and therefore non-present principles would be identified. The authors do not provide details on this point that could offer a better understanding.

In [11], emotion recognition was performed on spam emails. Their dataset consists of 343 sentences of a random sample sentence from emails labeled under six classes, each one associated with Cialdini's principles of persuasion. The basic idea is to identify principles of persuasion and associate them with emotions. For this, a transformer-based pretrained model called "Bidirectional Encoder Representations from Transformers" (BERT), and some other variants of BERT, were used. This work is based on a flawed premise: assuming that spam messages are the same as phishing messages. This premise is incorrect because, although both types of messages are morphologically similar, they do not express the same intentions semantically.

The work proposed by Karki et al. in [7] also evaluates ML models based on transformer networks. This work focuses on email classification using principles of persuasion. The goal is to find out if these principles are used in the construction of phishing emails and if it is possible to detect them automatically using Natural Language Processing (NLP) techniques. The models used to classify emails, into categories defined according to Cialdini's principles. Additionally, just as in [13], they use LDA for automated topic modeling to label the given emails. However, the results obtained show that LDA is not very effective for email classification. The topic modeling offered by LDA was too broad and generic, so it did not improved the classification results.

From the reviewed literature it has been observed that there are almost no labeled datasets for phishing detection available, and none for the classification of principles of persuasion. Since 2018, Rakesh Verma leaded the International Workshop on Security and Privacy Analytics Anti-Phishing Shared Task (IWSPA-AP). This workshop focused on identifying phishing emails. In addition to the basic contributions of this workshop, another contribution was the provision of a dataset composed of legitimate and phishing emails [14], which is also used in this work.

The discussed approaches have contributed to the comprehension and identification of principles of persuasion, but they entails some limitations. Manual extraction of persuasion principles is a time-consuming and subjective process that lacks automation. Li et al.'s method of associating words for labeling may lead to inaccuracies, as multiple principles can be linked to the same words. Pepe et al.'s assumption that spam and phishing messages are the same is flawed, as their semantic intentions differ. The ineffectiveness of LDA topic modeling, as observed by Karki et al., emphasizes the need for more robust techniques, which are explored in this research. Also, the literature review reveals that the detection of principles of persuasion in phishing messages has not been fully explored or thoroughly studied. Consequently, this research investigates various data representations and Machine Learning algorithms to determine the most effective combination for identifying persuasion principles as a main step for detecting phishing messages.

3 Data and Methodology

3.1 Principles of Persuasion Dataset

Given the absence of datasets specifically designed for the detection of principles of persuasion, it was necessary to develop one. To facilitate this endeavor, a comprehensive phishing dataset was required. The IWSPA-AP dataset, proposed by Rakesh Verma et al. [14], was selected for its inclusion of both phishing and legitimate emails[1].

[1] This dataset is available upon request to Rakesh Verma in the following link: https://www2.cs.uh.edu/~rmverma/.

Table 1. Details of PoP dataset.

PoP dataset	Positive	Negative	% of Positive
authority	681	432	61.18
commitment, integrity and reciprocation	141	972	12.66
distraction	201	912	18.05
liking, similarity and deception	39	1074	3.50
social proof	61	1052	5.48

Principles of persuasion are used in all kinds of communication, not only in phishing attacks, but considering that the success of such attacks largely depends on the use of Social Engineering, it can be concluded that the principles of persuasion are used more intensely in phishing attacks than in normal communication. In consequence, all the phishing emails from the IWSPA-AP dataset were considered for the creation of the Principles of Persuasion dataset (hereafter referred to as the "PoP dataset"). This resulted in a collection of 1113 confirmed phishing emails. Afterwards, the principles of persuasion of each data sample were labeled manually. To facilitate this process, 3 referees were instructed in the detection of principles of persuasion as proposed in [4]. The labels used corresponded to the principles of persuasion proposed by Ferreira et al. A "blind" methodology was employed during labeling, in which none of the referees were aware of the labels assigned by their colleagues. At the conclusion of the labeling process, the level of agreement between the 3 referees was 94.75%. A "majority vote" label assignment strategy was utilized, in which labels receiving the highest number of votes from referees were assigned. In cases where no consensus was reached among referees, the label was assigned by the authors. This occurred in 5.25% of cases. The obtained set is presented in Table 1. The resulting PoP dataset contains the text of the messages and five columns indicating the presence or absence of each five principle of persuasion within the messages.

3.2 Learning Phase

Once the PoP dataset was created, the next phase was to train a classifier that learns the patterns for detecting the principles of persuasion in each data sample. To accomplish this phase, a crucial issue is the selection of the data representation. A comprehensive literature review revealed that no single data representation method demonstrates superiority over others in detecting principles of persuasion within texts. Similarly, an examination of classification algorithms reported in the state of the art for detecting principles of persuasion in texts yielded comparable results. Therefore, the goal of this research is to identify a highly effective combination of data representation techniques and classifiers for accurately detecting principles of persuasion in texts. The strategy delineated in Pseudocode 1 endeavors to achieve this aim.

Given a dataset D of phishing messages (which were pre-processed in order to remove stop words, removed non alpha-numeric symbols and down-cased all characters), and given a set of principles of persuasion P composed of {"authority", "commitment, integrity and reciprocation", "distraction", "liking, similarity and deception", "social proof"}, a set of features extraction algorithms F that includes {Universal Sentence Encoder[2], LASER, RoBERTa, TF-IDF, Words Unigrams, Bigrams, Trigrams} was used to train a set of classification algorithms C composed of {Naïve Bayes, K-Nearest Neighbors, Random Forest, Support Vector Machines, BERT_base [2], RoBERTa [10]}. For storing the classification results obtained, a list L is used.

For each principle of persuasion $p \in P$, all messages in D are obtained and stored in d_p. D is composed of 6 columns: one column labeled "txt" that stores the text of the messages and 5 additional columns that store the voting of each message according the principle of persuasion p. Subsequently, for d_p, its corresponding data representation d_{p_f} is computed using each feature extraction algorithm $f \in F$ except for BERT_base and RoBERTa, which include their own feature extraction method. Each d_{p_f} is then used to train each classifier $c \in C$ using a 10-fold cross-validation process. Then the principle of persuasion p, the feature extraction algorithm f and the resulting classification model *model* are stored as a tuple in a list L. All of this processing is performed in parallel using Spark. Finally, the combination $< p, f, model >$ that achieves the best accuracy according to some pre-established metric (AUC-ROC in this research) will be returned as output of the proposed approach. After the processing, the combination of data representation and classification model that achieves the best results in detecting that principle of persuasion is determined.

4 Experimental Work

As explained above, this research focuses on obtaining a ML model capable of detecting the principles of persuasion contained in messages. To achieve this goal, a processing scheme is proposed in which each principle of persuasion is detected independently of the others. Considering the fact that principles of persuasion detection is a crucial stage for automatically detection of phishing attacks, three research questions arise:

- RQ1: Given the chosen set of data representations, which is best suited for detecting principles of persuasion regardless of classification algorithms?
- RQ2: Given the chosen set of classification algorithms, which is best suited for detecting principles of persuasion regardless of data representation?
- RQ3: Given the chosen set of data representations and classification algorithms, which combination of them is best suited for improving the detection rate of each principle of persuasion?

[2] Universal Sentence Encoder includes two feature extractor algorithms based on Deep Averaging Networks (DAN) and Transformers (TRANSF).

Algorithm 1: Principles of persuasion extraction method.

Input: D: PoP dataset of phishing messages.
Output: $< p, f, model >$: for each principle of persuasion p, this list contains the features extraction algorithm f and the model $model$ that obtains the best results in detecting principles of persuasion.

```
Procedure Train_Models(D, P, F, C)
    L = list()
    do in parallel
        foreach p ∈ P do
            d_p =< D[txt], D[p] >
            foreach f ∈ F do
                if (f ∈ {BERT_base, RoBERTa}) then
                    d_pf = d_p
                else
                    d_pf = f(d_p)
                foreach c ∈ C do
                    cross_val = True
                    folds = 10
                    model = c(d_pf, cross_val, folds)
                    L.append([p, f, model])
    return L
Procedure Get_Model_by_Principle(L)
    result = list()
    do in parallel
        foreach p ∈ P do
            model = argmax_{i=1}^{|L|}(AUC-ROC(∀L_i.model ∈
              L, if L_i.model has been trained for p))
            f = model_f
            result.append([p, f, model])
    return result
```

The platform used for conduct the experiment was an Intel(R) Xeon(R) Gold 6248 CPU @ 2.50 GHz equipped with 2 sockets, 20 cores per socket, 80 CPUs and 256 GB of RAM. Additionally, 8 GPUs Tesla V100-SXM2 with 32 GB of RAM was used.

4.1 Experiments Results

Several experiments were designed and conducted to answer the 3 proposed research questions. To do so, the messages in D were represented as a matrix of feature vectors using each feature extraction algorithm in F, resulting in eight different representations of D. Each data representation was then used to train each of the six classification algorithms in C using 10-fold cross-validation to mitigate over-fitting issues. This led to the training of 240 classification models using AUC-ROC as the performance evaluation metric, and the results obtained for each model were stored in L. Tables 2, 3, and 4 shows the obtained result. Furthermore, F is the set of features extractor algorithms used. Although AUC-ROC was selected as main evaluation metric, due to their well-known performance on unbalanced classification problems, other evaluation metrics were included such as the Macro Precision (Pr), the Macro Recall (Re), and the Macro F1 Score (F1 Score). These evaluation metrics were reported since they measure the behavior of the obtained classification models using other particular perspective. This allows to obtain other specific points of view.

Table 2. Best features extractor algorithm for detecting each principle of persuasion regardless of classification algorithm used.

Principle of Persuasion	F	Pr	Re	F1 Score	AUC-ROC
authority	DAN	0.76 ± 0.07	0.75 ± 0.09	0.75 ± 0.09	0.82 ± 0.08
commitment, integrity and reciprocation	RoBERTa	0.56 ± 0.09	0.62 ± 0.14	0.53 ± 0.07	0.76 ± 0.07
distraction	DAN	0.74 ± 0.11	0.68 ± 0.06	0.66 ± 0.08	0.80 ± 0.07
liking, similarity and deception	DAN	0.55 ± 0.15	0.58 ± 0.17	0.55 ± 0.14	0.75 ± 0.19
social proof	DAN	0.53 ± 0.14	0.55 ± 0.12	0.52 ± 0.1	0.77 ± 0.13

Best Features Extraction Algorithm for Each Principle of Persuasion. Table 2 describes the performance metrics obtained when each feature extractor in F is used to determine which of them is best suited to detect principles of persuasion regardless the classification algorithm used. In this experiment, the performance results obtained for classifiers in C were averaged for each feature extractor.

The obtained results indicate that there is no single data representation that consistently yields superior detection results for all principles of persuasion. Furthermore, the detection rate for the principles of persuasion varies between 0.75 and 0.82 for AUC-ROC. The principle "authority' was most effectively detected using the DAN feature extractor, achieving an AUC-ROC of 0.82 with 0.08 of standard deviation across all classifiers. The second most effectively detected principle was "distraction", with an AUC-ROC of 0.80 and a standard deviation of 0.07, also using the DAN feature extractor. "social proof" was the third most effectively detected principle with an AUC-ROC of 0.77 with 0.13 of standard deviation, while "commitment, integrity and reciprocation" was detected with AUC-ROC of 0.76 and a standard deviation of 0.07 using RoBERTa. Finally "liking, similarity and deception" was detected with 0.75 of AUC-ROC and a standard deviation of 0.19 using DAN.

Irrespective of the classification algorithm employed, DAN and RoBERTa were found to be the most effective feature extractors. In response to research question RQ1, the evidence collected suggests that DAN and RoBERTa are the two feature extractors that yield superior classification rates. Specifically, RoBERTa is recommended for detecting the principle of 'commitment, integrity and reciprocation,' while DAN is recommended for detecting the remaining principles.

Best Classifier for Each Principle of Persuasion. In this experiment, each classifier in C was used to determine which of them is best suited to determine the principles of persuasion regardless the data representation used. Similarly to the

Table 3. Best classifier for detecting each principle of persuasion regardless the feature extractor.

Principle of Persuasion	C	Pr	Re	F1 Score	AUC-ROC
authority	BERT_base	0.78 ± 0.08	0.77 ± 0.07	0.77 ± 0.08	0.83 ± 0.06
commitment, integrity and reciprocation	SVM	0.56 ± 0.15	0.58 ± 0.14	0.54 ± 0.1	0.72 ± 0.15
distraction	BERT_base	0.73 ± 0.08	0.71 ± 0.07	0.72 ± 0.07	0.80 ± 0.06
liking, similarity and deception	SVM	0.55 ± 0.15	0.56 ± 0.15	0.54 ± 0.12	0.75 ± 0.15
social proof	SVM	0.56 ± 014	0.57 ± 0.15	0.55 ± 0.12	0.75 ± 0.16

former experiment, the performance results obtained for the features extractors in F were averaged for each classifier. The obtained results are expressed in Table 3.

The best classification results concerning AUC-ROC were obtained for "authority", with 0.83 and a standard deviation of 0.06. This result was obtained using BERT_base. "distraction" was the second-highest rated principle of persuasion detected, with an AUC-ROC of 0.8 with a standard deviation of 0.06, also obtained using BERT_base. The third-highest value of AUC-ROC at 0.75 with a standard deviation of 0.15 was for "liking, similarity and deception", which was obtained using SVM. The "social proof" principle was detected also with 0.75 of AUC-ROC and 0.16 of standard deviation using SVM; while "commitment, integrity and reciprocation" was detected also using SVM with 0.72 of AUC-ROC and 0.15 of standard deviation.

The findings of this experiment indicate that BERT_base and SVM can be effectively utilized for the detection of principles of persuasion, irrespective of the feature extraction technique employed. Specifically, BERT_base is recommended for detecting the principles of "authority" and "distraction", while SVM is recommended for detecting the remaining principles. Consequently, research question RQ2 is addressed based on the results obtained in this experiment.

Best Combination of Features Extractor and Classifier for Each Principle of Persuasion. As result of this experiment,it can be noticed that there is no a single combination of feature extractor and classifier that detects all principles of persuasion. In consequence, each principle of persuasion should be detected using their own combination of feature extractor and classifier. Opposite to the previous experiments, Table 4 shows the detection results obtained without averaging any value to show the classification metrics obtained for each combination in each principle of persuasion. From this table it can be observed that the principle of "authority" achieves the highest AUC-ROC value with a value of 0.86 with an standard deviation of 0.07 when using DAN as the feature extractor and Random Forest as the classifier. This is obtained employing the optimal data representation (DAN) which was determined as conclusion of experiment described in Sect. 4.1. For the principle "authority", and considering the best data classification results described in Table 3, BERT_base was found to be the best classifier. This classifier employs its own feature extractor approach, and using it, an AUC-ROC value of 0.84 with a standard deviation of 0.07 was obtained. Considering the AUC_ROC values for "authority", the best combination of features extractor and data classifier is DAN with Random Forest.

A similar behavior is found for "distraction", which achieves an AUC-ROC value of 0.82 and a standard deviation of 0.08 when DAN and SVM are used. This result was obtained from Table 2, where DAN was determined to be the best data representation for detecting "distraction". Subsequently, the best classification result using DAN was achieved using SVM. With regard to the best classifier, according with Table 3, BERT_base achieves the best classification result. BERT_base employs its own feature extractor approach, and using this combination of feature extractor and classifier, an AUC-ROC value of 0.80 with a standard deviation of 0.07 is obtained. Then, it can be concluded that for detecting the "distraction", the best classification results are achieved using DAN and SVM.

The third principle of persuasion that is most effectively detected is "social proof", with an AUC-ROC value of 0.83 and a standard deviation of 0.11. These results were obtained when TRANSF and SVM were used. For detecting this principle of persuasion, the best results regarding the data representation (see Table 2) were achieved using DAN. Considering DAN, the best classification results were achieved using SVM with an AUC-ROC value of 0.79 and a standard deviation of 0.13 (see Table 3). Also considering Table 3, the best results were reported for SVM, but this time the best results for SVM were achieved using TRANSF as the data representation. Using this combination, the detection was 0.83 for AUC-ROC and 0.11 for standard deviation. As a conclusion, and concerning this principle of persuasion, the best classification results were obtained for the combination of TRANSF and SVM.

A different behavior is observed for the principle of "liking, similarity and deception". For this principle, according the Table 2, the best discrimination result is achieved using DAN. Considering DAN and according to Table 3, the best classification result was achieved using Naïve Bayes, with an AUC-ROC value of 0.80 and a standard deviation of 0.16. Also for "liking, similarity and deception", the best classification results with regard to the classifier were obtained for SVM, and these results were achieved using DAN as feature extractor, with an AUC-ROC value of 0.80 and a standard deviation of 0.16. Subsequently, the best detection rate according to the AUC-ROC values obtained for identifying "liking, similarity and deception" was achieved using LASER as features extractor and SVM as classifier, which was 0.82 with a standard deviation of 0.14. It was expected that the best classification results for "liking, similarity and deception" would be obtained using the best data representation (DAN) and the best classifier (SVM), but this was not the case.

Table 4. Best combination of features extractor algorithm and classifier for each principle of persuasion.

Principle of Persuasion	*F*	*C*	Pr	Re	F1 Score	AUC-ROC
*authority**	**DAN**	**RF**	0.79 ± 0.01	0.78 ± 0.08	0.78 ± 0.09	**0.86** ± **0.07**
authority+	–	BERT_base	0.78 ± 0.08	0.77 ± 0.07	0.77 ± 0.08	0.84 ± 0.07
*commitment, integrity and reciprocation**	**RoBERTa**	**NB**	0.58 ± 0.04	0.72 ± 0.09	0.53 ± 0.07	**0.78** ± **0.09**
commitment, integrity and reciprocation+	DAN	SVM	0.48 ± 0.11	0.51 ± 0.04	0.48 ± 0.06	0.77 ± 0.12
commitment, integrity and reciprocation#	RoBERTa	SVM	0.57 ± 0.04	0.65 ± 0.16	0.56 ± 0.04	0.73 ± 0.13
*distraction**	**DAN**	**SVM**	0.70 ± 0.10	0.67 ± 0.08	0.69 ± 0.09	**0.82** ± **0.08**
distraction+	–	BERT_base	0.74 ± 0.08	0.71 ± 0.07	0.72 ± 0.07	0.80 ± 0.07
*liking, similarity and deception**	DAN	NB	0.60 ± 0.12	0.71 ± 0.22	0.60 ± 0.12	0.80 ± 0.16
liking, similarity and deception+	**LASER**	**SVM**	0.48 ± 0.01	0.50 ± 0.0	0.49 ± 0.01	**0.82** ± **0.14**
liking, similarity and deception#	DAN	SVM	0.53 ± 0.16	0.55 ± 0.16	0.54 ± 0.16	0.80 ± 0.16
*social proof**	DAN	SVM	0.57 ± 0.22	0.56 ± 0.16	0.56 ± 0.17	0.79 ± 0.13
social proof+	**TRANSF**	**SVM**	0.62 ± 0.20	0.58 ± 0.17	0.57 ± 0.17	**0.83** ± **0.11**

* Combination of the best feature extractor algorithm and the best classifier associated with it.
+ Combination of the best classifier and the best feature extractor algorithm associated with it.
# Combination of the best individual feature extractor and classifier.
In **bold** text, the results of the combination of feature extractor and classifier that obtains the best overall detection results for each principle of persuasion

Finally, for detecting "commitment, integrity and reciprocation", the best detection rate concerning data representation (see Table 2), was achieved using RoBERTa. For RoBERTa, the best detection AUC-ROC value was achieved using Naïve bayes according to Table 3, with 0.78 and 0.09 standard deviation. Concerning the classifier, and according to Table 3, the best detection rate for "commitment, integrity and reciprocation" was achieved using SVM as classifier and, and were obtained using DAN as features extractor. With this combination it was obtained an AUC-ROC of 0.77 with 0.12 of standard deviation. At this point the best classification results using the best feature extractor (RoBERTa) and the best classificator (SVM) were used, was 0.73 of AUC-ROC and 0.13 of standard deviation. Similarly to "liking, similarity and deception", the best classification result is not achieved using the best data representation and the best classifier, but was achieve using RoBERTa and Naïve Bayes with 0.78 of AUC-ROC and 0.09 of standard deviation. Considering these results, the research question RQ3 is answered.

5 Conclusions

Phishing is a highly profitable and effective scam that exploits the human factor in information systems. In such attacks, messages are delivered with the intent of provoking emotions such as urgency, greed, and curiosity in their victims. In the literature reviewed, the majority of proposed approaches focused on detecting *what* is communicated in a phishing message rather than *how* the message is communicated. One approach to detecting *how* a phishing message is communicated is by identifying the principles of persuasion included in the messages. This article presents a study aimed at determining the data representation and classifier that improve the detection rate of each principle of persuasion, both independently and in combination. This approach is novel in that the Machine Learning models obtained in this research are specifically tailored for detecting principles of persuasion most commonly used in phishing attacks, rather than broader principles of persuasion addressed in the literature. The detection rate, as measured by AUC-ROC, ranges between 0.78 and 0.86.

Acknowledgement. This research was supported by the IBERO and InIAT through the project *"Detección de ataques de phishing en mensajes electrónicos mediante técnicas de Inteligencia Artificial"*. Additionally, the authors thank CONACYT for the computer resources provided through the INAOE Supercomputing Laboratory's Deep Learning Platform for Language Technologies.

References

1. Cialdini, R.B.: Influence: The Psychology of Persuasion, vol. 55. Collins New York (2007)
2. Devlin, J., Chang, M.W., Lee, K., Toutanova, K.: BERT: pre-training of deep bidirectional transformers for language understanding. arXiv:1810.04805v1 [cs.CL] (2018)
3. Ferreira, A., Coventry, L., Lenzini, G.: Principles of persuasion in social engineering and their use in phishing. In: Tryfonas, T., Askoxylakis, I. (eds.) HAS 2015. LNCS, vol. 9190, pp. 36–47. Springer, Cham (2015). https://doi.org/10.1007/978-3-319-20376-8_4
4. Ferreira, A., Teles, S.: Persuasion: how phishing emails can influence users and bypass security measures. Int. J. Hum.-Comput Stud. **125**, 19–31 (2019)
5. Gragg, D.: A multi-level defense against social engineering. SANS Reading Room **13**, 1–21 (2003)
6. Hogan, K.: The Psychology of Persuasion: How to Persuade Others to Your Way of Thinking. Pelican Publishing (2010)
7. Karki, B., Abri, F., Namin, A.S., Jones, K.S.: Using transformers for identification of persuasion principles in phishing emails. In: 2022 IEEE International Conference on Big Data (Big Data), pp. 2841–2848. IEEE (2022)
8. Koddebusch, M.: Exposing the phish: the effect of persuasion techniques in phishing e-mails. In: DG. O 2022: The 23rd Annual International Conference on Digital Government Research, pp. 78–87 (2022)
9. Li, X., Zhang, D., Wu, B.: Detection method of phishing email based on persuasion principle. In: 2020 IEEE 4th Information Technology, Networking, Electronic and Automation Control Conference (ITNEC), vol. 1, pp. 571–574. IEEE (2020)
10. Liu, Y., et al.: RoBERTa: a robustly optimized BERT pretraining approach. arXiv:1907.11692 (2019)
11. Pepe, E.: Human-centric approach to emails phishing detection. Ph.D. thesis, Dublin, National College of Ireland (2022)
12. Stajano, F., Wilson, P.: Understanding scam victims: seven principles for systems security. Commun. ACM **54**(3), 70–75 (2011)
13. Van Der Heijden, A., Allodi, L.: Cognitive triaging of phishing attacks. In: SEC 2019, pp. 1309–1326. USENIX Association (2019)
14. Verma, R.M., Zeng, V., Faridi, H.: Data quality for security challenges: case studies of phishing, malware and intrusion detection datasets. In: Proceedings of the 2019 ACM SIGSAC Conference on Computer and Communications Security, CCS 2019, pp. 2605–2607. Association for Computing Machinery, New York (2019)

Indirect Condition Monitoring of the Transmission Belts in a Desalination Plant by Using Deep Learning

Deivis Avila[1](✉), G. Nicolás Marichal[1], Yanelys Cuba Arana[2], and Ramón Quiza[2]

[1] INGEMAR Research Group, University of La Laguna, La Laguna, P.O. Box 456, 38200 Santa Cruz de Tenerife, Spain
davilapr@ull.edu.es

[2] Centre for Advanced and Sustainable Manufacturing Studies, University of Matanzas, Autopista a Varadero Km 3.5, 44740 Matanzas, MT, Cuba

Abstract. Condition monitoring is a basic technique in contemporary maintenance, since it can be used to identify problems in equipment and machinery before catastrophic failures occur. In the present work, an indirect monitoring system of the state of deterioration of the transmission belt of a water desalination plant is proposed. To achieve this goal, the mechanical vibrations in the three axes, measured at the bearing of the drive pulley, are taken as input signals. They are preprocessed by applying a fast Fourier transform and combining the respective outcomes into an image, where each basic channel corresponds to an axis. These images are used as the inputs of a two-block convolutional neural network, which is trained by using the Adam algorithm. The trained convolutional network allows the belts to be classified into three categories: new, medium used, and worn out. The proposed system was more than 90% effective for both the training and validation sets.

Keywords: Indirect condition monitoring · Transmission belt · Vibrations · Fast Fourier transform · Convolutional neural network

1 Introduction

In the desalination industry, as in any other, the equipment is subjected to high mechanical loads, which can cause breakage or unscheduled stoppages, so maintenance, and especially predictive maintenance, plays a fundamental role in its proper operation. This maintenance depends on the physical state of the equipment by measuring certain variables, with one of the most used methods being vibration analysis [1, 2]. The advantages of predictive maintenance are many, since it guarantees the reliability and availability of the equipment, improving its performance and productivity. This type of maintenance is gaining more and more traction, since it makes it possible to anticipate breakdowns, which reduces downtime and allows maintenance to be properly scheduled [3]. Currently, artificial intelligence techniques are very much present in predictive systems in

Y. Hernández Heredia et al. (Eds.): IWAIPR 2023, LNCS 14335, pp. 167–176, 2024.
https://doi.org/10.1007/978-3-031-49552-6_15

the industry, since they can more quickly identify patterns or anomalies that indicate possible failures or imminent problems [4, 5].

Transmission elements are an essential part of machines, and include transmission shafts, chains, sprockets and/or transmission belts, the latter of which is the focus of this work. During their life, belts can be exposed to different tension loads, wear due to friction and adverse environmental conditions, so it is usually a very important element to take into consideration in preventive maintenance, given its likelihood of deteriorating or breaking. Belt transmissions are systems that continue to be widely accepted in modern industry due to their ability to connect widely spaced shafts, being silent transmission elements, their low cost, and the possibility of acting as a mechanical fuse. These systems are also widely employed in the desalination industry, especially for use in high-pressure pumps for small and medium production systems [6]. These high-pressure pumps for desalination can be of various types, including piston pumps with a V-belt transmission.

In light of the above, monitoring the condition of transmission belts should be considered the most appropriate methodology to guarantee their proper operation and to prevent possible failures and/or malfunctions in these systems. Being a common element in transmission systems, belts condition monitoring has received a lot of attention from technical and scientific literature [7–9]. Some of the most popular techniques used for this purpose include deep transfer learning [10], expert systems [11] and convolutional neural networks [12].

It can be pointed out that convolutional neural networks were chosen for modelling, because it has several remarkable advantages over other alternatives, such as Kalman filters and autoregressive models. These advantages include ability to learn complex patterns, end-to-end learning, robustness to noise, scalability and transfer learning [13, 14]. This last reward is especially important for implementing a system with continuous learning capability [15].

The goal of this study is the development of a system that indirectly monitors the state of deterioration of the transmission belt of the high-pressure pump in an RO seawater desalination plant.

In the experimental phase, the mechanical vibrations measured at the bearing of the drive pulley of a laboratory set-up with a high-speed rotating machine will be taken as input signals. These signals will be processed using a fast Fourier transform applied to each signal corresponding to a coordinate axis, combining them in an image. With these images, a convolutional neural network will be trained that will categorize the belts into one of three possible conditions: new, medium used, and worn.

The paper is structured into four sections. After this introduction, the materials and methods section describes the desalination plant where the study was carried out, the mechanical vibration signal capture system used, the signal processing and the modelling by the convolutional neural network. In the third section, the results are analyzed, showing the effectiveness of the classification made. Finally, the conclusions are presented and the future continuation of the work is outlined.

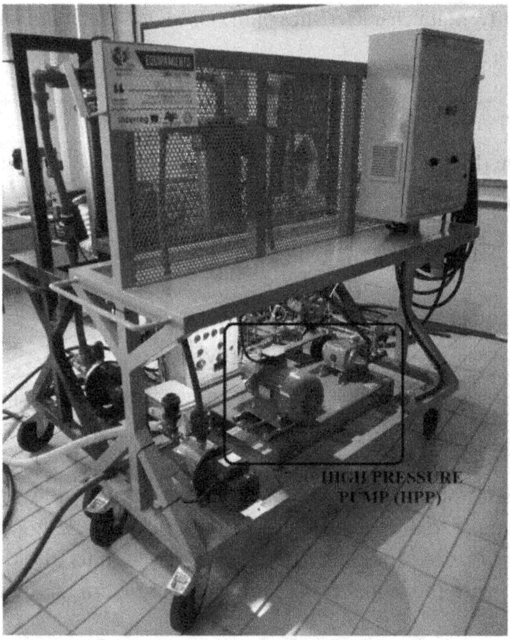

Fig. 1. Pilot RO desalination plant. E5DES (MAC2/1.1a/309) Project

2 Materials and Methods

Below is a brief description of the pilot desalination plant where the belt condition monitoring study is intended to be replicated, as well as the mechanical vibration signal capture system consisting of a triaxial piezoelectric accelerometer, a dynamic signal analyzer, and a laptop computer.

2.1 Pilot RO Desalination Plant Description

The experimental desalination plant (OSMOMAR-2) has a water production capacity of up to 3.0 m^3/day. It consists of three membranes for desalination. A low-pressure pump (LPP) transports the salt water to the device after it passes through a pre-filtration system. Once the water is filtered, it is transported to the membrane, where a high-pressure pump (HPP) supplies enough pressure to force the feed flow through the membranes, exceeding the osmotic pressure and separating out the salts present in the water (see Fig. 1).

Table 1 shows the main characteristics of the plant. The values shown in this table are approximate, since they can vary depending on different parameters: temperature and conductivity of the feed water, number of membranes used in the plant, etc.

2.2 Description of the Mechanical Vibration Signal Capture System

The data are collected on a test bench of a high-speed rotating machine. This test bench makes it easier to search for the key elements to detect failures in belt transmission systems. This test bench is described in Camacho et al. [16].

Table 1. Main characteristics of the OSMOMAR-2 pilot plant.

Characteristics	Value
Production capacity (l/day)	1,500 … 3,000
HPP working pressure (MPa)	5.5
HPP maximum pressure (MPa)	6.5
HPP velocity (min–1)	1,500
Feed flow rate (l/min)	16
Permeate recovery rate (%)	35 (3 membranes)
Electrical connection	400 V, 3 ph, 50 Hz
Membrane type	Cross-lined aromatic polyamide

In the experimental phase, the mechanical vibration signals were captured with a Brüel & Kjaer triaxial piezoelectric accelerometer, type 4504-A. A PHOTON+ dynamic signal analyzer is responsible for converting the analog signals into digital and transferring them to a laptop with the signal processing software from the Brüel & Kjaer branch (see Fig. 2).

The experimental measurements were carried out on 26 V-belts under operating conditions of 0, 12 000 and 24 000 h [17], corresponding to the states called "new", "medium used" and "worn out", respectively. For each condition, 10 consecutive measurements were taken, with a sampling frequency of 2.56 kHz and a sample time of 2.0 s.

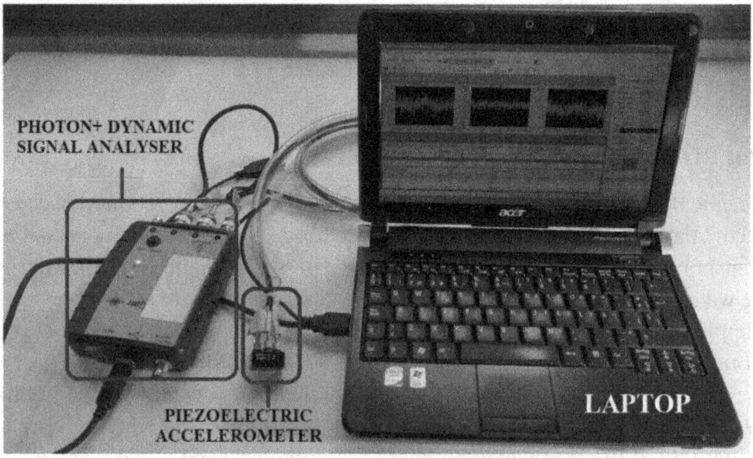

Fig. 2. Mechanical vibration signal capture system.

Figure 3 shows a segment of 100 ms of sample signals corresponding to three belts in the different states of use. As we can see, all three exhibit very similar behavior, without there being any notable differences, at first glance, between them.

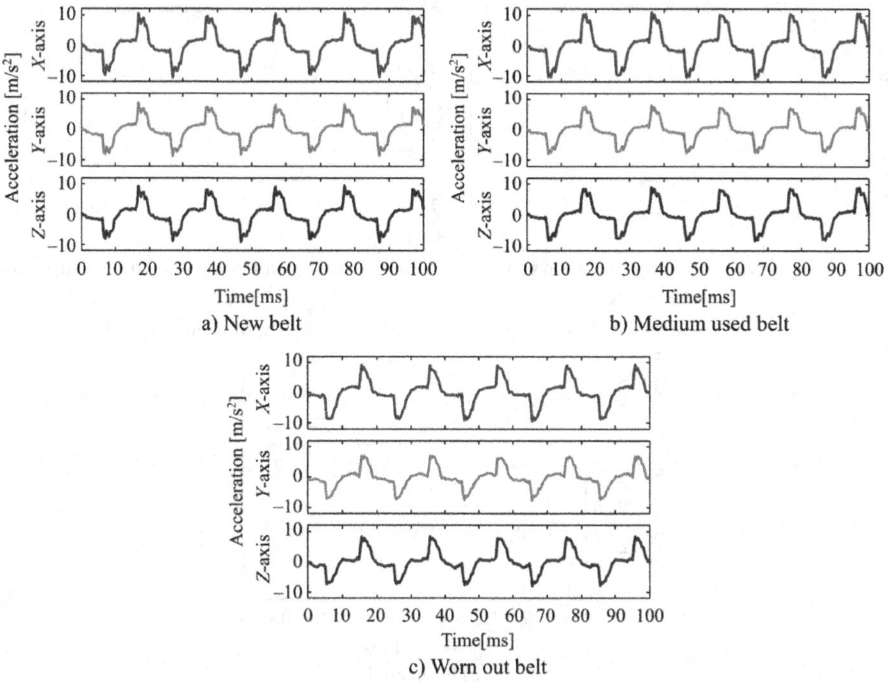

Fig. 3. Example of vibration signals measured by each channel

2.3 Signal Preprocessing

In the first stage of the indirect monitoring, the signals were preprocessed by applying a fast Fourier transform. Considering a factor of 2.56 for the Nysquist frequency, the frequency spectrum obtained was limited to the range from 0 to 1.0 kHz. As Fig. 4 shows, the 50 Hz harmonics stand out, especially the odd ones, which may be caused by the frequency of the motor supply current. In order to be usable as an input to the convolutional network, the frequency spectra of the three axes were consolidated into an image of 120 000 × 1 pixels, where each pixel is formed by the red, green and blue channels, whose intensity is proportional to the power values of each point of the frequency spectrum for the *X*, *Y* and *Z* axes, respectively. This power was normalized, with the upper limit corresponding to the maximum global power value for all the belts in the respective axis.

These images were resampled, using bicubic interpolation, to a size of 800 × 50 pixels, which served to filter the peaks, taking into account the power values in the peak environments. Figure 5 shows the images obtained for three sample belts.

2.4 Convolutional Neural Network Modeling

For training, the convolutional network whose architecture is shown in Table 2 was used. It consists of two convolutional blocks (each composed of four layers: convolution,

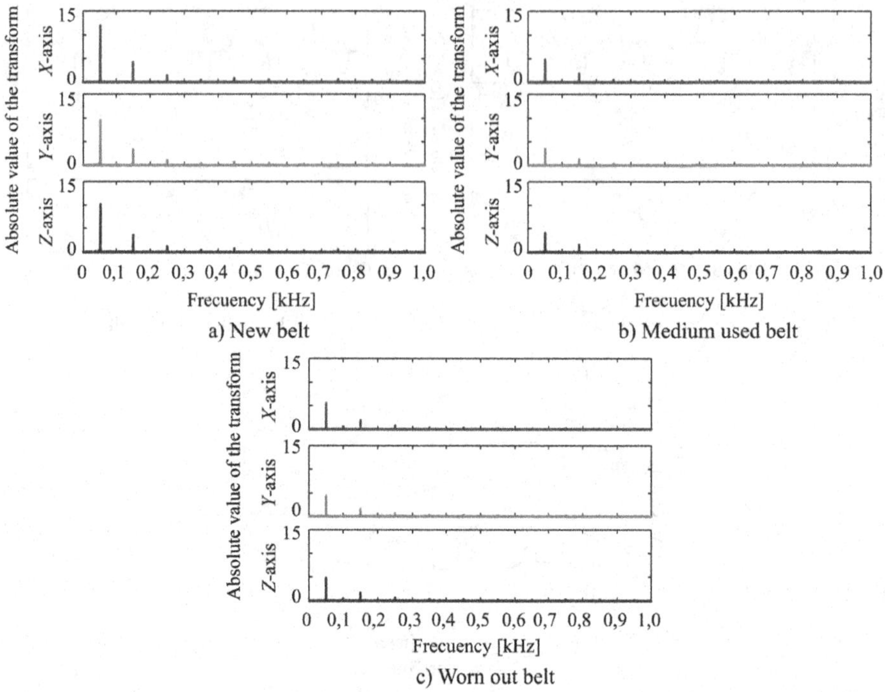

Fig. 4. Example of the FFT outcomes for each channel

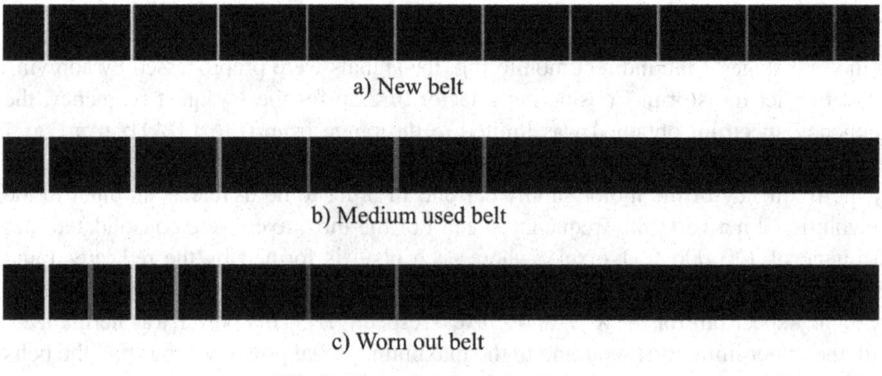

Fig. 5. Example of training images

linear rectification, undersampling and deactivation) and a fully connected, two-layer block with a final classification layer (in the three classes of the belt use condition).

For training, the 222 images generated in the preprocessing step were used: 94 of them correspond to the "New" class, 65 to the "Medium used" class and 63 to the "Worn out" class. The set of images was randomly divided into three subsets for training, validation and testing, each with 60%, 20% and 20%, respectively, of the total images.

Table 2. Layers of the convolutional neural network.

Layer	Type of layer	Parameters
1	Image input	50 × 800 × 3 images, with zero centered normalization
2	Convolution	20 10 × 10 convolutions with stride 1 and padding 0
3	Linear Rectification	---
4	Max Pooling	10 × 10 max pooling with stride 2 and padding 0
5	Dropout	10% dropout
6	Convolution	10 5 × 5 convolutions with stride 1 and padding 0
7	Linear Rectification	---
8	Max Pooling	5 × 5 max pooling with stride 2 and padding 0
9	Dropout	5% dropout
10	Fully connected	50 units
11	Dropout	5% dropout
12	Fully connected	3 units
13	Activation	Softmax function
14	Classification output	Cross-entropy

Training was performed using the Adam optimizer (with adaptive moment estimation), using as parameters a maximum number of iterations equal to 50; a validation frequency of 10; a validation patience of 50; a mini-batch factor of 1; an initial learning rate of 10^{-4}; a learning rate decay factor of 0.1; a learning rate decay period of 10; an L_2 regularization factor of 10^{-4}; a gradient moving average decay rate of 0.9; a gradient moving average squared gradient decay rate of 0.999; a denominator offset of 10^{-8}; and an infinite gradient threshold.

3 Results and Discussion

The training was concluded after 2 320 iterations. Figure 6 shows the change in the accuracy and losses during the training process for both the training and validation sets. As we can see, the accuracy rises as the losses decrease during the training, until the values stabilize somewhat at the end of the training process. Finally, the accuracy reached a value of 88.6% and the losses, 0.6%.

Once the convolutional neural network was trained, it was applied to the test set in order to verify its generalization capacity. As is evident from the resulting confusion matrix (see Table 3), 18 of the 19 cases of new belts, 10 of the 13 cases of medium-used belts, and the 13 cases of worn belts, were correctly classified. It is worth mentioning that in no case was the condition of a belt classified as having less use than it actually did, which is a guarantee of the safety of the proposed approach.

From the confusion matrix, the precision, sensitivity and F_1 metrics were determined for each of the classes (see Table 4). The lowest precision value (81%) corresponded

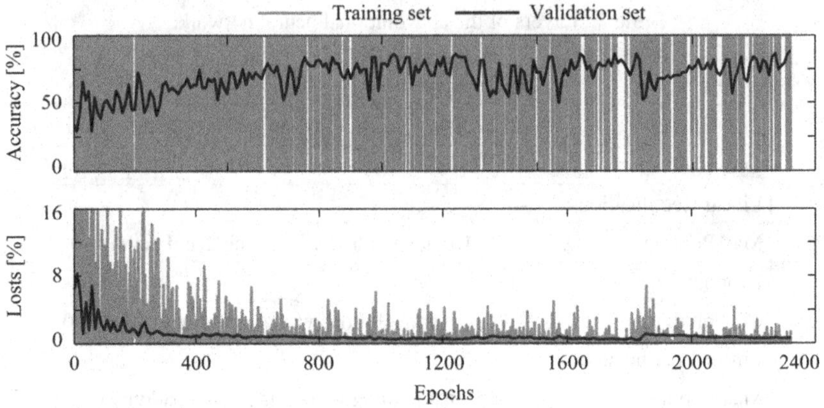

Fig. 6. Training process

Table 3. Confusion matrix of the classification in the test set

Observed classes	Predicted classes		
	New	Medium used	Worn out
New	18	1	0
Medium used	0	10	3
Worn out	0	0	13

to the class of worn belts, while the lowest values of sensitivity (77%) and F_1 metric (83%) corresponded to the half-worn belts. The averages calculated for these metrics, both macro and weighted, were in the range from 90 to 92%, with an overall accuracy value of 91%, slightly higher even than that achieved for the validation set.

Table 4. Ranking metrics in the test set

Class	Precision	Sensitivity	F1-metric	Support
New	1.00	0.95	0.97	19
Medium used	0.91	0.77	0.83	13
Worn out	0.81	1.00	0.90	13
Macro average	0.91	0.91	0.90	45
Weighted average	0.92	0.91	0.91	45
Accuracy	0.91			45

The values obtained for the metrics fully support the goodness of fit of the model and its generalization capacity, from which its practical introduction in the operation of the desalination plant can be assessed.

4 Conclusions

As a result of the work, a system for indirectly monitoring the condition of the belts of the high-pressure pump of a desalination plant was devised. The vibrations in the three spatial axes were used as signals, preprocessed by FFT and combined into a single image, using the three color channels. These images were used to train a convolutional neural network, which performed the classification according to the conditions. Based on the results, it was determined that the system was able to predict the belt condition with an accuracy of 91% for the test set, which showed a very high generalization capacity. It should be noted that, in every case, the estimation error was conservative, meaning the belt condition was estimated to be worse than it actually was, which, if accepted, increases costs, but also safety.

Due to the scalability of convolutional neural networks, which can be easily scaled to handle large amounts of data, making them well-suited for online monitoring applications where data is generated continuously over time, the proposed approach can be considered as a first step of a monitoring system were, after a first training, the model will be refined to successive minor trainings, as more data is measured and incorporated to the training dataset.

In a future iteration of the work, we plan, in the first place, to increase the number of belt condition classes, the goal being to have more reliable data, and to include other operating hours in order to increase the number of conditions of use. Different desalination plants may also be used to verify the generalizability of the system in other environments. Furthermore, in order to improve the effectiveness of the model, future works should include the optimization of the parameters of the convolutional neural networks. Comparison with other alternative approaches must be also carried out.

Acknowledgments. The work was funded by the R&D Program for the challenges of society, National project PID2020-116984RB-C21, of Spain, and by ERDF funds, INTERREGMAC Program 2014–2020 of the European Union, part of the E5DES project (MAC2/1.1a.309). It also received funds from the Office of Funds Management and International Projects, Cuba, under project code PN223LH004–024.

References

1. UNE [Asociación Española de Normalización]: UNE-EN 13306:2018. Mantenimiento: Terminología del mantenimiento. Madrid (Spain) (2018)
2. Marichal, G.N., Avila, D., Hernández, A., Padrón, I., Castejón, C.: Feature extraction from indirect monitoring in marine oil separation systems. Sensors **18**, 3159 (2018)
3. Zonta, T., da Costa, C.A., da Rosa Righi, R., de Lima, M.J., da Trindade, E.S., Pyng Li, G.: Predictive maintenance in the Industry 4.0: a systematic literature review. Comput. Ind. Eng. **150**, 106889 (2020)
4. Zhong, D., Xia, Z., Zhu, Y., Duan, J.: Overview of predictive maintenance based on digital twin technology. Heliyon **9**(4), e14534 (2023)
5. Meriem, H., Nora, H., Samir, O.: Predictive maintenance for smart industrial systems: a roadmap. Procedia Comput. Sci. **220**, 645–650 (2023)

6. Nabhan, A., El-Sharkawy M., Rashed, A.: Monitoring of belt-drive defects using the vibration signals and simulation models. In: 20th International Conference on Innovations in Engineering and Technology Research, Roma (Italia) (2019)
7. Xu, X., Yang, Z., Liu, Q., Yan, S., Ding, H.: Condition monitoring and mechanism analysis of belt wear in robotic grinding of TC4 workpiece using acoustic emissions. Mech. Syst. Signal Process. **188**, 109979 (2023)
8. Wan, Q., Zou, L., Han, C., Wang, W., Quian, K., Ou, J.: A U-net-based intelligent approach for belt morphology quantification and wear monitoring. J. Mater. Process. Technol. **306**, 117652 (2022)
9. Koch, Y., Weller, R., Welzbacher, P., Kirchner, E.: In-situ condition monitoring in timing belts for automation purposes-challenges and opportunities. Procedia CIRP **109**, 263–268 (2022)
10. Li, Z., Tan, Q., Wang, S., Zhang, P.: A deep transfer learning method for monitoring the wear of abrasive belts with a small sample dataset. J. Manuf. Process. **74**, 374–382 (2022)
11. Zarchi, M., Shahgholi, M.: An expert condition monitoring system via fusion of signal processing for vibration of industrial rotating machinery with unseen operational conditions. J. Vibr. Eng. Technol. (2022). https://doi.org/10.1007/s42417-022-00702-w
12. Qi, J., Chen, B., Zhang, D.: Multi-information fusion-based belt condition monitoring in grinding process using the improved-Mahalanobis distance and convolutional neural networks. J. Manuf. Process. **59**, 302–315 (2020)
13. Wang, J., Li, Z.: Wind speed interval prediction based on multidimensional time series of Convolutional Neural Networks. Eng. Appl. Artif. Intell. **121**, 105987 (2023)
14. Ong, P., Tan, Y.K., Lai, K.H., Sia, C.K.: A deep convolutional neural network for vibration-based health-monitoring of rotating machinery. Decis. Anal. J. **7**, 100219 (2023)
15. Wang, H., Liu, Z., Peng, D., Zuo, M.J.: Interpretable convolutional neural network with multilayer wavelet for Noise-Robust Machinery fault diagnosis. Mech. Syst. Signal Process. **195**, 110314 (2023)
16. Camacho, J., Marichal, G.N., Avila, D., Hernández, A. Aplicación de técnicas de Machine Learning para la predicción de posibles averías de correas en equipos rotatorios. In: XV Congreso Iberoamericano de Ingeniería Mecánica. Madrid (Spain) (2022)
17. Optibelt: Manual técnico para transmisiones por correas trapeciales. Sabadell (Spain) (2013)

A Novel Method for Filtering a Useful Subset of Composite Linguistic Summaries

Carlos R. Rodríguez Rodríguez[1,2(✉)], Marieta Peña Abreu[1], Denis Sergeevich Zuev[2], Yarina Amoroso Fernández[1,3], and Yeleny Zulueta Véliz[1]

[1] University of Informatics Sciences, Havana, Cuba
crodriguezr@uci.cu
[2] Kazan Federal University, Kazan, Russia
[3] National Union of Cuban Jurists, Havana, Cuba

Abstract. Selecting a subset of linguistic summaries and providing them in a user-friendly and compact form is a latent issue in the field of Linguistic Data Summarization. The paper proposes a method for filtering the most useful subset, for a given decision problem, from a set of composite linguistic summaries. Those summaries embody Evidence, Contrast or Emphasis relations, inspired by the Rhetorical Structure Theory. The summaries' usefulness is determined according to the relevance of the attributes contained in each one. The strategy followed is based on first finding the Evidence relation whose nucleus contains the better possible representation of the problem attributes, then searching for a Contrast relation and an Emphasis relation that share that nucleus. The method output is a scheme that synthesizes and combines the texts of the three relations. The paper provides an illustrative example in which the most useful relations are found from a dataset of 63 crimes to solve a case of bank document forgery.

Keywords: Linguistic descriptions of data · Linguistic data summarization · Natural language generation · Expressiveness of linguistic summaries

1 Introduction

Linguistic data summarization (LDS) is a descriptive knowledge discovery technique to produce summaries from a database using natural language [1]. Several authors have extended the original LDS approach [2, 3] by defining different stereotyped forms for structuring summaries, proposing new indicators to measure their quality, using different techniques to generate them, and applying these developments to a wide range of problems. Pupo et al. [4] provide a comprehensive review about these topics.

The structure of linguistic summaries (LS), and of any kind of information, is a key factor of their actual usefulness. The usefulness of LS depends, among other criteria, on their expressiveness [5]. Stereotyped forms for structuring LS, called protoforms, were initially proposed by Zadeh [6] and then presented as a hierarchy of abstract prototypes

Y. Hernández Heredia et al. (Eds.): IWAIPR 2023, LNCS 14335, pp. 177–189, 2024.
https://doi.org/10.1007/978-3-031-49552-6_16

[7]. The protoforms have been extended for different problems, but their original forms has been the most widespread [4, 8], which are defined as in (1) or (2):

$$T\left(QX \xrightarrow[have]{are} Y\right) \tag{1}$$

$$T\left(QFX \xrightarrow[have]{are} Y\right) \tag{2}$$

where ***Y*** is a summarizer (*e.g., have sentences from 24 to 42 months*); ***X*** is the object (*e.g., FBCD crimes*) ***Q*** is a quantity in agreement given as a fuzzy linguistic quantifier (*e.g., many*); and ***T*** is the truth degree of the summary in [0, 1]. In (Eq. 2), a qualifier ***F*** (*e.g., with circumstances 80.1(c) and 79.1(a)*) is added. ***F*** is a filter to get a specific data subset. The following is a summary like (Eq. 2): ***T (Many FBCD crimes with circumstances 80.1(c) and 79.1(a), have sentences from 24 to 42 months) = 1.***

These protoforms consist of quantified sentences that are said not to be delivered directly to the user due to their lack of expressiveness. Moreover, they are usually handled individually without taking into account the relationships between them [8]. For these reasons, several approaches aim to improve the expressiveness of LS [8–13]. Among these contributions, CLS-QD stands as a model for generating composite linguistic summaries from qualitative data [13]. All these proposals improve the LS understanding, but they do not propose ways to select the proper subset of LS for an instance of a decision problem. That is, they provide an improved description of data, but do not show how to filter those LS in a dynamic decision-making environment.

In order to address this issue, this paper proposes a method to select the three most useful summaries, for a given situation, from all those generated with the CLS-QD model [13]. For this purpose, Sect. 2 briefly reviews the CLS-QD model; Sect. 3 presents the model for selecting and assembling the most useful summaries; and Sect. 4 describes an illustrative example of its applicability.

2 A Short Overview of CLS-QD Model

CLS-QD model was formalized in [13] and presented in an implementable form in [14]. Those summaries embody relations of Evidence (P^e), Contrast (P^c) or Emphasis (P^h), inspired by the Rhetorical Structure Theory [15, 16]. A relation (P^r) involves at least two constituent statements, which can function as nuclei (P^N) or satellites (P^S), and which are semantically linked by a relation r, i.e., by a specific connector.

The constituent statements are the classical protoforms of LS (see Eq. (1) and Eq. (2)), which we will call type-I and type-II statements, respectively. X and Y can be simple or complex predicates. A simple predicate consists of a single pair (attribute: value), and a complex one comprises two or more pairs.

For measuring the quality of any relation P^r, CLS-QD defines three metrics: the truth degree $T(P^r)$, the relation strength $S(P^r)$ and the coverage degree $S(P^r)$.

An **Evidence relation** $\boldsymbol{P^e}$ provides one main statement (the nucleus, P^N) and one or more supporting statements (the satellites, P^S), which supply finer-grained information that validates the nucleus. Its general structure is:

$$P^e = P^N,\ \langle evidence\ connector\rangle\ P^S \tag{3}$$

The nucleus of P^e can be a type-I or type-II statement. The satellite can be one or more non-overlapping type-II statements. In P^e, the satellites semantically support the nucleus, i.e., all constituent statements of relation share the same consequent.

A **Composite relation** $\boldsymbol{P^c}$ consists of two nuclei, which provide contrasting information about the same attributes of the analyzed problem. Its general structure is:

$$P^c = P^{N_1}, \langle contrast\ connector \rangle\, P^{N_2} \quad (4)$$

Both nuclei can be type-I or type-II statements and can have complex predicates in their antecedents and consequents, but at least one pair of predicates must be different.

An **Emphasis relation** $\boldsymbol{P^h}$ combines two similar statements in which the second one (the satellite) has an additional predicate that specifies the main feature of the objects described by the first one (the nucleus). Its general structure is:

$$P^h = P^N, \langle emphasis\ connector \rangle\, P^S \quad (5)$$

In $\boldsymbol{P^h}$, the statement that functions as the nucleus is, in turn, the antecedent of the satellite, and the consequent of the satellite contains a different predicate that emphasizes a feature of the nucleus. The nucleus can be a type-I or type-II statement. Meanwhile, the satellite has been constrained to only one statement of type-II.

3 A Method for Filtering and Assembling the Most Useful Relations

The strategy for selecting the most useful composite relations aims at identifying those Evidence, Contrast and Emphasis relations (one per type), which, according to value of their attributes, are the most helpful for the specific situation addressed. Therefore, selecting these relations is not a simple search for those that maximize the values of $T(P^r)$, $S(P^r)$ and $C(P^r)$ metrics defined in [13] for measuring its quality. That is to say, a relation that is the most useful one for solving a problem instance may not be useful for another one, even if in both cases the same subset of attributes is involved. The method comprises five activities (see Fig. 1).

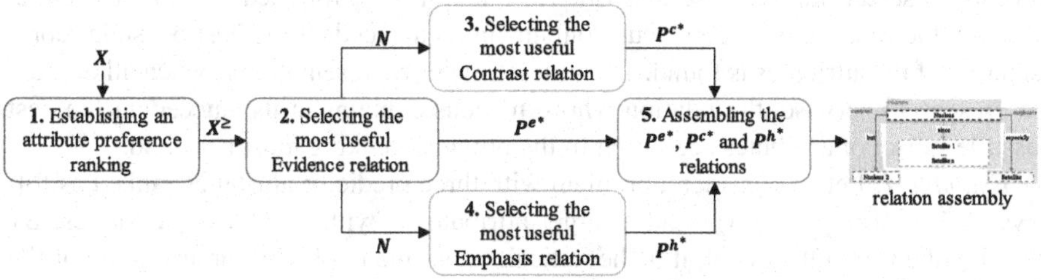

Fig. 1. Method flowchart.

The strategy focuses attention on the nucleus of Evidence relation because, by its self-definition, this relation exposes a main statement (the nucleus) and the satellite provides information that helps to increase the credibility of the nucleus. Therefore, finding the most representative nucleus of the attributes brings implicitly other information (the satellite) that supports it. At the same time, from that nucleus it is possible to find a Contrast relation that shares it and contains another nucleus in which the target attribute (summarizer) has a different value. Similarly, it is possible to find another Emphasis relation that shares the nucleus of the Evidence relation and that its satellite highlights an additional property of the cases described by the nucleus. We believe that this compendium, harmoniously assembled, could be useful to assist decision-makers.

Remark. The analysis and selection of the most useful relations works mainly with the relation's attributes, it does not take into account the Q values and the T values are considered only as a second resource for selecting. So, the constituent statements (Eq. (1) and Eq. (2)), will be handled as $X \rightarrow Y$ and $FX \rightarrow Y$, respectively, where X and FX comprise the set of predictor attributes and Y comprise the set of target attributes.

3.1 Establishing an Attribute Preference Ranking

The selection strategy takes into account that not all predictor attributes of the analyzed problem may be present in the same relation. For this reason, it is initially necessary to establish a ranking among these attributes according to its relevance, significance, or the intensity of its values for the specific situation to be solved. That is to say, given a set of n predictor attributes, $X = \{x_i | i \in (1, \ldots, n)\}$, it is necessary to obtain the ordered set $X^{\geq} = \left\{x_j \geq \ldots \geq x_n\right\}$ where $j \in (1, \ldots, n)$ and x_j denotes the *j-th* most relevant attribute. Knowing this ranking of preference, it is then possible to search for the relations that best represent such attributes.

Several approaches can be explored to set a ranking of attributes, including:

- Employing feature selection techniques.
- Using a ranking pre-established by domain experts.
- Obtaining the ranking after the decision makers assess the relevance of each attribute for the specific situation they are solving.

3.2 Selecting the Most Useful Evidence Relation

In order to select the most useful Evidence relation, $\boldsymbol{P^{e*}}$, for each value of the target attribute, the relation whose nucleus contains in its antecedent the best possible representation of the attributes is found. The best attributes representation is when all of them are present. Otherwise, the relation whose nucleus contains in its antecedent the best possible subset of attributes according to the previous ranking must be found.

Example 1: Let us consider a problem with three predictor attributes ranked as follows: $X^{\geq} = \{x_1 \geq x_2 \geq x_3\}$ and a target attribute, y, with four possible values. By applying the CLS-QD model, it is theoretically possible to obtain, for any value of the target attribute, y_*, the Evidence relations whose nuclei are shown in Fig. 2a). Such nuclei, with the form $FX \rightarrow Y$, are ordered as shown in Fig. 2b) according to the attributes ranking, i.e., $x_1, x_2, x_3 \rightarrow y_*$ is the most representative (useful) nucleus.

But in a real case it is unlikely that all relations would be obtained for a single value of the target attribute. Instead, it is usual to find relations for several or all values of the target attribute, as shown in Fig. 3. If the Evidence relations obtained were those whose nuclei are shown in Fig. 3a), the order of representativeness would be: $x_1, x_2, x_3 \rightarrow y_2 > x_1, x_2 \rightarrow y_1 > x_1, x_3 \rightarrow y_3 > x_2, x_3 \rightarrow y_4$, therefore, the most useful relation would be the one to which the nucleus $x_1, x_2, x_3 \rightarrow y_2$ belongs.

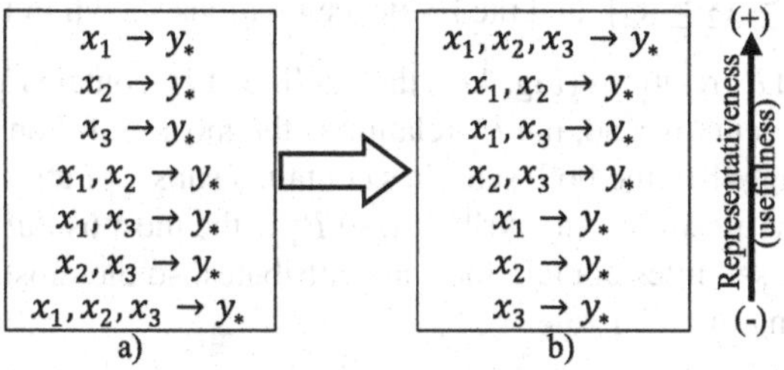

Fig. 2 Nuclei prototypes of all possible Evidence relations that contain at least one attribute in the antecedent for any value of the target attribute y_*.

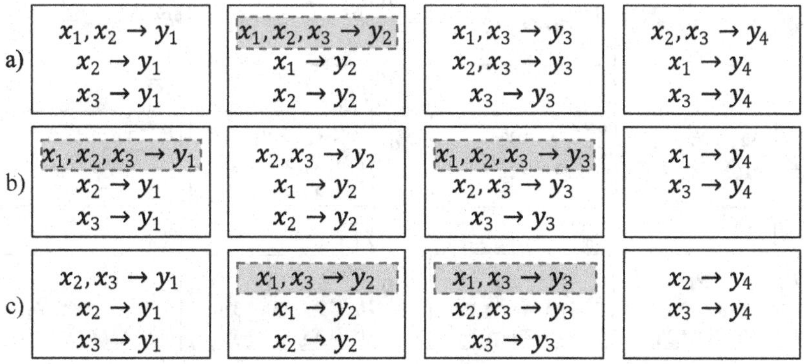

Fig. 3 Prototypes of Evidence relations nuclei that contain at least one attribute in the antecedent for the four possible values of the target attribute.

On the other hand, if the relations obtained were those whose nuclei are shown in Fig. 3b) or Fig. 3c), where several nuclei share the same antecedent, then it would be necessary to apply the following decision rules:

- **R1**. *If* the relations nuclei share the same antecedent, and it contains all the attributes (see Fig. 3b)), *then* select the one whose nucleus has the highest value of T.
  - **R1.1**. *If* the nuclei have the same value of T, *then* select the relation with the highest value of $T(P^e)$, and *if* these values are equal, *then* select the one with the highest value of $S(P^e)$.
- **R2**. *If* the relations nuclei share the same antecedent, but it does not contain all the attributes (see Fig. 4c)), *then* select the one that has the most representative satellite.

– **R2.1.** *If* the satellites share the same attributes (see Fig. 4c)), *then* select the relation with the highest value of $T(P^e)$, and *if* these values are equal, *then* select the one with the highest value of $S(P^e)$.

Example 2: Let us consider now a problem with three predictor attributes ranked as follows: $X^{\geq} = \{x_1 \geq x_2 \geq x_3\}$, and the Evidence relations shown in Fig. 4.

- Given the P_1^e and P_2^e relations (Fig. 4a)), the satellite of P_1^e contains all three attributes, is the most representative, so, the P_1^e relation is the most useful one.
- In P_3^e and P_4^e (Fig. 4b)), the both satellites contain a subset of attributes, the satellite of P_4^e has the two most relevant attributes, so P_4^e is the most useful relation.
- In Fig. 4c), both satellites contain the same attributes, so the most useful relation is found by applying the R2.1 rule.

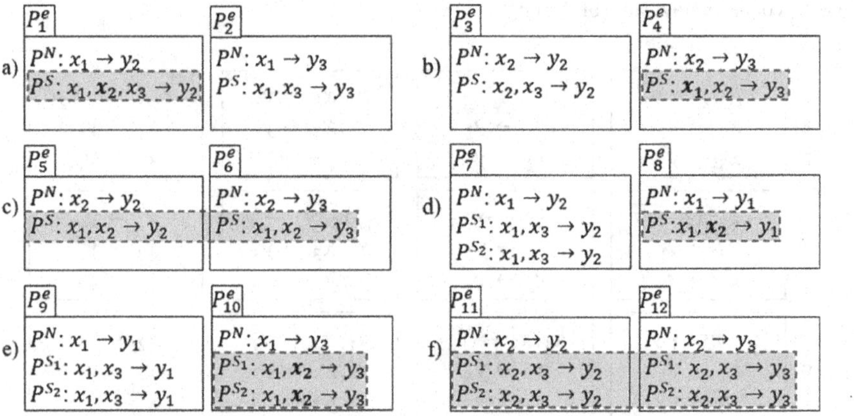

Fig. 4. Paired prototypes of Evidence relations with equal antecedents in its nuclei. The relations are compared according to its satellites.

On the other hand, it should be reminded that the Evidence relations may contain more than one satellite, but they share the same set of attributes, so:

- In Fig. 4d), the satellite of P_8^e contains a better representation of the attributes than satellites of P_7^e, so P_8^e is the most useful relation although it has only one satellite.
- In Fig. 4e), both relations contain two satellites, but the satellites of P_{10}^e include more representative attributes than the satellites of P_9^e, so P_{10}^e is the most useful relation.
- Finally, in Fig. 4f), both relations contain the same attributes in its satellites, so the most useful relation is found by applying the R2.1 rule.

3.3 Selecting the Most Useful Contrast Relation

Selecting the most useful Contrast relation, P^{c*}, depends on the nucleus of the previously selected Evidence relation, P^{e*}. This nucleus will be, in turn, the first nucleus of the Contrast relation, i.e., $P^{N_1} \in P^{c*} = P^N \in P^{e*}$. The aim of this dependence is to find another statement (second nucleus of the Contrast relation, $P^{N_2} \in P^{c*}$) that relates the same predictor attributes to another value of the target attribute.

In order to select the P^{c*} relation, the following tasks are performed:

1. Find all Contrast relations which contain the P^{e^*} nucleus and a second constituent statement with another value of the target attribute given some combination of the same attributes.

   Let $X \rightarrow Y$ be the nucleus of the P^{e*} relation and $A \rightarrow B$ be the other constituent statement that will compose the Contrast relation. The constraints to be met by the candidate Contrast relations are specified below:

$$(((A = X) \vee (A \subset X) \vee (X \subset A)) \wedge P\_Dif(Y, B)) \vee \\ (((X = B) \vee (B \subset X) \vee (X \subset B)) \wedge P\_Dif(Y, A)) \tag{6}$$

   where $P\_Dif(K, L)$ is a constraint which checks that the predicates $K \in P^{N_1}$ and $L \in P^{N_2}$ have at least one equal attribute, but with different values (see Eq. 7).

$$P\_Dif(K, L) = \exists (k_i \in K,\ l_j \in L) \Big| att_{k_i} = att_{l_j};\ val_{k_i} \neq val_{l_j};\ i = 1, 2, \ldots, n;\ j = 1, 2, \ldots, n \tag{7}$$

2. When there are several relations that meet such restrictions, then select the relation whose nucleus P^{N_2} better represents the attributes, operating in the same way as described for selecting the nucleus of the $\boldsymbol{P^{e*}}$ relation.
3. If in more than one relation the nucleus P^{N_2} have the same representation of the attributes, then select the relation with the highest value of $T(P^c)$.

3.4 Selecting the Most Useful Emphasis Relation

Selecting the most useful Emphasis relation, P^{h*}, also depends on the nucleus of the previously selected Evidence relation, P^{e*}. This nucleus will be, in turn, the nucleus of the Emphasis relation, i.e., $P^N \in P^{h*} = P^N \in P^{e*}$. The aim of this dependency is to find another statement (satellite of the Emphasis relation, $P^S \in P^{h*}$) that highlights the most common property among objects described by the nucleus.

In order to select the P^{h*} relation, the following tasks are performed:

1. Find all Emphasis relations whose nuclei are the same as that of the P^{e*} relation.
2. Among them, select the one with the highest value of $S(P^e)$.
3. If several relations have the same value of $S(P^e)$, then select the one whose satellite has the highest value of T.

3.5 Assembling the P^{e^*}, P^{c^*} and P^{h^*} Relations

Delivering linguistic summaries in a user-friendly way, which facilitates their understanding and, therefore, increases their usefulness in decision making, is still a latent need. For this reason, we first find the statement (nucleus) most representative of the problem attributes and around it we select the most useful P^{e*}, P^{c*} and P^{h*} relations.

These relations share the same nucleus. Therefore, in order to clean up the data to be delivered to the user, to facilitate its understanding, it is necessary to eliminate the fragments of information repeated in the three relations. To this end, the capabilities of graphic representation are used to provide information in a synthesized and logically structured manner. Thus, a knowledge graph (KG) representing the relationships between P^{e*}, P^{c*} and P^{h*} is create (see Fig. 5). The KG is based on the ⟨relation assembly⟩ section of the $\text{CNL}_{\text{Summaries}}$ language (available at http://bit.ly/CNL_Summaries). $\text{CNL}_{\text{Summaries}}$ is a controlled natural language specified for creating the constituent summaries, for generating the composite relations, and for assembling a subset of relations.

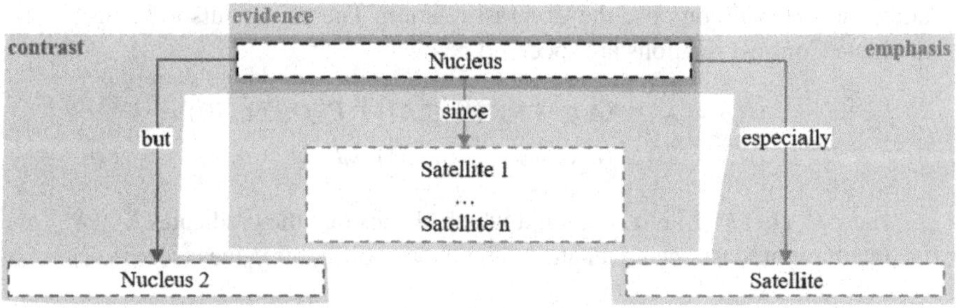

Fig. 5. Knowledge graph of the most useful relations.

4 Illustrative Example

To better understand how the method works, an illustrative example is developed using data from criminal cases. The procedure consists of three tasks:

1. Retrieving data and results of the experiment №3 reported in [17].
2. Generating candidate relations from a dataset of similar cases using CLS-QD [13].
3. Applying our proposal to the relation set obtained with CLS-QD taking as input the circumstances of experiment №3 [17] ranked according to their intensity.

Completing Task 1. The following relevant case information was retrieved:

- Crime: 333.1 – Forgery of banking or commercial documents (FBCD)
- Original punishment interval: 2–5 years (24–60 months)
- Mitigating circumstances: *79.1 (a)* and *79.1 (c)*
- Aggravating Circumstances: *80.1 (c)*
- Ranking of circumstances according to its intensity: *80.1 (c)* >*79.1 (a)* >*79.1 (c)*

Completing Task 2. A **dataset** of 98 similar previous cases judged in cassation by the Criminal Chamber of the Supreme People's Court was compiled. It comprises six attributes without missing values (see Table 1). Based on the case information retrieved in task 1, the dataset was preprocessed:

- Records of other crime types were eliminated, as well as FBCD offenses involving circumstances different from those of the analyzed case, finally leaving 63 cases.

- The attribute "punishment" was discretized as follows. First, the value expressed in years was translated into months. Then, since the original punishment interval foreseen in the CPC for the FDBC offense ranges from two to five years of imprisonment, the numerical values of the attribute "punishment" were transformed into one of the following four labels: $\{i_1 = [12 \text{ months}; 23 \text{ months}], i_2 = [24 \text{ months}; 42 \text{ months}], i_3 = [43 \text{ months}; 60 \text{ months}], i_4 = [61 \text{ months}; 90 \text{ months}]\}$.

Table 1. Attributes of the criminal case dataset.

№	Name	Description	Example
1	Crime	Crime code and denomination	333.1 – Forgery of banking or commercial documents
2	Mitigating circumstances	List of mitigating circumstance codes	From *79.1(a)* to *79.1(k)*
3	Aggravating circumstances	List of aggravating circumstance codes	From *80.1(a)* to *80.1(r)*
4	Response to appeal	Court response to defendant's appeal	Accepted / Rejected
5	Punishment	Length of penalty (in years)	3 years

Then, to obtain the composite relations from 63 cases obtained after data preprocessing, the CLS-QD model [13] was applied using the Java implementation developed in [14] and the $\text{CNL}_{\text{Summaries}}$ language, with the following settings:

- For generating the association rules, the Apriori algorithm (Weka version) were invoked using the following configuration: *numRules* = *100*, *metricType* = *Confidence*, *minMetric* = *0.5*, *delta* = *0.05*, *minSupport* = *0.05*.
- Parameters *minT* (Algorithms 1 and 2 in [14]) and *minConf* (Algorithm 1 in [14]) were set to 0.5.
- For computing $T(P^r)$, the *minimum* t-norm was used.
- The set of fuzzy linguistic quantifiers were modeled with trapezoidal fuzzy sets as follows: *Q* = *{About_half* = *[0.42, 0.48, 0.52, 0.58], Many* = *[0.52, 0.58, 1, 1], Most* = *[0.72, 0.78, 1, 1], Almost_all* = *[0.92, 0.98, 1, 1]}*.
- For creating the Contrast relations, the contrast degree between each pair of labels (l_i, l_j) for attribute *"punishment"* was set the unity, i.e., $\mu_R(l_i, l_j) = 1$.
- We discarded the relations were $S(P^r) < 0.5$.

As a result, four Evidence relations, seven Contrast relations and five Emphasis relations were generated, whose statistical values are shown in Table 2.

Completing Task 3. Our proposal was applied to the relations derived from task 2. Mitigating and aggravating circumstances were taken as predictor attributes and were ranked according to the intensity assigned by the judges: 80.1 (c) >79.1 (a) >79.1 (c).

Performing the activities defined in 3.2, the P^{e*} *relation selected was the following:*

P^N: *Many* FBCD (333.1) crimes in which circumstances *80.1(c)* and *79.1(a)* were met, have been sentenced with punishments from *24 to 42 months.*
P^S : *Almost all* FBCD (333.1) crimes in which circumstances *80.1(c), 79.1(a) y 79.1(c)* were met, have been sentenced with punishments from *24 to 42 months.*

$$T\left(P^e\right) = 1;\ S\left(P^e\right) = 0.87;\ C\left(P^e\right) = 0.61$$

By verbalization via the ⟨evidence relation⟩ section of $\text{CNL}_{\text{Summaries}}$, the relation is shown as:

> ***Many*** FBCD (333.1) crimes in which circumstances *80.1(c)* and *79.1(a)* were met, have been sentenced with punishments from *24 to 42 months, since **almost all*** FBCD (333.1) crimes in which circumstances *80.1(c), 79.1(a) and 79.1(c)* were met, have been sentenced with punishments from *24 to 42 months.*

Table 2. Statistical values of the composite relations generated in task 2.

Composite relations	Measures	$T(P^r)$	$S(P^r)$	$C(P^r)$
Evidence, P^e number: 4	Min	0.79	0.63	0.05
	Max	1	0,94	0.69
	Mean	0.9132	0.8832	0.4625
	StdDev	0.1163	0.1045	0.1564
Contrast, P^c number: 7	Min	0.68	0.5	0.21
	Max	1	0,75	0.78
	Mean	0.7864	0.6721	0.5430
	StdDev	0.1437	0.1889	0.1539
Emphasis, P^h number: 5	Min	0.71	0.61	0.05
	Max	1	0.91	0.69
	Mean	0.8949	0.8650	0.4807
	StdDev	0.1266	0.1343	0.1398

Performing the activities defined in 3.3, the P^{c*} *relation selected was the following:*

P^{N_1} : *Many* FBCD (333.1) crimes in which circumstances *80.1(c)* and *79.1(a)* were met, have been sentenced with punishments from *24 to 42 months.*

P^{N_2} : *About half* of FBCD (333.1) crimes in which circumstances *80.1(c)* was met, have been sentenced with punishments from *43 to 60 months.*

$$T(P^c) = 1; S(P^c) = 0.75; C(P^c) = 0.66$$

By verbalization via the ⟨contrast relation⟩ section of $\text{CNL}_{\text{Summaries}}$, the relation is shown as:

> ***Many*** FBCD (333.1) crimes in which circumstances *80.1(c)* and *79.1(a)* were met, have been sentenced with punishments from *24 to 42 months, but **about half*** of FBCD (333.1) crimes in which circumstances *80.1(c)* was met, have been sentenced with punishments from *43 to 60 months.*

Performing the activities defined in 3.4, the P^{h*} relation selected was the following:

P^N: *Many* FBCD (333.1) crimes in which circumstances *80.1(c)* and *79.1(a)* were met, have been sentenced with punishments from *24 to 42 months.*
P^S: In *most* of FBCD (333.1) crimes in which circumstances *80.1(c)* and *79.1(a)* were met and have been sentenced with punishments from *24 to 42 months*, the appeals were *rejected.*

$$T\left(P^h\right) = 0.93; S\left(P^h\right) = 0.88; C\left(P^h\right) = 0.61$$

By verbalization via the ⟨emphasis relation⟩ section of $\text{CNL}_{\text{Summaries}}$, the relation is shown as:

> ***Many*** FBCD (333.1) crimes in which circumstances *80.1(c) and 79.1(a)* were met, have been sentenced with punishments from *24 to 42 months, and specially* in ***most*** of them, the appeals were *rejected.*

Finally, the relations are mapped in the knowledge graph of the Fig. 6, which is the method output, i.e., the information delivered to the user. In it, it is easy to understand the most frequent behavior in the previous cases similar to the handled case.

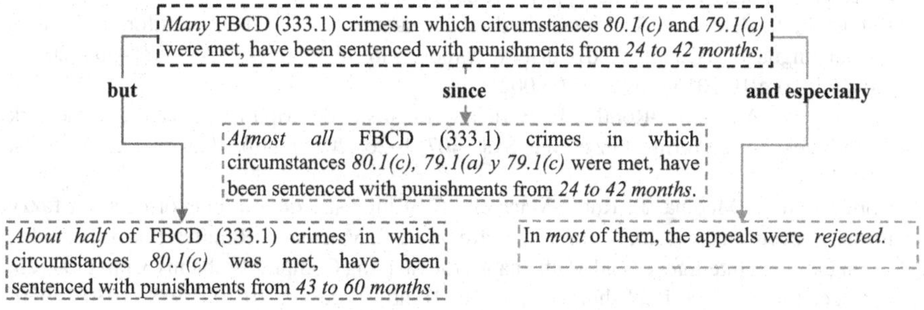

Fig. 6. Knowledge graph of P^{e*}, P^{C*} and P^{h*} relations.

5 Concluding Remarks

The proposed method addresses the problem of selecting a proper subset of LS for an instance of a decision problem. The described approach makes a better use, for a specific situation, of previous knowledge about similar cases. Its representation scheme improves the expressiveness and simplicity of the initially generated composite summaries, which increases their usefulness.

Defining an attribute preference ranking allows that, in the absence of an all-inclusive relation, priority is given to those ones that contain the most relevant attributes. For this reason, the metrics T, $T(P^r)$ and $S(P^r)$ are used as a second resource to select the most useful relations.

Focusing on the nucleus of Evidence relation allows to find first the most representative statement and then, for that nucleus, to identify the three most useful relations.

The proposed approach allows to rescan, for each instance of a dynamic decision-making problem, a set of composite relations previously mined from a dataset.

References

1. Yager, R.R., Reformat, M.Z., To, N.D.: Drawing on the iPad to input fuzzy sets with an application to linguistic data science. Inf. Sci. (Ny) **479**, 277–291 (2019). https://doi.org/10.1016/J.INS.2018.11.048
2. Yager, R.R.: A new approach to the summarization of data. Inf. Sci. (Ny) **28**, 69–86 (1982)
3. Zadeh, L.A.: A computational approach to fuzzy quantifiers in natural languages. Comput. Math. Appl. **9**(1), 149–184 (1983). https://doi.org/10.1016/0898-1221(83)90013-5
4. Pupo, I., Piñero, P.Y., Bello, R.E., García, R., Villavicencio, N.: Linguistic data summarization: a systematic review. In: Piñero Pérez, P.Y., Bello Pérez, R.E., Kacprzyk, J. (eds.) Artificial Intelligence in Project Management and Making Decisions, pp. 3–21. Springer International Publishing, Cham (2022). https://doi.org/10.1007/978-3-030-97269-1_1
5. Kuhn, T.: A survey and classification of controlled natural languages. Comput. Linguist. **40**(1), 121–170 (2014)
6. Zadeh, L.A.: A prototype-centered approach to adding deduction capability to search engines-the concept of protoform. In: 2002 Annual Meeting of the North American Fuzzy Information Processing Society Proceedings, pp. 523–525 (2002)
7. Kacprzyk, J., Zadrozny, S.: Linguistic database summaries and their protoforms: towards natural language based knowledge discovery tools. Inform Sci (Ny) **173**(4), 281–304 (2005). https://doi.org/10.1016/j.ins.2005.03.002
8. Ramos-Soto, A., Martin-Rodilla, P.: Enriching linguistic descriptions of data: a framework for composite protoforms. Fuzzy Sets Syst. **407**, 1–26 (2021). https://doi.org/10.1016/j.fss.2019.11.013
9. Cornejo, M.E., Medina, J., Rubio-Manzano, C.: Linguistic descriptions of data via fuzzy formal concept analysis. In: Harmati, I.Á., Kóczy, L.T., Medina, J., Ramírez-Poussa, E. (eds.) Computational Intelligence and Mathematics for Tackling Complex Problems 3, pp. 119–125. Springer International Publishing, Cham (2022). https://doi.org/10.1007/978-3-030-74970-5_14
10. To, N.D., Reformat, M.Z., Yager, R.R.: Question-answering system with linguistic summarization. In: 2021 IEEE International Conference on Fuzzy Systems (FUZZ-IEEE), pp. 1–8 (2021). https://doi.org/10.1109/FUZZ45933.2021.9494389.

11. Trivino, G., Sugeno, M.: Towards linguistic descriptions of phenomena. Int. J. Approx. Reason. **54**(1), 22–34 (2013). https://doi.org/10.1016/j.ijar.2012.07.004
12. Pérez, I., Piñero, P.Y., Al-subhi, S.H., Mahdi, G.S.S., Bello, R.E.: Linguistic data summarization with multilingual approach. In: Piñero Pérez, P.Y., Bello Pérez, R.E., Kacprzyk, J. (eds.) Artificial Intelligence in Project Management and Making Decisions, pp. 39–64. Springer International Publishing, Cham (2022). https://doi.org/10.1007/978-3-030-97269-1_3
13. Rodríguez, C.R., Peña, M., Zuev, D.S.: Extracting composite summaries from qualitative data. In: Heredia, Y.H., Núñez, V.M., Shulcloper, J.R. (eds.) Progress in Artificial Intelligence and Pattern Recognition: 7th International Workshop on Artificial Intelligence and Pattern Recognition, IWAIPR 2021, Havana, Cuba, October 5–7, 2021, Proceedings, pp. 260–269. Springer International Publishing, Cham (2021). https://doi.org/10.1007/978-3-030-89691-1_26
14. Rodríguez Rodríguez, C.R., Zuev, D.S., Peña Abreu, M.: Algorithms for linguistic description of categorical data. In: Piñero Pérez, P.Y., Bello Pérez, R.E., Kacprzyk, J. (eds.) UCIENCIA 2021. SCI, vol. 1035, pp. 79–97. Springer, Cham (2022). https://doi.org/10.1007/978-3-030-97269-1_5
15. Mann, W.C., Thompson, S.A.: Rhetorical structure theory: toward a functional theory of text organization. Text **8**(3), 243–281 (1988)
16. Hou, S., Zhang, S., Fei, C.: Rhetorical structure theory: a comprehensive review of theory, parsing methods and applications. Expert Syst. Appl. **157**, 113421 (2020)
17. Rodríguez, C.R., Amoroso, Y., Zuev, D.S., Peña, M., Zulueta, Y.: M-LAMAC: a model for linguistic assessment of mitigating and aggravating circumstances of criminal responsibility using computing with words. Artif. Intell. Law (2023). https://doi.org/10.1007/s10506-023-09365-8

Harnessing Key Phrases in Constructing a Concept-Based Semantic Representation of Text Using Clustering Techniques

Ali Mansour[1] (✉), Juman Mohammad[1], Yury Kravchenko[1], Daniil Kravchenko[1], and Nemury Silega[2]

[1] Department of Computer Aided Design, Southern Federal University, 347900 Taganrog, Russia
mansur@sfedu.ru
[2] Department of System Analysis and Telecommunications, Southern Federal University, 347900 Taganrog, Russia

Abstract. This paper introduces a modified approach for representing text as semantic vectors, building upon the Bag of Weighted Concepts (BoWC) method developed in previous research. The limitations of the BoWC method are addressed, and a proposed solution is presented. Instead of using unigrams, the authors propose extracting key phrases that best represent each document to generate high-quality concepts and reduce concept overlap. These unique key phrases are then used to construct the concept dictionary. Document vectors are created by mapping document key phrases to the concept dictionary using a modified concept weighting function that considers the weight of the key phrase within the document. To evaluate the effectiveness of the resulting vectors, they were employed in a clustering task and compared against robust baselines. Experimental studies demonstrate that the proposed modifications enhance the quality of document vector representation, as evidenced by a minimum 4% increase in clustering accuracy based on the V1 metric.

Keywords: text mining · concept extraction · keyword extraction · key phrase extraction · document vectorization · text clustering · CF-IDF

1 Introduction

The rapid growth of textual data on the web and social media platforms necessitates the use of automated text mining techniques to extract valuable information from unstructured text and enhance user experiences by providing relevant information. In the text mining process, two key factors play a crucial role: the representation of text and the choice of text mining algorithm. Document representation, in particular, is a fundamental aspect that significantly impacts performance. Its objective is to convert documents into a machine-readable format through a process known as vectorization [1].

Great efforts have been made for a long time. First of all, the most classical method is Vector Space Model (VSM) [2]. Methods that adopt this model such as Term Frequency

Y. Hernández Heredia et al. (Eds.): IWAIPR 2023, LNCS 14335, pp. 190–201, 2024.
https://doi.org/10.1007/978-3-031-49552-6_17

Inverse Document Frequency (TF-IDF) and Bag of Words (BoW) represent a document as a vector in the vector space where each word represents an independent dimension [3]. However, these methods don't consider semantic relations among different words the size of such vectors increases according to the number of words used in the documents. This affects the efficiency of text mining algorithms and makes it difficult to capture good text features.

To model the sematic relations between words, like synonymy and polysemy, improved methods are proposed. Latent Semantic Indexing (LSI) [4] approximates the source space with fewer dimensions which uses matrix algebra technique termed SVD. Latent Dirichlet Allocation (LDA) can recognize the latent topics of documents and use topic probability distribution for representations.

In recent years, a lot of efforts have been made in the field of text representation using machine learning algorithms. One well-known method for distributed representations of sentences and documents, Doc2Vec is proposed by [5]. It is based on Word2Vec [6], which trains a distributed representation in a skip-gram likelihood as the input for prediction of words from their neighbor words [7] while Doc2Vec learns distributed vector representations for variable-length fragments of texts, from a phrase or sentence to a large document.

Although the vectors produced by these embedding techniques are of low dimensions and despite the success it has achieved in some tasks, the resulting feature vectors are ambiguous and it is difficult to explain the logic of the mining algorithms based on the extracted feature vector.

In this context, the conceptual representation of documents appeared as a solution to these drawbacks. It represents the document as a vector in which each concept represents an independent dimension. Such representation is considered a linear transformation from the space of words to the space of the concept which allows controlling the size of vectors. However, the quality of the vectors depends strongly on the way concepts are extracted and weighted.

Following this approach several works have been presented, the most famous of which are the Bag of Concepts (BoC) [8], as well as our Bag of Weighted Concepts method (BoWC) presented in previous works [9, 10]. Both methods create concepts by clustering word vectors into concept clusters, then uses the frequencies of these clusters to represent document vectors. To reduce the influence of concepts that appear in most documents, BoC uses a weighting scheme similar to TF-IDF, replacing the frequency of the term TF with the frequency of the concept CF.

In contrast in BoWC authors proposed a new concept weighting function which achieves a relative balance between common and rare concepts.

Also, unlike "BoC" approach, our "BoWC" method adopts term filtering in the preprocessing stage to reduce noise in clusters when forming the concept dictionary. This, in turn, means that the cluster centroid vector will become an accurate representation of the cluster (the concept) and sufficient to calculate similarity to the document thus reducing the computational cost of the clustering process and mapping the document's words to the concept dictionary.

Thanks to this optimization, our method outperformed many strong baselines for only 200 features. This confirms that the concepts in BoWC have much greater discriminatory power than BoC.

However, these improvements in creating the concept dictionary did not prevent the existence of noisy concepts (overlap between concepts). In both methods, the concept is a cluster of words, which have been grouped together on the basis of the similarity of their embedding vectors. Although the formation of the concept on the basis of single words (unigrams) is simpler, it is considered problematic due to the word polysemy. Especially since the word will belong to one concept, although it may appear in contexts with different connotations.

Regarding these shortcomings, we propose some improvements to the BoWC method by applying a key phrase extraction algorithm to use n-grams terms instead of unigrams in document representation and concept extraction processes. The key phrase can be understood as confirming the meaning of the word and relatively revealing its ambiguity by expanding it with neighboring words from the context.

The extraction of n-grams is carried out according to the FBKE (Frequency and Bert based Keyword Extraction) method presented in [11]. The motive behind choosing FBKE method is that it produces keywords that are similar to the context of the document, which ensures that these keywords are an accurate and sufficient representation of the document. The use of key phrases in conceptual formation is expected to reduce noise in clusters and produce cleaner concepts, as well as reduce the number of matching operations between the dictionary of concepts and the document. These advantages are supposed to reflect positively on the performance of document mining algorithms.

The contributions of this article are twofold. Firstly, a pre-processing algorithm is introduced, which aims to enhance the quality of concepts generated by the concept dictionary building algorithm. This algorithm represents the document using its most significant key phrases, taking into account both frequency and semantic similarity. The goal is to improve the accuracy and relevance of the resulting concepts.

Secondly, a modified concept weighting function is proposed. This function incorporates a novel weighting coefficient that captures the relationship between the key phrase and both the document and the concept. This coefficient can be combined with other weighting functions, such as CF-EDF and CF-IDF, that follow a similar approach to the proposed method. By incorporating this new coefficient, the concept weighting function becomes more comprehensive and adaptable, allowing for more accurate and context-aware concept representation.

This paper is organized as follows. In the Materials section, an explanation of the basic BoWC method and then proposed modifications are provided, in addition to a description of the experiments that were performed to test the performance of the method against other baselines. The analysis of the results is shown in the Results section, followed by expectations and future plans in the Conclusions section.

2 Materials and Methods

The implementation of the original BoWC method includes two stages[1]: the first is the concepts extraction which includes the text processing, the unique terms extraction, the word embeddings process, and finally, the word clustering process, which creates a dictionary of concepts. The second stage is documents vectorization, which includes mapping documents into the concepts dictionary to generate the vectors. In the modified method, the concept extraction algorithm is modified to include key phrases extraction and using them instead of unigrams. In the following the stages of the original BoWC method will be explained, concerning the position of the modification (Fig. 1).

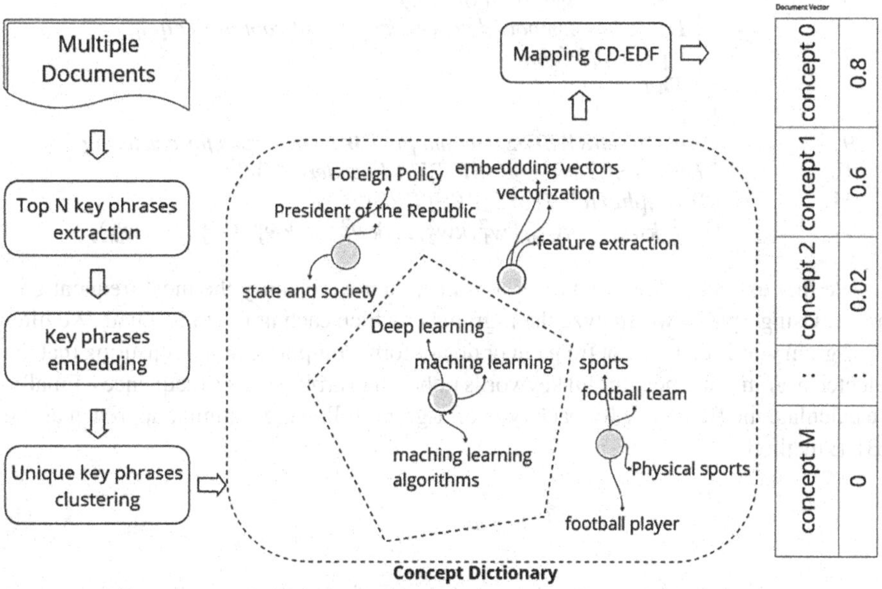

Fig. 1. General scheme of the modified BoWC method

2.1 Key Phrases Extraction

In "BoWC" each document is represented as a sequence of its words $d_i = \{w_1, w_2, w_3, \ldots, w_N\}$. The proposed modification in this work suggests that each document be represented by its most expressive key phrases. For this purpose, we apply the same methodology used in [11], which includes two phases: First, the selection of candidate key phrases, which is based on the frequency. The second stage is the weighting and ranking of the candidates using a function based on the semantic similarity between

[1] BoWC method implementation example with resources: BoWC-Method/codes/Github_FastText_BoWC.ipynb at main · Ali-MH-Mansour/BoWC-Method · GitHub.

the document and its key phrases. In this work, we will make a simple modification to improve the process of extracting key phrases, represented in the following algorithm.

Algorithm 1. *Text Preprocessing and document filtering*

```
Input     Set D = {d_1, d_2, ..., d_N} of N documents
Output    CD a concept dictionary
          D* = preprocessing(D)
          CKW = extract_n_grams(D*)
          Freq_UN = extract_frequent_unigrams(D*)
          Foreach kw in CKW do:
          | Kw_doc = parse_by_spacy(kw)
          | Kw_root = get_root(kw_doc)
          | If doc has compound dependency or kw_root in Freq_UN:
          |   | KWS [] ← kw
          | End
          End
          UKWS = set(KWS) //Select unique KW from corpus for clustering
          UKWS_VECTORS = FASTTEXT_Encoder(UKWS)
          CD = sphericl(UKWS_VECTORS) =
          (kw_1^1, kw_2^1, ..., kw_M^1, kw_1^2, kw_2^2, ..., kw_M^2, ..., kw_1^K, kw_2^K, ..., kw_M^K),
```

We first extract different types of n-grams, then we identify the most frequent unigrams. Using SpaCy, we analyze the n-grams in which each unigram is found. We filter out n-gram words that are not frequent or do not form compound nouns, ensuring that the selected n-grams are meaningful keywords rather than arbitrary word sequences. Finally, we calculate the frequency for each type of n-gram, following a similar approach as the FBKE method.

$$TF_{n-gram} = \frac{n_t^i}{\sum_k n_k^i}, \tag{1}$$

where $\boldsymbol{n_k}$ refers to the total count of a specific type of n-gram (with i elements) in, while $\boldsymbol{n_t}$ represents the count of occurrences of token t in the document.

After that we choose top-N keywords to represent the document. These keywords are then encoded by an appropriate embedding model. Here for simplicity, we apply Fasttext [12]. Then FBKE selects the most relevant keyword phrases in the context of the document using the following weighting functions:

$$rel\left(d, c^j\right) = 2 \cdot \frac{tf_{c^j} \cdot S_{norm}^{j,d}}{tf_{c^j} + S_{norm}^{j,d}}, \tag{2}$$

where $S_{norm}^{j,d} = S^j \cdot e^{S^j/|c^j|}$ is the normalized value for similarity of the candidate c^j of the document d. S^j is the cosine similarity of the j-th candidate with the document. Tf is the key phrases frequency.

2.2 Concept Extraction

Aer obtaining the key phrases and their vectors for each document, the spherical k-means clustering algorithm is applied to these vectors. The output is a collection of concepts, where each concept is represented by M key phrases with similar meaning, such as synonyms, hyponym and hypernyms, which have been grouped together on the basis of the similarity of their vectors. The concept dictionary is presented as follows:

$$C = \left(kw_1^1, kw_2^1, \ldots, kw_M^2, kw_1^2, kw_2^2, \ldots, kw_M^2, \ldots, kw_1^K, kw_2^K, \ldots, kw_M^K\right), \quad (3)$$

where kw_i^j is the jth cluster's (ith) key phrases. However, the concept vector is the centroid vector (the average vector of the concept's keyword vectors).

2.3 Document Representation

At this stage, the input data consists of the concepts dictionary and the documents represented by their embedding vectors. However, the extraction of key phrases during the concept extraction stage enables the modification of the CF-EDF weighting function, which can be expressed using the following formula:

$$BoWC_{c_i} = CF - EDF\left(c_i, d_j, D\right) \cdot e^{S_{c_i}} = \frac{n_{c_i}}{\sum_k n_k} \cdot e^{-\frac{|\{d \in D | c_i \in d\}|}{|D|}} \cdot e^{S_{c_i}}, \quad (4)$$

CF is concept frequency $\frac{n_{c_i}}{\sum_k n_k}$, where it is considered that the concept has appeared in the text when the value of similarity S_c between the centroid of the concept(s) with the document keyword exceeds a certain limit (ϴ).

$$(S_c) = \begin{cases} 1, & S_c > \Theta \\ 0, & otherwise \end{cases}. \quad (5)$$

In the original method, S_{c_i}. is the average degree of similarity of the document's words with the concept to which the words belong. However, since the key phrases of the document are selected on the basis of frequency and semantic similarity between the phrase and the context of the document, the author proposes to replace the term S_{c_i}. With the average weights of the document's key phrases that belong to the concept given by the following formula:

$$S_i^j = \frac{1}{N} \sum_{n=1}^{N} rel\left(c_i, kw_n^j\right), \quad (6)$$

where N is the number of key phrases of the document (j-th)hat appeared in the current concept c_i. The resulting weight expresses the relatedness between the key phrase and the document on the one hand, and between key phrase and the concept on the other hand. The final formulation of the concept weighting function according to BoWC becomes as follows:

$$BoWC_{c_i} = \frac{n_{c_i}}{\sum_k n_k} \cdot e^{-\frac{|\{d \in D | c_i \in d\}|}{|D|}} \cdot e^{S_i^j}, \quad (7)$$

As a result, the method generates a feature vector V for each given document d, where v_i^j reflects the importance (weight) of the i-th concept and k is the concepts quantity.

$$V^d = vectorization(C, d^*, D^*) = \left\{v_1^d, v_2^d, \ldots, v_K^d\right\}, \quad (8)$$

Thus, we have two versions of the modified BoWC method: the first is only by changing the pre-processing stage and using keywords (key phrases) instead of unigrams while maintaining the same weighting function. The second includes the modification of the weighting function. In addition, the proposed weight S_i^j to the function of the "BoWC" method can also be used to weight the concepts in the "BoC" method, which follows the same approach.

2.4 Experimental Research

These experiments aim to check the representativeness of the resulting vectors compared to the original BoWC method and to a set of reliable baselines, namely: Bag-of-words (BoW), TF-IDF, averaged Fasttext (pre-trained and self-trained), Bag-of-concepts (BoC) detailed in previous works [9, 10]. Baselines used the same settings as in previous studies, and k-means algorithm was employed as the document clustering algorithm.

Datasets

To accomplish the document clustering tasks and assess the improved BoWC method, five text datasets were used (see Table 1).

Table 1. Overview of the used datasets

Datasets	Dataset information	
	# Documents	*# Classes*
BBC	2225	5
REUTERS (RE)	8491	8
OHSUMED (OH)	5380	7
20Newsgroups (20NG)	18821	20
WebKB	4199	4

BBC data set [13], comprises 2225 documents sourced from the BBC news website, encompassing news stories across five distinct topical areas during the period of 2004–2005.

The Reuters (RE) data set consists of articles obtained from the Reuters news feed. For this study, the R8 partition of the Reuters data set was utilized, which includes a total of 8491 documents.

The 20Newsgroups (20NG) dataset consists of 18,821 documents that have been classified into 20 distinct newsgroup categories, ensuring a roughly equal distribution among the categories.

The OHSUMED (OH) dataset is derived from a subset of clinical paper abstracts sourced from the Medline database. For this study, a partition containing 5380 documents from the OHSUMED dataset was utilized.

The WebKB dataset comprises web pages obtained from different sections of computer science, gathered through the World Wide Knowledge Base (Web->Kb) project conducted by the CMU text learning group [14]. These web pages have been categorized into seven distinct classes, including students, faculty, staff, and more. For this study, a preprocessed version of the WebKB dataset was employed, consisting of four different classes and a total of 4199 documents [14].

For the BoC method, which follows the same approach as the BoWC method, two versions of it will be tested, the first applies the CF-IDF weighting function and it is denoted as "$\text{BoC}_{\text{CF-EDF}}$" in the Table 2. The second version applies a modified concept weighting function expanded by the key phrase weight function used in BoWC method and it is denoted as "$\text{BoC}_{\text{CF-EDF-FBKE}}$" in the Table 2.

Documents are processed by lowercasing and deleting stop-words, symbols and numbers. FBKE method is used to extract key phrases, so for that n grams are extracted (with a length of 2–4) and then these phrases are filtered using Spacy to get only nominal phrases whose root is a word with a high frequency (Spacy is applied to n grams and not to the sentences). The embedding vectors were generated using the FASTTEXT embedding model with 300-word vectors. The word embedding model is trained on the data itself with a window size 15. The FBKE weighting function (1) is applied to select the top 20 most important key phrases to represent the document. The second step is to generate the concept dictionary by applying a clustering algorithm to the vectors of the key phrases with a similarity threshold of 0.6. Results may vary depending on the clustering algorithm used. In this work we use spherical k-means algorithm.

As mentioned, each cluster represents a concept. The threshold of similarity of the key phrase with the centroid of the cluster was set experimentally to 0.42. Document vectors are generated using the mapping function eq. (6) using [100, 200] concepts for each dataset.

For the evaluation metric, the V-measure evaluation metric was utilized. It is computed as the harmonic mean of homogeneity (H) and completeness (C) calculations [15].

$$V - measure = \frac{(1 + \beta) \cdot \text{H} \cdot \text{C}}{(\beta \cdot \text{H}) + \text{C}}, \tag{9}$$

Here, completeness (C) represents the extent to which every member of a class is assigned to a single cluster, while homogeneity (H) indicates the degree to which each cluster exclusively contains members of a single class. The beta coefficient is set to one as the default value for this particular study.

3 Results and Discussion

This section discusses the test results that were performed with the aim of testing the quality of the vectors generated by our proposed methods as well as a set of robust baselines. Figure 2 shows the performance comparison of the original and modified

BoWC method when performing clustering tasks on five datasets. Overall, the modified BoWC (with only 100 concepts) is vastly superior to the original BoWC (with only 200 concepts).

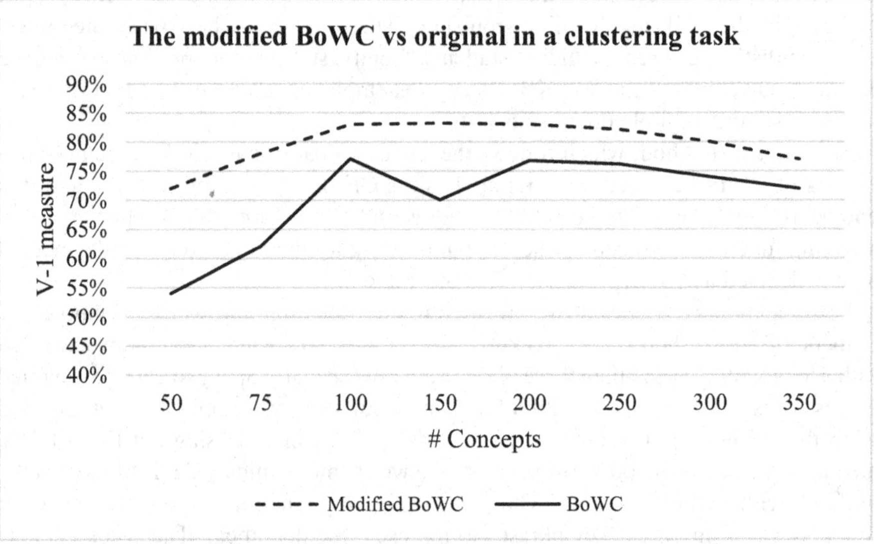

Fig. 2. The V1-score comparison between the modified and original methods in clustering tasks on BBC Dataset

It is also worth noting that the weighting of the concepts by means of the average weights of the keywords belonging to the concept led to the improvement of not only the "BoWC" method, but also the "BoC" method (Fig. 3, Table 2). This confirms the importance of this proposed coefficient in improving the quality of the resulting vectors and making them more discriminative.

Regarding the effect of the number of concepts on clustering accuracy, it is noted that BoWC begins to provide comparable performance to other methods for only 100 concepts (Fig. 2, Table 2). We can also notice that for a number of concepts greater than 200, the accuracy starts to decrease slightly, given that the concepts become overlapping and therefore non-discriminatory.

As a general note, the adjustments result in a significant improvement in clustering accuracy, which is up to 6% as with the BBC dataset.

Despite the good results achieved by our proposed encoding method compared to other approaches, it is still not efficiently applicable for encoding short texts. According to the findings in this research and previous studies that have addressed this method, it can be observed that the performance of the vectors generated by the BoWC method is better with longer texts. This is due to the ability to capture a larger number of distinctive concepts for each document and weigh them more effectively than in short texts.

However, the proposed concept extraction algorithm in this study offers applicability beyond document vectorization. It can be utilized in various fields, such as expanding

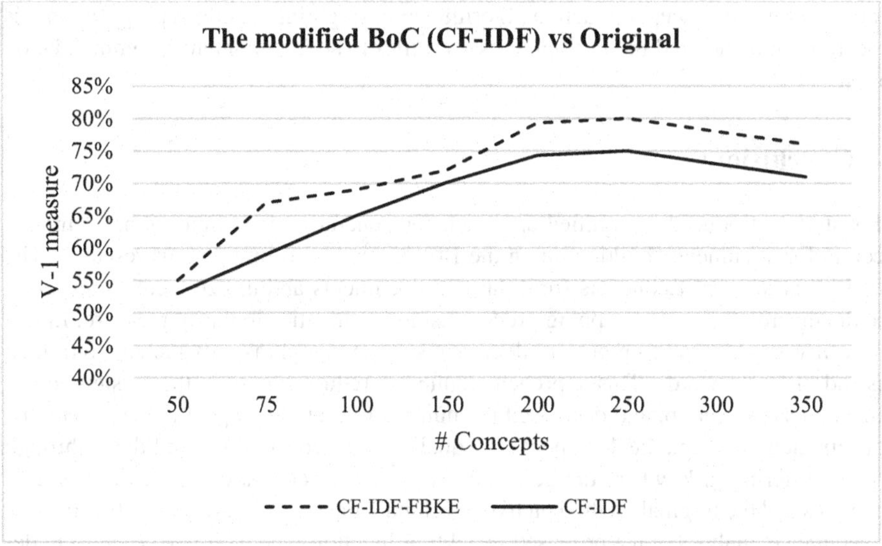

Fig. 3. The V1-score comparison between the modified and original BoC versions in clustering tasks on BBC Dataset

Table 2. The clustering results measured by v1-measure

	V1-score				
	BBC	RE	OH	20NG	WebKB
BoWC$_{\text{Fasttext}}$ (100)	0.768	0.591	0.129	0.316	0.318
BoWC$_{\text{Fasttext}}$ (200)	0.771	0.545	0.140	0.391	0.328
BoWC-FBKE (100)	0.830	0.623	0.154	0.414	0.390
BoWC-FBKE (200)	**0.832**	**0.64**	**0.155**	**0.426**	**0.391**
BoC$_{\text{CF_IDF}}$ (200)	0.743	0.527	0.1	0.394	0.088
BoC$_{\text{CF_IDF-FBKE}}$ (200)	0.793	0.59	0.13	0.400	0.2
TF-IDF	0.663	0.513	0.122	0.362	0.313
BoW	0.209	0.248	0.027	0.021	0.021
Averaged Fasttext (300)	0.774	0.481	0.109	0.381	0.219
self-trained Fasttext (300)	0.631	0.557	0.115	0.325	0.324

Self-trained vectors mean embedding models trained on the owned dataset (not pre-trained).

key phrases that describe a document by extracting keywords and phrases not explicitly mentioned in the text itself. Furthermore, the results obtained from the concept extraction algorithm can be employed in constructing interactive visualizations of document concepts, which prove valuable in tasks involving visual representation of documents and generating customized summaries for lengthy and multi-subject documents [16].

Additionally, the concept extraction algorithm and weighting functions proposed in this research can be utilized in developing user profiles to address content recommendation tasks.

4 Conclusions

This study introduced a modified approach for generating low-dimensional semantic vectors for documents, building upon the BoWC method from previous research. The key idea is to extract concepts from the text documents and utilize them to represent the documents through a mapping process using a semantic similarity measure. In this work, it was proposed to represent documents using key phrases extracted from them instead of single words. This approach resulted in reduced noise in the clusters, minimized concept overlap, and decreased the number of matching operations between the concept dictionary and the document. The quality of the concepts was validated through a text clustering task, where the generated vectors were compared against four strong baselines and the original method on five benchmark datasets. Future research will focus on a detailed analysis of the proposed weighting functions and their performance under different conditions. Additionally, efforts will be made to demonstrate the advantages and interpretability of the resulting vectors, highlighting their significance in solving document visualization tasks and other text mining tasks based on conceptual indexing.

Acknowledgment. The study was performed by the grant from the Russian Science Foundation № 23-21-00089, https://rscf.ru/project/23-21-00089/ in the Southern Federal University.

References

1. Bengforth, B., et al.: Applied analysis of text data in Python (2019)
2. Salton, G., Wong, A., Yang, C.-S.: A vector space model for automatic indexing. Commun. ACM **18**(11), 613–620 (1975)
3. Liu, Z., Lin, Y., Sun, M.: Representation Learning for Natural Language Processing. Springer Nature Singapore, Singapore (2020). https://doi.org/10.1007/978-981-15-5573-2
4. Deerwester, S., et al.: Indexing by latent semantic analysis. J. Am. Soc. Inform. Sci. **41**(6), 391–407 (1990)
5. Le, Q., Mikolov, T.: Distributed representations of sentences and documents. In: International Conference on Machine Learning (2014)
6. Mikolov, T., et al.: Distributed representations of words and phrases and their compositionality. In: Advances in Neural Information Processing Systems (2013)
7. Taddy, M.: Document classification by inversion of distributed language representations (2015)
8. Kim, H.K., Kim, H., Cho, S.: Bag-of-concepts: comprehending document representation through clustering words in distributed representation. Neurocomputing **266**, 336–352 (2017)
9. Mansour, A., Mohammad, J., Kravchenko, Y.: Text vectorization method based on concept mining using clustering techniques. In: 2022 VI International Conference on Information Technologies in Engineering Education (Inforino). IEEE (2022)
10. Mansour, A.M., Mohammad, J.H., Kravchenko, Y.A.: Text vectorization using data mining methods. Izvestia SFedU. Tech. Sci. (2), 154–167 (2021)

11. Мохаммад, Ж, et al.: Метод извлечения ключевых фраз на основе новой функции ранжирования. Информационные технологии **28**(9), 465–474 (2022)
12. Bojanowski, P., et al.: Enriching word vectors with subword information. Trans. Assoc Comput. Linguist. **5**, 135–146 (2017)
13. Greene, D., Cunningham, P.: Practical solutions to the problem of diagonal dominance in kernel document clustering. In: Proceedings of the 23rd international conference on Machine learning (2006)
14. Craven, M., et al.: Learning to construct knowledge bases from the World Wide Web. Artif. Intell. **118**(1–2), 69–113 (2000)
15. Casey, K.: The V Metric, Menopausal Hormone Therapy, and Breast Cancer Risk. Yale University (2020)
16. Zhang, X., et al.: ConceptEVA: Concept-Based Interactive Exploration and Customization of Document Summaries (2023)

A Comparative Study of Deep Learning Methods for Brain Magnetic Resonance Image Reconstruction

Eduardo Garea-Llano(✉), Evelio Gonzalez-Dalmau, and Carlos Cabal-Mirabal

Cuban Neuroscience Center, 190 No. 1520, Playa, 11600 Havana, Cuba
eduardo.garea@cneuro.edu.cu

Abstract. Deep Learning shows a high promise in the field of neuroimaging with the recent development of models for data acquisition, classification problems, segmentation, and image synthesis and reconstruction. Magnetic resonance has been in recent times a very effective tool in the studies of various brain pathologies such as tumors and neurodegenerative diseases, however in the field of neurosciences reducing the patient's exposure time has been very useful in patients who suffer from alterations in their nervous state whose movement can compromise the image quality for the execution of longer brain scan protocols. On the other hand, the high cost of high-field scanners has led to the development of portable low-field equipment with lower cost but lower performance that produce noisy images. In this work we present a comparative study between different techniques based on deep learning for image reconstruction in high and low field brain magnetic resonance images. We analyze methods based on convolutional networks, adversarial generative networks and propose a deep learning model for magnetic resonance image reconstruction based on the concepts of semantic genesis. The experiments developed in neuro-images taken by high and low field magnetic resonance scanners demonstrated a superior performance of the proposed architecture based on semantic genesis in terms of correlation and signal to noise ratio.

Keywords: Brain MRI · Deep Learning · Image Reconstruction

1 Introduction

The use of deep learning for medical image processing is relatively recent. However, long before, machine learning has been used for decades in radiology for detection, segmentation and classification [1–3]. Recent advances in computer vision, specifically deep learning convolutional neural networks (CNNs), have led to very promising advances in various areas of medical imaging in tasks such as disease classification, semantic segmentation of anatomical regions, lesions and tumors, image synthesis and reconstruction [4].

Y. Hernández Heredia et al. (Eds.): IWAIPR 2023, LNCS 14335, pp. 202–214, 2024.
https://doi.org/10.1007/978-3-031-49552-6_18

The process of transforming data contained in magnetic resonance imaging (MRI) measured in the frequency domain (k-space) to the image domain (MR image reconstruction) is the basis of how MR imaging works. It is an area in which intense research has been carried out since the appearance of this modality of medical imaging. Problems such as the variable trajectory of k-space, parallel images and compressed detection, among others, have been topics widely addressed by the scientific community [5]. Recent applications of deep learning-based tools to aid reconstruction problems are set to further revolutionize this area [6].

MR-based imaging produces images of high spatial resolution by capturing strong nuclear magnetic resonances, gradient fields, and hydrogen atoms within the human body. Although magnetic resonance is less invasive than X-rays in terms of harmful ionizing radiation received by the patient, the time that the patient must remain in the scanning station is much longer, this implies having the patient confined to a very small space, sometimes in uncomfortable positions for a considerable time [7].

In the case of brain studies using MR neuro-imaging, reducing the patient's exposure time has been very useful in patients who suffer from alterations in their nervous state whose movement can compromise the quality of the image. Or in other types of studies, for the execution of longer brain scan protocols with multiple sequences and study sessions that can increase the total scan time.

In [7] a deep learning method is presented for the restoration of MRI affected by the effect that occurs when reducing the k-space data with sampling strategies. To achieve the desired effect the authors perform uniform subsampling in the phase coding direction (a phase that requires a long time to capture high-resolution image information), while allowing for the image folding problem. To deal with the location uncertainty due to image folding, a small amount of low-frequency k-space data is added. Training of the Unet architecture CNN network involves input and output images that are pairwise Fourier transforms of the subsampled and fully sampled k-space data. The authors demonstrated in their experiments the remarkable performance of the proposed method as with only 29% of k-space data they can generate high-quality images with the same efficiency as standard MRI reconstruction with fully sampled data.

In [8] the authors proposed deep learning brain image reconstruction model that showed high performance in terms of maximum signal-to-noise ratio (SNR) over a wide range of intervals of decrease in patient exposure time.

An alternative approach based on unsupervised deep learning is presented in [9]. In this work, the authors applied the proposed method to a public data set composed of complex multi-coil images of healthy volunteers and images of patients with white matter lesions. The experimental results demonstrated that high visual quality reconstructions and low mean square error (MSE) values are obtained compared to other deep learning methods.

A major challenge in deep learning is how to best define the loss function. In MRI reconstruction problems, minimizing a loss metric such as MSE does not always result in clinically useful or optimally realistic-appearing images; for example, images can achieve a low overall MSE but also be diagnostically useless if they are highly accurate in all but small but anatomically critical regions. Using the deep learning reconstruction methods, the resulting images often appear too smooth. It is not yet clear if and how such differences may affect diagnosis; however, in practice this may lead to less confidence for the radiologist in terms of clinical interpretation and could hinder the adoption of these techniques in clinical practice.

To overcome or mitigate this problem, several authors have explored the use of so-called generative adversarial networks (GAN) in different architectures [10–12]. These types of networks use a learned loss function. In essence a GAN is composed of two interacting networks: a generator and a discriminator, where the generator is a network trained for the MRI reconstruction task and the discriminator is a network trained to compare the output of the generator and a real or ideal image without disturbances.

In this type of network, the error in the discriminator (contradictory loss) becomes an additional loss term in the optimization problem for the generation of images that more closely mimic the appearance of the ideal image. The generator and the discriminator are trained simultaneously. The goal of the generator is to simultaneously minimize the per-pixel loss metric while maximizing adversary loss, and the goal of the discriminator is to distinguish between generator output images and target images and minimize generator loss.

In [13], the Semantic Genesis framework was proposed, a self-supervised learning framework that allows models to directly learn common visual representation of image data, and take advantage of semantically-enriched representation of anatomical consistent and recurring patterns, taking into account the broad set of unique properties that medical imaging offers. This model introduced two novel components in the process of obtaining generic models: self-discovery and self-classification of the anatomy implicit in medical images. This self-supervised learning framework for medical imaging (2D and 3D), allows to train deep learning models from scratch on unlabeled images. Semantic Genesis is composed by an encoder-decoder structure with skip connections in the between and a classification head at the end of the encoder.

The goal of the model is to learn different sets of semantic-enriched representation from multiple perspectives. For this, the authors propose three important components: 1) self-discovery of anatomical patterns of similar patients; 2) self-classification of patterns; and 3) self-restoration of the transformed patterns. Once the set of self-discovered anatomical patterns is built, the classification and restoration branches are trained jointly on the model.

The results presented by these authors demonstrate that Semantic Genesis is superior to publicly available 3D models, previously trained by self-monitoring or even fully supervised, as well as 2D ImageNet-based transfer learning.

In this work we present a comparative study between different techniques based on deep learning for image reconstruction in high and low field brain MRI. We analyze methods based on convolutional networks, adversarial generative networks and propose a reconstruction model based on the concepts of semantic genesis.

The remainder of the paper is structured as follows. Section 2 describes the experimented models. Section 4, describes the experimental data, and presents the design of the experiment, the results achieved, and their discussion. Finally, conclusions are drawn.

2 Methods

2.1 Data Set

Data used in the preparation of this article were obtained from the Alzheimer's Disease Neuroimaging Initiative.[1] (ADNI) database (adni.loni.usc.edu). The ADNI was launched in 2003 as a public-private partnership, led by Principal Investigator Michael W. Weiner, MD. The primary goal of ADNI has been to test whether serial magnetic resonance imaging (MRI), positron emission tomography (PET), other biological markers, and clinical and neuropsychological assessment can be combined to measure the progression of mild cognitive impairment (MCI) and early Alzheimer's disease (AD). The latest information is available at http://adni.loni.usc.edu/about/.

2.2 Simulation of Aliasing and Blurring in MRI Images

Aliasing and blur are two of the most common effects that occur in MRI images due to patient movement or reduced scanning, but other mechanisms such as low-resolution scanning that occur in MRI low-field images lead to image blurring [15].

Aliasing effect is obtained by subsampling the low frequencies. To obtain the effect of the image subsampling, we use the implementation of the method proposed in [7] and publicly available (https://github.com/Corey-Zumar/MRI-Reconstruction). The implemented scheme simulates the aliasing effect that can occur as a consequence of reducing the patient's exposure time in the scanner. It begins with the transformation of the original image to the frequency domain or k-space by the fast Fourier transform, then an operation is performed to shift the zero frequency of the image towards its center to facilitate the subsampling process, next some low frequencies in the k-space are eliminated, this is done through two parameters that regulate the amount of frequencies to eliminate, the subsampling step (*substep*) and the percentage of low frequencies (*low_freq_percent*) to retain in the output image. Finally, the inverse Fourier transform is applied to the resulting image to obtain the subsampled image. In the case of our study we apply the same parameters used in the implementation of [7], *substep* = 4 and *low_freq_percent* = 0.04.

Gaussian blur describes the blur of an image using a Gaussian function. This is an effect widely used in computer vision, typically to reduce image noise and reduce details. The visual effect of this blur technique is a soft blur similar to viewing the image through a translucent screen.

[1] Data used in preparation of this article were obtained from the Alzheimer's Disease Neuroimaging Initiative (ADNI) database (adni.loni.usc.edu). As such, the investigators within the ADNI contributed to the design and implementation of ADNI and/or provided data but did not participate in analysis or writing of this report. A complete listing of ADNI investigators can be found at: http://adni.loni.usc.edu/wp-content/uploads/how_to_apply/ADNI_Acknowledgement_List.pdf.

In our study we used a Gaussian blurring filter to simulate the effect produced in the image by movement of the patient. In two dimensions, it is the product of two such Gaussians, one per direction (1), where x is the distance from the origin in the horizontal axis, y is the distance from the origin in the vertical axis, and σ is the standard deviation of the Gaussian distribution. Figure 1 show an example of effect of subsampling (b) and Gaussian blurring (c) in a MR image.

$$Gxy = \frac{1}{2\pi\sigma^2} e^{-\frac{x^2+y^2}{2\sigma^2}} \tag{1}$$

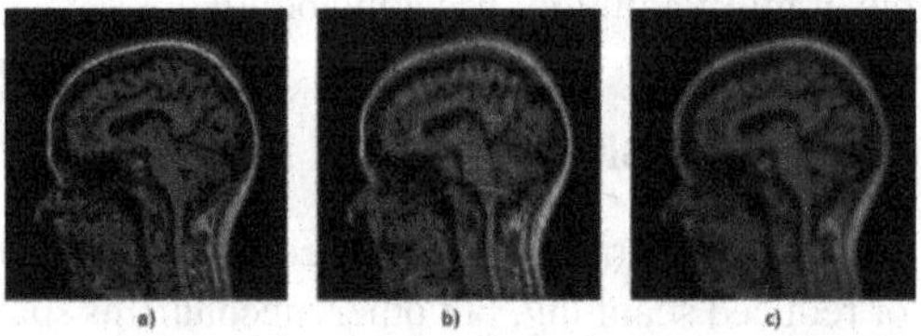

Fig. 1. Effect of subsampling (b) and Gaussian blurring (c) on a high field MR image (a)

2.3 Image Reconstruction Schemes

For the development of the comparative study, we propose two experimental schemes: The first scheme is designed for image reconstruction from the aliasing effect caused by the subsampling process described in Sect. 2.1. It is based on the scheme proposed in [7] (Fig. 2). The scheme consists of two main components: deep learning framework and k-space correction. As pre-processing, the unmeasured region of the subsampled data is first padded with zeros. Then, by means of the inverse Fourier transform, its absolute value is taken and the folded image is obtained. After this pre-processing the folded image is used as the input of the pre-trained network and produce the output. The network retrieves the zero-padded portion of the k-space data. The Fourier transform is obtained and the unpadded parts are replaced by the original k-space data to preserve the original measured data. Finally, the output image is obtained by applying the inverse Fourier transform and the absolute value.

In the second scheme, the simulation of the effect of blurring is carried out by means of the Gaussian filtering of the original image, the image resulting from the filtering is the input to the pretrained deep learning model (for the task of reconstruction from the blurred image), finally the output of the network is the reconstructed image (Fig. 3).

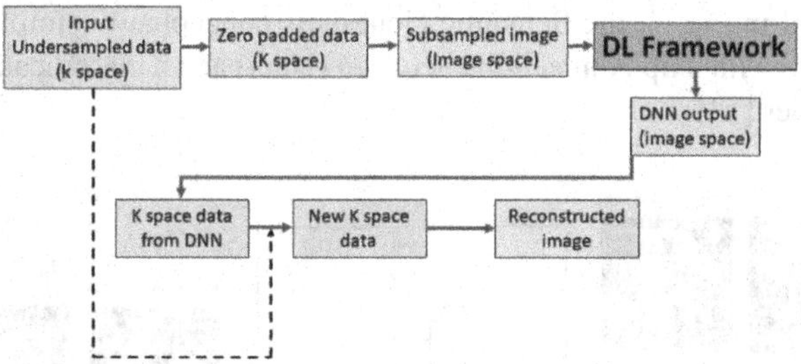

Fig. 2. Experimental scheme for MRI reconstruction from the aliasing effect based in [7]

Fig. 3. Experimental scheme for MRI reconstruction from blurring effect

2.4 Experimented Deep Neural Networks Frameworks

As the main baseline we use the Unet convolutional network, which is the one used in the original scheme proposed in [7].

Unet is a fully convolutional neural network model. This model was originally developed for medical images segmentation [16]. The Unet architecture consists of two "tracks". The first is that of contraction, also called the encoder. It is used to capture the context of an image. Actually, it is a set of convolutional layers and "max pooling" layers that allow to create a feature map of an image and reduce its size to reduce the number of network parameters.

As the second deep learning framework for this study we propose the Pix2pix architecture. It is a Generative Adversarial Network (GAN). Pix2Pix is a system formed by a generator network and a discriminator network based on conditional GAN [17]. In the training process, the generating network tries to learn an optimal mapping between pairs of noiseless images and their noisy equivalents in order to propose a reconstructed image similar to its original pair. The discriminator evaluates the degree of similarity between the image without noise and the reconstructed one. In order to increase the performance of the Pix2Pix model to generate noise-free images, we use the generator, which is modeled based on the previously described Unet architecture.

As a third framework to be evaluated, we propose the semantic genesis approach [13]. As we described in the introduction section the semantic genesis framework has as goal to learn different sets of semantic-enriched representation from multiple perspectives and use this learned representation in multiple tasks such as segmentation and classification of 2D and 3D medical images. In this work we propose the adaptation of this approach to the task of reconstruction of MRI (Fig. 4.). In this case, for a better description and simplification of terms, we will call as disturbed image the image to which the processes described above have been applied to obtain the effect of aliasing or blurring.

The framework consists of three components: 1) Pseudo-labeling of anatomical patterns, 2) Anatomical Pattern Classification, and 3) Restoration of anatomical patterns.

As illustrated in Fig. 4, the Semantic Genesis is conceptually simple: an encoder-decoder structure with skip connections between (Unet) and a classification head at the end of the encoder [13].

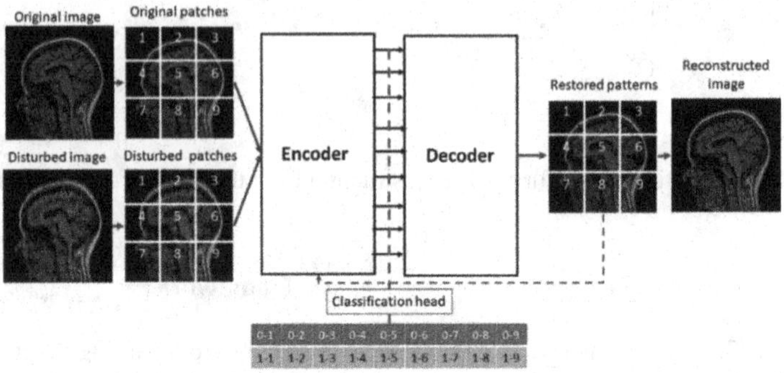

Fig. 4. Framework for MRI reconstruction based on Semantic Genesis [13]

Pseudo-labeling of Anatomical Patterns: In this first step, in the training process, a set of anatomical patterns is constructed from the original images and the disturbed images. To do this, we cut patches of a number of fixed coordinates for each pair of images (original and disturbed), which share similar semantics. Pseudo-labels are assigned to these patches based on their coordinates and the type of image from which it was extracted (disturbed, non-disturbed), resulting in a new data set, in which each patch is associated with one of the two classes. Since the coordinates are randomly selected, some of the anatomical patterns may not be very meaningful to radiologists; however, these patterns are associated with rich local semantics of the human brain [13]. In the reconstruction process, once the network has been trained, it only receives the patches of the disturbed image as input without labeling (Fig. 4).

Anatomical Pattern Classification: As illustrated in Fig. 4, the classification branch encodes the input anatomical pattern in a latent space, followed by a sequence of fully connected (FC) layers, and predicts the label associated with the pattern. As input, in the training process, it receives the patches obtained from the original image and the patches of its corresponding disturbed image and recursively classifies them and sends them to the decoder until classifying all patches as non-disturbed. In the reconstruction process, once the network has been trained, it only receives the patches of the disturbed image.

Restoration of Anatomical Patterns: The objective of the restoration is for the model to learn different visual representations by recovering original anatomical patterns (original image) from the disturbed ones. As shown in Fig. 4, the restoration branch encodes the input disturbed anatomical pattern in a latent space and decodes it to the original resolution to recover the original anatomical pattern.

For model training, we follow [13] and define the following loss functions for the multi-task (Restoration & classification) (2):

$$L = \gamma cl * Lcl + \gamma rc * Lrc \tag{2}$$

where γcl and γrc regulate the weights of classification and reconstruction losses, respectively. *Lcl* is the loss function of the classification process, in this case we adopt the binary cross entropy loss function expressed by expression 3, where *N* denotes the batch size; *y* is the class label (1 for non-disturbed patches and 0 for disturbed patches) and *p(y)* is the predicted probability of the patch being non-disturbed for all *N* patches.

$$Lcl = -\frac{1}{N}\sum_{i=1}^{N}(yi.\log(p(yi)) + (1 - yi).\log(1 - p(yi)) \quad (3)$$

Lrc is the distance L2 between the original pattern and the reconstructed pattern expressed as a loss function through the expression 4, where *N* is the batch size, *X* is the ground truth (original anatomical pattern) and X' is the reconstructed prediction.

$$Lcl = -\frac{1}{N}\sum_{i=1}^{N}\|Xi - Xi'2\|. \quad (4)$$

The adoption of *Lcl* based on [13] allows the model to learn a semantically enriched representation. Similarly, the use of the *Lrc* function encourages the model to learn from multiple perspectives by trying to restore original images from various image deformations.

3 Experimental Results and Discussion

3.1 Implementation and Training Details

The acquisition protocols of the 3D T1w images can be found in [14] for ADNI 1. ADNI 1 images were used in the training, validation and test sets. For our experiment we used a total of 2968 slides in dicom format corresponding to image sequences of 28 individuals.

In order to have an idea of the behavior of the compared methods in low-field images, a set of images in dicom format obtained in various studies carried out in our center were taken. The 100 low field, neuro-radiologist labeled images were obtained from a 0.36T scanner from a Havana hospital.

All the implementations of the experimental pipelines were carried out on the open source library Keras (with MIT license) written in Python. The objective of using this library was to facilitate the implementation of the compared models because Keras does not work as an independent framework, but rather as an intuitive user interface (API) that allows access to various machine learning frameworks such as TensorFlow. The implementation of the model based on [7] was taken from its official GitHub site (https://github.com/Corey-Zumar/MRI-Reconstruction).

For model training, the dataset obtained from ADNI1 cohort was divided into three sets with randomly selected images: Training: 1899. Validation: 594 and Test: 475. An additional test set was implemented with the 100 low-field images. Previously, their corresponding pairs of disturbed images by aliasing and blurring were obtained. Table 1 shows the different schemes trained and tested in the study.

All training sessions were carried out on a HPC with 5 nodes: HP Proliant XL230a Gen9 servers with 2 CPUs x node: Intel Xeon E5–2670 at 2.30GHz, 12C, for a total of 24 cores per node, 120 Computing Cores. RAM: 48 GB per node. All models were trained for 600 epochs in a 4-fold cross-validation scheme, so a total of 24 weight files were obtained (4 per model).

Table 1. Schemes experimented and compared in the study

No	Experimental scheme	Deep Learning Framework
1	MRI reconstruction from the aliasing effect (Fig. 1)	Unet
2		Pix2Pix
3		Semantic Genesis
4	MRI reconstruction from blurring effect (Fig. 2)	Unet
5		Pix2Pix
6		Semantic Genesis

3.2 Evaluation of the Performance of the Obtained Models

For the evaluation and comparison of the performance of the obtained models, two measurements were taken that are widely used to assess the performance of image reconstruction methods: Signal to noise ratio (SNR), is a measure that compares the level of a desired signal to the level of background noise. We estimated SNR for each original, disturbed and reconstructed image by region of interest (ROI) measurements. Let *Simg* be the ROI image intensity in an image and *Sbackground* be the ROI image intensity on the image background, then SNR can be calculated as [18]:

$$SNR = 0.665\frac{mean(S_{img})}{std\left(S_{\text{background}}\right)} \tag{5}$$

The factor 0.665 accounts for the Rayleigh distribution of the noise in the magnitude image. For experiments we compared the SNRs of original image (SNRo), disturbed image (SNRd) and reconstructed image (SNRr).

Normalized Correlation (NC). Has been chosen as it has proved to be a successful similarity measure for image comparison in the image space. For identical images it takes the maximum value equal to unity. The NC can be calculated by eq. (6), where the original image is *w(i,j)* and the reconstructed image is *w1(i,j)*.

$$NC = \frac{\sum_i \sum_j (w(i,j)w1(i,j)}{\sqrt{\sum_i \sum_j w(i,j)^2 \sum_i \sum_j w1(i,j)^2}} \tag{6}$$

Table 2 shows the average results obtained by each model in the 4-fold cross-validation scheme and the standard deviation for each measure. Figure 5 and 6 show some examples of the obtained results for each of the experimented frameworks. The white rectangles in the images indicate the ROI chosen according to eq. (5) for the calculation of the RSN.

Table 2. Results obtained in the 4-fold cross-validation scheme

No	Exp. Scheme	DL.Framew	SNRo	SNRd	SNRr	Std (SNRr)	NC	Std (NC)
High field MRI								
1	No.1 (Fig. 1)	Unet	0.872	0.977	1.052	0.030	0.715	0.074
2		Pix2Pix			**1.359**	0.074	0.696	0.004
3		Sem.Gen			1.288	**0.006**	**0.724**	**0.002**
4	No 2 (Fig. 2)	Unet		0.889	1.020	0.003	0.707	0.003
5		Pix2Pix			0.988	0.001	0.726	**0.002**
6		Sem. Gen			**1.124**	**0.0004**	**0.739**	0.003
Low field MRI								
1	No.1 (Fig. 1)	Unet	5.021	4.774	5.525	0.028	0.645	0.003
2		Pix2Pix			**6.216**	0.161	0.649	**0.002**
3		Sem.Gen			6.152	**0.003**	**0.674**	**0.002**
4	No 2 (Fig. 2)	Unet		6.521	5.165	0.064	0.683	0.029
5		Pix2Pix			5.816	0.024	0.658	0.005
6		Sem. Gen			**6.349**	**0.005**	**0.692**	**0.004**

As can be seen, all the methods studied have a good performance in the task of image reconstruction. However, the reconstruction methods that are developed in the k-space obtain a better recovery of the image with a NC above 0.70 in most of the cases. Regarding the SNR, all the methods achieve an increase in this parameter with respect to the disturbed image. On the other hand, the proposed scheme based on semantic genesis achieves the best results with greater stability of its values and with low standard deviations. The latter corroborates the theory of the authors of [13] regarding the ability of this approach to capture the intrinsic semantics in medical images.

Another interesting observation is about the results obtained in low-field MRI reconstruction. Although these images were not taken into account in any of the trainings carried out for this study, the results of the reconstruction using models trained only for high-field MRI nevertheless show a good performance, which demonstrates the extrapolation capacity of these types of network. A training process that mixes high-field and low-field MRI may undo a more robust MRI reconstruction system.

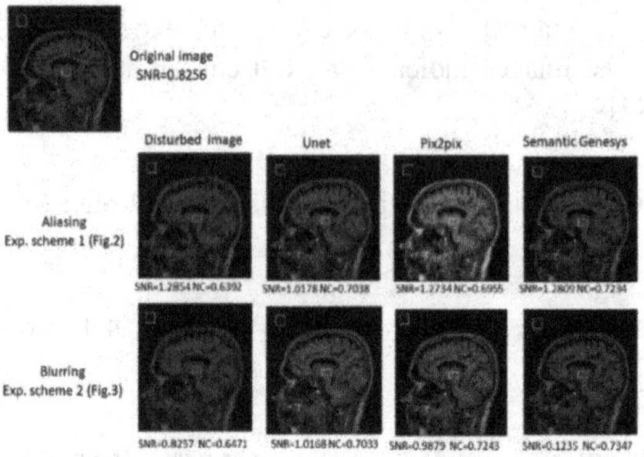

Fig. 5. Example of the obtained results for each of the experimented frameworks in a high field MRI.

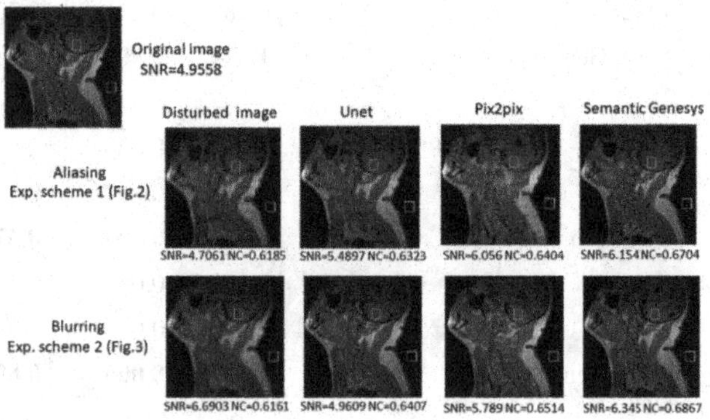

Fig. 6. Example of the obtained results for each of the experimented frameworks in a low field MRI.

4 Conclusions

In this work we presented a comparative study between different techniques based on deep learning for image reconstruction in high and low field brain MRI. We compared the performance of methods based on convolutional networks, adversarial generative networks and propose a deep learning model for MRI reconstruction based on the concepts of semantic genesis. The studied methods showed a good performance in the task of image reconstruction. The k-space based methods obtain a better performance with a NC above 0.70 in most of the experimented schemes. Regarding the SNR, all methods achieve an increase in this parameter with respect to the disturbed image.

The experiments on low field MRI shown that it is possible to obtain images with a low level of affectation and better visual quality than the images affected by aliasing and blurring. For a better study of this fact, as continuity of this research we will train the compared networks on a low filed image dataset.

Finally, in this work was proved that the semantic genesis approach is also effective for the task of MRI reconstruction showing a better performance.

References

1. Hosny, A., Parmar, C., Quackenbush, J., Schwartz, L.H., Aerts, H.: Artificial intelligence in radiology. Nat. Rev. Cancer **18**(8), 500–510 (2018)
2. McBee, M.P., Awan, O.A., Colucci, A.T., et al.: Deep learning in radiology. Acad. Radiol. **25**(11), 1472–1480 (2018)
3. Zaharchuk, G., Gong, E., Wintermark, M., Rubin, D., Langlotz, C.P.: Deep learning in neuroradiology. AJNR Am. J. Neuroradiol. **39**(10), 1776–1784 (2018)
4. Bash, S., Johnson, B., Gibbs, W., et al.: Deep learning image processing enables 40% faster spinal MR scans which match or exceed quality of standard of care. Clin. Neuroradiol. **32**, 197–203 (2022). https://doi.org/10.1007/s00062-021-01121-2
5. Wang, G., Ye, J.C., Mueller, K., Fessler, J.A.: Image reconstruction is a new frontier of machine learning. IEEE Trans. Med. Imaging **37**(6), 1289–1296 (2018)
6. Lin, D.J., Johnson, P.M., Knoll, F., Lui, Y.W.: Artificial intelligence for MR image reconstruction: an overview for clinicians. J. Magn. Reson. Imaging **53**, 1015–1028 (2021)
7. Hyun, C.M., Kim, H.P., Lee, S.M., Lee, S., Seo, J.K.: Deep learning for undersampled MRI reconstruction. Phys. Med. Biol. **63**(13), 135007 (2018). https://doi.org/10.1088/1361-6560/aac71a
8. Aggarwal, H.K., Mani, M.P., Jacob, M.: MoDL: model-based deep learning architecture for inverse problems. IEEE Trans. Med. Imaging **38**(2), 394–405 (2019)
9. Tezcan, K.C., Baumgartner, C.F., Luechinger, R., Pruessmann, K.P., Konukoglu, E.: MR image reconstruction using deep density priors. IEEE Trans. Med. Imaging **38**(7), 1633–1642 (2019)
10. J. Huang, Wu, Y., Wu, H., Yang, G.: Fast MRI reconstruction: how powerful transformers are? In: 2022 44th IEEE (EMBC), pp. 2066–2070 (2022). https://doi.org/10.1109/EMBC48229.2022.9871475
11. Laino, M.E., Cancian, P., Politi, L.S., Della Porta, M.G., Saba, L., Savevski, V.: Generative adversarial networks in brain imaging: a narrative review. J. Imag. **8**(4), 83 (2022). https://doi.org/10.3390/jimaging8040083
12. Xu, J., Bi, W., Yan, L., Du, H., Qiu, B.: An efficient lightweight generative adversarial network for compressed sensing magnetic resonance imaging reconstruction. IEEE Access **11**, 24604–24614 (2023). https://doi.org/10.1109/ACCESS.2023.3254136
13. Haghighi, F., Hosseinzadeh Taher, M.R., Zhou, Z., Gotway, M.B., Liang, J.: Learning semantics-enriched representation via self-discovery, self-classification, and self-restoration. In: Martel, A.L., et al. (eds.) Medical Image Computing and Computer Assisted Intervention – MICCAI 2020: 23rd International Conference, Lima, Peru, October 4–8, 2020, Proceedings, Part I, pp. 137–147. Springer International Publishing, Cham (2020). https://doi.org/10.1007/978-3-030-59710-8_14
14. Jack, C.R., et al.: The Alzheimer's disease neuroimaging initiative (ADNI): MRI methods. J. Magn. Reson. Imaging **27**, 685–691 (2008). https://doi.org/10.1002/jmri.21049
15. Mehta, D., Padalia, D., Vora, K., Mehendale, N.: MRI image denoising using U-Net and Image Processing Techniques. In: 2022 5th International Conference on Advances in Science and Technology (ICAST), Mumbai, India, pp. 306–313 (2022). https://doi.org/10.1109/ICAST55766.2022.10039653
16. Ronneberger, O., Fischer, P., Brox, T.: U-Net: convolutional networks for biomedical image segmentation. In: Navab, N., Hornegger, J., Wells, W., Frangi, A. (eds.) Medical Image Computing and Computer-Assisted Intervention – MICCAI 2015: 18th International Conference, Munich, Germany, October 5-9, 2015, Proceedings, Part III, pp. 234–241. Springer International Publishing, Cham (2015). https://doi.org/10.1007/978-3-319-24574-4_28

17. Odena, A., Olah, C., Shlens, J.: Conditional image synthesis with auxiliary classifier gans. In: Proceedings of the International Conference on Machine Learning, Sydney, NSW, Australia, 6–11 Aug 2017, pp. 2642–2651 (2017)
18. National Electrical Manufacturers Association: NEMA Standards Publication MS 1-2008, Determination of Signal-to-Noise Ratio (SNR) in Diagnostic Magnetic Resonance Imaging, pp. 1–19 (2008)

Enhancing Spanish Aspect-Based Sentiment Analysis Through Deep Learning Approach

Patricia Montañez Castelo[1], Alfredo Simón-Cuevas[1](✉), José A. Olivas[2], and Francisco P. Romero[2]

[1] Universidad Tecnológica de La Habana "José Antonio Echeverría", Havana, La Habana, Cuba
{pmontanez,asimon}@ceis.cujae.edu.cu

[2] Universidad de Castilla-La Mancha, Ciudad Real, Spain
{JoseAngel.olivas,FranciscoP.Romero}@uclm.es

Abstract. Aspect-based sentiment analysis is the task of monitoring user sentiment on textual opinions about the characteristics of a given entity. Recognizing the aspects present in the opinion and determining its sentimental orientation (positive or negative) in a similar way as if it were done by a human being continues to be a challenging task, but at the same time necessary. Achieving quality improvement of existing aspect-based sentiment analysis solutions remains a challenge and the vast majority of solutions reported in this task are focused on the English language, so further progress is needed in languages like Spanish. This paper presents an aspect-based sentiment analysis method which uses language models based on Transformers (BERT models) with a linear layer to extract aspects from opinions in Spanish and a similar model to perform Aspect Sentiment Classification, demonstrating that its use allows us to surpass the state of the art for said language. The proposed solution was evaluated using the Semeval2016 Task 5 dataset achieving promising results, respect those reported by other solutions.

Keywords: aspect-based sentiment analysis · deep learning · transformers-based language models · aspect extraction · polarity detection

1 Introduction

The vast amount of data, specifically opinions, available in various online spaces such as social media, blogs, chats, and e-commerce websites, represents a valuable asset for different companies. These companies are interested in understanding what their consumers think about their products [1]. Sentiment analysis, also known as opinion mining, is the process of analyzing the feelings, opinions, and emotions of users regarding a specific topic in textual form [2]. From a business perspective, monitoring and analyzing user or customer opinions becomes essential in a highly competitive environment. However, to varying degrees, companies face the challenge of analyzing a large volume of opinions about their own products or services, as well as, those of their competitors, from multiple sources. Manual analysis of the opinions is impractical, making it necessary to establish automated processes [3].

Y. Hernández Heredia et al. (Eds.): IWAIPR 2023, LNCS 14335, pp. 215–224, 2024.
https://doi.org/10.1007/978-3-031-49552-6_19

Opinion mining or sentiment analysis provides the opportunity to address the aforementioned problems by automating the process of monitoring what users think or feel about various topics [4]. This task is applicable to virtually any context, such as e-commerce, services, healthcare systems, politics, and the financial sector. Companies like Google and Microsoft have developed their own systems of this kind to enhance the quality of the products and services they provide [5]. Generally, the process of sentiment analysis in text is categorized into three levels: document-level, sentence-level, and aspect-level. This research is focused on aspect-level, which is concerned with identifying the sentiment towards specific aspects or features mentioned in the text [2]. Aspect-Based Sentiment Analysis (ABSA) focuses on identifying and analyzing the sentiment expressed towards specific aspects or features of a given entity, enabling a more fine-grained understanding of opinions and feedback. Aspects refer to attributes or components of an entity. For example, in the case of a phone (entity), aspects can include the camera, battery, and others.

This paper presents a Spanish-oriented aspect-based sentiment analysis method based on language models with Transformers architecture for aspect extraction and polarity classification tasks. In the proposed method a BERT (Bidirectional Encoder Representations from Transformers) model is used for aspect extraction and a RoBERTa (Robustly Optimized BERT Approach) model is used for polarity classification task. Through this approach we explored the modeling capabilities of contextual embeddings from the pre-trained BERT on the Spanish aspect extraction and polarity classification task. Specifically, we examined the incorporation of the BERT embedding component with a simple linear classification layer, for aspect extraction and sentiment classification. Our proposal was inspired by the solutions reported in [6, 7], but employing different representation mechanisms and a different workflow, as well as being conceived for the Spanish language. The proposed solution was evaluated with the Spanish-language dataset used in SemEval-2016 Task 5: Aspect Based Sentiment Analysis [8]. The obtained results were compared with those obtained by other reported works outperforming the results quality of these.

The remainder of the paper is structured as follows: Section 2 provides a background about ABSA; Section 3 describe the proposed solution in details; Section 3 presents the results of the evaluation process and the corresponding analysis; and conclusions arrived and future works are given in Sect. 4.

2 Background

ABSA plays a crucial role in applications such as customer reviews analysis, market research, and product/service improvement [9], and this new challenge has sparked increased interest among researchers worldwide. The aspect-based sentiment analysis task, usually is divide it into two subtasks, these are Aspect Extraction (AE) and Aspect Sentiment Classification (ASC) [10, 11]. The first part aims to identify and extract the aspect about which an opinion is being issued and the second part is responsible for detecting the polarity of sentiment associated with that aspect in the opinion [10]. Aspect identification is one of the most challenge tasks in this context.

Currently, supervised approaches dominate the ABSA field, including traditional methods such as Support Vector Machine (SVM) and Naive Bayes, where they are used for both polarity detection and aspect extraction [12]. In recent years, methods based on deep learning have gained particular popularity [13]. In several works [14, 15] it is proposed to use a Bidirectional Long-Short Term Memory (BLSTM) for aspect extraction, since it can analyze the text in both directions simultaneously. Then for the polarity classification process a Convolutional Neural Network (CNN) and a Graph Convolutional Network (GCN) are used respectively which yields a sentiment score with respect to a target. One problem with the use of convolutional networks is that it does not take into account the order of words in the sentence so it is difficult to extract appropriate meaning from them [16]. Although several solutions are reported in the literature, there are still many deficiencies in this field, including the language problem. The majority of existing works are designed for the English language, which limits their scope and applicability to other languages, such as the Spanish. Addressing these language limitations is crucial to broaden the reach and effectiveness of aspect-based sentiment analysis in diverse linguistic contexts [1]. Furthermore, existing systems are not entirely accurate in extracting the aspects being discussed in an opinion or detecting the associated polarity.

3 Proposed Method for Spanish ABSA

The proposed solution is conceived in four fundamental steps: preprocessing, aspect extraction, determining the polarity towards the aspect extracted from the opinions where it appears, and summarizing the number of positive and negative reviews per aspect. The general workflow is shown in Fig. 1.

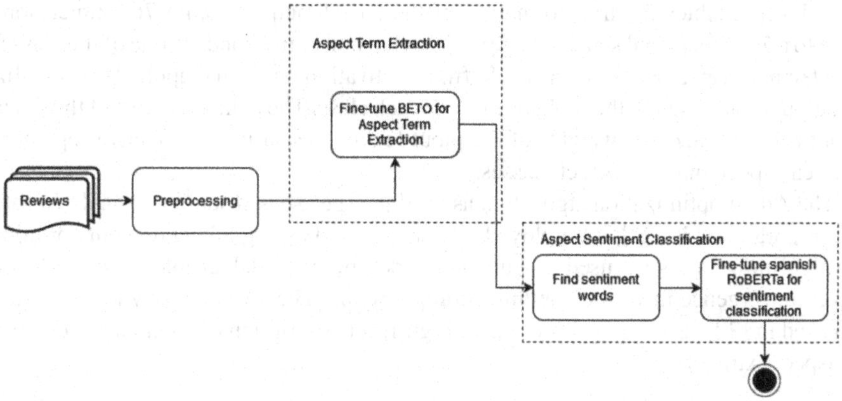

Fig. 1. Overview of the workflow of the proposed method

3.1 Preprocessing

The unstructured nature of texts requires the execution of preprocessing or normalization in most cases; however, these tasks differ depending on the objective. However, the use of pre-trained deep learning models reduces the number of pre-processing tasks that are usually carried out in other solutions that do not apply these technologies. For example, due to in this solution the use of bert-base-spanish-cased is adopted, to lowercase the text or remove punctuation marks was not necessary and nor are stop words extracted. An important part of this process is to bring the text to a structure understandable by the BERT model. Among these tasks are the elimination of special characters, bringing the outlines to a binary vector structure, among other tasks. Figures 2, 3 shows preprocessing tasks that are applied by the Transformers-based language models used.

3.2 Aspect Extraction

The aspect extraction from reviews is carried out through a pre-trained BERT model for Spanish, proposed by [17] and known as BETO. This model is employed for both representation and capturing the embedded semantics in the content, as well as for aspect extraction, for which specific fine-tuning adjustments were made. The use of BERT for aspect-based sentiment analysis has significantly improved the quality of aspect extraction in languages such as Arabic [18] and Portuguese [19], and this research also demonstrates its benefits for Spanish. The total size of the corpus used to train BETO is comparable to that used in the original BERT model called bert-base-uncased, with approximately 3 billion words and composed of 12 layers of transformers.

Subsequently, the token embeddings, segment embeddings, and position embeddings are fused together, forming a composite representation that is then passed through L transformer layers in order to optimize the features at the token level. In order to identify aspect terms in the opinions, word embeddings extracted from the BERT model are processed through a task-specific layer. This additional layer, known as a fully connected linear layer, enables the transformation of the BERT output from a 768-dimensional space to a 2-dimensional space, where each dimension corresponds to one of the classes: aspect or non-aspect. Subsequently, a Softmax activation function is applied to normalize the outputs and compute the probabilities for each class. The main objective of this linear output is to optimize the weights of the input features, ensuring an effective separation between aspect and non-aspect classes.

The Adam optimization algorithm, as used in aspect-based sentiment analysis solutions reported in [20–22], is employed. Adam is a stochastic gradient descent optimization algorithm commonly used in neural network training [23]. It enables faster and more stable convergence in various optimization problems. The cross-entropy loss function, also used in [20, 22]. Figure 2 provides a high-level description of the architecture used for aspect extraction.

3.3 Aspect Sentiment Classification

3.3.1 Sentiment Feature Selection

Once the aspects discussed in the text have been identified, it is necessary to determine the sentiment of the opinion towards each specific aspect. This requires a careful selection of the features or words used in the opinion to refer to a particular aspect. Various mechanisms exist for selecting features used to express an opinion. In this case, a word window technique is employed. The word window technique involves selecting a set of words surrounding a target word, in this case, the aspect, to determine its polarity. For instance, in the sentence "The food is excellent," the word window around "food" could include words such as "is excellent," depending on the defined window size. The window size defined in this study is 5 words around the aspect, based on experimental studies.

3.3.2 Sentiment Classification

Once the words used to express an opinion about a specific aspect have been selected, it is necessary to classify the review for that aspect as positive, negative, or neutral. For this process, a similar approach to aspect extraction was followed, employing pre-trained language models. The chosen model for Spanish was Bertin model based on RoBERTa architecture, as proposed by [24]. This model consists of 12 layers with 12 attention heads each, a hidden size of 768, and a total of 125 million parameters. It was trained from scratch using the Spanish portion of mC4 dataset [24].

The training data consists of text fragments containing the word window where the aspect is located, along with a polarity label. The polarity label is a numerical value indicating whether the class for that aspect is negative (0), positive (1), or neutral (2). The architecture of the aspect classification model is similar to the aspect extraction model, combining BERT with a linear layer and a softmax activation function to assign the output class to the text. In this case, the cross-entropy loss function was utilized, along with the Adam optimization algorithm and a learning rate of 1e-5. The overall architecture of the proposed model for aspect sentiment classification is depicted in Fig. 3.

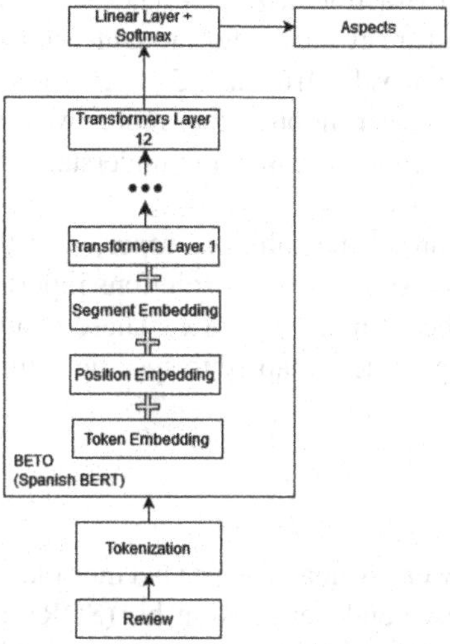

Fig. 2. Aspect extraction workflow

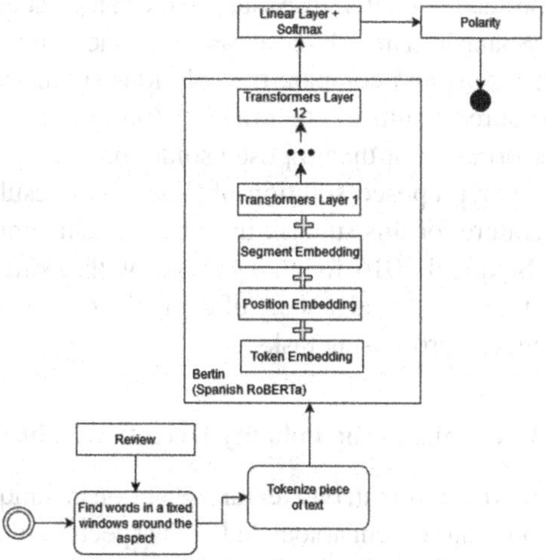

Fig. 3. Polarity detection workflow

4 Experimental Results and Discussions

The evaluation of the proposed solution was divided in two tasks: aspect extraction and polarity detection subtasks. The polarity is evaluated considering the opinions in which each extracted aspect appears. The experiments were carried out on a set of Spanish-language reviews used in SemEval-2016 Task 5: Aspect Based Sentiment Analysis [8], specifically, a set of restaurant reviews labeled with information about the aspects discussed in them (e.g., servicC4e, food, ambience, attention, among others.) and the polarity of the sentiment expressed towards those aspects. Results were measured using precision, recall, F1-score, and accuracy metrics. Table 1 shows the characterization of the test collection selected.

Table 1. Characterization of the test collection.

Dataset SemEval 2016 Spanish ABSA	Opinions for test	Opinions for train	Aspects	Polarity class
	627	2070	247	4

4.1 Results of the Aspect Extraction Subtask

Table 2 shows the results of evaluating different batch sizes with the selected models. The results indicate that the models with a smaller batch size (8) perform better than the models with a larger batch size (16), as well as that the bert-base-spanish-cased model performs better than the bert-base-multilingual-cased model. Table 3 shows the comparison of the results of our solution in aspect extraction task with other solutions reported in the literature that use the same dataset and are evaluated for the same subtask in Spanish. The F1-score was the one used in SemEval-2016 Task 5 to computing the results and compare the solutions submitted, however, in our experiments we also measured results of other metrics (precision and recall) in order to better understand the performance of the proposed solution.

The proposed solution obtains better results than all the solutions reported in the literature for this subtask in Spanish, achieving to be superior to all solutions reported in SemEval-2016 for this subtask with a difference of more than 8%. These results corroborate the advantage of using the deep learning models adapted to specific natural language processing tasks.

4.2 Results of the Polarity Detection Subtask

In this experiment, two feature selection techniques were evaluated to predict the polarity of opinion content associated with aspects: syntactic dependency relationship (SDR) and window of words (WW). The first one consists in the fact that given an aspect and a sentence where it appears, all those words that syntactically depend in the sentence on the target aspect are extracted. The second technique consists of extracting as features the words that are in the neighborhood of size 5 around the target aspect in the sentence where

Table 2. Comparison of different BERT models and different batch sizes.

Models	Batch Size	Precision	Recall	F1
bert-base-spanish-cased	8	**0,74**	**0,81**	**0,78**
bert-base-spanish-cased	16	0,73	0,8	0,76
bert-base-multilingual-cased	8	0,69	0,77	0,72
bert-base-multilingual-cased	16	0,69	0,79	0,73

Table 3. Comparison of the proposed solution for aspect extraction with the state of the art.

Solutions	Precision	Recall	F1
Henríquez Miranda & Buelvas [1]	-	-	0,730
GTI/C*	-	-	0,685
GTI/U*			0,683
IIT-T/U*			0,643
TGB/C*			0,557
SemEval-2016 – baseline			*0,519*
Solution proposal (bert-base-spanish-cased + Batch Size 8)	**0,736**	**0,815**	**0,767**

* Solutions submitted to SemEval-2016 Task 5 (results in Slot1: Aspect Category) (Pontiki et al. [8])

it appears. In addition, four classification models were evaluated: BERT, RoBERTa, RoBERTuito and GPT2. These deep learning-based language models have been shown to be very effective in a variety of natural language processing tasks, including sentiment analysis.

Table 4 shows the results obtained according to the feature selection technique and the classification model used. According the obtained results, when using SDR the values of the quality metrics are inferior to those obtained when using a WW (size 5), demonstrating that this sentiment word selection strategy is not the most appropriate.

On the other hand, it is observed that the solution that offers the best results is the combination of RoBERTa and WW (size 5). Table 5 compares the results of this solution with those obtained by other solutions reported in the literature, including those presented in SemEval-2016, where the highest result achieved was 83.5% of accuracy. Similar to the evaluation of the previous subtask, the accuracy metric was the one used in SemEval-2016 Task 5 to computing the results and compare the solutions submitted, and we also measured results of other metrics too.

These findings suggest that language models based on Transformers (deep learning approaches) offer improvements to the aspect-based sentiment analysis process, and that the selection of appropriate features is a critical factor to improving the accuracy of the prediction model.

Table 4. Polarity detection results according to several feature selection technique and classification models

Feature selection technics	Models	Precision	Recall	F1	Acc
WW (size 5)	BETO (BERT *model for Spanish*)	0,833	0,845	0,834	0,844
	RoBERTa	**0,836**	**0,864**	**0,848**	**0,866**
	GPT-2	0,751	0,773	0,748	0,772
	RoBERTuito	0,805	0,828	0,812	0,832
SDR	BETO (BERT *model for Spanish*)	0,745	0,745	0,745	0,745
	RoBERTa	0,700	0,780	0,730	0,770
	GPT-2	0,685	0,725	0,696	0,717
	RoBERTuito	0,730	0,770	0,745	0,785

Table 5. Comparación de la solución propuesta para clasificación de polaridad con estado del arte.

Solutions	Precision	Recall	F1	Acc
IIT-T/U*	-	-	-	0,835
TGB/C*	-	-	-	0,820
UWB/C*	-	-	-	0,813
INSIG/C*	-	-	-	0,795
Henriquez Miranda & Buelvas [1]	-	-	-	0,848
Martínez-Seis et al. [25]	-	-	-	0,796
SemEval-2016 - baseline	-	-	-	0,778
Solution proposal (RoBERTa + WW(size 5))	**0.836**	**0.864**	**0.848**	**0,866**

* Solutions submitted to SemEval-2016 Task 5 (results in Slot3: Sentiment Polarity) (Pontiki et al. [8])

5 Conclusions and Future Works

In this work, we explored the modeling capabilities of contextual embeddings from the pre-trained BERT on the Spanish aspect extraction and polarity classification task. Specifically, we examined the incorporation of the BERT embedding component with a simple linear classification layer, for aspect extraction and sentiment classification. Different experiments were performed on the only available Spanish dataset for this subtask proposed in Semeval2016 Task 5. The obtained results demonstrate that notwithstanding the simplicity of the model, with the utilization of language models with Transformer architecture surpasses the state-of-the-art for the Spanish language, this can be attributed to the ability of Transformer-based language models to obtain high-dimensional textual representations capable of capturing context.

In the future works, others Transformer-based language models will be evaluated in order to identifying the best model for both tasks. Based on this result, a new approach will be conceived which the same Transformer-based language model will be applied for both tasks.

Acknowledgments. This work has been partially supported by FEDER and the State Research Agency (AEI) of the Spanish Ministry of Economy and Competition under grant SAFER: PID2019-104735RB-C42 (AEI/FEDER, UE).

References

1. Miranda, C.H., Buelvas, E.: AspectSA: Unsupervised system for aspect-based sentiment analysis in Spanish. Prospectiva **17**, 87–95 (2019)
2. Mohammadreza, S., Khoshavi, N., Baraani-Dastjerdi, A.: Language-independent method for aspect-based sentiment analysis. IEEE Access **8**, 31034–31044 (2020)
3. García, S.R.: Minería de textos y análisis de sentimientos en sanidadysalud.com, Tesis de Master en Minería de Datos e Inteligencia de Negocios, Universidad Complutense de Madrid, Madrid (2016)
4. Aboelela, E.M., Gad, W., Ismail, R.: The impact of semantics on aspect level opinion mining. PeerJ Comput. Sci. **7**, e558 (2021)
5. Ambreen, N., Yuan, R., Wu, L., Ling, S.: Issues and challenges of aspect-based sentiment analysis: a comprehensive survey. IEEE Trans. Affect. Comput. **13**, 845–863 (2020)
6. Li, X., Bing, L., Zhang, W., Lam, W.: Exploiting BERT for end-to-end aspect-based sentiment analysis. In: Proceedings of the 5th Workshop on Noisy User-generated Text (W-NUT 2019), pp. 34–41 (2019)
7. Abdelgwad, M.M., Soliman, T.H.A., Taloba, A.I.: Arabic aspect sentiment polarity classification using BERT, arXiv:2107.13290v4 (2023)
8. Pontiki, M., Galanis, D., Papageorgiou, H., Androutsopoulos, I., Manandhar, S., Al-Smadi, M., et al.: Semeval-2016 task 5: aspect based sentiment analysis. In: Proceedings of the 10th International Workshop on Semantic Evaluation (SemEval-2016), pp. 19–30 (2016)
9. Liu, N., Shen, B., Zhang, Z., Zhang, Z., Mi, K.: Attention-based sentiment reasoner for aspect-based sentiment analysis. Hum.-Centric Comput. Inform. Sci. **9**, 1–17 (2019)
10. Karimi, A., Rossi, L., Prati, A.: Improving BERT performance for aspect-based sentiment analysis. In: Proceedings of the 4th International Conference on Natural Language and Speech Processing (ICNLSP 2021), pp. 39–46 (2021)
11. Minh Hieu, P., Ogunbona, P.O.: Modelling context and syntactical features for aspect-based sentiment analysis. In: Proceedings of the 58th Annual Meeting of the Association for Computational Linguistics, pp. 3211–3220 (2020)
12. López Ramos, D., Arco García, L.: Deep learning for aspect extraction in textual opinions. Revista Cubana de Ciencias Informáticas **13**(2), 105–145 (2019)
13. Liu, N., Shen, B., Zhang, Z., Zhang, Z., Mi, K.: Attention-based sentiment reasoner for aspect-based sentiment analysis. Hum.-Centric Comput. Inf. Sci. **9**, 35 (2019)
14. Jangid, H., Singhal, S., Rajiv Ratn, S., Zimmermann, R.: Aspect-based financial sentiment analysis using deep learning. In: Proceedings of WWW '18: Companion Proceedings of the The Web Conference 2018, pp. 1961–1966 (2018)

15. Peng, H., Xu, L., Bing, L., Huang, F., Lu, W., Si, L.: Knowing what, how and why: a near complete solution for aspect-based sentiment analysis. The Thirty-Fourth AAAI Conference on Artificial Intelligence (2020)
16. Mohammadi, A., Shaverizade, A.: Ensemble deep learning for aspect-based sentiment analysis. Int. J. Nonlinear Anal. Appl. **12**(Special Issue), 29–38 (2021)
17. Pathan, A.F., Prakash, Ch.: Cross-domain aspect detection and categorization using machine learning for aspect-based opinion mining. Int. J. Inf. Manag. Data Insights **2**(2), 100099 (2022)
18. Sivakumar, M., Uyyala, S.R.: Aspect-based sentiment analysis of mobile phone reviews using LSTM and fuzzy logic. Int. J. Data Sci. Analytics **12**, 355–367 (2021)
19. Afzaal, M., Usman, M., Fong, A.C.M., Fong, S., Zhuang, Y.: Fuzzy aspect based opinion classification system for mining tourist reviews. Adv. Fuzzy Syst. **2016**, 1–14 (2016)
20. Karimi, A., Rossi, L., Prati, A.: Improving BERT performance for aspect-based sentiment analysis. Int. J. Intell. Netw. (2021)
21. Abdelgwad, M.M., Soliman, T.H.A., Taloba, A.I.: Arabic aspect sentiment polarity classification using BERT. J. Big Data **9**, 115 (2022)
22. Pang, G., Lu, K., Zhu, X., He, J., Mo, Z., Peng, Z., et al.: Aspect-level sentiment analysis approach via bert and aspect feature location model. Wireless Commun. Mob. Comput. **2021**, 1–13 (2021)
23. Goodfellow, I., Bengio, Y., Courville, A.: Deep Learning. MIT Press (2016)
24. Rosa, J.d.l., Ponferrada, E.G., Villegas, P., González de Prado Salas, P., Romero, M., Grandury, M.: BERTIN: Efficient Pre-Training of a Spanish Language Model using Perplexity Sampling. arXiv:2207.06814 (2022)
25. Martínez-Seis, B.C., Pichardo-Lagunas, O., Miranda, S., Pérez-Cázares, I.-J., Rodríguez-González, J.-A.: Deep learning approach for aspect-based sentiment analysis of restaurants reviews in Spanish. Computación y Sistemas **26**(2), 899–908 (2022)

A Hybrid Approach for Spanish Emotion Recognition Applying Fuzzy Semantic Processing

Oscar M. González Parets[1](✉), Alfredo Simón-Cuevas[1], José A. Olivas[2], and José M. Perea-Ortega[3]

[1] Universidad Tecnológica de La Habana "José Antonio Echeverría", Havana, La Habana, Cuba
oscarmigo@tesla.cujae.edu.cu, asimon@ceis.cujae.edu.cu
[2] Universidad de Castilla-La Mancha, Ciudad Real, Spain
JoseAngel.olivas@uclm.es
[3] Universidad de Extremadura, Badajoz, Spain
jmperea@unex.es

Abstract. Emotion detection is a task in sentiment analysis that deals with the extraction and analysis of emotions in texts. Recognizing implicit emotions is one of the main challenges in keyword or lexicon-based approaches. This paper presents a hybrid emotion detection approach, which combines lexicon-based emotion-relevant feature selection with a classical learning approach to determine emotion. The proposed semantic feature selection process focuses on capturing the emotional meaning of the text by computing the semantic relationship between its content and the lexicon vocabulary using a fuzzy approach, with the goal of increasing implicit emotion recognition. The proposed solution was evaluated using AIT dataset used in SemEval-2018, obtaining better results than those obtained by other solutions reported.

Keywords: Emotion detection · semantic feature selection · machine learning · fuzzy aggregation operator

1 Introduction

Emotions are basic traits that characterize to the human beings and influence our actions, thoughts and, of course, our way of communicating. Despite not being considered strictly linguistic entities, emotions are expressed through language and, therefore, for several years they have been studied by researchers from different disciplines such as psychology, sociology, medicine, or computer science [1]. In recent years, the scientific community related to natural language processing has shown special interest in the automatic recognition of emotions in textual conversations, since its research can find several applications [2–4]. For example, in the field of customer service, social networks such as Twitter are gaining prominence and customers expect quick responses.

Y. Hernández Heredia et al. (Eds.): IWAIPR 2023, LNCS 14335, pp. 225–236, 2024.
https://doi.org/10.1007/978-3-031-49552-6_20

The automatic emotion detection task in texts grants an important challenge because it lacks the help that, in any visual communication, facial expressions and voice modulations provide. Moreover, the challenge of detecting emotions in a text is compounded by the difficulty of understanding some aspects related to communication, such as context, sarcasm, the ambiguity of natural language itself, or the growing jargon that is causing the massive use of instant messaging applications [5, 6]. In the literature there are several approaches to address this task. One of the most widely used is the rule-based approach [2, 7], which tries to exploit the use of keywords and their co-occurrence with other words that have a certain emotional or affective value associated with them. This value associated with certain words in the language is usually established from different existing lexical resources, some of which are well known, such as WordNet-Affect or SentiWordNet. For that reason, methods following this approach are also known as keyword-based or lexicon-based methods. More recently, approaches combining the use of lexicon with machine learning models are reported, which are recognized as hybrid approaches. Having a lexicon or keywords with a certain emotional or affective value allows determining with high efficiency the emotional state of texts, however, certain limitations are recognized in lexicon-based approaches that are related to the coverage of the textual content [8–10]. Processing vocabulary in a lexicon from a semantic perspective allows increasing its coverage to identify emotional features of a text, without the need to increase the size of the vocabulary. However, this semantic orientation of the use of lexicons, e. g. by computing underlying semantic relations between emotion words and the textual content to be processed, has been little exploited. Precisely, studies performed on solutions reported in the literature point out as limitations the non-use of semantic features in the detection of emotions in texts [11].

In this paper, a new method for emotion detection in texts is proposed, which is based on the combination of an emotion-oriented, lexicon-assisted semantic feature selection process with the application of supervised learning algorithms for emotion prediction. Our hypothesis focuses on the fact that if we manage to determine a good degree of emotional affinity of the feature of the opinion texts, we will achieve a more emotion-focused feature selection, which would mean a better learning process in the algorithm in charge of the classification. Therefore, the main novelty provided by this work is related to the proposed approach to capture the degree of semantic affinity between the opinion content and each of the vocabularies that characterize each emotion, which allows a selection of opinion features where the relevance analysis is more oriented to the problem domain (emotions), rather than to statistical aspects within the content, as is commonly adopted. Another contribution is the semantic approach proposed to deal with the vocabulary of the lexicon and its relation to the opinion text, which is based on combining several semantic relationship metrics through a fuzzy approach employed a compensatory aggregation. Our contribution provides a solution to the challenge of extending the coverage of this knowledge in the processing of textual content to classify and identify text features more relevant to predict emotion classes.

The remainder of the paper is structured as follows: the analysis of related works is presented in Sect. 2; Section 3 describe the proposed solution in details; Section 4 presents the results of the evaluation process and the corresponding analysis; and conclusions arrived and future works are given in Sect. 5.

2 Related Works

Different approaches to address the emotion detection task have been reported in the literature, being even classified into several categories by different researchers [8, 12–14]. The most generic classification is the one proposed in [12], which establishes two categories: those based on rules and those based on machine learning algorithms. The first category includes those methods that make use of lexical resources such as lexicons, bags of words and even ontologies. The second includes those methods that apply supervised algorithms based on linguistic features.

In rule-based approaches some methods exploit the use of keywords in texts and their co-occurrence with other keywords with explicit emotional/affective value [15]. For this purpose, several lexical resources such as WordNet-Affect [16] and SentiWordNet [17] for the English language are used. As for the availability of such resources in other languages, the number is very limited. For Spanish, the Spanish Emotion Lexicon (SEL) [18] and the Improved Spanish Opinion Lexicon (iSOL) [19] stand out. Other methods based on this approach also try to exploit the syntax of keywords by using POS taggers and, although they usually obtain good accuracy, they suffer from low (real) coverage because many texts do not contain affective words despite conveying emotions [13]. Most of the solutions presented in the well-known SemEval evaluation forum during the last years [3, 4], use affect lexicons and conclude that they are a very valuable source of information because they provide prior information about the type of emotion associated with each word. Moreover, in WASSA forum related to these tasks, it was also shown that the use of features from affect lexicons is useful for emotion mining tasks [3]. In this regard, Bandhakavi et al. [20] study the problem of emotion feature selection using domain-specific lexical resources and general-purpose emotion lexicons. Still, there are several recent reviews that highlight the limitations associated with the use of semantics found in these processes for detecting or classifying emotions in texts [8, 11].

In machine learning based approaches most methods rely on feature extraction, such as the presence of frequent n-grams, negation, punctuation, emoticons, hashtags, etc., to form a feature representation of the text which is then used as input by the classifiers to predict the output [21, 22]. These methods usually require an arduous feature selection process and do not achieve high coverage due to the various ways of representing emotions. Within these approaches, methods based on deep neural networks have been reported, which have had considerable success in various tasks applied to text, speech, and image. Variations of recurrent neural networks (RNN), such as LSTM and BiLSTM, have been effective in modeling sequential information. Meanwhile, the introduction of convolutional neural networks (CNNs) in the text domain has demonstrated their ability to classify emotion features [23]. Despite the good results, deep learning-based approaches present some disadvantages with respect to traditional learning models, which in some contexts may lead to discard their choice. Some of them are: demand for much larger amounts of well-labeled data for training, higher demands on computational capacity, and finally, their "black box" nature of operation, which does not allow an adequate understanding of the learning process [24].

The great success of traditional methods based on machine learning, together with the fact that lexical resources such as SEL provide very valuable information about the type of emotion associated with each word, has motivated us to test a combination of both approaches to detect emotions in order to conceived a hybrid approach. Based on the use of SEL, we propose to compute the semantic text-emotion relationship in order to achieve a more emotion-focused feature selection, which is supposed to result in a better learning of the classification algorithm.

3 Proposed Solution

This section describes the solution proposed in this work. First, the opinion texts are preprocessed and normalized. Next, the process of determining the emotional orientation of the texts is carried out, which consists of establishing a degree of affinity (semantic relationship) of each text with each emotion vocabulary in the SEL lexicon. Finally, the feature selection process is carried out, based on the degree of affinity obtained in the previous phase, which allows the generation of the feature vectors to be used by the supervised learning algorithm. The general workflow is presented in Fig. 1.

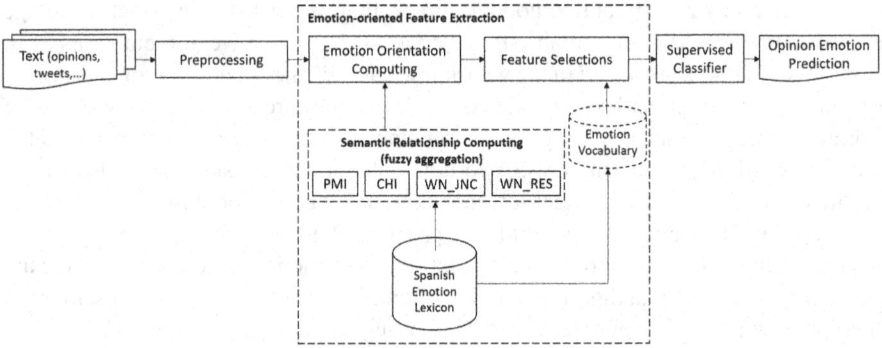

Fig. 1. Overview of the solution pipeline proposed.

3.1 Preprocessing

The unstructured nature of the texts, more so in the case of tweets and opinion texts, required the execution of preprocessing or normalization tasks. These tasks consisted of tokenizing the tweets using NLTK TweetTokenizer, converting all text to lowercase and removing stop words, punctuation marks and rare characters. No previous translation process was necessary because this tool supports working with Spanish texts.

3.2 Emotion Orientation Computing

3.2.1 Determining Emotional Orientation

In this task, the emotion affinity of the content includes in the opinion texts, according to the emotions vocabulary included in the lexicon is determined from a semantic processing approach. Specifically, the SEL lexicon is used, which contains a total of 2,036

Spanish words that are organized into 6 different emotions: anger, fear, sadness, joy, surprise, and disgust. Therefore, each emotion is represented through a vocabulary of terms, where each term is labeled with a PFA (Probability Factor of Affective) value [18]. Examples of words included in each category are: 'friendship', 'well-being', 'laughter', 'celebrate'.... (joy), 'angry', 'infuriated', 'enraged', 'wrath'.... (anger), 'creepy', 'phobia', 'fear', 'dread', 'terror'... (fear), 'disgusting', 'disgusting', 'fearful'... (fear), 'disgusting', 'loathsome', 'loathsome', filthy, disgusting... (disgust), 'disgusting', 'disgusting', 'disgusting', 'disgusting'... (repulsion), 'amazing', 'incredible', 'marvelous', 'perplexing'... (surprise), 'unhappy', 'unhappy', 'unbelievable', 'marvelous', 'perplexed'... (surprise), 'unhappy', 'mourning', 'grief', 'sorrow', 'lost'... (sadness). Determine the semantic affinity with the emotion allows to perform a more emotion-focused feature selection process (to the classification task), which is not possible when the frequency-based relevance models such as TF or TF-IDF is used, as was considered in Plaza.

The determination of the emotional affinity is based on the analysis of the semantic relationship between the content of the opinion texts and each emotion vocabulary of the lexicon. The semantic relationship between the opinion texts and the emotions in the lexicon is represented by an affinity matrix, which is constructed for each tweet or opinion to be processed. In this matrix, the rows identify each of the emotions in the SEL lexicon, and the columns identify the opinion words that constitute candidate features. The emotional orientation $EO(w_i, E_j)$ between each opinion word w_i and the emotion E_j in SEL lexicon, is calculated according to Eq. 1, where v_j is a term include in E_j vocabulary of SEL, and stored in the term-emotion intersection of the affinity matrix. This matrix forms the basis for the next phase (emotion-based feature selection) where the most relevant features (those most related to emotions) are selected.

$$EO(w_i, E_j) = \frac{\sum_{v_j \in E_j} sem\_rel(w_i, v_j)}{|E_j|} \tag{1}$$

In this process we consider and evaluates three approaches for computing opinion-emotion semantic relationship ($sem\_rel(w_i, v_j)$): (1) based on the corpus of opinions, and (2); based on an external semantic resource; (3) based on a fuzzy logic technique. Among the corpus-based measures that have been applied in the field of sentiment analysis are Pointwise Mutual Information (PMI) and chi-square (CHI), and in the case of the variant that relies on semantic resources, metrics based on WordNet [25] were used. Each of these measures offers advantages and disadvantages in their individual application, according to the strategy used in the computation of the semantic relationship between the terms, from which we hypothesize that if we combine these measures, we can achieve a more effective measurement process. In this sense, we propose to use fuzzy aggregation operators in this combination of measures.

3.2.2 Pointwise Mutual Information (PMI)

The PMI measure is derived from information theory and provides a formal way of modeling the mutual information between features (e. g. opinion words) and classes (e. g. emotions) [26]. In the field of text classification, this type of measures constitutes an alternative way to assess the relevance of potential text features with respect to specific classes. This pointwise mutual information between the word w_i and the emotion class E_j is defined on the basis of the cooccurrence between the words v_j of the emotion glossary E_j and the word w_i the opinion text (*coocurrence*(w_i, v_j)), and would be calculated according to Eq. 2, where *freq*(w_i) and *freq*(v_j) are de frequency of w_i and v_j, respectively. This approach is based on the assumption that affective words (included in the lexicon) that frequently cooccur with opinion words tend to be semantically related [27].

$$PMI(w_i, v_j) = \frac{cooccurrence(w_i, v_j)}{freq(w_i) * freq(v_j)} \tag{2}$$

3.2.3 Chi-Square (CHI)

The Chi-square (*CHI*(w_i, v_j)) statistical formula is related to feature selection functions which attempt to capture the best *K* terms for the class [28]. The CHI statistic measures the association between the term and the category and is defined by Eq. 3. In this Equation, *A* is the number of times the word w_i and the emotion word $v_j | v_j \in E_j$ appear in the same context; *B* is the number of times the w_i appears without v_j; *C* is given by the occurrence frequency of the words v_j; *D* is the number of times neither w_i nor v_j appears; *N* is the total number of comments.

$$CHI(w_i, v_j) = \frac{N * (A * D - C * B)^2}{(A + C) * (B + D) * (A + B) * (C + D)} \tag{3}$$

3.2.4 WordNet-Based Metrics

Unlike PMI, where the computation is based on the processing of text content alone, this type of measure exploits the topological structure formed by the synsets and their relations in WordNet, as an external semantic resource. Semantic relatedness is a concept that encompasses the relationship between two words, both by similarity between meanings and by contextual links (e. g. functional, association, part of, etc.) [29]. Several metrics have been defined to measure both types of relationships, the implementations of which are provided in the free software package WordNet::Similarity [26]. The availability of these metrics is an advantage, since different individual alternatives could be evaluated and also combined. However, it is recognized that the use of these metrics is limited by the fact that the words being compared are included in some synset in WordNet. In this approach, Resnik (WN_RES) and the JCN (WN_JCN) similarity metrics [30] are used for semantic relatedness assessment, then *rel_sem*(w_i, v_j) = *WN_RES*(w_i,v_j) and *rel_sem*(w_i, v_j) = *WN_JCN*(w_i, v_j), respectively.

3.2.5 Fuzzy-Based Semantic Relationship Measurement

In order to obtain a semantic relationship measure that representing the combination of the considered metrics, the compensatory aggregation function reported in [31] is applied, and defined as *fuzz_sem_agg*(e_1, e_2, ..., e_n) been $n = [1, 4]$ (see Eqs. 4–6). In these Equations, e_i represents the single obtained values of each i metrics PMI, CHI, WN_RES, and WN_JNC for measures de semantic relationship between w_i, v_j, γ is the degree of compensation provided and could be calculated according to Eq. 5 [32], and t-norm function $T(e_1,e_2,\ldots,e_n)$ that could be calculated according to Eq. 6, is applied to aggregate the numerical values (e_i).

$$fuzz\_sem\_agg(e_1, e_2, \ldots, e_n) = \left(\prod_{i=1}^{n} e_i\right)^{1-\gamma} * \left(1 - \prod_{i=1}^{n} (1 - e_i)\right)^{\gamma} \quad (4)$$

$$\gamma = \frac{T(e_1, e_2, \ldots, e_n)}{T(e_1, e_2, \ldots, e_n) + T(1 - e_1, \ldots, 1 - e_n)} \quad (5)$$

$$T(e_1, e_2, \ldots, e_n) = \prod_{i=1}^{n} e_i \quad (6)$$

3.3 Semantic Feature Selection

In this phase, the semantic features are selected based on the affinity matrix constructed in the previous phase and with the aim of generating the feature vectors that will be used by the supervised classifier. Initially, for each opinion Op_i a Semantic Affinity Degree ($SAD(Op_i, E_j)$) respect to each of emotion E_j is computed, according to Eq. 7. Then, the class of emotion with which the opinion has the highest affinity is selected, this being the one that yields the highest value of $SAD(Op_i, E_j)$. The emotion on which the highest affinity is expressed will determine which affective words that characterize the opinion.

$$SAD(Op_i, E_j) = \frac{\sum_{w_i \in Op_i} EO(w_i, E_j)}{|Op_i|} \quad (7)$$

After identifying the emotion E_j with the highest $SAD(Op_i, E_j)$, the affinity matrix of the opinion being processed is filtered, eliminating the rows corresponding to the remaining emotions. The feature vector of the opinion will be constructed with the words of the opinion that possess $EO(w_i, E_j) > 0$. In this approach, a feature selection process is achieved where the evaluation of its relevance takes more into account the semantics around the emotions, unlike other proposals where the fundamental weight of relevance is in frequency-based approaches [33]. This selection proposal favors the reduction of redundant features in the construction of feature vectors of opinion content, since the features are determined by a particular emotion. It also allows the reduction of non-informative (or uninformative) features that do not have a high discriminative power, due to irrelevance or redundancy with respect to the class (the same feature is relevant in different degrees for several classes). All this would be conducive to improving the results of lexicon-based emotion recognition.

After identifying the features of each opinion, we proceed to the last task for the construction of the opinion vector referring to the weighing the features. The weight value of each of the features should express its relevance degree, and as part of this work some weight alternatives were studied, such as $EO(w_i, E_j)$, as direct relevance of the feature

w_i in terms of the emotion that determined its selection; and the frequency of occurrence of that feature word within the corpus of opinions, since it is the most common alternative in supervised text classification solutions. However, partial experimental results showed that a binary model of vector representation obtained better results than these two alternatives, confirming what was reported in [34], where it is stated that, in the field of sentiment analysis, this type of model offers better results than the frequency-based one. In this sense, the binary representation model was adopted to construct the characteristic vector of the opinions, taking into account that the weight of a characteristic w_i has value 1 if $EO(w_i, E_j) \neq 0$, and 0 otherwise.

3.4 Emotion Prediction

After completing the semantic feature extraction phase, the constructed vectors of each opinion text pass to the supervised classifiers for predicting the emotion. In this approach, several machine learning algorithms were considered and evaluated, such as: Support sector Machine (SVM), Logistic Regression (LR), Multilayer Perceptron (MLP) and Naive Bayes (NB). It is important to note that these algorithms require training process, and from the magnitude and quality of the training data will be the quality of the results.

4 Experimental Results

The proposed solution was evaluated on the classification of four emotions (anger, fear, sadness, and joy) in tweets written in Spanish, using the AIT dataset used in SemEval-2018 Task 1: Affect in Tweets (subtask EI-oc) [3]. The experiments were performed applying SVM, LR, MLP and NB classification algorithms. The experiments performed were intended to evaluate the behavior of the four semantic relatedness measures PMI, CHI, WN_JNC, and WN_RES in an individual form, and the combination of them through the fuzzy semantic aggregation. The precision (P), recall (R), F-score (F1) and accuracy (Acc.) metrics were used for measuring the results, and the results of term frequency (TF)-based feature selection were adopted as baseline. Tables 1, 2, 3 and 4 shown the obtained results with each classifier, respectively. Table 5 shown a comparison between the best performing proposed solution and the state of the art, specifically, the reported in [33].

According the results, the semantic relatedness metrics PMI and CHI stand out with respect to the WordNet-based JCN and Resnik metrics, regardless of the classifier. Nevertheless, the results reflect the benefits of combining these metrics through a fuzzy aggregation operator, improving the semantic processing of the lexicon in the feature selection process. The best results are obtained when fuzzy aggregation is applied, regardless the classifier used, and the highest values are achieved when MLP is used, in both cases obtaining higher values than those reported in [33]. Compared to the results reported by Plaza, these experiments demonstrate the contribution of the semantic processing approach conceived for the use of the SEL lexicon in a hybrid approach for emotion detection. This comparison shows significant improvements in the results of the proposed solution.

Table 1. Results obtained with SVM classifier

Semantic feature extraction	Anger			Fear			Joy			Sadness			Acc
	P	R	F1	P	R	F1	P	R	F1	P	R	F1	
PMI	.76	.98	.86	**.90**	.86	.88	.96	.81	.88	.93	.85	.89	.88
CHI	.79	.98	**.88**	.90	.89	.89	.95	.82	.88	**.94**	**.86**	**.90**	**.89**
WN_JCN	.54	.95	.69	.83	.67	.74	.94	.63	.75	.86	.66	.75	.73
WN_RES	.54	.94	.69	.83	.68	.75	.93	.64	.76	.86	.65	.74	.73
fuzz_sem_agg	**.80**	**.98**	**.88**	**.90**	**.90**	**.90**	**.97**	**.83**	**.89**	**.94**	**.86**	**.90**	**.89**
baseline	*.33*	*.31*	*.31*	*.35*	*.28*	*.33*	*.36*	*.34*	*.38*	*.35*	*.31*	*.35*	*.34*

Table 2. Results obtained with the LR classifier

Semantic feature extraction	Anger			Fear			Joy			Sadness			Acc
	P	R	F1	P	R	F1	P	R	F1	P	R	F1	
PMI	.84	**.97**	.90	**.90**	.90	**.90**	**.95**	.84	**.89**	.92	**.89**	.90	**.90**
CHI	.85	.96	.90	**.90**	.90	**.90**	.94	.84	.89	.91	.88	.90	**.90**
WN_JCN	.52	.87	.65	.76	.62	.68	.83	.59	.69	.76	.60	.67	.67
WN_RES	.52	.87	.65	.76	.64	.69	.84	.60	.70	.76	.59	.66	.67
fuzz_sem_agg	**.86**	**.97**	**.91**	**.90**	**.91**	**.90**	.94	**.85**	**.89**	**.93**	**.89**	**.91**	**.90**
baseline	*.33*	*.35*	*.37*	*.35*	*.30*	*.35*	*.35*	*.36*	*.39*	*.34*	*.33*	*.35*	*.36*

Table 3. Results obtained with the MLP classifier

Semantic feature extraction	Anger			Fear			Joy			Sadness			Acc
	P	R	F1	P	R	F1	P	R	F1	P	R	F1	
PMI	.94	.99	.96	**.90**	.97	**.93**	**.98**	.87	.92	.98	**.96**	**.97**	**.95**
CHI	**.95**	**1**	**.97**	.89	**.98**	.93	**.98**	.87	.92	.98	**.96**	**.97**	**.95**
WN_JCN	.60	.93	.73	.85	.74	.79	.92	.69	.79	.89	.74	.81	.78
WN_RES	.60	.94	.73	.85	.74	.79	.91	.71	.80	.89	.71	.79	.77
fuzz_sem_agg	**.95**	.99	**.97**	**.90**	**.98**	**.93**	**.98**	**.88**	**.93**	**.99**	**.96**	**.97**	**.95**
baseline	*.24*	*.29*	*.26*	*.24*	*.26*	*.31*	*.35*	*.30*	*.33*	*.32*	*.29*	*.31*	*.31*

Table 4. Results obtained with the NB classifier

Semantic feature extraction	Anger			Fear			Joy			Sadness			Acc
	P	R	F1	P	R	F1	P	R	F1	P	R	F1	
PMI	.62	**1**	.77	**.90**	.55	.68	.85	**.62**	.72	**.70**	**.74**	**.72**	.73
CHI	.61	**1**	.76	.85	.63	.72	.97	.53	.69	.66	.72	.69	.72
WN_JCN	.41	.99	.58	.84	.39	.53	.96	.36	.53	.63	.46	.53	.55
WN_RES	.42	.99	.59	.86	.40	.55	.97	.35	.51	.59	.48	.53	.55
fuzz_sem_agg	**.64**	**1**	**.78**	.86	**.66**	**.75**	**.98**	.58	**.73**	.69	**.74**	**.72**	**.74**
baseline	*.28*	*.27*	*.25*	*.25*	*.26*	*.23*	*.33*	*.30*	*.34*	*.32*	*.25*	*.32*	*.30*

Table 5. Comparison with other work reported in the literature

Solutions		Anger			Fear			Joy			Sadness		
		P	R	F1	P	R	F1	P	R	F1	P	R	F1
Plaza et. al 2019 [33]	SVM (Acc: .76)	.78	.76	.77	.76	.68	.72	.73	.88	.80	.76	.68	.72
	NB (Acc: .69)	.62	.77	.69	.67	.68	.67	.84	.63	.72	.68	.68	.68
	MLP (Acc: .66)	.64	.66	.65	.62	.62	.62	.78	.72	.75	.59	.64	.62
Proposed solution: fuzz_sem_agg	MLP (Acc: **.95**)	**.95**	**.99**	**.97**	**.90**	**.98**	**.93**	**.98**	**.88**	**.93**	**.99**	**.96**	**.97**

5 Conclusions and Future Works

This paper addresses the task of emotion detection in texts using a hybrid approach, which combines a lexicon-based feature selection process with a classical machine learning approach. The novelty of the proposal les in the semantic approach proposed to capture the degree of affiniity between the opinion content and the vocabulary characterizing each emotion, so that an emotion-oriented feature selection in opinions is achieved that is more suitable for the target classification task. In the semantic analysis process, it was shown that the combination of semantic relation metrics through a fuzzy aggregation operator provided higher quality results. To evaluate the proposed solution, several experiments were conducted using the AIT corpus of emotions in Spanish tweets. In the experiments, different alternatives for calculating the degree of text-emotion semantic affinity were evaluated and several classification algorithms were tested. As a main conclusion, it is considered that the proposed approach is quite promising when it comes to perform a more appropriate feature selection, i.e., more focused on emotions, the good results obtained support this, being these superior to those obtained by other works of the state of the art.

As future work, other semantic relatedness metrics and aggregation operators will be evaluated, and we intend to extend this approach to train classification models that take into account other linguistic information from the opinion context such as, for example, negation. On the other hand, we will evaluate the combination of classifiers through classifier assembly architectures.

Acknowledgments. This work has been partially supported by FEDER and the State Research Agency (AEI) of the Spanish Ministry of Economy and Competition under grant SAFER: PID2019-104735RB-C42 (AEI/FEDER, UE) and the Regional Government of Extremadura (GR18135).

References

1. Ekman, P.: An argument for basic emotions. Cogn. Emot. **6**(34), 169–200 (1992)
2. Strapparava, C.: Emotions and NLP: future directions. In: Proceedings of NAACL-HLT 2016 (2016)
3. Mohammad, S.M., Bravo-Márquez, F., Salameh, M., Kiritchenko, S.: SemEval-2018 Task 1: affect in tweets. In: Proceedings of International Workshop on Semantic Evaluation (SemEval-2018), pp. 1–17. New Orleans, LA, USA. (2018)
4. Chatterjee, A., Narahari, K.N., Joshi, M., Agrawal, P.: SemEval-2019 Task 3: EmoContext contextual emotion detection in text. In: Proceedings of the 13th International Workshop on Semantic Evaluation, ACL, pp. 39–48 (2019)
5. Khan, M.T., Durrani, M., Ali, A., Inayat, I., Khalid, S., Khan, K.H.: Sentiment analysis and the complex natural language. Complex Adapt. Syst. Model. **4**(1), 1–19 (2016). https://doi.org/10.1186/s40294-016-0016-9
6. Shivhare, S.N., Khethawat, S.: Emotion detection from text. ArXiv abs/1205.4944 (2012) 371–377
7. Sykora, M.D., Jackson, T.W., O'Brien, A., Elayan, S.: Emotive ontology: extracting fine-grained emotions from terse, informal messages. In: Proceedings of the IADIS International Conference Intelligent Systems and Agents 2013 (2013)
8. Acheampong, F., Wenyu, C., NunooMensah, H.: Text-based emotion detection: advances, challenges, and opportunities. Eng. Rep. **2**(7), 1–24 (2020)
9. Chakriswaran, P., Vincent, D.R., Srinivasan, K., Sharma, V., Chang, C.-Y., Reina, D.G.: Emotion AI-driven sentiment analysis: a survey, future research directions, and open issues. Appl. Sci. **9**(24) (2019)
10. Hemmatian, F., Sohrabi, M.K.: A survey on classification techniques for opinion mining and sentiment analysis. Artif. Intell. Rev. **52**(3), 1495–1545 (2019)
11. Alswaidan, N., Menai, M.: A survey of state-of-the-art approaches for emotion recognition in text. Knowl. Inf. Syst. **62**(8), 2937–2987 (2020)
12. Cambria, E.: Affective computing and sentiment analysis. IEEE Intell. Syst. **31**(2), 102–107 (2016)
13. Gupta, U., Chatterjee, A., Srikanth, R., Agrawal, P.: A sentiment and semantic based approach for emotion detection in textual conversations. arXiv (2017)
14. Sailunaz, K., Dhaliwal, M., Rokne, J., Alhajj, R.: Emotion detection from text and speech: a survey. Soc. Netw. Anal. Min. **8**(1), 1–26 (2018)

15. Strapparava, C., Mihalcea, R.: Learning to identify emotions in text. In: Proceedings of the 2008 ACM Symposium on Applied Computing, pp. 1556–1560 (2008)
16. Strapparava, C., Valitutti, A.: WordNet-Affect: an affective extension of WordNet. In: Proceedings of the 4th International Conference on Language Resources and Evaluation, pp. 1083–1086 (2004)
17. Esuli, A., Sebastiani, F.: SentiWordNet: a publicly available lexical resource for opinion mining. In: Proceedings of LREC 2006, pp. 417–422 (2006)
18. Sidorov, G., et al.: Empirical study of opinion mining in Spanish tweets. LNAI **7629**, 1–14 (2012)
19. Molina-González, M.D., Martínez-Cámara, E., Martín-Valdivia, M.T., Perea Ortega, J.M.: Semantic orientation for polarity classification in Spanish reviews. Expert Syst. Appl. **40**(18), 7250–7257 (2013)
20. Bandhakavi, A., Wiratunga, N., Padmanabhan, D., Massie, S.: Lexicon based feature extraction for emotion text classification. Pattern Recogn. Lett. **93**, 133–142 (2017)
21. Canales, L., Martínez-Barco, P.: Emotion detection from text: a survey. In: Proceedings of the Workshop on Natural Language Processing in the 5th Information Systems Research Working Days (JISIC), ACL, pp. 37–43 (2014)
22. Liew, J.S.Y., Turtle, H.R.: Exploring fine-grained emotion detection in tweets. In: Proceedings of the NAACL Student Research Workshop, pp. 73–80 (2016)
23. Mundra, S., Sen, A., Sinha, M., Mannarswamy, S., Dandapat, S., Roy, S.: Fine grained emotion detection in contact center chat utterances. Lect. Notes Comput. Sci. **10235**, 337–349 (2017)
24. Kowsari, K., Jafari Meimandi, K., Heidarysafa, M., Mendu, S., Barnes, L., Brown, D.: Text classification algorithms: a survey. Information **10**(4) (2019)
25. Pedersen, T., Patwardhan, S., Michelizzi, J.: WordNet::Similarity – measuring the relatedness of concepts. In: Proceedings of the National Conference on Artificial Intelligence, pp. 1024–1025 (2004)
26. Aggarwal, C.C.: Mining text data. In: Data Mining, pp. 429–455. Springer, Cham (2015). https://doi.org/10.1007/978-3-319-14142-8_13
27. Agrawal, A., An, A.: Unsupervised emotion detection from text using semantic and syntactic relations. In: Proceedings of the 2012 IEEE/WIC/ACM International Conference on Web Intelligence, pp. 346–353 (2012)
28. Bahassine, S., Madani, A., Al-Sarem, M., Kissi, M.: Feature selection using an improved Chi-square for Arabic text classification. J. King Saud Univ. – Comput. Inf. Sci. **32**(2), 225–231 (2020)
29. Budanitsky, A., Hirst, G.: Evaluating WordNet-based measures of lexical semantic relatedness. Comput. Linguist. **32**(1), 13–47 (2006)
30. Jiang, J.J., Conrath, D.W.: Semantic similarity based on corpus statistics and lexical taxonomy. In: Proceedings of the 10th Research on Computational Linguistics International Conference, pp. 19–33 (1997)
31. Zimmermann, H.J., Zysno, P.: Latent connectives in human decision making. Fuzzy Sets Syst. **4**(1), 37–51 (1980)
32. Yager, R.R., Rybalov, A.: Full reinforcement operators in aggregation techniques. IEEE Trans. Syst. Man Cybern. B Cybern. **28**(6), 757–769 (1998)
33. Plaza-del Arco, F.M., Martín-Valdivia, M.T., Ureña-López, L.A., Mitkov, R.: Improved emotion recognition in Spanish social media through incorporation of lexical knowledge. Futur. Gener. Comput. Syst. **110**, 1000–1008 (2020)
34. Agarwal, B., Mittal, N.: Prominent feature extraction for sentiment analysis. Prominent Feature Extraction for Sentiment Analysis (2016) 21–45

A Knowledge-Based User Feedback Classification Approach for Software Support

Vladimir Milián Núñez[1(✉)], Thalía Blanco Martín[2], Alfredo Simón-Cuevas[2(✉)], Héctor González Diéz[1], and Anaisa Hernández González[2]

[1] Universidad de Las Ciencias Informáticas (UCI), Havana, La Habana, Cuba
{vmilian,hglez}@uci.cu
[2] Universidad Tecnológica de La Habana "José Antonio Echeverría", Havana, La Habana, Cuba
{tblanco,asimon,anaisa}@ceis.cujae.edu.cu

Abstract. The analysis of the textual content of user opinions on social networks about software applications in use can provide valuable information to the development and support teams, in terms of errors, dissatisfactions, new functional requirements, among others. The paper presents a solution based on intelligent technologies to automatically classify whether or not the content of a review is relevant to a software support team. This solution combines machine learning algorithms, with the use of a domain-specific glossary for feature selection, in predicting the relevance of reviews. The proposed solution was evaluated experimentally with three datasets, specifically Facebook, Tapfish and SwiftKey, and the results obtained were very promising.

Keywords: Opinion mining · text classification · machine learning · natural language processing

1 Introduction

The role of Requirements Engineering (IR) in software development requires the analyst team to make the sources for requirements extraction as rich in information as possible. Currently, there is a high accumulation of relevant content, described in natural language of interest to IR, such as user comments in application stores, social networks, discussion forums, version control systems, error tracking, among others [19]. On the other hand, recent advances in IR methods have seen an increase in the use of machine learning algorithms to solve different problems. This has led to a growing interest in the use of Natural Language Processing (NLP) techniques combined with the analysis of large volumes of data and machine learning (ML) techniques, to extract useful information for IR, which is known as data-driven IR [11, 17]. Thus, the problem posed in this paper arises: How to determine whether the content of a user opinion is relevant or not for software development support?

The analysis of user opinions on social networks about a software in use allows to identify which new feature should be included in the next version of the product, which functionalities to avoid or improve, as well as the errors present in the applications [6, 7,

Y. Hernández Heredia et al. (Eds.): IWAIPR 2023, LNCS 14335, pp. 237–247, 2024.
https://doi.org/10.1007/978-3-031-49552-6_21

16, 23]. It is important to note that the unstructured nature of the textual content of the opinions requires the use of NLP tools for their standardization and subsequent analysis. During this analysis process, the authors [19] recommend filtering out those opinions that are irrelevant or do not contribute to the improvement of application requirements. This first step is essential, as it represents approximately 70% of the opinions expressed by users. Other studies show encouraging results in similar filtering processes when using domain knowledge, as reported in [10].

In this paper, we propose a method for the automatic classification of user opinions according to whether their content is relevant (informative) or not for a development or software support team. The proposed workflow combines the potential of machine learning technologies in solving requirements engineering problems with the use of a glossary of domain-specific terms to improve efficiency in selecting relevant features in reviews. The glossary of terms used was constructed from what was reported in ISO/IEC/IEEE of 2017 [13]. The proposed method was evaluated experimentally using the Facebook, Tapfish, and SwiftKey datasets, and Precision, Recall, F1-Score, and Accuracy metrics, with 5 classification algorithms: SVM, NB, MLP, LR and k-NN. The results obtained were compared with several approaches, the most commonly used, which do not use external knowledge to select characteristics (BoW, TF-IDF and n-gram), as well as those reported in other works in the literature, and the analysis of them led to very promising conclusions.

2 Automatic Classification of Textual Content

The unstructured nature of texts, even more so in the case of opinion texts, requires the execution of preprocessing or standardization tasks. It is one of the most important phases, where it is about eliminating the noise of the data that is held in the input opinions. Initially opinions are segmented into sentences, since, within an opinion, some sentences may be "relevant" and others may not. This level of granularity can help more accurately distinguish "relevant" information and non-relevant information or "noise" [19].

Natural Language Processing (NLP) is an automatic translation of natural language such as speeches, texts, with the help of software. Mostly all documents can be written in the form of natural language, therefore, the analysis and processing of that data on a computer will be done with the help of natural language techniques. Several natural language techniques are present in aiding in data processing, such as text mining, tokenization, lemmatization, or semantic analysis [20].

2.1 Machine Learning Algorithms

Supervised learning is a technique for inferring a function from training data. The training data consists of input data and expected output. The objective of this learning is to create a function capable of predicting the value corresponding to any input object after having seen examples (the training data). That is, supervised learning pursues the objective of obtaining a result from a data input after having been trained with data from which the expected output is already known. Solutions that involve working with supervised learning are developed in two phases: Training and Testing.

Supervised or predictive algorithms predict the value of an attribute (label) of a dataset, known other attributes (descriptive attributes). From data whose labels are known, a relationship is induced between that tag and another set of attributes. These relationships are used to predict data whose label is unknown.

2.2 Feature Extraction Techniques

Machine learning algorithms operate in a space of numerical features, expecting a two-dimensional array as input where rows are instance and columns are featured. To perform machine learning on text, you need to transform instances, documents, into vector representations so that numerical machine learning can be applied. The process of encoding texts in a numerical vector space is known as feature extraction, or simply, vectorization, and is an essential first step in text analysis [3].

Among the techniques used in the research are Bag of Words (BoW), Term frequency – Inverse document frequency (TF IDF), N-Grams, Pointwise Mutual Information (PMI) and one based on the occurrence of the word that will be explained later in the article.

2.3 Analysis of Related Works

Supervised learning is one where you try to learn from examples as if they were a teacher. It is assumed that each of these examples includes characteristics that define which category or class it belongs to, from a set of predefined categories or classes, in this way each example is associated with its class. This type of learning is called supervised by the presence of the examples to guide the learning process. The set of examples from which you are trying to learn is called a training set [2].

The study [19] proposes a supervised learning solution for the prediction of requirement categories using the Functional, Error or Other categories. The results are analyzed with the Facebook and Tapfish datasets for the BoW, TF-IDF and N-Grams feature extraction techniques. Of the algorithms proposed by the study, greater precision is observed in the data with the ExtraTrees algorithm. Kurtanović et al. [15] classify needs into Functional Requirements (FR), Non- Functional Requirements (NFRs) and non-functional requirements categories using the Support Vector Machine technique. The authors employed the PROMISE repository, which is known to have a set of functional and non-functional criteria. User feedback on Amazon items was incorporated into the main dataset to help balance the database. As a feature extraction technique, it uses N-G rams.

Another study [21] uses Support Vector Machine to offer an automated approach to the categorization requirement. The authors used two Mercedes-Benz vehicle specifications to test machine learning. The findings of this study demonstrated that automated categorization of requirements is significant and provides a satisfactory degree of Accuracy. As a feature extraction technique, it uses N-G rams.

Jindal et al. [14] used a single machine learning method to perform an automated analysis of the multiple specifications needed from a software in the PROMISE repository and introduce binary categorization into various types of security requirement categories (decision tree). Tokenization, lemmatization and elimination of empty words were used as preprocessing techniques, while vectorization was performed using TF-IDF. The authors [1] propose a solution for the classification of functional and non-functional requirements from a dataset built from different sources, which is analyzed after the preprocessing and feature extraction phase by the Logistic Regression and Multinomial Naive Bayes classifiers.

Semi-supervised learning is the combination of supervised and unsupervised learning. In this one you learn with the help of two sets. One that contains data associated with a class, and the other that contains data not associated with a class. The idea is to learn with the data associated with your class and associate a class with the data that does not contain a class associated [2]. To classify NFRs automatically, a semi-supervised automated technique was used. The authors of the study [5] aimed to assist requirements analyzers in categorizing requirements. Getting started, the requirements analysis team selected and ranked a collection of requirements to serve as the training set of the system. After that, the machine was able to identify the remaining unclassified needs. Using a common set of requirements documents, the authors employed some supervised machine learning methods. Vectorization was performed using TF-IDF. The study [2] proposes a semi-supervised method for the classification of textual content. It uses BoW and N-G rams vector models and classifiers such as Naive Bayes, k-nn and SVM. For the evaluation of the proposed solution, the dataset proposed in [22].

The prediction model proposed by Malhotra and Khanna [18] uses hybrid search-based techniques. This study analyzes and compares the predictive performance of five hybrid search-based techniques and four machine learning techniques, as well as a statistical technique for predicting change-prone classes in six Android operating system application packages.

The work [10] proposes a hybrid method for the analysis of opinions. Their solution includes the use of n-grams for feature extraction, and linear classifiers, SVM, regression and neural networks. For the evaluation of his study, he used the AIT SemEval 2018 and TASS 2020 datasets. The research carried out by [24] proposes a hybrid solution for text classification using the n-grams technique for feature extraction. The evaluation of the proposed solution was made with the Reuters-21578 collection and classifiers such as k-nNN.

3 Proposed Solution

The solution is proposed for the prediction of the software domain relevance of user opinions in social networks, using a supervised, domain-specific knowledge-driven classification approach. Figure 1 shows the overall workflow of the proposed solution.

3.1 Pre-processing

The unstructured nature of texts, especially in the case of opinion texts, requires the implementation of pre-processing or standardization procedures. It is one of the most important phases, where it is about eliminating the noise of the data that is held in the input opinions. Initially opinions are segmented into sentences, since, within an opinion, some sentences may be "relevant" and others may not. This level of granularity can help more accurately distinguish "relevant" information and non-relevant information. Subsequently, on each sentence, a process of word selection or tokenization is carried out and all the text is converted to lowercase. Before continuing, a process of expansion of contractions is carried out and subsequently the stop-words are eliminated, as well as tags, punctuation marks, and rare characters. Finally, a process of lemmatization is carried out on each of the extracted tokens and those opinions that after the described process remain with no tokens left are eliminated.

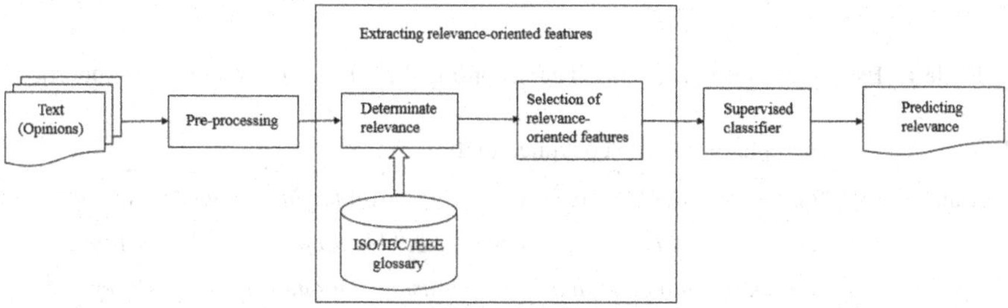

Fig. 1. Workflow of the proposed solution

3.2 Extracting Relevance-Oriented Features

An approach based on the occurrence of the word is proposed, which consists of establishing a comparison between each of the words of the opinion with those that are collected in the proposed thesaurus. In this way, if a correspondence is established between the words, either a total or partial coincidence, this word is considered a characteristic of relevance within the opinion. A full match between words occurs when the opinion word is inside the glossary, for example: install (opinion word) – install (glossary word). However, a partial match occurs when a portion of the opinion word corresponds to the word in the glossary, for example: installing (opinion word) – install (glossary word).

The binary representation model was adopted to construct the characteristic vector of opinions, taking into account that the weight of a characteristic w_i has value 1 if the value of the semantic relationship calculated was greater than 0, and value 0 otherwise as proposed by the study [10]. It is considered with this representation that the relevant characteristics are those with weight 1. The characteristic vector is then represented in the form of a Python dictionary list, where each review is a dictionary that counts its words or tokens as keys and its value (0 or 1) as an item. For example, a review: ['takes', 'forever', 'load', 'photos'] as a vector would be expressed: 'takes': 0, 'forever': 0, 'load': 1, 'photos': 0, where there is only one relevance feature.

The domain-specific glossary used is constructed from the vocabulary reported in [13], gathering 3176 terms from the software domain. Among them are acronyms, simple and compound terms that reach a length of up to 2 words. Not only those proposed as terms, but also part of those exposed as meaning in the ISO/IEC/IEEE vocabulary [13] taken as a basis were included as terms in the glossary.

3.3 Predicting Relevance

After completing the characteristic extraction stage, the constructed vectors pass to the supervised classifiers that will determine the relevance. A review is considered Relevant when it contains information that could be related to the Software domain, and not otherwise relevant. See Table 1 The solution uses for the prediction of relevance a total of 58 algorithms proposed in the solution [19]. Among them are: k-NN, Logistic Regression (LR), Naive Bayes (NB), Multi-Layer Perceptron (MLP) and Support Vector Machine (SVM), which were selected for this work.

Table 1. Examples of opinions classified according the relevance for software support.

Class	Example of opinion contained in datasets
Relevant	*"i hate that i cant change my cover photo on the app" (from Facebook)*
	"great game, but too many repetitive bubble tip pop-ups." (from Tapfish)
	"I think it could do with a bit more customization..." (from SwiftKey)
Not relevant	*"facebook needs some major work!" (from Facebook)*
	"fun game to play" (from Tapfish)
	"It is the best thing I ever payed for on the play store." (from SwiftKey)

4 Results and Discussion

The evaluation of the proposed solution is carried out experimentally using the Facebook (social app), Tapfish (casual game), and SwiftKey (smart touchscreen keyboard app) datasets [6], which characterizations is shown in Table 2. These datasets collects the raw user reviews of these 3 apps from Google Play roughly in the period from Oct, 2012 to Feb, 2013 [6]. The following 5 classification algorithms were selected for analysis: SVM, NB, MLP, LR and k-NN. In the experiments was proposed an approach based on the use of the glossary in the selection of characteristics with the non-use of glossary, considering in the latter three alternatives of selection of characteristics: BoW, TF-IDF and n-gram. Results were measured using the metrics Precision (Eq. 1), Recall (Eq. 2), F1-Score (Eq. 3) and Accuracy (Eq. 4). These metrics are computed by comparing the predictions obtained by the proposed classification method, with the correct results included in the dataset [8]. Cross-validation is applied in 5 rounds.

$$\text{Precision} = \frac{TP}{TP + FP} \tag{1}$$

$$\text{Recall} = \frac{TP}{TP + FN} \tag{2}$$

$$\text{F1 - score} = \frac{2TP}{2TP + FP + FN} \tag{3}$$

Table 2. Characterization of datasets.

	Facebook	Tapfish	SwiftKey
Relevant	1661	710	862
Not relevant	1330	1865	2054
% Relevant	55.5%	27.6%	29.6%
Total	2991	2575	2916

$$\text{Accuracy} = \frac{TP + TN}{TP + FP + TN + FN} \quad (4)$$

It is defined as true positives (TP) all those opinions have been classified as relevant and are. Then false positives (FP), are those opinions that have been classified as relevant, but are not. True negatives (TN) are opinions that the system determines are not relevant and actually are and false negatives (FN) are all those classified as not relevant, but are actually relevant.

4.1 Deployment Technologies

The proposed solution is implemented using Python as programming language, whose elegant Python syntax and dynamic typing, together with its interpreted nature make it an ideal language for scripting and rapid application development in many areas, for most platforms [9]. There are a lot of libraries available for use in Python, which is why Scikitlearn [12], one of the most widely used and popular free use machine learning libraries today for machine learning, was selected. NLTK (Natural Language Toolkit) was used as a library for Natural Language Processing, which is a platform for creating Python programs for text analysis. As it was created for educational purposes in 2001, it allows the realization of projects with different purposes and varied scope. It provides step-by-step demonstrations of different algorithms [4].

4.2 Experimental Results

The experimental results obtained in Tables 3, 4, 5 and 6 are presented below. The highest values obtained from the metrics are highlighted in bold, and associated with each of them is the average value to check their behavior regardless of the classifier used. Table 7 includes the comparison of the proposed solution with those obtained by other work reported in the literature; the only one identified so far with which to compare. Finally, the results will be analyzed according to the Accuracy measure (Table 6). The experiment included the use of five learning algorithms which are classics in this field, and commonly used in this type of comparisons, namely: SVM, Naive Bayes (NB), MLP, Logistic Regression (LR), and k-NN.

The analysis of Tables 3, 4 and 5 shows that the results obtained by the proposed solution when using glossary, for the F1-score measure are superior, which represents an improvement in the quality of the selection of characteristics. In addition, this solution

Table 3. Results obtained with the Facebook dataset.

Learning algorithms	Feature selection without using ISO/IEC/IEEE GLOSSARY									Using ISO/IEC/IEEE GLOSSARY		
	BoW			TF-IDF			N-Grams					
	Prec	Rec	F1	Prec	Rec	F1	Prec	Rec	F1	Prec	Rec	F1
SVM	.883	.909	.896	.865	.921	.892	.867	.443	.587	**.891**	**.925**	**.908**
NB	.91	.842	.874	**.93**	.804	.862	.864	.488	.57	.906	**.865**	**.885**
MLP	.874	.913	.893	.856	.875	.866	.676	.894	.77	**.875**	**.925**	**.9**
LR	**.859**	.939	.897	**.859**	.917	.887	.838	.372	.515	**.859**	**.940**	**.898**
k-NN	.728	.917	.811	**.79**	.823	.806	.463	**1**	.633	.737	.917	**.817**
Ave	.851	.904	.874	**.860**	.868	.863	.742	.639	.615	.854	**.914**	**.882**

Table 4. Results obtained with the Tapfish dataset.

Learning algorithms	Feature selection without using ISO/IEC/IEEE GLOSSARY									Using ISO/IEC/IEEE GLOSSARY		
	BoW			TF-IDF			N-Grams					
	Prec	Rec	F1	Prec	Rec	F1	Prec	Rec	F1	Prec	Rec	F1
SVM	**.889**	.967	**.926**	.858	.978	.914	.768	**.989**	.865	**.889**	.962	.924
NB	**.914**	.86	.886	.846	.978	.907	.784	**.997**	.878	.906	.925	**.917**
MLP	.892	.932	.912	.883	.932	.907	.812	**.989**	.892	**.902**	.938	**.922**
LR	**.887**	.951	**.918**	.839	.983	.906	.758	**.991**	.859	.867	.960	.911
k-NN	.8	.989	.884	.86	.957	**.906**	.728	**1**	.842	.794	.989	.881
Ave	**.876**	.940	.905	.857	.966	.908	.770	**.993**	.867	.872	.955	**.911**

offers a better and more balanced balance between Precision and Recall, which is a desired behavior in text classification solutions. Table 6 also shows the improvement in efficiency with the use of the glossary, since regardless of the classifier used, the average Accuracy values are higher for the three datasets. Taking into account that both metrics synthesize a general behavior of the solutions, it is possible to establish that the results demonstrate that the use of glossary is promising. Finally, as shown in Table 7, the values obtained with the proposed solution are higher than those reported by Chen et al. [6], and in two datasets the difference between the results stands out.

Table 5. Results obtained with the SwiftKey dataset.

Learning algorithms	Feature selection without using ISO/IEC/IEEE GLOSSARY									Using ISO/IEC/IEEE GLOSSARY		
	BoW			TF-IDF			N-Grams					
	Prec	Rec	F1	Prec	Rec	F1	Prec	Rec	F1	Prec	Rec	F1
SVM	.845	.948	.894	.815	.98	.89	.719	**1**	.837	**.847**	.944	**.899**
NB	**.912**	.883	.897	.797	.985	.881	.721	**.997**	.837	.894	.922	**.908**
MLP	**.868**	.929	**.897**	.861	.919	.889	.78	**.953**	.858	.865	.934	.831
LR	.865	.951	**.906**	.798	.98	.879	.712	**1**	.831	**.849**	.956	**.906**
k-NN	.737	**.992**	.846	**.802**	.968	.877	.703	**1**	.826	.739	**.99**	.896
Ave	***.845***	*.941*	***.888***	*.815*	*.966*	*.883*	*.727*	***.990***	*.838*	*.839*	*.949*	***.888***

Table 6. Results obtained for the Accuracy measure.

Learning algorithms	Feature selection without using ISO/IEC/IEEE GLOSSARY									Using ISO/IEC/IEEE GLOSSARY		
	BoW			F-IDF			N-Grams					
	FB	TP	CS	FB	TP	CS	FB	TP	CS	FB	TP	CS
SVM	.906	**.889**	**.842**	.901	.867	.83	.722	.776	.726	**.917**	.885	.841
NB	.893	.840	.857	.886	.8	.813	.672	.8	.727	**.9**	**.876**	**.868**
MLP	.903	.869	**.851**	.879	.862	.839	.762	.827	.779	**.908**	**.882**	**.851**
LR	.904	**.877**	**.861**	.896	.852	.811	.689	.765	.715	**.905**	.864	.849
k-NN	.811	.813	.746	.824	**.856**	.809	.485	.730	.703	**.818**	.806	**.747**
Ave	*.883*	*.858*	*.831*	*.877*	*.847*	*.820*	*.666*	*.780*	*.730*	***.890***	***.863***	***.831***

Table 7. Comparison with results of related works reported, from F1-score measure

Solutions	SwiftKey	Facebook	Tapfish
Chen et al. [6]	0.764	0.877	0.761
Proposed solution	**0.888**	**0.882**	**0.911**

5 Conclusions

The present work proposes a solution for the prediction of the relevance of textual content incorporating the use of external knowledge in the form of a glossary. This solution uses as a characteristic extraction technique an experimental approach based on the occurrence of the words of the glossary within the opinion. The prediction stage is carried out with 58 supervised learning algorithms. The preliminary results are presented after an evaluation of the solution with the datasets: Facebook, Tapfish and SwiftKey, which allow corroborating the accuracy of the results according to the four computed metrics: Precision, Recall, F1-score and Accuracy. For the analysis, five of which obtained the most promising results were selected from the total algorithms used in the solution.

The analysis of the data shows that on average better results are obtained with the incorporation of external knowledge. The highest value of Precision is obtained with the TF-IDF feature extraction technique, for the Recall measurement it is achieved with the n-grams technique, techniques that do not use glossary. However, the F1-score and Accuracy measures both reach their highest value with the technique proposed using the glossary. The classifier algorithm that reports the best results according to the four metrics and the three datasets is SVM, followed by MLP.

For future work, it is proposed to include in the selection of characteristics the evaluation of the semantic relationship between the words of the glossary and the opinion using metrics such as Pointwise Mutual Information (PMI). Likewise, it is proposed to include in the same phase the use of N-grams that allows to cover more information within the glossary and the analysis of the slogan of the words.

References

1. Abdulmunim, A., Younis, Y.S.: Supporting classification of software requirements system using intelligent technologies algorithms. Technium **3**(11), 32–39 (2021)
2. Araujo Arredondo, N.P.: Método Semisupervisado para la Clasificación Automática de Textos de Opinión. Tesis de Maestría en Ciencias Computacionales, INAOE (2009)
3. Bengfort, B., Bilbro, R., Ojeda, T.: Applied Text Analysis with Python: Enabling Language-Aware Data Products with Machine Learning. O'Reilly Media (2018)
4. Bird, S.: Nltk: the natural language toolkit. In: Proceedings of the COLING/ACL on Interactive Presentation Sessions,pp. 69–72 (2006)
5. Casamayor, A., Godoy, D., Campo, M.: Identification of non-functional requirements in textual specifications: a semi-supervised learning approach. Inf. Softw. Technol. **52**(4), 436–445 (2010)
6. Chen, N., Lin, J., Hoi, S.C., Xiao, X., Zhang, B.: Ar-miner: mining informative reviews for developers from mobile app marketplace. In: Proceedings of the 36th International Conference on Software Engineering, pp. 767–778. Hyderabad, India (2014)
7. Ciurumelea, A., Schaufelbühl, A., Panichella, S., Gall, H.C.: Analyzing reviews and code of mobile apps for better release planning. In: 2017 IEEE 24th International Conference on Software Analysis, Evolution and Reengineering (SANER), pp. 91–102. Klagenfurt, Austria (2017)
8. Dias Canedo, E., Cordeiro Mendes, B.: Software requirements classification using machine learning algorithms. Entropy 1057 **22**(9), 1–20 (2020)
9. Foundation, P.S.: Python 3.11.1 documentation, April (2023)
10. González Guerra, P.S.: Hybrid method of emotion detection with semantic approach in feature selection (2021)
11. Groen, E.C., Doerr, J., Adam, S.: Towards crowd-based requirements engineering a research preview. In: Requirements Engineering: Foundation for Software Quality: 21st International Working Conference, REFSQ 2015, pp. 247–253. Essen, Germany (2015)

12. Hao, J., Ho, T.K.: Machine learning made easy: a review of scikit-learn package in python programming language. J. Educ. Behav. Stat. **44**(3), 348–361 (2019)
13. ISO/IEC/IEEE. International standard. Systems and software engineering — vocabulary (2017)
14. Jindal, R.R., Malhotra, R., Jain, A.: Automated classification of security requirements. In: 2016 International Conference on Advances in Computing, Communications and Informatics (ICACCI), pp. 2027–2033. Jaipur, India, (2016)
15. Kurtanovićand, Z., Maalej, W.: Automatically classifying functional and non-functional requirements using supervised machine learning. In: 2017 IEEE 25th International Requirements Engineering Conference (RE), pp. 490–495. Lisbon, Portugal (2017)
16. Maalej, W., Nabil, H.: Bug report, feature request, or simply praise? on automatically classifying app review. In: 2015 IEEE 23rd International Requirements Engineering Conference (RE), pp. 116–125. Ottawa, Canada (2015)
17. Maalej, W., Nayebi, M., Johann, T., Ruhe, G.: Toward data-driven requirements engineering. IEEE Softw. **33**(1), 48–54 (2015)
18. Malhotra, R., Khanna, M.: An exploratory study for software change prediction in object oriented systems using hybridized techniques. Autom. Softw. Eng. **24**, 673–717 (2017)
19. Milián Núñez, V., González Diez, H., Simón Cuevas, A.: Predicting the evolution of software requirements based on user reviews. In: 6th International Conference on Computer Science (CICCI' 2022), Proceedings of 18th International Convention and Fair INFORMATICA 2022, Havana, Cuba (2022)
20. Nagpalnjm, M.D., Kalia, A.: A comprehensive analysis of requirement engineering utilizing machine learning techniques. Design Engineering 2662–2678 (2021)
21. Ott, D.: Automatic requirement categorization of large natural language specifications at mercedes-benz for review improvements". In: Requirements Engineering: Foundation for Software Quality: 19th International Working Conference, REFSQ 2013, pp. 50–64. Essen, Germany (2013)
22. Pang, Lee, L.: Seeing stars: exploiting class relationships for sentiment categorization with respect to rating scales. In: Proceedings of the 43rd Annual Meeting of the Association for Computational Linguistics (ACL'05), pp. 115–124 (2005)
23. Villarroel, L., Bavota Russo, G.B., Oliveto, R., di Penta, M.: Release planning of mobile apps based on user reviews. In: Proceedings of the 38th International Conference on Software Engineering, pp. 14–24. Austin, USA (2016)
24. Villena Román, J., Collada Pérez, S., Lana Serrano, S., González Cristóbal, J.C.: Hybrid method for categorization of text based on learning and rules. Nat. Lang. Process. **46**, 35–43 (2011)

A Metaphorical Text Classifier to Compare the Use of RoBERTa-Large, RoBERTa-Base and BERT-Base Uncased

Ericka Ovando-Becerril(✉) and Hiram Calvo

Centro de Investigación en Computación del IPN, Laboratorio de Ciencias Cognitivas Computacionales, Av. Juan de Dios Bátiz S/N, 07738 Ciudad de México, CDMX, Mexico
erid.ovando@gmail.com

Abstract. This work presents a literal and metaphorical language classifier for the Trofi corpus (Gao G. et al. 2018), through LSTM cells, comparing the results for the use of three pretrained language models RoBERTa-large, RoBERTa-base and BERT-base uncased. Through this article, it is proposed to address three fundamental points of the study of metaphorical language: the different tools for its vectorial representation, the use of LSTM cells to work metaphorical language and the impotence of the central task presented, its classification. Finally the results are compared against the state of the art and that work presents some observations as a conclusion.

Keywords: Classifier · BERT · Language models · LSTM · RoBERTa

1 Introduction

The relevance of metaphorical language in the field of computational linguistics has been increasing. Considering the relevance of metaphorical expressions in everyday use, and their fundamental linguistic and cognitive human processes that are carried out naturally, this offers new perspectives for addressing the issue, specifically one area of focus is the classification of metaphorical text.

The phrases "life as a journey", "marriage as slavery", and even "the human body as a mechanism" represent cognitive concepts that are transformed into metaphorical expressions. These expressions persist not only as a sequence of words or signs but as ideas, images and concepts that are part of our linguistic-cognitive model, and in turn are present in our daily lives.

This phenomenon, complex, which is inherent, is a reflect our capacity for creativity as humans and extends beyond the language itself; it represent even in the way we build and conceive our environment. The implications of metaphor are fundamental elements to consider for proposing this study. In general, the metaphorical expressions "arises from the insertion in a certain context of a note that comes from a different one" [1], the process of interpreting metaphorical language involves a complex exercise. For example "My car drinks gasoline" prompts questions about which characteristics of ***gasoline*** are associated of with the verb ***drink*** and, in turn, with a ***car***?

Y. Hernndez Heredia et al. (Eds.): IWAIPR 2023, LNCS 14335, pp. 248–259, 2024.
https://doi.org/10.1007/978-3-031-49552-6_22

According to Lakoff G. and Jhohnson M. (2008) we can find two fundamental perspectives on the metaphorical phenomenon [1]:

1. "Metaphors permeate everyday language, forming a complex and interrelated network to which both newer creations and 'fossilizations' are relevant".
2. The existence of this metaphorical networks affects the internal representations, and worldview of the speaker.

These two perspectives are crucial for this project: the first pertains to identifying the characteristics and elements that govern the interrelationships that make up the metaphorical phenomenon, and the second pertains to how this interrelationship relates to the internal representations of individuals and their collective interactions within a given group.

Given the significance of metaphorical text, its study is essential for Natural Language Processing (NLP); this involves understanding the role and relevance of metaphor in natural language and its impact on comprehending the message conveyed by a sender. From a computational perspective is crucial to assess the available for addressing these tasks, defining objectives and implementing effectively before evaluating results.

Metaphors play a significant role in natural language, making their computational processing indispensable for real-world applications of NLP that address semantic tasks [2]. Metaphorical expressions can lead misinterpretations in algorithms such as machine translation or sentiment analysis [3].

The complexity of the metaphor underscores the three different tasks involved in its computational processing terms: classification, generation and interpretation of metaphorical text with a focus on concepts and definitions for its implementation. The intricacy of these tasks requires an exhaustive review of concepts, corpora, computational tools and algorithms developed to date, aimed at gaining a more accurate understanding of natural language. In this context, the study of non-literal language entails, within the framework of the study of language, a more accurate understanding of the complex communication system, likewise, from the cognitive area, it proposes a more accurate understanding of the relationship between language and thought and finally from the computational field, it presents a more accurate approach to the study of natural language.

The complexity of metaphor highlights the different perspectives from which the classification, generation and interpretation of a metaphorical text can be approached in computational terms. This project starts from the need to classify metaphorical text, as a task hierarchically related to the interpretation and generation of text; it also addresses from an experimental perspective the usefulness of three pre-trained language models: RoBERTa-large, RoBERTa-base and BERT-base uncased. The selected models share an important characteristic in common that they consider the context and the context is a key element in the metaphor.

This work allows to evaluate new perspectives in the study of metaphorical language, particularly it proposes an evaluation of the pre-trained language models (RoBERTa-base, RoBERTa-large and BERT-base uncased) and the consideration of a metaphor language classifier that stands out before the state of the art.

1.1 Metaphor Classification

Numerous authors and recent works have proposed valuable methods for metaphor detection, understanding metaphor detection in general, as the classification or ability to distinguish between literal and non-literal language.

Some of these relevant works on the metaphor detection task [4] propose the use of Graph Convolutional Networks (GCN) for metaphor identification using the ELMO language model; [5] propose a detection algorithm from VerbNet and WordNet; [6] evaluate the uses the BERT and Word2Vec models taking into account concreteness and implements a multilayer perceptron-type model; and finally [7] focus on reviewing and proposing word embeddings models. Together, the authors [4–7] demonstrate the variety of approaches and tools available for developing algorithms that can detect and classify metaphorical language, ranging from graph convolutional networks to language models like ELMO and BERT, to word embeddings and vector representations. This highlights the potential of combining different techniques and models to improve the accuracy and effectiveness.

Throughout this section, some tools have been identified, some of which were mentioned in the works cited, while others are considered part of the state of the art in text classification. These tools include neural networks, convolutional neural networks, generative neural networks, the Naive Bayes algorithm, graph representations, and recurrent neural networks in their various configurations and combinations. These elements and tools can be considered for future works in this field.

Metaphors could be considered omnipresent in natural language, and detecting them requires challenging contextual reasoning about whether specific situations can actually happen [11]. This article proposes to review some main features should be considered and some of the available resources like preprocessing process and pre-training language models to work on computational metaphor. Finally, this work focuses on presents a metaphor classification model using LSTM cells.

2 Materials and Methods

2.1 LSTM and NLP

There are several tools to address the problem of non-literal text classification, in this work we consider the LSTM (Long Short Term Memory) networks proposed in 1997 by Hochreiter and Schmidhuber and the GRU (Gated recurrent unit) networks developed in 2014 [10].

Describing in detail each of these models, would imply extending this section considerably so we will only review the performance of LSTM networks for their application in this work. LSTM cells offer several advantages such as a larger memory capacity, which, particularly in the field of NLP allows working with longer texts; additionally, LSTM networks are a solution to the leakage gradient problem that RNNs usually present.

Returning to the basic operation of LSTM cells, it is possible to consider the structural difference of LSTM cells as compared to traditional RNNs. Firstly, a new element is introduced, which corresponds to the state of the corresponding cell. In general, the main difference of LSTMs is the use of two vectors: one corresponding to long-term memory and the one corresponding to short-term memory.

According to the above, the functioning of LSTMs can be summarized in three main processes: the forgetting gate, which corresponds to the long-term memory that is forgotten; the input gate that evaluates new information to update the memory; and the output gate that controls which information in the long-term memory will be displayed. According to the above, this project proposes the use of LSTM cells and sentence embedding of pre-training models to consider the metaphor contextual and semantic features to develop a metaphor classification model; in that proposal the sequential perspective of a sentence is preserved at the sequential characteristic of the sentence embedding.

2.2 Corpus of Metaphorical Language

This subsection presents the main datasets identified in the literature on metaphorical language for study in English. These datasets are:

1. MOH-X: it contains 646 sentences and doesn't contain a predetermined training and test set. This dataset is derived from the MOH set and the verbs are used as metaphors.
2. The VUA sequence set: it contains 5323 sentences and has a predetermined training and test set. It represents text extracted from 117 British National Corpus fragments from four genres: academic, news, conversation and fiction; and corresponds to texts written between 1985–1994.
3. TroFi database: it contains 3737 sentences and doesn't contain a given training and test set. It corresponds to excerpts from the Wall Street Journal Corpus from the years 1987–1989.

For this work, the TroFi database was considered for the implementation of the metaphorical text classifier, proposed in this article.

The Corpus does not contain a particular training and testing set, which allows decide the training and testing set. TroFi database works with different topics that enrich this project and that allows to clearly exemplify the use of literal and non-literal language.

TroFi database is used as it is a reference in the study of metaphorical language within computational linguistics. This corpus was chosen because its annotation is based on the metaphorical use of the 50 English verbs and their relation with the close nouns and this allows a better idea of the metaphorical phenomenon; that focuses on grouping sentences about the use of the following verbs:

absorb	drink	flow	**pass**	sleep	assault	drown	
fly	plant	smooth	attack	eat	grab	play	step
besiege	escape	grasp	plow	stick	cool	evaporate	
kick	pour	strike	dance	examine	kill	pump	
destroy	fill	knock	rain	target	stumble	die	fix
lend	rest	touch	dissolve	flood	melt	ride	
vaporize	drag	flourish		miss	roll	wither	

2.3 Pre-processing

The task of classifying literal and non-literal language focuses on the Trofi Dataset corpus [11]. Pre-processing comprises 2,146 metaphorical sentences and 1,593 literal sentences of 50 verbs in English.

The corpus pre-processing stage, shown in Fig. 1, involved generating three sets of sentences based on the corpus tags:

1. Literal: 1592 sentences
2. Non-literal: 2145 sentences
3. No annotations: 2699 sentences

For this project is proposed two types of preprocessing that be compared (Fig. 1) a) Punctuation marks and stop words were removed from all sentences and all text was converted to lower case.

Second, as part of experimentation b) Punctuation marks and all text were converted to lower case.

2.4 Description of the Proposed Solution to the Problem Posed

In this section, a proposed solution is presented that uses two LSTM cells to analyze each sentence as a sequence of words, where the interaction between these elements results in a particular meaning. In other words, it is the interrelation between the sequence of words in a sentence that gives rise to the classification and interpretation of the text.

In this sense, to illustrate the importance of the memory element present in LSTM cells, we can consider the difference in the interpretation of two sentences:

(1) The shirts are articles of clothing.
(2) The shirts are terrible articles of clothing.

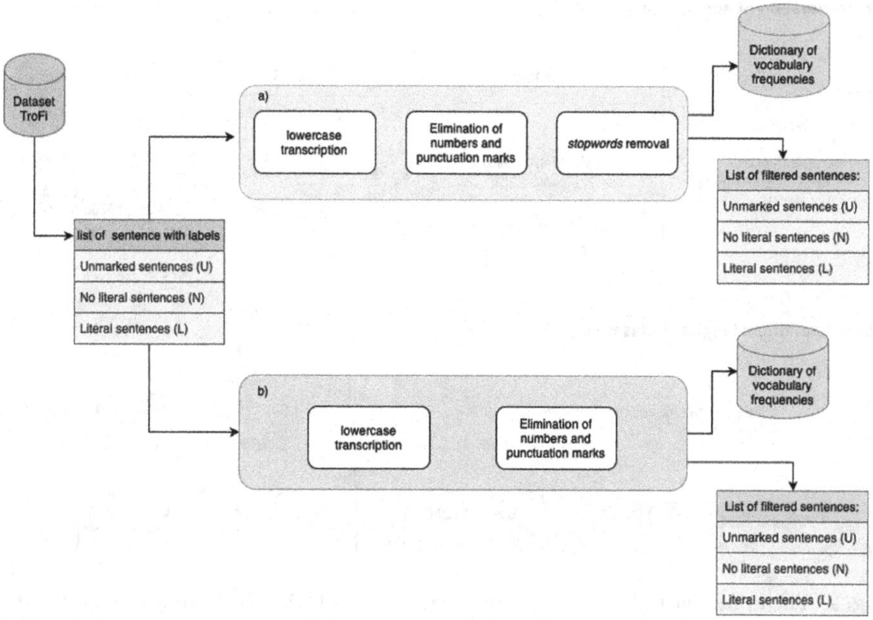

Fig. 1. Diagram of the general pre-processing for a metaphorical language classifier using the TroFi corpus.

The subject doesn't work without the predicate, and in turn, the predicate doesn't work without the verb. To generate the interpretation of such a sentence, it is necessary to consider the relationship between all the words.

From this perspective, a classifier model is presented below, using three different pre-training language models: RoBERTa-base, RoBERTa-large and BERT-base uncased. By understanding the vectors of each sentence, the *sentence embeddings* generated by means of *sentence transformers* correspond to a sequence related to the interaction between words, taking into account the context of the sentence.

As shown in Fig. 2, these models developed in *keras* comprise two LSTM cells connected in series followed by a densely connected layer that outputs a p-value that determining the class to which the sentence belongs, according to the Eq. 1:

$$f(p) = \begin{cases} \text{if } p > 0.50 \; class = 0 \\ \text{if } p \leq 0.50 \; class = 1 \end{cases} \tag{1}$$

The models presented in Fig. 2 use two LSTM cells connected in series and a densely connected layer that outputs a p-value to determine whether the sentence belongs to class 0 (metaphorical text) or class 1 (literal text). The Adam algorithm is used for optimization and cross-entropy for loss. These classifier models demonstrate the importance of using and evaluating pre-trained RoBERTa-large, RoBERTa-base, and BERT-base uncased models. These models, as already men-

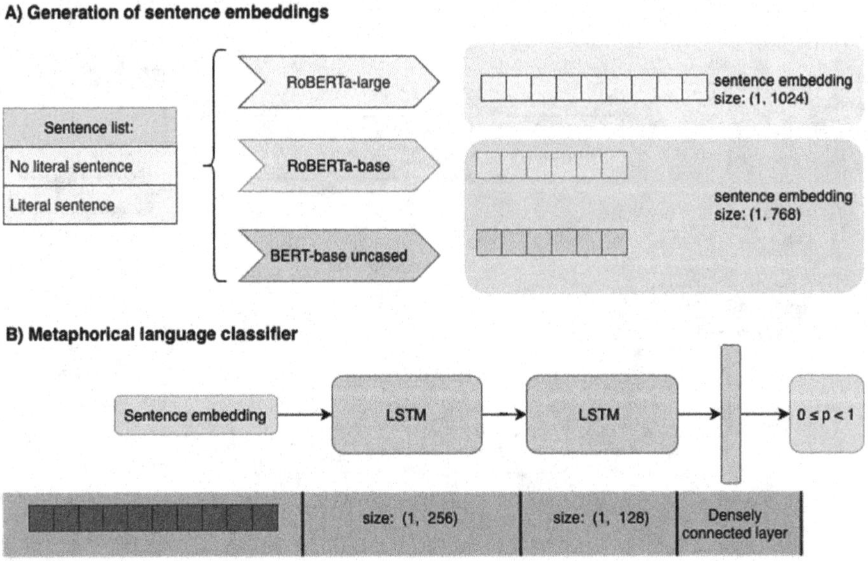

Fig. 2. The upper part of the figure shows the process of **A) Generation of sentence embeddings** according to the pre-trained model of the language and the dimensions of the vectors. At the lower part the model is shown **B) Metaphorical language classifier model** is shown using two LSTM cells and a densely connected layer with the the dimensions of the exits of the cells

tioned, allow considering the context as well as the power of the broad vocabulary due to the nature of its training. The classifier models also highlight the hierarchical nature of metaphor processes and the need to consider word interrelation through memory; this solution achieves the objective of the proposed task and provides a strong foundation for exploring the generation and interpretation of metaphors beyond independent tasks, but as interconnected processes.

2.5 Evaluation

In this section we present and analyze the corresponding results of the models presented based on their performance. In the first instance. For the evaluation of the models we consider, the following indices, which are considered for their usefulness to understand the model and fully evaluate its operation:

$$Accuracy = \frac{TrueMetaphore + TrueLiteral}{TrueMetaphore + TrueLiteral + FalseMetaphore + FalseLiteral} \tag{2}$$

$$Precision = \frac{TrueMetaphore}{TrueMetaphore + FalseMetaphore} \tag{3}$$

$$Recall = \frac{TrueMetaphore}{TrueMetaphore + FalseLiteral} \tag{4}$$

$$F1 = 2 * \frac{precision + recall}{precision * recall} \tag{5}$$

Based on these formulas, the classifiers' performance is evaluated, taking the state of the art as a reference, evaluation is a crucial aspect of understanding the model and proposing future work and new perspectives.

Particularly, relevant works that are considered for comparison of results are Gao G. et al. (2018) [11] which proposes the use of LSTM structures; Mao et al. (2019) [8] which experiments with ELMO and GloVe models and two deep learning models; and Rohanian et al. (2020) [9] which proposes a neural network.

The following models were evaluated using 10-fold cross validation with *StratifiedKFold* from *Sklearn* for each iteration k of the test and training sets the performance metrics of Accuracy, Recall, Precision, and F1-score were reported. Finally, the means of these metrics were calculated to evaluate the overall performance of the models.

3 Results

In this section is presented six tables to show the results of the experimentation. First, below are three tables showing the results of the LSTM model proposed in Fig. 2, using pretrained RoBERTa-large, RoBERTa-base and BERT-base uncased pre-trained models, respectively with the pre-processing a) punctuation marks and stop words were removed from all sentences and all text was converted to lower case:

Table 1. Results of the LSTM-based classifier model using RoBERTa-large. Each iteration (k) of the 10-fold cross validation set is represented in the table.

Results LSTM- classifier RoBERTa-large				
k	Accuracy	Recall	Precision	F1-score
0	0.783	0.845	0.789	0.816
1	0.761	0.817	0.777	0.796
2	0.719	0.737	0.762	0.749
3	0.761	0.812	0.779	0.786
4	0.775	0.831	0.787	0.808
5	0.751	0.775	0.786	0.780
6	0.753	0.822	0.764	0.792
7	0.775	0.817	0.795	0.806
8	0.791	0.826	0.811	0.819
9	0.761	0.822	0.774	0.797
Mean	0.763	0.810	0.782	0.795

Table 2. Results of the LSTM-based classifier model using RoBERTa-base. Each iteration (k) of the 10-fold cross validation set is represented in the table.

Results LSTM- classifier RoBERTa-base				
k	Accuracy	Recall	Precision	F1-score
0	0.818	0.859	0.828	0.843
1	0.839	0.911	0.826	0.866
2	0.820	0.850	0.838	0.844
3	0.831	0.883	0.812	0.822
4	0.820	0.836	0.848	0.834
5	0.847	0.887	0.851	0.869
6	0.845	0.883	0.851	0.866
7	0.769	0.930	0.736	0.822
8	0.820	0.836	0.848	0.842
9	0.847	0.878	0.858	0.868
Mean	0.826	0.875	0.829	0.847

Table 3. Results of the LSTM-based classifier model using BERT-base uncased. Each iteration (k) of the 10-fold cross validation set is represented in the table.

Results LSTM- classifier BERT-base uncased				
k	Accuracy	Recall	Precision	F1-score
0	0.778	0.822	0.795	0.808
1	0.786	0.817	0.809	0.813
2	0.778	0.812	0.801	0.807
3	0.780	0.826	0.796	0.811
4	0.780	0.826	0.796	0.811
5	0.769	0.822	0.785	0.803
6	0.767	0.812	0.786	0.799
7	0.772	0.793	0.805	0.799
8	0.794	0.826	0.815	0.821
9	0.783	0.831	0.797	0.814
Mean	0.779	0.819	0.799	0.809

3.1 Comparison of Classifier Performance Using the Three Pre-trained Language Models

Tables 4 and 5 compare in the first place the performance of the model with the two different pre-processing step proposal and the the performance of the proposed classifier with LSTM cells using the three different pre-trained language models.

In the Table 4 is stand out the results of the model, that uses the RoBERTa-base model with the first proposed method for pre-processing achieve the highest scores for this table in all four evaluation metrics: accuracy, recall, precision, and F1-score. In a general consideration of Tables 4 and 5 that model (RoBERTa-base model with first pre-processing method) could be consider the best although there are close of some independent high metrics like the results of the BERT-base model with second proposed way for pre-processing.

Table 4. Comparison of the classifier results using the three pre-trained language models with pre-processing a) Punctuation marks and stop words were removed from all sentences and all text was converted to lower case.

Results LSTM-classifier			
	RoBERTa-large	RoBERTa-base	Bert-base
Accuracy	0.763	**0.826**	0.773
Recall	0.810	**0.875**	0.821
Precision	0.782	**0.829**	0.790
F1-score	0.795	**0.847**	0.804

Table 5. Comparison of the classifier results using the three pre-trained language models with pre-processing b) Punctuation marks were removed from all sentences and all text was converted to lower case.

Results LSTM-classifier			
	RoBERTa-large	RoBERTa-base	Bert-base
Accuracy	0.813	0.810	**0.821**
Recall	**0.811**	0.804	0.818
Precision	0.809	**0.803**	**0.817**
F1-score	0.810	**0.804**	**0.820**

3.2 Comparison with State-of-the-Art Models

Based on the above analysis, this subsection presents a comparison between the proposed model using the RoBERTa-base pre-trained model as shown in Fig. 2 and state-of-the-art models. The results are presented in Table 6.

The performance of the classifier in Table 6 shows a clear difference in terms of accuracy, recall, precision, and F1-score when compared to the state of the art. The proposed model using the pre-trained RoBERTa-base model outperforms the state of the art in all four metrics.

Table 6. Comparison of the classifier with LSTM cells using RoBERTa-base against the state of the art.

Comparison of results against the state of the art				
	Model-RoBERTa-base	Gao G. (2018)	Mao R. (2019)	Rohanian O.(2020)
Accuracy	**0.826**	0.750	0.750	0.730
Recall	**0.875**	0.720	0.770	0.710
Precision	**0.829**	0.710	0.690	0.740
F1-score	**0.847**	0.710	0.720	0.720

4 Conclusions and Future Work

One of the main ideas of this article is to show some of the important results of the experimentation and talk about experimentation around non-literal language with more information about the different tools that have been presented throughout this work.

Tables 1, 2 and 3 show the main experimentation results that focus in the different pre-trained models. Then, the fist three tables results are compared with the Tables 4 and 5 to understand and evaluate the relevance of consider some language features at the pre-processing process.

Last, the Table 6 demonstrates the importance of the results of this work by proposing a better classification model than previously reported. This justifies the importance of considering models with memory such as the LSTM, since it is so necessary due to the syntactic, grammatical, semantic and contextual characteristics of language, particularly metaphorical language, that is, the importance of the interrelationship of words in a statement as part of the meaning of the text.

On the other hand, experimentation in pre-processing is allows to evaluate the value of stopwords in pre-processing using the pre-trained models and thus consider optimizing this step when working with non-literal language or in general with this language models.

As future work is important to consider the formal key points and models of each of the characteristics related of language and the relation with natural language processing techniques and tools. This work evaluate with a interesting results the use of the pre-trained languages models (RoBERTa-base, RoBERTa-large and BERT-base uncased) for work with metaphorical language and consider some important features and tools to the future work with metaphorical language.

In particular, this project demonstrates the usefulness of the RoBERTa pre-trained model and opens new perspectives in the study of metaphorical text by highlighting the importance of its vector representation. The presented model and results provide a foundation for evaluating new perspectives on metaphorical language. This work generate new perspectives about the relevance to consider the metaphor at the natural language processing tasks.

Moreover, as future work, the performance of the classifier can be evaluated using other corpora with non-literal language, and the relationship between the classification task and text generation and interpretation can be further explored. Finally, it is important to make it clear that the results presented in this project correspond to the first part of the evaluation of the algorithm, which must be subjected to a rigorous evaluation of the particular test cases.

References

1. Lakoff, G., Johnson, M.: Metaphors We Live By. University of Chicago press, Chicago (2008)
2. Shutova, E., Teufel, S., Korhonen, A.: Statistical metaphor processing. Comput. Linguist. **39**(2), 301–353 (2013)
3. Mohammad, S., Shutova, E., Turney, P.: Metaphor as a medium for emotion: an empirical study. In Proceedings of the Fifth Joint Conference on Lexical and Computational Semantics, pp. 23–33 (2016)
4. Le, D., Thai, M., Nguyen, T.: Multi-task learning for metaphor detection with graph convolutional neural networks and word sense disambiguation. In Proceedings of the AAAI Conference on Artificial Intelligence, vol. 34(05), pp. 8139–8146) (2020)
5. Wilks, Y., Dalton, A., Allen, J., Galescu, L.: Automatic metaphor detection using large-scale lexical resources and conventional metaphor extraction. In Proceedings of the First Workshop on Metaphor in NLP, pp. 36–44 (2013)
6. Maudslay, R.H., Pimentel, T., Cotterell, R., Teufel, S.: Metaphor detection using context and concreteness. In Proceedings of the Second Workshop on Figurative Language Processing, pp. 221–226. Association for Computational Linguistics (2020)
7. Ruder, S., Vulić, I., Søgaard, A.: A survey of cross-lingual word embedding models. J. Artif. Intell. Res. **65**, 569–631 (2019)
8. Mao, R., Lin, C., Guerin, F.: End-to-end sequential metaphor identification inspired by linguistic theories. In Proceedings of the 57th Annual Meeting of the Association for Computational Linguistics, pp. 3888–3898 (2019)
9. Rohanian, O., Rei, M., Taslimipoor, S., Ha, L.: Verbal multiword expressions for identification of metaphor. ACL (2020)
10. Pilehvar, M.T., Camacho-Collados, J.: Embeddings in Natural Language Processing: Theory and Advances in Vector Representations of Meaning. Morgan and Claypool Publishers, San Rafael (2020)
11. Gao, G., Choi, E., Choi, Y., Zettlemoyer, L.: Neural metaphor detection in context. arXiv preprint arXiv:1808.09653 (2018)

Improvements to the IntiGIS Model Related to the Clustering of Consumers for Rural Electrification

Mirelys Torres-Pérez[1], Marieta Peña Abreu[2(✉)], and Javier Domínguez[3]

[1] University of Las Tunas, Avenida 30 de Noviembre S/N, Reparto Aurora, 75100 Las Tunas, Cuba
mtperez@ult.edu.cu

[2] University of Informatics Sciences, Carretera a San Antonio de los Baños Km 2 ½, Torrens, 19370 Boyeros, La Habana, Cuba
mpabreu@uci.cu

[3] CIEMAT, Centro de la Moncloa, Complutense, 40, 28040 Madrid, Spain

Abstract. Providing access to electricity in rural areas remains a challenge in many developing countries, where the lack of infrastructure, low population density, and high costs hinder the implementation of conventional electrification schemes. In this context, off grid solutions (microgrid and individual systems) have emerged as a promising solution, allowing the integration of local renewable energy resources and providing electricity to communities that are not connected to the main power grid. The IntiGIS model has been proposed as a tool to allow the evaluation and comparison of the various electrification technology options. However, some limitations and challenges have been identified in the original model, particularly related to the level of consumer aggregation and the distribution network layout. In this paper, we present improvements to the IntiGIS model related to the clustering of consumers for rural electrification, based on a modified agglomerative clustering algorithm and a set of performance metrics to form the clusters. We also present a comparison with the IntiGIS II version in a case study in Guamá, Santiago de Cuba to demonstrate the effectiveness of the proposed improvements. The results show that the modified IntiGIS model can generate clusters that meet the technical and economic requirements for microgrid and grid extensions systems, with better accuracy and efficiency than the original model. These improvements can contribute to the implementation of sustainable and reliable electricity access in rural areas, promoting social and economic development in these regions.

Keywords: Clustering Algorithm · Semisupervised Learning · IntiGIS · Geospatial Analysis · Rural Electrification · Energy Access · Sustainable Development

Y. Hernández Heredia et al. (Eds.): IWAIPR 2023, LNCS 14335, pp. 260–272, 2024.
https://doi.org/10.1007/978-3-031-49552-6_23

1 Introduction

Access to electricity is a critical factor for socio-economic development, particularly in rural areas of developing countries. The lack of electricity in these areas is a significant obstacle for improving the living conditions of their inhabitants, who rely on traditional and inefficient energy sources. Therefore, rural electrification is a key strategy to reduce poverty, promote education, and enhance the overall quality of life [1].

However, rural electrification planning presents a number of challenges, including the high cost of extending the national grid to remote areas, the low population density typified by scattered settlements, and limited financial resources. That is why to make an informed decision, decision-makers rely on energy planning tools and models.

Among the literature studied, stand out the models for techno-economic and geospatial planning of large-scale rural electrification, also referred to as LCEM (Least-Cost Electrification Models) [2]. These models evaluate rural electrification alternatives based on Levelized Cost of Electricity (LCOE), making it possible to compare different electrification technologies without incurring the costs of physically building infrastructures, and by using geospatial planning, they also determine the location of each technology within the study area.

Examples of the aforementioned models are IntiGIS I [3], REM [4], ONSSET [5], RE2nAF [6], Mahapatra & Dasappa [7], Van Ruijven et al. [8], Dagnachew et al. [9], Sahai [10], Blechinger & Bertheau et al. [11, 12], Abdul-Salam & Phimiste [13, 14], Zeyringer et al. [15], Network Planner [16], Deichmann et al. [17], Levin and Thomas [18], GEOSIM[19] and Banks et al. [20].

One of the key inputs of these model is the map that represents the location of consumers[1] with their respective demands of energy. The consumer layer forms the foundation for all other geospatial data and dictates the spatial coverage of the analysis. There are several levels of consumer aggregation: individual consumers, communities, or cells. When a model operates at the level of villages or cells, the cells themselves are considered viable microgrids[2] or grid extensions. This fact reduces the computational complexity of the model by aggregating a large number of households into a smaller number of communities or grid cells. However, it will not be able to calculate the network layout that connects each consumer to the power source, whether it be the main grid or the generation site of the microgrid.

At the other hand, working with a high level of resolution like consumer level, requires an algorithm for clustering consumers with to identify areas with sufficient demand density to ensure the construction of a larger energy delivery system, such as a microgrid or the electrical network [2].

Clustering algorithms can provide insights into the underlying factors that contribute to electricity access disparities in rural areas, helping the decision-makers to identify the

[1] For the purposes of this investigation, the term "consumer" refers to a household or building that needs to be electrified.

[2] Also referred as mini-grids in literature, a microgrid refers to a small-scale electricity generation and distribution system that can operate independently or in conjunction with the main grid. It often includes renewable energy sources and energy storage and can serve as a reliable and cost-effective solution to provide electricity to remote or off-grid rural areas.

most suitable electrification solutions (isolated, microgrids, and grid extensions) for each group and allocate resources accordingly. The aforementioned models, except for REM, doesn't work at consumer level and therefore calculate LCOEs considering only the cost of connecting a cell or community with a single technology.

IntiGIS is a geospatial model that allows the evaluation and comparison of various technology options for electrifying rural areas.

This paper presents improvements to the IntiGIS model related to the clustering of consumers for rural electrification. Specifically, we focus on the RElect_MGEC algorithm, designed to create microgrid and grid extension clusters. The proposed improvements aim to enhance the accuracy and efficiency of the clustering process, resulting in more reliable and cost-effective electrification solutions.

The rest of the paper is organized as follows: Sect. 2 provides an overview of the IntiGIS Model an presents the proposed improvements to the model. Section 3 describes the results of the evaluation of the new clustering algorithm, including a comparison with the previous version. Finally, Sect. 4 concludes the paper and provides directions for future research.

2 IntiGIS Model

In Fig. 1, the evolution of IntiGIS is summarized (dates are approximate), where three stages can be seen: a first one corresponding to SolarGIS and SolarGIS II, a second one where versions of IntiGIS I and IntiGIS II emerged, and a third one that marks the starting point of the present investigation [21, 22] and upgrades made to the model. The current version of the tool, unlike the previous ones, was implemented in a QGIS free software environment. Highlights that allow the calculation and comparison of the LCOE of seven electrification alternatives: individual (based on photovoltaic, wind, diesel), microgrid (based on diesel, wind-diesel, photovoltaic-diesel), and grid connection. Additionally, it is possible to work at the consumer level, assigning different values of demand and power, and group them into microgrid and grid extensions clusters.

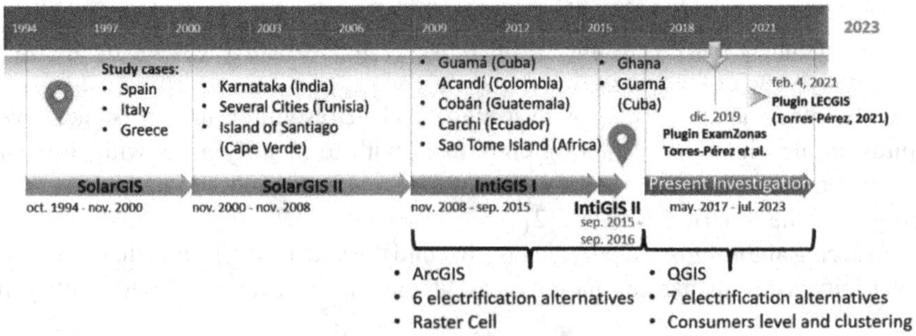

Fig. 1. Evolution of IntiGIS model.

The new version of the model consists of three components: 1. Territorial ordering analysis, 2. Geospatial clustering, and 3. Technical-economic analysis. Figure 2 shows an overview of the components with the interrelation and outputs of each one.

C1 carries out an analysis from the perspective of territorial ordering, with the aim of determining sensitive areas (non-viable) or barriers that should not be crossed by the layout of Low Voltage (LV) distribution lines. Some barriers may be associated with municipal limits or other administrative borders. These barriers can be used as input to C2 to support the clustering of consumers and allow the user to have different options to influence the way clusters are formed. C1 is based on the functionality to determine sensitive areas (barriers) of the ExamZonas plugin [22].

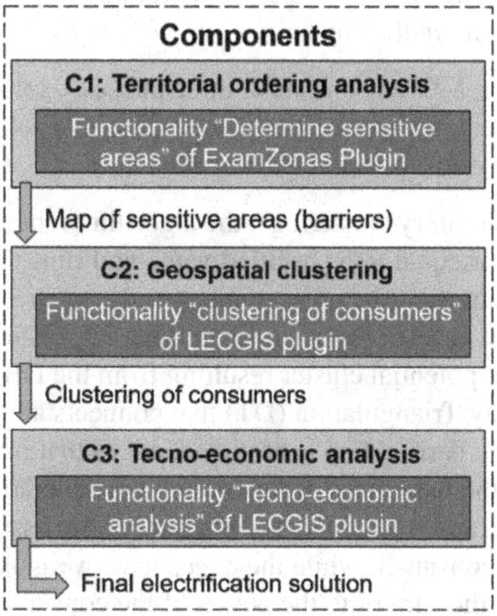

Fig. 2. Diagram components of the new version of IntiGIS model

The objective of C2 is to determine if there is sufficient demand density to guarantee the construction of a larger energy delivery system such as a microgrid or the electrical network [2]. This component will be described in more detail in the next section. The clustering solution generated by C2 is used as input to C3. This last component performs a techno-economic analysis of electrification alternatives using the "Techno-Economic Analysis" functionality of the LECGIS plugin described in [21].

2.1 The Proposed Geospatial Clustering Strategy

The proposed clustering strategy, named RElect_MGEC (Rural Electrification Microgrid and Grid Extension Clustering) fallows the approach of constrained clustering as a form of semisupervised learning, to clustering data while incorporating domain knowledge in the form of constraints. With this in mind the following metrics were stablished for the formation of the clusters[3]:

[3] The distribution infrastructure for microgrids and electrical grid extensions consists of a generation center and the branches connecting the center to a group of consumers. For this research, the term "cluster" refers to this distribution infrastructure with low-voltage lines.

- MinCons: Minimum number of consumers for a cluster to be considered valid.
- Radius: Search radius in which the MinCons must be found.
- MaxLongC: Denotes the maximum permissible distance between the generation center of the cluster and its associated branches that connect the consumers. This metric aims to restrict the energy losses that may occur during distribution. The generation center is assumed to be the location of the consumer with the smallest value of MaxLongC. Accordingly, the distance of a branch is determined by the sum of the widths of the path originating from the generation center till the leaf nodes.
- PotMax: Maximum power of the cluster (W). Obtained from the sum of the energy powers of the consumers in the cluster.

The algorithm RElect_MGEC consists of three phases: exploratory clustering, evaluation of potential clusters, and generating the results. The following are the steps to create the microgrid and grid extension (MGE) clusters:

1. In the phase one "exploratory clustering", the algorithm removes the consumers with PotMax greater than or equal to a specified value and runs the DBSCAN algorithm on the remaining consumers. The noise points that do not meet the minimum number of consumers required to form a cluster are labeled as isolated consumers.
2. In the phase two, each potential cluster resulting from the DBSCAN is evaluated by:
   a. Creating a Delaunay Triangulation (DT) that connects all the consumers.
   b. If a sensitive area or barrier map is provided, edges that intersect with these areas or are longer than the maximum distance from the generation center are removed.
   c. Build a weighted graph from the DT, where nodes are assigned weights based on the power of each consumer, while the edges have weights calculated as the ratio of their length and the sum of to the power of the consumers they connect.
   d. Computing the minimum spanning tree (MST)[4].
   e. If the tree is connected and satisfy the metrics MaxLongC, PotMax and MinCons it is added to the list of MGE clusters. Otherwise, for each connected component, the same evaluation is applied, and if the component satisfies the requirements, it is also added to the list of MGE clusters.
   f. If the clusters do not satisfy these conditions, the RElect-BUC algorithm (see **Algorithm 1**) is used to further cluster the consumers.
3. Finally, in the third phase, the algorithm generates the results by creating shapefiles for the resulting clustering of consumers and LV distribution lines for each cluster.

The density-based spatial clustering algorithm presented by authors [23] shares some similarities with the RElect_MGEC algorithm. Their approach utilized a DT with edge length constraints to generate a network of connected vertices, which was subsequently analyzed using a modified density-based strategy to identify spatial clusters.

RElect-BUC algorithm is based on graph theory to perform agglomerative clustering that ensures the obtained clusters meet the established metrics. First, all the edges of the graph are sorted according to their weight from smallest to largest. Initially, all edges are considered inactive. In this sense, the edges of the graph correspond to the clustering

[4] A MST is the set of connections between customers so that all customers are connected directly or through other customers and the sum of the lengths of the connections are minimized. To create the MST, we use the minimum_spanning_tree function in the NetworkX library.

decisions. An edge can be activated to merge the consumers on both sides of the edge into a single cluster, or remain inactive to leave them in separate clusters. This decision is based on whether they meet the previously defined metrics. Finally, once all the edges have been considered, the series of interconnected consumers that meet the metrics will be the clusters of microgrids and network extensions.

Algorithm 1. RElect_BUC

```
Input: T, a weighted connected graph
Input: MaxLongC, the maximum length from the generation center
Input: PotMax, the maximum power of a cluster
Input: MinCons, the minimum number of consumers for a cluster
Output: Lr, a resulting list of microgrid and network exten-
sion clusters
1:Sort the edges of T by their weight
2:Create an empty graph, T'
3:For each edge i in T do
// The nodes that connect the edge will be automatically added
if they are not already in the graph T'
4:     Add edge i to the graph T'
5:     For each connected component c in T' do
6:       If edge i exists in c then
7:         If graph_MaxLongC(c) >= MaxLongC or graph_to-
tal_power(c) >= PotMax then
8:           Remove edge i from graph T'
9:         End if
10:      End if
11:    End for
12:End for
13:For each connected component cn in T' do
14:    If number_of_nodes(cn) >= MinCons then
15:      Add cn a Lr
16:    End if
17:End for
18:Return Lr
```

3 Application and Results Analysis

To evaluate the influence of the improvements introduced to the model as part of the geospatial clustering component II, it was proposed a comparison with the case study conducted by [24] in the Guamá municipality. The maps from the original case study can be accessed through the geoportal: http://arcg.is/2ffrzAY. The same technical-economic parameters presented in Annex V of the thesis were employed, but with the consumers grouped using the proposed clustering strategy, in contrast to the original analysis that was performed at the raster cell level to represent consumers. This approach will also allow for a comparison between the current version and the IntiGIS II version.

For the application of the clustering proposal, the next experiments were design:

- E1: execution of RElect_MGEC with the parameters MinCons = 5, Radius = 200 m, MaxLongC = 1000 m, and PotMax = 46200W.
- E2: execution of RElect_MGEC, with Radius = 250 m and the same rest parameters.
- E3: direct application of RElect_BUC without using the DBSCAN algorithm in Phase 1. This approach began by calculating the DT that connects all consumers in the study area. With the input parameters MinCons = 5, MaxLongC = 1000 m, and PotMax = 46200 W.

The "Clustering of Consumers" functionality (C2 in Fig. 2), was implemented using the QGIS API functions and the NetworkX library [25]. It is part of the upgrades made to the LECGIS plugin described in [21], which was also updated to work with version 3.x of QGIS.

To establish a reference value for PotMax, we analyzed the demand raster used as input for IntiGIS II in search of the highest cell density. The maximum number of households per cell found was 14, and considering that the contracted power per household is Ph = 3300 W, the resulting aggregated power would be 46200 W. The value of MaxLongC was recommended by energy specialist we consulted. The Radius was set between 200 and 250 m, considering the raster resolution of the consumers layer in the original study, which was 400 m. Also, with the purpose of facilitating the comparison between the two different versions of IntiGIS, we did not use the barriers layer, to recreate similar conditions to the original case. Figure 3 displays the layer used as input for the experiments E1–E3, with the 3535 consumers located in the study area.

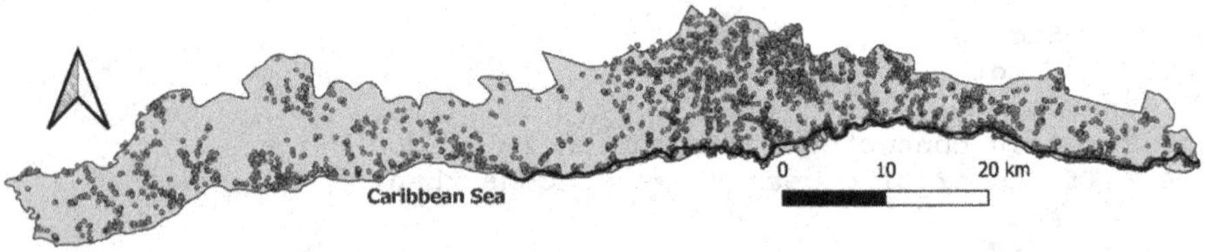

Fig. 3. Layer of consumers from the Guamá municipality

The result from each experiment (E1, E2 and E3) using the clustering of consumer (C2 in Fig. 2) is inputted into C3 to calculate the LCOE of the same electrification alternatives as in the original Guamá case study. The electrification alternatives considered include individual (based on photovoltaic, wind, diesel), microgrid (based on diesel, wind-diesel), and grid connection. The experiments were conducted on a workstation with Intel(R) Core(TM) i7-8750H CPU @ 2.20GHz, NVIDIA GeForce GTX 1050 GPU with 4GB of DRAM and 24 GB RAM. The comparison of results obtained after the execution of the three clustering experiments over the map of consumers in Guamá municipality is presented in Table 1.

Table 1. Results comparison of clustering proposal experiments

Experiment	Average of clusters size				Total Execution Time
	Total of consumers	MaxLongC (m)	PotMax (W)	Total LV lines (m)	
E1	9	375.15	26154.7	755.34	35 s, 394 ms
E2	8	430.284	27053.6	860.51	51 s, 382 ms
E3	9	678.669	29563.7	1350.66	4 min, 11 s

Note: PotMax value match with the total power of the consumers in the cluster.

In Table 2, the comparison of results for the entire study area of Guamá municipality is shown. By observing the fourth column, it is noted that the number of cells in IntiGIS II with 1410 is much higher than those generated by the proposed clustering strategies. This is due to the fact that in the original case study, the layer of 3535 consumers was rasterized to a resolution of 500 m.

Table 2. Comparison of LECGIS and IntiGIS II tools for Guamá municipality study area

Tool	Spatial Resolution	Clustering variant	Nº of clusters or cells/Tot. Consumers	Total LV lines (m)	Nº of consumers or cells for recommended Technology		Total LCOE (cts. €/kWh)
					Photovoltaics	Grid	
IntiGIS II	Cells of 500 m	-	1410/3535	275975	1275*	291*	126976
LECGIS	Consumers	E1	148/1173	111792	3004	531	308647
		E2	207/1697	178127	2851	684	287289
		E3	339/3037	457873	2641	894	287294

* Value obtained from a raster layer of 400 m resolution from a total of 1566 cells.

Figure 4 illustrates the contrast between representing consumers as point vectors versus raster cells in a grid format, in a portion of the study area. The image displays LV line length values (in light blue) for each pixel, and highlights three clusters in green, blue, and pink, respectively. The black line represents the total line length value computed from the MST. IntiGIS II divided the consumers contained in the three clusters into 5 cells, resulting in smaller partitions that require shorter line lengths. However, these partitions are impractical from an energy point of view.

Cell number 6 (counting from left to right and top to bottom) has only one consumer (white point) and a value of 316.38 m. For IntiGIS II, this cell represents a viable micro-grid or grid extension, and therefore it will calculate all the centralized electrification alternatives for that cell, even though designing a system with those characteristics is impractical. On the other hand, the clustering algorithm has labeled that consumer as isolated and has therefore discarded it for the calculation of centralized alternatives. Lastly, regarding to the total LV lines E1 and E2 yielded lower count than IntiGIS II.

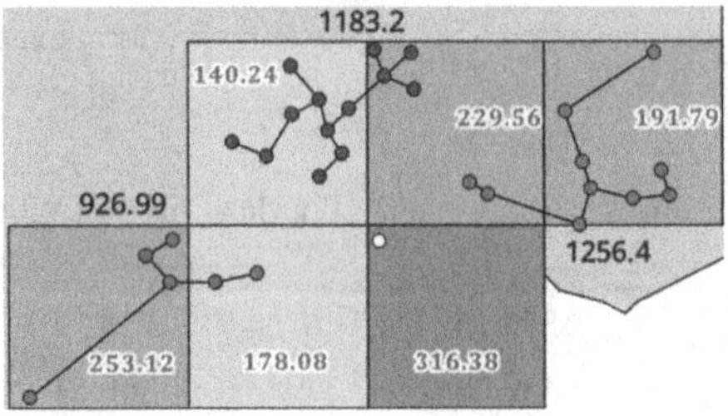

Fig. 4. Overlap of raster map of low voltage line and a clustering of consumer's layers (Color figure online)

Additionally, one of the advantages of working at the consumer level in the new version of the tool is that it is not necessary to transform vector shapes to raster format.

The comparison of the total LCOE cost was difficult because inconsistencies were found in the resolution of the input (500 m) and output (400 m) rasters, provided by the Geographic Information Technologies and Renewable Energies (gTIGER) units from CIEMAT. It was found that the layers sent by gTIGER correspond to those in the thesis document [24]. Since we did not have access to an installation of IntiGIS II, it was not possible to run the tool and determine whether the discrepancies we observed were due to a software malfunction or to human error on the part of the thesis author, who may have selected inappropriate output layers when conducted different experiments. In addition to the difference in raster resolution, it was found that the output raster is missing pixels in areas where consumers exist in the vector map.

It can be observed in the total cost column of Table 2 that IntiGIS II has lower values, but this may be due to the missing pixels. Furthermore, due to the fact that the IntiGIS II program automatically assigns grid connection as the most profitable option for settlements located less than 800 m from the medium voltage line (visualized in Fig. 5), these values are not calculated and therefore are not available in the LCOE results maps.

Among the experiments conducted using the new version, E2 demonstrated the lowest total cost, followed closely by E3. Figures 5, 6, 7 and 8 display maps showing the spatial distribution of the final electrification solutions obtained. To better visualize the differences between the solutions, a zoomed-in view of the existing electrical network area (represented by a solid black line) is displayed, as this is where the differences are concentrated. Each map displays consumers or cells in red to indicate the recommendation of implementing individual photovoltaic systems, while those in green indicate the recommendation of extending the electrical grid. For the remaining consumers not shown in the zoomed-in region, the recommended system was individual photovoltaic in all cases.

Figures 6, 7 and 8 correspond to the solutions that employed the clustering of consumers, and demonstrate that it is possible to recommend individual systems for places located less than 800 m from the electrical network. This finding provides valuable insights for energy distribution and access in the study area, as it suggests that clustering can be an effective strategy for improving the efficiency and cost-effectiveness of electrification efforts.

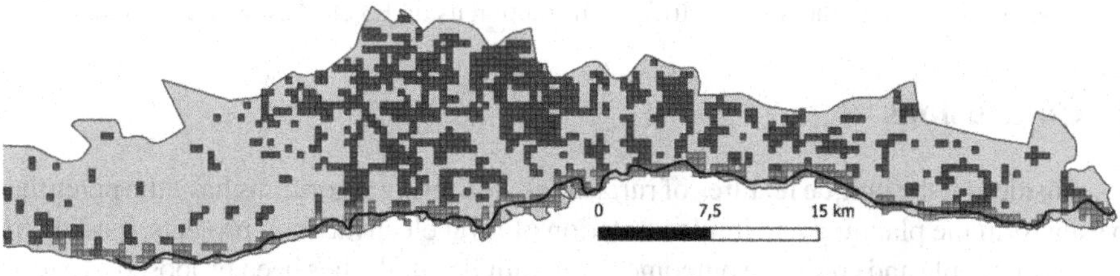

Fig. 5. Zoom in to the final electrification solution with IntiGIS II

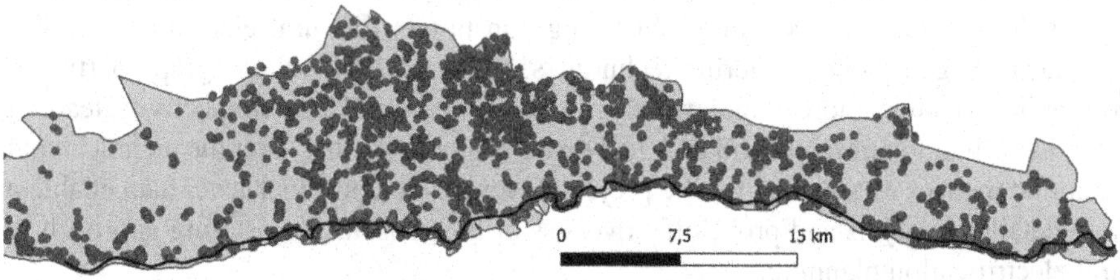

Fig. 6. Zoom in to the final electrification solution using E1 clustering of consumers

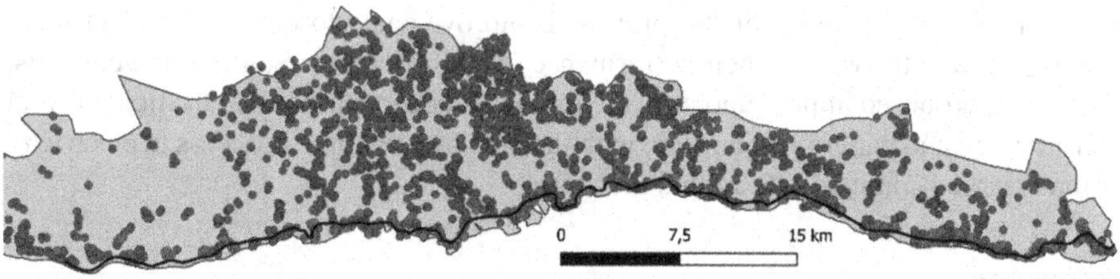

Fig. 7. Zoom in to the final electrification solution using E2 clustering of consumers

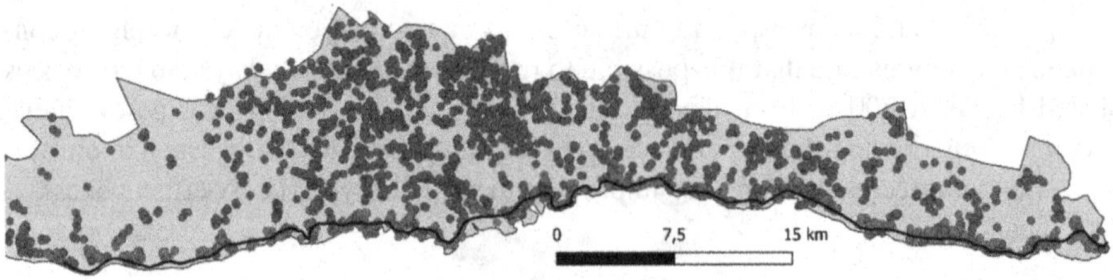

Fig. 8. Zoom in to the final electrification solution using E3 clustering of consumers

4 Conclusions

By considering the unique features of rural areas, clustering algorithms have the potential to transform the planning and implementation of rural electrification projects, leading to more sustainable and equitable outcomes. The IntiGIS model has been proposed as a tool to support the planning and design of microgrid systems, using a geospatial clustering approach to group consumers and optimize the distribution network.

In conclusion, the proposed improvements to the IntiGIS model have shown promising results in terms of accurately clustering consumers for rural electrification. The integration of geospatial clustering techniques, such as DBSCAN and graph partitioning, has allowed for a more granular analysis of consumers and their connectivity, leading to the identification of microgrid and grid extension clusters that meet the technical and economic metrics established for the project. Overall, the consumer-level data enable a more detailed analysis and prove effectiveness of the geospatial clustering approach in rural electrification planning.

The results obtained from applying the RElect_MGEC algorithm to a case study in the Guamá municipality demonstrate the effectiveness of the proposed approach in comparison to the IntiGIS model version based on raster. Further research can be conducted to explore the applicability of the proposed improvements to other rural electrification projects and to evaluate their performance under different conditions and contexts. Overall, the proposed improvements to the IntiGIS model contributes to the field of rural electrification and pattern recognition, with the potential to improve access to electricity for underserved communities around the world.

References

1. IEA: SDG7: Data and Projections – Access to electricity. https://www.iea.org/reports/sdg7-data-and-projections/access-to-electricity. Last accessed 14 Apr 2023
2. Morrissey, J.: Achieving universal electricity access at the lowest cost: a comparison of published model results. Energy Sustain. Dev. **53**, 81–96 (2019). https://doi.org/10.1016/j.esd.2019.09.005
3. Pinedo-Pascua, I.: IntiGIS: propuesta metodológica para la evaluación de alternativas de electrificación rural basada en SIG, p. 240. Universidad Politécnica de Madrid: Madrid (2010) https://dialnet.unirioja.es/servlet/tesis?codigo=185480
4. Ciller, P., et al.: Optimal electrification planning incorporating on-and off-grid technologies: the reference electrification model (REM). (2019). https://doi.org/10.1109/JPROC.2019.2922543

5. Korkovelos, A.: Advancing the state of geospatial electrification modelling: new data, methods, applications, insight and electrification investment outlooks. KTH Royal Institute of Technology. (2020) https://www.diva-portal.org/smash/record.jsf?pid=diva2:1431484
6. Moner-Girona, M., et al.: Universal access to electricity in Burkina Faso: scaling-up renewable energy technologies. Environ. Res. Lett. **11**(8), 084010 (2016). https://doi.org/10.1088/1748-9326/11/8/084010
7. Mahapatra, S., Dasappa, S.: Rural electrification: optimising the choice between decentralised renewable energy sources and grid extension. Energy Sustain. Dev. **16**(2), 146–154 (2012). https://doi.org/10.1016/j.esd.2012.01.006
8. Van Ruijven, B.J., Schers, J., van Vuuren, D.P.: Model-based scenarios for rural electrification in developing countries. Energy **38**(1), 386–397 (2012). https://doi.org/10.1016/j.energy.2011.11.037
9. Dagnachew, A.G., et al.: The role of decentralized systems in providing universal electricity access in Sub-Saharan Africa–a model-based approach. Energy **139**, 184–195 (2017). https://doi.org/10.1016/j.energy.2017.07.144
10. Sahai, D.: Toward universal electricity access: renewable energy-based geospatial leastcost electrification planning (No. 84314). The World Bank. (2013). https://www.esmap.org/sites/default/files/esmap-files/ASTAE_Indonesia_TUEA_Brief_1.pdf
11. Blechinger, P., Cader, C., Bertheau, P.: Least-cost electrification modeling and planning—a case study for five Nigerian federal states. Proc. IEEE **107**(9), 1923–1940 (2019). https://doi.org/10.1109/JPROC.2019.2924644
12. Bertheau, P., et al.: Visualizing national electrification scenarios for Sub-Saharan African Countries. Energies **10**(11), 1899 (2017). https://doi.org/10.3390/en10111899
13. Abdul-Salam, Y., Phimister, E.: The politico-economics of electricity planning in developing countries: a case study of Ghana. Energy Policy **88**, 299–309 (2016). https://doi.org/10.1016/j.enpol.2015.10.036
14. Abdul-Salam, Y., Phimister, E.: How effective are heuristic solutions for electricity planning in developing countries. Socioecon. Plann. Sci. **55**, 14–24 (2016). https://doi.org/10.1016/j.seps.2016.04.004
15. Zeyringer, M., et al.: Analyzing grid extension and stand-alone photovoltaic systems for the cost-effective electrification of Kenya. Energy Sustain. Dev. **25**, 75–86 (2015). https://doi.org/10.1016/j.esd.2015.01.003
16. Kemausuor, F., et al.: Electrification planning using network planner tool: the case of Ghana. Energy Sustain. Dev. **19**, 92–101 (2014). https://doi.org/10.1016/j.esd.2013.12.009
17. Deichmann, U., et al.: The economics of renewable energy expansion in rural Sub-Saharan Africa. Energy Policy **39**(1), 215–227 (2011). https://doi.org/10.1016/j.enpol.2010.09.034
18. Levin, T., Thomas, V.M.: Least-cost network evaluation of centralized and decentralized contributions to global electrification. Energy Policy **41**, 286–302 (2012). https://doi.org/10.1016/j.enpol.2011.10.048
19. IED: GEOSIM – Geospatial Rural Electrification Planning, https://www.ied-sa.com/en/products/planning/geosim-gb.html. Last accessed 25 Jul 2023
20. Banks, D., et al.: Electrification planning decision support tool, in Domestic Use of Energy Conference. Citeseer (2000) http://citeseerx.ist.psu.edu/viewdoc/download?doi=10.1.1.195.2137&rep=rep1&type=pdf
21. Torres-Pérez, M., et al.: Freeware GIS tool for the techno-economic evaluation of rural electrification alternatives. Acta Sci. Pol. Administratio Locorum. **20**(1), 47–58 (2021). https://doi.org/10.31648/aspal.5821
22. Torres-Pérez, M., et al.: Tool for the planning of rural electrification taking into account criteria of the territorial ordering. Revista Cubana de Ciencias Informáticas. **13**(3) (2019). https://rcci.uci.cu/?journal=rcci&page=article&op=view&path%5B%5D=1886

23. Liu, Q., et al.: A density-based spatial clustering algorithm considering both spatial proximity and attribute similarity. Comput. Geosci. **46**, 296–309 (2012). https://doi.org/10.1016/j.cageo.2011.12.017
24. Romero Otero, L.: Sistemas de Información Geográfica y electrificación rural. Analisis, desarrollo y estudio de caso con IntiGIS, in Geografía-. Universidad Complutense de Madrid: Madrid. p. 98 (2016) http://eprints.ucm.es/41911/
25. NetworkX Developers: Software for Complex Networks, https://networkx.org/documentation/stable/index.html. Last accessed 01 May 2023

Diagnosis of Alzheimer Disease Progression Stage from Cross Sectional Cognitive Data by Deep Neural Network

Eduardo Garea-Llano(✉), Sheyla León Pino, and Eduardo Martinez-Montes

Cuban Neuroscience Center, 190 No. 1520, 11600 Playa, Havana, Cuba
eduardo.garea@cneuro.edu.cu

Abstract. The use of deep learning in diagnostic and modeling the progression of neurodegenerative diseases has had a significant boom in the last years. The model complexity, due to the large quantity and diversity of data necessary for their training, do not make them affordable in conditions where obtaining clinical data and magnetic resonance imaging are expensive and complex. However, under these conditions it is feasible using scores from cognitive functions. These techniques are cheap and do not require the use of sophisticated equipment. In this work we propose a deep learning based model for classification of cognitive vectors collected from each patient taking into account the labels corresponding to the disease stage (normal, mild cognitive impairment, and diseased). Experiments on ADNI cohorts shown that our proposal maintained an average accuracy of 0.968 with a standard deviation of 0.01, which is higher than the obtained by the compared methods. The experiments demonstrated the feasibility of the proposed model.

Keywords: Deep Learning · Alzheimer Disease · Progression Stage · Classification

1 Introduction

Alzheimer's disease (AD), as one of the most common forms of dementia, is a neurodegenerative disease that causes progressive cognitive decline and memory loss. In terms of neuropathology, it causes neurons and synaptic loss in the cerebral cortex and specific subcortical regions, ultimately leading to death [1]. The prevention and treatment of Alzheimer's disease is a key challenge in today's aging society.

Due to its nature and long evolution, the care and treatment of patients with AD adds more economic burden to their family members. In addition, the psychological burden of caring for people with AD is very severe and, as a result, many families or caregivers experience high levels of emotional stress and depression.

For now, there is no cure for AD, and the available treatments offer relatively little symptomatic benefit and are palliative in nature. Therefore, achieving effective and efficient intervention through early detection and diagnosis of AD is of great importance

Y. Hernández Heredia et al. (Eds.): IWAIPR 2023, LNCS 14335, pp. 273–284, 2024.
https://doi.org/10.1007/978-3-031-49552-6_24

to ensure a better quality of life for patients and adequate tools for their management to family members and caregivers. On the other hand, there is a need to have tools that allow specialists to assess the effectiveness of new treatments and drugs that are being developed in our country to face the high prevalence of this disease in an aging population [2]. AD can be diagnosed, but not predicted in its early stages, since the prediction is only applicable before the disease manifests itself.

Despite being a very recent area of research, a large number of advanced techniques are currently reported in the literature [3]. Cognitive function assessment techniques have been described as important indicators of dementia [4–6], such as the Mini Mental State Examination (MMSE), the cognitive subscale of the AD (ADAS) and the Rey Auditory Verbal Learning Test (RAVLT), which are used as preliminary screening tools in the detection of collaboration and vocabulary memory in patients with AD. The brain scan technique [7] is very popular, and is based on a magnetic resonance imaging (MRI) machine to obtain tomographic images with the aim of identifying structural and functional brain abnormalities, including dementia, and which allows estimating the volume and density of the brain components of the patient with AD [8].

In [3] a study of the state of the art of modeling techniques for AD progression is carried out. The authors report that among the key techniques for the care of patients with AD, a fundamental aspect is to understand the progress of the disease and try to identify stable and sensitive biomarkers for accurate monitoring of AD progression. For example, atrophy of the temporal structures is considered a valid diagnostic marker in the stage of mild cognitive impairment. On the other hand, as the disease progresses in AD patients, changes in their cerebral cortex can be captured on magnetic resonance images.

Regression models [7, 9, 10] have previously been used in AD studies to explore correlations between cognitive measurement and magnetic resonance imaging changes. Therefore, the way to establish a model of AD progression on cognitive scores has drawn attention due to its importance in the early diagnosis of AD.

The latest advances in machine learning techniques provide another opportunity to train disease progression models for AD. This trend leads to explore and design new machine learning techniques for a multimodal health and medical dataset with the aim of predicting occurrences and modeling the progression of AD.

Currently, the accurate diagnosis of AD can only be postmortem [1]. However, based on clinical observations a working diagnosis of the AD evolutionary stage can be made. The use of deep learning in diagnostic tasks and modeling the progression of AD has had a significant boom in the last 5 years [11]. The great complexity of the proposed models in the literature [12, 13], due to the large quantity and diversity of data necessary for their training, do not make them affordable in conditions where obtaining clinical laboratory data and magnetic resonance brain imaging are expensive and complex. However, under these conditions it is feasible using scores from the assessment of cognitive functions. These widely used techniques are cheap and do not require the use of sophisticated equipment, in addition to being minimally invasive and quick to perform.

In the specialized literature, several of them are described as important biomarkers of the disease [14].

In this work we present a model based on deep neural networks for the classification of Alzheimer Disease progression stage from cross sectional cognitive data and carry out a comparative study of the performance of various machine learning architectures in this task. To the study and validation of the proposed model under realistic conditions, we performed classification experiments on the Alzheimer's disease Neuroimaging Initiative (ADNI) cohort (http://adni.loni.usc.edu).

The remainder of the paper is structured as follows. Section 2 describes the experimental data and the proposed algorithm. In Sect. 3, we present the design of the experiment, the results achieved, and their discussion. Finally, conclusions are drawn.

2 Methods

Data used in the preparation of this article were obtained from the Alzheimer's Disease Neuroimaging Initiative[1] (ADNI) database (adni.loni.usc.edu). The ADNI was launched in 2003 as a public-private partnership, led by Principal Investigator Michael W. Weiner, MD. The primary goal of ADNI has been to test whether serial magnetic resonance imaging (MRI), positron emission tomography (PET), other biological markers, and clinical and neuropsychological assessment can be combined to measure the progression of mild cognitive impairment (MCI) and early Alzheimer's disease (AD). The latest information is available at http://adni.loni.usc.edu/about/.

The current study comprised all participants enrolled in the four ADNI cohorts (ADNI1, ADNI2, ADNIGO, and ADNI3). It included 14,451 records from 2,234 participants. For the experiments, data from the ADNI neuropsychological battery was taken. These scores are robust and outperform individual domain-specific measures. During follow-up, participants were classified as Normal/ Mild Cognitive Impairment (MCI)/AD following published standards.

2.1 Study of the Degree of Correlation of Cognitive Variables

For this first study, a manual, patient-to-patient process was performed to merge the cognitive data tables of the ADNI1 cohort (https://adni.loni.usc.edu/). For this, the dates of the visits where the tests were performed were compared and collated. The scores that describe the results of each of the tests were taken from each table. In Table 1 we present the merged tables and the scores taken by each of them.

As a result, a database of the fused 15 scores was obtained for each of the ADNI1 patients and for each of the visits made by each patient. The database consists of 3873 patient records comprising ADNI1. The records are labeled according to the diagnosis made by the specialists at the time the tests were carried out.

[1] Data used in preparation of this article were obtained from the Alzheimer's Disease Neuroimaging Initiative (ADNI) database (adni.loni.usc.edu). As such, the investigators within the ADNI contributed to the design and implementation of ADNI and/or provided data but did not participate in analysis or writing of this report. A complete listing of ADNI investigators can be found at: http://adni.loni.usc.edu/wp-content/uploads/how_to_aply/ADNI_Acknowledgement_List.pdf.

The three classes that make up the cohort are well balanced with 1132 records labeled as normal, 1606 records labeled as MCI and 1135 records labeled as AD.

Feature reduction among selected scores was performed on the training set using a Wilcoxon rank-sum test, Student's t-test, or a maximum relevance minimum redundancy approach [15]. Highly correlated features (Pearson correlation threshold = 0.9) were removed to reduce redundancy.

The extracted features correspond to the 3 ADAS cognitive scores (COT1SCOR, COT2SCOR, COT3SCOR), the 2 ADAS total scores (TOTAL11, TOTALMOD), Total score of functional assessment questionnaire (FAQTOTAL), and score mini-mental state exam (MMSCORE).

Table 1. Tables and merged scores of ADNI1 cohort

Description	Score name	ADNI file
Cognitive behavior		
Alzheimer's Disease Assessment Scale (ADAS) Subscores and Total Scores	COT1SCOR	ADAS_ADNI1.csv
	COT2SCOR	
	COT3SCOR	
	TOTAL11	ADASSCORE.csv
	TOTALMOD	
Clinical Dementia Rating		
Memory score	CDMEMORY	CDR.csv
Orientation score	CDORIENT	
Judgment and Problem Solving Score	CDJUDGE	
Community Affairs Score	CDCOMMUN	
Home and Hobbies Score	CDHOME	
Personal Care Score	CDCARE	
Global Clinical Dementia Rating	CDGLOBAL	
Functional Assessment Questionnaire		
Total Score	FAQTOTAL	FAQ.csv
Geriatric Depression Scale		
Total Score	GDTOTAL	GDSCALE.csv
Mini-mental state examination		
Total Score	MMSCORE	MMSE.csv

Figures 1 and 2 show a graphic analysis of the distribution of the values of the 7 characteristics that were most discriminative for each class.

As can be seen in Fig. 1, the three parameters of cognitive behavior are capable of separating patients in a normal state well, however they mix those patients in MCI and AD states. The parameters of the total score of the ADAS (TOTAL11 and TOTALMOD) and the FAQTOTAL are good descriptors of the EA class, however they mix the rest of the classes. Finally, we see in Fig. 2 that the MMSCORE parameter makes it possible to define the three classes with a certain degree of clarity.

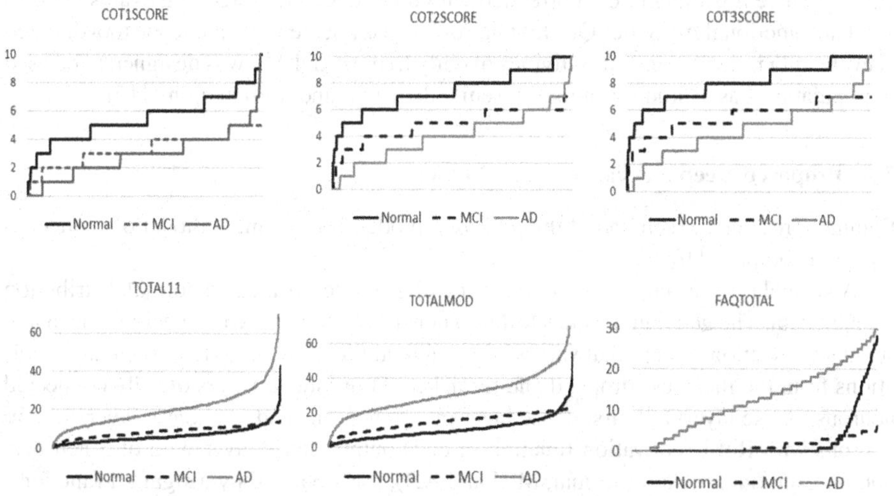

Fig. 1. Distribution of values in ADNI1 cohort corresponding to ADAS-Cognitive behavior and Functional Assessment Questionnaire. The x-axis shows the number of records analyzed, the y-axis shows the values of each parameter

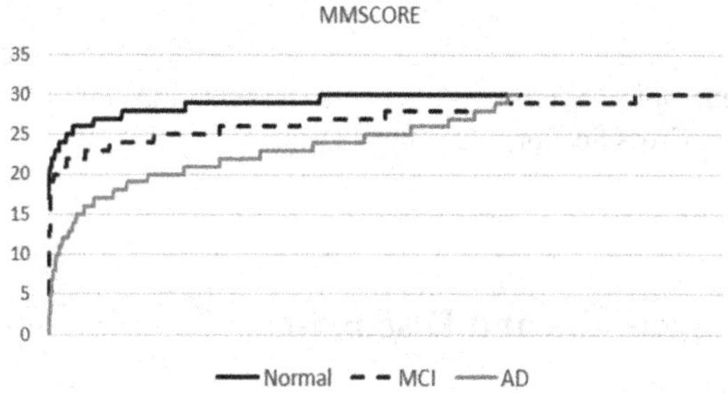

Fig. 2. Distribution of values in ADNI1 cohort corresponding to Mini-mental state examination. The x-axis shows the number of records analyzed, the y-axis shows the values of MMSCORE

The Alzheimer's Disease Assessment Scale [16] is made up of two parts: cognitive and non-cognitive testing. The ADAS-Cog consists of items from the following areas chosen for their sensitivity to Alzheimer's disease: language; memory; praxis; and orientation. The test takes 30–35 min to administer and the item scores generally range from 1–5. The total ADAS-Cog score ranges from 0–70 with higher scores suggesting greater impairment.

Mini–Mental State Examination (MMSE) is a tool that can quickly diagnose if a person suffers from mild cognitive impairment (MCI) through answering questions in different cognitive domains. The MMSE demonstrates moderately high levels of reliability. It has been reported to be internally consistent. The MMSE has been found to have short-term test–retest reliability in patients with dementia, as well as long-term reliability in cognitively intact individuals. The MMSE has been shown to have construct validity, since it is moderately correlated with other dementia screening exams [16].

The Functional Activities Questionnaire (FAQ) is a screening diagnostic tool directed at evaluating independence in activities of daily living (ADL). It was designed to be used in population-based studies on mildly senile dementia and normal aging [16].

2.2 Proposed Deep Neural Network Model

Figure 3 presents the scheme of the proposed model. It is a simple model of sequential type and composed by:

A normal type initializer. This function will generate a truncated normal distribution of input data. The generated values follow a normal distribution with specified mean and standard deviation, except that values whose magnitude is more than two standard deviations from the mean are dropped and re-picked. Four hidden layers of fully connected neurons (dense layers). A first dense layer of 128 neurons and two dense layers of 256 neurons with ReLU activation function. It ends output dense layer with of 3 neurons, one for each output class (normal, MCI and AD), it is obtained by a sigmoid function.

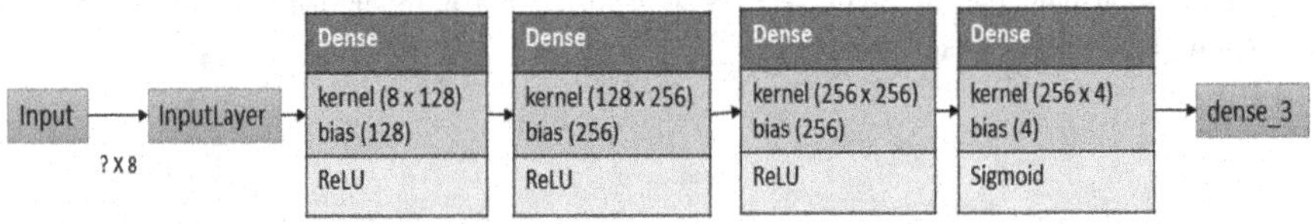

Fig. 3. General scheme of the proposed network for classification of Alzheimer Disease Progression Stage from Cross Sectional Cognitive Data.

3 Experimental Results and Discussion

For the validation of the proposed model, it was compared with the performance of 4 other architectures, 2 based on classic machine learning methods and 2 based on CNN-type networks.

3.1 Implementation Details

The architectures were chosen based on criteria based on the volume of data needed for training, validation and testing of the models, as well as the length of the feature vectors.

Random Forest (RF). This algorithm creates multiple decision trees and combines them to obtain a prediction. In this algorithm additional randomness is added to the model, as the trees grow, instead of looking for the most important characteristic when dividing a node, it looks for the best characteristic among a random subset of characteristics, this results in a wide diversity that generally results in a better model [17].

Linear Discriminant Analysis (LDA). Consists in finding the projection hyperplane that minimizes the interclass variance and maximizes the distance between the projected means of the classes. Similarly to PCA, these two objectives can be solved by solving an eigenvalue problem with the corresponding eigenvector defining the hyperplane of interest. This hyperplane can be used for classification, dimensionality reduction and for interpretation of the importance of the given features [18].

U-net. One of the most widely used neural networks for image segmentation is U-net. It is a fully convolutional neural network model. This model was originally developed in 2015 for the segmentation of medical images [19]. The U-net architecture consists of two "tracks". The first is that of contraction, also called the encoder. It is used to capture the context of an image. Actually, it is a set of convolution layers and "max pooling" layers that allow to create a feature map of an image and reduce its size to reduce the number of network parameters.

ResNet50. It is a convolutional neural network that is 50 layers deep. ResNet, short for Residual Networks, is a classic neural network used as the backbone for many computer vision tasks. The fundamental advance with ResNet was that it allowed us to train extremely deep neural networks with more than 150 layers [20].

The implementation of the necessary pipelines was developed in python language. In the case of the RF and LDA algorithms, the implementations available in the scikit-learn package (https://scikit-learn.org/stable/) were used. For the implementation of CNN networks and the proposed model, the Keras framework (https://keras.io/) was used.

3.2 Model Training

For model training, the dataset obtained from ADNI1 cohort was divided into three sets with randomly selected records: Training: 2796. Validation: 693 and Test: 384.

In order to verify the observations made in the process carried out in 2.1, all the models were trained with three different schemes, a first scheme considers all the characteristics of Table 1 (15), the second takes the 7 characteristics that resulted discriminative in the feature reduction process and the third takes 4 features resulting from the graphic analysis carried out in 2.1 (COT3SCORE, TOTALMOD, FAQTOTAL and MMSCORE).

To carry out the training of the CNN networks, we adapted the input feature vectors to the data entry form of the CNN architectures. For this, the data of each vector corresponding to each patient visit were normalized to values from 0 to 1 in a 1xn one-dimensional matrix, where n is the number of characteristics used in each scheme. By means of concatenation operations, 150 X 150 arrays were then created with the values of each matrix.

All models were trained with the same training set. In the case of the RF and LDA, 50 training iterations were carried out on the training set. For CNNs and the proposed model the training process was carried out for 100 epochs using categorical cross entropy (*Lcl*) as loss function and the Adam optimizer.

Lcl is the loss function of the classification process, in this case we adopt the categorical cross entropy loss function expressed by expression 1, where N denotes the batch size; y is the class label (0 for Normal, 1 for MCI and 2 for AD) and p(y); is the predicted label probability.

$$Lcl = -\frac{1}{N}\sum_{i=1}^{N}(yi.\log(p(yi)) + (1 - yi).\log(1 - p(yi)) \quad (1)$$

For the evaluation of the obtained classifiers, the Accuracy (acc) measure was used, which is the number of true hits obtained by the classifier over the total number of samples in the test set. The obtained results are shown in Table 2. Two Accuracy values were measured. The first (*Val_acc*), obtained on the validation set in the training process and second (*Test_acc*), the one obtained on the test set using the trained model.

Table 2. Results obtained in the training and evaluation process

Model	15-features		7-features		4-features	
	Val_acc	Test_acc	Val_acc	Test_acc	Val_acc	Test_acc
RF	0.754	0.732	0.776	0.757	0.773	0.756
LDA	0.762	0.725	0.791	0.775	0.789	0.773
U-net	0.773	0.745	0.833	0.791	0.812	0.783
ResNet50	0.796	0.788	0.878	0.869	0.854	0.807
Proposed	0.912	0.892	0.993	0.987	0.991	0.984

The results of the training and first evaluation shown that our proposal maintained an average acc = 0.987 which is higher than the obtained by the compared methods.

The difference caused by the use of the different schemes in terms of the used number of features is notable. The 15-features scheme achieves the worst results in all the models, however the 7-features and 4-features schemes achieve very close results, observing a slight decrease in the 4-features scheme, which indicates that the feature reduction process carried out was correct and that the exclusion of the three characteristics in the latter scheme causes a negative influence on the result.

3.3 Validation of the Obtained Classifier

To check the validity and robustness of the proposed model, cross-validation experiments were performed. In this sense, a process of comparison of the results obtained in the classification on the test set was carried out with the other two CNN networks that obtained the best results in the first training and testing process, U-net and ResNet50.

To scale up the experiments, we developed a cross-validation scheme. The dataset was divided into 10 sets of 387 samples each, and the model was trained and tested using 10-fold cross-validation scheme and the 7-features vector scheme.

Figure 4 shows the results. It is observed that our proposal maintained an average accuracy = 0.968 with a standard deviation of 0.01 higher than that obtained by the compared methods.

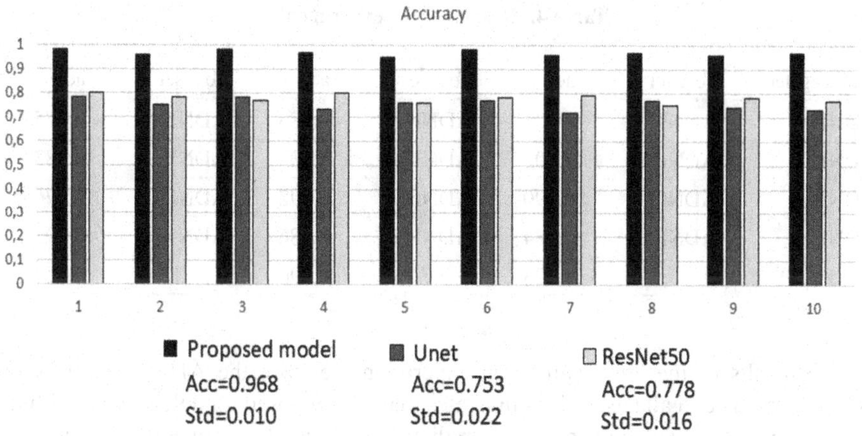

Fig. 4. Results obtained in the 10 fold cross-validation process

3.4 Extension of the Validation Experiments to the ADNI2, ADNIGO and ADNI3 Cohorts

In order to carry out a more complete validation of the results, we developed a cross-validation process on the four cohorts that comprise the ADNI database.

In the same way as with ADNI1, a manual process was carried out, patient by patient, for the fusion of cognitive data from the ADNI2, ADNIGO and ADNI3 cohorts, but only the characteristics included in the 7-features scheme were selected. In total, the three cohorts consist of 7379 records.

The extension of the experiments consisted in the validation of the results previously obtained on the ADNI1 cohort on the ADNI2, ADNIGO and ADNI3 cohorts. For this, a cross-validation scheme was designed, which we show in Table 3. The scheme takes each of the cohorts from the ADNI database and performs the training and test of each of them crosswise, so that only one cohort is used in training while the rest are used as test set. As can be seen, four training processes of the proposed network and 12 classification tests were carried out on the proposed model.

Table 3. Cross-validation scheme used in the development of the experiments.

Training set	Test set 1	Test set 2	Test set 3
ADNI1	ADNIGO	ADNI2	ADNI3
ADNI2	ADNI1	ADNIGO	ADNI3
ADNIGO	ADNI2	ADNI1	ADNI3
ADNI3	ADNI2	ADNI1	ADNIGO

Each classifier was trained for 100 epochs using categorical cross entropy as loss function and the Adam optimizer. For the evaluation of the obtained classifiers, the Accuracy (acc) measure was used. The results obtained are shown in Table 4.

Table 4. Results of the experiments

Training set	Test set 1	acc	Test set 2	acc	Test set 3	acc
ADNI1	ADNIGO	1.00	ADNI2	0.983	ADNI3	0.975
ADNI2	ADNI1	1.00	ADNIGO	1.00	ADNI3	0.983
ADNIGO	ADNI2	0.990	ADNI1	0.992	ADNI3	0.976
ADNI3	ADNI2	0.984	ADNI1	0.986	ADNIGO	0.993
Average		0.993		0.990		0.982

The results of the cross-validation experiment between the ADNI cohorts show high performance in all cases. This indicates that the proposed model together with the selected characteristics are capable of predicting with great accuracy the evolutionary stage of the disease in which the patient is at the time of the cognitive tests.

4 Conclusions

In this work we presented a deep neural network based model for diagnosis of Alzheimer disease progression stage. Experiments on ADNI1 cohort shown that our proposal obtained better results than other methods of the state of the art with which it was compared. The extension of the experiments to the rest of the cohorts of ADNI database in a cross-validation scheme demonstrated the robustness and reliability of the model and of the selected features to predict the evolutionary stage of Alzheimer's disease. The model should be tested in populations with cognitive impairment due to other neurological problems to study the specificity that can be achieved in the diagnosis of Alzheimer Disease.

Acknowledgement. Data collection and sharing for this project was funded by the Alzheimer's Disease Neuroimaging Initiative (ADNI) (National Institutes of Health Grant U01 AG024904) and DOD ADNI (Department of Defense award number W81XWH-12-2-0012). ADNI is funded by the National Institute on Aging, the National Institute of Biomedical Imaging and Bioengineering, and through generous contributions from the following: AbbVie, Alzheimer's Association; Alzheimer's Drug Discovery Foundation; Araclon Biotech; BioClinica, Inc.; Biogen; Bristol-Myers Squibb Company; CereSpir, Inc.; Cogstate; Eisai Inc.; Elan Pharmaceuticals, Inc.; Eli Lilly and Company; EuroImmun; F. Hoffmann-La Roche Ltd and its affiliated company Genentech, Inc.; Fujirebio; GE Healthcare; IXICO Ltd.; Janssen Alzheimer Immunotherapy Research & Development, LLC.; Johnson & Johnson Pharmaceutical Research & Development LLC.; Lumosity; Lundbeck; Merck & Co., Inc.; Meso Scale Diagnostics, LLC.; NeuroRx Research; Neurotrack Technologies; Novartis Pharmaceuticals Corporation; Pfizer Inc.; Piramal Imaging; Servier; Takeda Pharmaceutical Company; and Transition Therapeutics. The Canadian Institutes of Health Research is providing funds to support ADNI clinical sites in Canada. Private sector contributions are facilitated by the Foundation for the National Institutes of Health (www.fnih.org). The grantee organization is the Northern California Institute for Research and Education, and the study is coordinated by the Alzheimer's Therapeutic Research Institute at the University of Southern California. ADNI data are disseminated by the Laboratory for Neuro Imaging at the University of Southern California.

This work was also founded by the Cuban Center for Neurosciences through project PN305LH013-015. Development of disease progression models for brain dysfunctions.

References

1. Khachaturian, Z.S.: Diagnosis of Alzheimer's disease. Arch. Neurol. **42**(11), 1097–1105 (1985). Nov.
2. Almaguer-Melian, W., Mercerón-Martínez, D., Bergado-Rosado, J.: A unique erythropoietin dosage induces the recovery of long-term synaptic potentiation in fimbria-fornix lesioned rats. Brain Research **1799**, 148178 (2023). https://doi.org/10.1016/j.brainres.2022.148178
3. Wang, X., Qi, J., Yang, Y., Yang, P.: A Survey of Disease Progression Modeling Techniques for Alzheimer's Diseases. In: 2019 IEEE 17th International Conference on Industrial Informatics (INDIN), pp. 1237–1242 (2019). https://doi.org/10.1109/INDIN41052.2019.8972091
4. Folstein, M.F., Folstein, S.E., McHugh, P.R.: Mini-mental state. A practical method for grading the cognitive state of patients for the clinician. J. Psychiatr Res. **12**(3), 189–98 (1975)
5. Schmidt, M.: Rey Auditory Verbal Learning Test: A Handbook RAVLT (1996)
6. Chu, L.W., et al.: "The reliability and validity of the Alzheimer's Disease Assessment Scale Cognitive Subscale (ADAS-Cog) among the elderly" Chinese in Hong Kong. Ann Acad. Med. Singapore **29**(4), 474–85 (Jul. 2000)
7. Frisoni, G.B., Fox, N.C., Jack, C., Scheltens, M., Thompson,P.P.: The clinical use of structural MRI in Alzheimer disease. Nature Reviews Neurology (2010)
8. Baskaran, K.R., Sanjay, V.: Deep learning based early Diagnosis of Alzheimer's disease using Semi Supervised GAN. Annals of the Romanian Society for Cell Biology, 7391–7400 (2021)
9. Wan, J., et al.: Sparse Bayesian multi-task learning for predicting cognitive outcomes from neuroimaging measures in Alzheimer's disease. IEEE Conference on Computer Vision and Pattern Recognition **2012**, 940–947 (2012). https://doi.org/10.1109/CVPR.2012.6247769
10. Wan, J., et al.: Identifying the neuroanatomical basis of cognitive impairment in Alzheimer's disease by correlation- and nonlinearity-aware sparse bayesian learning. IEEE Trans. Med. Imaging **33**(7), 1475–1487 (2014). https://doi.org/10.1109/TMI.2014.2314712. July
11. Al-Shourky, S., Rassem, T.H., Makbol, N.M.: "Alzheimer's Diseases Detection by Using Deep Learning Algorithms": A Mini-Review. IEEE Access **8** (2020)
12. Jain, R., Aggarwal, A., Kumar, V.: Chapter 1 - A review of deep learning-based disease detection in Alzheimer's patients. In: Jude, H.D. (ed.) Handbook of Decision Support Systems for Neurological Disorders, pp. 1–19. Academic Press (2021). https://doi.org/10.1016/B978-0-12-822271-3.00004-9
13. Ghada, M., Fadhl, A., Algaphari, G.H.: Machine learning and deep learning-based approaches on various biomarkers for Alzheimer's disease early detection: A review. IJSECS **7**(2), 26–43 (2021). https://doi.org/10.15282/ijsecs.7.2.2021.4.0087
14. Monfared, T., Byrnes, A.A., White, M.J., et al.: Alzheimer's Disease: Epidemiology and Clinical Progression. Neurol Ther **11**, 553–569 (2022). https://doi.org/10.1007/s40120-022-00338-8
15. Peng, H., Long, F., Ding, C.: Feature selection based on mutual information criteria of max-dependency, max-relevance, and min-redundancy. IEEE Trans. Pattern Anal. Mach. Intell. **27**, 1226–1238 (2005)
16. Lichtenberg, P.A., (ed.): Handbook of Assessment in Clinical Gerontology, 2nd Edition, pp. 179–210. Academic Press (2010). ISBN 9780123749611, https://doi.org/10.1016/B978-0-12-374961-1.10007-7
17. Gelbowitz, A.: Decision Trees and Random Forests Guide: An Overview of Decision Trees and Random Forests: Machine Learning Design Patterns. Independently Published (2021)

18. Xanthopoulos, P., Pardalos, P.M., Trafalis, T.B.: Linear discriminant analysis. In: Robust Data Mining. SpringerBriefs in Optimization. Springer, New York, NY. https://doi.org/10.1007/978-1-4419-9878-1_4
19. Ronneberger, O., Fischer, P., Brox, T. U-net: convolutional networks for biomedical image segmentation. In: Navab, N., Hornegger, J., Wells, W., Frangi, A. (eds.) Medical Image Computing and Computer-Assisted Intervention – MICCAI 2015. MICCAI 2015. Lecture Notes in Computer Science(), vol 9351. Springer, Cham (2015). https://doi.org/10.1007/978-3-319-24574-4_28
20. He, K., Zhang, X., Ren, S., Sun, J.: Deep Residual Learning for Image Recognition, 770–778 (2016). https://doi.org/10.1109/CVPR.2016.90

Robust MCU Oriented KWS Model for Children Robotic Prosthetic Hand Control

Alejandro Perdomo-Campos[1(✉)], Jorge Ramírez-Beltrán[2], and Arturo Morgado-Estevez[3]

[1] Center for Microelectronics Research, Technological University of Havana "José Antonio Echeverría", 114 Street e/Ciclovía & Rotonda, Marianao, Havana, Cuba
aperdomoc@tele.cujae.edu.cu

[2] Center for Hydraulic Research, Technological University of Havana "José Antonio Echeverría", 114 Street e/Ciclovía & Rotonda, Marianao, Havana, Cuba

[3] School of Engineering, Av. Universidad de Cádiz, 10, University of Cadiz, Puerto Real, Cadiz, Spain
arturo.morgado@uca.es

Abstract. There are few models of prosthetic hands in literature designed for children. The use of speech commands as control method was not found to be used in any of them. Control by voice based on Keyword Spotting (KWS) is a non-invasive method that offers many advantages over others. KWS based on Deep Learning models have proved to be the most accurate, but their implementation in microcontrollers (MCUs) is challenging due to MCUs low hardware resources. In this paper, a robust KWS model based on log-Mel spectrograms and CNNs is presented for deployment on MCUs. The model is trained to recognize 5 keywords using the Multilingual Spoken Words Corpus and UrbanSound8k datasets, including a large number of non-keywords and background noise in training to provide robustness. Some popular MCU platforms are evaluated to implement the model, and STM32 was chosen for its advantages. Inference time simulations were made on some model-compatible STM32 boards.

Keywords: Keyword Spotting · Deep Learning · microcontrollers · children prosthetic hand

1 Introduction

Prosthetic hands are one of the most complex types of prostheses to design. Hands give humans the ability to perform specific grips and movements that require a high level of precision. Few models of hand prostheses have been found in the literature to be designed for children. Children hand prostheses are characterized for being small, which makes difficult the integration of some kinds of hardware elements in their design.

Y. Hernndez Heredia et al. (Eds.): IWAIPR 2023, LNCS 14335, pp. 285–296, 2024.
https://doi.org/10.1007/978-3-031-49552-6_25

Ribeiro et al. offer a literature review on the different methods used for the control of robotic prostheses in upper-limbs through Man-Machine interfaces [13]. The most frequently used method is based on the acquisition of superficial electromyographic signals (sEMG). This method has the disadvantage of the acquisition of sEMG signals being greatly affected by high levels of noise. An alternative to avoid this has been implanting the electrodes into the muscles to obtain intramuscular electromyographic signals (iEMG). Another method that has been used is the implementation of Brain-Machine interfaces for the acquisition of electrocardiographic signals (ECoG). However, the methods of iEMG and ECoG signals are invasive and require surgical interventions, which makes them unsuitable for children. Attempts have been made to find non-invasive methods not having the appointed drawbacks of sEMG signals. One that has given good results is the obtention of ultrasound images of the forearm muscles, but its implementation requires specialized equipment, which is difficult to integrate into small dimension hardware solutions. Another approach that has also been used is the control by speech commands. The latter does not have the disadvantages of sEMG signals and in relation to the ultrasound images demands much simpler hardware for data acquisition, i.e. a microphone, which can be small enough for easy integration into the available space in most children prosthetic hands. Multiple implementations of prostheses and medical devices being controlled by speech commands can be found in the literature. However, no children oriented robotic prosthetic hand controlled by speech was found.

Some of the most used hardware platforms for automatic speech recognition (ASR) systems are Single Board Computers (SBC) and FPGAs for the great development possibilities they offer due to their powerful hardware resources, but they are difficult to embed into size-limited devices. Microcontrollers (MCUs) on the other hand, can be easily embedded, but their limited resources make their use for ASR a challenging task due to the computational complexity of ASR techniques. Nevertheless, a lot of research has been done since the beginnings of ASR for embedding these models into MCUs [14].

It was not until the rise of Deep Learning approaches that speech recognition became possible with high levels of accuracy in real scenarios. Deep keyword spotting (KWS) involves unique inherent issues compared to general-purpose ASR. López-Espejo et al. offer a review on deep KWS [6].

One of the main issues when designing and training a deep KWS model is the availability of datasets. Spoken keywords datasets require significant manual effort to collect. This is why much of the work found in literature relies on existing public datasets. These datasets are usually monolingual and contain only a handful of keywords in controlled low-noise environments. The selection of the most significant speech datasets employed for training and validating deep KWS systems offered by López-Espejo et al. shows the lack of datasets in Spanish language [6]. In 2021, Mazumder et al. presented the Multilingual Spoken Words Corpus (MSWC), a large audio dataset of spoken words in 50 languages collected from 5 billion people for academic and commercial purposes [8]. The MSWC outperforms other popular public datasets like GSC in the number of word utterances and is publicly available. It contains recordings of over 24800 words in Spanish made in natural environments to achieve the presence of common levels of noise, which makes a difference when compared to other public datasets. For background noise, UrbanSound8K dataset is a good alternative. It is also publicly available, containing 8732 labeled slices divided into ten different classes [18].

TinyML has emerged as a popular approach for embedded intelligence, making Deep Learning available to MCUs [12], so deep KWS have been easier to embed into MCU edge devices. Many recent works implement KWS in MCUs by using TinyML approaches [1].

In 2022 Osman et al. trained a Convolutional Neural Network (CNN) for KWS with the Google Speech Commands (GSC) dataset, benchmarking two popular TinyML frameworks: Tensorflow Lite Micro (TFLM) on the Arduino Nano BLE and CUBE AI on the STM32-NUCLEOF401RE board [10]. Saifullah et al. used a CNN with the GSC dataset on the STM32-NUCLEOG474RE board for KWS in the same year [15]. However, in these works models were trained only with recordings of the keywords to identify, not considering audio streams containing non-keywords. Miah and Wang also in 2022, did include non-keywords for training a model based on CNNs, but did not include non-speech audio signals containing background noise, which may lead to false positives if models are not trained to deal with them [9].

In this paper, a model for speech commands recognition is presented. The main contribution is the obtention of a robust deep KWS model with 91.49% of accuracy in Spanish language, suitable for embedding into MCUs. Implementing these models in MCUs implies great limitations in memory and processing. The deep KWS model obtained will be used in the design of a voice control module for a children robotic prosthetic hand. It is more robust for real environments than others found in literature, as it includes non-keywords and background noise in training by using the MSWC and UrbanSound8k datasets.

2 Deep KWS Model for Evaluation

Figure 1 shows the general architecture of a deep KWS model.

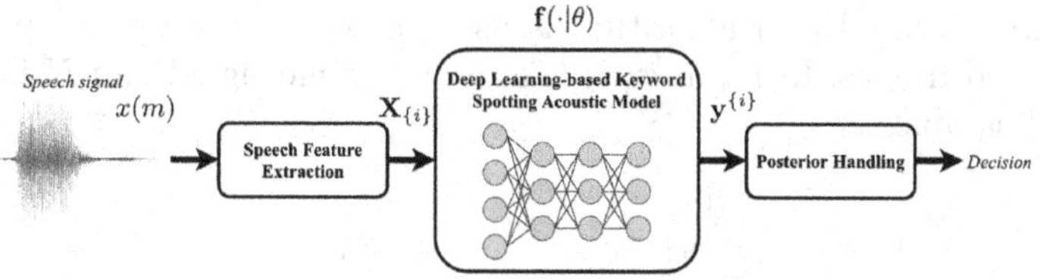

Fig. 1. General architecture of a KWS model based on Deep Learning [6]

As it can be seen, audio signals must be passed through a feature extraction block that converts them into feature vectors. These features are used by the

Deep Learning acoustic models to obtain sequences of predicted labels for the decision logic to determine the possible existence of keywords [6]. Subsections 2.1 and 2.2 state the techniques evaluated for the implementation of these blocks.

2.1 Speech Feature Extraction

Mel-scale related features, commonly Mel-frequency Cepstral Coefficients (MFCC) and log-Mel spectrograms, are still nowadays the most widely used speech features in Deep Learning based KWS models [6]. Figure 2 depicts the classical Mel-scale based feature extraction pipeline.

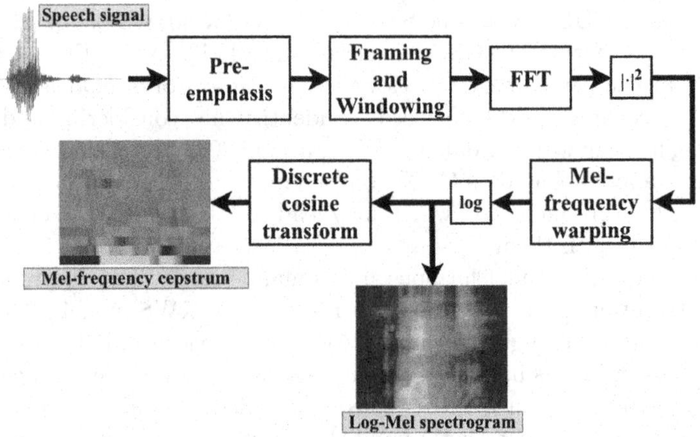

Fig. 2. Classical pipeline for extracting log-Mel spectrogram and MFCC [6]

At first, the signal is passed through a pre-emphasis stage generally consisting of a digital high-pass filter, and then it is split into overlapping frames that are windowed to reduce spectral leakages. Over these windowed frames is that feature extraction is made.

A Discrete Fourier Transform (DFT) (see Eq. 1) computed by the Fast Fourier Transform (FFT) algorithm is used to obtain the power spectrum of the windowed frames. In Eq. 1, $x(n)$ is a discrete-time signal and N is the total number of samples.

$$X(k) = \sum_{n=0}^{N-1} x(n) e^{-\frac{2\pi jnk}{N}} \qquad k = 1, 2, 3...N-1 \tag{1}$$

Power spectrum is then passed through a Mel band-pass filter, which is a bank of filters based on the Mel frequency scale. Mel filters have triangular transfer functions $H_m(k)$. The transfer function for the $m-th$ filter is defined in Eq. 2.

$$H_m(k) = \begin{cases} 0 & \text{if } k < f(m-1) \\ \frac{k-f(m-1)}{f(m)-f(m-1)} & \text{if } f(m-1) \leq k < f(m) \\ 1 & \text{if } k = f(m) \\ \frac{f(m+1)-k}{f(m+1)-f(m)} & \text{if } f(m) < k \leq f(m+1) \\ 1 & \text{if } k > f(m+1) \end{cases} \tag{2}$$

Where $f(m)$ is the central frequency for the $m - th$ triangular filter and $\sum_{m}^{M-1} H_m(k) = 1$. Equation 3 and Eq. 4 show the relationship between the Mel and linear frequency scales.

$$m = 2595\ log_{10}\left(1 + \frac{f}{700}\right) \tag{3}$$

$$f = 700\left(10^{\frac{m}{2595}} - 1\right) \tag{4}$$

At this point, a Mel spectrogram of the signal is obtained, which can be turned into a log-Mel spectrogram by taking it to the logarithmic scale. To complete the obtention of the MFCC a Discrete Cosine Transform (DCT) is applied for compression. Equation 5 shows the tipically used DCT, where $x(n)$ is a discrete-time signal and N is the length of the signal.

$$X(k) = \sum_{n=0}^{N-1} x(n) \cos\left(\frac{2\pi jnk}{N}\right) \qquad k = 1, 2, 3 ... N - 1 \tag{5}$$

Deep Learning models are able to exploit spectro-temporal correlations. This is why when facing Deep Learning models, the latter step has been shown to be unnecessary or unwanted, since it removes information and destroys spatial relations [11]. Researchs referenced in [9,15] use MFCC for feature extraction. In this research, log-Mel spectrograms are used.

2.2 Deep Learning Model Architectures

Models based on CNNs have been widely used with great results in KWS tasks since its adoption for acoustic modelling in 2015, thanks to exploiting local speech time-frequency correlations [16]. Later, Long Short-Term Memory (LSTM) models and Gated Recurrent Units (GRUs) outperformed CNNs and conventional fully-connected models. Sainath et al. showed that a cascade of convolutional, LSTM and fully-connected layers defined as Convolutional, Long Short-Term Memory Deep Neural Network (CLDNN), improved performance over LSTM-only models [17]. In 2020, Dridi and Ouni improved CLDNN models by using GRU layers instead of LSTM layers, in what they called a Convolutional Gated Recurent Unit, Deep Neural Network (CGDNN) [3]. Despite transformers and similar models have currently outperformed these approaches, their memory footprint and high latency are prohibitive for efficient deployment and inference on resource-limited devices [2]. CNN, CLDNN and CGDNN general models are shown in Fig. 3.

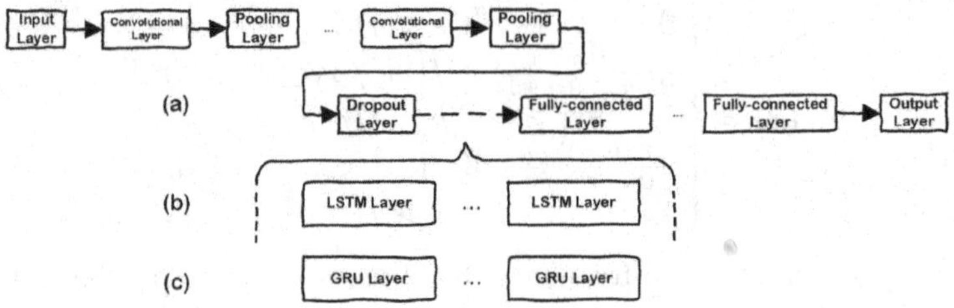

Fig. 3. DNN models considered for evaluation. (a) CNN model (b) CLDNN model (c) CGDNN model

The general models in Fig. 3 were considered for evaluation in order to select the most suitable for the KWS system implementation. Section 3 explains how these models were trained and compares the results obtained with every one of them.

3 Experimentation and Results Discussion

The MATLAB Deep Learning Toolbox was used for the evaluation of the Deep Learning models discussed in Subsect. 2.2. Tests were made for detecting five keywords consisting of the Spanish digits from 1 to 5. No tests were made for a larger number of keywords as it was not necessary for the application.

Log-Mel spectrograms were used for feature extraction. Models were designed to process 1-second recordings, split into 20 ms frames with a 10 ms overlapping. The Hann function was used for windowing. For power spectrum computing, 512 point FFTs were used.

The number of filter-bank channels in the works summarized by López-Espejo et al. ranges from 20 to 128, but experience suggests that deep keyword spotting performance is not significantly sensitive to the value of this parameter [7]. This fact allows the use of a lower number of channels without compromising accuracy in order to limit the computational complexity. This is why the number of channels used for the Mel filter-bank was 40, which is the most common value.

For the CNN model, five 2-D convolutional layers were used, followed by a single fully-connected layer targeting output classification. For each convolutional layer, batch normalization layers were used for normalizing convolution outputs to have zero mean and unit variance; Rectified Linear Unit (ReLU) layers were used for activation to introduce non-linearity and max-pooling 2-D layers were used for downsampling. At the output of the fully-connected layer, a softmax layer was used for classification.

For the CLDNNs model, a flatten layer and one single LSTM layer was introduced at the output of the group of 2-D convolutional layers and before the fully-connected layer. Only one LSTM layer was used considering the computational complexity and memory usage of LSTM models. For the CGDNN model, the LSTM layer was substituted by a GRU layer.

For training, Adam algorithm was used with an initial learning rate of 3×10^{-4}. Models were trained in 100 epochs using the Spanish subset of the MSWC. The MSWC Spanish subset and UrbanSound8K recordings were downsampled to 16 kHz, this being the sample rate expected to be used for audio acquisition. Data was split into training, testing and validation sets for every keyword class. Non-keywords were labeled as an "unknown" class. The use of this additional class with recordings of over 24800 spanish words gives robustness to the model, allowing to learn the presence of non-keywords. UrbanSound8K recordings were labeled as a background noise class, to give the model the ability to learn when there is no speech present in audio signals.

Table 1 summarizes the results obtained from training the three models discussed.

Table 1. Results obtained from training the KWS models

Model	Accuracy	Training error	Validation error	Memory size
CNN	91.49%	1.53%	8.51%	278.24 kB
CLDNN	92.41%	0.58%	7.59%	2850.60 kB
CGDNN	92.56%	0.21%	7.44%	2207.53 kB

As it can be seen, the CLDNN slightly outperformed the CNN model, whereas the CGDNN model only increased the accuracy over the CLDD in 0.15 %. The CLDNN and CGDNN models may be able to improve their performance if more LSTM and GRU layers are respectively added. However, it can be seen that one single layer of these types hugely increased memory size compared to the CNN, so adding more layers is not suitable for the purposes of this research. CLDNN and CGDNN models memory sizes achieved are incompatible with most microcontrollers. In most cases, external RAM or Flash memories would be needed to support them. The CNN model only uses 278.24 kB, which is acceptable for embedding into many microcontrollers without the need for external memories. Figure 4 shows the confusion matrix obtained for validation data used on the CNN model.

The confusion matrix shows that for all keywords high recognition rates were obtained. The lowest recognition rate was obtained for the keyword "uno", which gave 25 % of false negative predictions. However, it must be observed that for all keywords, false negatives are mostly associated to the "unknown" class, which means that failures are mostly related to "pure" false negatives and not to confusion among keywords. On the other hand, the false positive predictions rate was 8.1 % for the "unknown" class, which can be considered to be low taking into account the amount of non-keywords involved in the validation. Background noise classification was extremely accurate, with only one non-accurate prediction. As it can be seen, the model also proves to be speaker independent, as validation data contains a great number of speakers included in the MSWC dataset.

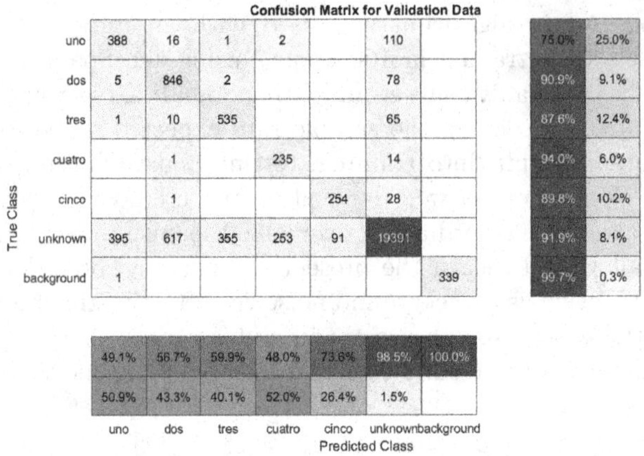

Fig. 4. Confusion matrix for validation data in the CNN model

4 MCU Selection for Model Deployment

Many frameworks and tools have emerged in recent years to embed Machine Learning models into MCUs. All these tools have been born under the concept of TinyML. Saha et al. and Ray offer reviews on the main existing frameworks and tools [12,14].

TinyML software suites are very useful tools to use pre-trained high-level models, optimize them and provide conversion to low-level MCU oriented drivers. Most of them support neural networks, making them suitable for embedding Deep Learning models. In the case of TensorFlow Lite Micro, uTensor, uTVM, SONIC and TAILS, CMSIS-NN and FANN-on-MCU, neural networks are the only supported models.

Most TinyML suites support ARM Cortex-M based microcontrollers. The suites TensorFlow Lite Micro, EON Compiler (Edge Impulse) and EloquentML support the Espressif's ESP32 system-on-modules. In the case of SONIC and TAILS, it is oriented to Texas Instruments MSP430 microcontrollers family. Based on Saha et al. and Ray reviews, Table 2 summarizes some of the most microcontroller-based development platforms with their compatible suites [12,14].

Arduino is one of the most popular development platforms in the developers community. Despite the simplicity of the MCUs in most Arduino boards, efforts have been made to take Deep Learning models into these platforms with results. The incorporation of ARM Cortex-M processors into some of the Arduino latest boards has been a major contribution to this cause. Gimenez et al. perform a comparison between the Arduino Nano 33 BLE Sense and the Arduino Portenta H7 boards in the implementation of deep KWS tasks [4].

Table 2. Some popular microcontroller-based platforms and compatible TinyML suites

Platform	CPU	TinyML compatible suites
Arduino	AVR	EloquentML
	ARM Cortex-M	TensorFlow Lite Micro
ESP8266	Tensilica Xtensa L106	EloquentML
ESP32	Tensilica Xtensa LX6	TensorFlow Lite Micro
		EON Compiler (Edge Impulse)
		EloquentML
STM32	ARM Cortex-M	STM32Cube.AI
		NanoEdge AI Studio
MSP430	MSP430 CPU	SONIC and TAILS

Espressif's ESP32 and ESP8266 system-on-modules are among the most popular platforms for IoT development. Their embedded Wi-Fi and Bluetooth peripherals makes them especially useful for the development of edge devices in IoT networks. Compared to most Arduino boards, these platforms have higher processing and memory resources. However, very little research has been made on their use for Machine Learning applications. Zim studied the performance of Xtensa LX6 processors for the implementation of neural networks in ESP32 [19].

On the other hand, STM32 and MSP430 are known to be robust MCU platforms for real-time digital signal processing (DSP) applications. In the case of STM32 MCUs, their DSP instruction set and their Floating Point Arithmetic Unit (FPU) along with their 32-bit architecture makes them powerful tools to perform DSP tasks with high-resolution data.

MSP430 MCUs, despite having a 16-bit architecture, are famous for their extremely low power consumption rates and for their Low Energy Accelerator (LEA), a coprocessor designed for the execution of high-speed complex math operations with ultra-low power consumption and independence from the CPU. Research on Machine Learning algorithms deployed on MSP430 MCUs is also poor. Heller and Woias studied the implementation of different algorithms including neural networks, with low power consumption, in MSP430 MCUs [5].

For interfacing I2S output digital microphones, STM32 is preferred over MSP430 due to the presence of I2S hardware peripherals. If MSP430 were to be used, some hardware adaptation would be needed to turn one of the integrated SPI hardware interfaces into an I2S interface. However, in high-resolution applications audio data is commonly sampled with 24-bit resolution or higher, which would be very difficult for MSP430 to deal with.

According to these elements, STM32 was chosen for deploying the deep KWS model. STM32Cube.AI was used as TinyML software suite to make the previously trained deep KWS model adaptation. It was exported from MATLAB environment to the STM32Cube.AI Cloud via the ONNX standard. Balanced optimization was made to optimize for both RAM memory usage and inference time. Table 3 summarizes the results obtained from inference simulations made for some model-compatible STM32 boards suggested by STM32Cube.AI.

Table 3. Inference time simulation for some model-compatible STM32 boards

Board	CPU (Freq.)	RAM	Flash	Inf. time
STM32H735G-DK	ARM Cortex-M7 (550 MHz)	564 kB (Int.) 16 MB (Ext.)	1024 kB (Int.) 64 MB (Ext.)	83.82 ms
STM32 NUCLEO-H743ZI2	ARM Cortex-M7 (480 MHz)	1024 kB	2048 kB	96.97 ms
STM32H747I-DISCO	ARM Cortex Dual M7+M4 (400 MHz)	1024 kB (Int.) 8 MB (Ext.)	2048 kB (Int.) 16 MB (Ext.)	115.5 ms
STM32H7B3I-DK	ARM Cortex-M7 (280 MHz)	1184 kB (Int.) 16 MB (Ext.)	2048 (Int.) 64 MB (Ext.)	166.3 ms
STM32F769I-DISCO	ARM Cortex-M7 (216 MHz)	512 kB (Int.) 16 MB (Ext.)	2048 kB (Int.) 64 MB (Ext.)	215.1 ms
B-U585I-IOT02A	ARM Cortex-M33 (160 MHz)	786 kB	2048 kB (Int.) 64 MB (Ext.)	410.5 ms
STM32F469I-DISCO	ARM Cortex-M4 (180 MHz)	384 kB (Int.) 16 MB (Ext.)	2048 kB (Int.) 16 MB (Ext.)	471.7 ms
STM32 NUCLEOG474	ARM Cortex-M4 (170 MHz)	128 kB	512 kB	529.2 ms
STM32L4R9I-DISCO	ARM Cortex-M4 (120 MHz)	640 kB	2048 (Int.) 16 MB (Ext.)	780.0 ms

As can be seen from Table 3, the STM32H735G-DK board is capable of making inferences with the lowest time delay. This board, uses the STM32H735IG MCU chip, which belongs to the H-7 series of ST high-performance MCUs. It contains a powerful ARM Cortex-M7 processor running at 550 MHz. Figure 5 shows a picture of the STM32H735-DK board.

Fig. 5. STM32H735G-DK board front and backfront views

5 Conclusions and Future Work

In this work, a speaker independent deep KWS model has been obtained for embedding onto an MCU to identify keywords in Spanish language. The embedded deep KWS model is intended to be used in the control module of a robotic prosthetic hand for children. Different models were trained and tested. The best results were obtained with a model based on CNN, reaching an accuracy of 91.49% by using the MSWC and UrbanSound8K datasets for training and validation. Several MCU-based platforms were evaluated for deployment. STM32 was chosen due to its hardware advantages over other MCUs for DSP and audio acquisition. Simulations were made for some STM32 boards. The best results were obtained for the STM32H735G-DK board, with an estimated inference time of 83.82 ms.

As future work, practical implementation must be made and several tests must be carried out to check the accuracy of the embedded model in real human environments, taking into account the decrease in accuracy that may take place when the model is quantized and optimized in the process of embedding. For physical mounting onto the prosthetis, a small hardware PCB module must be designed, containing the digital microphone and the STM32H735IG chip running the KWS model. The collection of an own dataset from children speakers for the model training would also be appropriate to increase the effectiveness of the model on children as well as to change the keywords to identify from Spanish digits to other selected words.

Acknowledgements. The authors would like to thank the Academic Interchange and Mobility Program (PIMA) held by the University of Cadiz, that made possible authors collaboration for the development of this research. This research was partially funded by the FEDER research project "Sistemas multimodales avanzados para prótesis robóticas de miembro superior (PROBOTHAND)" (FEDER-UCA18-108407) from Junta de Andalucía, Spain.

References

1. Alajlan, N.N., Ibrahim, D.M.: TinyML: enabling of inference deep learning models on ultra-low-power IoT edge devices for AI applications. Micromachines **13**(6), 851 (2022). https://doi.org/10.3390/mi13060851
2. Bondarenko, Y., Nagel, M., Blankevoort, T.: Understanding and overcoming the challenges of efficient transformer quantization (2021). https://doi.org/10.48550/arXiv.2109.12948
3. Dridi, H., Ouni, K.: Towards robust combined deep architecture for speech recognition: experiments on TIMIT. Int. J. Adv. Comput. Sci. Appl. **11**, 525–534 (2020). https://doi.org/10.14569/IJACSA.2020.0110469
4. Giménez, N.L., Freitag, F., Lee, J., Vandierendonck, H.: Comparison of two microcontroller boards for on-device model training in a keyword spotting task. In: 2022 11th Mediterranean Conference on Embedded Computing (MECO), pp. 1–4 (2022). https://doi.org/10.1109/MECO55406.2022.9797171

5. Heller, S., Woias, P.: Microwatt power hardware implementation of machine learning algorithms on MSP430 microcontrollers. In: 2019 26th IEEE International Conference on Electronics, Circuits and Systems (ICECS), pp. 25–28 (2019). https://doi.org/10.1109/ICECS46596.2019.8964726
6. López-Espejo, I., Tan, Z.H., Hansen, J.H.L., Jensen, J.: Deep spoken keyword spotting: an overview. IEEE Access **10**, 4169–4199 (2022). https://doi.org/10.1109/ACCESS.2021.3139508
7. López-Espejo, I., Tan, Z.H., Jensen, J.: Exploring Filterbank learning for keyword spotting. In: 2020 28th European Signal Processing Conference (EUSIPCO), pp. 331–335 (2021). https://doi.org/10.23919/Eusipco47968.2020.9287772
8. Mazumder, M., et al.: Multilingual spoken words corpus. In: Thirty-Fifth Conference on Neural Information Processing Systems Datasets and Benchmarks Track (Round 2) (2021)
9. Miah, M.N., Wang, G.: Keyword spotting with deep neural network on edge devices. In: 2022 IEEE 12th International Conference on Electronics Information and Emergency Communication (ICEIEC), pp. 98–102 (2022).https://doi.org/10.1109/ICEIEC54567.2022.9835061
10. Osman, A., Abid, U., Gemma, L., Perotto, M., Brunelli, D.: TinyML platforms benchmarking. In: Saponara, S., De Gloria, A. (eds.) ApplePies 2021. LNEE, vol. 866, pp. 139–148. Springer, Cham (2022). https://doi.org/10.1007/978-3-030-95498-7_20
11. Purwins, H., Li, B., Virtanen, T., Schlüter, J., Chang, S.Y., Sainath, T.: Deep learning for audio signal processing. IEEE J. Sel. Top. Sig. Process. **13**(2), 206–219 (2019). https://doi.org/10.1109/JSTSP.2019.2908700
12. Ray, P.P.: A review on TinyML: state-of-the-art and prospects. J. King Saud Univ. Comput. Inf. Sci. **34**(4), 1595–1623 (2022). https://doi.org/10.1016/j.jksuci.2021.11.019
13. Ribeiro, J., et al.: Analysis of man-machine interfaces in upper-limb prosthesis: a review. Robotics **8**(1), 16 (2019). https://doi.org/10.3390/robotics8010016
14. Saha, S.S., Sandha, S.S., Srivastava, M.: Machine learning for microcontroller-class hardware: a review. IEEE Sens. J. **22**(22), 21362–21390 (2022). https://doi.org/10.1109/JSEN.2022.3210773
15. Saifullah, K., Quaiser, R.M., Akhtar, N.: Voice keyword spotting on edge devices. In: 2022 5th International Conference on Multimedia, Signal Processing and Communication Technologies (IMPACT), pp. 1–5 (2022). https://doi.org/10.1109/IMPACT55510.2022.10029228
16. Sainath, T., Parada, C.: Convolutional neural networks for small-footprint keyword spotting (2015)
17. Sainath, T.N., Vinyals, O., Senior, A., Sak, H.: Convolutional, long short-term memory, fully connected deep neural networks. In: 2015 IEEE International Conference on Acoustics, Speech and Signal Processing (ICASSP), pp. 4580–4584 (Apr 2015). https://doi.org/10.1109/ICASSP.2015.7178838
18. Salamon, J., Jacoby, C., Bello, J.P.: A dataset and taxonomy for urban sound research. In: Proceedings of the 22nd ACM International Conference on Multimedia, pp. 1041–1044. MM '14, Association for Computing Machinery, New York, NY, USA (2014). https://doi.org/10.1145/2647868.2655045
19. Zim, M.Z.H.: TinyML: analysis of Xtensa LX6 microprocessor for neural network applications by ESP32 SoC (2021). https://doi.org/10.13140/RG.2.2.28602.11204

Detection of Malicious Bots Using a Proactive Supervised Classification Approach

Daniel Pardo Echevarría[1], Nayma Cepero-Perez[1], Mailyn Moreno-Espino[2](✉), Helder J. Chissingui[3], and Humberto Díaz-Pando[1]

[1] Universidad Tecnológica de La Habana José Antonio Echeverría, CUJAE. 114 No.11901, e/ Ciclovía y Rotonda, Marianao, La Habana, Cuba
{dpardo,ncepero}@ceis.cujae.edu.cu, humbe80@gmail.com

[2] Centro de Investigación en Computación, Instituto Politécnico Nacional. Av. Juan de Dios Bátiz, esq. Miguel Othón de Mendizábal, Col. Nueva Industrial Vallejo, C.P. 07738 Alcaldía Gustavo A. Madero, Mexico
moreno.espino.mailyn@gmail.com, mmorenoe2022@cic.ipn.mx

[3] Departamento de Electrotecnia, Instituto Superior Técnico Militar - ISTM, Avenida Deolinda Rodrigues Km 9, Luanda, Angola

Abstract. Malicious bots are one of the most commonly used tools by cybercriminals today to carry out security breaches. These malicious programs can simulate human activity, which is the reason why they affect t a large number of websites. Different techniques have been developed to ensure the detection of malicious bots, highlighting the application of Machine Learning algorithms and the meta-learning branch, for improving their performance. The present work proposes the application of the Proactive Forest algorithm as the main element of a module that allows the detection of malicious bots, based on Machine Learning. An experimental study was carried out to measure its performance, based on a comparison with the Random Forest algorithm. The results showed that 99.93% of instances were correctly classified and 99.96% were correctly classified as malicious bots out of the total, as the best results achieved.

Keywords: Bots detection · Machine Learning · Decision Forest

1 Introduction

The Internet has become a necessity for human beings, which is why its use is increasing and with it, the risk of compromising information. This leads to an increase in computer security attacks, and to achieve this, cybercriminals use various tools. One of the most prominent today are bots [1].

A bot is a computer program that simulates human activity and acts automatically; therefore, it is constantly evolving [2, 3]. Bots are usually classified into two types: benign bots and malicious bots [2]. A benign bot is characterized by being employed to perform activities for the benefit of many websites. On the other hand, cybercriminals employ malicious bots as a tool to execute computer security attacks [3, 4].

Y. Hernández Heredia et al. (Eds.): IWAIPR 2023, LNCS 14335, pp. 297–309, 2024.
https://doi.org/10.1007/978-3-031-49552-6_26

Bots have a great impact nowadays. According to [5] they accounted for 42.3% of total user traffic in 2022, of which 27.7% was comprised of traffic by malicious bots. For this reason, malicious bots are a problem that affects many web services [2]. The most prominent attacks by these malicious programs are price scraping, content scraping, user account creation, and denial of service, among others [2].

To counteract the action of these malicious bots, several techniques are used, where Machine Learning is of great relevance [6]. The use of Supervised Learning algorithms to obtain models that allow for the classification of a user as a human or malicious bot stands out above all [1, 7]. To achieve this, the importance of the application of algorithms that generate a Decision Forest as a classification model is pointed out in the literature [1, 6].

Algorithms based on Decision Forests build a collection of Decision Trees, giving rise to a Decision Forest model, with the particularity that each new tree must be as different as possible from the previous ones, so that there is diversity in the forest, but each one must be individually as accurate as possible [8]. Of these algorithms, Random Forest stands out as one of the most widely used for bot detection [6]. However, its main disadvantage is the loss of the diversity generated in the forest, due to the random approach used to build each tree [9]. To make up for this disadvantage, the Proactive Forest algorithm is presented in [9], to achieve a controlled diversity in the generated forest.

This paper presents the application of the Proactive Forest algorithm as the main component of a module for detecting malicious bots. An experimental study of its performance is performed, using different evaluation metrics, based on a comparison with the Random Forest algorithm.

2 Related Works

The impact of malicious bots is a danger to websites, and different techniques have been developed to ensure their detection. For this reason, there has been an increase in the elements of the State-of-the-art, oriented to the study, application, methodologies, and mechanisms to detect bots [6].

This is evident in the work presented in [6], where the authors provide a general overview of the techniques used in the detection of bots, emphasizing the importance of Machine Learning algorithms, particularly those belonging to Supervised Learning. Their point is supported by studies such as [1, 10, 11], which applied several of these algorithms to detect bots and achieved significant results. In [3, 4], the authors employ several Supervised Learning algorithms, focused on the detection of bots in an e-commerce context, achieving relevant results in classifying users as human or malicious bots.

In [1, 7, 12], Decision Forest algorithms are used as classification models to efficiently identify malicious bot users. Random Forest is one of the most commonly used algorithms in bot detection, as stated in [6]. It is worth highlighting the results achieved by [7] when applying the Random Forest algorithm for the detection of bots in e-commerce sites, obtaining the best result of 99.88% correctly classified instances. The importance of the CTU-13 bot attack database in training classification algorithms and evaluating their performance is emphasized in [6, 11, 13].

3 Malicious Bot Detection Module Based on Machine Learning

The need for constant analysis of malicious bots and their similarity to human users poses a problem in malicious bot detection. These are the factors that give way to the Machine Learning-based malicious bot detection module presented in this paper. This module integrates a classification algorithm based on Decision Forests and a meta-learning component, which according to [14], improves classification results. Figure 1 shows, through the Erikson Penker diagram, the architecture of the presented module, which according to [15], is called process view.

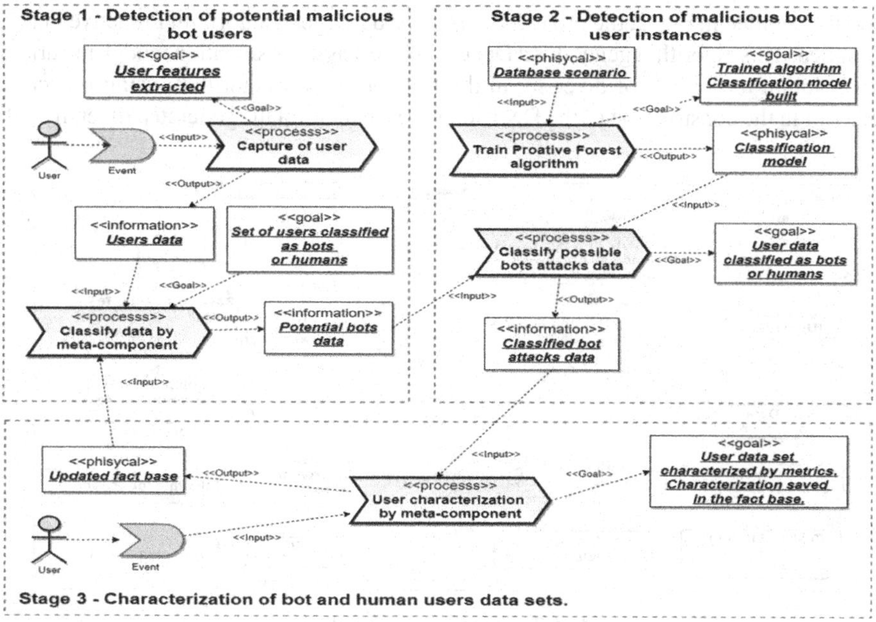

Fig. 1. Malicious bot detection module process diagram.

As shown in Fig. 1, the malicious bot detection module is comprised of three stages, which are described below:

- **Stage 1- Detection of potential malicious bot users:** The characteristics of the users accessing a website are extracted. To detect whether a given set of users are potentially malicious bots or not, meta-learning is used. This improves the results of user classification at an early stage [14]. Users considered as potential malicious bots are analyzed in the next stage.
- **Stage 2- Detection of malicious bot user instances:** In this stage, individual user instances are classifying into malicious bot or human. This is done using a classification model trained on a database of malicious bot attacks and a dataset of potential malicious bot users received from stage 1.
- **Stage 3 - Characterization of bot and human user data sets:** The instances of users interacting with the web platform, being inside it, are characterized. Using the data

already classified in the previous stage and applying different complexity measures. The results of this characterization are stored in a fact base. For this purpose, a meta-learning approach is used, which allows the characterization of data and, applying an analysis based on metrics [14].

This work focuses on the development of the second stage, using the proactive Supervised Learning algorithm, Proactive Forest [9].

3.1 Stage 2- Detection of Malicious Bot User Instances

As part of the proposed solution, for the second stage of the malicious bot detection module, detailed in Fig. 2, the proactive Supervised Learning algorithm Proactive Forest is applied. This algorithm generates a Decision Forest as a classification model and arises as a solution to the loss of diversity in the Random Forest algorithm, using proactive behavior in the construction of the Decision Forest to control the generated diversity [9].

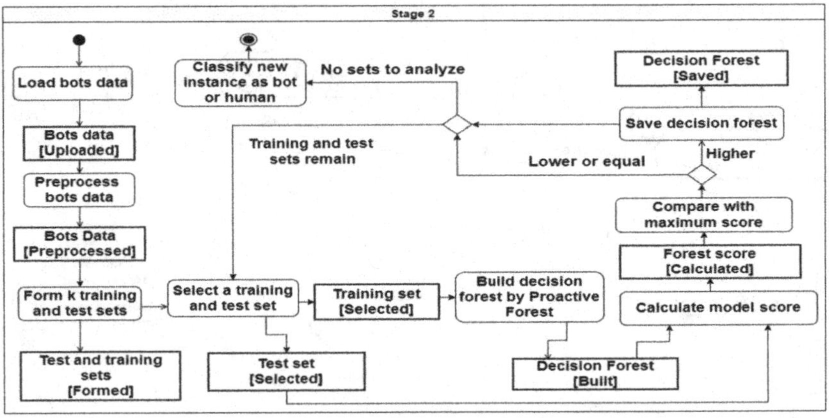

Fig. 2. Stage 2 execution flow

In this algorithm, each new tree is trained by analyzing the attributes that were least taken into account in the construction of the previous ones [9]. This analysis is performed at the time of constructing each node of each tree by taking a subset of attributes from the total, to select the one that best divides the sample data. The attributes that are part of this subset are chosen based on a probability, which is updated after the construction of each tree, increasing its value for those attributes that are less important in the construction of a tree. The classification result is obtained based on the class that resulted the most from each tree that makes up the forest [9].

As shown in Fig. 2 with the execution flow of this stage, to build the Proactive Forest model, the cross-validation technique was employed by training the algorithm on multiple training and test subsets formed by dividing the data into *k* sets of equal size. The algorithm builds models on *k-1* sets and tests on the remaining one, training and evaluating each Decision Forest constructed on all the analyzed data, and selecting the best-performing model as the result [16]. It is noteworthy that 250 trees were used to build the model since the results do not improve beyond this number. Moreover, $\log_2 n + 1$ was selected by default in [9], to form the subset to be analyzed at each level of each tree for the construction of the forest.

4 Experimental Study

This section defines the strategy to validate the results of applying the Proactive Forest algorithm through an experimental study. First, the database to be used and the preprocessing performed are described. Subsequently, the configuration used in the experimental study is discussed. Finally, the results of the experiments are shown.

4.1 Database Description

To validate the results of the present work, the CTU-13 database [1] was selected [1]. It consists of thirteen scenarios, which contain labeled data of bot attacks, obtained in real time. Each scenario contains fourteen attributes representing user network characteristics and half of these are numeric [1]. The description of each of these attributes is given in table 1.

Table 1. Description of CTU-13 attributes

Atribute	Desciption
StartTime	Start time of the attack, each record with a different timestamp with the format: 2011/08/10 12:30:13.516854
Dur	Duration of attack in seconds
Proto	Five types of protocols called: ‘tcp’, ‘udp’, ‘rtp’, ‘pim’, ‘icmp’, ‘arp’, ‘ipx/spx’, ‘rtcp’, ‘igmp’, ‘ipv6-icmp’, ‘ipv6’, ‘udt’, ‘esp’, ‘unas’, ‘rarp’
SrcAddr	Source Ip Address
Sport	Port of origin from which the traffic originated
Dir	Direction of traffic represented as: ‘- > ‘, ‘ ? > ‘, ‘ < - > ‘, ‘’, ‘ who’, ‘ < -’, ‘ < -?’
DstAddr	Recipient Ip
Dport	Destination port to which traffic is directed
State	Transaction status according to protocol, contains 231 unique values
sTos	Type of field service origin: 0, 1, 2, 3, 192, NaN
dTos	Type of field service destination: 0, 1, 2, 3, 192, NaN
TotPkts	Total packet transactions with a range of 1 to 2686731
TotBytes	Total byte transactions with a range from 60 to 2689640464
SrcBytes	Total byte transactions from origin to destination with a range of 0 to 2635366235

The database is comprised of instances belonging to three classes: normal, botnet, and back-ground [1]. Instances in the normal class correspond to actions performed by human users on the web, while instances in the botnet class represent malicious bot users. On the other hand, instances in the back-ground class represent the network's characteristics when there is no human or bot activity [1]. Table 2 shows the percentage of instances for each class relative to the total number of instances in each scenario. The amount of data present in the thirteen scenarios varies [1]. According to [7], the scenarios are categorized as large, containing more than one million instances, and small, containing less than one million instances.

Table 2. Data number of each class, for each CTU-13 scenario, taken from [1]

Scenario	Back-ground (%)	Normal (%)	Botnet (%)	Total
1	97,47	1.07	1,41	2.824.636
2	98,33	0,50	1,15	1,808,122
3	96,94	2,48	0.561	4.710.638
4	97,58	2,25	0,154	1.121.076
5	95,70	3.60	1,68	129,832
6	97,83	1,34	0,82	558,919
7	98,47	1,47	1,50	114,077
8	97,32	2,46	2,57	2,954,230
9	91,70	1,57	6,68	2,753,884
10	90,67	1.20	8.112	1,309,791
11	89,85	2,53	7.602	107,251
12	96,99	2,34	0,657	325,471
13	96,26	1,65	2,07	1.925.149

4.2 Preprocessing of Data

To preprocessing the data of the database is carried out, taking into account [17]. In this process, all the data are transformed into numerical type, since they are the majority in the scenarios to be worked. The class labels are also treated with numerical values, assigning the value 0 to the examples of background and normal label, which will be treated as examples of human users, and assigning the value 1, to those of botnet label. In addition to treating the case of rows with empty attribute values, assigning the value 0, avoiding the loss of information by not deleting examples.

As in [17], a normalization of the data and a subsequent dimensionality reduction is performed by applying the Principle Component Analysis (PCA) technique, presented in [18] and used in recent studies by [19]. However, in this work, the normalization is performed to maintain the values of the attributes within the scale of 0 to 1, facilitating better comparison between instances. Consequently, PCA dimensionality reduction with a cumulative explanatory variance of 99% is applied, resulting in a total of 7 principal components in all scenarios.

Due to the few examples of malicious bots (positive botnet class with value 1) in the scenarios, the Synthetic Minority Over-sampling Technique (SMOTE) for class balancing, presented in [20], was applied. This involved creating synthetic examples of the minority class, until reaching the same amount of the majority class [20]. This was done for all scenarios in the database, before separating the data into training and test sets, considering that synthetic examples created in the test sets can be included. Otherwise, there would be insufficient botnet data to train the model or to evaluate its performance.

To evaluate the model's performance, only the first 5000 instances of each class in the corresponding scenario were considered. The cross-validation technique was used to create the test and training sets by dividing the data sample into k equal parts, taking one of those parts to test the model and the rest to train it.

4.3 Description of Experiments

To validate the proposed solution, an experimental study is conducted to evaluate the performance of the Proactive Forest algorithm for the detection of malicious bots, compared to the Random Forest algorithm. The performance will be measured using several metrics that allow the evaluation of classification models, which according to [6], are among the most used to evaluate the results obtained in the detection of bots. These metrics measure performance based on the correct classification of malicious bots (True Positives with positive class of value 1) and non-threats (True Negatives with negative class of value 0), as well as instances that are misclassified as malicious bots but do not pose a threat (False Positives) and actual malicious bots that are not classified as such (False Negatives). The metrics employed are [6]:

1. **Accuracy:** This measures the percentage of instances that are correctly classified out of the total instances. However, it may have issues with class imbalance.
2. **Precision:** This measures the percentage of instances correctly classified as malicious bots out of the total instances classified as malicious bots by the model.
3. **Recall:** This measures the percentage of instances correctly classified as malicious bots out of the total actual malicious bots instances.
4. **F1:** This metric combines the results of precision and recall to provide an idea of the errors made in misclassifying malicious bot instances. A high percentage indicates a balance in the total number of instances correctly classified as malicious bots, out of the total classified by the model and the actual ones.

To conduct the experimental study, two scenarios, a large and a small one, will be used, as described in Sect. 4.1 and established in [1]. These scenarios are chosen due to the significant difference in the total number of instances they contain. Therefore, it is necessary to verify whether this amount of data influences the algorithms' performance by making a comparison. We will examine how each algorithm performs in the context of a large dataset and a small dataset in the opposite case. Scenario number 11 is selected as the small one because it has the fewest instances, while scenario number 3 is chosen as the large one due to its substantial amount of data. Each algorithm will be run a total of ten times.

4.4 Discussion of the Results

This section of the paper shows and analyzes the results achieved in the experimental study. The results are first discussed for the runs in the large scenario and then in the small scenario.

Results on Large Scenario.
Table 3 shows the results achieved by executions of the Proactive Forest (PF) and Random Forest (RF) algorithms, for each of the metrics evaluated. From the analysis, it can be concluded that both algorithms have a similar performance, achieving a score above 99% in all metrics. However, the following results stand out: the Proactive Forest algorithm reached a maximum of 99.92% for both Accuracy and F1 metrics, while both algorithms reached a maximum of 99.88% in the Recall metric. Additionally, the Random Forest algorithm reached a maximum of 99.98% in the Precision metric.

Table 3. Percentage results, achieved for both algorithms in the large scenario

Executions	Proactive Forest				Random Forest			
	Accuracy	Recall	Presicion	F1	Accuracy	Recall	Presicion	F1
1	99,91	99,86	99,96	99,9	99,91	99,86	99,96	99,91
2	99,91	99,86	99,96	99,91	99,9	99,84	99,96	99,9
3	99,91	99,88	99,96	99,9	99,88	**99,88**	99,88	99,88
4	99,86	99,82	99,9	99,86	99,91	99,88	99,94	99,91
5	99,91	99,86	99,96	99,91	99,91	99,88	99,94	99,91
6	99,9	99,86	99,94	99,9	99,89	99,84	99,94	99,89
7	99,88	99,82	99,94	99,87	99,9	99,86	99,94	99,9
8	**99,92**	**99,88**	99,96	**99,92**	99,89	99,84	99,94	99,89
9	99,9	99,86	99,94	99,9	99,9	99,82	**99,98**	99,9
10	99,88	99,82	99,93	99,88	99,89	99,82	99,96	99,89

To verify whether significant differences exist in the results achieved by both algorithms in each of the evaluation metrics, a non-parametric statistical test will be performed. This is due to the small sample size of ten runs for each algorithm. The selected test is Mann-Whitney test, which allows for the comparison of two data samples based on their median values [21]. It also determines whether there are significant differences between them, and if so, which of the algorithms performs better, as stated in [21]. A significance level $\alpha = 0.05$ was used, and the following hypotheses were posed:

$$H_0 : \eta_{PF} - \eta_{RF} = 0$$

$$H_1 : \eta_{PF} - \eta_{RF} > 0$$

As a result of the test, p-values of 0.339, 0.515, 0.515, and 0.530 were obtained for the Accuracy, Recall, Accuracy and F1 metrics, respectively. These values are above the significance level. Therefore, there is insufficient evidence to reject the null hypothesis, which states that there is no significant difference in the performance of both algorithms when used for detecting malicious bots. Despite this, the Proactive Forest algorithm showed slightly superior performance, in terms of the median analysis, for the Accuracy, Recall and Precision metrics, as can be seen individual value graphs in the Fig. 3. The results obtained from the precision and recall metrics are worth noting, indicating that the Proactive Forest algorithm effectively classifies instances of malicious bot users. These results show a slight improvement compared to those obtained by the Random Forest algorithm, which is one of the most used algorithms in the literature for detecting malicious bots.

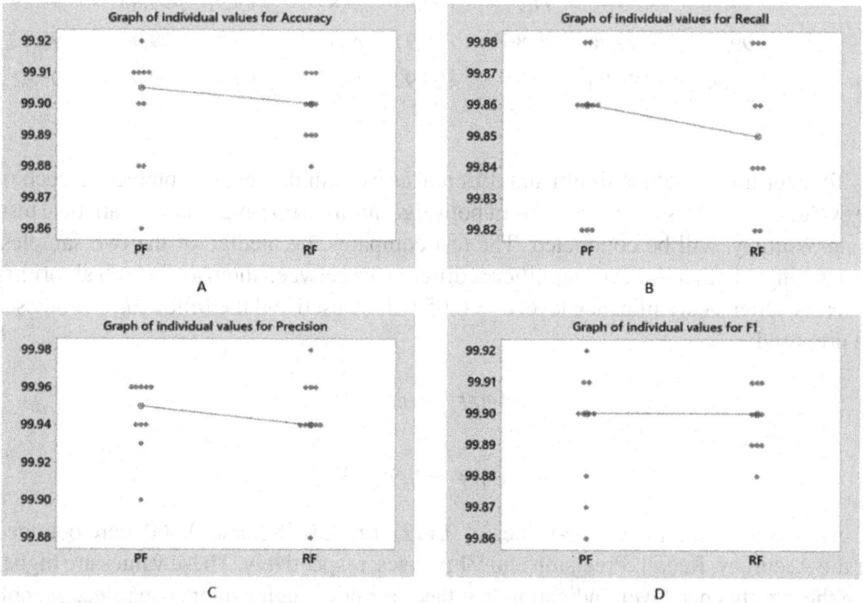

Fig. 3. Plots of individual values for the Accuracy (A), Recall (B), Precision (C) and F1 (D) metrics. In the large scenario

Results in Small Scenario

Table 4 shows the results achieved in the executions of the Proactive Forest (PF) and Random Forest (RF) algorithms, for each of the metrics evaluated.

Analyzing Table 4, it can be concluded that both algorithms demonstrate a similar performance, obtaining a score higher than 99% in all metrics. Although the results are comparable, it is worth noting that both algorithms achieved a maximum of 99.93% for the Accuracy and F1 metrics, as well as a maximum of 99.96% and 99.9% for the Recall and Precision metrics, respectively.

Table 4. Percentage results, reached for both algorithms in the small scenario

Executions	Proactive Forest				Random Forest			
	Accuracy	Recall	Presicion	F1	Accuracy	Recall	Presicion	F1
1	**99,93**	**99,96**	**99,9**	**99,93**	99,91	99,92	**99,9**	99,91
2	99,91	99,92	99,9	99,9	99,88	99,94	99,82	99,88
3	99,87	99,92	99,82	99,87	99,89	99,92	99,86	99,89
4	99,9	99,9	99,9	99,9	99,92	99,94	99,9	99,92
5	99,92	99,94	99,9	99,92	99,91	99,92	99,9	99,91
6	99,91	99,96	99,86	99,9	99,9	99,94	99,86	99,9
7	99,92	99,94	99,9	99,92	**99,93**	**99,96**	99,9	**99,93**
8	99,93	99,96	99,9	99,93	99,89	99,92	99,86	99,89
9	99,91	99,96	99,86	99,91	99,92	99,94	99,9	99,92
10	99,92	99,94	99,9	99,92	99,91	99,92	99,9	99,91

To determine whether significant differences exist in the results obtained in each of the evaluation metrics for the ten runs of both algorithms, a non-parametric statistical test, Mann-Whitney, will be conducted. The test compares the median of the two samples, determining whether there are significant differences between them and which algorithm performs better. A significance level $\alpha = 0.05$ will be used and the following hypotheses are proposed:

$$H_0 : \eta_{PF} - \eta_{RF} = 0$$

$$H_1 : \eta_{PF} - \eta_{RF} > 0$$

After conducting the test, p-values of 0.172, 0.154, 0.381, and 0.260 were obtained for the Accuracy, Recall, Precision and F1 metrics, respectively. These values are higher than the significance level, indicating that there is not enough evidence to reject the null hypothesis, that there are no significant differences in the results of both algorithms for each metric. However, as shown in Fig. 4, with displays individual value diagrams, upon analyzing the median value, the Proactive Forest algorithm demonstrated slightly superior performance for the Accuracy, Recall and F1 metrics. It is worth noting the results obtained by both algorithms when analyzing the performance based on the number of correctly classified malicious bot users, using the precision and recall metrics. Although the Proactive Forest algorithm performs slightly better than Random Forest in terms of the recall metric.

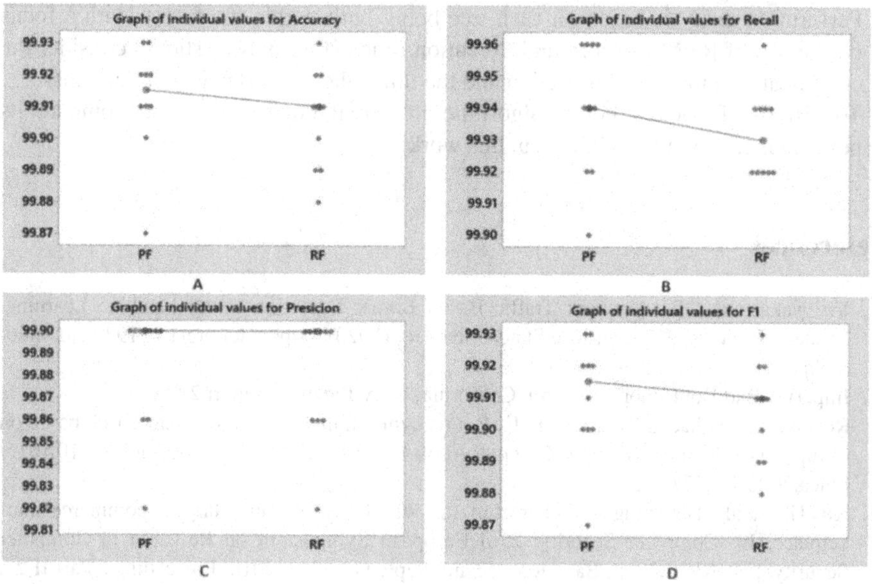

Fig. 4. Individual value plots for Accuracy (A), Recall (B), Precision (C) and F1 (D) metrics. in the small scenario

5 Conclusions

At the end of the present work, it can be concluded that:

- The Proactive Forest algorithm used in the malicious bot detection module, effectively classifies human users and malicious bots obtained from the CTU-13 database. The results are comparable or even superior to those of the widely used Random Forest algorithm.
- In a large database scenario, the Proactive Forest algorithm performs slightly better than the Random Forest algorithm in terms of correctly classified instances and instances classified as malicious bots. However, the difference is not significant.
- In a small database scenario, there is no significant difference in the performance of the Proactive Forest and Random Forest algorithms. Nevertheless, the Proactive Forest algorithm is slightly better in terms of the percentage of correctly classified instances and instances classified as malicious bots. It also achieves a better balance between correctly classified malicious bots and those classified by the model.

6 Future Work

As a future research direction, we propose the following:

- To continue evaluating the remaining stages of the malicious bot detection module and conducting a detailed analysis of the results obtained in each of them. Moreover, the overall performance of the module can be evaluated and compared with other algorithms and techniques used for malicious bot detection.

- Perform an analysis based on each tree being built within the forest, with a focus on the use of RAM memory and execution time. This analysis should consider the classification model's construction and the time taken to make new predictions.
- To test the Proactive Forest algorithm in a real environment and compare its performance with that achieved in this work.

References

1. Vishwakarma, A.R.: Network Traffic Based Botnet Detection Using Machine Learning, Master's Projects, 917. San Jose State University (2020). https://doi.org/10.31979/etd.4nd6-m6hp
2. Imperva: Bad Bot Report, Imperva, California, USA Technical report 2020
3. Rovetta, S., Suchacka, G., Masulli, F.: Bot recognition in a web store: an approach based on unsupervised learning. J. Netw. Comput. Appl. **157**, 102577 (2020). https://doi.org/10.1016/j.jnca.2020.102577
4. Xu, H., et al.: Detecting and characterizing web bot traffic in a large e-commerce marketplace. In: Computer Security: 23rd European Symposium on Research in Computer Security, ESORICS 2018, Barcelona, Spain, September 3–7, 2018, Proceedings, Part II 23, pp. 143–163. Springer (2018). https://doi.org/10.1007/978-3-319-98989-1_8
5. Imperva: Imperva Bad Bot Report - Evasive Bots Drive Online Fraud. Imperva, Technical Report 2022
6. Chissingui, H.J., Pando, H.D., Espino, M.M., Pérez, N.C.: Bot detection algorithms: a systematic literature review. Revista Cubana de Ciencias Informáticas **16**(4) (2022)
7. Pardo, D., Moreno, M., Diaz, H., Chissingui, H.J.: Random forest para la detección de bots en el comercio electrónico. In: Presented at the X Congreso Internacional de Tecnologías, Comercio Electrónico y Contenidos Digitales (2022)
8. Rokach, L.: Decision forest: twenty years of research. Information Fusion **27**, 111–125 (2016). https://doi.org/10.1016/j.inffus.2015.06.005
9. Cepero-Pérez, N., Denis-Miranda, L.A., Hernández-Palacio, R., Moreno-Espino, M., García-Borroto, M.: Proactive forest for supervised classification. In: International Workshop on Artificial Intelligence and Pattern Recognition, pp. 255–262. Springer, Cham (2018). https://doi.org/10.1007/978-3-030-01132-1_29
10. Doran, D., Gokhale, S.S.: Web robot detection techniques: overview and limitations. Data Min. Knowl. Disc. **22**(1), 183–210 (2011). https://doi.org/10.1007/s10618-010-0180-z
11. Haq, S., Singh, Y.: Botnet detection using machine learning. In: Presented at the In 2018 Fifth International Conference on Parallel, Distributed and Grid Computing (PDGC) (2018). https://doi.org/10.1109/PDGC.2018.8745912
12. Rout, R.R.L., Somayajulu, D.V.: Detection of malicious social bots using learning automata with url features in twitter network. IEEE Transactions on Computational Social Systems **7**(4), 1004–1018 (2020). https://doi.org/10.1109/TCSS.2020.2992223
13. Velasco-Mata, J., González-Castro, V., Fidalgo, E., Alegre, E.: Efficient detection of botnet traffic by features selection and decision trees. IEEE Access **9**, 120567–120579 (2021). https://doi.org/10.1109/ACCESS.2021.3108222
14. Hospedales, T., Antoniou, A., Micaelli, P., Storkey, A.: Meta-learning in neural networks: a survey. IEEE Trans. Pattern Anal. Mach. Intell. **44**(9), 5149–5169 (2021). https://doi.org/10.1109/TPAMI.2021.3079209
15. Kruchten, P.B.: The 4+ 1 view model of architecture. IEEE Softw. **12**(6), 42–50 (1995). https://doi.org/10.1109/52.469759

16. Orallo, J.H., Quintana, J.R., Ramírez, C.F.: Introducción a la Minería de Datos. Madrid, 680 (2004)
17. Chissingui, H.J., Pérez, N.C., Humberto, D., Espino, M.M.: Multiclasificador homogéneo para detección de Bots en el comercio electrónico. Revista Cubana de Transformación Digital **4**(1), e200–e200 (2023)
18. Hotelling, H.: Analysis of a complex of statistical variables into principal components. J. Educ. Psychol. **24**(6), 417 (1933). https://doi.org/10.1037/h0071325
19. Kurita, T.: Principal component analysis (PCA). Computer Vision: A Reference Guide, 1–4 (2019). https://doi.org/10.1007/978-3-030-03243-2_649-1
20. Chawla, N.V., Bowyer, K.W., Hall, L.O., Kegelmeyer, W.P.: SMOTE: synthetic minority over-sampling technique. J. Artif. Intel. Res. **16**, 321–357 (2002). https://doi.org/10.1613/jair.953
21. Nachar, N.: The mann-whitney U: a test for assessing whether two independent samples come from the same distribution. Tutori. Quantit. Methods Psychol. **4**(1), 13–20 (2008)

Hybrid Selection of Breast Cancer Risk Factors in Cuban Patients

José Manuel Valencia-Moreno[1,2(✉)], Everardo Gutiérrez López[1], José Ángel González Fraga[1], Juan Pedro Febles Rodríguez[2], Yanio Hernández Heredia[2], and Ramón Santana Fernández[1]

[1] Universidad Autónoma de Baja California, Ensenada, México
{jova,everardo.gutierrez,angel_fraga}@uabc.edu.mx, ramonsf29@gmail.com

[2] Universidad de las Ciencias Informáticas, Havana, Cuba
{febles,yhernandezh}@uci.cu

Abstract. Breast cancer is a worldwide public health problem, a disease that, although its risk factors are recognized by international health institutions, may vary from region to region. Knowing which risk factors are relevant for a certain type of population is one of the main challenges for early diagnosis and prevention of the disease. In this work, a hybrid selection of features was performed by integrating the voting of filter and wrapper techniques on a set of risk factors of 1,697 Cuban patients. With the Pareto principle on the voting of the different feature selection techniques, 8 out of 15 features were selected: number of biopsies, family history of breast cancer, tobacco use, breastfeeding, number of children, atypical hyperplasia, alcohol consumption, and obesity. The precision with which the features were selected reached an AUC of 0.999 and 99.2% accuracy. The experimental results showed that the identified risk factors have a significant effect, which can be used to develop more accurate breast cancer prediction models and improve prevention and early diagnosis in Cuban patients.

Keywords: Feature selection · Machine learning · breast cancer · risk factors

1 Introduction

Breast cancer is a very common disease in women that affected more than two million people in 2020. It represents one of the leading causes of cancer mortality [1] and is considered a public health problem as it is the type of cancer with the highest incidence and mortality among women. It has affected more than two million and caused the death of more than 680 thousand patients in 2020 [1]. A set of factors called risk factors are involved in the appearance of the disease. The identification of these risk factors is essential for prevention and timely decision making, which increases the chances of surviving the disease. This is why analyzing risk factors is an important task that has been studied from different angles in the computational sciences.

In Cuba, breast cancer ranks first in incidence and second in mortality, which means the death of approximately 6 women daily [2]. To address this problem, the Ministry

Y. Hernández Heredia et al. (Eds.): IWAIPR 2023, LNCS 14335, pp. 310–322, 2024.
https://doi.org/10.1007/978-3-031-49552-6_27

of Public Health promotes programs for prevention and early detection of this cancer, periodic screening is encouraged in women of certain ages with specific risk factors. These programs may include the assessment of individual breast cancer risk, which could involve the use of risk estimation models based on the specific risk factors of that population, to identify women who are at increased risk of developing this disease and who could benefit from more intensive surveillance and follow up.

The entire analysis is based on knowledge of the risk factors that play a role in the onset of the disease and which, once attenuated, may give a better chance of not developing the disease. To this end, various computational techniques can help to determine, based on historical data, which risk factors are most present in people who have developed the disease. In the present work we propose a hybrid feature selection based on the voting of several techniques grouped in the filter and wrapper methods, whose results can be analyzed by medical and machine learning specialists. The methods section describes the feature and data selection methods and techniques used. The results obtained are described in the results section and the discussion section compares the results with other related work.

2 Materials and Methods

2.1 Feature Selection for Breast Cancer

The number of publications addressing the application of machine learning to support the fight against breast cancer has increased significantly in recent years. In classical machine learning methods, it is necessary to have a good selection of functionalities to train the algorithms. The feature selection for machine learning focused on breast cancer prediction, was the criteria in the literature analyzed [3–18].

In these papers, data sets, techniques of filtering, wrapping and embedded variable selection methods were identified. The datasets were: Wisconsin Diagnostic Breast Cancer (WDBC), Wisconsin Breast Cancer Original (WBC) and Breast Cancer Surveillance Consortium (BCSC). As filter techniques: Extra-trees (eTrees), Feature Importance Measure (VIM), Pearson's Correlation (Pearson), Mutual information gain (Mutual), Relief-F (Relief), Chi-Square (Chi), Spearman correlation (Spearman), Gini index (Gini). Among the wrapper techniques were reported: Recursive feature elimination (RFE), Forward selection (FW), Backward elimination (BW). Embedded methods were reported with algorithms such as: Support Vector Machines (SVM), Random Forests (RF), Logistic Regression (LR), Naive Bayes (NB), k nearest neighbors (kNN), Artificial Neural Networks (ANN), Decision Trees (DT), Hierarchical Clustering Random Forest (HCRF), Ridge Regression (RR), Gradient Boosting (GB), Linear (LDA) and Quadratic Discriminant Analysis (QDA), and Multi-layer Perceptron (MLP) among others.

The effectiveness of the various feature selection techniques is different, but they can improve the performance of classical machine learning classifiers in breast cancer diagnosis. Feature selection identifies which variables have a major impact on the disease. The proposal in this work is to explore different feature selection techniques on a set of Cuban breast cancer patients, which have been little studied from the machine learning perspective. Each technique obtains a different result, so a hybrid feature selection could help to obtain a consensual result. In the works analyzed, the use of this technique was not identified for a population of Cuban women, and knowing the risk factors that affect them could be useful to create a specific risk estimation model for this population.

2.2 Dataset and Preprocessing Process

For the development of the experiments, a data set of patients who attended breast cancer consultation in a second level hospital in Cuba was used. It contains data on 23 risk factors, an identifier and 1,697 patient cases. The features contained quantitative and qualitative values. The data complied with the Helsinki Agreement, maintaining the privacy of the patients [19]. With the advice of medical specialists, the features: weight, emotion and depression were eliminated.

During data cleaning, 537 missing values were detected, since the data were captured only in case of a positive diagnosis, so they were eliminated. Seven missing values in BMI and one in the feature Biopsies were imputed via arithmetic mean. The data set contains a mixture of qualitative and quantitative values, features with qualitative and multivariate values were transformed to quantitative values through a mapping function as shown in Table 1.

Table 1. Profile of the preprocessed data set of Cuban patients. The dependent feature is Cancer, with the classes "yes" and "no".

Feature	Description	Type	Values
Age	Patient age	Quantitative	20–90
Menarche	Age of Menarche	Quantitative	8–17
Menopause	Age of Menopause	Quantitative	0, 30–60
Birth1	Age of first successful birth	Quantitative	0, 9–46
Children	Number of children born alive	Quantitative	0–6
Breastfeeding	Time breastfed in months	Quantitative	0–72
FHistory	Number of positive first-degree relatives with breast cancer	Quantitative	0–2
Biopsies	Number of breast biopsies	Quantitative	0–5
Hyperplasia	Atypical hyperplasia	Qualitative	no, yes
Race	Patient race	Qualitative	white, mixed, black
BMI	Body mass index	Quantitative	5.0–88.0
Exercise	Weekly physical exercise	Quantitative	0–7
Alcohol	Alcohol consumption	Qualitative	no, yes
Tobacco	Tobacco consumption	Qualitative	no, yes
Allergies	Number of Allergies suffered	Quantitative	0–4
Cancer	Breast cancer diagnosis	Qualitative	no, yes

2.3 Feature Selection Process

Feature, variable or attribute selection aims to reduce data size by eliminating irrelevant or redundant features [20]. The various feature selection techniques used in machine learning can be classified into three main categories [3, 21]. **Filter methods**. The relevance of the characteristics is established through statistical measures to assess the relationship between each independent feature and the objective feature. **Wrapper methods.** They use the predictor as a black box and the performance of a classifier as the objective function that evaluates the subset of features.

In this work, a hybrid feature selection process is implemented, which consists of counting the votes of the techniques used and then defining the selected set through the Pareto principle [22]. In the case of the filter method, the arithmetic mean of the IGR [23], COR [24], CHI [25], GINI [26], REL [27] techniques and the Pareto principle were used. For the filter method and the wrapper method, the following algorithms were used: RF [28], kNN [20], SVM [29], NB [29] and ANN [30]. The results of the wrapper method selection with BW and FW were based on area under the curve (AUC) and accuracy of each one [31].

3 Experimental Results

Four experiments were conducted: the first included the filter method with non-standardized weights; the second the filter method with standardized weights; the third the wrapper method and the backward elimination technique; and the fourth the wrapper method and the forward selection technique. Cross validation and stratified sampling were used in the last two experiments.

3.1 First Experiment. Filter Method with Non-standardized Weights

The filter techniques (IGR, COR, CHI, GINI and REL) were used for the development of this experiment. With the average of the results represented in Table 2, the Pareto principle was used to determine the main features: Biopsies, Tobacco, Family members, Allergies, Exercise, Age and Breastfeeding.

Table 2. Results of the first experiment. Filter methods with non-normalized weights, sorted by the arithmetic mean in descending order.

Attribute	IGR	COR	CHI	GINI	REL	Mean
Biopsies	0.897	0.714	1576.439	0.402	2.552	316.201
Tobacco	0.229	0.545	554.408	0.128	3.247	111.711
FHistory	0.260	0.519	530.510	0.135	1.646	106.614

(continued)

Table 2. (*continued*)

Attribute	IGR	COR	CHI	GINI	REL	Mean
Allergies	0.251	0.011	503.314	0.024	0.114	100.743
Exercise	0.018	0.029	430.080	0.006	0.608	86.148
Age	0.244	0.348	356.353	0.072	0.254	71.454
Breastfeeding	0.320	0.460	329.891	0.101	0.163	66.187
Children	0.226	0.430	328.965	0.067	0.517	66.041
Menopause	0.216	0.292	299.638	0.050	0.169	60.073
Hyperplasia	0.207	0.503	138.733	0.110	2.557	28.422
Birth1	0.164	0.174	137.911	0.022	0.205	27.695
BMI	0.257	0.146	129.114	0.040	0.125	25.936
Menarche	0.216	0.116	88.546	0.012	0.525	17.883
Race	0.003	0.084	67.629	0.003	0.486	13.641
Alcohol	0.258	0.572	12.003	0.141	4.282	3.451

3.2 Second Experiment. Filter Method Using Normalized Weights

In this experiment the weights obtained by each technique were normalized and the filter methods described in Subsect. 3.1 were used. Using the Pareto principle, the features Alcohol, Biopsies, Tobacco, Hyperplasia, Family members, Children, Breastfeeding and Age were selected, the results are shown in Fig. 1.

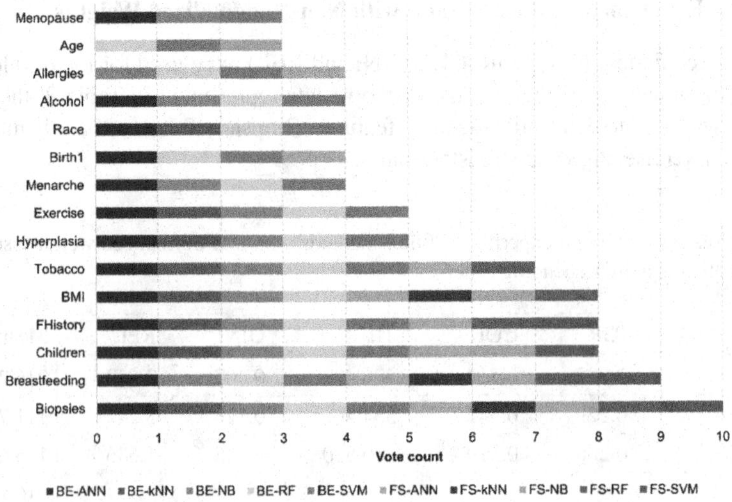

Fig. 2. Voting of features by counting backward elimination and forward selection techniques.

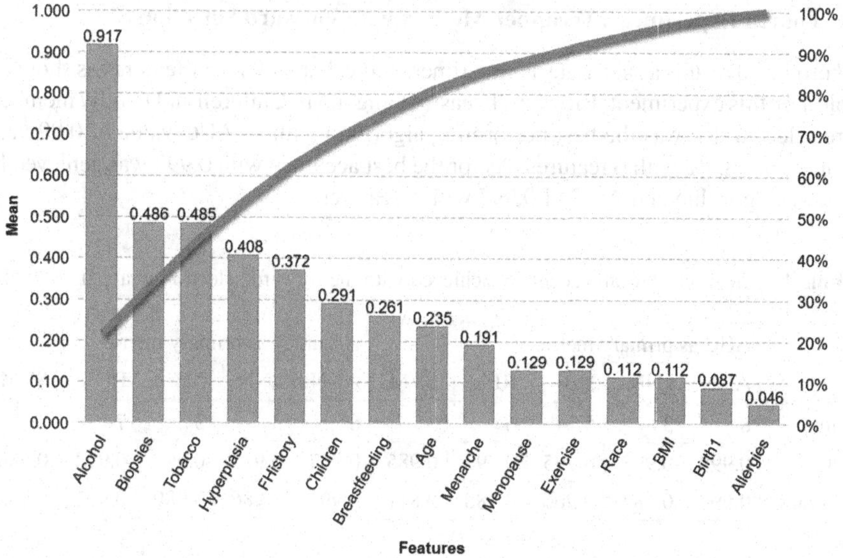

Fig. 1. Results of the second experiment using the filter method and normalized weights with blue line Pareto.

3.3 Third Experiment. Wrapper Method with Backward Elimination

Feature selection with the wrapper method was performed by vote counting. One vote was assigned to each feature used by each algorithm (ANN, KNN, NB, RF, SVM). The features selected were those with the highest votes: Biopsies, Children, Family members, Tobacco, Hyperplasia and Exercise. Table 3 presents the best selection AUC and accuracy metrics versus number of features, sorted by AUC in descending order and sorted by accuracy in descending order. The algorithm that achieved the best performance in both metrics was RF with AUC of 0.999 and accuracy of 0.992 selecting 14 of the 15 independent features.

Table 3. Selection AUC and accuracy achieved with backward elimination wrapper method.

	AUC as primary metric					Accuracy as primary metric				
	ANN	kNN	NB	RF	SVM	ANN	kNN	NB	RF	SVM
Features	13	8	12	14	14	12	8	14	15	14
AUC	0.997	0.997	0.997	0.999	0.994	0.996	0.994	0.996	0.999	0.994
Accuracy	0.989	0.980	0.986	0.992	0.952	0.990	0.986	0.986	0.992	0.952

3.4 Fourth Experiment. Wrapper Method with Forward Selection

FW produced results as accurate as experiment three, but with fewer features as shown in Table 4. In this experiment, Biopsies, Breastfeeding, BMI, Children and Family members were selected. RF was the best performing algorithm with an AUC value of 0.999 and accuracy of 98.8% with 6 features. As for the best accuracy with 0.992 was achieved by the ANN algorithm and AUC of 0.997 with 8 features.

Table 4. Selection AUC and accuracy achieved with the forward-selection wrapper method.

	AUC as primary metric					Accuracy as primary metric				
	ANN	kNN	NB	RF	SVM	ANN	kNN	NB	RF	SVM
Features	8	3	5	6	3	8	3	3	7	4
AUC	0.998	0.993	0.995	0.999	0.985	0.997	0.985	0.993	0.998	0.980
Accuracy	0.990	0.984	0.966	0.988	0.811	0.992	0.986	0.989	0.991	0.923

In voting for the wrapper methods (backward elimination and forward selection), the features selected were those that had a vote count greater than half of the possible votes Biopsies, Breastfeeding, Children, AFamilies, BMI, and Tobacco as shown in Fig. 2. As for the performance of the algorithms by selection AUC and accuracy, in Fig. 3 the results were ordered in descending order by selection AUC, while Fig. 4 presents the results ordered by selection accuracy in descending order.

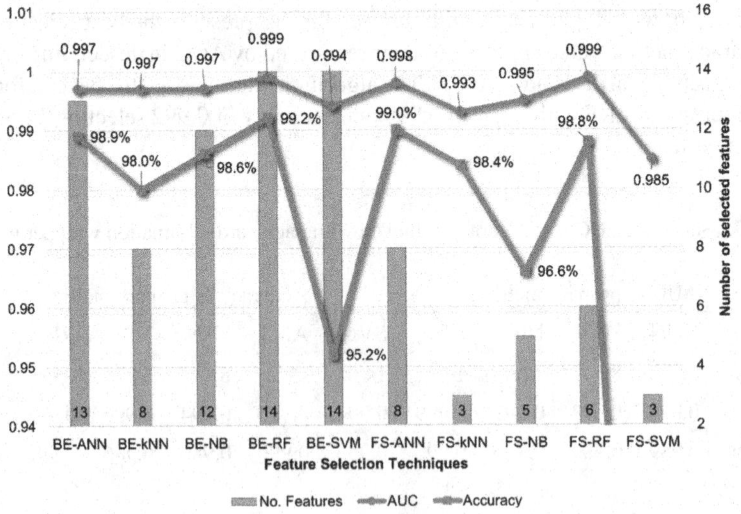

Fig. 3. Comparison of selection AUC, selection accuracy, and number of features resulting from envelope selection methods, sorted by AUC in descending order.

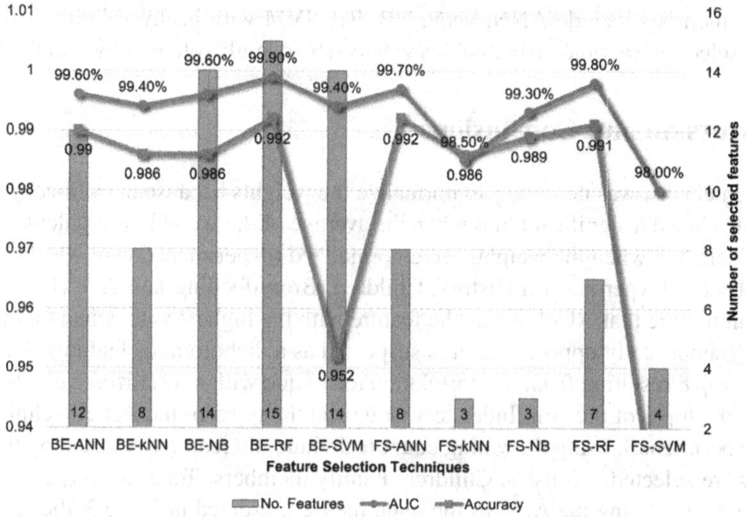

Fig. 4. Comparison of accuracy, AUC and number of features resulting from wrapper selection methods, sorted by accuracy in descending order.

3.5 General Voting

The general voting table of the hybrid selection was generated from the results obtained for the filter and wrapper methods. Filter methods include IGR, CORR, CHI, GINI, RELIEF with standardized weights and non-standardized weights (10 possible votes).

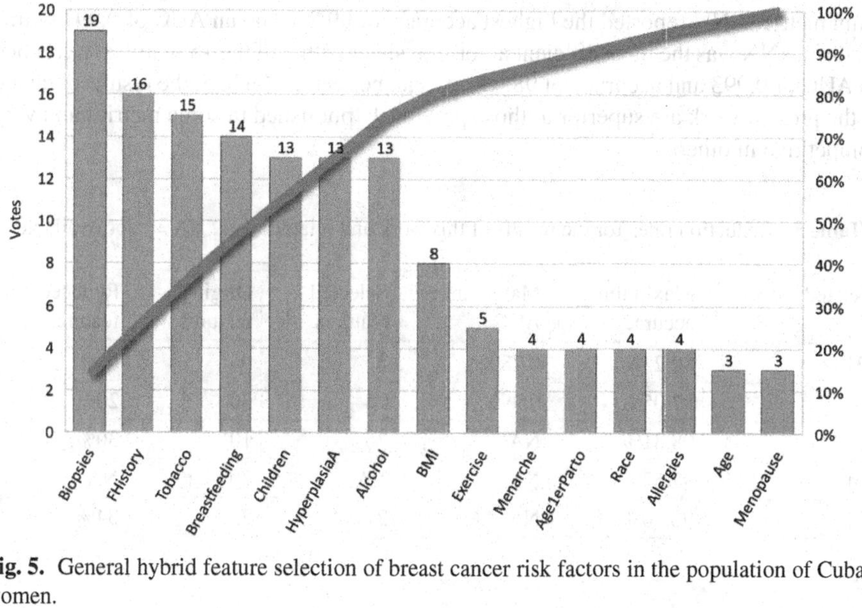

Fig. 5. General hybrid feature selection of breast cancer risk factors in the population of Cuban women.

Wrapper methods include ANN, kNN, NB, RF, SVM with backward elimination and forward selection (another 10 possibles votes). The overall vote is shown in the Fig. 5.

4 Discussion and Conclusions

In experiment 1 it was necessary to normalize the weights because the Chi-square technique introduced a significant bias when the average of the weights was calculated. The features selected when the weights were normalized (experiment 2) are Alcohol, Biopsies, Tobacco, Hyperplasia, FHistory, Children, Breastfeeding and Age (Fig. 1). It is important to note that Alcohol was the feature with the highest vote, when in Table 2 it was the diametrically opposite (so it is suspected as a dichotomous feature). This set is the same top 8 resulting from the correlation technique with normalized weights, it also contains the top 6 of the Gini Index technique and the top 5 of the Relief technique.

In experiment 3, using the voting count technique the features selected by the algorithms were selected: Biopsies, Children, Family members, Tobacco, Hyperplasia and Exercise. Considering the AUC as the main metric presented in Table 3, the set of features would be the 14 selected by RF reaching an AUC of 0.999 and accuracy of 99.2%. When considering accuracy as the main metric, in this experiment it turned out to be the same set of features with RF, since the accuracy was 99.2% and AUC of 0.999. The most efficient algorithm was kNN which, with 8 of the 15 independent features, obtained an AUC of 0.997 and accuracy of 98%.

In experiment 4 with the wrapper and FW method (Table 4), considering the same ways to select features as in experiment 3, the features Biopsies, Breastfeeding, BMI, Children and AFamily were obtained through vote counting, which were voted by 5, 4 and 3 algorithms. The algorithm that achieved the highest AUC was RF with 98.8% accuracy selecting 6 of the 15 independent features. When considering accuracy as the main metric, ANN reported the highest accuracy of 99.2% and an AUC of 0.997 with 8 features. kNN was the most efficient algorithm since with 3 of the 15 features, it reached an AUC of 0.993 and accuracy of 98.4%. As can be seen in Table 5, the results obtained in the present work are superior to those previously published in some metrics and very competitive in others.

Table 5. Reduction rates for the results of this work and related work. NA = Not Available.

Related work	Maximum accuracy	Maximum AUC	Selected features	Original features	Reduced features
[3]	80.23%	0.780	3	9	67%
[4]	97.05%	0.990	24	30	20%
[5]	98.31%	NA	7	10	30%
[6]	97.53%	NA	NA	30	NA
[7]	98.20%	NA	21	32	34%

(*continued*)

Table 5. (*continued*)

Related work	Maximum accuracy	Maximum AUC	Selected features	Original features	Reduced features
[8]	91.00%	NA	15	22	32%
[9]	98.33%	0.980	11	25	56%
[10]	99.91%	0.990	9	11	18%
[11]	96.20%	0.996	20	32	38%
[12]	97.40%	NA	15	32	50%
[13]	99.90%	NA	6	16	63%
[14]	98.07%	NA	NA	10	NA
[15]	97.36%	NA	16	32	50%
This work	99.20%	0.999	6	16	63%

Depending on the practical application of feature selection, a metric (AUC or accuracy) should be chosen, and the minimum number of features should be considered to improve the training and performance of classifiers in supervised learning. In this work, an AUC of 0.999 was achieved with 14 and with 6 features; to obtain the maximum accuracy value, 14 or 8 features were required, and the best reduction percentage was 81% when selecting 3 out of 16 features (Table 4).

Conclusions. Not all risk factors have a significant incidence of disease, so a subset of them can be used to estimate the risk of breast cancer in that population. The selection of that subset of features is a critical step in the analysis of breast cancer risk factors. The results of this study indicate that is a set of features that significantly affect breast cancer in the population of Cuban patients analyzed, being consistent with international health organizations.

According to the general vote of the results obtained in the four experiments (Fig. 5), this study identified that the characteristics of Biopsies, FHistory, Tobacco, Breastfeeding, Children, Hyperplasia, Alcohol and BMI, is a set of 8 features that significantly affect breast cancer in the population of Cuban patients analyzed, being consistent with international health organizations.

The results obtained were, selection AUC of 0.999 and 99.2% accuracy, which indicates that the identified risk factors have a significant effect in the prediction of breast cancer in Cuban patients. The Forward Selection wrapper method proved to be more efficient than Backward Elimination as it always selected fewer features. FW was the most effective as it selected 6 of the above features (excluding Hyperplasia and Alcohol), to achieve the highest AUC. As an algorithm, RF yielded the best results regardless of whether it was applied in FW or BW. The risk factors identified in this study can be used to develop more accurate breast cancer estimation models and improve prevention and early diagnosis of the disease in Cuban patients.

In the future, more data will be incorporated, and a set of algorithms will be trained with the results of each experiment to analyze their behavior and evaluate the proposal to develop an application that contains the selected features and supports the public health service in Cuba.

Acknowledgments. To the Hospital Universitario Clínico Quirúrgico Comandante "Manuel Fajardo" of Havana Cuba and the physicians: Dr. Dalsy Torres Ávila (Director of the Hospital in 2020); Dr. Manuel Ortega Soto (Secretary of the Scientific Council); Dr. Hugo Alexis Cantero Ronquillo (Creator and director of the health project Wings for Life, in support of breast cancer patients in Cuba); Dr. Heydi Bustamante Abreu (Specialized in the support of breast cancer patients in Cuba). Hugo Alexis Cantero Ronquillo (Creator and director of the health project Wings for Life, in support of breast cancer patients in Cuba and President of the Mastology Section of the Cuban Society of Surgery); Dr. Heydi Bustamante Abreu (First Degree Specialist in General Comprehensive Medicine and General Surgeon Resident).

References

1. Ferlay, J., et al.: Cancer statistics for the year 2020: an overview. Int. J. Cancer 149 (2021). https://doi.org/10.1002/ijc.33588
2. Ministerio de Salud Pública: Estadísticas de Salud – Anuario Estadistico de Salud 2020. https://temas.sld.cu/estadisticassalud/2021/08/11/anuario-estadistico-de-salud-2020/
3. Alfian, G., et al.: Predicting breast cancer from risk factors using SVM and extra-trees-based feature selection method. Computers. **11**, 136 (2022). https://doi.org/10.3390/computers11090136
4. Huang, Z., Chen, D.: A breast cancer diagnosis method based on VIM feature selection and hierarchical clustering random forest algorithm. IEEE Access **10**, 3284–3293 (2022). https://doi.org/10.1109/access.2021.3139595
5. Sachdeva, R.K., Bathla, P., Rani, P., Kukreja, V., Ahuja, R.: A systematic method for breast cancer classification using RFE feature selection. In: 2022 2nd International Conference on Advance Computing and Innovative Technologies in Engineering (ICACITE) (2022). https://doi.org/10.1109/icacite53722.2022.9823464
6. Tounsi, S., Kallel, I.F., Kallel, M.: Breast cancer diagnosis using feature selection techniques. In: 2022 2nd International Conference on Innovative Research in Applied Science, Engineering and Technology (IRASET) (2022). https://doi.org/10.1109/iraset52964.2022.9738334
7. Algherairy, A., Almattar, W., Bakri, E., Albelali, S.: The impact of feature selection on different machine learning models for breast cancer classification. In: 2022 7th International Conference on Data Science and Machine Learning Applications (CDMA) (2022). https://doi.org/10.1109/cdma54072.2022.00020
8. Agaal, A., Essgaer, M.: Influence of feature selection methods on breast cancer early prediction phase using classification and regression tree. In: 2022 International Conference on Engineering & MIS (ICEMIS) (2022). https://doi.org/10.1109/icemis56295.2022.9914078
9. Macaulay, B.O., Aribisala, B.S., Akande, S.A., Akinnuwesi, B.A., Olabanjo, O.A.: Breast cancer risk prediction in African women using Random Forest Classifier. Cancer Treat. Res. Commun. **28**, 100396 (2021). https://doi.org/10.1016/j.ctarc.2021.100396
10. Haq, A.U., et al.: Detection of breast cancer through clinical data using supervised and unsupervised feature selection techniques. IEEE Access **9**, 22090–22105 (2021). https://doi.org/10.1109/access.2021.3055806

11. Mate, Y., Somai, N.: Hybrid feature selection and bayesian optimization with machine learning for breast cancer prediction. In: 2021 7th International Conference on Advanced Computing and Communication Systems (ICACCS) (2021). https://doi.org/10.1109/icaccs51430.2021.9441914
12. Bahrami, M., Vali, M.: Wise feature selection for breast cancer detection from a clinical dataset. In: 2021 28th National and 6th International Iranian Conference on Biomedical Engineering (ICBME) (2021). https://doi.org/10.1109/icbme54433.2021.9750287
13. Nouira, K., Maalej, Z., Rejab, F.B., Ouerfelly, L., Ferchichi, A.: Analysis of breast cancer data: a comparative study on different feature selection techniques. In: 2020 International Multi-conference on: "Organization of Knowledge and Advanced Technologies" (OCTA) (2020). https://doi.org/10.1109/octa49274.2020.9151824
14. Nurhayati, Agustian, F., Lubis, M.D.I.: Particle swarm optimization feature selection for breast cancer prediction. In: 2020 8th International Conference on Cyber and IT Service Management (CITSM) (2020). https://doi.org/10.1109/citsm50537.2020.9268865
15. Dhanya, R., Paul, I.R., Sindhu Akula, S., Sivakumar, M., Nair, J.J.: A comparative study for breast cancer prediction using machine learning and feature selection. In: 2019 International Conference on Intelligent Computing and Control Systems (ICCS) (2019). https://doi.org/10.1109/iccs45141.2019.9065563
16. Dheeru, D., Casey, G.: UCI Machine Learning Repository: Breast Cancer Wisconsin (Diagnostic). https://archive.ics.uci.edu/ml/datasets/Breast+Cancer+Wisconsin+(Diagnostic)
17. Wolberg, Wi.H., Mangasarian, O.: UCI Machine Learning Repository: Breast Cancer Wisconsin. https://archive.ics.uci.edu/ml/datasets/Breast+Cancer+Wisconsin+(Original)
18. Barlow, W.E., et al.: Prospective breast cancer risk prediction model for women undergoing screening mammography. JNCI: J. Natl. Cancer Inst. **98**, 1204–1214 (2006). https://doi.org/10.1093/jnci/djj331
19. World Medical Association: World medical association declaration of Helsinki. JAMA **310**, 2191 (2013). https://doi.org/10.1001/jama.2013.281053
20. Orallo, J.H., Quintana, M.J.R., Ramírez, C.F.: Introducción a la minería de datos. Pearson Prentice Hall, Madrid (2004)
21. Chandrashekar, G., Sahin, F.: A survey on feature selection methods. Comput. Electr. Eng. **40**, 16–28 (2014). https://doi.org/10.1016/j.compeleceng.2013.11.024
22. Kiremire, A.R.: The application of the pareto principle in software engineering (2011). http://www2.latech.edu/~box/ase/papers2011/Ankunda_termpaper.PDF
23. Quinlan, J.R.: Induction of decision trees. Mach. Learn. **1**, 81–106 (1986). https://doi.org/10.1007/bf00116251
24. Pearson, K.: Note on regression and inheritance in the case of two parents. Proc. R. Soc. Lond. **58**, 240–242 (1895). https://doi.org/10.1098/rspl.1895.0041
25. Cochran, W.G.: The X2 test of goodness of fit. Ann. Math. Stat. **23**, 315–345 (1952). https://doi.org/10.1214/aoms/1177729380
26. Ceriani, L., Verme, P.: The origins of the Gini index: extracts from Variabilità e Mutabilità (1912) by Corrado Gini. J. Econ. Inequal. **10**, 421–443 (2012). https://doi.org/10.1007/s10888-011-9188-x
27. Kira, K., Rendell, L.A.: A practical approach to feature selection. In: Proceedings of the Ninth International Workshop on Machine Learning, pp. 249–256 (1992)
28. Breiman, L.: Random forests. Mach. Learn. **45**, 5–32 (2001). https://doi.org/10.1023/a:1010933404324
29. Bishop, C.M.: Pattern Recognition and Machine Learning. Springer (2006). https://link.springer.com/book/9780387310732

30. McCulloch, W.S., Pitts, W.: A logical calculus of the ideas immanent in nervous activity. Bull. Math. Biophys. **5**, 115–133 (1943). https://doi.org/10.1007/bf02478259
31. Kumar, R., Indrayan, A.: Receiver operating characteristic (ROC) curve for medical researchers. Indian Pediatr. **48**, 277–287 (2011)

Good Negative Sampling for Triple Classification

Yoan Antonio López-Rodríguez(✉), Orlando Grabiel Toledano-López, Yusniel Hidalgo-Delgado, Héctor González Diéz, and Rey Segundo-Guerrero

Universidad de las Ciencias Informáticas (UCI), Havana, La Habana, Cuba
{yalopez,ogtoledano,yhdelgado,hglez,reysgp}@uci.cu

Abstract. Knowledge graphs are large and useful sources widely used for natural question answering, Web search and data analytics. They describe facts about a certain domain of interest by representing them using entities interconnected via relations in the way of triples. However, due to the fact that they are created under the Open World Assumption, they are incomplete. Knowledge graph completion includes the triple classification task, for discerning correct from incorrect triples. In this regard, knowledge graph embedding models have been proposed for the knowledge graph completion tasks. However, knowledge graphs include only positive triples and training models with only positive triples over generalize, therefore, these models require negative examples. A random negative sampling generates low-quality negative triples which give rise to the zero loss problem during training. In this work, Good Negative Sampling, which is a negative sampling strategy that aims to improve the negative generation process by using background ontological knowledge is put forward. We prove our strategy on a state-of-the-art embedding model - KG-BERT for the triple classification task - on a benchmark dataset - FB13. As result, we demonstrate that the Good Negative Sampling strategy overcomes other state-of-the-art negative strategies, with significant differences.

Keywords: knowledge graph completion · KG-BERT · negative sampling · ontological knowledge · triple classification

1 Introduction

Knowledge graphs (KGs) are large and useful repositories widely used for natural question answering, Web search, data analytics, and so on [8,11,16, 17,25]. They describe facts about a certain domain of interest by representing them using entities interconnected via relations in the way of triples <*head_entity*, *relation*, *tail_entity*> [8,9]. A standardized data model for KGs is the Resource Description Framework (RDF), which has been recommended by the W3C. The RDF model defines different types of entities and relations [8]. The schema for an RDF knowledge graph (KG onwards) can be defined as an

Y. Hernndez Heredia et al. (Eds.): IWAIPR 2023, LNCS 14335, pp. 323–334, 2024.
https://doi.org/10.1007/978-3-031-49552-6_28

ontology, which shows the properties of a specific domain and how they are related [16]. Prominent examples of large KGs are Freebase [4] depicted in Fig. 1, Yago [18], DBpedia [3], and WikiData [21]. KGs are constructed under the Open World Assumption (OWA) semi-automatically or using crowdsourcing methods, therefore, they are often bound to be incomplete [9,11]. Knowledge graph completion includes the triple classification task, for discerning correct from incorrect triples with respect to the KG [7]. In this regard, knowledge graph embedding models have been proposed for the knowledge graph completion tasks.

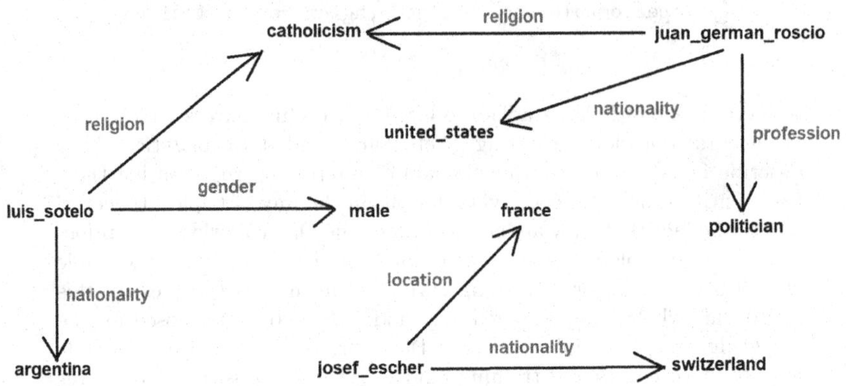

Fig. 1. Freebase knowledge graph subset

However, KGs include only positive triples, and training on all-positive data is tricky, because the model might easily over generalize [14]. For inducing KG embeddings, using negative instances leads to better models [11]. The goal of the embedding models is to rank every positive triple higher than all its negative alternatives. Hence, the quality of embedding models is heavily impacted by the generated negative triples [9]. Negative sampling was initially proposed to approximate the Softmax Cross Entropy loss function and reduce the computational cost in learning word representation [13]. Since then, it has been used to train learning models where there are only positive examples [26]. Negative sampling in KGs aims to generate negative triples by replacing entities in the triples of the graph [12].

Given a KG G, where E and R are the sets of entities and relations belonging to it respectively, all possible triples T is constructed through their Cartesian product $T = E \times R \times E$. G is a subset of all possible triples, $G \subseteq T$ [1]. Given G is the observed set of triples, we denote the remaining triples of T as $G\complement$, $T \backslash G = G\complement$. In the triple corruption process under OWA where triples that belong to $G\complement$ are not false but unknown, $G\complement$ is composed of three kinds of triples: 1) false negatives (FN), which despite not being present in the current version of the KG dataset, are really positive triples; 2) low-quality negatives (LQN), which do not fit into the constraints of the underlying ontological model; and the remaining are: 3) high-quality negatives (HQN). According to the Freebase KG subset depicted in Fig. 1, an example of a FN triple could be: <*josef_escher, religion, catholicism*>, an example of an LQN triple would be: <*josef_escher, religion, male*>, and an example of a HQN triple would be: <*luis_sotelo, nationality, switzerland*>.

There exist several models to learn entity and relation embeddings in KGs such as: TransE [5], Rescal [15], ComplEx [19], DistMult [23] and KG-BERT [24], and all these models require negative examples during training [11]. Traditional KG embedding models generate negative triples randomly through the Uniform Negative Sampling (UNS) [12]. Unfortunately, this approach is not ideal because it generates a lot of LQN triples. LQN triples are effective at the beginning of training since most negative triples are still within the range of positive triples. However, when the training process goes on, it is very likely that those examples will fall outside the range of positive triples, which gives rise to the zero loss problem. Therefore, those trivial negative examples do not provide learning for the model. Indeed, LQN examples contribute semantically to the fact that the model does not learn to distinguish the entities. On the other hand, HQN examples do contribute to the model learning by pushing it to its limits [26].

Knowledge Graph Bidirectional Encoder Representations from Transformer (KG-BERT) [24] is a KG embedding model based on the Transformer Architecture [20]. It can achieve state-of-the-art performance in the knowledge graph completion tasks, including triple classification. KG-BERT as most KG embedding models, generates negative triples randomly through the UNS approach. According to the Freebase KG subset depicted in Fig. 1, we realize that LQN triples such as: <*luis_sotelo, gender, argentina*> or <*luis_sotelo, gender, josef_escher*> can be generated by corrupting triple entities randomly. Hence, this work goes on the line of analyzing the impact of the negative sampling in KG-BERT with the goal of improving it, thus, we stated the first research question of this work as follows: How to improve the negative sampling of the KG-BERT model to avoid the injection of LQN triples during training?

One way to deal with that issue is using background ontological knowledge [7,9,11]. Previous works in this vein: i) Pseudo Typed Negative Sampling (PTNS) generates relevant negative candidates (sources or targets) by constraining the entities that are in the same position as that of the source (or target) [11]. ii) TransOWL leverages ontological axioms to get consistent negative triples using reasoners [7]; and iii) ReasonKGE with its Iterative Negative Sampling (INS) identifies dynamically via symbolic reasoning, inconsistent predictions produced by a given embedding model, and feeds them as negative samples for retraining the model [9]. As of the progress in the KG negative sampling supported by ontological knowledge, it is significant to go further, providing experimental evidences on this topic to KG completion researchers, with emphasis on Transformers-based recent models.

In this work, we put forward Good Negative Sampling (GNS), which is a negative sampling strategy supported by ontological axioms to generate HQN triples. Unlike PTNS, GNS also aims at decreasing the number of FN triples. Instead of retraining the model like INS [9], GNS is a static negative sampling approach, which generates the negative set in only one model training. Test triples should be also checked with the background ontological knowledge in order to belong to the set. Otherwise, they are classified as not belonging to the graph beforehand. RDF model includes general object relations and object type relations ($rdf : type$). Unlike other strategies, GNS allows to corrupt triples with both kinds of relations.

We suspected that KG-BERT with the GNS strategy would improve its accuracy in the triple classification task. Hence, in order to prove it, we stated the second research question of this work as follows: Will the KG-BERT model trained with GNS increase its accuracy in the triple classification task? As the hypothesis of this work, we defined: KG-BERT model trained with GNS will achieve a greater accuracy in the triple classification task than when trained with other state-of-the-art negative sampling strategies. The source code is available at https://github.com/yalopez84/Good-Negative-Sampling. The salient contributions of this work are the following.

- We put forward GNS, which is a negative sampling strategy for knowledge graph completion models that uses underlying ontological knowledge.
- We proved that KG-BERT model trained with GNS increases its accuracy with significant differences if compared to other state-of-the-art negative sampling strategies.
- This work goes further in the vein of joining symbolic and neural learnings in the KG completion tasks. While, KG-BERT's authors injected textual descriptions of entities and relations in the original model training, with GNS, KG ontological patterns are also injected.

The remaining of this paper is organized as follows: First, in Sect. 2, related work is described. Then, we present GNS in Sect. 3. The evaluation of our strategy is given in Sect. 4. Finally, the conclusions and future work are given.

2 Related Work

For training a KG completion model, several elements must be taken into account: scoring function, loss function, negative sampling and hyperparameters [10]. In recent years, the construction of new scoring functions has attracted the most attention, while other elements, e.g. negative sampling strategies, have been less explored [10]. Since KGs store explicitly only positive triples, proper negative triple generation is acknowledged to be a challenging problem [9]. Next, we analyze some state-of-the-art strategies.

2.1 Traditional Negative Sampling

Given the set of triples observed in the graph, represented as G, the simplest form of sampling negative instances is to assume a Closed World Assumption (CWA) and all triples that are not in G are false [9]. However, since the number of false facts is much larger than the number of true facts, this way can lead to scalability issues if all negative examples are used in the model training. Traditional KG embedding models randomly generate a small number of examples using the Uniform Negative Sampling (UNS) strategy [12].

To avoid FN triples, TransH [22] introduced the application of the Bernoulli probability distribution to decide the entity (head or tail) to corrupt. This strategy is called Bernoulli Negative Sampling (BNS).

Moreover, a Local-Closed World Assumption (LCWA) [11] assumes a KG to be only locally complete. For an observed particular subject-predicate pair (s_i, p_k), assuming that any non-existing triple $(s_i, p_k, *)$ is indeed false. It generates negative instances by corrupting positive instances: for every relation p, it collects the sets:
$S = \{s|(s, p, *) \in G\}$ and $O = \{o|(*, p, o) \in G\}$,
and produces sets of corrupted triples:
$S' = \{(s', p, o)|s' \in S, (s', p, o) \notin G\}$ and $O' = \{(s, p, o')|o' \in O, (s, p, o') \notin G\}$
This strategy is called Pseudo Typed Negative Sampling (PTNS). It is focused on generating relevant negative candidates (sources or targets) with the entities that are in the same position as that of the source (or target).

2.2 Ontology-Based Negative Sampling

Wrong negative information may be generated and used when training and learning the embedding models because of the negative sampling [7]. Hence, one relevant line of work, concerns the integration of ontological knowledge to the negative sampling.

The first attempt to use ontological knowledge is the Pseudo Typed Negative Sampling (PTNS) strategy seen above [11]. However, restricting entity corruption by its position in the triple rather than its type of class does not allow the model to learn to semantically differentiate entities by classes.

ReasonKGE [9] with its Iterative Negative Sampling (INS) identifies dynamically via symbolic reasoning inconsistent predictions produced by a given embedding model and feeds them as negative samples for retraining the model. To address the scalability problem that arises when integrating ontological reasoning into the training process of embedding models, it considers ontologies as an extension of the Description Logic (DL) DL-Lite [2]. So that consistency checking and the generalization procedure can be performed efficiently.

TransOWL [7] leverages ontological axioms in order to inject knowledge to the model. Specifically, it modifies the scoring function according to those axioms. This model uses prior knowledge both during learning and triple corruption processes to improve the quality of the low-dimensional representation of KGs.

2.3 Pykeen Negative Sampling

In addition to the above, it is noteworthy to review how KG embedding libraries like Pykeen [1], have tailored and implemented negative sampling strategies.

Pykeen negative sampling is made up of three strategies mentioned above: 1) Uniform Negative Sampling (UNS), 2) Bernoulli Negative Sampling (BNS) and 3) Pseudo Typed Negative Sampling (PTNS). UNS generates corrupted triples from a known positive triple $<s, p, o> \in G$, by uniformly randomly either using the corrupted head operation or the corrupted tail operation.

BNS is an implementation of the Bernoulli probability distribution [22]. It generates corrupted triples from a known positive triple $<s, p, o> \in G$ similarly to UNS, but it sets different probabilities for replacing the head or tail entity when corrupting the triple, which depends on the mapping property of the relation i.e., one-to-many, many-to-one or many-to-many. The aim is to give more chance of replacing the head entity if the relation is one-to-many, and give more chance of replacing the tail entity if the relation is many-to-one, and, in this way, the chance of generating FN triples is reduced.

PTNS accounts for which entities co-occur with a relation. It generates a corrupted head entity for triple $<s, p, o>$, only those entities are considered which occur as a head or tail entity in a triple with the relation.

3 Good Negative Sampling

With the goal of generating HQN triples, we put forward Good Negative Sampling (GNS), which is a negative sampling strategy supported by ontological axioms.

GNS aims to be neither as narrow as PTNS nor as broad as UNS, but a trade-off in between. To deal with the FN triples, GNS proposes to include the BNS strategy and thus, corrupting triples according to the cardinalities of relations. In order to generate HQN triples, light-weight ontological axioms such as: relation domain and range, functional and inverse relations, equivalent and disjoint classes are proposed. Instead of retraining the model like INS, GNS is a static negative sampling approach, which generates the negative set based on the ontological axioms just once during the model training. Test triples are also checked to be consistent with the background ontological knowledge in order to belong to the set. Otherwise, they are classified as not belonging to the graph beforehand. RDF model includes general object relations and object type relations ($rdf : type$). Unlike other strategies, GNS allows to corrupt triples with both kinds of relations. Main definitions of GNS are given next.

3.1 Formal Definitions

Let C, P and I, three disjoint sets of class names (types), property names (relations) and individuals (entities) respectively. Each individual $i \in I$ has a type $T_i \in C$. Each property $p \in P$ has a domain $D_p \in C$ and a range $R_p \in C$, if $p \neq rdf : type$; $D_p \in rdfs : Resource$ and $Rp \in rdfs : Class$ otherwise ($rdfs$ is the prefix of RDFS (RDF language schema)).

Definition 1 ***(Knowledge Graph):*** A knowledge graph G is a finite set of triples of the form $<s(head\_entity), p(relation), o(tail\_entity)>$, where $s \in I, p \in P$ and $o \in I$, if $p \neq rdf : type$; $o \in C$ otherwise.

Definition 2 ***(Ontology):*** An ontology O is a finite set of axioms expressed in a certain Description Logic (DL). In this work, we focus on light-weight ontologies with the axioms: *property domain, property range, disjoint with, functional property, equivalent class, equivalent property, inverse of* and *subclass of.*

Definition 3 ***(Triple corruption process):*** When corrupting a triple, to pick the head or tail entity to be replaced, the Bernoulli probability distribution should be used. To corrupt the head of the triple $<s, p, o>$ per $<s', p, o>$, let T_s be the type of s and T'_s the type of s', if $p \neq rdf : type$, then $T_s = T'_s = D_p; T_s \neq T'_s$ otherwise. To corrupt the tail of the triple $<s, p, o>$ per $<s, p, o'>$, let T_o be the type of o and T'_o the type of o', if $p \neq rdf : type$, then $T_o = T'_o = R_p$; o disjointWith o' otherwise.

Algorithm 1.1 describes how to generate the negative examples through the GNS strategy. The *Good_Neg* function checks whether the corrupted triple is a HQN triple or not. Test set should be also checked through that function before being evaluated with the model.

4 Experiments

Triple classification aims to judge whether a given triple $<s, p, o>$ is correct or not with respect to the KG [7]. Negative examples are needed to avoid the overfitting during training. In this section, we evaluate our GNS strategy on the KG-BERT model [24].

4.1 Baselines

We compare GNS to: 1) UNS, the simpler negative sampling strategy used in most KG embedding models including KG-BERT; and 2) PTNS, which was the first attempt to use ontological knowledge in the KG negative sampling. Since, GNS includes the BNS strategy to select the entity to corrupt, in order to achieve a fairer comparison we also implemented BNS in the UNS and PTNS strategies. The hypothesis of this work was defined as: KG-BERT model trained with GNS will achieve greater accuracy in the triple classification task than when trained with other state-of-the-art negative sampling strategies.

4.2 KG-BERT

KG-BERT [24] treats triples in KGs as textual sequences. It borrows the idea from language model pretraining and takes Bidirectional Encoder Representations from Transformer model (BERT) [6] as an encoder for entities and relations in graphs. The only new parameters introduced during KG-BERT triple classification fine-tuning are classification layer weights $W \in R^{2 \times H}$. The scoring function for a triple $T = <s, p, o>$ is $S_T = f(s, p, o) = sigmoid(CW^T)$, $S_T \in R^2$ is a 2-dimensional real vector with $S_{T0}, S_{T1} \in [0, 1]$ and $S_{T0} + S_{T1} = 1$. C is

Algorithm 1.1: Good negative sampling

Input: X dataset, E entities, R relations
Output: Ex positive and negative examples
/* Data initializations */
Data: $E_x \leftarrow []$ examples, $R_i \leftarrow \emptyset$ triple relation, $Dom\_R_i \leftarrow \emptyset$ relation domain, $Ran\_R_i \leftarrow \emptyset$ relation range, $Head\_or\_Tail \leftarrow$ "*Head*" flag, $E_i \leftarrow \emptyset$ entity to corrupt, $new\_triple \leftarrow \emptyset$ corrupted triple, $good\_Neg\_Triple \leftarrow false$ flag to validate
CALCULATE *tph* tail entities per head and *hpt* head entities per tail from X
$R \leftarrow$ **CALCULATE** Bernoulli_Probabilities through $p_r = \frac{tph}{tph+hpt}$
for *triple* in X **do**
    $R_i \leftarrow$ **Get** $Relation\_with\_Bernoulli\_Probability(triple)$
    $Dom\_R_i \leftarrow$ **Get** $Domain\_of\_Relation(R_i)$
    $Ran\_R_i \leftarrow$ **Get** $Range\_of\_Relation(R_i)$
    $Head\_or\_Tail \leftarrow$ **Determine** $Which\_To\_Corrupt\_From\_Bern(R_i)$
    if $Head\_or\_Tail ==$ "*Head*" **then**
        while true **do**
            $E_i \leftarrow$ **Get** $New\_Entity\_To\_Corrupt(E)$
            $new\_triple \leftarrow$ **Get** $New\_Triple\_with\_Corrupted\_Head(E_i)$
            if *new_triple* exist_in X **then**
                continue
            end if
            $good\_Neg\_Triple \leftarrow$ **Validate** $Good\_Neg(new\_Triple, Dom\_R_i, X)$
            if $good\_Neg\_Triple == false$ **then**
                continue
            end if
            break
        end while
        add *triple* to Ex
        add *new_triple* to Ex
    else
        while true **do**
            $E_i \leftarrow$ **Get** $New\_Entity\_To\_Corrupt(E)$
            $new\_triple \leftarrow$ **Get** $New\_Triple\_with\_Corrupted\_Tail(E_i)$
            if *new_triple* exist_in X **then**
                continue
            end if
            $good\_Neg\_Triple \leftarrow$ **Validate** $Good\_Neg(new\_Triple, Ran\_R_i, X)$
            if $good\_Neg\_Triple == false$ **then**
                continue
            end if
            break
        end while
        add *triple* to Ex
        add *new_triple* to Ex
    end if
end for
return Ex

the final hidden vector of the BERT special [CLS] token. Given the positive triple set G and a negative triple set G^- constructed accordingly, they compute a cross-entropy loss with S_T and triple labels. In the original implementation of

KG-BERT, G^- is simply generated by the UNS strategy by replacing the head entity s or tail entity o in a positive triple $<s, p, o> \in G$ per a random entity s' or o'.

4.3 Datasets

Table 1 gives the statistics of the datasets. We evaluated GNS on FB13 [17] that is a subset of Freebase [4]. Freebase is a large knowledge graph of general world facts. FB13 was used in the experiments of the KG-BERT model. We picked a subset of 11082 triples for training and 2253 triples for tests. The strategy to select subsets for training and tests was similar to [17] in order to achieve that entities in the test set were contained in the training set. Columns R and E are the number of relations and entities, while UNS, PTNS and GNS are the number of negative triples generated for training KG-BERT with each negative sampling strategy respectively. In total (positive and negative triples), each training set had around 24000 triples. The test set has a class balance of 50%.

Table 1. The statistics for base line datasets

Dataset	R	E	Train	UNS	PTNS	GNS	Test (+)	Test (−)
FB13 (FB13_reduced)	13	89146	11082	13050	13050	13050	1128	1125

4.4 Results and Discussion

KG-BERT uses pre-trained BERT-Base model with 12 layers, 12 self-attention heads and hidden state size H =768. KG-BERT fine-tuning has the following hyperparameters: batch size: 32, learning rate: $5e^{-5}$ with Adam optimizer implemented in BERT, dropout rate: 0.1, 3 epochs and 1 negative triple per positive triple, which can ensure class balance in binary classification.

We trained KG-BERT model 30 times for each negative sampling strategy. The rows of the Table 2, corresponding to the negative sampling strategies, show the average of the training loss for each epoch carried out. As expected, UNS produces the least training loss due to the fact that it generates a lot of LQN triples. Those triples are too easy to be classify and give rise to the zero loss. On the other hand, semantic-based strategies like PTNS and GNS generate more HQN triples which do produce losses greater than zero and learning. To answer the first research question, we state that it is possible to improve the KG-BERT model negative sampling by avoiding the injection of LQN triples during training, with semantic-based negative sampling strategies like PTNS and GNS.

Table 2. Training Loss

FB13 (FB13_reduced)	Epoch 1	Epoch 2	Epoch 3
UNS	**42.5166**	**10.2094**	**3.2385**
PTNS	161.7024	83.8646	45.7079
GNS	170.2427	86.1006	45.5844

Each trained model was directly tested on the test set. Table 3 shows the mean of the accuracies and standard deviations of the models evaluated on the test set and grouped by each negative sampling strategy. KG-BERT trained with GNS achieves the best accuracy.

Table 3. Triple classification outcomes (accuracy, standard deviation)

FB13 (FB13_reduced)	Acc	Std-dev
UNS	0.5182	0.0045
PTNS	0.8972	0.0041
GNS	**0.9013**	0.0026

To find significant statistical differences between the negative strategies, normality tests were performed on the results using the Shapiro-Wilk test. Due to some samples did not have a normal distribution, we performed nonparametric tests using the Friedman ranking test considering the accuracy. Table 4 shows the results of chi-square statistic (χ^2), $p - value$, and degree of freedom (df). We perform a Bonferroni -Dunn post-hoc test for the one-versus-all comparison using the best result (GNS strategy). We can notice statistical differences with a confidence interval of 95%, concerning UNS and PTNS strategies. Hence, we accepted the research hypothesis that was defined as: KG-BERT model trained with GNS will achieve greater accuracy in the triple classification task than when trained with other state-of-the-art negative sampling strategies.

Table 4. Results of the Friedman Test and Post-Hoc procedure

FB13 (FB13_reduced) ($\chi^2 = 141.8674$, $p - value = 1.1102e^{-16}$, $df = 2$)			
	UNS	PTNS	GNS
Average ranking	3.0	1.7833	**1.2166**
Bonferroni Dunn	$4.9564e^{-12}$	0.0282	–

5 Conclusions and Future Work

Training models for triple classification requires negative examples. Traditional KG embedding models generate negative triples randomly through the Uniform Negative Sampling. Unfortunately, this approach generates a lot of low-quality negative triples which are trivial examples that give rise to the zero loss problem. One way to cope that issue is using background ontological knowledge. Throughout this work, we presented GNS, which is a negative sampling strategy that takes into account ontological axioms to generate high-quality negative examples. Our strategy also deals with false negative triples through the Bernoulli probability distribution. The investigated hypothesis was to study whether KG-BERT model trained with GNS achieves greater accuracy in the triple classification task than when trained with other state-of-the-art negative sampling strategies. Experimental results on Freebase dataset proved our strategy outperforms the other strategies with significant statistical differences. This is a work in progress, further experiments on other datasets are planned later on.

Acknowledgments. This research has been partially sponsored by VLIR-UOS Network University Cooperation Programme-Cuba.

References

1. Ali, M., et al.: PyKEEN 1.0: a python library for training and evaluating knowledge graph embeddings. J. Mach. Learn. Res. **22**(1), 3723–3728 (2021)
2. Artale, A., Calvanese, D., Kontchakov, R., Zakharyaschev, M.: The DL-Lite family and relations. J. Artif. Intell. Res. **36**, 1–69 (2009)
3. Auer, S., Bizer, C., Kobilarov, G., Lehmann, J., Cyganiak, R., Ives, Z.: DBpedia: a nucleus for a web of open data. In: Aberer, K., et al. (eds.) ASWC/ISWC -2007. LNCS, vol. 4825, pp. 722–735. Springer, Heidelberg (2007). https://doi.org/10.1007/978-3-540-76298-0_52
4. Bollacker, K., Evans, C., Paritosh, P., Sturge, T., Taylor, J.: Freebase: a collaboratively created graph database for structuring human knowledge. In: Proceedings of the 2008 ACM SIGMOD International Conference on Management of Data, pp. 1247–1250 (2008)
5. Bordes, A., Usunier, N., Garcia-Duran, A., Weston, J., Yakhnenko, O.: Translating embeddings for modeling multi-relational data. In: Advances in Neural Information Processing Systems, vol. 26, 2013
6. Devlin, J., Chang, M.-W., Lee, K., Toutanova, K.: BERT: pre-training of deep bidirectional transformers for language understanding. arXiv preprint arXiv:1810.04805 (2018)
7. d'Amato, C., Quatraro, N.F., Fanizzi, N.: Injecting background knowledge into embedding models for predictive tasks on knowledge graphs. In: Verborgh, R., et al. (eds.) ESWC 2021. LNCS, vol. 12731, pp. 441–457. Springer, Cham (2021). https://doi.org/10.1007/978-3-030-77385-4_26
8. Hogan, A., et al.: Knowledge graphs. ACM Comput. Surv. (CSUR) **54**(4), 1–37 (2021)

9. Jain, N., Tran, T.-K., Gad-Elrab, M.H., Stepanova, D.: Improving knowledge graph embeddings with ontological reasoning. In: Hotho, A., et al. (eds.) ISWC 2021. LNCS, vol. 12922, pp. 410–426. Springer, Cham (2021). https://doi.org/10.1007/978-3-030-88361-4_24
10. Kamigaito, H., Hayashi, K.: Comprehensive analysis of negative sampling in knowledge graph representation learning. In: International Conference on Machine Learning, pp. 10661–10675. PMLR (2022)
11. Kotnis, B., Nastase, V.: Analysis of the impact of negative sampling on link prediction in knowledge graphs. arXiv preprint arXiv:1708.06816 (2017)
12. Liu, H., Kairong, H., Wang, F.-L., Hao, T.: Aggregating neighborhood information for negative sampling for knowledge graph embedding. Neural Comput. Appl. **32**, 17637–17653 (2020). https://doi.org/10.1007/s00521-020-04940-5
13. Mikolov, T., Sutskever, I., Chen, K., Corrado, G.S., Dean, J.: Distributed representations of words and phrases and their compositionality. In: Advances in Neural Information Processing Systems, vol. 26 (2013)
14. Nickel, M., Murphy, K., Tresp, V., Gabrilovich, E.: A review of relational machine learning for knowledge graphs. Proc. IEEE **104**(1), 11–33 (2015)
15. Nickel, M., Tresp, V., Kriegel, H.-P., et al.: A three-way model for collective learning on multi-relational data. In: ICML, vol. 11, pp. 3104482–3104584 (2011)
16. Peng, C., Xia, F., Naseriparsa, M., Osborne, F.: Knowledge graphs: opportunities and challenges. Artif. Intell. Rev. **56**, 13071–13102 (2023). https://doi.org/10.1007/s10462-023-10465-9
17. Socher, R., Chen, D., Manning, C.D., Ng, A.: Reasoning with neural tensor networks for knowledge base completion. In: Advances in Neural Information Processing Systems, vol. 26 (2013)
18. Suchanek, F.M., Kasneci, G., Weikum, G.: Yago: a core of semantic knowledge. In: Proceedings of the 16th International Conference on World Wide Web, pp. 697–706 (2007)
19. Trouillon, T., Welbl, J., Riedel, S., Gaussier, É., Bouchard, G.: Complex embeddings for simple link prediction. In: International Conference on Machine Learning, pp. 2071–2080. PMLR (2016)
20. Vaswani, A., et al.: Attention is all you need. In: Advances in Neural Information Processing Systems, vol. 30 (2017)
21. Vrandečić, D., Krötzsch, M.: Wikidata: a free collaborative knowledgebase. Commun. ACM **57**(10), 78–85 (2014)
22. Wang, Z., Zhang, J., Feng, J., Chen, Z.: Knowledge graph embedding by translating on hyperplanes. In: Proceedings of the AAAI Conference on Artificial Intelligence, vol. 28 (2014)
23. Yang, B., Yih, W., He, X., Gao, J., Deng, L.: Embedding entities and relations for learning and inference in knowledge bases. arXiv preprint arXiv:1412.6575 (2014)
24. Yao, L., Mao, C., Luo, Y.: KG-BERT: BERT for knowledge graph completion. arXiv preprint arXiv:1909.03193 (2019)
25. Zhang, J., Chen, B., Zhang, L., Ke, X., Ding, H.: Neural, symbolic and neural-symbolic reasoning on knowledge graphs. AI Open **2**, 14–35 (2021)
26. Zhang, Y., Yao, Q., Chen, L.: Simple and automated negative sampling for knowledge graph embedding. VLDB J. **30**(2), 259–285 (2021). https://doi.org/10.1007/s00778-020-00640-7

Polarity Prediction in Tourism Cuban Reviews Using Transformer with Estimation of Distribution Algorithms

Orlando Grabiel Toledano-López[1(✉)], Miguel Ángel Álvarez-Carmona[2], Julio Madera[3], Alfredo Simón-Cuevas[4], Yoan Antonio López-Rodríguez[1], and Héctor González Diéz[1]

[1] Universidad de las Ciencias Informáticas (UCI), Habana, Cuba
{ogtoledano,yalopez,hglez}@uci.cu

[2] Centro de Investigacion en Matemáticas, Sede Monterrey, México
miguel.alvarez@cimat.mx

[3] Universidad de Camagüey, Camagüey, Cuba
julio.madera@reduc.edu.cu

[4] Universidad Tecnológica de La Habana "José Antonio Echeverría", Habana, Cuba
asimon@ceis.cujae.edu.cu

Abstract. The tourism sector has benefited from recent research in the area of natural language processing, where digital platforms on the web offer the opportunity for people to express their opinions about the services and places they visit. The texts of the reviews are unstructured data characterized by high dimensionality, variable size, and complex semantic relationships between words, which has led to the development of neural architectures with a larger number of parameters to optimize. The training of deep neural networks has been approached by methods based on partial derivatives of the objective function and presents several theoretical and practical limitations, such as the probability of convergence to local minima. In this paper, a hybrid method based on Distribution Estimation Algorithms is proposed for fine-tuning an mT5-based Transformer for polarity prediction. For this purpose, a new Spanish dataset is proposed for polarity classification compiled from TripAdvisor reviews of Cuba. Different preprocessing variants are applied and compared in the solution and data imbalance is treated by back translation. The proposed method combined with back translation decreases the mean of the absolute error in the mT5-based Transformer for polarity prediction.

Keywords: mT5-based Transformer · Estimation of Distribution Algorithms · Polarity prediction

1 Introduction

Tourism in Cuba turns out to be a fundamental line in the economy, since the early 1990s Cuba began to focus its investments in this sector to increase

Y. Hernndez Heredia et al. (Eds.): IWAIPR 2023, LNCS 14335, pp. 335–346, 2024.
https://doi.org/10.1007/978-3-031-49552-6_29

the number of rooms and income from foreign visitors, creating the necessary conditions for it [12]. Considering the TripAdvisor platform, more than 1,200,000 opinions on hotels, restaurants, and tourist attractions have been issued about the country. In this sense, the opinions issued promote existing businesses in the country, are a source of complaints and suggestions, and share real experiences of the people who visit the places. However, this information constitutes a source of data for the development of supervised learning models for the classification of reviews in Spanish and has not been sufficiently exploited.

Recent research has improved deep learning architectures for Natural Language Processing (NLP) by introducing self-attention mechanisms with transformers, allowing features extraction and learning complex relationship among words [13]. However, basic approaches for training these deep learning architectures are the methods based on partial derivatives of the objective function, such as Stochastic Gradient Descent (SGD) [5], Adam [6] and AdamW [9]. These methods have theoretical-practical limitations that are evident in their probability of convergence to local minima, which results in a significant effect on the accuracy of the final model [11].

Continuous and discrete optimization has been addressed via meta-heuristic algorithms in NLP [1,3,10]. In [1], Genetic Programming (GP) is used to obtain an optimal multi-task topology in feed-forward neural networks for text classification and the Seq2Seq model for conversational systems. In [3], Particle Swarm Optimization (PSO), Artificial Bee Colony (ABC), Ant Colony Optimization (ACO), and Firefly Algorithm (FA) are introduced for feature selection from documents represented by Latent Semantic Analysis (LSA), and general machine learning approaches are subsequently used. Swarm intelligence and Genetic Algorithms (GA) have allowed optimizing the initial weight matrix in Long Short-Term Memory (LSTM) neural network for text classification [10]. However, these evolutionary algorithms employ general search operators that do not consider relationships between the variables of the optimization problem. In this respect, the Estimation of Distribution Algorithms (EDA) modify the search operator through a probabilistic model that can learn these dependency relationships, thus contributing to the exploitation of local information [7]. In contrast to GA, they do not require the classical crossover and mutation operators [8].

Text classification is a problem of high dimensionality, and fine-tuning transformers for these purposes requires a large number of parameters to be optimized. As consequence, this leads to a high computational cost of the training process, so some population meta-heuristics are limited to obtaining good results with a reasonable population size. In addition, polarity analysis from online reviews is characterized by a marked imbalance in the data.

Based on this, our contribution in this paper is as follows:

- Propose a new dataset from TripAdvisor reviews of hotels, hostels, and vacation rentals in Cuba for polarity prediction.
- A new hybrid method that combines AdamW with EDA for fine-tuning an mT5-based transformer [14] in polarity prediction.

– Analyze the effect of considering different preprocessing techniques for denoising, lemmatization, and data augmentation.

In the next, we present the design of an mT5-based transformer model for polarity prediction and introduce a hybrid method for fine-tuning this model that combines AdamW and EDA. For this purpose, we present the theoretical basis related to EDA, through the study of three variants of these algorithms: Estimation of Multivariate Normal Algorithm (EMNA) [8], Univariate Marginal Distribution for the continuous domain (UMDAc) [8], and Covariance Matrix Adaptation-Evolution Strategy (CMA-ES) [2]. The compiled dataset is described and we address the problem of data imbalance through data augmentation using back translation. We discuss the comparison between the different approaches used in the solution considering the metrics Accuracy (Acc), Macro F-measure (Macro F), Mean Absolute Error (MAE), and Recall (R). Finally, some conclusions and recommendations are given.

2 Computational Methodology

Giving a text sequence in the input space $\mathbf{x} \in \mathcal{X}$, the classification model can be considered as a function, i.e. $f(\mathbf{x}) = C$ for measuring the conditional probability distributions over all possible labels in the pre-defined category set $C = \{c_1, c_2, c_3, ..., c_L\}$. Text classification works in a instance of the input space. Hence, let $X = \{\mathbf{x}_1, \mathbf{x}_2, \mathbf{x}_3, ..., \mathbf{x}_N\}$ be the training set, an each input text sequence $\mathbf{x}_i = (t_1, t_2, t_3, ..., t_P)$, represents a sequence of tokens. $Y = \{y_1, y_2, y_3, ..., y_N\}$ the set of categories in which each document $\mathbf{x}_i$ is classified, each $y_i \in C$.

The model will be trained for the set which represents the parameter matrices Θ minimizing the cross-entropy loss in the Eq. 1a:

$$\Theta = \underset{\Theta \in \mathbb{R}^{\mathcal{M} \times \kappa}}{\operatorname{argmin}} F(\Theta, X) \tag{1a}$$

$$F(\Theta, X) = -\sum_{i=1}^{N} \sum_{c=1}^{L} \Upsilon_{\mathbf{x}_i|c} \log(P_{\mathbf{x}_i|c}(\Theta)) \tag{1b}$$

$$\Upsilon_{\mathbf{x}_i|c} = \begin{cases} 1 \; if \; y_i = c \\ 0 \; EOT \end{cases} \tag{1c}$$

where $P_{\mathbf{x}_i|c}(\Theta)$ is the predicted conditional probability of $\mathbf{x}_i$ given class c. $\Theta = \{W_1, W_2, W_3, ..., W_\kappa\}$ is the set of parameter matrices in the space $\mathcal{M}$ of the Deep Neural Network of κ layers. Each $W_k \in \mathbb{R}^{d_k \times h_k}$, such that $0 \leq k < \kappa$, is the parameter matrix of the k-th deep neural network of dimensions d_k and h_k. Computational operations on the model from an input are performed between contiguous layers W_k and W_{k+1}.

2.1 Model Description

In this section, we propose an mT5-based transformer model for text classification, shown in Fig. 1 that receives an input token sequence. For mT5 model, an input sequence can be represented in two ways by using special tokens, such as a single sequence $\mathbf{x}_1$ </s> or a pair of sequences $\mathbf{x}_1$ </s> $\mathbf{x}_2$ </s>. The special token </s> indicates the end of the sequence. As mT5 is a massive multilingual T5 (Text-to-Text Transfer Transformer) [14] model, it can be used for multiple tasks in NLP, which leads to the input sequence being specified as a task prefix. For the problem addressed, we will use the prefix *"multilabel classification:"*. An example of input is formatted as: $\{multilabel, classification, :\}$ $\mathbf{x}$ </s>. mT5 model is an encoder-decoder architecture, in our proposal, we will use the encoder part of the architecture, whose output is the input to a fully-connected head on top.

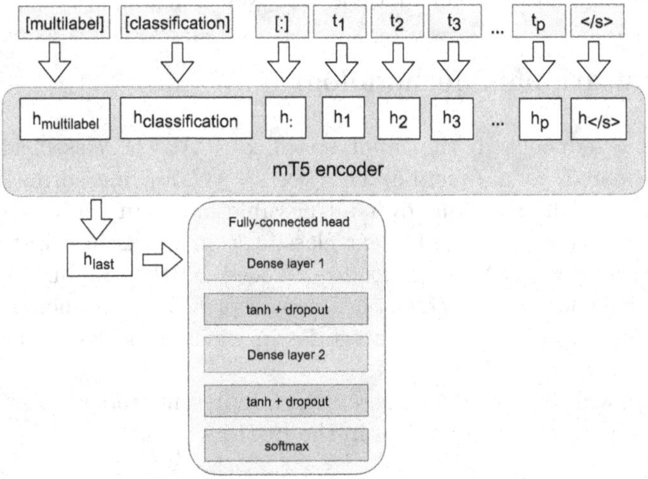

Fig. 1. MT5 encoder model overview with additional fully-connected head

The encoder part consists of a stack of blocks formed by a self-attention layer followed by a small feed-forward network [14]. Only using the encoder part, the complexity of the model is reduced to less than half of the parameters compared to using both encoder and decoder parts.

In our design, we add a head formed by a dense layer of 64 neurons and the output layer whose neurons correspond to the number of classification labels. The first dense layer receives a vector of size 512 that represents the last hidden state h_{last}, both layers have as activation function the hyperbolic tangent (*tanh*), and dropout is applied to both at the output. Finally, the softmax function is applied to the output of the last layer.

The output on the fully-connected head is a simple softmax classifier on top of the mT5 encoder. Let Θ be the set of trainable parameters of the model, the fully-connected head turns the vector $\mathbf{h}_{last}$ from input sequence $\mathbf{x}_i$ into the conditional probability distributions $P(c_l|\mathbf{h}_{last}, \Theta)$ over all categorical labels C as follows:

$$P(c_l|\mathbf{h}_{last},\Theta) = softmax(\tanh(W_2^T \tanh(W_1^T \mathbf{h}_{last}))) = \frac{exp(P(c_l|\mathbf{h}_{last},\Theta))}{\sum_{c=1}^{L} exp(P(c_l|\mathbf{h}_{last},\Theta))} \tag{2}$$

where $W_1 \in \mathbb{R}^{|\mathbf{h}_{last}|\times K}$ and $W_2 \in \mathbb{R}^{K\times L}$ are the trainable parameters of the first dense layer and second dense layer. K is amount of neurons of the first dense layer, both W_1 and W_2 are subset of Θ such that $W_1 \cup W_2 = \Theta \backslash W_e$ being W_e trainable parameters of mT5 encoder.

Hence, the final prediction of the model $\hat{y}$ giving input $\mathbf{x}$ is taken with the maximum label value of the conditional probability distributions:

$$\hat{y}_{\mathbf{x}} = \operatorname{argmax} P(c_l|\mathbf{h}_{last},\Theta) \tag{3}$$

2.2 Estimation of Distribution Algorithms and Hyper-parameters

In our proposal, we use three strategies in continuous domains: UMDAc, EMNA, and CMA-ES. For estimating distribution we sort the individuals by increasing fitness function $F_1 < F_2 < F_3 < ...F_\Lambda$ and select M best individuals for CS.

Algorithm 1.1 describes how to use a hybrid EDA-based method for fine-tuning our custom mT5-based transformer model. The algorithm receives as input the set of training patterns X and the set of categories Y of each input. We proposed a combination of the training process in two stages. First, we train the mT5 encoder body via the AdamW method, and after we train the fully-connected head via EDA optimization. In this, an individual represents the set of parameters in W_2, and the fitness function is evaluated for Θ that represents all trainable parameters in the mT5-based transformer model. The fitness function is computed for all trainable parameters in the model as we show in Eq. 1a.

An individual $W_2 = (u_1, u_2, u_3, ..., u_\gamma)$ is a configuration that corresponds to a distribution $p(W_2) = [P_0 = u_1, P_1 = u_2, P_3 = u_3, ..., P_\gamma = u_\gamma]$. Optimization problem consists to find a minimum configuration W_2 where $F(.) : \mathbb{R}^\gamma \rightarrow \mathbb{R}$.

UMDAc is an EDA for the continuous domain as a modified version of UMDA [8]. A selection method is needed to identify the subset of good solutions from which to calculate univariate marginal probabilities and to use the probabilities to influence the probabilistic selection of components in the component-wise construction of new candidate solutions. For each generation g, we obtain new individuals using random sampling with normal distribution with mean zero and variance one as we show in Eq. 4:

$$W_{2,\lambda}^{(g+1)} = \sigma^{(g)} \mathcal{N}_\lambda(0,1) + CS_{avg}^{(g)} \tag{4}$$

EMNA is an EDA for the continuous domain [8], which uses a multivariate normal distribution to generate the new solutions. The parameters of this distribution are estimated from the best solutions of a given generation, and the next generation is obtained by simulating the distribution with these parameters. EMNA needs an initial centroid vector Ω and each individual per generation is given by Eq. 5:

$$W_{2,\lambda}^{(g+1)} = \sigma^{(g)} \mathcal{N}_\lambda(0,1) + \Omega^{(g)} + CS_{avg}^{(g)} \tag{5}$$

Algorithm 1.1: General approach for fine-tuning mT5-based transformer via EDA

Require: Set of training pattern $X = \{\mathbf{x}_1, \mathbf{x}_2, \mathbf{x}_3, ..., \mathbf{x}_N\}$.
Require: Random initialization of Θ.
Require: Fitness function $F(\Theta, X)$.
* *STAGE 1: Learning parameters of the mT5 encoder by AdamW method.* *\
while Criterion not fulfilled **do**
  for *batch in X* **do**
    Forward pass in *batch* to get output $\hat{y}$.
    Backforward propagation to compute gradients.
    Update parameters Θ with computed gradients.
  end for
end while
* *STAGE 2: Learning fully-connected head by EDA optimization.* *\
Initialize $g \leftarrow 1$.
Keep parameters for mT5 encoder W_e and W_1.
Generate initial population $Z = \{W_{2,1}, W_{2,2}, W_{2,3}, ..., W_{2,\Lambda}\}$.
while Criterion not fulfilled **do**
  for $W_{2,\lambda} \in Z$ **do**
    Evaluate the fitness function $F(W_e \cup W_1 \cup W_{2,\lambda}, X)$
  end for
  Select an intermediate set CS from M individuals.
  Estimate distribution from CS through $p^{CS} = p(W_2, g)$.
  Generate new individuals from $p(W_2, g+1) \approx p^{CS}(W_2, g)$.
  $g = g + 1$.
end while
return Best individual W_2^* in the population.

where $1 \leq \lambda \leq \Lambda$. Finally, in the next generation Ω is updated as follows in Eq. 6:

$$\Omega^{(g+1)} = \Omega^{(g)} + CS_{avg}^{(g)} \tag{6}$$

EMNA uses two hyper-parameters such as initial centroid Ω and initial variance σ for generating a random initial population with the initial distribution. Initial Ω is the estimation of the location of the optimum for each parameter in an individual, variance σ defining the speed of convergence of the algorithm when the number of individuals that resolve the problem increase, and a determinate value can produce a premature convergence of the algorithm. For UMDAc, the initial variance σ is considered as a hyper-parameter.

For CMA-ES, the covariance matrix $Cov \in \mathbb{R}^{\gamma \times \gamma}$ is initialized in identity matrix $Cov = I$, this matrix is symmetric and positive definite. We fix the initial centroid $\Omega \in \mathbb{R}^{\gamma}$ and the initial step-size $\sigma \in \mathbb{R}$ that corresponds to initial variance. Initial Ω is the estimation of the location of the optimum for each parameter in an individual and indicates where to start the evolution. For each generation, we obtain new individuals following Eq. 7:

$$W_{2,\lambda}^{(g+1)} = \Omega^{(g)} + \sigma^{(g)} \mathcal{N}(0, Cov^{(g)}) \tag{7}$$

The matrix Cov has an orthonormal basis of eigenvectors defined as B as results of eigenvalue decomposition of $Cov = BD^2B^T$, being B an orthogonal matrix, where $B^TB = BB^T = I$. $D^2 = diag(d_1^2, ..., d_\gamma^2)$ is a diagonal matrix with eigenvalues of Cov as diagonal elements. Hence, $D = diag(d_1, ..., d_\gamma)$ is a diagonal matrix with square roots of eigenvalues of D as diagonal elements [2].

Using previous eigenvalue decomposition of Cov, $\mathcal{N}(0, Cov^{(g)})$ can be computed as following Eq. 8:

$$\mathcal{N}(0, Cov^{(g)}) = BD\mathcal{N}(0, I) \tag{8}$$

where $\mathcal{N}(0, I)$ represents a standard normally distributed vector which is a realization from a multivariate normal distribution with zero mean and identity covariance matrix. Selection and recombination are important steps in the evolution strategy to adjust of initial centroid Ω, taking into account initial weights for each point of distribution. Moreover, σ is considered a step-size and we perform its control using the matrix decomposition Cov and initial evolution path $p \in IR^\gamma$. Finally, we perform the covariance matrix adaptation step as described in [2].

2.3 Dataset for Polarity Detection in Cuban Opinion Reviews

In this section, a compilation of the data available on TripAdvisor concerning hotels, villas, hostels, and rental houses in Cuba is carried out. The data collected consisted of raw texts in the Spanish language from 2006 to 2022. The opinions of 429 facilities out of a total of 878 were covered, since the rest, despite being registered on TripAdvisor, did not have registered opinions. The data were collected by the web scraping technique using the library Selenium and BeautifulSoup4, available for Python.

The dataset has a total of 17988 examples and is structured in the following fields:

- **Title:** The title that the tourist himself gave to his opinion. *Data type:* Text
- **Opinion:** The opinion issued by the tourist. *Data type:* Text
- **Polarity:** The label that represents the polarity of the opinion. *Data type:* [1, 2, 3, 4, 5]
- **Date:** Date the opinion was issued. *Data type:* Date

Figure 2 (right) illustrates the distribution of opinions by category for the database collected, hereafter referred to by the name Cuba Hotels Sentiment (CHS)[1] It can be seen that there is an imbalance in the distribution of examples by class. The database is partitioned into a 70% training set and 30% test set. On the right, the cumulative histogram of the words in the vocabulary for the CHS database is shown. The distribution information is shown in a logarithmic scale and in descending order. The rest of the database statistics are shown in Table 1.

[1] Available at: https://drive.google.com/drive/folders/1pZVxp5DgpD7UEgOnWXKhLm5-pX0YYlNo?usp=sharing.

Table 1. Statistic summarization for the dataset

Cuba Hotels Sentiment	
Vocabulary length	44 609 tokens
Train set	12 591 reviews
Test set	5 397 reviews
Labels	5
Stop-words	1 012 405 tokens
Punctuation marks	237 492 tokens

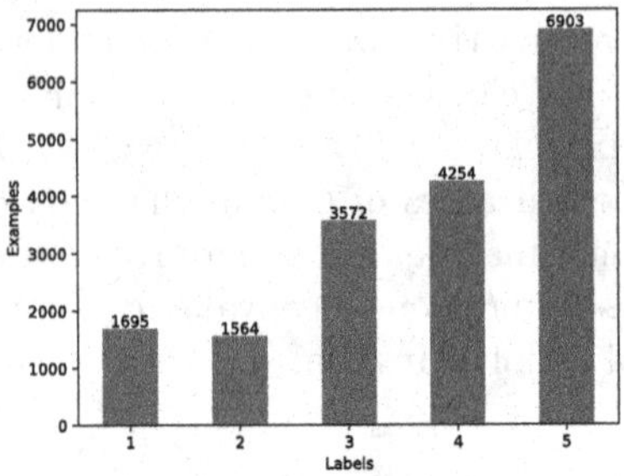

Fig. 2. Distribution of examples per labels

2.4 Pre-processing and Data Augmentation

For data preprocessing, the data is normalized by tokenization, the text is capitalized (all the tokens are lowercased), stop-words and punctuation marks are removed. In addition, words are brought to their basic form by Lemmatization in order to reduce noise from the use of certain terms or words in different contexts, where the meaning may be ambiguous.

For the treatment of data imbalance, back translation will be used as a technique of data augmentation, for which the MarianMT [4] language model based on Transformers is used. It is a model for low-resource machine translation, each translation model occupies a disk size less than 300 MB and supports 1440 language pairs for translation[2]. For this database, English is used as the auxiliary language, so each opinion is translated first into English and then into Spanish.

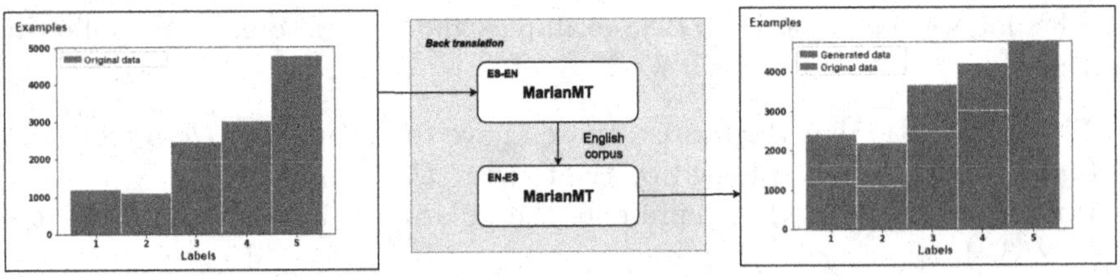

Fig. 3. Overview for back translation process in the dataset

The Fig. 3 shows how the MarianMT model was applied in the back translation process. It was used for the language pair the model **Helsinki-NLP/opus-mt-en-en**[3] and for the language pair the model **Helsinki-NLP/opus-mt-en**[4] For classes 1 and 2 the data were duplicated, while for classes 3 and 4 1200

[2] A language pair refers to a translation from a source language to a target language. Example: *EN-ES*, which indicates translating from English to Spanish.

[3] Available at: https://huggingface.co/Helsinki-NLP/opus-mt-es-en.

[4] Available at: https://huggingface.co/Helsinki-NLP/opus-mt-en-es.

opinions per class were chosen by random sampling without replacement. Thus, the initial imbalance between the classes with the lowest number of examples (1 and 2) was reduced utilizing of new synthetic examples, keeping the number of examples balanced in the rest of the labels.

3 Results and Discussion

This section presents the results of the opinion ranking process from the collected database. To perform the experiments, the Grid Search Cross-Validation algorithm was applied, with $k = 10$ to adjust the hyper-parameter learning rate (α) in the AdamW training algorithm, thereby setting $\alpha = 6e - 05$. A total of 3 training epochs were performed for the selected database due to over-fitting the model to a larger number of epochs. In the experimental results, we seek to analyze the effect of applying different preprocessing techniques and the influence of data augmentation for the treatment of the imbalance. We further considered weight decay (wd) and dropout (dp) as hyper-parameters, taking the following values: $wd = 0.01$, and $dp = 0.1$.

Our model is implemented with Pytorch[5]. For performing the EDA algorithm we use the Deap library as an evolutionary computation framework that includes implementations of meta-heuristic algorithms. We run the experiments in Google COLAB using a GPU environment.

Table 2. Test set results for AdamW in polarity prediction using different preprocessing techniques

Polarity prediction				
Pre-processing	Acc	MAE	Macro F	R
Normalization	0,6472	0,4073	0,5739	0,6472
Normalization, Lemmatization	0,6468	0,4137	0,5618	0,6468
Normalization, Data augmentation	**0,6535**	**0,4030**	**0,5981**	**0,6535**
Normalization, Data augmentation, Lemmatization	0,6463	0,4065	0,5776	0,6463

Table 2 shows the results of the test set across the Acc, MAE, Macro F and R metrics. Since there is an imbalance in the data, MAE will be considered as a metric to estimate the generalization error. Applying data augmentation improves the results compared to the rest of the combinations.

Figure 4 shows that with the four preprocessing variants used, the classification of opinions in each of the classes is achieved. It is evident that applying data augmentation increases the number of correctly classified examples in the minority classes without affecting the overall efficiency. However, applying data

[5] Available at: https://colab.research.google.com/drive/1QdhSMLSOq1jXC4OPJfK6PKsmvc1-RrQa?usp=sharing.

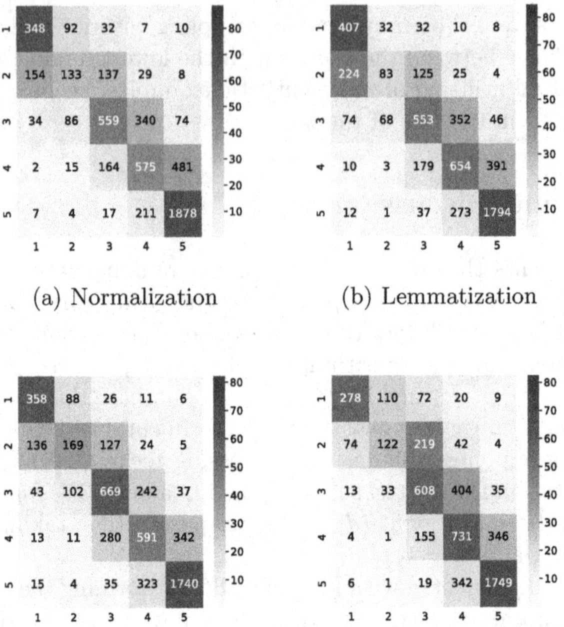

(a) Normalization

(b) Lemmatization

(c) Normatization and Data augmentation

(d) Normatization, Data augmentation, and Lemmatization

Fig. 4. Confusion matrix for AdamW in polarity prediction using different preprocessing techniques.

Table 3. Test set results in polarity prediction via EDA optimization

Polarity prediction				
Algorithm	Acc	MAE	Macro F	R
AdamW	0,6535	0,4030	0,5981	0,6535
Variant 1	0,6555	0,3965	0,5962	0,6555
Variant 2	**0,6593**	**0,3919**	0,6097	**0,6593**
Variant 3	0,6543	0,3956	**0,6136**	0,6543

augmentation and lemmatization together only improves the results in classes 3 and 4. The confusion matrix for each combination shows that the architecture based on the encoder mT5 achieves that, for data augmentation, 30.39% of the instances that were not correctly classified are around the main diagonal of the matrix. This indicates that there is an overlap of opinions in the database; this behavior can be seen in the rest of the preprocessing techniques applied.

We compare the results with AdamW regarding the combination of algorithms as hybrid proposals: AdamW+UMDAc (Variant 1), AdamW+EMNA (Variant 2), AdamW+CMA-ES (Variant 3). Combinations are represented by a plus symbol separating the gradient-based algorithm used in the first stage, and the EDA evolutionary strategy used in the second stage. Table 3 shows the results of applying the EDA algorithms in the second phase of the proposed method, taking the best combination between preprocessing and imbalance treatment (Normalization and Data augmentation). At this point, it is shown how EDAs can be applied as a second level of improvement in the generalization capability of the neural network. In training, a total of 20 generations were applied, and 20 individuals were set as the population size. For UMDAc and EMNA a $\sigma = 0.095$ was used, while for CMA-ES a $\sigma = 0.096$ was used. For EMNA and CMA-ES, the initial centroid was set as $\Omega = 0.03$.

Experimental results show that applying data augmentation for imbalance improves the generalization of the model. However, applying lemmatization has no effect on learning in either case, suggesting that bringing words into their basic form or lemma for Spanish affects the way the transformer learns the context, and thus the meaning, by tracking relationships in the sequence of words.

The last dense layer optimization of the fully-connected head, using the proposed meta-heuristics, enables the interpretation of the extracted features from the mT5 encoder in terms of a predictive output. Experimental results indicate the influence of learning parameters distribution in this part of the model through the EDAs, to find parameters close to the global optimum and obtain a model with greater generalization capacity. Considering our mT5 encoder design in Fig. 1, the number of network parameters for a five-class classification problem (polarity prediction) is 146 973 765, with only 325 parameters for the last dense layer of the fully-connected head. This takes advantage of what the network learned in the first stage, and with the last hidden state produced by the mT5 encoder, refines the weights of the last layer in the fully-connected head which is a simpler network part.

4 Conclusions and Further Work

In this paper, we present a hybrid gradient-based method and EDA together for fine-tuning the mT5-based transformer in polarity prediction. The use of AdamW as an optimizer in the first phase takes advantage of the speed of these methods for learning parameters of the mT5 encoder, something that would not be appropriate to apply through population meta-heuristics due to the over-parameterization of this type of deep learning model. Experimental results show that applying back translation improves model performance with imbalanced data. Further study should be conducted to analyze other techniques to overcome the imbalance and the introduction of additional features through lexicons or ontology enrichment.

Acknowledgments. This work has been partially funded by VLIR-UOS Network University Cooperation Programme-Cuba. We gratefully acknowledge the computing time granted through UCI-HPC and Computational Mathematics Study Center at the University of Informatics Sciences supercomputer resources.

References

1. Chaturvedi, I., Su, C.L., Welsch, R.E.: Fuzzy aggregated topology evolution for cognitive multi-tasks. Cogn. Comput. **13**(1), 96–107 (2021). https://doi.org/10.1007/s12559-020-09807-4
2. Hansen, N., Ostermeier, A.: Completely derandomized self-adaptation in evolution strategies. Evol. Comput. **9**(2), 159–195 (2001)
3. Janani, R., Vijayarani, S.: Automatic text classification using machine learning and optimization algorithms. Soft. Comput. **25**(2), 1129–1145 (2021). https://doi.org/10.1007/s00500-020-05209-8
4. Junczys-Dowmunt, M., et al.: Marian: fast neural machine translation in C++. In: ACL 2018–56th Annual Meeting of the Association for Computational Linguistics, Proceedings of System Demonstrations, pp. 116–121 (2015)
5. Kiefer, J., Wolfowitz, J.: Stochastic estimation of the maximum of a regression function. Ann. Math. Stat. **23**(3), 462–466 (1952)
6. Kingma, D.P., Ba, J.L.: Adam: a method for stochastic optimization. In: 3rd International Conference on Learning Representations, ICLR 2015 - Conference Track Proceedings, pp. 1–15 (2015)
7. Larrañaga, P.: A review on estimation of distribution algorithms. In: Larrañaga, P., Lozano, J.A. (eds.) Estimation of Distribution Algorithms. GENA, vol. 2, pp. 57–100. Springer, Boston (2002). https://doi.org/10.1007/978-1-4615-1539-5_3
8. Larrañaga, P., Lozano, J.A.: Estimation of Distribution Algorithms: A New Tool for Evolutionary Computation, vol. 2. Springer, New York (2002). https://doi.org/10.1007/978-1-4615-1539-5
9. Loshchilov, I., Hutter, F.: Decoupled weight decay regularization. In: 7th International Conference on Learning Representations, ICLR 2019, pp. 1–8 (2019)
10. Khataei Maragheh, H., Gharehchopogh, F.S., Majidzadeh, K., Sangar, A.B.: A new hybrid based on long short-term memory network with spotted hyena optimization algorithm for multi-label text classification. Mathematics **10**(3), 488 (2022)
11. Rojas-Delgado, J., Trujillo-Rasúa, R., Bello, R.: A continuation approach for training artificial neural networks with meta-heuristics. Pattern Recogn. Lett. **125**, 373–380 (2019)
12. Salinas Chávez, E., Salinas Chávez, E., Mundet i Cerdan, L.: Tourism in Cuba: development, challenges, perspectives. Revista Rosa dos Ventos - Turismo e Hospitalidade **11**(1), 23–49 (2019)
13. Vaswani, A., et al.: Attention is all you need. In: Advances in Neural Information Processing Systems, NIPS, pp. 5999–6009 (2017)
14. Xue, L., et al.: mT5: a massively multilingual pre-trained text-to-text transformer. In: Proceedings of the 2021 Conference of the North American Chapter of the Association for Computational Linguistics: Human Language Technologies, pp. 483–498 (2021)

Biometrics, Image, Video and Signals Analysis and Processing

SqueezerFaceNet: Reducing a Small Face Recognition CNN Even More via Filter Pruning

Fernando Alonso-Fernandez[1](✉), Kevin Hernandez-Diaz[1], Jose Maria Buades Rubio[2], and Josef Bigun[1]

[1] School of Information Technology, Halmstad University, Halmstad, Sweden
{feralo,kevin.hernandez-diaz,josef.bigun}@hh.se

[2] Computer Graphics and Vision and AI Group, University of Balearic Islands, Palma, Spain
josemaria.buades@uib.es

Abstract. The widespread use of mobile devices for various digital services has created a need for reliable and real-time person authentication. In this context, facial recognition technologies have emerged as a dependable method for verifying users due to the prevalence of cameras in mobile devices and their integration into everyday applications. The rapid advancement of deep Convolutional Neural Networks (CNNs) has led to numerous face verification architectures. However, these models are often large and impractical for mobile applications, reaching sizes of hundreds of megabytes with millions of parameters. We address this issue by developing SqueezerFaceNet, a light face recognition network which less than 1M parameters. This is achieved by applying a network pruning method based on Taylor scores, where filters with small importance scores are removed iteratively. Starting from an already small network (of 1.24M) based on SqueezeNet, we show that it can be further reduced (up to 40%) without an appreciable loss in performance. To the best of our knowledge, we are the first to evaluate network pruning methods for the task of face recognition.

Keywords: Face recognition · Mobile Biometrics · CNN pruning · Taylor scores

1 Introduction

The widespread use of smartphones as all-in-one platforms has led to more people relying on them for accessing online services such as e-commerce and banking. This makes it crucial to implement robust user authentication mechanisms to ensure secure device unlocking and protected transactions. Here, we address face recognition (FR) for mobile applications, where biometric verification is increasingly employed for the mentioned purposes. As with many other vision tasks, Convolutional Neural Networks (CNNs) have become a very popular tool for biometrics, including FR [19]. Nevertheless, the high-performing models proposed

Y. Hernndez Heredia et al. (Eds.): IWAIPR 2023, LNCS 14335, pp. 349–361, 2024.
https://doi.org/10.1007/978-3-031-49552-6_30

Table 1. Proposed lightweight models in the literature for face recognition.

Network	Input size	Parameters	Vector Size	Base Architecture
LightCNN (18) [21]	128 × 128	12.6M	256	
MobileFaceNets (18) [6]	112 × 112	0.99M	256	MobileNetv2
MobiFace (19) [9]	112 × 112	n/a	512	MobileNetv2
ShuffleFaceNet (19) [15]	112 × 112	0.5–4.5M	128	ShuffleNet
SeesawFaceNets (19) [23]	112 × 112	1.3M	512	
VarGFaceNet (19) [22]	112 × 112	5M	512	VarGNet
SqueezeFacePoseNet [2]	113 × 113	0.86–1.24M	1000	SqueezeNet
PocketNet (21) [4]	112 × 112	0.92–0.99 M	128–256	PocketNet
MixFaceNets (21) [3]	112 × 112	1.04–3.95M	512	MixNets
SqueezerFaceNet (ours)	113 × 113	0.65–0.94M	1000	SqueezeNet

in the literature, e.g. [7], usually entail extensive storage and computational resources due to their millions of parameters. This poses a significant challenge for deploying them on resource-limited devices.

Across the years, several light CNNs have been presented, mainly for common visual tasks in the context of the ImageNet challenge [17]. Examples include SqueezeNet [11] (1.24M parameters), MobileNetV2 [18] (3.5M), ShuffleNet [25] (1.4M), MixNets [20] (5M), or VarGNet [24] (13.23M). They employ different techniques to achieve fewer parameters and faster processing, such as point-wise convolution, depth-wise separable convolution, variable group convolution, mixed convolution, channel shuffle, and bottleneck layers. Some works (Table 1) have adapted these networks for FR purposes [2,3,6,9,15,22]. Instead of adapting existing common architectures, the work [4] suggested applying Neural Architecture Search (NAS) to design a family of light FR models, named PocketNets.

In this paper, we follow another strategy, consisting of applying network compression to existing architectures. Common techniques include knowledge distillation, quantization, or pruning. A number of them have been used to reduce the size of general image classification models, and some works recently started to apply them for face detection [13] or ocular recognition [1]. Here, we use a pruning method based on importance scores of network filters [16] to reduce an already small FR network of 1.24M parameters that uses a modified SqueezeNet architecture [2,11]. Thus, we call our network SqueezerFaceNet. The importance score of a filter is obtained considering its effect on the error if it is removed. This is computed by first-order Taylor approximation, which only requires the elements of the gradient computed during training via backpropagation.

To the best of our knowledge, we are the first to evaluate network pruning methods for the task of FR. We test SqueezerFaceNet on a face verification scenario over VGGFace2-Pose, a subset of the VGGFace2 database [5] with 11040 images from 368 subjects on three poses (frontal, three-quarter, and profile). We show that the number of filters of the network can be reduced up to 15% without a significant loss of accuracy in one-to-one comparisons for any given pose. If we allow five images per user to build an identity template, accuracy is not significantly affected until a 30–40% reduction in the number of filters.

2 Network Pruning Method

We apply the method of [16], which iteratively estimates the importance scores of individual elements based on their effect on the network loss. Then, elements with the lowest scores are pruned, leading to a more compact network.

Given a network with parameters $\mathbf{W} = \{w_0, w_1, ..., w_M\}$ and a training set $\mathcal{D}$ of input (x_i) and output (y_i) pairs $\mathcal{D} = \{(x_0, y_0), (x_1, y_1), ..., (x_K, y_K)\}$, the aim of network training is to minimize the classification error E by solving $\min_{\mathbf{W}} E(\mathcal{D}, \mathbf{W}) = \min_{\mathbf{W}} E(y|x, \mathbf{W})$. The importance of a parameter w_m can be defined by its impact on the error if it is removed. Under an *i.i.d.* assumption, the induced error can be quantified as the squared difference of the prediction error E with and without the parameter:

$$\mathcal{I}_m = \Big(E(\mathcal{D}, \mathbf{W}) - E(\mathcal{D}, \mathbf{W}|w_m = 0)\Big)^2 \tag{1}$$

However, computing $\mathcal{I}_m$ for each parameter using Eq. 1 would demand to evaluate M versions of the network, one for each removed parameter, making the process expensive computationally. This is avoided by approximating $\mathcal{I}_m$ in the vicinity of $\mathbf{W}$ by its first-order Taylor expansion $\mathcal{I}^1_m(\mathbf{W}) = (g_m w_m)^2$, where $g_m = \frac{\partial E}{\partial w_m}$ are the elements of the gradient g. A second-order expansion is also proposed [16], but it demands computing the Hessian of E, so we employ the first-order approximation for a more compact and fast computation. The gradient g is available from backpropagation, so $\mathcal{I}_m$ can be easily computed. To compute the joint importance of a set of parameters $\mathbf{W}_S$ (e.g. a filter), we apply:

$$\mathcal{I}^1_S(\mathbf{W}) \triangleq \sum_{s \in S} (g_s w_s)^2 \tag{2}$$

The algorithm starts with a trained network, which is pruned iteratively over the same training set. Given a mini-batch, the gradients are computed, and the network weights are updated by gradient descent. Simultaneously, the importance of each filter is computed via Eq. 2. At the end of each epoch, the importance scores of each filter are averaged over the mini-batches, and the filters with the smallest importance scores are removed. The pruning process is then stopped after a certain number of epochs. The resulting network can be then fine-tuned again over the training set to regain potential accuracy losses due to filter removal.

3 SqueezerFaceNet Architecture and Database

As the backbone for SqueezerFaceNet, we employ SqueezeNet [11]. This is among the smallest generic CNNs proposed in the context of the ImageNet challenge, and one of the early networks designed to reduce the number of parameters and size. It has only 18 convolutional layers, 1.24M parameters, and 4.6 MB in its uncompressed version. To reduce the network size, it uses fire modules, which

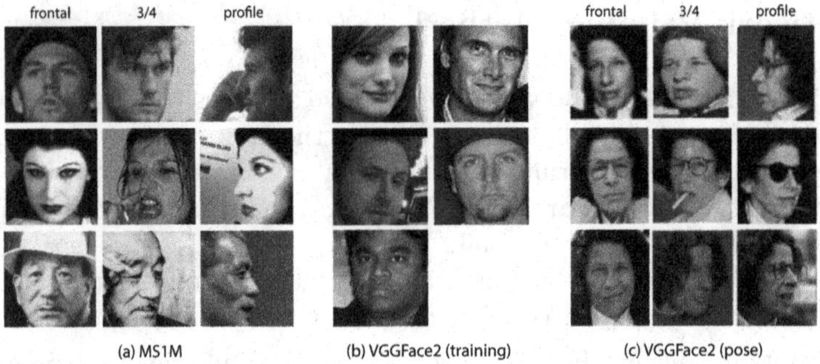

Fig. 1. Example images of the databases used. (a) MS1M from three users (by row) and three viewpoints (column). (b) VGGFace2 training images with a random crop. (c) VGGFace2 pose templates from three viewpoints (by column).

first reduce the input channel dimensionality via 1 × 1 point-wise filters (*squeeze* phase), to be then processed with a larger amount of (more costly) 3 × 3 and 1 × 1 filters in a lower dimensional space (*expand* phase). Another strategy is late downsampling, so convolution layers are presented maps as large as possible. According to its authors, it should lead to higher accuracy.

In the present paper, we adopt the SqueezeNet implementation previously proposed for FR using light CNNs in [2], referred to as SqueezeFacePoseNet. In particular, the network employs an input of 113 × 113, instead of the original 227 × 227 of SqueezeNet. This is achieved by changing the stride of the first convolutional layer from 2 to 1, while keeping the rest of the network unchanged, which allows to reuse ImageNet parameters as starting model. Such transfer learning strategy from ImageNet has been shown to provide equal or better performance than if initialized from scratch, while converging faster [14]. In the present paper, we have also added batch normalization between convolutions and ReLU layers. This is missing in the original SqueezeNet and in [2], but batch normalization is commonly used before non-linearities to aid in the training of deep networks [12]. Compared to [2], we observe that it also leads to increased recognition accuracy, with a small overhead of parameters.

The database for training and evaluation is VGGFace2, with 3.31M images of 9131 celebrities (363.6 images/person on average) [5]. The images, downloaded from the Internet, show significant variations in pose, age, ethnicity, lightning and background. The protocol contemplates 8631 training classes (3.14M images) and the remaining 500 classes for testing. For cross-pose experiments, a subset of 368 subjects from the test set is defined (called VGGFace2-Pose), having 10 images per pose (frontal, three-quarter, and profile) and a total of 11040 images.

To further improve recognition performance, we also pre-train Squeezer-FaceNet in the RetinaFace cleaned set of the MS-Celeb-1M database [10] (MS1M for short), with 5.1M images of 93.4K identities. The release contains 113 × 113 images of MS1M cropped with the five facial landmarks provided by RetinaFace [8]. While MS1M has a more significant number of images, its intra-identity variation is limited due to an average of 81 images/person. Following previous research [2,5], we first pre-train SqueezerFaceNet on a dataset with a large number of images (MS1M) and then fine-tune it with more intra-class diversity (VGGFace2). This has been shown to provide better performance than training the models only with VGGFace2. Some example images are shown in Fig. 1.

4 Experimental Protocol

SqueezerFaceNet is trained for biometric identification using the soft-max function and ImageNet as initialization. We follow the training/evaluation protocol of VGGFace2 [5]. For training, the bounding boxes of VGGFace2 images are resized, so the shorter side has 129 pixels, and a random crop of 113 × 113 is taken. A random crop is not possible with MS1M, since images are directly at 113 × 113. We also apply horizontal random flip to both databases. The optimizer is SGDM with a mini-batch of 128. The initial learning rate is 0.01, which is decreased to 0.005, 0.001, and 0.0001 when the validation loss plateaus. Two percent of images per user in the training set are set aside for validation. Users in MS1M with fewer than 70 images are removed to reduce the parameters of the fully connected layer dedicated to under-represented classes and ensure at least one image per user in the validation set. This results in 35016 users and 3.16M images. We train with Matlab r2022b and use the ImageNet pre-trained model that comes with such release.

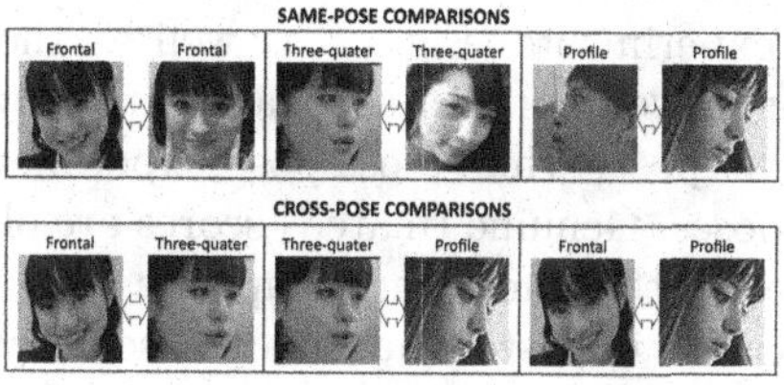

Fig. 2. Same-pose (top) and cross-pose comparisons (bottom).

Verification experiments are done with VGGFace2-Pose following the protocol of [5]. A center crop of 113 × 113 is taken after the shortest image side is resized to 129 pixels. Identity templates per user are created by combining five faces with the same pose, resulting in two templates available per user and pose. To test the robustness of the network and the pruning method in more adverse conditions, we also do experiments using only one image as template. A template vector is created by averaging the descriptors of the faces in the template set, which are obtained from the layer adjacent to the classification layer (i.e., the Global Average Pooling). With SqueezeNet, this corresponds to a descriptor of 1000 elements. To further improve performance against pose variation, we also average the descriptor of an image and its horizontally flipped counterpart, which is hypothesized to help to minimize the effect of pose variation [9]. The cosine similarity is then used to compare two given templates.

Table 2. Face verification results on the VGGFace2-Pose database (EER %) without pruning. F = Frontal View. 3/4 = Three-Quarter. P = Profile.

Network	One face image per template (1-1)							Five face images per template (5-5)						
	Same-Pose			Cross-Pose			Over-all	Same-Pose			Cross-Pose			Over-all
	F-F	3/4-3/4	P-P	F-3/4	F-P	3/4-P		F-F	3/4-3/4	P-P	F-3/4	F-P	3/4-P	
SqueezerFaceNet (ours)	5.32	4.87	7.36	5.09	7.32	6.47	6.07	0.27	0.3	0.85	0.23	0.74	0.75	0.52
SqueezeFacePoseNet [2]	6.39	5.47	7.88	6.09	8.15	7.02	6.34	0.27	0.06	0.54	0.2	1.23	0.88	0.52

Table 3. Number of biometric verification scores.

Template	SAME-POSE		CROSS-POSE	
	Genuine	Impostor	Genuine	Impostor
1 image (1-1)	368 × (9+8+...+1) = 16560	368 × 100 = 36800	368 × 10 × 10 = 36800	368 × 100 = 36800
5 images (5-5)	368 × 1 = 368	368 × 100 = 36800	368 × 2 × 2 = 1472	368 × 100 = 36800

5 Results

We first report the verification accuracy of SqueezerFaceNet without any pruning in Table 2. This will be the baseline to which we will compare after pruning. We also give the results of SqueezeFacePoseNet from [2]. We detail the results of both same- and cross-pose experiments (Fig. 2), as well as the overall performance across all poses. Same-pose comparisons are made with only templates generated with images of the same pose, while cross-pose experiments are done between templates of different poses. Genuine (mated) scores are obtained by comparing each template of a user to the remaining templates of the same user, avoiding symmetric comparisons. For impostor (non-mated) scores, the first template of a user is used as the enrolment template and compared with the second template of the next 100 users. Table 3 shows the total number of scores.

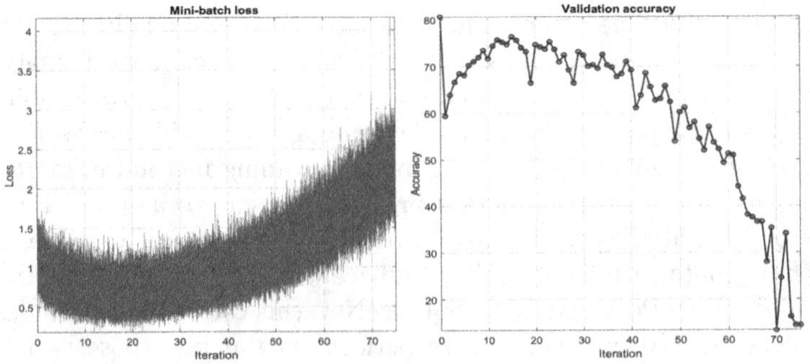

Fig. 3. Mini-batch loss and validation accuracy during the pruning of SqueezerFaceNet. One iteration removes 1% of the filters with the lowest importance scores.

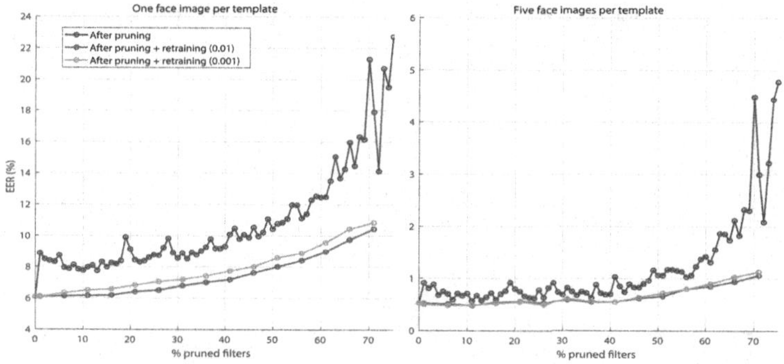

Fig. 4. Face verification results on the VGGFace2-Pose database (EER %) during the pruning of SqueezerFaceNet (overall accuracy across all pose comparison types). One iteration removes 1% of the filters with the lowest importance scores. (Color figure online)

One observation from Table 2 is that SqueezerFaceNet improves the results of [2]. The main differences of the present paper are that we have added batch normalization to the network, we apply random horizontal flip to the training images, we use cosine similarity instead of χ^2 distance to compare vectors, and we compute an image descriptor by averaging the descriptor of the original image and its horizontally flipped counterpart [9]. These modifications seem to have an overall positive effect. Regarding pose comparison types, it can be seen that the worst performance is given by the most difficult ones, either when the image is only visible from one side (Profile vs. Profile) or when there is a maximum difference between query and test templates (Frontal vs. Profile). It is also worth noting the substantial improvement observed when five images are used to generate user's templates (5-5) in comparison to using one (1-1).

We then apply the pruning of Sect. 2 to SqueezerFaceNet. On each iteration, we use a random 25% of the VGGFace2 training set to compute the importance score of each convolution filter. After each iteration, we remove 1% of the filters with the lowest scores. The optimizer is SGDM with a mini-batch of 128 and a learning rate of 0.01. Figure 3 shows the mini-batch loss and validation accuracy across different iterations. An interesting observation is that the loss decreases a bit until ~15% of the filters have been pruned and then increases again (the validation loss shows the opposite behavior, as expected). However, after removing just 1% of the filters (first iteration), the validation accuracy decreases sharply from ~80% to ~60%, and then it is regained again as the network is pruned up to ~15% of the filters. Figure 4 (blue curves) shows the overall verification accuracy of the pruned network on the VGGFace2-Pose database. The origin of the x-axis ($x = 0$) corresponds to SqueezerFaceNet without pruning. As can be seen also here, after removing just 1% of the filters, there is a jump towards a worse performance, after which performance is regained a bit until the network is pruned approximately by 10–15%. In five-to-five comparisons (right plot), performance is kept more stable until 30–40% of the network has been pruned,

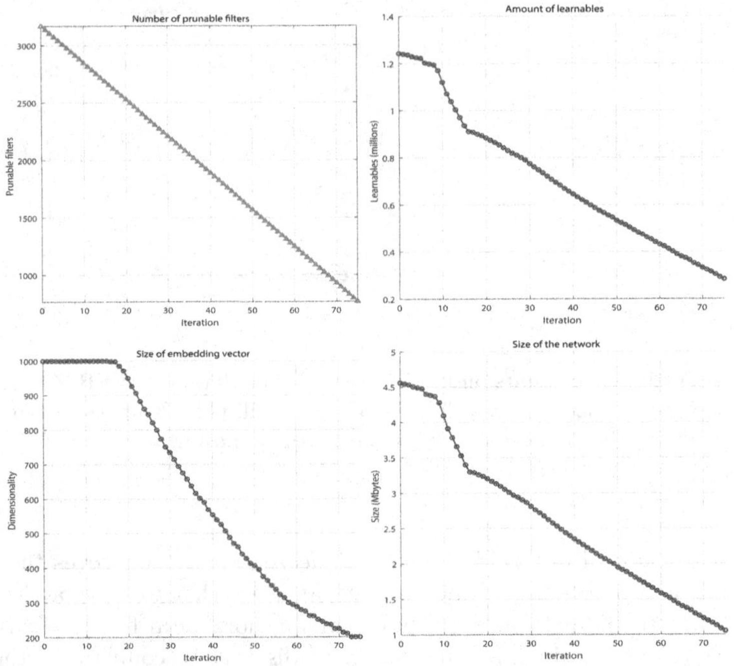

Fig. 5. Effect of pruning in: number of filters (top left), learnables (top right), embedding size (bottom left) and size (bottom right) of SqueezerFaceNet.

suggesting that combining several face images to create a user template can be a method to counteract the effect of eliminating convolution filters. In one-to-one comparisons, however, accuracy decreases quicker.

After pruning the network with different percentages, we retrain it over VGGFace2 according to the same protocol of the original unpruned network (Sect. 4) in order to regain the accuracy lost during pruning. Given the time that it takes to train the network over the entire VGGFace2, we do the retraining only every 5 iterations of the pruning algorithm (starting at 1%). The results are given in Fig. 4 as well. The network is retrained either with a starting learning rate of 0.01 (red curve) or 0.001 (orange). The rationale between these two options is that even if the network is pruned, it has already been trained once over the same database, so starting with a high learning rate may be counterproductive. However, as seen in Fig. 4, this is not the case. Indeed, in one-to-one comparisons, the best accuracy is given by starting with 0.01. Regarding the accuracy lost after pruning, it can be seen that training the pruned network again is able to recover the original accuracy up to a certain percentage of pruned filters. In one-to-one comparisons, performance remains stable until ~15% of the filters have been eliminated. Then, accuracy worsens exponentially. In five-to-five comparisons, on the other hand, performance remains at the same level as the unpruned network until about 30–40%. A remarkable result, in any case, is

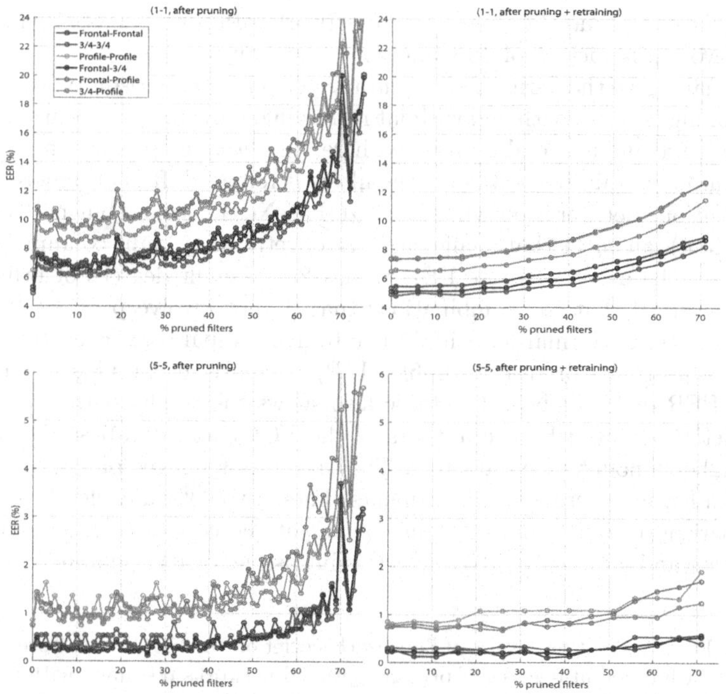

Fig. 6. Face verification on VGGFace2-Pose (EER %) during the pruning of SqueezerFaceNet per pose comparison type (retraining with a starting rate = 0.1). Each iteration removes 1% of the filters with the lowest importance scores.

that after 70% of the filters have been removed, the EER is less than double, so a certain reduction in the number of filters does not translate to accuracy in the same proportion. In five-to-five comparisons, the EER goes from 0.52% (unpruned network) to 1.06% (network pruned at 71%).

We then analyze the effect on the network of the pruning process (Fig. 5). Obviously, the number of filters decreases linearly on each iteration (by 1%), since we have designed the experiments that way. However, the amount of learnables or the size of the network first decreases slowly until about 10% of the filters are removed. Between 10 and 15%, there is a significant drop in learnables, and then the decrease is stabilized again at a slower pace. This suggests that the filters that are removed first are not big and/or do not affect a high amount of channels, but then, the pruning algorithm removes filters having a larger amount of parameters. Regarding the size of the embedding vector, it is maintained constant until a pruning of about 18%, indicating that the filters that are removed first do not affect the last layer of the network. If we set 15% as the optimal pruning (from Fig. 4), it translates to a reduction in parameters from 1.24M to 0.94M (by 24%) and in size from 4.6MB to 3.4MB (by 26%). This is without losing accuracy significantly. In five-to-five comparisons, we could go even higher and prune about 40% of the network, resulting in 0.65M parameters and 2.35MB (a reduction of 48% and 49%, respectively).

We finally give the verification accuracy per pose comparison type after network pruning (Fig. 6), with and without retraining. Obviously, the same accuracy gains after retraining are also observed here, and how the performance is maintained until a certain percentage of the filters is removed. It is also more evident the oscillations per iteration when SqueezerFaceNet is pruned but not retrained (left column), an effect that is alleviated after retraining (right column). Table 4 also details the exact per-pose EER values for different degrees of pruning. It can be observed that the combinations that do not involve profile (P) images result in better performance. Still, in five-to-five comparisons, even the difficult profile-profile (P-P) or frontal-profile (F-P) comparisons provide a very competitive EER of 1% or less. The table also shows the results with two variants of ResNet50 deployed by the authors of the VGGFace2 database [5] having a much higher amount of parameters. They use input images of 224 × 224 and produce a feature vector of 2048 elements. These two networks clearly stand out in comparison to our SqueezeNet model but at the cost of a larger number of parameters and size (∼150 MB), which is infeasible for mobile applications.

Table 4. Face verification results of SqueezerFaceNet on the VGGFace2-Pose database (EER %) with different degrees of pruning (pruned networks retrained with a starting rate = 0.01). F = Frontal View. 3/4 = Three-Quarter. P = Profile. Results with two large networks (ResNet50 variants [5]) are also shown.

Network	Parameters	One face image per template (1-1)							Five face images per template (5-5)						
		Same-Pose			Cross-Pose			Over-all	Same-Pose			Cross-Pose			Over-all
		F-F	3/4-3/4	P-P	F-3/4	F-P	3/4-P		F-F	3/4-3/4	P-P	F-3/4	F-P	3/4-P	
No pruning	1.24M	5.32	4.87	7.36	5.09	7.32	6.47	6.07	0.27	0.3	0.85	0.23	0.74	0.75	0.52
Pruning 16%	0.91M	5.53	4.87	7.38	5.16	7.52	6.64	6.18	0.27	0.31	0.89	0.21	0.75	0.78	0.54
Pruning 31%	0.76M	6.19	5.3	8.2	5.71	8.13	7.26	6.80	0.27	0.33	1.08	0.2	0.81	0.83	0.59
Pruning 46%	0.58M	6.86	5.94	9.17	6.29	9.28	8.19	7.62	0.27	0.27	1.09	0.27	0.97	0.83	0.62
Pruning 51%	0.52M	7.21	6.27	9.63	6.74	9.7	8.48	8.01	0.32	0.29	1.08	0.29	1.03	0.95	0.66
ResNet50ft [5]	25.6M	4.14	3.13	5.16	3.68	4.99	4.25	4.23	0.01	0.02	0.27	0.07	0.14	0.14	0.11
SENet50ft [5]	28.1M	3.86	2.87	4.16	3.36	4.48	3.71	3.74	0.02	0.02	0.2	0.07	0.14	0.2	0.12

6 Conclusions

This paper deals with the task of developing SqueezerFaceNet, a lightweight deep network architecture for mobile face recognition. For such purpose, we apply a CNN pruning method based on Taylor scores which assigns an importance measure to each filter of a given network. Such importance metric is based on the impact on the error if the filter is removed, and it only requires the back-propagation gradient for its computation. The method starts with a network trained for the target task (here: face recognition). Then, it is iteratively pruned by removing filters with the smallest importance. To regain potential accuracy losses, the pruned network is finally retrained again for the target task. The method is applied to an already light model (1.24M parameters) based on a modified SqueezeNet architecture [11]. As training sets, we use the large-scale MS-Celeb-1M (3.16M images, 35K identities) [10] and VGGFace2 (3.31M images, 9.1K identities) [5] datasets. We evaluate two verification scenarios, consisting of using a different number of images to create a user template. In one case, a template consists of five face images with the same pose, following the evaluation protocol of [5]. In the second case, we consider the much more difficult case of only one image to generate a user template. Different pose combinations between enrolment and query templates are tested too (Fig. 2).

Our experiments show that the pruning method is able to further reduce the number of filters of SqueezerFaceNet without decreasing accuracy significantly. This is especially evident if we employ a sufficient number of images to create a user template (five in our experiments). In such case, the number of filters can be reduced up to 40% without an appreciable accuracy loss. In one-to-one comparisons, a more difficult case, a reduction of up to 15% is also feasible. The resulting network in each case has 0.65M and 0.94M parameters, respectively. As future work, we are looking into evaluating the employed pruning method in more powerful CNN architectures which are widely used in face recognition, such as ResNet [7]. If the same effects as in the present paper are observed, it would allow to lower error rates in comparison to the ones obtained in this paper (Table 4), for a fraction of the size of such large networks. We are also considering other alternatives for network compression to evaluate if they are capable of producing even more reductions in network size [1].

Acknowledgements. This work was partly done while F. A.-F. was a visiting researcher at the University of the Balearic Islands. F. A.-F., K. H.-D., and J. B. thank the Swedish Research Council (VR) and the Swedish Innovation Agency (VINNOVA) for funding their research. Author J. M. B. thanks the project EXPLAINING - "Project EXPLainable Artificial INtelligence systems for health and well-beING", under Spanish national projects funding (PID2019-104829RA-I00/AEI/10.13039/501100011033). We gratefully acknowledge the support of NVIDIA Corporation with the donation of the Titan V GPU used for this research. The data handling in Sweden was enabled by the National Academic Infrastructure for Supercomputing in Sweden (NAISS).

References

1. Almadan, A., Rattani, A.: Benchmarking neural network compression techniques for ocular-based user authentication on smartphones. IEEE Access **11** (2023)
2. Alonso-Fernandez, F., Barrachina, J., Hernandez-Diaz, K., Bigun, J.: SqueezeFacePoseNet: lightweight face verification across different poses for mobile platforms. In: Del Bimbo, A., et al. (eds.) ICPR 2021. LNCS, vol. 12668, pp. 139–153. Springer, Cham (2021). https://doi.org/10.1007/978-3-030-68793-9_10
3. Boutros, F., Damer, N., Fang, M., Kirchbuchner, F., Kuijper, A.: MixFaceNets: extremely efficient face recognition networks. In: IEEE International Joint Conference on Biometrics, IJCB (2021)

4. Boutros, F., Siebke, P., Klemt, M., Damer, N., Kirchbuchner, F., Kuijper, A.: PocketNet: extreme lightweight face recognition network using neural architecture search and multistep knowledge distillation. IEEE Access **10**, 46823–46833 (2022)
5. Cao, Q., Shen, L., Xie, W., Parkhi, O.M., Zisserman, A.: VGGFace2: a dataset for recognising faces across pose and age. In: 13th IEEE International Conference on Automatic Face and Gesture Recognition, FG (2018)
6. Chen, S., Liu, Y., Gao, X., Han, Z.: MobileFaceNets: efficient CNNs for accurate real-time face verification on mobile devices. CoRR abs/1804.07573 (2018). http://arxiv.org/1804.07573
7. Deng, J., Guo, J., Xue, N., Zafeiriou, S.: ArcFace: additive angular margin loss for deep face recognition. In: IEEE/CVF Conference on Computer Vision and Pattern Recognition, CVPR (2019)
8. Deng, J., Guo, J., Zhou, Y., Yu, J., Kotsia, I., Zafeiriou, S.: RetinaFace: single-stage dense face localisation in the wild. CoRR abs/1905.00641 (2019). http://arxiv.org/1905.00641
9. Duong, C.N., Quach, K.G., Jalata, I.K., Le, N., Luu, K.: MobiFace: a lightweight deep learning face recognition on mobile devices. In: IEEE 10th International Conference on Biometrics Theory, Applications and Systems, BTAS (2019)
10. Guo, Y., Zhang, L., Hu, Y., He, X., Gao, J.: MS-Celeb-1M: a dataset and benchmark for large-scale face recognition. In: Leibe, B., Matas, J., Sebe, N., Welling, M. (eds.) ECCV 2016. LNCS, vol. 9907, pp. 87–102. Springer, Cham (2016). https://doi.org/10.1007/978-3-319-46487-9_6
11. Iandola, F.N., Moskewicz, M.W., Ashraf, K., Han, S., Dally, W.J., Keutzer, K.: SqueezeNet: AlexNet-level accuracy with 50x fewer parameters and <1mb model size. CoRR abs/1602.07360 (2016). http://arxiv.org/1602.07360
12. Ioffe, S., Szegedy, C.: Batch normalization: accelerating deep network training by reducing internal covariate shift. In: 32nd International Conference on Machine Learn, ICML (2015)
13. Jiang, N., et al.: PruneFaceDet: pruning lightweight face detection network by sparsity training. Cogn. Comput. Syst. **4**(4), 391–399 (2022)
14. Kornblith, S., Shlens, J., Le, Q.V.: Do better ImageNet models transfer better? In: Proceedings of the IEEE/CVF Conference on Computer Vision and Pattern Recognition, CVPR (2019)
15. Martinez-Díaz, Y., Luevano, L.S., Mendez-Vazquez, H., Nicolas-Diaz, M., Chang, L., Gonzalez-Mendoza, M.: ShuffleFaceNet: a lightweight face architecture for efficient and highly-accurate face recognition. In: Proceedings of the IEEE/CVF International Conference on Computer Vision Workshop, ICCVW (2019)
16. Molchanov, P., Mallya, A., Tyree, S., Frosio, I., Kautz, J.: Importance estimation for neural network pruning. In: IEEE/CVF Conference on Computer Vision and Pattern Recognition, CVPR (2019)
17. Russakovsky, O., et al.: ImageNet large scale visual recognition challenge. Int. J. Comput. Vision **115**(3), 211–252 (2015)
18. Sandler, M., Howard, A., Zhu, M., Zhmoginov, A., Chen, L.: MobileNetV 2: Inverted residuals and linear bottlenecks. In: IEEE/CVF Conference on Computer Vision and Pattern Recognition, CVPR (2018)
19. Sundararajan, K., Woodard, D.L.: Deep learning for biometrics: a survey. ACM Comput. Surv. **51**(3), 1–34 (2018)
20. Tan, M., Le, Q.V.: Mixconv: Mixed depthwise convolutional kernels. In: 30th British Machine Vision Conference, BMVC (2019)
21. Wu, X., He, R., Sun, Z., Tan, T.: A light CNN for deep face representation with noisy labels. IEEE Trans. Inf. Forensics Secur. **13**(11), 2884–2896 (2018)

22. Yan, M., Zhao, M., Xu, Z., Zhang, Q., Wang, G., Su, Z.: VarGFaceNet: an efficient variable group convolutional neural network for lightweight face recognition. In: IEEE/CVF International Conference on Computer Vision Workshop, ICCVW (2019)
23. Zhang, J.: SeesawFaceNets: sparse and robust face verification model for mobile platform. CoRR abs/1908.09124 (2019). http://arxiv.org/1908.09124
24. Zhang, Q., et al.: VarGNet: variable group convolutional neural network for efficient embedded computing. CoRR abs/1907.05653 (2020). arxiv.org/abs/1907.05653
25. Zhang, X., Zhou, X., Lin, M., Sun, J.: ShuffleNet: an extremely efficient convolutional neural network for mobile devices. In: IEEE/CVF Conference on Computer Vision and Pattern Recognition, CVPR (2018)

Drone Navigation and License Place Detection for Vehicle Location in Indoor Spaces

Moa Arvidsson[1], Sithichot Sawirot[1], Cristofer Englund[1], Fernando Alonso-Fernandez[1](✉), Martin Torstensson[2], and Boris Duran[2]

[1] School of Information Technology, Halmstad University, Halmstad, Sweden
{cristofer.englund,feralo}@hh.se
[2] RISE Viktoria, Gothenburg, Sweden
{martin.torstensson,boris.duran}@ri.se

Abstract. Millions of vehicles are transported every year, tightly parked in vessels or boats. To reduce the risks of associated safety issues like fires, knowing the location of vehicles is essential, since different vehicles may need different mitigation measures, e.g. electric cars. This work is aimed at creating a solution based on a nano-drone that navigates across rows of parked vehicles and detects their license plates. We do so via a wall-following algorithm, and a CNN trained to detect license plates. All computations are done in real-time on the drone, which just sends position and detected images that allow the creation of a 2D map with the position of the plates. Our solution is capable of reading all plates across eight test cases (with several rows of plates, different drone speeds, or low light) by aggregation of measurements across several drone journeys.

Keywords: Nano-drone · License plate detection · Vehicle location · UAV

1 Introduction

The business of transporting vehicles is constantly expanding. Millions of cars are transported in different ways, such as by truck, air, rail, or vessel [6]. The most cost-effective method is by boat [15]. Today there are ocean vessels built to carry up to 8000 vehicles. There are currently about 1400 vessels globally [5], and an estimated 7 million cars carried on vessels around the world every year.

Due to the high density of packed vehicles on decks, finding and identifying specific ones can be challenging. The mixed storage of combustion engines and electric vehicles or vehicles of different sizes further complicates the situation. Accurate knowledge of vehicle locations is crucial for safety reasons, such as in the event of a fire, as different measures are needed with electric vehicle batteries.

A simple way to identify them is to detect the license plate or identification number. This is possible via CCTV cameras, but plates are usually small and maybe obstructed due to tightly parked vehicles. Therefore, a solution based

Y. HernÃąndez Heredia et al. (Eds.): IWAIPR 2023, LNCS 14335, pp. 362–374, 2024.
https://doi.org/10.1007/978-3-031-49552-6_31

on a nano drone is investigated, since it can fit in narrow spaces. An onboard camera can carry out plate detection simultaneously. The proposed solution uses a wall-following strategy for navigation, treating rows of packed vehicles as walls. The images and drone position are sent to a remote client, which builds a 2D map that depicts the drone's path and detection results. This solution offers a promising method for efficiently identifying vehicles in crowded storage areas.

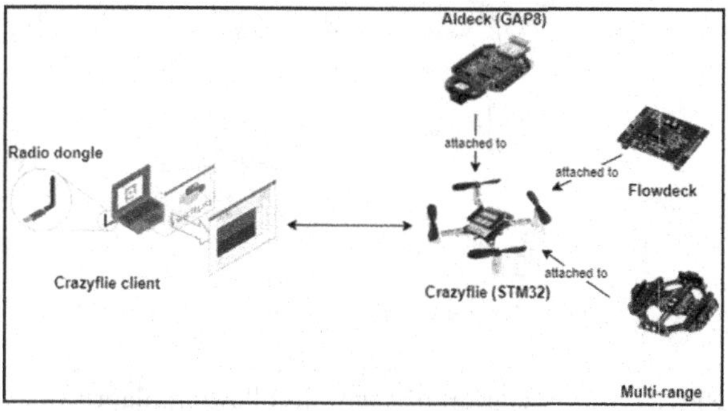

Fig. 1. System overview.

2 Related Works

We describe existing methods for navigation and object detection with drones. One gap is the limited size, weight, and computation onboard, making the use of predominant deep learning solutions a challenge [9].

2.1 Navigation

Unmanned Aerial Vehicles (UAVs) or drones require a navigation system to determine their position and trajectory. GPS navigation is feasible outdoors, but not indoors. An indoor positioning system like Bitcraze's Loco Positioning system can be employed [3]. It includes anchors, similar to GPS satellites, and a tag that acts as a receiver. It provides absolute positioning in 3D with a range of 10 m. However, in large areas like ship decks, with dozens/hundreds of meters, equipping the entire space with anchors becomes costly.

When GPS or tags are not available, cameras can be used to navigate unknown spaces. Simultaneous Localization and Mapping (SLAM) is a well-established technique, researched for many years [4]. The first SLAM on a small drone was achieved with a residual Convolutional Neural Network (CNN) called DroNet [10], followed by PULP-DroNet [12], which enabled onboard computation on a nano drone like ours. However, they only provide collision probability and recommended steering angle to avoid collisions. Additionally, they are trained with outdoor data from car driving, as they are designed for autonomous navigation on streets. For indoor environments, the swarm gradient bug algorithm

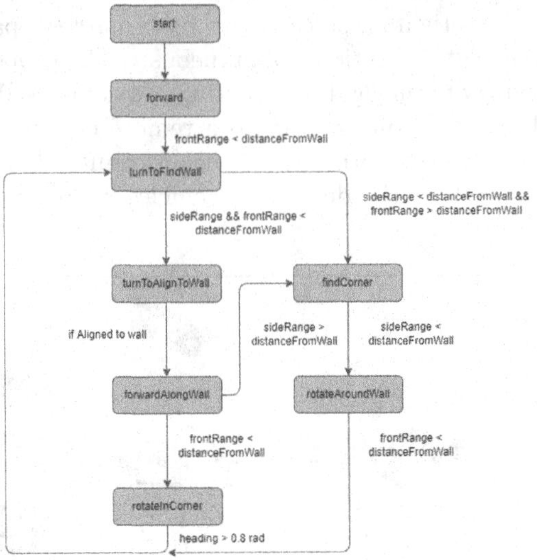

Fig. 2. State diagram of the wall-following algorithm.

(SGBA) [11] was proposed. It is a minimal solution to explore an unknown environment autonomously using a 'wall-following' behavior. Unlike SLAM, SGBA requires less processing power, making it more suitable for our requirements. A row of vehicles can be considered walls, with the drone following along with the camera facing them while scanning for plates. This simplifies the navigation while still achieving the goal of identifying vehicles in a crowded storage area.

2.2 Object Detection

For object detection, the state-of-the-art is given by region proposal networks (RPN), such as region-based Convolutional Neural Networks (R-CNN) [1], or Single-Shot Detection networks (SSD), such as YOLO [14]. RPNs require two stages, one for generating region proposals, and another for object detection. SSDs predict position and object type in a single stage, making them faster and more efficient, at the cost of less accuracy. However, the size of the networks behind any of these models (e.g. Darknet or EfficientNet) is too large for a nano drone. To address this, Greenwaves Technologies, the manufacturer of the GAP8 processor used by our drone, offers several SSD classification CNNs based on different architectures of the much lighter MobileNet [8].

Detection of objects such as vehicles, people, fruits, pests, etc., from UAVs, is gaining attention [13]. However, it mostly involves drones of bigger size than ours. Another difference is that studies mostly use aerial images taken from a certain height and with the objects appearing small compared to the background. Here, the problem is reversed. The UAV will fly relatively close to the target object, making that, for example, vehicles do not fit entirely into the image.

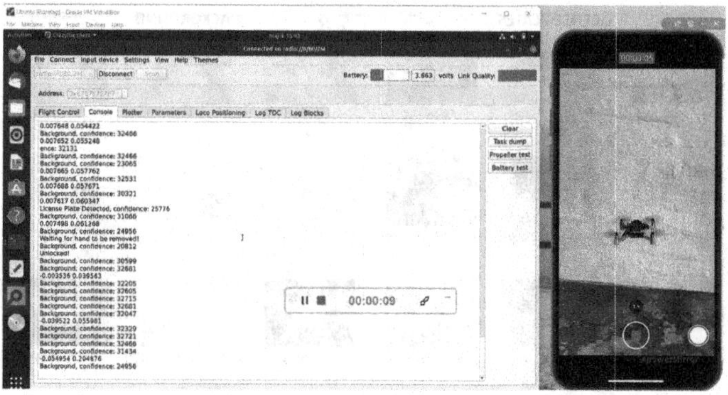

Fig. 3. Screenshot of system recording.

3 Methodology

3.1 Hardware

The system has several components (Fig. 1). At the core is the **CrazyFlie drone**, which utilizes an MCU (STM32) for autonomous flight control, position estimation, sensor data collection, and communication with other components. The CrazyFlie, manufactured by Bitcraze, is a nano quadrotor with a small 10 cm wingspan, classified as nano due to its small size and low power. Weighing 27 g, it features low latency and long-range radio capabilities, Bluetooth LE, onboard charging via USB, and expansion decks for additional features. The flight time is 7 min, and the max recommended payload is 15 g. Bitcraze offers a range of expansions, with the relevant ones for this research described next.

An **AI deck** (of weight 4.4 g) allows for AI computations onboard to manage, for example, autonomous navigation. It is equipped with a GreenWaves Technologies GAP8 system-on-chip processor [7], featuring a CNN accelerator optimized for image and audio algorithms. The AI deck also includes I/O peripherals to support devices such as cameras and microphones. Additionally, an integrated ESP32 chip provides WiFi connectivity to stream images from a grayscale ultra-low-power Himax camera. The AI deck sends the computation result to the CrazyFlie, which relays the information along with the drone's estimated position to the CrazyFlie client's console via radio.

A **Flow deck** keeps track of the drone's movements. A VL53L1x ToF sensor measures the distance to the ground and a PMW3901 optical flow sensor measures ground movement. These sensors allow the CrazyFlie to be programmed to fly distances in any direction or hover at a certain altitude. The flow deck can measure up to 4 m and weights 1.6 g.

A **MultiRanger deck**, of weight 2.3 g, detects any object around the CrazyFlie. It measures the distance to objects in 5 directions: front, left, right, back, and up. The maximum distance is 4 m with millimeter precision.

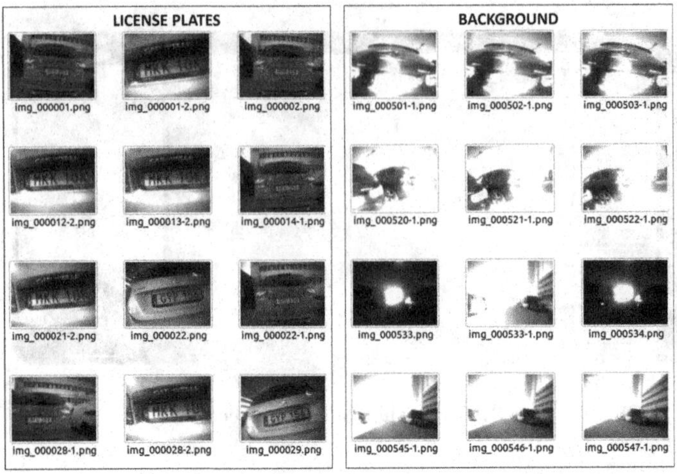

Fig. 4. Collected images of license plates and background with HIMAX camera.

3.2 Software and Data

When creating a system that navigates and detects objects onboard a nano-drone, the computing capabilities can be a challenge. The software components of our system are divided into three tasks: navigation, detection, and mapping, which are explained next.

Considering a row of parked cars as a wall due to their tight packing, we use the SGBA's wall-following algorithm [11] as a lighter and more power-efficient **navigation** solution compared to SLAM. The original algorithm was modified to have the drone face the walls while flying sideways, allowing the camera to scan for license plates. The MultiRanger deck is used to detect obstacles, while the Flow deck helps maintain the drone's stability at a specific height and measures the distance and direction of movement. The implemented wall-following algorithm, shown in Fig. 2, involves the drone moving forward until a wall is detected in front. It then aligns itself with the wall and continues moving forward along it. If the side range sensor loses sight of the wall, the drone seeks a corner and rotates around it. The drone then aligns itself to the new wall and moves forward along it. If it finds a wall from the front range sensor instead, it will rotate in the corner, align with the new wall, and move along it.

For **detection**, a binary approach is followed, where the system outputs either 'license plate' or 'background' as a result. Real-time computation is crucial since the drone needs to simultaneously fly and perform classification. To meet the computational constraints, MobileNet v2 is chosen as the classification backbone, as it reduces complexity costs and network size compared to other models, making it suitable for mobile devices like drones [16]. Bitcraze provides a demo for classifying Christmas packets [2] using the AI deck of the CrazyFlie, which serves as the basis for this research, although it needs adaptation to our particular scenario and data. The provided model is trained for a different task

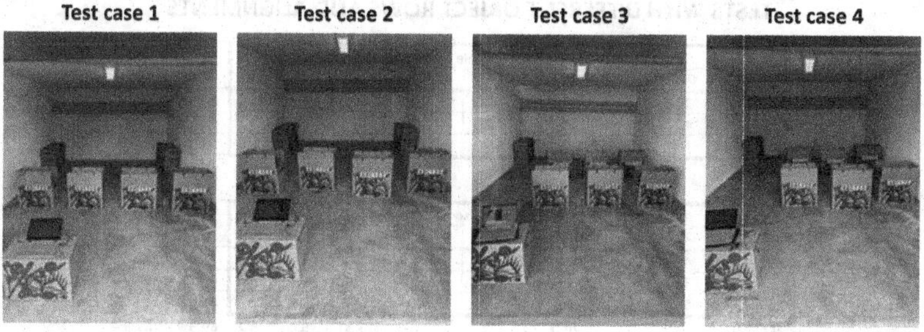

Fig. 5. Setup of different flight test cases (Sect. 4.1).

(Christmas packets) and their data is collected from just one position. To use it for our intended purposes, we captured our own customized **database** of 'license plates' and 'background' (Fig. 4) with the HIMAX camera attached to the AI deck. The dataset consists of training/validation images with 747/180 license plate samples and 743/183 backgrounds, all grayscale and at a resolution of 320×320. The detection model is trained using the captured samples for 100 epochs. To deploy the deep learning model on the GAP8 processor, we use the GAP flow tool provided by GreenWaves Technologies inside the GAP8 SDK [7].

Mapping plays a crucial role in monitoring the target objects and keeping track of their positions. This is achieved by sending the drone position and the classification result to a remote client console. When navigating, the CrazyFlie captures images with the HIMAX camera at 2 Hz, which are classified in real-time, generating a confidence score for each. The results, along with the drone's current position, are transmitted to a remote client (Fig. 3). The client connects to the CrazyFlie using a USB radio dongle. This allows the client to display the classification results, drone position, and path on a scaled figure. The classification results can be color-coded for easier interpretation (e.g. Fig. 7).

4 Experiments and Results

To evaluate the system, precision (P) and recall (R) are used to measure the classification performance. Precision measures the proportion of positive classifications (said to be a license plate), which are actually an image with a license plate. Recall, on the other hand, measures the proportion of actual positive cases (images with a license plate) which are correctly classified as positive (said to have a license plate). A summarizing metric is the F1-score, the harmonic mean of P and R, computed as $F1 = 2*(P*R)/(P+R)$.

4.1 Test Cases

To simulate vehicles, we employ moving boxes with printed-out standard-size license plates (Fig. 5) on a garage of size 6 × 3.6 m. A fixed start point will be used so that the drone starts in the same position every time. We define four

TESTS WITH DIFFERENT OBJECT ROWS AND ALIGNMENTS

TEST 1		True Positives					False Negatives							Preci	Re	
Round	Time	O1	O2	O3	O4	Sum	O1	O2	O3	O4	Sum	TN	FP	sion	call	F1
1	00:01:05	1	2	3	3	9	2	1	4	1	8	17	5	64.3%	52.9%	**58.1%**
2	00:01:03	3	4	4	4	15	2	3	1	0	6	14	9	62.5%	71.4%	**66.7%**
3	00:01:08	3	1	1	2	7	1	5	4	3	13	22	6	53.8%	35.0%	**42.4%**
	Average:					**10.3**					**9**	**17.7**	**6.7**	**60.2%**	**53.1%**	**55.7%**

TEST 2		True Positives					False Negatives							Preci	Re	
Round	Time	O1	O2	O3	O4	Sum	O1	O2	O3	O4	Sum	TN	FP	sion	call	F1
1	00:00:51	9	4	5	6	24	0	2	0	0	2	5	8	75.0%	92.3%	**82.8%**
2	00:00:58	5	4	4	6	19	1	2	2	1	6	4	10	65.5%	76.0%	**70.4%**
3	00:00:55	4	5	4	4	17	1	0	0	1	2	6	8	68.0%	89.5%	**77.3%**
	Average:					**20.0**					**3.3**	**5.0**	**8.7**	**69.5%**	**85.9%**	**76.8%**

TEST 3		True Positives							False Negatives									Preci	Re	
Round	Time	O1	O2	O3	O4	O5	O6	Sum	O1	O2	O3	O4	O5	O6	Sum	TN	FP	sion	call	F1
1	00:02:20	6	2	1	3	0	1	13	2	7	7	0	5	7	28	54	7	65.0%	31.7%	**42.6%**
2	00:02:32	1	0	2	3	2	3	11	5	4	3	0	5	0	17	34	26	29.7%	39.3%	**33.8%**
3	00:02:32	0	0	0	0	0	0	0	5	5	5	5	4	5	29	50	11	0%	0%	**0%**
	Average:							**8.0**							**24.7**	**46**	**14.7**	**31.6%**	**23.7%**	**25.5%**

TEST 4		True Positives							False Negatives									Preci	Re	
Round	Time	O1	O2	O3	O4	O5	O6	Sum	O1	O2	O3	O4	O5	O6	Sum	TN	FP	sion	call	F1
1	00:02:50	4	1	0	0	0	2	7	2	7	7	0	5	7	28	37	16	30.4%	20.0%	**24.1%**
2	00:03:15	0	1	0	6	4	3	14	6	6	8	2	1	2	25	27	9	60.9%	35.9%	**45.2%**
3	00:02:48	4	3	2	5	6	5	25	3	2	4	0	0	1	10	22	30	45.5%	71.4%	**55.6%**
	Average:							**15.3**							**21.0**	**28.7**	**18.3**	**45.6%**	**42.4%**	**41.6%**

Fig. 6. Classification results and flying time of different test cases (Sect. 4.1).

different setups for testing with different paths and placements of the objects. Each case will be evaluated three times (i.e. the drone will be deployed on three different occasions). The test cases are set up to evaluate the performance of the wall following algorithm and license plate detection, including when the drone has to proceed across several walls. We also aim at evaluating situations where the objects with license plates are not in a straight line. The following test cases are thus considered, shown in Fig. 5:

1. One row with 4 moving boxes in a straight line, with a gap of 25 cm between each. The row is 2 m away from the starting navigation point.
2. The same previous setup, but the boxes were not placed in a straight line.
3. Two rows with 3 moving boxes each in a straight line and separated 25 cm, leaving space for the drone to turn around. The first row is 2 m away from the starting navigation point, and the second is 1.37 m behind the first one.
4. The same previous setup, but the boxes were not placed in a straight line.

Figure 6 gives the classification results and the flying time of each round across the different tests cases, whereas Fig. 7 shows the 2D grid with the drone path and classification output of selected rounds during the journey (the worst and the best round, based on the F1-score).

Since the drone classifies continuously, there are more true positives (TP) than objects, because the same object is captured in different frames. TP indicates how many true ‘license plates detected’ the drone prints out when flying past the boxes. For example, in test case 1, with four objects tested, there are between 7 and 15 true positives (depending on the round). It can also be seen

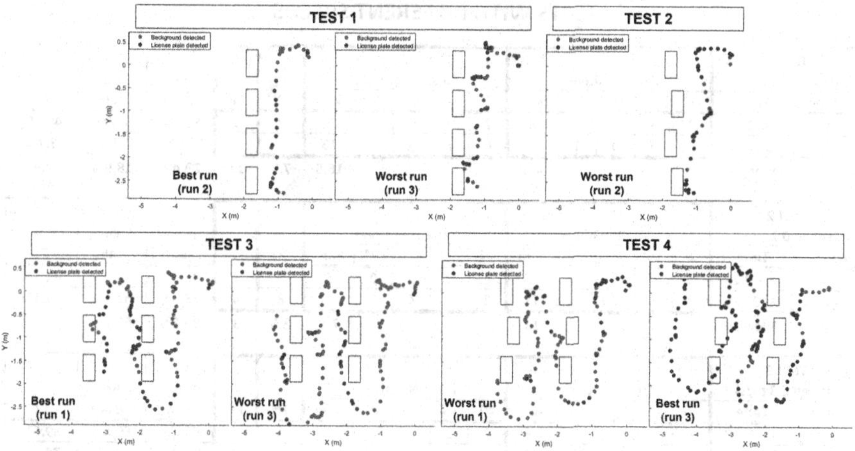

Fig. 7. Drone paths on different flight test cases (Sect. 4.1).

that in all tests, all objects are detected at least once in some of the rounds. This means that all license plates are captured if the drone is allowed to do two or three rounds of navigation. At the remote client, the actual plate number could be extracted (not implemented in this work), making possible to consolidate the different true positives of the same number into one single instance. These results indicate that the implemented system is able to work across the different layouts and object alignment tested.

The system also shows false negatives (FN), meaning that the drone classifies as 'background' an image containing a license plate. On average, the false negatives are less than the true positives in the single-row experiments (tests 1 and 2), but in the two-rows experiments (tests 3 and 4), it is the opposite. In tests 3 and 4, there are more objects to classify (six vs. four) and the drone is navigating more time, which obviously results in more available images with positives. But having to navigate and deal with wall/row corners (Fig. 7) may produce many of those images showing a license plate from a very difficult perspective, impacting the capability to detect them. However, based on the previous considerations about the true positives, this should not be an issue because the drone is able to capture all license plates in several images across different journeys. The system is not free of false positives (FP) either (i.e. background frames said to have a license plate), an issue that could also be resolved at the remote client with a more powerful classifier that concentrates only on the selected frames sent by the drone and discards erroneous cases. The number of true negatives (TN) is also usually higher than the false positives, meaning that a high proportion of background images are labeled correctly.

When analyzing if boxes are in a straight line or not (case 1 vs. 2, and 3 vs. 4), it is interesting to observe that the performance is better when they are not forming a straight line (observe P, R, and F1-score). The drone does not seem to have difficulties in following the 'wall' of boxes even if they are not completely

TESTS WITH DIFFERENT SPEEDS

TEST 1 (speed 0.1 m/s)		True Positives					False Negatives							Precision	Recall	
Round	Time	*O1*	*O2*	*O3*	*O4*	Sum	*O1*	*O2*	*O3*	*O4*	Sum	TN	FP	Precision	Recall	F1
1	00:01:00	3	3	1	1	8	2	2	6	7	17	7	7	53.3%	32.0%	**40.0%**
2	00:00:58	0	0	0	1	1	6	3	4	3	16	8	17	5.6%	5.9%	**5.7%**
	Average:					**4.5**					**16.5**	**7.5**	**12**	**29.4%**	**18.9%**	**22.9%**

TEST 2 (speed 0.2 m/s)		True Positives					False Negatives							Precision	Recall	
Round	Time	*O1*	*O2*	*O3*	*O4*	Sum	*O1*	*O2*	*O3*	*O4*	Sum	TN	FP	Precision	Recall	F1
1	00:00:28	3	4	3	5	15	0	2	3	0	5	9	2	88.2%	75.0%	**81.1%**
2	00:00:29	5	3	2	1	11	2	3	4	1	10	8	4	73.3%	52.4%	**61.1%**
	Average:					**13**					**7.5**	**8.5**	**3**	**80.8%**	**63.7%**	**71.1%**

TEST 3 (speed 0.3 m/s)		True Positives					False Negatives							Precision	Recall	
Round	Time	*O1*	*O2*	*O3*	*O4*	Sum	*O1*	*O2*	*O3*	*O4*	Sum	TN	FP	Precision	Recall	F1
1	00:00:28	4	3	3	6	16	2	2	3	0	7	5	7	69.6%	69.6%	**69.6%**
2	00:00:29	4	3	5	7	19	3	1	0	1	5	4	8	70.4%	79.2%	**74.5%**
	Average:					**17.5**					**6**	**4.5**	**7.5**	**70.0%**	**74.4%**	**72.0%**

Fig. 8. Classification results and flying time of speed test cases (Sect. 4.2).

aligned, as seen in the paths of Fig. 7, and this indeed produces better detection results overall. On the other hand, the two-row tests (cases 3 and 4) show worse performance overall than the single-row tests (cases 1 and 2), an issue that could be attributed to the mentioned imaging perspective of the two-rows navigation that causes a greater amount of false negatives and false positives. Also, the flight time obviously differs. Two rows demand extra time for the drone to turn around, find the way and navigate across a bigger amount of objects. As seen in Fig. 7, the drone navigates each row of boxes on the two sides, as expected from the wall following algorithm, which increases flying time to well beyond double.

When analyzing the drone paths in Fig. 7, it can be seen that in several cases, the drone has difficulties flying following a straight line. This is, very likely, a limitation of employing a wall-following algorithm, since we use objects that have some gap among them (25 cm). Sometimes, the drone has a tendency to move toward the gap between the boxes, although it is not always the case. In the two-row setup, it is capable of moving along wall corners and row ends without issues. Together with the fact that the system does not miss any license plate if several rounds are allowed, these results validate our overall approach. In a few runs, the paths show that the drone flies over the boxes, but it did not happen in any run. The drone was flying correctly, close to the boxes, but it seems that it was estimating its position incorrectly.

4.2 Speed Factor

Three different speeds of the drone (0.1, 0.2, and 0.3 m/s) have also been tested across two rounds per speed to see how it impacts performance. This experiment is carried out on scenario 1 of the previous sub-section (a single row of 4 boxes

Fig. 9. Setup of the low light test case (garage door closed) (Sect. 4.3).

TESTS WITH LOW ILLUMINATION

TEST 1		True Positives					False Negatives							Preci	Re	
Round	Time	01	02	03	04	Sum	01	02	03	04	Sum	TN	FP	sion	call	F1
1	00:00:43	1	2	1	2	6	6	3	6	5	20	15	2	75.0%	23.1%	**35.3%**
2	00:00:51	7	6	5	6	24	0	0	2	0	2	0	8	75.0%	92.3%	**82.8%**
	Average:					**15.0**					**11.0**	**7.5**	**5.0**	**75.0%**	**57.7%**	**59.0%**

Fig. 10. Classification results and flying time of low light test cases (Sect. 4.3).

in a straight line). Figure 8 gives the classification results and the flying time of each round.

Also, here, all license plates are captured across the two rounds, regardless of the speed. An interesting result is that the worst results are given at the slowest speed, with the system missing many plates as false negatives, and producing many false positives as well. At 0.2 or 0.3 m/s, the amount of false negatives and false positives is significantly less, with a conversely higher amount of true positives. Comparatively, a higher speed does not imply worse results in general. This could be exploited to complete the expedition faster, counteracting the battery issue mentioned in the previous sub-section.

4.3 Light Factor

This test was conducted with the garage door closed, so the environment is darker and only illuminated by some ceiling lamps (Fig. 9). The test is done over two rounds with a single row of 4 boxes in a straight line. Figure 10 gives the results and the flying time of each round. As in the previous cases, all license plates are captured across the two rounds, so the evaluated light conditions do not have an impact on the detection either. One possible effect of the lower light is the dispar results between the two rounds in detecting plates. The first round has many false negatives, whereas the second round has many true positives. Also, in round two, no background is detected correctly (true negatives = 0). It must be stated as well that the navigation is not be affected by darkness, since the sensors of the Flow and MultiRanger decks are not based on visible illumination.

Only the classification would need cameras and software adaptation capable of working in very low light conditions, such as infrared cameras.

5 Conclusions

This work has presented a system that makes use of a camera on-board a nano drone to navigate across rows of vehicles tightly parked and find their license plate. We apply a navigation solution based on wall-following, and a MobileNet-based CNN trained to detect license plates. The solution is fully executed onboard a CrazyFlie drone, with just 10 cm wingspan. The drone position and images are used on a remote client to build a 2D map of the path and license plates detected without relying on positioning systems (e.g. GPS) or tagging. Our application scenario is transportation, where vehicles are packed closely together, and knowing the exact position of each one and its features (e.g. electric or combustion) can help to mitigate security issues, such as fires.

We have carried out several tests simulating objects with license plates. Different scenarios are considered, such as several rows (demanding the drone to turn around and find the next row), objects not stacked across a straight line, different drone speeds, or lightning. In any of them, even if the plates are not detected in every frame, all are captured by aggregation after the drone carries out 2–3 rounds of navigation. This is feasible e.g. on-board vessels after all vehicles have been parked. The wall-following algorithm, which is less computationally demanding than SLAM [4], correctly navigates across all objects despite a small gap between them. It also works well if the objects are not perfectly aligned.

Our solution assumes that the rows of objects are connected to a wall. It would need extra tweaking if, for example, they do not have a wall on any of their ends. Also, we only send the drone position and image with a plate detected, but the actual number could be read, either at the drone with additional software or at the remote console. Processing or sending only images with high detection confidence would allow to save resources at the drone while completing the navigation mission. The drone path with color codes (Fig. 7) would also allow obtaining a map with the exact position of each object, as long as at least one image per object is sent eventually. When several true positives of a license plate are captured, the actual number could be used to group them and filter multiple detections. In the same manner, checking the extracted number against a list of expected vehicles (a manifesto) would also allow to filter out errors.

Our garage is of size 6×3.6 m and the drone covers it in 1–3 min, depending on the number of rows (Fig. 6). The maximum flying time declared by the CrazyFlie is 7 min, so one single charge is able to cover the three rounds of tests 1 and 2, but not of tests 3 and 4. This must be considered when deploying a system like this to a larger space like garages or ships, either by stocking several batteries or more than one drone. Adding more tasks to the drone itself (e.g. reading the license plate number) would also have an impact on the battery time. However, if the drone is capable of filtering out several true positives or other errors (at the cost of extra processing), it would transmit fewer images to the remote client, which would reduce battery consumption as a contraposition.

Another possibility is to relieve the drone of detecting plates, and just send the camera stream and position. Detection and number reading would then be done in a more powerful remote client, which could include a larger CNN detector [14] for a more precise result.

Acknowledgements. This work has been carried out by M. Arvidsson and S. Sawirot in the context of their Master Thesis at Halmstad University (Computer Science and Engineering). The authors acknowledge the Swedish Innovation Agency (VINNOVA) for funding their research. Author F. A.-F. also thanks the Swedish Research Council (VR).

References

1. Abbas, S.M., Singh, D.S.N.: Region-based object detection and classification using faster R-CNN. In: 4th International Conferencee on Computational Intelligence Communication Technology (CICT) (2018)
2. Bitcraze: Classification Demo. https://www.bitcraze.io/documentation/repository/aideck-gap8-examples/master/ai-examples/classification-demo/
3. Bitcraze: Loco positioning system. https://www.bitcraze.io/documentation/system/positioning/loco-positioning-system/
4. Cadena, C., et al.: Past, present, and future of simultaneous localization and mapping: toward the robust-perception age. IEEE Trans. Robot. **32**(6), 1309–1332 (2016)
5. Council, W.S.: Liner shipping vessels. https://www.worldshipping.org/about-liner-shipping/container-roro-ships
6. Friedrich, L.: How are cars shipped? https://www.uship.com/guides/how-are-cars-shipped/
7. GreenWaves-Technologies: Gap8 iot application processor. https://greenwaves-technologies.com/wp-content/uploads/2021/04/Product-Brief-GAP8-V1_9.pdf
8. GreenWaves-Technologies: Image classification models on GAP. https://github.com/GreenWaves-Technologies/image_classification_networks
9. Huo, Z., Xia et al.: Vehicle type classification and attribute prediction using multi-task RCNN. In: Proceedings of CISP-BMEI (2016)
10. Loquercio, A., Maqueda, A.I., del Blanco, C.R., Scaramuzza, D.: Dronet: learning to fly by driving. IEEE Robot. Autom. Lett. **3**(2), 1088–1095 (2018)
11. McGuire, K.N., et al.: Minimal navigation solution for a swarm of tiny flying robots to explore an unknown environment. Sci. Robot. **4**, eaaw9710 (2019)
12. Niculescu, V., et al.: Improving autonomous nano-drones performance via automated end-to-end optimization and deployment of DNNs. IEEE J. Emerg. Sel. Top. Circ. Syst. **11**(4), 548–562 (2021)
13. Ramachandran, A., Sangaiah, A.K.: A review on object detection in unmanned aerial vehicle surveillance. Int. J. Cognitive Comput. Eng. **2**, 215–228 (2021)

14. Redmon, J. et al.: You only look once: unified, real-time object detection. In: IEEE Conference on Computer Vision and Pattern Recognition (CVPR) (2016)
15. RoadRunner Auto Transport: The history of car shipping. https://www.roadrunnerautotransport.com/news/1401/the-history-of-car-shipping
16. Tsang, S.H.: Review: Mobilenetv2-light weight model (image classification). https://towardsdatascience.com/review-mobilenetv2-light-weight-model-image-classification-8febb490e61c

Comparison of Root Mean Square Index and Hilbert-Huang Transform for Detection of Muscle Activation in a Person with Elbow Disarticulation

Leonardo Antonio Bermeo Varon[1(✉)], Edgar Francisco Arcos Hurtado[1], Katherin Nathalia Ortiz Ortega[1], Luisa Maria Poveda Londoño[1], and John Jairo Villarejo-Mayor[2]

[1] Faculty of Engineering, Universidad Santiago de Cali, Street 5 # 62-00, Cali, Colombia
leonardo.bermeo00@usc.edu.co

[2] School of Public Health, Physiotherapy and Sports Science, University College Dublin, 4 Stillorgan Rd, Belfield, Dublin, Ireland

Abstract. An active prosthesis is a device developed to substitute an absent limb of the human body supplying its functionalities without neglecting the patient's body image. The development of these devices includes the signal acquisition process, signal conditioning, onset/offset detection, classification algorithms that determine which movement is being realized, and actuators that executed the motion. One of the important aspects, and with few studies are the techniques of onset/offset detection which allow performing the movement with the minimum delay and stop executing the movement to then proceed to the classification stage. Normally, this stage is not considered due to the design of the prosthesis a part of the signal is taken by suppressing the start and the end of the contraction considering only the isotonic component. In this study, the comparison of two techniques, the root means square index and the Hilbert-Huang Transform concerning the visual inspection technique for the onset/offset detection is realized. Statistical analysis is performed by considering the median, maximum value, minimum value, mean, standard deviation, and dispersion of the data to determine which technique is more adequate. Additionally, a protocol is proposed to acquire signals for the performance of 6 movements: elbow flexion, elbow extension, pronation and supination of the forearm, and opening and closing of the hand. The study was performed on a person with elbow disarticulation and a healthy person. The results indicate that the most appropriate technique for onset/offset detection in a person with elbow disarticulation is the Hilbert-Huang transform indicating greater accuracy.

Keywords: myoelectric signals · active prosthesis · elbow disarticulation · onset/offset detection · myoelectric signal processing

Y. Hernández Heredia et al. (Eds.): IWAIPR 2023, LNCS 14335, pp. 375–386, 2024.
https://doi.org/10.1007/978-3-031-49552-6_32

1 Introduction

Active prostheses are devices that replace a missing limb to recover its functionality. These external devices are constructed using various materials, taking into account weight and ergonomics. They also contain motorized mechanisms that realize the movement, activated by myoelectric signals. Detectable action potentials are required on the skin surface when the residual limb muscle (stump) contracts. The myoelectric signal is obtained through these potentials, allowing the resulting electrical activity from muscle fiber excitability to be observed [1].

The use of prostheses is becoming increasingly popular among individuals who have undergone upper limb amputations, as they enhance the patient's performance in daily activities and substantially improve their functionality [2]. The development of prostheses is of great significance to individuals who have experienced limb loss, as they not only restore aesthetic harmony but also offer emotional benefits by facilitating the patient's reintegration into social environments.

In the implementation of prosthetic devices, several factors and tasks must be considered in order for the prostheses to be functional. Among these factors are (i) signal acquisition, (ii) signal conditioning, where an electronic system is included for the acquisition and implementation of algorithms that allow its conditioning, and (iii) identification of the activation/deactivation threshold for the subject to execute a certain movement. These processes are performed with a large number of signals from the person using the prosthesis taking into account its specificity. (iv) A decision system that allows the prosthesis to perform the movement that the subject executes, (v) motorized mechanisms to execute the movement, and (vi) Computer Assisted Design (CAD) for the construction of the prosthesis.

In recent years different studies have independently developed processes for the construction of active prostheses, which include signal conditioning and processing for classification and deciding which movement the subject is performing. However, most studies are oriented to motion classification by means of pattern recognition [1, 3–6]. Likewise, identifying activation thresholds is a critical step in the development of prosthesis, as it aids in the prompt onset/offset detection of muscle. This phase can significantly enhance the response and intuition of myoelectric control [7].

Staude and collaborators [8] performed an objective performance analysis to compare different methods for detecting the onset of motion. They tested various onset detection techniques, as well as statistically optimized algorithms, using simulated EMG data with known signal parameters. The results revealed a high level of dependence on EMG parameters, including muscle activity onset time, signal-to-noise ratio, and activity level. In terms of robustness, statistically optimized algorithms generally fared better and produced superior outcomes.

Tabie and Kirchner [9] conducted a study to compare three preprocessing methods for motion prediction based on EMG signals obtained from the right upper extremity of 8 subjects without pathology. The three methods that were compared are the Teager Kaiser Energy Operator (TKEO) and two other methods based on signal variance and standard deviation calculations. An adaptive threshold was applied for onset detection after preprocessing, and the team analyzed the performance in motion prediction as well as the early onset detection. The study also investigated the impact of different motion speeds on prediction time and performance. The results indicated significant differences in the preprocessing methods in terms of the prediction time limit, and the authors demonstrated that motion speeds also have a considerable influence on prediction time.

Several researchers have suggested algorithms for detecting muscle activation using EMG, which have yielded excellent results with high detection rates [10–13]. However, most of these studies have been conducted with simulated signals or on individuals without any medical conditions. Yang et al. [13] are among the few who have conducted research on subjects with pathologies, but they indicate that a low signal-to-noise ratio is required for accurate detection.

Previous studies have provided evidence of reliable threshold detection methods that allow for adequate analysis of EMG signals, highlighting the importance of precise activation threshold detection in myoelectric prosthesis control. However, many of these investigations did not implement the methods in real signals, or they were conducted solely on signals from individuals with upper or lower limb pathologies. Furthermore, some studies did not capture signals from individuals with amputations, which poses a challenge due to the absence of muscles required to perform specific movements.

Considering the significance of muscle activation in the development and implementation of active myoelectric prostheses, this paper compares two techniques for detecting the onset/offset thresholds of a group of muscles. The effectiveness of the root mean square (RMS) and Hilbert-Huang transform methods are evaluated to determine their accuracy. The study is conducted using myoelectric signals obtained from six movements: elbow flexion and extension, hand opening and closing, and forearm pronation and supination. Signals were collected from both a healthy individual and an individual with elbow disarticulation. These signals underwent conditioning and processing stages before statistical analysis and comparison of the onset/offset accuracy levels in muscle contraction.

2 Determination of the Onset/Offset Thresholds

The analysis used for the onset/offset detection of muscle is based on the signal obtained from the patient's indication of the start and end of the movement (i.e., muscle contraction and relaxation). It is crucial to accurately and automatically identify the onset of a voluntary muscle contraction for active control, especially in real-time myoelectric control systems.

Onset/offset detection of muscle can be performed through visual inspection [14]. However, this technique is subjective and dependent on the experience of the operator and familiarity with EMG signal characteristics. Visual inspection can be used to evaluate different detection algorithms, where an operator visually identifies landmarks and calculates the error of the process. The most commonly used technique for contraction onset/offset detection is based on the EMG amplitude definition, which is simple and fast to implement [15]. Other advanced techniques to determine these instants utilize more complex adaptive methods, considering the variation in muscle activation levels according to factors such as movement type, musculature type, and underlying pathological conditions.

2.1 Root Mean Square (RMS)

Equation (1) describes in a general way the root mean square. In this case, the square root of the data (x) is calculated, where the mean power of the previously rectified EMG signal is reflected, where N corresponds to the number of signal samples, and k is the number of the data segment. This technique is used to determine the activation threshold, which considers the time of the selected window and the phase change in the contractions that present a strong increase in the signal amplitude. The RMS index describes a characteristic in voltage amplitude that allows reflecting the muscle activation, where the higher the amplitude, the greater the muscle innervation, thus being possible to identify which muscle reacts to a given movement.

$$RMS_k = \sqrt{\frac{1}{N}\sum_{i=1}^{N} x_i^2} \tag{1}$$

2.2 The Hilbert-Huang Transform

The Hilbert-Huang transform analysis is based on the empirical mode decomposition (EMD) which decomposes the signal into a limited number of time series composed of characteristic oscillations called intrinsic mode functions (IMF). These IMF capture the oscillatory behaviors of the signal enabling the analysis of non-stationary signals useful in pattern recognition [16]. Each IMF function is composed of a signal modulated in amplitude and frequency satisfying two conditions: (i) the number of maximum and zero crossings must be equal or not different more than one; (ii) the mean between the outlines of the interpolations of local maxima and local minima must be zero. The original signal can be expressed adaptively into the sum of IMF components with different time scales. The first components are related to smaller time scales related to faster signal changes. After, the Hilbert-Huang Transform is applied for each component to express the signal in a phasorial form. The extraction o statistical moments from the Hilbert spectrum allow an adaptive representation through features of the signal. For computing the analytical signal, the HHT function of Matlab Mathworks® was used following Eq. 2.

$$z_i(t) = x_i(t) + jH\{x_i(t)\} \tag{2}$$

where $z_i(t)$, represents the analytical signal; $x_i(t)$ represents the real part (it is the original data); $jH\{x_i(t)\}$ is the imaginary part containing the Hilbert-Huang transform (the imaginary part is a version of the original real sequence with a phase shift of 90°). The Hilbert-Huang transformed series has the same amplitude and frequency content as the original sequence. The transform includes phase information that depends on the phase of the original.

3 Methodology

3.1 Subjects

The myoelectric signals (MES) data set was obtained from a healthy person 21-year-old and an individual with right elbow disarticulation 37-years-old. The time elapsed since the upper limb amputation is 13 years. This study was conducted following the Helsinki

Declaration and was approved by the Ethics Committee of the Universidad Santiago de Cali - Colombia act number 010 session 003. The subjects voluntarily signed an informed consent form before the experiments were performed.

3.2 Data Acquisition

Covidien H124SG electrodes were used to capture the MES, connected to a MyoWare sensor (AT-04–001). MES were digitized on a Beaglebone board at a sampling frequency of 1 kHz and scaled in a voltage range from 0 (GND) to 1.8 V. The BeagleBone has six analog input pins with a 12-bit analog-to-digital converter (ADC) that converts the analog input voltage to a digital voltage reading and can only accept up to 1.8 V maximum.

Four electrodes were placed on the biceps brachii (short head), deltoid (middle head), triceps brachii (lateral head), and triceps brachii (long head). The pattern movements recorded were elbow flexion, elbow extension, forearm pronation, forearm supination, hand opening, hand closing, and resting. The participant was in a seated position with the back erect and the amputated arm perpendicular to a table at the same height. During six sessions on different days, thirteen trials were recorded during 65 s. Each movement was repeated for 5 s with rest periods of 5 s between trials, starting with 5 s of limb relaxation. Between each activity, the participant had a 3-min rest to avoid muscle fatigue.

3.3 Signal Processing

Signal processing involved a two-stage procedure - preprocessing and processing - to detect the onset/offset threshold of muscle during movement. Preprocessing included a filtering stage with a second-order non-shifted high-pass Butterworth filter at a cutoff frequency of 25 Hz to remove wire movements or electrode resistance artifacts, a low-pass 10th-order Butterworth filter with a cutoff frequency of 300 Hz; and a Notch filter to reduce 60-Hz power-line interference. In the processing stage, a threshold of 0.1 V for the RMS index was defined, while for the Hilbert-Huang transform, an analytical signal was generated by taking the envelope and smoothing the signal. An adaptive threshold was used to detect signal activity, ensuring a minimum number of samples remained above the threshold. The threshold, based on the signal noise and activity level, was continually updated online. Signal processing used Matlab Mathworks® with a window size of 200 ms (segment) and 100 ms overlap.

3.4 Data Analysis

The effectiveness of the RMS index and Hilbert-Huang transform techniques in the onset/offset detection of the muscles was compared with the visual identification of an expert by the percentage of correct detections. Also, the time difference of onset/offset detection with the visual technique was analyzed. Then, the median, maximum, minimum, mean, and standard deviation for the differences between the RMS index and Hilbert-Huang transform concerning the visual inspection were calculated to know the dispersion of the data. This analysis provided insights into which technique was more suitable for the task. The entire dataset was analyzed without categorizing the data by movement types, as the objective was to identify the onset and offset detection of muscles in a broad range of data that may include characteristics from various movements.

4 Results and Discussion

Figures 1–6 show a sample for each movement of the subject with a disability. In all cases, it is observed that the Hilbert-Huang transform presents better results in terms of onset/offset detection of the signal, as well as the instant of onset/offset of the muscle.

Figure 1 shows an EMG obtained from the elbow flexion movement, which is divided into 13 segments of 5 s, 6 of which correspond to muscle activation and 7 to rest. The inferior part shows the result of the RMS index and Hilbert-Huang Transform for the determination of onset/offset windows. This particular signal indicates that for activation there are no perceptible differences between the two techniques. For offset the Hilbert-Huang transform technique presents early offset in most of the contractions.

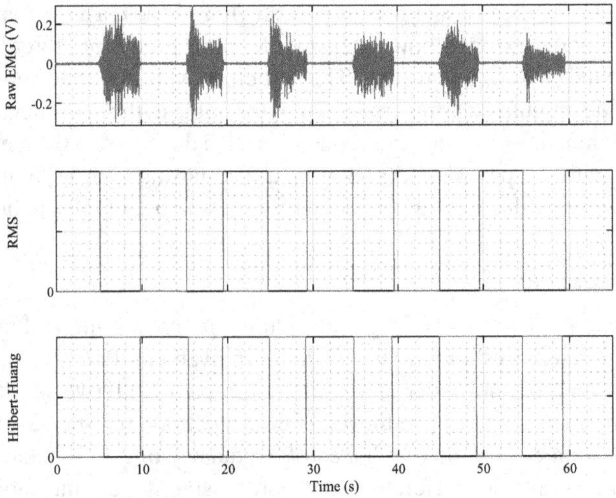

Fig. 1. Elbow flexion movement

In Fig. 2, the signal corresponding to elbow extension movement is depicted. It can be observed that both techniques exhibit a similar onset behavior. However, for the offset, the Hilbert-Huang Transform technique detects the first contraction with greater precision compared to the RMS technique, which takes only the higher amplitude part as the activation window. From the second contraction onwards, both techniques coincide in the offset detection.

Figure 3 displays the signal for the hand opening movement. The potential signal decrease and involuntary contraction are evident, which may be a result of muscular effort or subject fatigue. Concerning the onset/offset detection, the RMS index only adequately detects two contractions, and it only detects the activation for one. In contrast, the Hilbert-Huang transform accurately detects all contractions. One possible cause for the failure of the RMS index is the fixed threshold at 0.1 V, where the raw EMG signal falls below this value. This behavior is considered normal because the disabled person lacks the primary muscles required for this movement.

Figure 4 shows the signal corresponding to the hand closing movement. Note that the Hilbert-Huang transform detects adequately the six contractions, while the RMS index

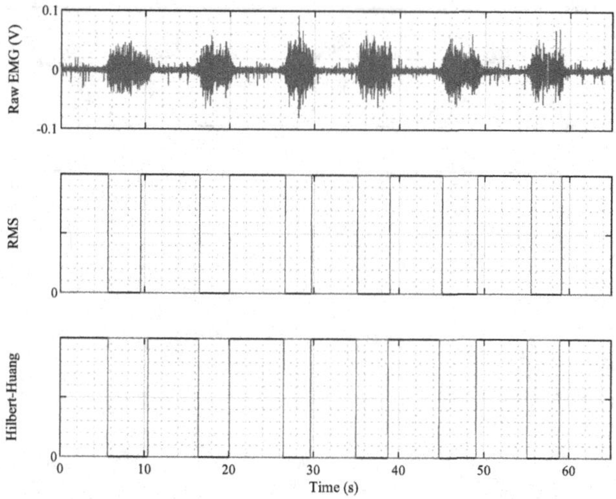

Fig. 2. Elbow extension movement

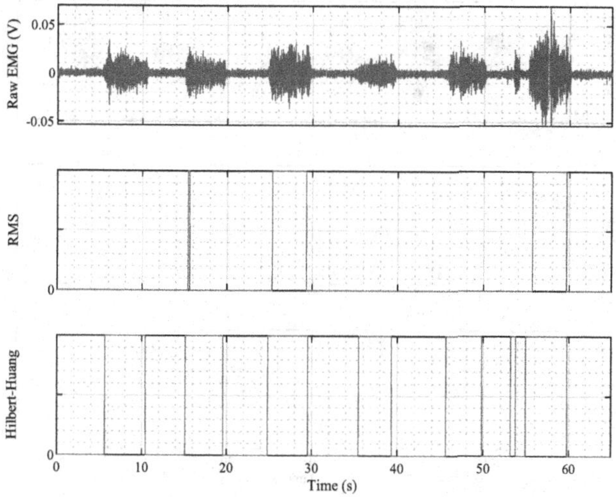

Fig. 3. Hand opening movement

only detects two contractions. This behavior is similar to the previous case and is mainly due to the low amplitude of the signal.

In Fig. 5, the signal for the forearm pronation movement is illustrated. Both the RMS index and the Hilbert-Huang transform exhibit similar behavior, with the detection of the onset/offset in all cases.

Figure 6 shows the signal corresponding to the forearm supination movement, which has a low amplitude. Notice that in all contractions, the detection of the onset is similar. However, in some cases, the RMS index does not detect the offset of the contractions.

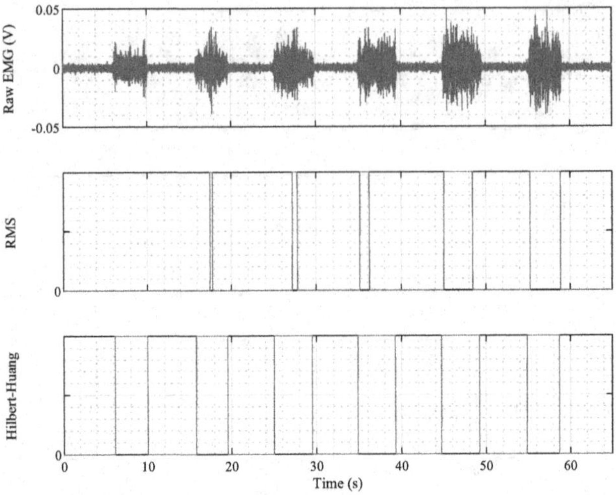

Fig. 4. Hand closing movement

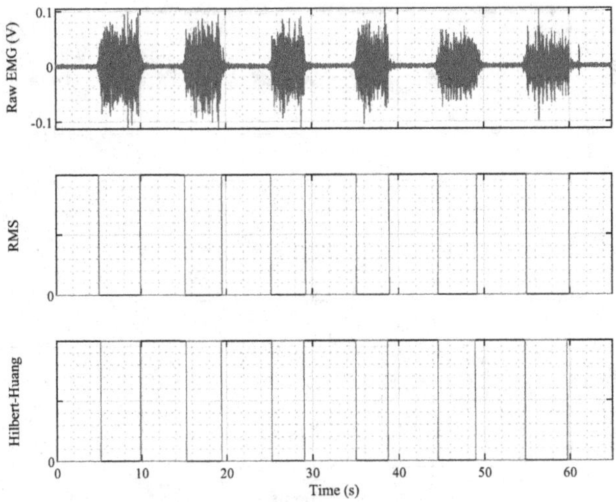

Fig. 5. Forearm pronation movement

The success rate of the onset/offset detection in 216 samples is presented in Table 1. The samples were obtained by executing 6 movements, each of which was performed 6 times. Each movement had 6 onsets and 6 offsets. The EMG signal processed corresponded to the primary muscle involved in each movement. Specifically, for elbow flexion and hand closing, the biceps brachii signal was taken; for elbow extension and forearm pronation, the triceps brachii (short head) signal was taken; and for forearm supination and hand opening, the triceps brachii (long head) signal was taken.

It is worth noting that the Hilbert-Huang transform outperforms other methods for both subjects. This could be attributed to the RMS index, which only detects muscle

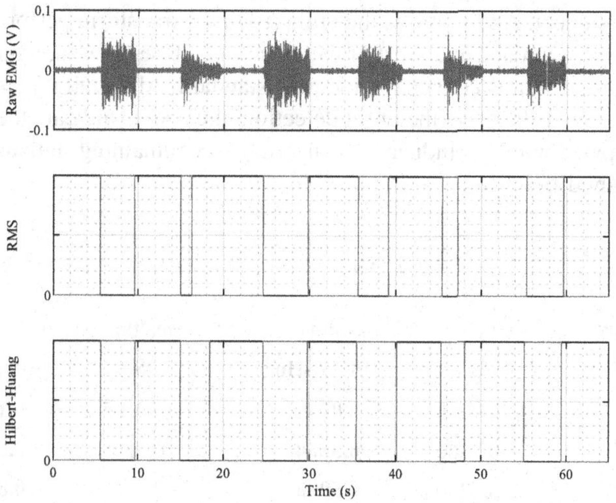

Fig. 6. Forearm supination movement

contractions with amplitude greater than the mean, including those close to the highest voltage amplitude.

It is worth comparing the subjects and noting that healthy individuals tend to have a higher success rate due to their well-conditioned muscles, which allow the acquisition system to pick up an appropriate signal for each movement. Additionally, it is important to mention that deactivation for the typical subject is more pronounced when using the RMS index, as the signal amplitude is adequate for detection.

Table 1. Percentage of successes of the onset/offset detection

Techniques	Person with a disability		Healthy person	
	Onset	Offset	Onset	Offset
RMS Index	33.33%	24.54%	77.78%	**68.06%**
Hilbert-Huang Transform	**68.52%**	**73.15%**	**88.43%**	59.26%

In order to study the timing of onset/offset detection, the instants are compared with the visual inspection. A summary of statistical variables obtained from the onset/offset time of the test subjects is presented in Tables 2 and 3. For the subject with a disability, the onset instant was calculated in 72 out of 216 samples, and the offset instant was calculated in 56 out of 216 samples. For the healthy subject, the onset instant was calculated in 189 out of 216 samples, and the offset instant was calculated in 165 out of 216 samples. Negative values indicate an early onset/offset detection.

Table 2 shows that the median has negative values indicating early onset detection in all cases. Regarding mean, it is observed that for the subject with a disability, the Hilbert-Huang technique detects the onset first, while the RMS index has better results for the healthy subject. Additionally, the Hilbert-Huang transform performs better as it has less variation in its data, and most of the values are closer to zero, which is closer to the visual technique that is considered the gold standard. Although it is not possible to conclude which one is better at the onset detection, the results indicate that the subjects cannot be compared with this indicator. Concerning the remaining statistical data, there are no significant differences.

Table 2. Onset detection instant

Statistical variables	Person with a disability		Healthy person	
	RMS	Hilbert-Huang	RMS	Hilbert-Huang
Median	−0.0045	**−0.0780**	−0.0335	**−0.1667**
Maximum	0.7360	**0.5664**	0.8365	**0.6274**
Minimum	−0.8250	**−0.5982**	−0.9648	**−0.8041**
Mean	0.2137	**0.1464**	**0.1974**	0.2213
Standard deviation	0.2150	**0.1394**	0.1938	**0.1781**

Table 3 shows that the median has positive values indicating a delay in offset detection in all cases. Regarding mean, it is observed that for the subject with a disability, the Hilbert-Huang technique detects the offset first, while the RMS index has better results for the healthy subject. Moreover, the Hilbert-Huang transform performs better with less variation in data, having values closer to zero, which is closer to the visual technique, considered the gold standard. In the case of the healthy subject, the RMS index presents better performance, consistent with the onset detection that shows better results.

Table 3. Offset detection instant

Statistical variables	Person with a disability		Healthy person	
	RMS	Hilbert-Huang	RMS	Hilbert-Huang
Median	0.1004	**0.0823**	**0.1007**	0.2410
Maximum	0.9205	**0.7431**	**0.9911**	0.9961
Minimum	**−0.3999**	−0.7204	−0.9500	**−0.4790**
Mean	0.2504	**0.2157**	**0.3000**	0.3320
Standard deviation	0.2086	**0.1896**	0.2669	**0.2665**

The study made a quantitative comparison of two techniques for onset/offset detection in a person with elbow disarticulation and a healthy person. The results show that the Hilbert-Huang transform offers better results, with a higher number of successful onset/offset detections, faster detection, and less statistical data dispersion. All of these indicate that the Hilbert-Huang transform is suitable for an automatic detection process.

The results obtained with the RMS index are better in the healthy subject because the MES signals have greater amplitude and are easily detected, while the Hilbert-Huang Transform can adapt to signals of less amplitude as in the case of the subject with a disability, since the latter have decreased muscle activity in the residual part of their limb.

5 Conclusions

The Hilbert-Huang Transform technique is found to be effective at detecting onset and offset, even when there is a drastic decrease in the amplitude of the muscle electrical signal (MES), unlike the RMS index. However, the RMS index is more effective at detecting onset/offset signals in healthy individuals.

Conversely, the Hilbert-Huang Technique is more effective for detecting signals obtained from individuals with disabilities. Precise onset/offset detection is crucial for controlling prosthetic devices accurately because inaccurate activation or deactivation thresholds can result in a delayed or non-causal response. Nevertheless, it is essential to stress that this protocol should be implemented in a larger group of subjects, including both those who are healthy and those with disabilities.

These techniques can be used for classifying EMG signal patterns. Visual inspection is traditionally used for this purpose, but it can lead to delays in the start of the contraction and premature deactivation at the end of the contraction. By contrast, these methods offer a more precise and automated approach to classification. This makes them particularly useful for prosthetic devices, where precise control is essential.

Acknowledgments. This research has been funded by Dirección General de Investigaciones of Universidad Santiago de Cali under call No. 02-2023.

References

1. Parajuli, N., et al.: Real-Time EMG Based Pattern Recognition Control for Hand Prostheses: A Review on Existing Methods, Challenges and Future Implementation. Sensors **19** (2019). https://doi.org/10.3390/s19204596
2. Ju, N., Lee, K.-H., Kim, M.-O., Choi, Y.: A user-driven approach to prosthetic upper limb development in Korea. Healthcare. **9**, 839 (2021). https://doi.org/10.3390/healthcare9070839
3. Rodriguez, W.A., et al.: Real-time detection of myoelectric hand patterns for an incomplete spinal cord injured subject. IFMBE Proceedings **83**, 1879–1885 (2022). https://doi.org/10.1007/978-3-030-70601-2_274
4. Blana, D., Kyriacou, T., Lambrecht, J.M., Chadwick, E.K.: Feasibility of using combined EMG and kinematic signals for prosthesis control: a simulation study using a virtual reality environment. J. Electromyogr. Kinesiol. **29**, 21–27 (2016). https://doi.org/10.1016/j.jelekin.2015.06.010
5. Calderon, C.A., Ramirez, C., Barros, V., Punin, G.: Design and deployment of grasp control system applied to robotic hand prosthesis. IEEE Lat. Am. Trans. **15**, 181–188 (2017). https://doi.org/10.1109/TLA.2017.7854610

6. Mastinu, E., et al.: An alternative myoelectric pattern recognition approach for the control of hand prostheses: a case study of use in daily life by a dysmelia subject. IEEE J. Translat. Eng. Heal. Medi. **6**, 2600112 (2018). https://doi.org/10.1109/JTEHM.2018.2811458
7. Zecca, M., Micera, S., Carrozza, M.C., Dario, P.: Control of multifunctional prosthetic hands by processing the electromyographic signal. Crit. Rev. Biomed. Eng. **30**, 459–485 (2002). https://doi.org/10.1615/critrevbiomedeng.v30.i456.80
8. Staude, G., Flachenecker, C., Daumer, M., Wolf, W.: Onset detection in surface electromyographic signals: a systematic comparison of methods. EURASIP J. Appl. Sign. Proc. **2**, 67–81 (2001)
9. Tabie, M., Kirchner, E.A.: EMG onset detection - comparison of different methods for a movement prediction task based on EMG. In: International Conference on Bio-inspired Systems and Signal Processing (2013)
10. Kang, K., Rhee, K., Shin, H.: Applied sciences event detection of muscle activation using an electromyogram. Appl. Sci. **10**, 5593 (2020). https://doi.org/10.3390/app10165593
11. Merlo, A., Farina, D., Merletti, R.: A fast and reliable technique for muscle activity detection from surface EMG signals. I.E.E.E. Trans. Biomed. Eng. **50**, 316–323 (2003). https://doi.org/10.1109/TBME.2003.808829
12. Xu, Q., Quan, Y., Yang, L., He, J.: An adaptive algorithm for the determination of the onset and offset of muscle contraction by EMG signal processing. IEEE Trans. Neural Syst. Rehabil. Eng. **21**, 65–73 (2013). https://doi.org/10.1109/TNSRE.2012.2226916
13. Yang, D., Zhang, H., Gu, Y., Liu, H.: Accurate EMG onset detection in pathological, weak and noisy myoelectric signals. Biomed. Signal Process. Control **33**, 306–315 (2017). https://doi.org/10.1016/j.bspc.2016.12.014
14. Vasseljen, O., Dahl, H.H., Mork, P.J., Torp, H.G.: Muscle activity onset in the lumbar multifidus muscle recorded simultaneously by ultrasound imaging and intramuscular electromyography. Clin. Biomech. **21**, 905–913 (2006). https://doi.org/10.1016/j.clinbiomech.2006.05.003
15. Hodges, P.W., Bui, B.H.: A comparison of computer-based methods for the determination of onset of muscle contraction using electromyography. Electroencephalogr. Clin. Neurophysiol. **101**, 511–519 (1996). https://doi.org/10.1016/s0013-4694(96)95190-5
16. Huang, N.E., et al.: The empirical mode decomposition and the Hilbert spectrum for nonlinear and non-stationary time series analysis. In: Proc. R. Soc. Lond. A, 903–993 (The Royal Society, 1998). In: Royal Society A. pp. 903–993 (1998)

MinimalAI: Brain Hemorrhage Detection in Images Through Minimalist Machine Learning Approach

José-Luis Solorio-Ramírez(✉)

Centro de Investigación en Computación, Instituto Politécnico Nacional, CDMX 07700, México
rjoseluiss2021@cic.ipn.mx

Abstract. Pattern classification encompasses a wide range of algorithms, such as Multi-Layer Perceptron, Support Vector Machine, K-Nearest Neighbors, Naïve Bayes, Adaboost, and Random Forest, catering to diverse applications. However, a new trend, eXplainable-Artificial Intelligence, aims to enhance the user-friendliness and understandability of Machine Learning algorithms. This study introduces a novel pattern classification approach, incorporating the Minimalist Machine Learning paradigm and the dMeans feature selection algorithm. It is evaluated against Multi-Layer Perceptron, Naïve Bayes, K-Nearest Neighbors, Support Vector Machine, Adaboost, and Random Forest classifiers for CT brain image classification. The dataset includes grayscale images divided into two categories: CT without Hemorrhage and CT with Intra-Ventricular Hemorrhage. Most models achieved 50–75% accuracy with sensitivity and specificity ranging from 58% to 86%. Notably, the proposed methodology achieved remarkable accuracy of 86.50%, matching the top-performing classifier and surpassing state-of-the-art algorithms. This performance is attributed to its simplicity and practicality, aligning with the trend of generating easily interpretable algorithms. Overall, the study contributes to eXplainable-Artificial Intelligence advancement by presenting a high-accuracy pattern classification methodology that outperforms existing algorithms in specificity. The methodology's practicality makes it suitable for real-world applications, promoting transparency and interpretability in Machine Learning algorithms.

Keywords: minimalist machine learning · pattern classification · explainable artificial intelligence

1 Introduction

Detecting early signs of hemorrhage is challenging, as the symptoms are often subtle or imperceptible. This lack of awareness can worsen the condition for those affected. Therefore, addressing this issue is of utmost importance to improve healthcare outcomes and mitigate the burden of these diseases. Medical specialists often rely on diagnostic imaging techniques like Magnetic Resonance Imaging (MRI) and Computed Tomography (CT) for initial evaluations of organic anomalies. Although MRI requires more complex

Y. Hernández Heredia et al. (Eds.): IWAIPR 2023, LNCS 14335, pp. 387–399, 2024.
https://doi.org/10.1007/978-3-031-49552-6_33

preparation, it is commonly used for patients who have suffered injuries. In acute phases, CT remains the preferred choice for brain injury cases [1–3]. Unfortunately, these imaging techniques may not always provide enough information to determine brain anomalies definitively. Cerebral hemorrhages can arise from different causes like cranioencephalic trauma, hypertension, or intracranial tumors. Typically, these hemorrhages are classified into five types based on their specific location within the brain [4]: Intracerebral Hemorrhage (ICH), Subarachnoid Hemorrhage (SAH), Epidural Hemorrhage (EDH), Subdural Hemorrhage (SDH), and Intraventricular Hemorrhage (IVH).

Advanced imaging techniques like MRI and CT, combined with AI and engineering, enable the development of computer vision applications. These applications integrate intelligent computation with medical images to aid accurate disease detection [1]. Algorithms such as ANN, SVM, and DL are commonly used for visual pattern recognition, including identifying brain hemorrhages. DL algorithms have high accuracy but lack interpretability, creating a need for eXplainable AI (XAI) [5]. Deep Learning algorithms have a notable drawback in that they perform optimally when trained with a vast number of instances or examples [6], especially as the depth of the network increases, leading to improved accuracy. Nonetheless, this creates a challenge as it becomes exceedingly difficult to comprehend how these algorithms reach a solution, rendering them as "Black Boxes" in practice.

Naturally, a significant inquiry arises: under what conditions can an algorithm be deemed explainable? Extensive deliberations have resulted in the identification of five essential criteria that these models must meet: Intelligibility (I), Transparency (T), Consistency (C1), Causality (C2), and Verifiability (V) [7, 8]. These characteristics aim to ensure that the algorithm's reasoning is understandable, transparent, and justifiable, enabling users to trust and comprehend its outputs. In response to the need for transparent and explainable Machine Learning models, we have undertaken this work with the recognition that image classification is a complex and extensive task. Our motivation led us to develop a methodology that incorporates two significant measures within an image and utilizes an unconventional approach known as Minimalist Machine Learning [9].

The Minimalist Machine Learning (MML) paradigm is commonly used for classification tasks in Pattern Recognition. One notable feature of this paradigm is its ability to visually represent data and results on a Cartesian plane. To achieve this representation, statistical measures such as Arithmetic Mean and the pattern index are employed to identify different classes. These statistical properties are highlighted in the article "Toward the Bleaching of the Black Boxes: Minimalist Machine Learning" as important tools for understanding and analyzing the data [9].

The process of defining a pattern classifier involves selecting an appropriate algorithm or model architecture that is suitable for the given task [10]. The choice of algorithm depends on the nature of the data, the complexity of the patterns to be recognized, and the desired performance metrics.

2 Materials and Methods

The paper addresses the problem of CT image classification for intracerebral hemorrhage detection and proposes a comprehensive approach. The methodology includes image enhancement techniques, attribute selection algorithm, and the implementation of a classification algorithm based on the MML paradigm.

2.1 Image Processing

Contrast enhancement. Contrast Limited Adaptive Histogram Equalization (CLAHE) is an image enhancement technique that aims to improve the contrast and enhance the details of an image. It is a variant of the traditional Histogram Equalization method, but with an additional limitation to prevent over-amplification of noise in localized regions [11].

Image filter: mean. The mean filter, also known as the average filter, is a common type of image filter used in image processing. It belongs to the category of linear filters, which means that the output pixel value is computed as a weighted average of the neighboring pixel values [12]. Mathematically, let's denote the input image as I and the mean-filtered output image as I'. Suppose the kernel size is $(n \times n)$, centered at each pixel position (x, y) in the image. The mean filter operation at pixel (x, y) can be represented as follows:

$$g(x, y) = \frac{1}{n^2} \sum_i \sum_j f(x + i, y + j) \tag{1}$$

Here, i and j are indices ranging from $-n/2$ to $n/2$, representing the relative positions within the kernel.

2.2 Morphological Operations

In image processing, dilation and erosion are fundamental morphological operations used to modify the shape and structure of objects within an image. These operations are commonly applied to binary or grayscale images, where each pixel has a certain intensity or value [13].

Dilation. Dilation is a morphological operation that expands the boundaries of objects in an image. It involves convolving the image with a structuring element or kernel, which defines the shape and size of the neighborhood around each pixel. Dilation is useful for tasks such as object detection, boundary detection, and image enhancement. It helps to enlarge or thicken the objects, fill in gaps, and merge adjacent regions [14].

Erosion. Erosion is a morphological operation that shrinks or erodes the boundaries of objects in an image. Similar to dilation, it involves convolving the image with a structuring element or kernel. Erosion helps in tasks such as noise reduction, object separation, and boundary extraction. It erodes or removes small details, breaks apart connected components, and refines the shape of objects [14]. Both dilation and erosion are basic morphological operations that can be combined with other operations, such as opening and closing, to achieve specific image processing goals [15].

2.3 Permutation of Relevance: *dMeans*

The dMeans transformation is an algorithm designed to improve the distinguishability of classes within a dataset. It involves a series of operations that prioritize class separability [16]. The operation that allows to distinguish that difference is: the arithmetic mean.

Algorithm 1: *dMeans*

Input: S_{Train} training, with two mutually exclusive classes $C = \{C_1, C_2\}$. The features are formed by a set of features $F = \{F_1, F_2, \ldots, F_n\}$.

Step 1: For each feature *F_i*:

I. Compute the mean M_{1i} of the values of the feature F_i of all the patterns belonging to Class C_1.

II. Compute the mean M_{2i} of the values of the feature F_i of all the patterns belonging to Class C_2.

III. Compute the difference $M_{1i} - M_{2i}$ and store that result in ***d_i***.

Step 2: Generate the Relevance Permutation (RP) sorting the d_i array from high to low.

Output: n positions, which are sorted in descending order, due to its relevance.

2.4 Minimalist Machine Learning Paradigm

In the Minimalist Machine Learning (MML) paradigm, a crucial step is to ensure that every image within the dataset undergoes a flattening process. This process involves converting each image into a two-dimensional array with dimensions $m \times n$, where m represents the number of patterns and n denotes the number of attributes for each pattern. According to the principles of the MML paradigm, the patterns undergo a transformation where their original n attributes are reduced to only two attributes [9]. These two attributes, represented as real numbers, are obtained by calculating the mean of each pattern. Consequently, the dataset is transformed into a matrix of size $m \times 2$ [9]. The first attribute corresponds to the corresponding to the value of the pattern number, while the second attribute represents the calculated mean value. Through these calculations, the behavior of each pattern can be visualized on a 2D plane. The x-axis represents to the pattern number (index), while the y-axis is determined by the mean value. The Figs. 1 and 2 are a representation of what is desired to observe in order to represent the training set.

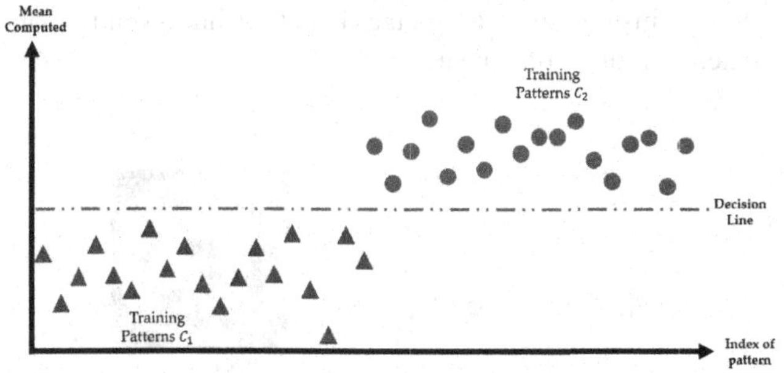

Fig. 1. Location of each pattern on the 2D plane. Total separation of classes.

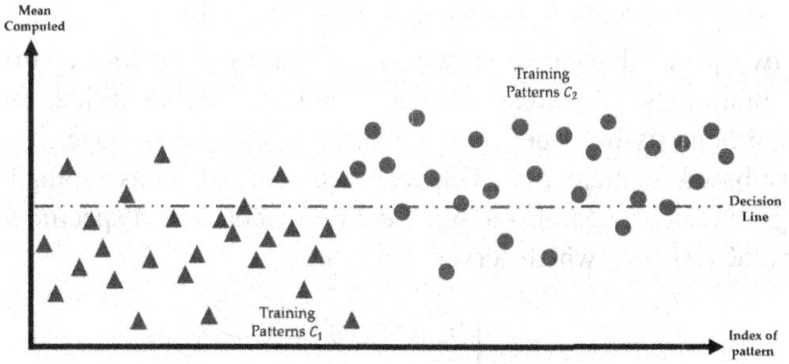

Fig. 2. Location of each pattern on the 2D plane. Optimal separation of classes.

3 Proposed Methodology

This section presents the methodology utilized in this study. Section 3.1 provides a brief overview of the image enhancement techniques proposed. Section 3.2 outlines the MinimalAI algorithm, including the dMeans algorithm and its decision boundary. Lastly, Sect. 3.3 illustrates a series of examples that aim to enhance understanding of the learning and testing phases of the developed model.

3.1 TC Scans Enhancement

Contrast Limited Adaptive Histogram Equalization (CLAHE). The alternative method used in this study is Contrast Limited Adaptive Histogram Equalization (CLAHE) implemented through the adapthisteq function in MATLAB [17].

Mean filter. After the extraction of bone tissue from the image, 9×9 pixels mean filter is applied to reduce additive noise and achieve image smoothing [18]. The selected filter serves two purposes: firstly, it smooths the image, and secondly, it functions as a low-pass filter to effectively remove the additive noise that is present.

Hard tissue removal. Various types of tissue can be observed in a brain CT image, each distinguished by its characteristic solidity. For example, the encephalic mass and the bone structure (skull) exhibit different levels of solidity. Figure 3 demonstrates this distinction, where the histogram of an image depicting Intra-Ventricular Hemorrhage reveals the presence of four distinct peaks (v).

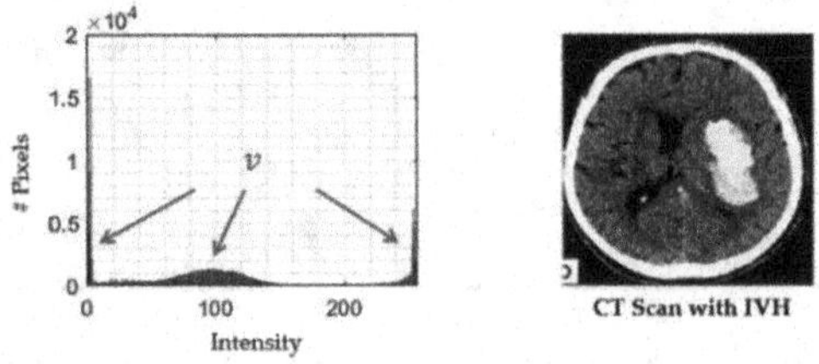

Fig. 3. Pre-processed histogram of a class IVH image.

The first two peaks that make up the group v are related to the soft tissues that conforms the brain mass; the areas of greater intensity are identified: intensities that characterize the bone tissue. Due to the characteristics of the image, it is possible to apply intensity-based segmentation. This technique consists of assigning binary values to a specific gray scale image, this assignment corresponds to a specific value, known as threshold value (α) [19], which serves as a limit.

$$g(x, y) = \begin{cases} 0 & \text{if } f(x, y) > \alpha \\ f(x, y) & \text{if } f(x, y) \le \alpha \end{cases} \tag{2}$$

The equation represents an intensity-based segmentation process, where the resulting image $g(x, y)$ is obtained by applying the segmentation to the source image $f(x, y)$ using a threshold value α. In this case, the threshold value α is calculated as the average intensity value of a subset of images.

Segmentation of suspicious tissue. Global thresholding can be expanded to incorporate multiple thresholds, allowing specific gray level ranges to be assigned a single value for enhanced identification of regions of interest. This involves defining lower (α_1) and upper (α_2) limits. Any elements within the range of $\alpha_1 \le f(x, y) \le \alpha_2$ are assigned a value that emphasizes them [20]. The reassignment of values for each image element can be described using the following expression.

$$g(x, y) = \begin{cases} 0 & \text{if } f(x, y) < \alpha_1 \\ 255 & \text{if } \alpha_1 \le f(x, y) \le \alpha_2 \\ 0 & \text{if } f(x, y) \ge \alpha_2 \end{cases} \tag{3}$$

The resulting image, $g(x, y)$, is obtained by applying intensity-based segmentation to the source image, $f(x, y)$, using lower limit α_1 and upper limit α_2 for assigning specific values.

In this study, the segmented binary images were created, and then they were overlaid on the equalized grayscale images. This overlaying process enhances the areas of interest without losing the properties provided by the original grayscale images.

3.2 Minimalist Machine Learning

In this subsection, Figs. 4 and 5 visualize the learning and testing phase applied to the MinimalAI classifier, based on the MML paradigm.

Learning Phase

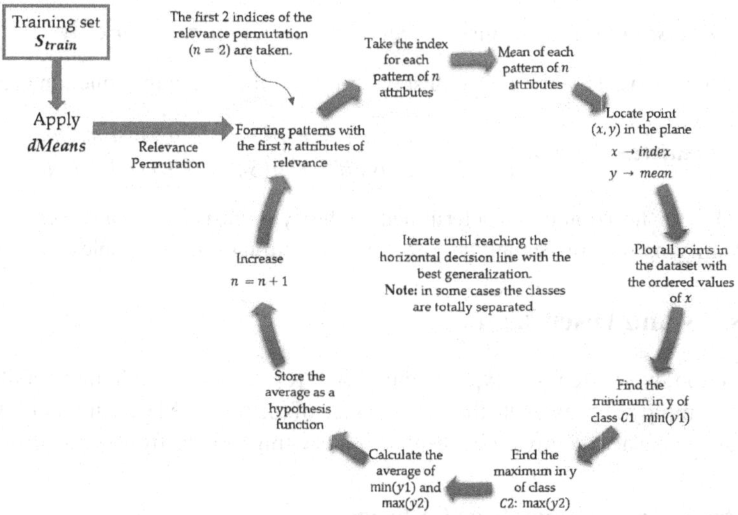

Fig. 4. Diagram of the training phase according to MinimalAI classifier [16].

Test Phase

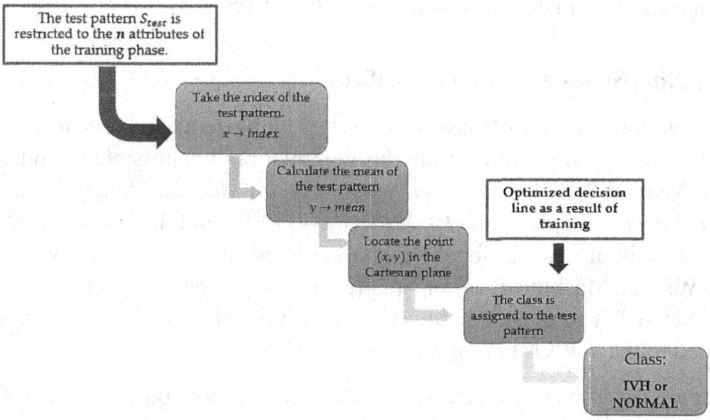

Fig. 5. Diagram of the test phase according to MinimalAI classifier [16].

Decision Line. The classifier design based on the new MML paradigm involves creating a decision line or boundary that effectively separates two classes within a dataset. The mean is calculated for each pattern in the dataset, which serve as important measures for this process. Using these measures, a function can be defined that aims to generalize the separation of classes by establishing a horizontal line according to the principles of the MML paradigm [9]. This decision line can partially or completely separate the classes, resulting in a decision boundary that achieves optimal performance in pattern classification. This calculation is represented by the following equation:

$$\boldsymbol{Decision\,Line} = \text{mean}\left[\max(\mathit{inferior\ Class}), \min(\mathit{superior\ Class})\right] \tag{4}$$

To assign a class label to a given test pattern S_{test}, the following function is applied:

$$\boldsymbol{Predicted\ Class} = \begin{cases} \mathit{Normal\ Class\ if\ mean}(S_{test}) < \mathit{Decision\,Line} \\ \mathit{IVH\ Class\ if\ mean}(S_{test}) > \mathit{Decision\,Line} \end{cases} \tag{5}$$

Visually, the horizontal line determined by the hypothesis function serves as a visual aid in identifying the correct and incorrect classification of test examples.

4 Results and Discussion

In this section, we present the experimental setup for our study, including details about the dataset employed to evaluate the performance of the proposed paradigm in CT image classification. We also compare the results with existing models from the state of the art.

4.1 Dataset: Brain Hemorrhage CT Scans

The dataset consisted of 128 x 128 pixel-sized CT images obtained from individuals aged between 15 and 60 years [21]. For this specific experiment, we focused on the IVH and Non-Hemorrhage classes, resulting in a final dataset of 252 images. Among these, 129 images belonged to the IVH class, and 123 images belonged to the Normal class, resulting in an approximate imbalance rate of $IR = 1.05$.

4.2 Competing State-of-the-Art Classifiers

There is a large compendium of classification algorithms frequently used to solve the task of medical image classification, within this compilation it is possible to find classifiers [22–27]: *K-Nearest Neighbors (K-NN), Support Vector Machine (SVM), Random Forest (RF), Multi-Layer Perceptron (MLP), Naïve Bayes (NB),* and *Adaboost*.

All the algorithms, except for the proposed algorithm in this study, were executed using the WEKA Machine Learning platform. The proposed algorithm was developed in MATLAB. The specific parameters employed for each classification algorithm implemented in the WEKA platform are presented below.

I. *K-NN:* K = 1; Distance Function = Euclidean Distance; Batch size = 100.
II. *RF:* Iters = 100; Batch size = 100; Features = log2(predictors) + 1; Depth = Unlimited.
III. *SVM:* Kernel = RBF; Batch size = 100; Kernel degree = 3; g = 1/max(index).
IV. *Adaboost:* Batch size = 100; Classifier = Decision Stump; Iterations = 10.
V. *Naïve Bayes:* Batch size = 100.
VI. *MLP:* Layers: 20; Learning rate = 0.3; momentum = 0.2; Epochs = 500.

4.3 Comparative Analysis

By employing validation methods and splitting the data into training and test sets, we can effectively evaluate the performance and reliability of classification models, ensuring they are robust and capable of accurately classifying new instances. In this work the Leave-One Out Cross Validation was implemented in all the experiments.

Performance metrics. To evaluate and compare the performance of a model, it is crucial to utilize metrics that provide insights into its effectiveness [28]. In this study, a two-class confusion matrix is employed, distinguishing between the positive and negative classes. The four cells of the matrix correspond to True Positive (TP), True Negative (TN), False Positive (FP), and False Negative (FN), arranged as follows (Table 1):

Table 1. Confusion matrix for a two-class problem.

Confusion Matrix			
		Predicted Class	
		Positive	Negative
Real Class	Positive	TP	FN
	Negative	FP	TN

The performance measure that will allow establishing a reference of the quality of the model will be the accuracy, since under this condition, it can be evaluated with full reliability of the model [29]. Furthermore, the model's reliability will be assessed by calculating Specificity and Recall measures.

$$Accuracy = \frac{TP + TN}{TP + TN + FP + FN} \tag{6}$$

$$Recall = \frac{TP}{TP + FN} \tag{7}$$

$$Specificity = \frac{TN}{TN + FP} \tag{8}$$

The obtained results from the classifiers on the BHCT dataset are presented in Table 2, showcasing their performance across three distinct measures: Accuracy, Recall, and Specificity.

In terms of classification results, the MLP and SVM models show poor performance, while the RF-based classifier obtains good results on all evaluation measures, making it a strong competitor to our proposed approach. The level of explainability required may vary depending on the specific application, user requirements and domain knowledge. What is considered sufficiently explainable in one context may not be so in another, making it difficult to create a universally applicable measure. It is for this reason that a way of representing non-quantitative performance, based on compliance with the characteristics set out in the X-AI discipline, is set out in Table 3.

Table 2. Performance achieved for classifiers in BHCT Images Dataset. [1] In seconds.

Classifier	Training Time[1]	Accuracy	Recall	Specificity
K-NN	6	0.7341	0.5890	0.8862
RF	203	0.8650	0.8600	0.8700
SVM	752	0.5198	1.0000	0.0162
MLP	101	0.6071	0.6590	0.5528
NB	116	0.7420	0.7440	0.7400
Adaboost	623	0.7341	0.6590	0.8130
MinimalAI	252	0.8650	0.8280	0.9160

Table 3. Non-quantitative performance related to the X-AI of the proposed algorithms.

Classifier	I	T	C1	C2	V	Accuracy
K-NN	✓	✓	✓	×	×	⋆
RF	×	×	×	×	✓	⋆⋆⋆⋆
SVM	✓	✓	×	✓	✓	⋆
MLP	×	×	×	✓	×	⋆
NB	✓	✓	✓	✓	✓	⋆⋆⋆
Adaboost	×	×	×	×	×	⋆⋆⋆
MinimalAI	✓	✓	×	✓	✓	⋆⋆⋆⋆

The proposed MinimalAI algorithm demonstrates competitive performance, achieving the highest accuracy value on a balanced dataset, matching in performance one of the most robust classifiers such as RF. Meanwhile, for the recall measure, MinimalAI achieves a second place only being surpassed by SVM. It is worth mentioning that deep learning algorithms were not included in the comparative study since the aim was to contemplate those algorithms with a better explanatory capacity, and at the same time compete in their performance. Finally, the specificity reaches the maximum reported. It is of utmost relevance to reveal that this performance was achieved with only 893 of the 16,384 total attributes. This implies only 5.45% of the total attributes, and that to be represented in a two-dimensional plane they were transformed into only two: mean and pattern index (it is clear that the index is only necessary for plotting) (Figs. 6 and 7).

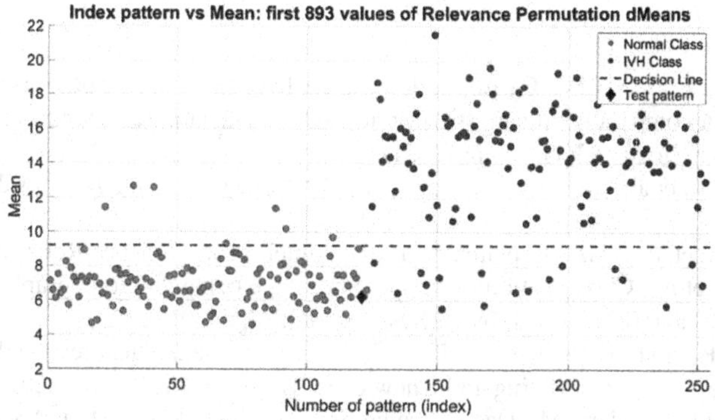

Fig. 6. Final plot of the training and testing result of the MinimalAI classifier. The plot represents a correct classification on Normal Class.

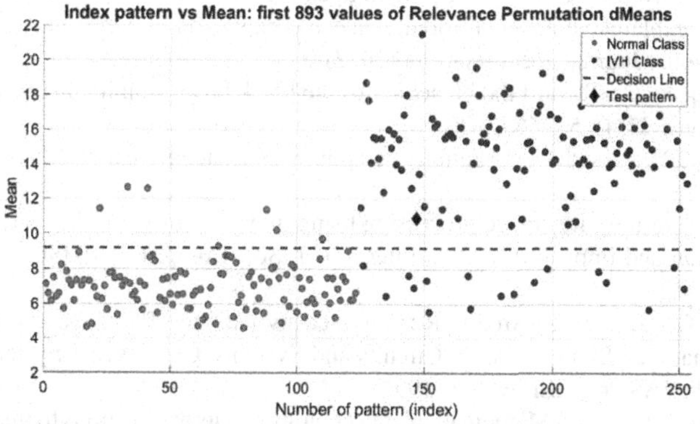

Fig. 7. Final plot of the training and testing result of the MinimalAI classifier. The plot represents a correct classification on IVH Class.

4.4 Conclusions

This paper presents a novel MML-based classification algorithm for CT brain image classification. It shows competitive performance compared to other algorithms, ranking second on two measures. The algorithm offers easy visualization and feature reduction using the dMeans method. However, it has a limitation of long training time with a small number of images. The decision line may change based on test set composition. Dimensionality is reduced by 94%. The MinimalAI algorithm allows graphical representation of results. The methodology is applicable to mobile and embedded systems. The proposed model aligns with Explainable Artificial Intelligence attributes, being highly explainable, transparent, justifiable, and open to scrutiny through graphical representations.

References

1. Alabousi, M., et al.: MRI vs. CT for the detection of liver metastases in patients with pancreatic carcinoma: a comparative diagnostic test accuracy systematic review and meta-analysis. J. Magne. Reson. Imag. **53**(1), 38–48 (2021)
2. Erickson, B.J., et al.: Machine learning for medical imaging. Radiographics **37**(2), 505–515 (2017)
3. Gunning, D., et al.: XAI—Explainable artificial intelligence. Science Robotics **4**(37) (2019)
4. Ozaltin, O., et al.: Classification of brain hemorrhage computed tomography images using OzNet hybrid algorithm. Int. J. Imag. Sys. Technol. **33**, 69–91 (2023)
5. Angelov, P.P., et al.: Explainable artificial intelligence: an analytical review. Wiley Interdisciplinary Reviews: Data Mining and Knowledge Discovery **11**(5), 1424 (2021)
6. Zohuri, B., Moghaddam, M.: Deep learning limitations and flaws. Mod. Approaches Mater. Sci **2**, 241–250 (2020)
7. Tjoa, E., Guan, C.: A survey on explainable artificial intelligence (xai): toward medical xai. IEEE Trans. Neural Netw. Learn. Sys. **32**(11), 4793–4813 (2020)
8. Singh, V., Konovalova, I., Kar, A.K.: When to choose ranked area integrals versus integrated gradient for explainable artificial intelligence–a comparison of algorithms. Benchmarking: An International Journal ahead-of-print (2022)
9. Yáñez-Márquez, C.: Toward the bleaching of the black boxes: minimalist machine learning. IT Professional **22**(4), 51–56 (2020)
10. Bishop, C.M., Nasrabadi, N.M.: Pattern recognition and machine learning. New York: springer **4**, 4 (2006)
11. Gupta, G.: Algorithm for image processing using improved median filter and comparison of mean, median and improved median filter. Int. J. Soft Comp. Eng. (IJSCE) **1**(5), 304–311 (2011)
12. Zurbach, P., Gonzalez, J.G., Arce, G.R.: Weighted myriad filters for image processing. In: 1996 IEEE International Symposium on Circuits and Systems. Circuits and Systems Connecting the World. ISCAS 96, IEEE, vol. 2 (1996)
13. Serra, J., Soille, P., (eds.): Mathematical morphology and its applications to image processing. Springer Science & Business Media **2** (2012)
14. Nandi, A.: Detection of human brain tumour using MRI image segmentation and morphological operators. In: 2015 IEEE international conference on computer graphics, vision and information security (CGVIS), IEEE (2015)
15. Yu-Qian, Z., et al.: Medical images edge detection based on mathematical morphology. In: 2005 IEEE engineering in medicine and biology 27th annual conference, IEEE (2006)
16. Solorio-Ramírez, J.-L., et al.: Brain hemorrhage classification in CT scan images using minimalist machine learning. Diagnostics **11**(8), 1449 (2021)
17. Mittal, N.: Automatic Contrast Enhancement of Low Contrast Images using MATLAB. Int. J. Adv. Res. Comp. Sci. **3**(1) (2012)
18. Techavipoo, U., et al.: Implementation of asymmetric kernel median filtering for real-time ultrasound imaging. In: 2018 11th Biomedical Engineering International Conference (BMEiCON), IEEE (2018)
19. Kohler, R.: A segmentation system based on thresholding. Comput. Graph. Image Process. **15**(4), 319–338 (1981)
20. Fan, Z., Wang, C., Ma, X.: Double-threshold image segmentation method based on gray gradient. In: 2009 International Conference on Optical Instruments and Technology: Optical Systems and Modern Optoelectronic Instruments, SPIE, vol. 7506 (2009)
21. Shahangian, B., Pourghassem, H.: Automatic brain hemorrhage segmentation and classification algorithm based on weighted grayscale histogram feature in a hierarchical classification structure. Biocybern. Biomed. Eng. **36**, 217–232 (2016)

22. Kim, J., Kim, B.-S., Savarese, S.: Comparing image classification methods: K-nearest-neighbor and support-vector-machines. In: Proceedings of the 6th WSEAS international conference on Computer Engineering and Applications, and Proceedings of the 2012 American conference on Applied Mathematics (2012)
23. Chandra, M.A., Bedi, S.S.: Survey on SVM and their application in image classification. Int. J. Info. Technol. **13**, 1–11 (2021)
24. Xu, B., Ye, Y., Nie, L.: An improved random forest classifier for image classification. In: 2012 IEEE International Conference on Information and Automation, IEEE (2012)
25. Lv, T., Bai, C., Wang, C.: Mdmlp: Image classification from scratch on small datasets with mlp. arXiv preprint arXiv:2205.14477 (2022)
26. Boiman, O., Shechtman, E., Irani, M.: In defense of nearest-neighbor based image classification. In: 2008 IEEE conference on computer vision and pattern recognition, IEEE (2008)
27. Zharmagambetov, A., Gabidolla, M., Carreira-Perpinán, Miguel A.: Improved multiclass AdaBoost for image classification: The role of tree optimization. In: 2021 IEEE International Conference on Image Processing (ICIP), IEEE (2021)
28. Li, J., Sun, H., Li, J.: Beyond confusion matrix: learning from multiple annotators with awareness of instance features. Mach. Learn. **112**(3), 1053–1075 (2023)
29. Hasan, S.M.M., et al.: Comparative analysis of classification approaches for heart disease prediction. In: 2018 International Conference on Computer, Communication, Chemical, Material and Electronic Engineering (IC4ME2), IEEE (2018)

Enhancing License Plate Recognition in Videos Through Character-Wise Temporal Combination

Carlos Quiala[1], Milton García-Borroto[2](✉), Rubén Sánchez-Rivero[3], and Annette Morales-González[3]

[1] Universidad Tecnologica de La Habana, Havana, Cuba
[2] Centro de Sistemas Complejos, Facultad de Física, Universidad de La Habana, Havana, Cuba
milton.garcia@gmail.com
[3] Advanced Technologies Application Center (CENATAV), Havana, Cuba

Abstract. License Plate Recognition (LPR) in videos is a critical task in various domains such as parking management, traffic control, and security. This study focuses on exploring the significance of temporal information in LPR systems to improve their accuracy. Previous research has not fully leveraged temporal information, resulting in multiple prediction results for the same vehicle. Unlike other tasks, LPR generates a sequence of characters per frame, necessitating a distinct approach for combining these outputs. To address this, we conducted a comprehensive investigation of LPR pipelines and different frame combination techniques. Our study introduces a new strategy for character-wise temporal sequence combination, enhancing the accuracy of license plate recognition. The proposed approach was evaluated using a new dataset of Cuban license plates captured in parking lot scenarios showing superior results in most cases. This study can serve as guide for future research and applications in the field of LPR in videos.

Keywords: License Plate Recognition (LPR) · Temporal Information · Video Frame Combination

1 Introduction

License Plate Recognition (LPR) in videos is the process of automatically detecting and recognizing license plates from video footage captured by cameras. LPR has a wide range of applications that can improve efficiency, security, and safety in various domains. Some examples are parking management, traffic management, toll collection, border control, security in public places such as airports, train stations, and government buildings by detecting and tracking suspicious vehicles [17].

LPR in images involves a series of steps [17], including license plate detection, character segmentation (not always necessary), and character recognition. In

Y. Hernndez Heredia et al. (Eds.): IWAIPR 2023, LNCS 14335, pp. 400–411, 2024.
https://doi.org/10.1007/978-3-031-49552-6_34

license plate detection, the algorithm searches for license plates in each image or frame. This is typically done using object detection techniques such as YOLO [12,19] or Faster R-CNN [3,13]. Character recognition is usually done using OCR techniques, being the most common ones Tesseract [21] and image processing techniques like template matching or YOLO to detect and classify individual characters [17].

In a system employing video streams, license plate detection and character recognition occur in every frame, which can lead to multiple prediction results for the same vehicle [1]. Various factors, including the camera's distance, viewing angle, sunlight, shadow, and dust, cause noise, resulting in different interpretations of the same vehicle number. As a consequence of these factors, the recognition result may include the correct license plate, along with many false-positive license plates. This is why in video scenarios, temporal and redundant information from different frames can be used to improve the recognition accuracy, as proven in other similar tasks [5]. However, there is a significant difference between license plate recognition (LPR) and other tasks such as face recognition or person re-identification in videos. In LPR, the processing of each frame results in a sequence of characters, where some characters may be correct while others may not. In contrast, other related tasks typically yield a single output per frame. Consequently, the approach for combining these outputs needs to be different in LPR due to the sequential nature of the characters and the potential variations within the sequence.

Most works of LPR in videos found in the literature do not use the temporal information of video sequences to improve LPR. Very few use some form of selection or combination of recognition results across frames. Within this context, the main objective of our work is to conduct a study of several licence plate recognition pipelines and different frame combination approaches in order to evaluate the impact of temporal information in the LPR final result. This may help as guide for future researches and applications in this topic. We also propose a new strategy to make a character-wise combination of the temporal sequence in order to improve the results.

Since different countries have distinct specifications for license plates (LPs), it is challenging to develop a universal automatic license plate recognition (ALPR) system that performs well for all types of LPs. In our case, our goal is to develop a parking lot control access system, based on the acquisition and registration of Cuban license plates. This is why we created a video dataset of Cuban licence plates in such scenario.

In summary, the main contributions of our work are: (1) a comprehensive study of different LPR pipelines with different temporal information combination and (2) a new proposal for character-wise frame combination to improve LPR consistency in video sequences.

2 Related Work

Two primary surveys have been conducted to summarize the current state-of-the-art techniques for license plate (LP) recognition. The first one [2], published in

2008, comprehensively covers the methods developed prior to the Deep Learning era. The second one [17], published in 2021, provides an updated review of works that have emerged since, with a particular focus on those utilizing Deep Learning techniques. However, neither of these surveys presents approaches for obtaining a consensus output of a license plate from a sequence of video frames. In the first survey, some remarks are made on the use of video-based approaches, but they are all concentrated on detection and tracking in videos.

Several LPR proposals employ video-based data, but they use frames independently, disregarding the relation among them [14,15]. There are few works in the literature that explicitly address the use of temporal or redundant information provided by video sequences. These are the ones presented and contrasted in this section.

One approach is to implicitly merge or combine raw frames in order to obtain a single representative image of all frames. This is the case of [21], which uses a super-resolution algorithm to enhance the quality of Brazilian license plates in low-quality videos by utilizing a sequence of frames (multi-frame super resolution). Subsequently, two state-of-the-art OCR methods (Tesseract and OCRopus) are applied for recognition of the license plate characters from the final high resolution image.

Another approach involves combining the results of processing each frame individually in a sequence. Most of the related works belong to this category.

The authors of [9] utilized parking lot videos and proposed a method for license plate detection and character recognition, employing state-of-the-art techniques. To obtain the final predicted license plate for a sequence of frames, they selected the plate with the highest frequency in each sequence.

The system proposed in [4] is designed for use in parking lots. In their pipeline, after the licence plate detection using a MobileSSD network, they employ a best frame selection strategy based on the highest detection confidence values and store only the top 3 cropped images for a single vehicle. The OCR is then applied to those cropped images without considering the temporal information or redundancy among them.

The approach in [1] involves using two-stage convolutional neural networks (CNNs) - Yolov3 for detection and a new CNN proposed for character recognition. The proposed method utilizes temporal information from various frames to eliminate false predictions. They group similar recognized license plates to select the most accurate ones. The Edit-distance (EDIT) metric is used to assess the similarity of two strings. By employing this similarity value, they cluster all license plate numbers coming from a video sequence and choose the one with the highest frequency in the cluster as the final decision.

The approach of [12] involves detecting and recognizing license plates in every frame of a video utilizing state-of-the-art convolutional neural networks (CNNs). To introduce temporal redundancy, all frames pertaining to the same vehicle are combined. The final recognition outcome is based on the most frequently predicted character at each license plate position (majority vote). The authors demonstrate a significant improvement in the results by incorporating this temporal information. The same temporal redundancy was used in [6]. The work of [8] uses a character-wise temporal redundancy by employing traditional algorithms (not deep learning) to detect and segment characters in license plates.

Those temporal redundancy strategies [8,11,12] are closely related to our proposal. However, a key distinction is that, to the best of our knowledge, existing works in license plate recognition (LPR) in videos predominantly employ character-based OCR methods. These methods involve detecting or segmenting individual characters and recognizing them separately [8]. With this approach, it is very easy to determine the position of each character within the sequence. Nevertheless, character-based OCR has several disadvantages for complex real scenarios. They are very sensitive to variations, they rely on accurate character segmentation and recognition, which can be challenging when dealing with low-quality or noisy images, thus they have limited tolerance to noise and distortions. In contrast, new end-to-end OCR methods are very robust to variations, they have a simplified pipeline (no character detection or segmentation) and they can leverage contextual information from the entire input image or sequence [22]. The problem in this case is that they output the entire sequence of characters, but it can be challenging to align among different outputs in order to combine them in a character-wise way. Our work takes advantage of accurate end-to-end OCR methods and proposes a novel approach for the alignment and combination of the sequence results.

Several public datasets exists for testing LP processing steps (either detection, character recognition or both) [11,17], but most of them consist on still images sets. There are very few datasets containing video sequence of license plates available, and most of the time, they are not accessible. Due to the significant variability in license plates across different countries, most studies create their datasets, as it is challenging to develop general methods that can account for this variability.

This is the case of [12] which proposed the UFPR-ALPR dataset, containing videos from non-static cameras capturing Brazilian license plates. In Brazil, license plates come in different sizes and colors depending on the type of vehicle and its category. The researchers in [4] developed both an image dataset and a video dataset comprising license plates from Bangladesh. These datasets are not suitable for Latin license plates due to the presence of conjunct consonants and grapheme roots in the Bangla language. Additionally, the license plate information in Bangla is displayed in two rows. In [21], the authors compiled their own video dataset of Brazilian license plates, which is not publicly accessible. The authors of [9] also generated their own video dataset of Indian license plates in a parking lot scenario to evaluate the effectiveness of their approach and the work of [1] presents a Jordanian license plate dataset, with its specific characteristics, including Arabic characters.

Due to the specific characteristics of Cuban license plates and the conditions of the parking lot scenario, none of the existing datasets mentioned earlier were suitable for our study. As a result, we made the decision to create our own dataset that aligns with our specific requirements and objectives.

3 Proposal

3.1 Detection and OCR Methods for LPR

Our main goal is to evaluate the influence of temporal information, specifically the combination of video frames, in the license plate recognition pipeline. To achieve this, we employ different techniques for each step of the pipeline, including image pre-processing methods, license plate detectors, and OCR algorithms. For detection, we employ deep-learning-based detectors Yolov3 [20] and MobileNetSSD [16] models. For the MobileNetSSD case we use a pre-trained model provided by OpenVino ModelZoo[1], in the following we refer to it as OpenVino-MobileSSD. To create the Cuban license plate detector, we leveraged a pre-existing privately trained Yolo3 model. We utilize two OCR detectors, namely PaddleOCR [7] and Tesseract [10]. This enables us to assess the individual contributions of different components and analyze the overall performance of the combined approach.

We generated several pipelines involving these different techniques. They are described below:

Affine-MobileSSD-Paddle. The plate detection process involves using the OpenVino-MobileSSD model to detect license plates. We extract the plate border from the predicted bounding box. However, due to image distortions caused by the plate's viewing angle, the extracted plate border might not perfectly match the bounding box. To address this, an affine transformation is applied to remove the distortions and align the plate correctly. Finally, the Paddle OCR algorithm is employed to perform optical character recognition on the transformed plate image, resulting in the extraction of the license plate characters.

Affine-Smooth-MobileSSD-Paddle. Similar to the Affine-MobileSSD-Paddle pipeline, an additional preprocessing step is performed before executing the OCR. This preprocessing involves applying a grayscale transformation to convert the image to grayscale, followed by the application of a Gaussian filter. The grayscale transformation helps to simplify the image by removing color information, while the Gaussian filter smooths the image and reduces noise. These preprocessing steps aim to enhance the clarity and quality of the image before feeding it into the OCR algorithm.

Smooth-MobileSSD-Tesseract. The plate image detected by OpenVino-MobileSSD is improved by applying a grayscale transformation to convert the image to grayscale, followed by the application of a Gaussian filter, before running the Tesseract OCR.

Equalized-MobileSSD-Tesseract. The plate image detected by OpenVino-MobileSSD is improved by histogram equalization, before running the Tesseract OCR.

[1] https://docs.openvino.ai/latest/omz_models_model_vehicle_license_plate_detection_barrier_0106.html.

Yolov-Paddle. We utilize the Yolov3 licence plate detector. Once a license plate is detected, we directly apply the Paddle OCR algorithm to the extracted bounding box without any additional preprocessing steps.

MobileSSD-Paddle. This method utilizes the Paddle OCR algorithm directly on the license plate detected by the OpenVino detector.

While numerous pipelines involving these algorithms are possible, presenting all of them would be excessive. Hence, we focus on describing the pipelines that generated more diverse results in our experiments. By using diverse approaches (and not only the best ones) we can better showcase the influence of adding the temporal information under different scenarios and configurations.

3.2 Video Frame Combination Strategies

For each car sequence, we obtain a collection of identified license plates along with their respective confidences as returned by each of the pipelines described in the previous section. These identified plates may have varying levels of confidence, reflecting the OCR system's estimation of the accuracy or reliability of the recognized characters on each plate. An example of the obtained results appears in Table 1.

Table 1. Examples of automatically extracted plates for a single car sequence.

Video frame	Plate ground-truth	Extracted plate	Confidence
1	P137471	101376	0.53
2	P137471	P137471	0.76
3	P137471	13747	0.54
4	P137471	P110	0.54
5	P137471	P11701	0.50
6	P137471	P137471	0.72
7	P137471	P17161	0.52
8	P137471	P137471	0.85
9	P137471	11901	0.58
10	P137471	P137471	0.72

We conducted tests on various strategies for combining individual license plates across a given video sequence. These strategies are the following:

Maximum confidence (max-conf). The plate with the highest confidence is selected as the final result. In cases where multiple plates have the same highest confidence, one of them is randomly chosen as the output.

Majority vote (max-total-vote). Each detected plate contributes a vote, and the plate with the highest total number of votes is selected as the final result.

Weighted majority vote (max-w-total-vote). Each detected plate contributes a vote equal to its confidence score, and the plate with the highest total vote is selected as the final result.

Average weighted majority vote (max-w-avg-vote). Each detected plate emits a vote equal to its confidence score, and the plate with the highest average vote is selected as the final result.

For each strategy, we also tested a variation which exclusively considers for combination plate candidates with a valid plate pattern. For Cuban plates, this pattern consists of a letter followed by six digits. For example, in Table 1, we would only take into account the license plates candidates predicted in frames 2, 6, 8 and 10. We added the suffix "-valid" after each of the previously presented strategies names in order to refer to this strategy modification.

3.3 Proposed Character-Based Combination Strategy

To obtain the final plate from a collection of inferred plate values, we introduce Fig. 1. The algorithm starts with Step 1, which cleans all the input plates by replacing non-alphanumeric characters with underscores, ensuring consistent formatting and removing unwanted characters. Then, Step 2 computes the total weighted edit distance between each plate, enabling the identification of the plate that is most similar to others in the collection in Step 3. This similarity assessment takes into account the penalization of plates based on the difference between their number of characters and the expected count of 7, favoring plates with complete character detection. Next, Step 4 aligns all the plates with respect to the selected plate, ensuring consistent positioning of the characters for further processing. Finally, Step 5 integrates the aligned plates and calculates the resultant plate by combining the characters from each aligned position. These logical and sequential steps provide a systematic approach to derive the estimated plate from the collection of inferred plate values, considering similarity, alignment, and character presence.

Algorithm 1: Algorithm to Calculate Plate

Input : collection of inferred plate values
Output: calculated plate

Step 1: Clean all the input plates by replacing any non-alphanumeric characters with underscore (_)

Step 2: Calculate the total weighted edit distance from every plate to the other plates to determine similarity

Step 3: Select the most similar plate based on the total weighted distance. A penalty is introduced for plates having less or more than 7 characters

Step 4: Align the plates with respect to the selected plate

Step 5: Integrate the aligned plates and calculate the resultant plate

Fig. 1. Plate Calculation Algorithm

To perform Step 2, it is essential to determine the specific costs attributed to character insertions, deletions, and replacements in the edit distance calculation. This entails utilizing a collection of pairs (real-plate, inferred-plate) obtained from images not present in the dataset. The main objective is to compute the probabilities associated with character insertion, removal, and substitution. Consequently, each cost is derived by taking the reciprocal of the corresponding probability. This approach facilitates a comprehensive evaluation of the weighted edit distance, enabling effective comparison and analysis of the inferred plates.

The alignment algorithm employed in Step 4 is based on the Ratcliff/Obershelp algorithm [18], which calculates the similarity ratio between two sequences. This algorithm conducts a line-by-line comparison of the input sequences, identifying the longest contiguous matching subsequence. By employing this algorithm, we can determine the subsequences that require addition, deletion, or replacement in order to align two strings.

In the context of our process, we compare each inferred plate with the plate selected in Step 3, utilizing the transformations obtained from the Ratcliff/Obershelp algorithm to achieve alignment. These transformations guide the adjustments necessary to align the characters of the inferred plates with the selected plate. By applying this alignment procedure, we ensure consistent positioning and enable further analysis of the plates.

In Step 5, the objective is to determine the most probable character for each position in the plate. This selection process takes into account two factors: the repetitions of each candidate character in that position and the probabilities of character replacement between candidate pairs, which were calculated in Step 2.

By analyzing the repetitions of each candidate character in a specific position, we can assess their frequency and identify the most common character in that context. Additionally, the probabilities of character replacement computed in Step 2 provide insights into the likelihood of substituting one character with another. This information is crucial in determining the most probable character for each position in the plate.

4 Experiments

4.1 Cuban License Plate Dataset

The initial step involves strategically placing cameras at key locations within the parking lot to capture videos of vehicles entering and exiting the area. Careful consideration is given to positioning the cameras for clear views of the license plates. The recorded videos (944 × 1080 resolution) capture vehicles as they approach the payment area, pause or slow down to pay the fee, and then continue towards the exit. This captures a range of license plate images with varying angles, distances, and lighting conditions. Frames are extracted from the input video at a rate of 25 frames per second.

In the subsequent step, a vehicle detection pre-trained model from the OpenVINO Model Zoo[2] is employed to localize vehicles. This algorithm accurately

[2] https://docs.openvino.ai/latest/omz_models_model_vehicle_detection_0202.html.

identifies the boundaries of the vehicles in the captured videos. To track the car detections, a basic intersection-over-union tracker is implemented, enabling the extraction of precise bounding boxes for each passing car.

In the resultant dataset, we obtained 1528 sequences of 1414 different cars. The number of images per sequence ranges from 57 to 2223, with an average of 408. No frame selection was performed to mimic real-world conditions for the deployed system. The dataset consists of individual car images with widths ranging from 85 to 530 pixels, and an average width of 297 pixels. The heights of the car images range from 200 to 959 pixels, with an average height of 524 pixels. A sample sequences of this dataset can be seen in Fig. 2.

Fig. 2. Examples of selected frames from car sequences in the dataset. These samples, captured in a parking lot scenario, showcase various viewing angles as well as challenges related to illumination and resolution. Images are resized to fit the figure bounds.

4.2 Results

We performed our experiments for the 6 LPR pipelines presented in Sect. 3.1 in combination with the 8 frame combination strategies described in Sect. 3.2 (4 without using valid plates and 4 selecting valid plates) and our character-based combination proposal (with and without the selection of valid plates). The overall results can be seen in the graph presented in Fig. 3. The x-axis show the 6 pipelines, and for each pipeline, 10 bars display the accuracy obtained with each frame combination strategy. The first thing to notice is that the best pipelines are Yolov3-Paddle and MobileSSD-Paddle. Within each pipeline, the selection of valid plates largely improves the results in the majority of cases. Also, our proposal shows superiority in all cases with and without the selection of valid plates. In this particular point is interesting to note that the results of our proposal with and without selecting valid plates is very similar, which shows its robustness to missing and noisy information.

In order to display in more detail these results, we show in Table 2 a subset of the results, showing only the best temporal combination strategies. In this table

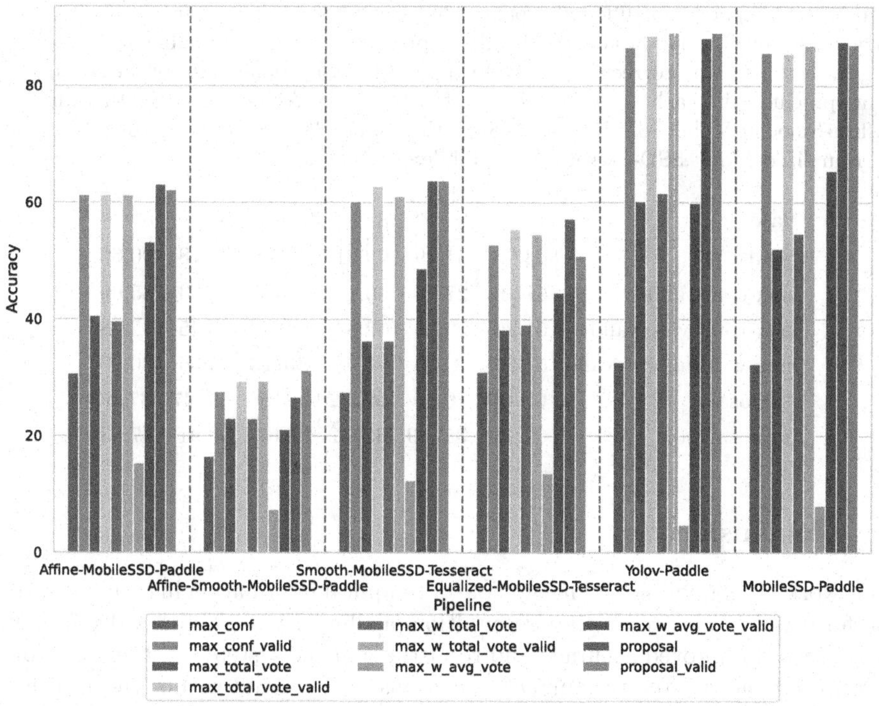

Fig. 3. Comparison among different pipelines and frame combination strategies

we included the row labeled as Ideal*. This row shows the best possible accuracy of each pipeline taking as reference the sequences where at least one of the frames has a correct prediction of the plate. It should be noted that a character-based combination approach could obtain better results than this Ideal*, since for a given sequence, the character combination might output the correct plate which is not entirely predicted in any of the frames. As can be seen in Table 2, our proposed combination strategy is consistently better than the other approaches in most cases. In Sect. 2 we described that most state-of-the-art works employ majority vote as frame combination strategy. Table 2 shows that this strategy (**max-total-vote-valid**) is outperformed by our proposals for all the pipelines.

Table 2. Comparison of different pipelines (columns) using different frame combination strategies (rows). The row labeled "Ideal*" represents the best achievable result, assuming the complete and correct license plate appears in at least one frame of the sequences. The pipelines in each column are the following: 1- Affine-MobileSSD-Paddle, 2- Affine-Smooth-MobileSSD-Paddle, 3- Smooth-MobileSSD-Tesseract, 4- Yolov3-Paddle, 5- Equalized-MobileSSD-Tesseract, 6- MobileSSD-Paddle.

Base	1	2	3	4	5	6
Ideal*	63.96	31.19	69.91	93.04	58.18	90.66
max-conf-valid	61.26	27.52	60.18	86.61	52.73	85.69
max-total-vote-valid	61.26	29.36	62.83	88.54	55.45	85.48
max-w-total-vote-valid	61.26	29.36	61.06	**89.13**	54.55	86.90
proposal	**63.06**	26.61	**63.72**	88.20	**57.27**	**87.57**
proposal-valid	62.16	**31.19**	**63.72**	89.07	50.91	87.03

5 Conclusion

Our work highlights the significant role of temporal information in enhancing the performance of the license plate recognition pipeline. By combining video frames, we observed improved accuracy and robustness in the system. Furthermore, our research demonstrates the impact of various components within the pipeline, such as image pre-processing techniques, license plate detectors, and OCR algorithms. The careful selection and optimization of these components are crucial for achieving optimal results. We found that the utilization of state-of-the-art OCR detectors, namely PaddleOCR and Tesseract, contributed to accurate and reliable license plate recognition. Our proposed character-wise frame combination outperformed other approaches based on the analysis of the entire plate.

Our study of 6 LPR pipelines and 10 frame combination strategies can guide future improvements and optimizations in the field. It can also serve to enhanced LPR applications in areas such as traffic management, parking systems, and law enforcement.

References

1. Alghyaline, S.: Real-time Jordanian license plate recognition using deep learning. J. King Saud Univ. Comput. Inf. Sci. **34**(6), 2601–2609 (2022)
2. Anagnostopoulos, C.N.E., Anagnostopoulos, I.E., Psoroulas, I.D., Loumos, V., Kayafas, E.: License plate recognition from still images and video sequences: a survey. IEEE Trans. Intell. Transp. Syst. **9**(3), 377–391 (2008)
3. Ap, N., Vigneshwaran, T., Arappradhan, M., Madhanraj, R.: Automatic number plate detection in vehicles using faster R-CNN. In: 2020 International Conference on System, Computation, Automation and Networking (ICSCAN), pp. 1–6 (2020)
4. Ashrafee, A., Khan, A.M., Irbaz, M.S., Nasim, M.A.A.: Real-time Bangla license plate recognition system for low resource video-based applications. In: 2022 IEEE/CVF Winter Conference on Applications of Computer Vision Workshops (WACVW), Waikoloa, HI, USA, pp. 479–488. IEEE (2022)

5. Becerra-Riera, F., Morales-González, A., Méndez-Vázquez, H., Dugelay, J.: Demographic attribute estimation in face videos combining local information and quality assessment. Mach. Vis. Appl. **33**(2), 26 (2022)
6. Dominguez, D.H.S., Sandoval, S.C.Q., Morocho-Cayamcela, M.E.: End-to-end license plate recognition system for an efficient deployment in surveillance scenarios. In: Rocha, Á., Ferrás, C., Méndez Porras, A., Jimenez Delgado, E. (eds.) ICITS 2022. LNNS, vol. 414, pp. 697–704. Springer, Cham (2022). https://doi.org/10.1007/978-3-030-96293-7_59
7. Du, Y., et al.: PP-OCR: a practical ultra lightweight OCR system. arXiv preprint arXiv:2009.09941 (2020)
8. Gonçalves, G.R., Menotti, D., Schwartz, W.R.: License plate recognition based on temporal redundancy. In: 2016 IEEE 19th International Conference on Intelligent Transportation Systems (ITSC), pp. 2577–2582. IEEE Press (2016)
9. Hashmi, S.N., Kumar, K., Khandelwal, S., Lochan, D., Mittal, S.: Real time license plate recognition from video streams using deep learning. Int. J. Inf. Retrieval Res. **9**, 65–87 (2019)
10. Hegghammer, T.: OCR with tesseract, amazon textract, and google document AI: a benchmarking experiment. J. Comput. Soc. Sci. **5**(1), 861–882 (2022)
11. Laroca, R., Cardoso, E.V., Lucio, D.R., Estevam, V., Menotti, D.: On the cross-dataset generalization in license plate recognition. In: Proceedings of the 17th International Joint Conference on Computer Vision, Imaging and Computer Graphics Theory and Applications, pp. 166–178 (2022). arXiv:2201.00267 [cs]
12. Laroca, R., et al.: A robust real-time automatic license plate recognition based on the YOLO detector. In: 2018 International Joint Conference on Neural Networks (IJCNN), Rio de Janeiro, Brazil, pp. 1–10. IEEE (2018)
13. Lee, D., Yoon, S., Lee, J., Park, D.S.: Real-time license plate detection based on faster R-CNN. KIPS Trans. Softw. Data Eng. **5**(11), 511–520 (2016)
14. Lee, Y., Jun, J., Hong, Y., Jeon, M.: Practical License Plate Recognition in Unconstrained Surveillance Systems with Adversarial Super-Resolution (2019)
15. Lee, Y., Yun, J., Hong, Y., Lee, J., Jeon, M.: Accurate license plate recognition and super-resolution using a generative adversarial networks on traffic surveillance video. In: 2018 IEEE International Conference on Consumer Electronics - Asia (ICCE-Asia), JeJu, Korea, South, pp. 1–4. IEEE (2018)
16. Liu, W., et al.: SSD: single shot multibox detector. In: Leibe, B., Matas, J., Sebe, N., Welling, M. (eds.) ECCV 2016. LNCS, vol. 9905, pp. 21–37. Springer, Cham (2016). https://doi.org/10.1007/978-3-319-46448-0_2
17. Lubna, Mufti, N., Shah, S.A.A.: Automatic number plate recognition: a detailed survey of relevant algorithms. Sensors **21**, 3028 (2021)
18. Nalawati, R.E., Yuntari, A.D.: Ratcliff/obershelp algorithm as an automatic assessment on e-learning. In: 2021 4th International Conference of Computer and Informatics Engineering (IC2IE), pp. 244–248. IEEE (2021)
19. Oublal, K., Dai, X.: An advanced combination of semi-supervised Normalizing Flow & Yolo (YoloNF) to detect and recognize vehicle license plates (2022). arXiv:2207.10777 [cs]
20. Redmon, J., Farhadi, A.: YOLOv3: an incremental improvement, pp. 1–6 (2018)
21. Seibel, H., Goldenstein, S., Rocha, A.: Eyes on the target: super-resolution and license-plate recognition in low-quality surveillance videos. IEEE Access **5**, 20020–20035 (2017)
22. Subramani, N., Matton, A., Greaves, M., Lam, A.: A survey of deep learning approaches for OCR and document understanding. CoRR abs/2011.13534 (2020)

A Comparison of Some Gradient Threshold Estimators for the Nonlinear Diffusion of Perona-Malik. A Novel Proposal to Improve Edges Detection in Mammography Images

Reinaldo Barrera Travieso[1], Angela M. León-Mecías[2], José A. Mesejo-Chiong[2](✉), and Richard M. Méndez-Castillo[3]

[1] Instituto de Geofísica y Astronomía, Havana, La Habana, Cuba
[2] Facultad de Matemática y Computación, Universidad de la Habana, San Lázaro y L, Habana 4, 10400 Havana, Cuba
{angela,mesejo}@matcom.uh.cu
[3] Union de Informáticos de Cuba, Havana, La Habana, Cuba

Abstract. In this work, based on the nonlinear Perona-Malik anisotropic diffusion (AD) model, we develop an efficient smoothing algorithm for mammography images that preserves edges and provides valuable information for any segmentation process. AD is believed to enhance image edges by a diffusion process with a variable diffusion coefficient including a gradient or contrast threshold parameter to which it is highly sensitive. This work proposes an algorithm, named AD-KMLS2, to estimate the gradient threshold of the diffusion coefficient in a way tailored for mammography images. AD-KMLS2 is compared with two other known methods for gradient threshold parameter estimation. When AD-KMLS2 is used, the results are better for 45% of the analyzed images in terms of two quality measures: Pratt's figure of merit and the Root Mean Square Error. In the cases where AD-KMLS2 does not reach the best results, it is only 5×10^{-5} away from these with respect to the metrics used. In this work the anisotropic diffusion smoothing process is performed by region using the superpixel segmentation technique called simple linear iterative clustering (SLIC).

Keywords: Perona-Malik model · KMLS2-gradient threshold estimator · mammography images

1 Introduction

Mammograms are images with low contrast and a complicated structured background generally contaminated by some noise. At the same time, mammograms are a very important non-invasive tests for early detection of breast cancer, a disease that, according to the World Health Organization, affects more than 2

Y. HernÃ¡ndez Heredia et al. (Eds.): IWAIPR 2023, LNCS 14335, pp. 412–423, 2024.
https://doi.org/10.1007/978-3-031-49552-6_35

billion women every year. It is considered, after lung cancer, the second leading cause of death from cancer among women [9]. In 2018 in Cuba 1519 of the 3748 women diagnosed were fatal victims of the disease. This represents the 40% of the cases diagnosed that year[1]. Therefore, it is important to develop algorithms that improve the quality of mammograms so that specialists can make accurate diagnoses. Image smoothing is one of the most common tasks in image processing. It is performed with the aim of improve image quality by some criteria, mostly to remove noise within the image. In this work, we are interested in image-smoothing algorithms able to remove noise while preserving edges defining the boundaries of objects at small and large scales. This is particularly important as a previous step for edge detection and image segmentation.

Among the partial differential equations (PDE) based image smoothing methods, Perona and Malik [11] proposed a nonlinear diffusion-based algorithm that overcomes the disadvantages of linear diffusion, such as blurring or dislocating the edges in the image. Nonlinear anisotropic diffusion is an image smoothing method (filtering) that preserves the position of edges. In the seminal work [11], a nonlinear PDE with a variable diffusion coefficient was proposed to model the diffusion process. The diffusion coefficient $c(x, y, t) = g(\|\nabla I(x, y, t)\|)$ was chosen as an appropriate function of the gradient of the pixel intensity function $\nabla I(x, y, t)$.

Different expressions for the diffusion coefficient have been proposed in order to achieve better performance in edge preservation, see for instance Table 1 in [3]. All the given expressions for c depend on a parameter k, called the contrast or gradient threshold parameter, which has great influence on edge preservation. Few studies have focused on estimating the contrast parameter k. The simplest approach is to use a constant k, with the disadvantage of applying smoothing with equal intensity at each iteration. Some methods to decrease k in each iteration and thus maintain the condition $\|\nabla I\| > k$ to preserve the edges, can be consulted in [3,7,13].

Closely related to our work is the proposal in [3] where a new method, based on Partition and Adjustment, to estimate k for grayscale images is presented. This method, called KMLS, uses the clustering K-means algorithm to partition the set of pixels P in the images according to the magnitude of the gradient of the intensity function in each of them. Given a specific expression of the diffusion coefficient and considering this partition an appropriate value for the parameter k is obtained using the least-squares curve fitting method. However, KMLS does not behave well for all types of images, including mammograms [7].

In this work a new method, which is a modification of the one presented in [3], for gradient threshold parameter estimation is proposed. Different methods for estimating the gradient threshold parameter and their influence on edge detection are also compared. The Simple Linear Iterative Clustering (SLIC) algorithm is used as a first step to partition the set of pixels in the images allowing to consider local changes of the intensity function gradient.

---

[1] https://salud.msp.gob.cu/un-diagnostico-a-tiempo-puede-establecer-la-diferencia/.

2 Image Smoothing by Diffusion

Diffusion is a physical process that balances concentration differences without creating or destroying mass. In image processing, we can identify the concentration with the intensity of the gray value at a certain pixel. Isotropic or *homogeneous* diffusion is defined by a constant diffusion coefficient over the entire image domain. Homogeneous diffusion smoothing changes the intensity of every pixel in the same way, independent of the gradient of the intensity function at its location. This has a similar effect as the application of a Gaussian filter $G_\sigma(x,y) = (1/(2\pi\sigma^2))e^{-(x^2+y^2)/2\sigma^2}$ with successively larger σ values. It is known that Gaussian smoothing, besides reducing noise, also blurs edges making identification of them difficult [14].

The Gaussian smoothing of images may also be viewed as the evolving solution of a PDE

$$\frac{\partial I\left(x,y,t\right)}{\partial t} - c\Delta I\left(x,y,t\right) = 0$$

where the time-scale relationship is given by $\sigma = \sqrt{t}$ [14]. To avoid the blurring of the edges that occurs when performing isotropic diffusion over an image Perona and Malik [11] proposed the non linear PDE model given by

$$\frac{\partial I\left(x,y,t\right)}{\partial t} - \operatorname{div}\left(c\left(x,y,t\right)\nabla I\left(x,y,t\right)\right) = 0, \text{ in } \Omega \times (0,T) \tag{1}$$

$$c\left(x,y,t\right)\left(\nabla I\left(x,y,t\right)\cdot \mathbf{n}\right) = 0, \text{ in } \partial\Omega \times (0,T) \tag{2}$$

$$I\left(x,y,0\right) = I_0\left(x,y\right), \text{ in } \Omega \tag{3}$$

where $\Omega \subset \mathbb{R}^2$, div represents the divergence operator, $I(x,y,0)$ and $I(x,y,t)$ are respectively the original and in time t smoothed image intensity function and $\mathbf{n}$ is the normal direction. In the following $I(x,y,t) = I_t(x,y)$.

The diffusion coefficient in (1) is chosen as $c(x,y,t) = g(\|\nabla I_t(x,y)\|)$ where g is a function of the gradient of the intensity function suitable to control the diffusion near the edges. In [11] $g_1(s) = \frac{1}{1+\frac{s^2}{k^2}}$, $g_2(s) = e^{(\frac{-s^2}{2k^2})}$, $s = \|\nabla I_t(x,y)\|$ were proposed. Both functions g_1 and g_2 depend on the parameter k, the contrast or gradient threshold parameter.

As Perona and Malik remark, their model is ill posed [5,11]. However, the authors in [15] proved that a standard spatial finite-difference discretization is sufficient to transform the model into a well-posed system of nonlinear ordinary differential equations.

2.1 The Gradient Threshold in the Diffusion Coefficient

Many interesting variations of the Perona-Malik model have been proposed, most of them related to the regularization of the model considering the introduction of new expressions for the diffusion coefficient, see for instance [6,14]. This coefficient characterizes the diffusion process and the goal is to carry on the smoothing preferentially inside regions defined by edges. The diffusion coefficient also works as a time stopping function. All known expressions for it depend on the gradient threshold k in such a way that in those regions of the image where $\|\nabla I\| > k$, the smoothing effect is weaker and therefore the edges are preserved. Where $\|\nabla I\| < k$ the smoothing effect is stronger.

It can be stated that k is a parameter with great influence in edge preserving. With the same number of iterations the result of the diffusion process for different values of k is also different. If we increase the value of k, the diffusion process blurs the image, removing the details. During diffusion, as the image gets smoothed, the norm of the gradient decreases. Then the parameter k that controls the diffusion rate must be readjusted at each iteration to avoid smoothing over edges. At the same time, for low contrast images as mammograms, k has to be chosen considering not only global but local changes of the intensity function gradient.

Considering the previous facts in this work we propose a diffusion process by regions dividing the image using the SLIC segmentation algorithm [2]. As proposed in [3], where a method based on K-means clustering and least square fitting (KMLS) to estimate k was introduced, the gradient threshold k should also depends on time (iteration). Although the method in [3] shows good results for Natural Images, its performance for mammograms is very poor [7]. The goal of the present paper is to overcome the limitations of the KLMS method for gradient threshold selection of [3] for mammogram images. We also compare our method with others for k estimation.

3 Estimating the Gradient Threshold for Mammograms

In the literature there are different methods for gradient threshold k estimation customized for different classes of images. In this article we select some of them with the aim of verifying their effectiveness for mammograms and comparison with our proposal.

In order to decrease the value of k for each iteration and thus maintain the condition $\|\nabla I\| > \kappa$ to preserve edges, two alternative methods are presented in [13]. The first is known as the p-norm, where the threshold value is calculated as $\kappa = \sigma \cdot \|I_t(x,y)\|_p/(n \cdot m)$ and σ is a constant proportional to the average intensity of the image. Because this value is too high, adaptive scaling of an image with n rows and m columns is used. The second method presented in [13] was based on a morphological approach. If the "open-close" difference is considered as the quantization parameter, then κ must be at least equal to the averaged noise amplitude value.

Given an image I_t with n rows and m columns, and given a structuring element st (usually 3×3 or 5×5), we can estimate κ as follows:

$$\kappa = \sum_{(x,y)\in I_t} \frac{(I_t(x,y) \circ st)}{n \cdot m} - \sum_{(x,y)\in I_t} \frac{(I_t(x,y) \bullet st)}{n \cdot m},$$

where the symbols "$\circ$" and "$\bullet$" represent the open and close operation respectively.

Another method to estimate k is the noise estimator (noise), initially described by [4] and later used by [11]. In this method, a histogram of the absolute values of the gradient in the entire image is calculated, and k is set to be equal to 90% of its integral value at each iteration.

The algorithm called KMLS in [3] updates the gradient threshold in each iteration. By applying K-means clustering, the set of pixels P is partitioned into three subsets: P_1, a subset of pixels that do not belong to the edges of the image; P_3 subset of pixels belonging to the edges of the image; and $P_2 = P \backslash (P_1 \cup P_3)$, a subset of pixels called a fuzzy set because its elements can be weak or not edges at all. From these sets, the points used to approximate the contrast parameter k are selected through a least-squares curve fitting of the curve defined by the diffusion coefficient $g_2(s)$ given above. Let i_{21} and i_{31} be the minimal values of the intensity gradients at pixels that belong to P_2 and P_3 respectively. To control the smoothing strength, two thresholds are defined: *wep* and *sep* for weak and strong edge preservation, respectively. In practice, these thresholds are the values of the diffusion coefficient $g_2(s)$ that we want to correspond to the values of the gradient of intensities i_{21} and i_{31}. The pixels in P_3 (strong edges) are smoothed with a strength less than *sep* and the pixels of weak edges are smoothed with a strength less than *wep*; therefore, *sep* should be taken as close as possible to zero.

On the other hand, the threshold *wep* should be selected by taking information from the image. Nevertheless, this seems to be a pretty hard work and requires experimenting in a specific image class to obtain some values from statistics. With the points (i_{21}, wep) and (i_{31}, sep), the contrast parameter k is obtained using Least Square fitting [3]. As already mentioned this estimator has problems with mammogram images [7].

3.1 Problems with the Gradient Threshold Estimator KMLS for Mammogram Images

The KMLS algorithm in [3] develops the process of image partitioning according to K-means with $K = 3$. Two of the clusters are defined by the minimum and maximum values of the intensity gradient of the $I_t(x, y)$ image. The centroid of the third cluster is defined as the mean of the centroids of the minimum and maximum clusters. Mammograms are low contrast images owing to the low doses of radiation to which the patient is subjected, in this case the third cluster can be empty. Under such conditions, the performance of the KMLS method is very poor. This problem is even worse if the KMLS method is applied in a separated way by regions of the image.

The low contrast is also a problem for any global (on the entire image) gradient threshold estimation method. Being k a unique value for the whole image such methods cannot discern between regions within which differences in intensity values are small but which greatly differ from each other on the global scale. Therefore, in one of the areas with subtle differences in pixels intensity values, the diffusion process will be strong, thus eliminating edges apparently weak on a global scale but strong on a local one. This fact led to the idea of using a simple image partitioning method other than K-means as a first step before running the diffusion process. For this purpose the SLIC algorithm will be used [7]. Based on this algorithm some other modifications to the KMLS algorithm are proposed.

3.2 KMLS2, a Modified Version of KMLS for AD Smoothing of Mammogram Images

Preserving the original ideas of Partitioning and Fitting we develop a new algorithm called KMLS2. To obtain the partition of the set of pixels of the image, K-means will be executed for $K = 2$ in order to solve the previously stated problem. Thus, there are only two non empty clusters of the intensity gradient set P, denoted as G_1 and G_2. The method of selecting the magnitudes of the gradient to perform the least-squares fitting for the function $g_2(s)$ is also modified. The gradient magnitude values i_{21} and i_{31} are selected as the values of the final centroid of the K-means for sets G_1 and G_2 respectively. To illustrate this procedure, we estimate the contrast parameter for the coefficient expression g_2 as in [3] (see Sect. 3).

Step1: Apply K-means to get the partition in two clusters, $\{G_1, G_2\}$ of the set P of pixels of the image, where:

- Initial Means

$$\mu_1 = min\{\|\nabla I\|_{(x,y)} \ : \ (x, y) \in P\} \text{ for } G_1,$$

$$\mu_2 = max\{\|\nabla I\|_{(x,y)} \ : \ (x, y) \in P\} \text{ for } G_2,$$

- Operations

  (i) Distance: $d((x, y), \mu_i) = |\|\nabla I\|_{(x,y)} - \mu_i|,\ i = 1, 2.$
  (ii) Add:$a((x_1, y_1), (x_2, y_2)) = \|\nabla I\|_{(x_1,y_1)} + \|\nabla I\|_{(x_2,y_2)}$.

Step2: Make the Least Squares fitting of $g_2(\|\nabla I_t(x, y)\|) = e^{-\left[\frac{\|\nabla I_t(x,y)\|}{k}\right]^2}$. By linearization we obtain

$$S = \| \ln f - G\|_2 = \min_k \sum_{j=1}^{n} \left[\ln f(x_j) - \left(\frac{-x_j^2}{k^2}\right)\right]^2 \tag{4}$$

where $G = \ln g_2$, $x_j = \|\nabla I_t(x_j, y_j)\|$, $n = 2$, having the points (i_{21}, wep) and (i_{31}, sep). The gradient magnitude values i_{21} and i_{31} are selected as the value of the final centroid of K-means for the set G_1 and G_2 respectively. Then, solving the equation $\frac{dS}{dk} = 0$, we obtain the following expression for the contrast parameter k

$$k = \sqrt{\frac{-(i_{21}^4 + i_{31}^4)}{\ln(wep)i_{21}^2 + \ln(sep)i_{31}^2}}. \tag{5}$$

Because the diffusion process will be carried out by regions, one of these regions may also have very low contrast, that is, the values of the intensity gradient are almost identical. In this case, the initial centroids of the clusters in K-means are equal ($\mu_1 = \mu_2$). The fitting phase is then performed using only one point, $(i_0^{'}, g_2(i_0^{'}))$, with $i_0^{'} = \mu_1 = \mu_2$. To choose $g_2(i_0^{'})$ we take $MaxG$ and $MinG$ as the largest and lowest gradients of the entire image, respectively. Then, if $MaxG - i_0^{'} < i_0^{'} - MinG$ holds, the *sep* threshold is used to fit $g_2(s)$ to create a weak smoothing process. In contrast, *wep* was used for a strong smoothing process. In the case $i_0{'} = 0$ then $k = 0$ and the function $g_2(s)$ is undefined. However, because $i_0{'} = 0$ the coefficient $c(x, y, t) = 1$ and we do not need to fit the curve. This is equivalent to isotropic diffusion in a homogeneous image (without contrast or edges), which is fine because there are no characteristics to preserve.

4 Experimental Environment and Results

In this section, we use the Perona-Malik AD model with different methods to estimate the contrast parameter, using the diffusion coefficient given by g_2 to smooth the mammogram images. After that the classical edge detector Scharr [12] is applied to obtain an edge image. This edge detector was chosen based on previous experimentation with 20 images from the Inbreast database [10] as shown in Table 1. The Perona-Malik equation (1) is solved by applying the same finite difference scheme as in [11].

The aim is to show how the previous filtering of the mammography image using AD significantly improves the subsequent edge images. Choosing a contrast parameter estimator with a better performance is also a goal. Because ground-truth edge images are only available for lesions known as masses, the images of the INbreast [10] database chosen for comparison are those where this anomaly appears.

To assess the quality of our AD-KMLS2 method we used two quantitative performance error measures based on distance: i) the well-known Root Mean Square Error (RMSE) [8] and ii) an alternative formulation of Pratt's figure of merit (PFoM*) [3]. PFoM* is defined as $PFoM{*}(RI, GT) = 1 - PFoM(RI, GT)$, see [1] for PFoM.

For the experimentation with AD-KMLS2 we use a combination of values $sep = 0.05$ and $wep = 0.3$ alternatively fixed. In Fig. 1 and Fig. 2, we can see the evolution of the objective performance measures as a function of the values of *sep* and *wep* respectively for the Scharr edge detector. Figure 1 shows, for the fixed value $wep = 0.3$, the Pratt and RMSE measures as a function of *sep* values, for 10 of the images in the database Inbreast. As can be seen, for some images, the variation in the measured values is very soft, and its differences for different values of *sep* are very small. However, for other fixed images, the variation in the measured values can be very different in general, and between different images it also changes slightly. The shapes of the graphs of Pratt and the RMSE measures as a function of *sep* values for a fixed value of *wep* are very similar. Nevertheless, the value $sep = 0.05$ provides a good value of the measure for nine of the 10 images. In Fig. 2 we show the objective performance measures as a function of

Table 1. Comparison of four edge detectors based on RMSE and PFoM quality measures on 20 Inbreast images.

ImageID	RMSE				PFoM			
	Scharr	Sobel	Farid	Prewitt	Scharr	Sobel	Farid	Prewitt
53586896	0.7089	0.709	0.7093	0.709	0.0528	0.0528	0.0528	0.0528
50997515	0.6885	0.6886	0.6886	0.6887	0.0499	0.0499	0.0499	0.0499
53582656	0.4825	0.4829	0.4858	0.4831	0.0251	0.0251	0.0251	0.0251
53580804	0.6972	0.6973	0.6975	0.6974	0.0511	0.0511	0.0511	0.0511
50999008	0.7372	0.7372	0.7384	0.7372	0.0567	0.0567	0.0568	0.0567
51049053	0.5267	0.5267	0.5273	0.5267	0.0298	0.0298	0.0298	0.0298
51048738	0.6613	0.6613	0.6625	0.6613	0.0462	0.0462	0.0462	0.0462
51049107	0.4943	0.4943	0.495	0.4943	0.0264	0.0264	0.0264	0.0264
50999432	0.5355	0.5356	0.5355	0.5356	0.0308	0.0308	0.0308	0.0308
53581406	0.7899	0.7899	0.7921	0.79	0.0645	0.0645	0.0646	0.0645
50999459	0.7724	0.7726	0.7727	0.7727	0.0619	0.0619	0.062	0.0619
53582683	0.5619	0.5623	0.5652	0.5626	0.0338	0.0338	0.0338	0.0338
53587014	0.6152	0.6152	0.6155	0.6152	0.0402	0.0402	0.0402	0.0402
53586960	0.608	0.6081	0.6083	0.6082	0.0394	0.0394	0.0394	0.0394
53587663	0.4204	0.4205	0.4215	0.4205	0.0192	0.0192	0.0192	0.0193
51048765	0.6625	0.6625	0.6633	0.6625	0.0463	0.0463	0.0464	0.0463
53580858	0.7747	0.7749	0.7749	0.7749	0.0623	0.0623	0.0623	0.0623
53586869	0.6427	0.6427	0.6433	0.6427	0.0438	0.0438	0.0438	0.0438
53581460	0.6871	0.6871	0.6885	0.6872	0.0497	0.0497	0.0497	0.0497
50998981	0.7159	0.716	0.7171	0.716	0.0537	0.0537	0.0537	0.0537

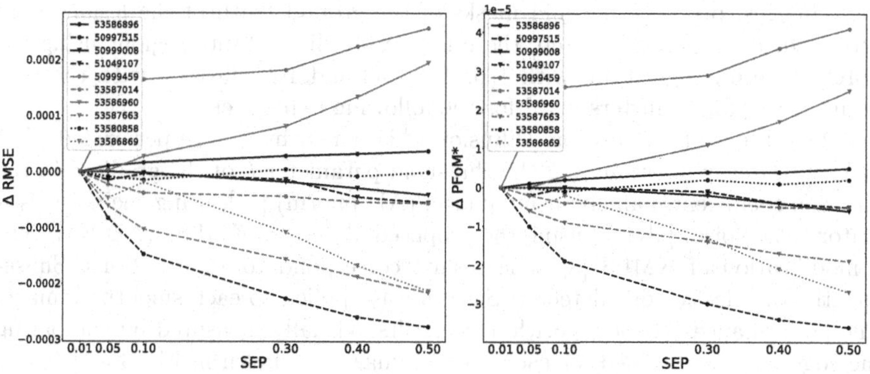

Fig. 1. Evolution of the objective performance measures as a function of sep values, for a fixed value $wep = 0.3$. Results of the Scharr edge detector for ten images of INbreast. Left: RMSE measure. Right: PFoM* measure.

the values of *wep*, for a fixed value $sep = 0.05$. Again, the graphs of the Pratt and RMSE measures were very similar. Reasoning in the same way, we choose $wep = 0.3$.

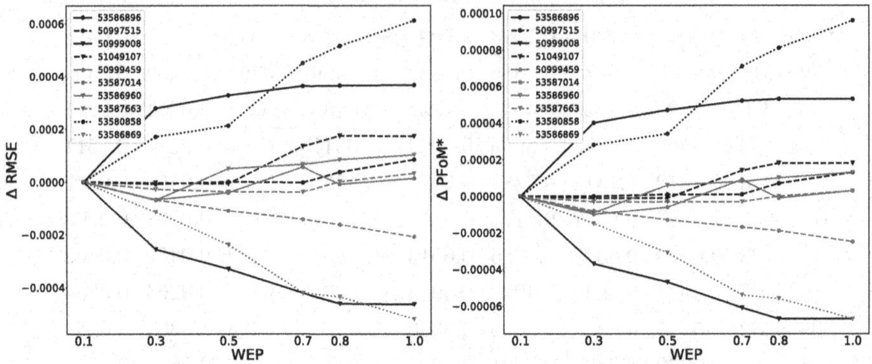

Fig. 2. Evolution of the objective performance measures as a function of wep values, for a fixed value $sep = 0.05$. Results of the Scharr edgedetector for ten images of INbreast. Left: RMSE measure. Right: PFoM* measure.

4.1 Results and Discussion

Using the same 20 images from the Inbreast database [10], the crop function was applied to each image to reduce unwanted external areas of the breast. These are the only images in the database that can be used to assess the influence of AD with our method of gradient threshold estimation, since they are the only ones that provide us with the edges of lesions, in this case those known as masses. For these images, pixel meshes and masks of the ground truth of the lesions were extracted. In the previous step, the images were divided into regions using the SLIC clustering algorithm, with $1, 6, 12, 20, 30$ and 100 clusters, with the best results being for 6 clusters, used for the following experiments.

Three types of Anisotropic Diffusion (AD) smoothing were performed, that differ in the way of estimating the threshold parameter k of the gradient in the diffusion coefficient, namely: using pnorm (AD-pnorm) [13], using the noise estimator (AD-Noise) [4], and using the proposed algorithm KMLS2 (AD-KMLS2), a modification of KMLS [3]. The results correspond to 10 iterations. Subsequently, the classic edge detector, Scharr, was applied to each smoothed image. The performances of the algorithms were first visually measured by comparing the edge images obtained for each filtered image, as shown in Fig. 3 and Fig. 4. The quality of the edge images using AD was always better than that when pre-smoothing was not applied. In both figures, the difference between AD-KMLS and AD-Noise is visually the same; in the latter, the edges are thicker. However, using objective quality measures, the image ID53586896 AD-KMLS has a better

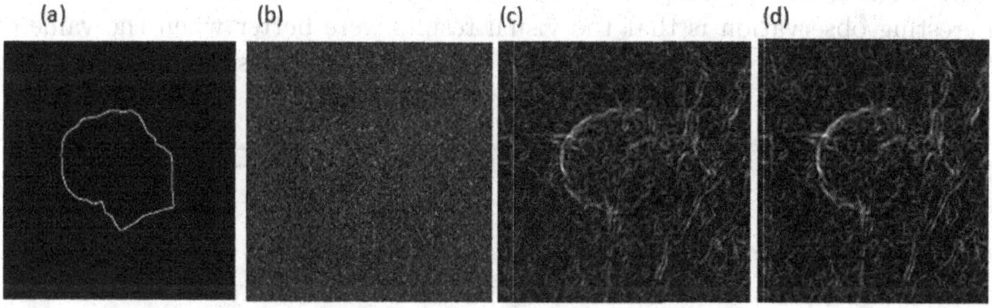

Fig. 3. Mammogram ID53586896 (a) Mask of the anomaly ground truth edge image, edge images: (b) without smoothing (c) and(d) after AD-KMLS2 and AD-Noise respectively.

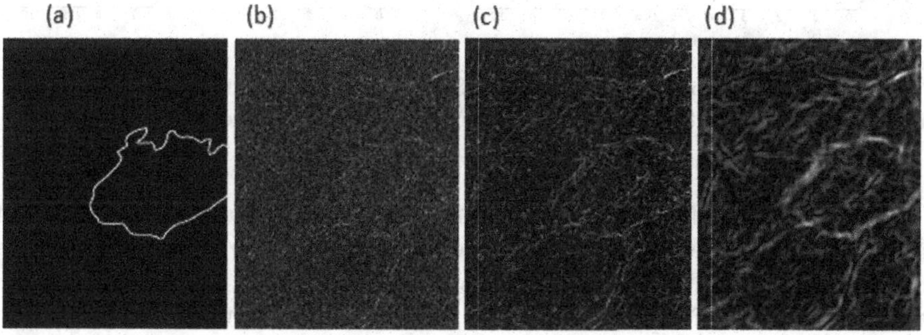

Fig. 4. Mammogram ID53587663 (a) Mask of the anomaly ground truth edge image, edge images: (b) without smoothing (c) and(d) after AD-KMLS2 and AD-Noise respectively.

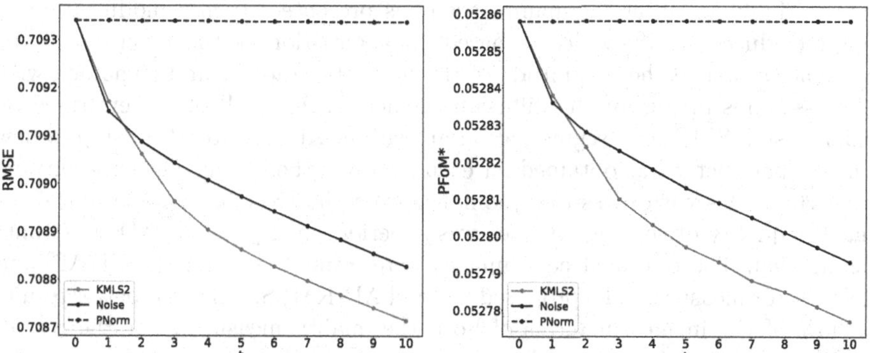

Fig. 5. Objective performance measure RMSE(left), PFoM*(right), applied to the edge image of ID53586896. Smoothing by AD-KMLS2, AD-pnorm and AD-Noise.

result (Fig. 5), and for image ID53587663, the better result is for AD-Noise. An interesting observation is that the visual results were better when the value of the objective measures was close to 0.06 for PFoM* and close to 0.7 for RMSE.

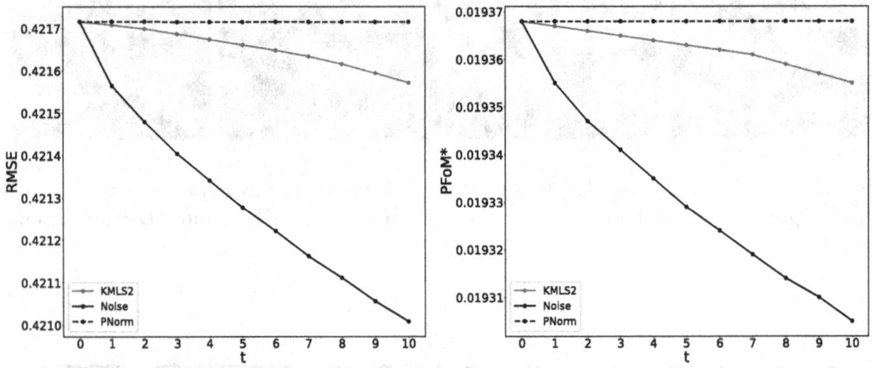

Fig. 6. Objective performance measure RMSE(left), PFoM*(right), applied to the edge image of ID53587663. Smoothing by AD-KMLS2, AD-pnorm and AD-Noise.

If we apply our algorithm (AD-KMLS2), we obtain better results for 45% of the images in terms of the two quality measures. However, when the results with AD-KMLS are not the best, the difference is of the order of least equal 5×10^{-5} compared with AD-Noise, which is the other estimator with good results (see Fig. 6).

5 Conclusions

In this paper, a method for estimating the gradient threshold KMLS2 in the Perona-Malik AD filter for mammograms is presented. It is a modification to that introduced in [3], which is based on a partition of the pixel set of the image according to the magnitude of the intensity gradient and combined with a least-squares fitting for the diffusion coefficient. AD-KMLS2 is performed by regions using SLIC as a segmentation algorithm. At each iteration step, a new contrast parameter was obtained for each region of the image. The experiments, using 20 images with mass-like anomalies from the INbreast database, showed that the quality of the edge images was superior when previous AD smoothing was applied. The obtained edge images were evaluated using the PFoM* and RMSE error measures. The proposed method AD-KMLS2 achieved better results for 45% of the images in terms of both the quality measures. For the rest of the images, AD-Noise worked better, although the difference according to the measurements was of the order of least equal 5×10^{-5} and visually the differences were barely perceptible. The best results were achieved using the Scharr edge detector.

Acknowledgements. We thank the Research Project "Métodos numéricos para problemas en múltiples escalas", Ciencias Básicas y Naturales, CITMA, Cuba.

References

1. Abdou, I.E., Pratt, W.K.: Quantitative design and evaluation of enhancement/thresholding edge detectors. Proc. IEEE **67**(5), 753–763 (1979)
2. Achanta, R., Shaji, A., Smith, K., Lucchi, A., Fua, P., Süsstrunk, S.: Slic superpixels compared to state-of-the-art superpixel methods. IEEE Trans. Pattern Anal. Mach. Intell. **34**(11), 2274–2282 (2012)
3. Borroto-Fernández, M., González-Hidalgo, M., León-Mecías, A.: New estimation method of the contrast parameter for the Perona-Malik diffusion equation. Comput. Methods Biomechan. Biomed. Eng. Imaging Vis. **4**(3–4), 238–252 (2016)
4. Canny, J.: A computational approach to edge detection. IEEE Trans. Pattern Anal. Mach. Intell. **6**, 679–698 (1986)
5. Catté, F., Lions, P.L., Morel, J.M., Coll, T.: Image selective smoothing and edge detection by nonlinear diffusion. SIAM J. Numer. Anal. **29**(1), 182–193 (1992)
6. Gilboa, G., Sochen, N., Zeevi, Y.Y.: Forward-and-backward diffusion processes for adaptive image enhancement and denoising. IEEE Trans. Image Process. **11**(7), 689–703 (2002)
7. Hidalgo-Gato, E.: Estimación del pámetro de contraste para el suavizado por Difusión Anisotrópica aplicado por regiones. Bachelor's thesis, University de La Habana (2015)
8. Hodson, T.O.: Root-mean-square error (RMSE) or mean absolute error (MAE): when to use them or not. Geoscientific Model Dev. **15**(14), 5481–5487 (2022)
9. McGuire, S.: World cancer report 2014. Geneva, Switzerland: world health organization, international agency for research on cancer, who press, 2015. Adv. Nutrition **7**(2), 418–419 (2016)
10. Moreira, I.C., Amaral, I., Domingues, I., Cardoso, A., Cardoso, M.J., Cardoso, J.S.: INbreast: toward a full-field digital mammographic database. Acad. Radiol. **19**(2), 236–248 (2012)
11. Perona, P., Malik, J.: Scale-space and edge detection using anisotropic diffusion. IEEE Trans. Pattern Anal. Mach. Intell. **12**(7), 629–639 (1990)
12. Scharr, H.: Optimal operators in digital image processing. Ph.D. thesis, Ruprecht-Karls-Universität Heidelberg (2000)
13. Voci, F., Eiho, S., Sugimoto, N., Sekibuchi, H.: Estimating the gradient in the Perona-Malik equation. IEEE Signal Process. Mag. **21**(3), 39–65 (2004)
14. Weickert, J.: Anisotropic Diffusion in Image Processing, vol. 1. Teubner Stuttgart (1998)
15. Weickert, J., Benhamouda, B.: A semidiscrete nonlinear scale-space theory and its relation to the Perona—Malik paradox. In: Solina, F., Kropatsch, W.G., Klette, R., Bajcsy, R. (eds.) Advances in Computer Vision. ACS, pp. 1–10. Springer, Vienna (1997). https://doi.org/10.1007/978-3-7091-6867-7_1

Offline Writer Identification and Verification Evaluation Protocols for Spanish Database

Ernesto Carballea Alonso, Yoanna Martínez-Díaz, and Heydi Méndez-Vázquez(✉)

Advanced Technology Application Center (CENATAV), 7A ♯21406, Siboney, Playa, Havana, Cuba
{ecarballea,ymartinez,hmendez}@cenatav.co.cu

Abstract. Writer identification based on text images is a well studied topic in Biometrics. Several methods have been proposed for this task. Despite the results achieved, current methods are limited in their ability to handle diverse languages, writing styles, and document types. In this work, we proposed relevant verification and open/closed-set evaluation protocols to assess the performance of writer identification methods on CENATAV-HTR dataset, containing Spanish handwritten documents. Under these evaluation protocols, we evaluate and analyze the effectiveness of a state-of-the-art Recurrent Neural Network originally proposed for English writer identification. The obtained results demonstrated that the models trained on English are not suitable to recognize writers in Spanish and thus they need to be adjusted or finetuned for this particular language. All text images and evaluation protocols are made available for future research in this topic.

Keywords: writer identification · writer verification · Spanish dataset

1 Introduction

Automatic writer identification is a biometric behavioral technique that enables the identification of an author or writer of a document by analyzing the patterns in their writing style. It has been widely used in forensic document examination [7,14] and historical document analysis [5,6]. Several approaches have been proposed to automatically identify authors of documents [15]. They can be classified into two categories: (1) online and (2) offline methods. Online writer identification depends on a touchscreen, mouse or electronic pen, and analyze factors such as angle, pressure and writing speed [19]. On the other hand, offline writer identification aims at identifying the writer from scanned images, dealing with spatial attributes like words, paragraphs, characters and lines, and it is considered a more challenging task [16].

Earlier methods for offline writer identification are based on texture and statistical features, including stroke width, angle of inclination, letter or word

Y. HernÃąndez Heredia et al. (Eds.): IWAIPR 2023, LNCS 14335, pp. 424–432, 2024.
https://doi.org/10.1007/978-3-031-49552-6_36

frequency, which require a large number of samples per writer in order to obtain a reliable recognition [2,4,12]. In recent years, deep learning techniques have gained a lot of attention for automatic writer identification. Different well-known architectures such as CaffeNet, AlexNet, VGG and ResNet have been used and evaluated on this task with promising results [5,8,17]. In particular, Recurrent Neural Networks (RNNs) have shown to be effective for automatic writer identification [9,22,23]. RNNs can capture long-term dependencies in the input sequence [20], thus they are well suited for sequential data such as handwriting samples, where the order of the strokes or characters is crucial.

Most of existing writer identification methods have been tested mainly on English, Arabic and Chinese documents [15], but there is a lack of standard datasets and evaluation protocols on more varied languages. Although it is claimed that deep learning based methods can be used for writer identification regardless of the language, the accuracy of the models can be affected by the handwriting styles of different languages. Different languages have variation in handwriting styles, and the models may need to be adjusted to capture the unique handwriting features specific to a particular language. To the best of our knowledge, no studies have been conducted on the performance of state-of-the-art writer identification methods on Spanish, the third most used language in the world. Recently, a first version of a Spanish handwritten text database, CENATAV-HTR, was introduced in [3], and made available upon request. The original database was proposed for handwriting text recognition. In this paper, we propose relevant evaluation protocols for CENATAV-HTR dataset, supporting writer verification and open/closed-set writer identification tasks. Under these protocols, we evaluate the performance of the recently proposed Global-Context Residual Recurrent Neural Networks (GR-RNN), that achieves state-of-the-art results on English datasets [9]. Experimental results show that existing methods are dependant to the language at hand.

2 Recurrent Neural Networks for Writer Identification

Recurrent neural networks have become popular for writer identification [9,22, 23]. They are designed to handle sequential data, which is precisely the nature of handwriting involving a continuous, temporal sequence of strokes that creates each character, word, and sentence. This sequential nature of handwriting makes it challenging for traditional machine learning methods to directly extract features from it. Recurrent neural networks, on the other hand, can capture the temporal dependencies between the sequential strokes, learn the complex relationships between the inputs, and produce high-level representations that make writer identification possible. Additionally, recurrent neural networks allow for the processing of variable-length sequences, thus they can handle varying lengths of text, which is common in real-life scenarios.

Long Short-Term Memory (LSTM) networks are ones of the most widely used for sequence-to-sequence learning. They have been applied to represent temporal patterns in handwriting, in order to identify writers [22]. Gated Recurrent Units

(GRUs), an improved version of the simple RNN, are also specialized for handling sequential data and have been used to extract features from stacks of input images in the context of writer identification [21]. Bidirectional Recurrent Neural Networks (Bi-RNNs) process input sequentially, in both forward and backward directions, in order to capture context information from both, past and future surrounding strokes [1].

Recently, the Global-Context Residual Recurrent Neural Network (GR-RNN) framework was proposed for writer identification [9]. It jointly employs global features from the entire character and contextual information from neighboring characters in a handwritten text. The method uses residual connections and convolution layers in a recurrent neural network architecture, to build a model capable of extracting significant features from the handwriting. It then applies multi-stage attention mechanisms that allows the model to selectively attend to relevant information, effectively highlighting unique characteristics of the style of each writer. The network consists of four blocks and each block has two convolutional layers and one max-pooling layer. It receives as input an image of a written word normalized to 64×128 pixels. The obtained feature vector has a dimension of 256. GR-RNN has demonstrated robust performance in identifying writers across multiple datasets, surpassing the accuracy of previous state-of-the-art approaches. In this paper, we have selected this method to evaluate and analyze their performance under the proposed evaluation protocols for writer verification and identification in Spanish handwritten documents.

3 Database and Evaluation Protocols

The CENATAV-HTR Spanish dataset was firstly introduced in [3]. The current version of the dataset[1] contains 930 document images, segmented into 60,996 handwritten words in Spanish, from 170 writers. The documents were filled on two sessions, with more than one week of difference between both sessions. Each author wrote three pages on every session. Every text contains about three to six sentences with at least 50 words. The filled documents were scanned with an HP scanner at a resolution of 300 dpi and a color depth of 24 bits. The images were saved in JPG format. There are 30 writers who complete only one session (3 documents), and the rest of them, 140, complete both sessions (6 documents). In Fig. 1 sample images for the same writers and different writers are illustrated.

Documents from 150 writers were used to conform the training set, including the ones which correspond to the 30 writers with only 3 pages. From those subjects that have 6 documents, 4 pages were randomly selected for training, leaving the two remaining pages for testing (one from each session). In the case of writers with a single session, one page was used for training and the other two were reserved for testing. In total, 31,523 words extracted from 510 pages were used for training. Verification and Identification evaluation protocols were designed using the remaining documents.

[1] https://github.com/ecarballea/CENATAV-HTR.

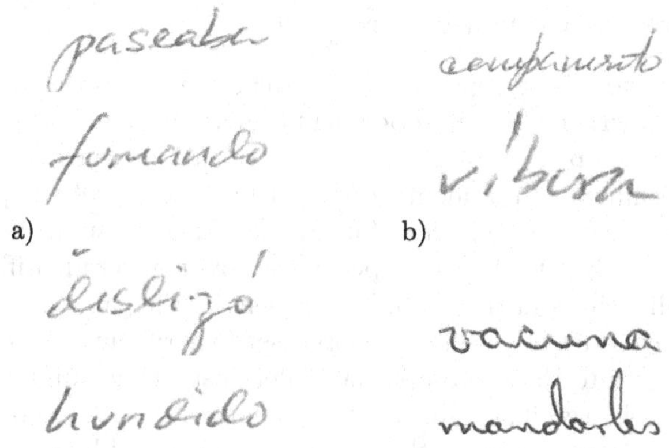

Fig. 1. Sample images from a) the same writer and b) different writers.

3.1 Verification Evaluation Protocol

Writer verification is the process of determining whether two documents or words have been written by the same author. The defined evaluation protocol considers two possible scenarios: "seen" and "unseen" writers, which relies on whether the word samples to be compared, correspond to writers that were used for training or not. In the case of the "seen" scenario, the experiment is splitted also into two cases, taking into account if the compared words were written under the "same session" or on "different sessions".

We conform all possible comparisons among all available words from each writer, and we have randomly selected a number of genuine and impostor comparisons for each experiment as summarized on Table 1.

Table 1. Summary of the number of genuine and impostor comparisons on all verification experiments.

	same session	different sessions
seen scenario	5000	5000
unseen scenario	320	

The Area Under the Curve (AUC) and the Equal-Error Rate (EER) were used as performance measures for writer verification experiments. The EER is the point where false acceptance rate and false rejection rate are equal. The AUC is the area under the Receiver Operating Characteristic (ROC) curve, which is a graphical representation of the true positives and false positives values at different threshold settings for a given model. It provides a single scalar value that represents the overall performance of the model across different threshold settings, the higher the best.

3.2 Identification Evaluation Protocol

Writer identification is the process of searching for suspected writers in a database of handwritten sample documents, given a questioned document. It can be divided into open-set or closed-set identification. Open-set identification consists of determining if the identity of a writer in the probe is present in the gallery or not and, if it is the case, find the top-k most similar writers in the gallery. Closed-set identification is a special case of open-set identification, which assumes that all writers in the probe are present in the gallery.

In order to conduct open-set and closed-set experiments, we randomly partition the test set into three subsets: the gallery set, the genuine probe set, and the impostors probe set. The gallery set is conformed by 170 writers (150 "seen" and 20 "unseen"). Every writer in the gallery is represented by the average vector obtained by six words, the most representative ones from each of its documents. The genuine probe set is composed by 5100 word images from the same subjects included in the gallery, but with different samples: 3 random words from every document of the 150 "seen" writers (2700) and 20 random words from every document of the 20 "unseen" writers (2400). The impostor probe set, consists of 1380 word images from 16 additional writers that are not present in the gallery.

In the closed-set identification protocol, genuine probe set is evaluated against gallery, while in the open-set identification protocol, impostor probe set is also tested. For evaluating closed-set recognition performance, Rank-1, Rank-5 and Rank-10 is reported. In the case of the open-set scenario, we adopt the Detection and Identification Rate (DIR), at a fixed value of False Acceptance Rate (FAR). DIR measures the combined efficiency of detect the presence and correctly identify a biometric trait of a registered user. The higher DIR, the more effectively the system detects and identify a registered user.

4 Experimental Evaluation

In this section we evaluate the performance of GR-RNN on the defined Verification and Identification evaluation protocols for CENATAV-HTR dataset.

4.1 Implementation Details

The original implementation of GR-RNN model, on PyThorch framework, was used [9]. It was trained with the Adam optimizer. The weight decay was set to 0.0001 and the mini-batch size to 16. The initial learning rate was set to 0.0001 and a decay schedule (reduce to half) was applied at every 10 epochs. The model was trained with 50 epochs.

All word images were resized to a fixed size of 64×128 pixels, by keeping the aspect ratio without distortions. Padding is used if it is necessary and a simple translation augmentation method was applied to avoid positional bias in the data during training.

4.2 Model Training

In order to evaluate the generalization ability of GR-RNN method, besides the model trained on the CENATAV-HTR Spanish dataset, we have evaluated the same model trained on IAM [13], CVL [11], Firemaker [18] and CERUG-EN [10] English datasets, which were all evaluated in [9] and were made public available. The number of word images used for training in each case is summarized in Table 2.

Table 2. Number of training word images used on each dataset.

Training Dataset	Number of writers	Number of training images
IAM	657	56,432
CVL	310	62,406
Firemaker	250	25,256
CERUG-EN	105	5,702
CENATAV-HTR	170	31,523

4.3 Verification Results

In Table 3 we present the performance achieved by the GR-RNN in the Spanish dataset by using the proposed verification evaluation protocol. In order to analyze the impact of using models trained on different languages, we also evaluate the performance of GR-RNN trained on the IAM, CVL, Firemaker and CERUG-En datasets. As can be seen from the table, the best results are achieved with the model trained in the Spanish dataset (CENATAV-HTR). For the models trained on English datasets all writers are unseen, thus one expect a performance similar to the one obtained in the "unseen" scenario, however it can be seen that there is a drop-off on the performance. This indicates us that, the method is language dependent. As expected, the results obtained when the compared samples belong to the same session are better. From the results achieved it is also evident that the number of writers and images used for training have a great impact on the model performance.

Table 3. AUC (%) and EER (%) obtained under the proposed Verification evaluation protocol for the CENATAV-HTR dataset.

Training Dataset	IAM		CVL		Firemaker		CERUG-EN		CENATAV	
	AUC	EER	AUC	EER	AUC	EER	AUC	EER	AUC	EER
"seen" - same session	92.62	14.88	82.57	25.20	72.73	33.52	66.83	37.50	**97.64**	**7.97**
"seen" - different sessions	81.16	26.00	72.84	33.28	77.45	29.76	76.63	30.42	**91.16**	**16.74**
"unseen" - same session	85.60	21.87	72.40	37.18	72.76	31.87	76.29	30.62	**91.99**	**15.13**

4.4 Identification Results

Tables 4 and 5 present the performance on closed-set and open-set identification evaluation protocols, respectively. It can be seen in Table 4 that although the results at Rank-1 and Rank-5 are not so good, the model trained on the CENATAV-HTR database achieves a 93.25% of Recognition Rate at Rank-10. Also in this case the performance is degraded for the models trained on English datasets. The best results for the models trained on English are achieved for IAM, which contains the largest number of writers.

Table 5 shows impact of including impostor comparisons in the identification experiments, which is not usually considered on existing databases and evaluation protocols. Open-set identification performance significantly drops for low FAR values, but there is a remarkable difference between the model trained on Spanish with respect to those trained on English.

Table 4. Recognition Rates (%) at Rank-1, Rank-5 and Rank-10 under the proposed closed-set Identification evaluation protocol for CENATAV-HTR database.

Training Database	Rank-1	Rank-5	Rank-10
IAM	34.43	65.57	78.31
CVL	31.26	56.63	67.67
Firemaker	19.57	46.00	59.12
CERUG-EN	11.53	33.12	45.39
CENATAV-HTR	**59.35**	**85.98**	**93.25**

Table 5. DIR at Rank-1 for 1% and 10%FAR, under the proposed open-set Identification evaluation protocol for CENATAV-HTR database

Training Database	DIR@FAR = 1%	DIR@FAR = 10%
IAM	8.22	15.23
CVL	2.88	7.24
Firemaker	3.29	6.63
CERUG-EN	1.25	3.43
CENATAV-HTR	**19.25**	**36.43**

5 Conclusion

In this work, we designed relevant evaluation protocols for writer identification and verification in CENATAV-HTR, a database containing Spanish handwritten documents. A state-of-the-art writer identification method is evaluated under the proposed evaluation protocols and it is shown that existing methods need to be trained or finetuned on particular languages. It is also demonstrated the impact of the number of writers and word images used on models training. The proposal allows the research community to advance writer recognition methods under both unconstrained writer verification and open/closed-set identification scenarios. The evaluation protocols are made publicly available with this purpose.

References

1. Adak, C., Chaudhuri, B.B., Blumenstein, M.: Impact of struck-out text on writer identification. In: 2017 International Joint Conference on Neural Networks (IJCNN), pp. 1465–1471. IEEE (2017)
2. Bulacu, M., Schomaker, L.: Text-independent writer identification and verification using textural and allographic features. IEEE Trans. Pattern Anal. Mach. Intell. **29**(4), 701–717 (2007)
3. Carballea, E., Becerra-Riera, F., Martinez-Diaz, Y., Mendez-vazquez, H.: Reconocimiento automatico de textos manuscritos en idioma español basado en aprendizaje profundo. In: Conferencia Internacional en Ciencias Computacionales e Informaticas (CICCI'2022), pp. 1–9. InformaticaHabana (2022)
4. Christlein, V., Bernecker, D., Hönig, F., Maier, A., Angelopoulou, E.: Writer identification using GMM supervectors and exemplar-SVMs. Pattern Recogn. **63**, 258–267 (2017)
5. Cilia, N.D., De Stefano, C., Fontanella, F., Molinara, M., di Freca, A.S.: What is the minimum training data size to reliably identify writers in medieval manuscripts? Pattern Recogn. Lett. **129**, 198–204 (2020)
6. De Stefano, C., Maniaci, M., Fontanella, F., di Freca, A.S.: Layout measures for writer identification in mediaeval documents. Measurement **127**, 443–452 (2018)
7. Dhieb, T., Njah, S., Boubaker, H., Ouarda, W., Ayed, M.B., Alimi, A.M.: Towards a novel biometric system for forensic document examination. Comput. Secur. **97**, 101973 (2020)
8. Fiel, S., Sablatnig, R.: Writer identification and retrieval using a convolutional neural network. In: Azzopardi, G., Petkov, N. (eds.) CAIP 2015. LNCS, vol. 9257, pp. 26–37. Springer, Cham (2015). https://doi.org/10.1007/978-3-319-23117-4_3
9. He, S., Schomaker, L.: GR-RNN: global-context residual recurrent neural networks for writer identification. Pattern Recogn. **117**, 107975 (2021)
10. He, S., Wiering, M., Schomaker, L.: Junction detection in handwritten documents and its application to writer identification. Pattern Recogn. **48**(12), 4036–4048 (2015)
11. Kleber, F., Fiel, S., Diem, M., Sablatnig, R.: CVL-DataBase: an off-line database for writer retrieval, writer identification and word spotting. In: 2013 12th International Conference on Document Analysis and Recognition, pp. 560–564. IEEE (2013)
12. Lai, S., Zhu, Y., Jin, L.: Encoding pathlet and SIFT features with bagged VLAD for historical writer identification. IEEE Trans. Inf. Forensics Secur. **15**, 3553–3566 (2020)
13. Marti, U.V., Bunke, H.: The IAM-database: an English sentence database for offline handwriting recognition. Int. J. Doc. Anal. Recogn. **5**, 39–46 (2002). https://doi.org/10.1007/s100320200071
14. Pervouchine, V., Leedham, G.: Extraction and analysis of forensic document examiner features used for writer identification. Pattern Recogn. **40**(3), 1004–1013 (2007)

15. Purohit, N., Panwar, S.: State-of-the-art: offline writer identification methodologies. In: 2021 International Conference on Computer Communication and Informatics (ICCCI), pp. 1–8. IEEE (2021)
16. Rehman, A., Naz, S., Razzak, M.I.: Writer identification using machine learning approaches: a comprehensive review. Multimed. Tools Appl. **78**, 10889–10931 (2019). https://doi.org/10.1007/s11042-018-6577-1
17. Rehman, A., Naz, S., Razzak, M.I., Hameed, I.A.: Automatic visual features for writer identification: a deep learning approach. IEEE Access **7**, 17149–17157 (2019)
18. Schomaker, L., Vuurpijl, L., Schomaker, L.: Forensic writer identification: a benchmark data set and a comparison of two systems (2000)
19. Shivram, A., Ramaiah, C., Porwal, U., Govindaraju, V.: Modeling writing styles for online writer identification: a hierarchical Bayesian approach. In: 2012 International Conference on Frontiers in Handwriting Recognition, pp. 387–392. IEEE (2012)
20. Trinh, T., Dai, A., Luong, T., Le, Q.: Learning longer-term dependencies in RNNs with auxiliary losses. In: International Conference on Machine Learning, pp. 4965–4974. PMLR (2018)
21. Wang, Z.R., Du, J.: Fast writer adaptation with style extractor network for handwritten text recognition. Neural Netw. **147**, 42–52 (2022)
22. Zhang, X.Y., Xie, G.S., Liu, C.L., Bengio, Y.: End-to-end online writer identification with recurrent neural network. IEEE Trans. Hum.-Mach. Syst. **47**(2), 285–292 (2016)
23. Zhang, X.Y., Yin, F., Zhang, Y.M., Liu, C.L., Bengio, Y.: Drawing and recognizing Chinese characters with recurrent neural network. IEEE Trans. Pattern Anal. Mach. Intell. **40**(4), 849–862 (2017)

Authenticity Assessment of Cuban Banknotes by Combining Deep Learning and Image Processing Techniques

Rubén Sánchez-Rivero[1,2], Yasmany Febles-Espinosa[1,2], Francisco José Silva-Mata[1,2], and Annette Morales-González[1,2](✉)

[1] Advanced Technologies Application Center, CENATAV, Havana, Cuba
{rsanchez,fjsilva,amorales}@cenatav.co.cu
[2] DATYS, Havana, Cuba
yasmani.febles@datys.cu

Abstract. The rapid evolution of technology has significantly increased the production and circulation of counterfeit currency, particularly high denomination bills, posing a detrimental impact on society's commercial and economic sectors. The continuous advancement of domestic technology makes it increasingly challenging to differentiate between genuine and counterfeit printed money. Despite the development of computational tools for detecting counterfeit currency in various countries, no such tools currently exist for Cuban banknotes. This study proposes methods that combines deep learning techniques and other classifiers based on shape, color, and texture features applied to regions of interest, as determined by forensic experts who consider their security measures and characteristics. The evaluation of the proposed methods shows their effectiveness in detecting counterfeit currency, even with the limited availability of both fake and genuine specimens.

Keywords: banknote authenticity · counterfeit Cuban currency · deep learning

Introduction

Identifying counterfeit banknotes solely by their appearance is a well-known challenge. Most consumers are unaware of the encryption and security techniques used in paper currency [14]. Even when they are aware, manually verifying these features can be difficult due to the nature of security measures and limited time. Subjective factors during verification can also introduce assessment errors. This challenge can be addressed automatically or semi-automatically through the development of computer applications that help identify counterfeits by analyzing images captured using cameras, scanners, and/or mobile phones.

Due to the phenomenon of counterfeit banknotes circulating in today's society, the relevance of automatic systems for currency recognition has grown in recent years. These recognition systems use mainly two approaches. The first

Y. Hernndez Heredia et al. (Eds.): IWAIPR 2023, LNCS 14335, pp. 433–444, 2024.
https://doi.org/10.1007/978-3-031-49552-6_37

approach usually analyzes local regions of banknotes. It employs basic image processing methodologies [1], such as image capture, pre-processing, detection, segmentation, feature extraction and classification. The second approach takes advantages of recent developments of deep learning (DL) to design end-to-end models that process the entire banknote images in a global way [15].

Currently, deep learning methods lead the field of image analysis technologies. In particular, for counterfeit money detection, they offer numerous advantages due to their high efficiency and effectiveness [7,8]. However, the development of these methods requires extensive data collections for training or tuning [6]. Obtaining samples of genuine currency for training purposes is often feasible. However, acquiring a significant number of counterfeit bills or coins for training is challenging due to their illegal nature or strict control by authorized organizations responsible for currency verification and circulation [12].

Due to this primary reason, many state-of-the-art approaches focus on developing classical image processing methods and algorithms rather than deep learning-based techniques. When appropriately adapted and combined, those classical algorithms enable efficient and effective analysis of security features, aiding in determining the authenticity or falsity of banknotes.

Inspection of certain security measures in banknotes often requires specialized lighting conditions (ultraviolet or infrared light), or specific observation angles under transmitted light. Manual verification of these features requires expertise and specialized knowledge. However, automatic methods need to be compatible with images captured by various digital devices, including mobile phones, which lack the capability to provide specialized lighting like UV and IR [2].

While current statistical data may not be readily accessible, the production of counterfeit money is a global issue, including incidents reported in Cuba [9]. The diverse nature of currencies, evolving counterfeit techniques, legal frameworks, and country-specific challenges make it necessary for each country to implement their own counterfeit currency detection methods that align with their unique currency characteristics, legal requirements, and operational considerations.

In this context, the main goal of the present work is to propose a method for counterfeit Cuban banknote detection. Our proposal includes the combination of state-of-the-art deep learning models with classical image processing techniques that can be customized for analyzing Cuban banknote security measures.

1 Related Work

Various state-of-the-art methods have been developed for fake currency detection. These methods can be broadly divided into two fundamental categories: those employing traditional image processing and classification techniques, and those using DL models, particularly Convolutional Neural Networks (CNNs).

Among the methods of the first category, we found the work of [1], where Indian currency notes are verified by analyzing images captured under ultraviolet light. The process involves edge detection, image segmentation, and the determination of authenticity based on thresholded intensities of extracted features. This method has been tested on individual specimens of 500 and 2000 denomination notes. Another method [3] focuses on visible light images of Indian currency notes. It employs edge detection, segmentation, and an authenticity decision based on visual comparison with model banknotes. However, this method only presents visual results without formal testing. Another technique [2] compares real and test Indian banknotes by evaluating the correlation and standard deviation of equivalent intensities. Applying a threshold allows for the determination of authenticity, and the method has been tested on a single banknote.

Regarding the methods employing DL solutions, we found that transfer learning using the AlexNet model has been employed [8], utilizing a database of 100 images per currency denomination (2000, 500, 200, 50) with augmentation techniques. For counterfeit currency detection in India's banking channels, a CNN model has been created [7] using a self-generated dataset of 10,000 images per category, including data augmentation. Additionally, there are methods that utilize deep learning models like VGG19 [14] and Mobilenet V2 [15] for authenticity classification of Indian currency notes. These methods create their own datasets, combining images found on the web and employing data augmentation techniques to increase dataset diversity. Other approaches include utilizing techniques like Faster Region Recurrent Neural Network (FRCNN) for naira detection [13] and developing intelligent systems for Pakistani banknotes using three-layer classification [17]. A more detailed review regarding deep learning methods for counterfeit currency detection can be found in [12].

A comparative study has been conducted [11] on the security features of various currencies such as the Indian Rupee, Australian Dollar, British Pound, Euro, American Dollar, and Renminbi. However, this study does not propose an automatic counterfeit detection method.

Overall, these methods showcase the diversity of approaches used worldwide for currency recognition systems in different countries. Creating general counterfeit currency detection methods is challenging given that different countries have unique currencies with distinct security features, designs, and printing techniques [11]. These variations make it difficult to develop a general approach that can accurately detect counterfeit currency across multiple currencies.

In this work, we propose new image processing pipelines specifically designed for the security measures of Cuban banknotes. It is worth noting that there are currently no public applications available in Cuba for determining the authenticity of money, nor are there any applications that perform this task automatically, although there are references to applications developed for individuals with visual impairments [21]. The effective utilization of deep learning methods relies on a large number of training samples and images. However, the scarcity of counterfeit samples presents a major challenge, limiting the broader application of deep learning methods in this research area. This is why we discarded DL end-to-end approaches for counterfeit detection, and instead, we decided to take advantage of pre-trained CNNs for specific tasks in combination with image processing techniques.

2 Security Measures and Features in Cuban Banknotes

Special security measures incorporated during the banknote manufacturing process include holograms, security threads, and textile fibers. These features, unique to each denomination, encompass dimensions, colors, texts, watermarks, and more. They are visually or automatically examined using specialized equipment to verify the authenticity of banknotes. This study focuses on measures observable or verifiable under visible light, excluding features requiring specialized light sources like ultraviolet (UV) or infrared (IR) light.

The following security measures and/or features have been listed according to their importance and usage:

1) **Unique Dimensions:** Banknotes feature distinct shapes and sizes, which facilitate easy identification of counterfeiting attempts.
2) **Textile Fibers:** Randomly embedded fibers in the paper during production provide an additional layer of security.
3) **Windowed Security Thread:** A partially embedded metallic thread appears as a continuous line when held against light, enhancing the banknote's security.
4) **Watermarks:** Semi-transparent designs become visible when the banknote is held up to light, making replication difficult.
5) **Electrotyped Printing:** The denomination is printed using a specialized technique that becomes visible when held against light, offering an extra security measure.
6) **Latent Images:** Hidden images are only visible at specific viewing angles, further complicating counterfeiting attempts.
7) **Braille Code:** Tactile markings enable blind or visually impaired individuals to identify the denomination of the banknote.
8) **Checkered Background:** A background pattern created by specific printing techniques adds complexity to the banknote's design.
9) **Micro-texts:** Extremely small printed texts, which may include the denomination or other information, are strategically placed to deter counterfeiting.
10) **Specially Designed Portraits:** Images of prominent patriots are incorporated into the banknote's design, adding a layer of national pride and security.
11) **Filigrees:** Intricate printing patterns contribute to the overall complexity and security of the banknote's design.

Automating the authenticity verification of banknotes requires examining specific security measures. However, various factors such as image capture quality, lighting conditions, contextual variations, wear and tear of banknotes, and external contaminants can introduce complexities into the verification process. To address this, it is practical to utilize a criterion that assigns a probability or similarity score to classify banknotes as authentic or counterfeit [3].

3 Proposed Pipeline

Our proposal involves utilizing deep learning methods to detect, segment, and perform optical character recognition on various objects, such as faces. These methods are combined with supervised and unsupervised processing and classification techniques based on shape, color, and/or texture descriptors. The objective is to verify and analyze the specific security marks or measures present in the designated regions of banknotes. The general pipeline is presented in Algorithm 1. Details of each step of this pipeline will be provided in the remainder of this section.

Algorithm 1: Counterfeit Currency Detection

Input : Image capture of the banknote (on a table, scanned, etc.)
Output: Counterfeit or Genuine banknote classification

1. Detection and segmentation: Obtain the banknote region with marked edges;

2. Verification of specimen dimensions: Calculate area, perimeter and aspect ratio;

3. Selection of interesting regions: Identification of coordinates of regions containing security features;

4. Determination of the denomination: Apply Optical Character Recognition (OCR) techniques to the value region;

5. Security measures processing: For each security measure in Cuban banknotes, perform the corresponding processing and obtain classification of Counterfeit/Genuine;

6. Decision output: If any result is False, consider the banknote possibly Counterfeit; otherwise, it is Genuine (as per the requested criterion of forensic experts);

3.1 Detection and Segmentation

Detection and segmentation is performed using deep learning with a retrained version of the UNET [16] network for banknotes. The output is a cropped image of the banknote. This cropped image is normalized, and the aspect ratio, dimensions, and features are analysed and compared to the standard pattern.

3.2 Selection of Interesting Regions

The Regions of Interest (ROI) are obtained through a combination of fine-tuned object detectors for these regions, such as YOLOv7 [18] (region 7 in Fig. 1), face detectors like RetinaFace [5] (region 10 in Fig. 1), text detectors like DB [10]

Fig. 1. The regions of interest (ROI) on the front view of the banknote, for example, the 1000 pesos banknote, have been outlined in rectangles of different colors. Each region has been assigned a reference number that corresponds to the figure number during the description of the processes.

(Region 11b in Fig. 1). The coordinates of the remaining regions are computed using positions relative to those detected with the previous deep learning-based detectors.

3.3 Security Measures Processing

For each specific security measure in Cuban banknotes, we have developed dedicated processing pipelines that provide a classification value indicating whether each region is Counterfeit or Genuine. The details of these pipelines will be provided below.

Banknote Border Analysis. The outer border of banknotes contains critical security features for determining authenticity. Key geometric attributes like length, width, area and aspect ratio are extracted and compared to denomination specifications using a Bayesian Network classifier. By analyzing multiple dimensional properties, the classifier can reliably output a probability that the border matches an authentic specimen to support automated decision making on currency validity.

Detection and Segmentation of Textile Fibers. The textile fiber detection method is applied to the ROI labeled with number 3 in Fig. 1. Although textile fibers are distributed along all the banknote surface, this specific zone has been selected due to the clarity of the background, which improves their detection and analysis (See Fig. 2 above). The proposed method involves a two-step process for the chromatographic separation of elements in the region of interest. Firstly, images are converted from RGB to HSV. This conversion allows for a more feasible chromatographic separation of elements based on their color. In the second step, edge detection is performed on each textile fiber present in the region. The method utilizes specific parameter settings that define the ranges of color values in the H (hue), S (saturation), and V (value) planes corresponding to the blue and red colors of the textile fibers. These two steps enable the effective separation and identification of textile fibers within the region.

The method's output is a boolean value (True or False) that responds to the detection of separated spots using contours. If the spots are textile fibers, the area and perimeter values are almost equal due to their narrowness, establishing a threshold. The True condition is obtained when at least one textile fiber is detected.

Windowed Security Thread. The detection and segmentation method is similar to the previous one for detecting textile fibers, with the particularity that once the image is binarized, a method for extracting heatmaps with the probability of textual character presence [4](CRAFT) is applied. This results in particular patterns that coincide with the presence of each character (See Fig. 2 below) in the area where microtexts or texts exist. The similarity percentage with the pattern corresponding to that banknote is determined directly, as well as the detection of the letters BCC and denomination numbers using OCR [20].

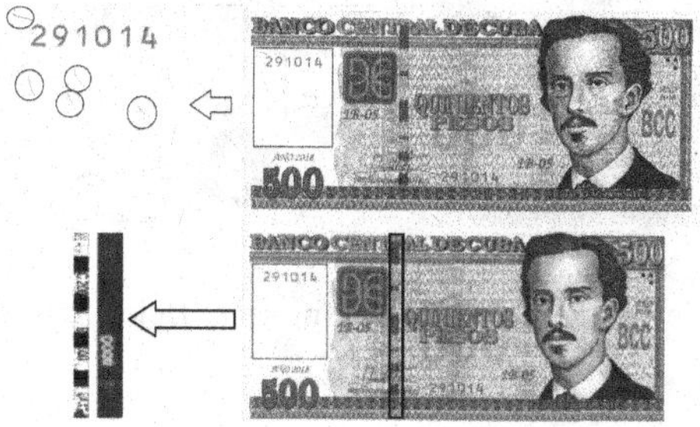

Fig. 2. Above: Textile fibers in a Cuban banknote. Below: windowed thread and correspondent heatmap.

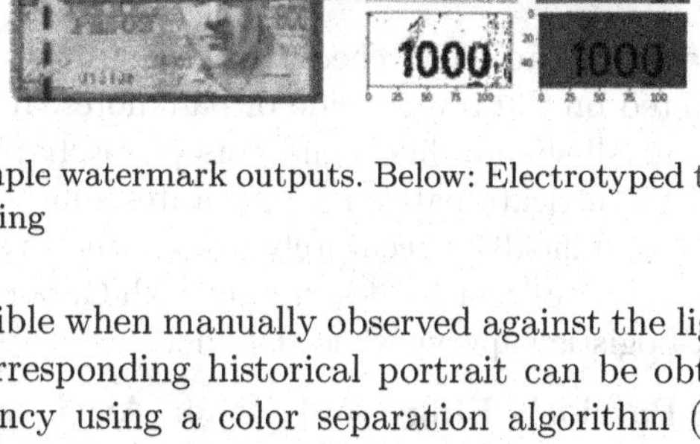

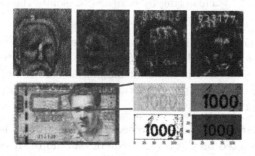

Fig. 3. Above: Example watermark outputs. Below: Electrotyped text with the denomination after processing

Watermarks. Visible when manually observed against the light, the watermark image with the corresponding historical portrait can be obtained without the need for transparency using a color separation algorithm (similar to the one used in the detection of textile fibers), described in ROI number 3. Once the watermark with the portrait is detected, the image is smoothed and a facial detection method [19] is applied. Some examples of the detection results are shown in Fig. 3 above. The facial detection algorithm, when properly trained, is capable of detecting the output images as faces.

Electroyped Denomination Print. In the final image obtained using chromatic separation, a deep learning-based text detector [4] and recognition algorithm [20] is applied, and the measurement consists of a boolean value True or False as a result of the match between the recognized number and the corresponding denomination. See Fig. 3 below, for denomination detection in the corresponding region.

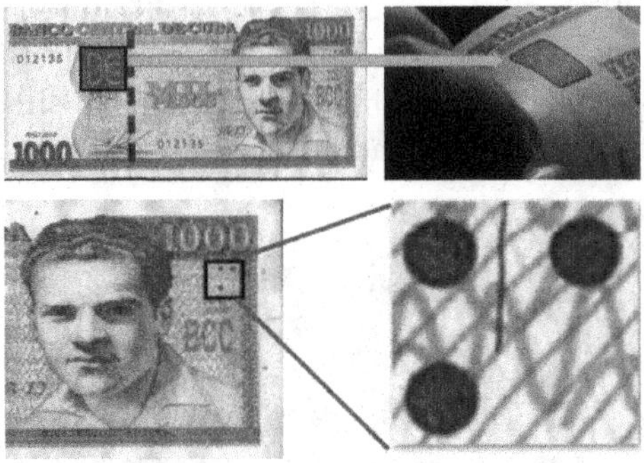

Fig. 4. Above: Viewing angle for latent images. Below: Braille code region

Latent Images. These can only be observed directly at a certain viewing angle, as shown in Fig. 4 above. The detection method used contains four steps: (1) Gaussian smoothing of the image, (2) we apply a Gabor kernel for the detection of different textures, (3) clustering by KMeans to isolate the desired denomination.

Braille Code. This type of region is used by the blind and visually impaired. These marks appear as circular dots that possess a distinct texture (See Fig. 4 below), and can be detected in a similar manner as described for latent images. The result is verified through the extraction of texture descriptors and a Logistic supervised classifier.

Checkerboard Background. The checkered background is a sophisticated security pattern printed on the reverse side of banknotes. It consists of a complex arrangement of small shapes, lines, and dots precisely positioned in a non-repeating fashion. This intricate pattern incorporates subtle variations in color and ink density that are difficult to accurately reproduce. Its authenticity is verified through the extraction of texture descriptors with Gabor kernel and Kmean segmentation and a Logistic supervised as classifier.

Sharpness of the Patriot's Effigy and Other Areas with Filigree. For the evaluation of this aspect, a descriptor that characterizes the sharpness of the drawing was used. An output value of this descriptor (Laplacian value) proved effective in determining the sharpness or print quality of these elements, which were found to be distinguishable between counterfeit and genuine banknotes.

Verification of the Presence and Location of Microtexts. The microtexts (See Fig. 5) were verified using the heatmaps method, followed by a counting of closed edges containing them. Within the sign with the letters BCC, a process is performed to detect and threshold the microtexts, which are subsequently read using OCR (Optical Character Recognition) method.

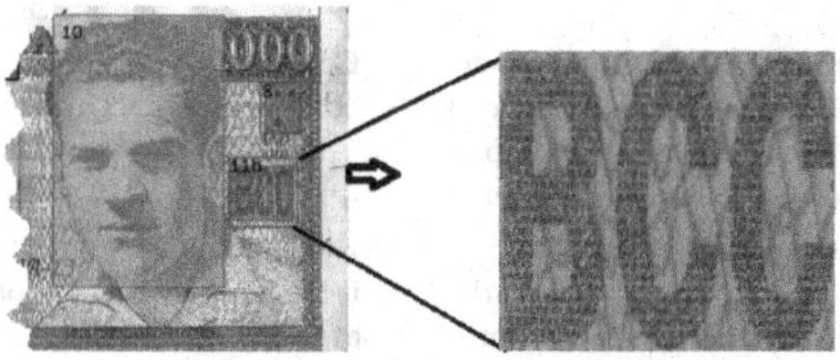

Fig. 5. Microtexts example in Cuban banknotes

3.4 Counterfait/Genuine Decision

All of the security measures are detected/classified for each test banknote. The final decision over its authenticity was suggested by forensic experts. The criterion employed is that if at least one of the individual measures yields a counterfeit (False) result, the overall banknote is classified as counterfeit. This means that for a banknote to be considered genuine, all the security measures must be classified as genuine (True).

4 Experimental Evaluation

For the evaluation of the results, we created a dataset of Cuban banknotes. It consists of 20 genuine specimens and five counterfeit specimens from five different denominations was used. The main objective was to determine the effectiveness of the methods applied to the different regions of interest. Therefore, the number of real test images reached 300. Each measure or feature was evaluated independently in specific regions, with 25 images for each region (from 1 to 9, excluding region 2), and 50 images for regions 10a, 10b, 11a, and 11b.

However, due to the limited availability of counterfeits, we employed data augmentation techniques on the genuine samples to expand the dataset. This included rotations, cropping, skew, and minor filtering or compression artifacts.

For training, sets of genuine banknotes were used, with varying numbers of specimens depending on availability during the experiments. Due to the scarcity of counterfeit cases, two strategies were employed for augmenting the false cases. First, the inclusion of regions from genuine banknotes whose ROIs did not match the respective denominations (non-matching denomination with the region). Second, in some cases, genuine regions were adulterated using filters, particularly

Table 1. Results of processing each individual security measure

Security Measure	Image Processing	Classification Strategy	Accuracy
Banknote border analysis	9-attribute vector: centroid coordinates, aspect ratio, area, perimeter, bounding box coordinates, convexity	Bayesian network	92%
	7-attribute vector: 7 normalized Hu moments	Bayesian network	96%
Textile Fibers	Determination of fibers by color ranges (chromatic separation), edge detection, relationship between area and perimeter	Count of closed contours compared to a threshold	93%
Windowed Security Thread	Separation of 3 HSV color channels, chromatic separation and thresholding. Detection of texts using heat maps and OCR	Heatmap pattern count. If there is at least one valid pattern and at least one of the letters or numbers is correct, the banknote specimen is considered as genuine	100%
Watermarks	Separation of 3 HSV color channels, smoothing of the image using Gaussian filter, detection of face presence. Comparison of the detected face with the corresponding pattern for each denomination	If the face is detected and correctly matches the corresponding pattern, the banknote is considered as genuine	82%
Electroyped denomination print	Separation of 3 HSV color channels, chromatic separation and thresholding. Detection of texts using OCR	If the detected number matches the banknote denomination, it is considered as genuine	96%
Latent Images	Gaussian smoothing of the ROI. Gabor kernel for texture detection. Segmentation based on pixel clustering using unsupervised KMeans algorithm. OCR	If the detected number matches the banknote denomination, it is considered as genuine	96%
Braille Code	24-attribute vector: composed by texture descriptors such as contrast, homogeneity, dissimilarity, ASM, energy, and correlation	Logistic classifier	100%
Checkerboard background	Gaussian smoothing of the ROI. Gabor kernel for texture detection. Segmentation based on pixel clustering using unsupervised KMeans algorithm. Edge detection. 7-attribute vector: 7 normalized Hu moments of the extracted contours	Contour classification using Logistic classifier. If the number of contours correctly classified is larger than a threshold, the banknote is considered as genuine	85%
Sharpness of the patriot's effigy and other areas with filigree	Calculation of the Laplacian of the region and comparison with a threshold. This value is directly related to the image sharpness	Comparison with a threshold	100%
Microtext verification	Detection and localization of the presence of microtext letters using heatmaps, followed by the detection of closed edges of a certain size	Count of closed edges compared to a threshold	100%

useful when texture played a crucial role in classification. All supervised classifiers underwent cross-validation (10-fold).

We evaluated all the methods for analyzing security measures on this Cuban banknote dataset and the results are provided in Table 1. With the aim of summarizing all the information, in this table we added a brief description of the image processing techniques employed for each security measure and the classification strategy to obtain the final decision of counterfeit or genuine.

Although each region of interest is processed independently, some of the processing methods are repeated, with only the data being changed. This reduces the burden of the application. The combination of DL methods yielded high effectiveness values in the experimental results, despite not being trained with specific data from this research.

It is important to notice that in several cases, the results were affected by the deterioration and wear of the banknotes, which adds an additional challenge to this problem.

5 Conclusions

In this work we proposed new methods based on image processing to address the specific security measures of Cuban banknotes. The study focused on observable features under visible light, considering factors such as dimensions, colors, texts, watermarks, and other elements unique to each denomination. It is important to note that there are currently no publicly available applications in Cuba for determining the authenticity of money, highlighting the need for automated solutions in this area.

The use of pre-trained deep learning methods combined with image processing techniques proved to be effective in achieving high accuracy in the experiments conducted. Also the approach of processing each region of interest independently allows for more specificity taking into account its characteristics.

Overall, this work lays the foundation for further research and development in automated banknote authentication methods, particularly in the context of Cuban currency. The findings and methodologies presented here contribute to the advancement of technology for detecting counterfeit banknotes and enhancing the security of monetary transactions.

References

1. Agasti, T., Burand, G., Wade, P., Chitra, P.: Fake currency detection using image processing. In: IOP Conference Series: Materials Science and Engineering, vol. 263, p. 052047. IOP Publishing (2017)
2. Alekhya, D., Prabha, G.D.S., Rao, G.V.D.: Fake currency detection using image processing and other standard methods. Int. J. Res. Comput. Commun. Technol. **3**(1), 128–131 (2014)
3. Atchaya, S., Harini, K., Kaviarasi, G., Swathi, B.: Fake currency detection using image processing. Int. J. Trend Res. Dev. 72–73 (2016)

4. Baek, Y., Lee, B., Han, D., Yun, S., Lee, H.: Character region awareness for text detection. In: Proceedings of the IEEE/CVF Conference on Computer Vision and Pattern Recognition, pp. 9365–9374 (2019)
5. Deng, J., Guo, J., Ververas, E., Kotsia, I., Zafeiriou, S.: RetinaFace: single-shot multi-level face localisation in the wild. In: Proceedings of the IEEE/CVF Conference on Computer Vision and Pattern Recognition (CVPR) (2020)
6. Ghonge, M., Kachare, T., Sinha, M., Kakade, S., Nigade, S., Shinde, S.: Real time fake note detection using deep convolutional neural network. In: 2022 Second International Conference on Computer Science, Engineering and Applications (ICCSEA), pp. 1–6. IEEE (2022)
7. Kamble, K., Bhansali, A., Satalgaonkar, P., Alagundgi, S.: Counterfeit currency detection using deep convolutional neural network. In: 2019 IEEE Pune Section International Conference (PuneCon), pp. 1–4. IEEE (2019)
8. Laavanya, M., Vijayaraghavan, V.: Real time fake currency note detection using deep learning. Int. J. Eng. Adv. Technol. (IJEAT) **9** (2019)
9. Leonard, J.E.P.: Delito de falsificacion de documentos en cuba, el. Rev. Der. PR **41**, 143 (2002)
10. Liao, M., Wan, Z., Yao, C., Chen, K., Bai, X.: Real-time scene text detection with differentiable binarization. In: Proceedings of the AAAI Conference on Artificial Intelligence, vol. 34, no. 07, pp. 11474–11481 (2020). https://doi.org/10.1609/aaai.v34i07.6812. https://ojs.aaai.org/index.php/AAAI/article/view/6812
11. Mann, M., Shukla, S., Gupta, S.: A comparative study on security features of banknotes of various countries. Int. J. Multidiscip. Res. Dev. **2**, 83–91 (2015)
12. Muhamad, S., Ahmed, T.: Counterfeit currency recognition using deep learning: a review. Technium: Romanian J. Appl. Sci. Technol. **3**(7), 14–26 (2021)
13. Ogbuju, E., Usman, W., Obilikwu, P., Yemi-Peters, V.: Deep learning for genuine naira banknotes. FUOYE J. Pure Appl. Sci. **5** FJPAS (2021)
14. Pallavi, S., Pooja, N., Yashaswini, H.R., Varsha, N.: Fake currency detection. Int. Res. J. Modernization Eng. Technol. Sci. (06) (2022)
15. Potluri, T., Jahnavi, S., Motupalli, R.: Mobilenet V2-FCD: fake currency note detection. In: Luhach, A.K., Jat, D.S., Bin Ghazali, K.H., Gao, X.-Z., Lingras, P. (eds.) ICAICR 2020. CCIS, vol. 1393, pp. 274–282. Springer, Singapore (2021). https://doi.org/10.1007/978-981-16-3660-8_26
16. Ronneberger, O., Fischer, P., Brox, T.: U-net: convolutional networks for biomedical image segmentation. In: Navab, N., Hornegger, J., Wells, W.M., Frangi, A.F. (eds.) MICCAI 2015. LNCS, vol. 9351, pp. 234–241. Springer, Cham (2015). https://doi.org/10.1007/978-3-319-24574-4_28
17. Sarfraz, M., Bux Sargano, A., Ul Haq, N.: An intelligent system for paper currency verification using support vector machines. Scientia Iranica **26**(Special Issue on: Socio-Cognitive Engineering), 59–71 (2019). https://doi.org/10.24200/sci.2018.21194
18. Wang, C.Y., Bochkovskiy, A., Liao, H.Y.M.: YOLOv7: trainable bag-of-freebies sets new state-of-the-art for real-time object detectors (2022)
19. Wu, W., Peng, H., Yu, S.: YuNet: a tiny millisecond-level face detector. Mach. Intell. Res. 1–10 (2023)
20. Yu, D., et al.: Towards accurate scene text recognition with semantic reasoning networks. In: Proceedings of the IEEE/CVF Conference on Computer Vision and Pattern Recognition, pp. 12113–12122 (2020)
21. Zaldivar, M.S., Pérez, R.H.: Asistencia a discapacitados visuales para reconocer billetes mediante aplicación móvil. Revista Cubana de Ciencias Informáticas (2021)

A Robust Preprocessing Method for Measuring Image Visual Quality Using Log-Polar FFT Features

Guang Yi Chen[1], Adam Krzyzak[1(✉)], and Ventzeslav Valev[2]

[1] Department of Computer Science and Software Engineering, Concordia University, Montreal, QC H3G 1M8, Canada
krzyzak@cse.concordia.ca

[2] Institute of Mathematics and Informatics, Bulgarian Academy of Sciences, 1113 Sofia, Bulgaria
valev@math.bas.bg

Abstract. To register two images, existing methods normally estimate the parameters of an affine transform, and then perform an inverse affine transform to the test image by using the estimated parameters. Any metric can then be applied to the reference image and the normalized image. In this paper we propose a new method for measuring visual image quality which circumvents the need to estimate the parameters of the affine transform. Instead, we use the log-polar transform and the fast Fourier transform (FFT) to extract features that are invariant to translation, rotation, and scaling. We apply the existing structural similarity index measure (SSIM) to the two invariant feature images, where no inverse transform is needed. Experimental results show that our proposed method outperforms the standard metric, the mean SSIM (MSSIM), significantly in terms of visual quality scores.

Keywords: translation invariance · rotation invariance · scale invariance · image visual quality · quality metrics

1 Introduction

Measuring visual quality of an image is an important task. The aim of the quality assessment (QA) is to develop methods, which can automatically assess the quality of images in a perceptually consistent manner. Image QA methods usually interpret image quality as fidelity or similarity to a reference image in some perceptual space. Such full reference QA methods can achieve consistency in quality prediction by modeling salient physiological and psychovisual features of the human visual system. There exist some unsupervised and no-reference QA approaches, however the are not considered in this paper.

We briefly review several metrics for measuring image visual quality here. Wang et al. [1] proposed the structural similarity index measure (SSIM) by comparing local correlations in luminance, contrast, and structure between reference and distorted images. The

Y. Hernández Heredia et al. (Eds.): IWAIPR 2023, LNCS 14335, pp. 445–454, 2024.
https://doi.org/10.1007/978-3-031-49552-6_38

SSIM index is defined as

$$SSIM(x, y) = \frac{2\mu_x\mu_y + C_1}{\mu_x^2 + \mu_y^2 + C_1} \cdot \frac{2\sigma_x\sigma_y + C_2}{\sigma_x^2 + \sigma_y^2 + C_2} \cdot \frac{\sigma_{xy} + C_3}{\sigma_x\sigma_y + C_3}$$

where μ_x and μ_y are sample means; ${\sigma_x}^2$ and ${\sigma_y}^2$ are sample variances, and σ_{xy} is the sample cross-covariance between x and y. The constants C_1, C_2 and C_3 stabilize SSIM when the means and variances become small. The mean SSIM (MSSIM) over the whole image gives the final quality measure. In [1] a more sophisticated SSIM is studied with exponents α, β, γ. It this paper we consider its simplified version. Rezazadeh and Coulombe ([2, 3]) proposed a discrete wavelet transform framework for full-reference image quality assessment, while Qian and Chen [4] developed four reduced-reference metrics for measuring the visual quality of hyperspectral images after spatial resolution enhancement. Keller et al. [5] proposed a pseudo polar-based method to estimate the large translation, rotation, and scaling in images. This algorithm used only 1D fast Fourier transform (FFT) calculations whose overall complexity is significantly lower than prior works. Chen and Coulombe [6] developed an FFT-based visual quality metric robust to spatial shift. This was achieved by taking advantage of the fact that the Fourier spectrum is invariant to spatial shifts. Chen and Coulombe [7] proposed an image visual quality assessment method based on scale-invariant feature transform (SIFT) features. In this method, the authors estimated translation, rotation, and scaling factors for the purpose of image registration. Ding et al. [8] provided a comparison of full-reference image quality models for optimization of image processing systems. They performed a large-scale comparison of image quality assessment (IQA) models in terms of their use as objectives for the optimization of image processing algorithms. Specifically, they used eleven full-reference IQA models to train deep neural networks for four low-level vision tasks: denoising, deblurring, super-resolution, and compression. Zhai and Min [9] performed a survey on perceptual image quality assessment where they provided an up-to-date and comprehensive review of these studies. Specifically, the frequently used subjective image quality assessment databases are first reviewed, as they served as the validation set for the objective measures. Okarma et al. [10] combined full-reference image quality metrics for objective assessment of multiply distorted images. Two techniques for the combination of metrics had been analyzed, which are based on the weighted product and the proposed weighted sum with additional exponential weights. Liu et al. [11] studied pseudo-log-polar Fourier transform for estimating large translations, rotations, and scaling in images. Experimental results had verified the robustness and high accuracy of this method. In work [13], the authors proposed an image normalization technique so that it is translation, rotation, and scale invariant.

All cited methods in this paper are good at measuring image visual quality when the images have no deformations such as translations, rotations, and scaling. As a result, the calculated scores with these metrics will be low in the presence of these deformations. Nevertheless, our new method proposed in this paper can do a very good job for measuring image visual quality even if small amount of deformation is introduced.

In this paper, we propose a new FFT-based MSSIM, which is invariant to translation, rotation, and scaling of the images. We take a forward Fourier transform (FFT) of the reference and test images. We then apply a log-polar transform to the magnitude of the Fourier coefficients. Another FFT is applied to the log-polar images. We apply the MSSIM onto the magnitude of the generated Fourier coefficients. Experimental results show that our proposed method improves the quality scores significantly for the LIVE image quality assessment database release 2 [14].

The rest of this paper is organized as follows. Section 2 proposes a new metric that is invariant to translation, rotation, and scaling of the input images. Section 3 conducts experiment to show the advantages of the proposed method over standard image quality metrics MSSIM without pre-processing. Finally, Section 4 presents conclusions.

2 Proposed Method

In this paper, we propose a new metric that is invariant to translation, rotation, and scaling of the input images. We utilize the property that the Fourier spectra are invariant to spatial shifts, and the log-polar transformation convert rotation and scaling into spatial shifts [12]. Let image x be the translated, rotated, and scaled version of image y, then their Fourier magnitude spectra F_1 and F_2 in polar coordinates are related as indicated in Eqs. (1)-(3) below:

$$F_1(r, \theta) = F_2(r/a, \theta - \theta_0) \tag{1}$$

$$F_1(\log(r), \theta) = F_2(\log(r) - \log(a), \theta - \theta_0) \tag{2}$$

$$F_1(\xi, \theta) = F_2(\xi - d, \theta - \theta_0) \tag{3}$$

where

$$\xi = \log(r)$$

$$d = \log(a)$$

Therefore, taking another forward Fourier transform and obtaining their Fourier spectra will be invariant to translation, rotation, and scaling of the input images. We use these normalized images as input to the MSSIM, and we obtain improved visual quality scores.

The proposed method can be summarized as follows:

1. Take the Fourier transform of both the reference image x and the test image y and obtain the magnitude of the Fourier coefficients F_1 and F_2. Assume the images are of size M $\times$ N.
2. Perform the log-polar transform on the two generated images, and we obtain $F_1(\xi, \theta)$ and $F_2(\xi - d, \theta - \theta_0)$
3. Take another forward Fourier transform on the two log-polar images, and calculate their Fourier spectra, S_1 and S_2.
4. Extract the center regions:

$\text{Im}_1 = S_1$(M/4:3M/4, N/4:3N/4)

$Im_2 = S_2(M/4{:}3M/4, N/4{:}3N/4)$

5. Use MSSIM to measure the visual quality of the images Im_1 and Im_2.

Figure 1 shows the original image (upper-left), its log operation of the Fourier spectra (upper-right), the log-polar image (lower-left), and the Fourier spectra of the log-polar image (lower-right).

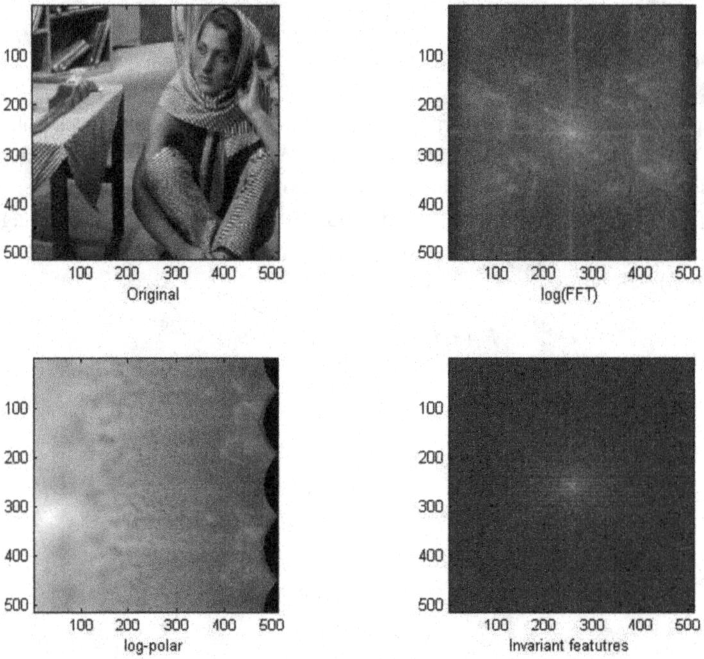

Fig. 1. The original image (upper-left), its log operation of the Fourier spectra (upper-right), the log-polar image (lower-left), and the Fourier spectra of the log-polar image (lower-right).

The major advantage of the method proposed in this paper is that we do not need to estimate translation, rotation, and scaling parameters in the input images. This can save computation time and at the same time avoid errors introduced in parameter estimation. The second advantage of our proposed method is that it does not need to align the spatial origins of the input images, whereas the alignment is crucial to the log-polar technique [12]. Since the magnitude of the Fourier coefficients is invariant to spatial shifts, the origin of step 1 in our proposed method is always at the center of the Fourier spectra images. This will make our proposed method more accurate than existing methods.

In paper [13], the authors proposed a normalization technique to an image so that it is translation, rotation, and scale invariant. The method uses 6 forward FFT and 6 inverse FFT, which is time consuming and error prone. In this paper, we recommend to apply the forward FFT to both the reference and test images, conduct a log-polar transform to the spectra of the FFT coefficients, and then apply the forward FFT to the log-polar coefficients. In this way, the obtained coefficients are translation, rotation, and scale invariant. We propose to use MSSIM to measure the visual quality of the two generated log-polar FFT coefficient images. Our method will use only 4 forward FFT and it is faster than the technique in [13], which preprocesses the input images. Existing metrics can then be applied to the reference and normalized images.

The major difference between our proposed method in this paper and the existing methods is that we do not estimate the parameters of translation, rotation, and scaling. We extract invariant features from the reference and test images by means of the Fourier transform and log-polar transform, and the metric MSSIM is applied to the extracted invariant features images. On the other hand, existing methods in the literature will register the test image with the reference image by estimating the parameters of translation, rotation, and scaling, and then apply MSSIM to the reference image and the normalized test image.

By introducing invariant properties in this paper, the measured scores will be higher for images with small amount of translation, rotation, and scaling, which is desirable in image processing. The MSSIM works on local windows, which is very effective in measuring image visual quality. Our new method also takes advantages of local windows in the transformed feature space with better scores compared to the standard MSSIM. We measure image visual quality based on the transformed feature images which are translation, rotation, and scaling invariant. Our new method takes the same approach as standard MSSIM for measuring image visual quality. The mean, variance, and cross-variance can be calculated from the transformed feature images the same way as the standard MSSIM. The MSSIM measures visual quality of similar images, so it is meaningless to test dissimilar images with our newly introduced method in this paper.

Our experimental results show that our proposed method is much better than the standard MSSIM without any preprocessing.

3 Experimental Results

We performed some experiments on the LIVE Image Quality Assessment Database Release 2 [14], which consists of 779 distorted images derived from 29 original images using five types of distortions. The distortions include JPEG compression, JPEG2000 compression, Gaussian white noise (GWN), Gaussian blurring (GBlur), and the Rayleigh fast fading (FF) channel model. We consider three measures of performance, namely, the correlation coefficients (CC) between the difference mean opinion score (DMOS) and the objective model outputs after nonlinear regression, the root mean square error (RMSE), and the Spearman rank order correlation coefficient (SROCC) in this experiment. The SROCC is a nonparametric rank-based correlation metric, independent of any monotonic nonlinear mapping between subjective and objective score.

Subjective results are frequently used as a benchmark for establishing a relationship between DMOS and a specific objective quality metric. The scores produced by the objective video quality metric must be correlated with the viewer scores in a predictable and repeatable fashion. The relationship between predicted and DMOS need not be linear as subjective testing can have nonlinear quality rating compression at the extremes of the test range. The linearity of the relationship is thus not so critical, but rather the stability of the relationship and a dataset's error variance determine predictive usefulness.

Table 1 gives the MSSIM scores for the LIVE image database. Our proposed method outperforms the original MSSIM in this case. Table 2 tabulates the results when every distorted image in the LIVE database is distorted furthermore by scaling factor 0.9, rotation angle $0.1 \times 180/\pi$ degrees, spatial shifts 4 pixels in the horizontal direction, and 4 pixels in the vertical direction. In the table, the standard metric MSSIM gets very low-quality scores, whereas the proposed method gives much better visual quality scores. We hypothesize that we have the same DMOS scores for the original images in the LIVE image database and their distorted versions. Since scaling leads to loss of image detail, shifting discards rows and columns of pixels, and rotation creates some artifacts, we see lower scores in the original MSSIM.

Figure 2 shows the scatter plots of DMOS versus MSSIM for all distorted images in the LIVE image database, whereas Fig. 3 shows the scatter plots of DMOS versus MSSIM for the LIVE image database for a combination of translation, rotation, and scaling. In addition, Figs. 4–6 present the experimental results of distorting one image in the LIVE database with translation, rotation, and scaling, respectively. It is easy to see that our proposed method is very robust against different kinds of distortion, whereas the existing MSSIM performs poorly in these cases.

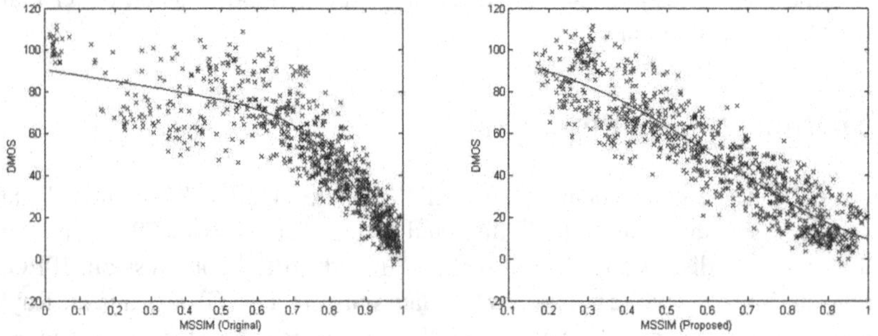

Fig. 2. Scatter plots of DMOS versus the original MSSIM (left) and the proposed method (right) for all distorted images in the LIVE image database.

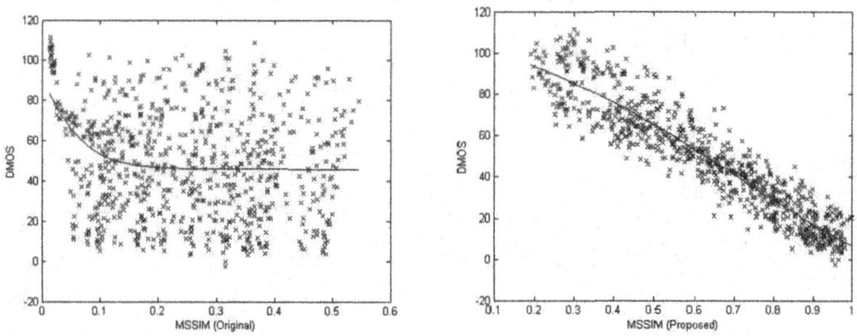

Fig. 3. Scatter plots of DMOS versus the original MSSIM (left) and the proposed method (right) for all distorted images in the LIVE image database. Every image in the LIVE database is distorted by scaling factor 0.9, rotation angle $0.1 \times 180/\pi$ degrees, spatial shifts 4 pixels in the horizontal direction, and 4 pixels in the vertical direction.

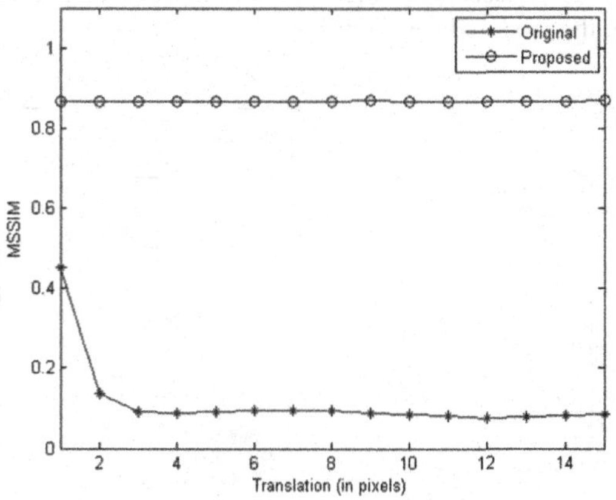

Fig. 4. The MSSIM scores for spatial shifts in both the horizontal and vertical directions by distorting one image in the LIVE image database. At an exceedingly small spatial shift of 1 pixel, the score difference between the original metric and the proposed method is noticeably big.

In future work more configurations will be tested and comparisons will be done with related works described in references [5, 7] and [13].

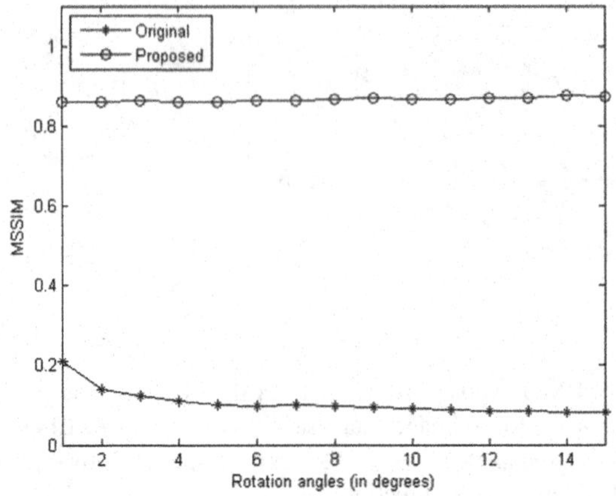

Fig. 5. The MSSIM scores for different rotation angles obtained by distorting one image in the LIVE image database. At an exceedingly small rotation angle of 1°, the score difference between the original metric and the proposed method is big.

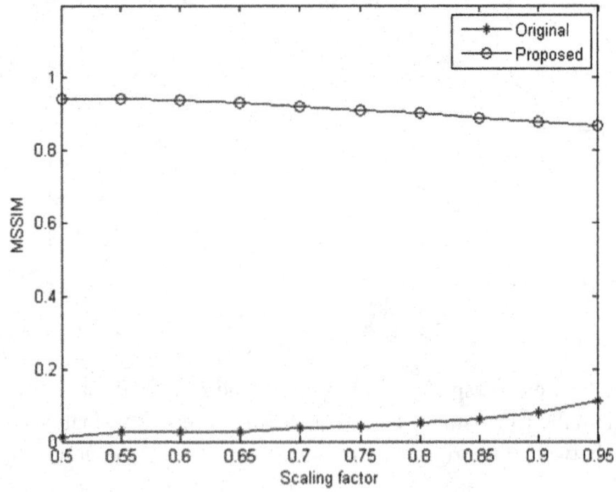

Fig. 6. The MSSIM scores for different scaling factors obtained by distorting one image in the LIVE image database. At a small scaling factor of 0.95, the score difference between the original metric and the proposed method is excessively big.

Table 1. Overall performance comparison of image quality assessment for all distorted images in the LIVE image database. The best performing method is highlighted in bold font.

MSSIM	Method	CC	SROCC	RMSE
	Original	0.9042	0.9104	11.67
	Proposed	**0.9059**	**0.9114**	**11.57**

Table 2. Overall performance comparison of image quality assessment for every image in the LIVE image database, which is distorted by scaling factor 0.9, rotation angle $0.1 \times 180/\pi$ degrees, spatial shifts 4 pixels in the horizontal direction, and 4 pixels in the vertical direction. The best performing method is highlighted in bold font.

MSSIM	Method	CC	SROCC	RMSE
	Original	0.3346	0.1675	25.81
	Proposed	**0.9327**	**0.9398**	**9.85**

4 Conclusions

Image visual quality metrics play very important role in many real-life applications. The obvious approach for measuring quality is to use assessment of human observers. Nevertheless, such subjective evaluations are usually cumbersome and expensive, and they cannot be incorporated into automatic systems that adjust themselves in real-time based on the feedback of output quality. The aim of visual quality assessment is to develop methods for objective evaluation of quality in such a way that is consistent with subjective human evaluation.

In this paper we proposed a new metric for measuring image visual quality, which is invariant to the translation, rotation, and scaling of the images. We propose to apply the forward FFT to both the reference and test images, perform a log-polar transform to the spectra of the FFT coefficients, and then apply the forward FFT to the log-polar coefficients. Thus the extracted coefficients are translation, rotation, and scale invariant. We select the MSSIM to measure the visual quality of the two generated FFT coefficient images. Experimental results demonstrate that the proposed method outperforms the standard metric MSSIM significantly under different kinds of distortion.

We are currently developing new visual quality metrics for video sequences, which are invariant to different kinds of distortions. We will also use the dual-tree complex wavelet transform (DTCWT) [15] to propose a new kind of metric that is invariant to spatial shifts. In the future other variants of MSSIM such as multi-scale MSSIM and weighted MSSIM will be considered.

References

1. Wang, Z., Bovik, A.C., Sheikh, H.R., Simoncelli, E.P.: Image quality assessment: from error visibility to structural similarity. IEEE Trans. Image Process. **13**(4), 600–612 (2004)
2. Rezazadeh, S., Coulombe, S.: Novel discrete wavelet transform framework for full reference image quality assessment. Signal, Image and Video Processing **7**, 559–573 (2011)
3. Rezazadeh, S., Coulombe, S.: A novel discrete wavelet domain error-based image quality metric with enhanced perceptual performance. Int. J. Comp. Electr. Eng. **4**(3), 390–395 (2012)
4. Qian, S.E., Chen, G.Y.: Four reduced-reference metrics for measuring hyperspectral images after spatial resolution enhancement, pp. 204–208. ISPRS International Archives of the Photogrammetry, Remote Sensing and Spatial Information Sciences, Vienna, Austria (2010)
5. Keller, K., Averbuch, A., Israeli, M.: Pseudo polar-based estimation of large translations, rotations, and scalings in images. IEEE Trans. Image Proc. **14**(1), 12–22 (2005)

6. Chen, G.Y., Coulombe, S.: An FFT-Based Visual Quality Metric Robust to Spatial Shift. In: The 11th International Conference on Information Science, Signal Processing and their Applications (ISSPA), Montreal, Quebec, Canada, pp. 372–376 (2012)
7. Chen, G.Y., Coulombe, S.: An image visual quality assessment method based on SIFT features. J. Pattern Recogn. Res. **1**, 85–97 (2013)
8. Ding, K., Ma, K., Wang, S., Simoncelli, E.P.: Comparison of full-reference image quality models for optimization of image processing systems. Int. J. Comput. Vision **129**, 1258–1281 (2021)
9. Zhai, G., Min, X.: Perceptual image quality assessment: a survey. Sci. China Inf. Sci. **63**, 211301 (2020)
10. Okarma, K., Lech, P., Lukin, V.V.: Combined full-reference image quality metrics for objective assessment of multiply distorted images. Electronics **10**, 2256 (2021)
11. Liu, H., Guo, B., Feng, Z.: Pseudo-log-polar Fourier transform for image registration. IEEE Signal Process. Lett. **13**(1), 17–20 (2006)
12. Wolberg, G., Zokai, S.: Robust image registration using log-polar transform. In: Proceedings of the IEEE International Conference on Image Processing (ICIP), pp. 493–496 (2000)
13. Reddy, B.S., Chatterji, B.N.: An FFT-based technique for translation, rotation and scale-invariant image registration. IEEE Trans. Image Process. **5**(8), 1266–1271 (1996)
14. Sheikh, H.R., Wang, Z., Cormack, L., Bovik, A.C.: LIVE image quality assessment database release 2, http://live.ece.utexas.edu/research/quality
15. Kingsbury, N.G.: Complex wavelets for shift invariant analysis and filtering of signals. J. Appl. Comput. Harmon. Anal. **10**(3), 234–253 (2001)

Effectiveness of Blind Face Restoration to Boost Face Recognition Performance at Low-Resolution Images

Yoanna Martínez-Díaz[1], Luis S. Luévano[2], and Heydi Méndez-Vázquez[1](✉)

[1] Advanced Technology Application Center (CENATAV), 7A #21406, Havana, Cuba
{ymartinez,hmendez}@cenatav.co.cu
[2] Tecnológico de Monterrey, School of Engineering and Science, Monterrey, Mexico
luis.s.luevano@tec.mx

Abstract. This paper studies the effectiveness of Blind Face Restoration methods to boost the performance of face recognition systems on low-resolution images. We investigate the use of three blind face restoration techniques, which have demonstrated impressive results in generating realistic high-resolution face images. Three state-of-the-art face recognition methods were selected to assess the impact of using the generated high-resolution images on their performance. Our analysis includes both, synthesized and native low-resolution images. The conducted experimental evaluation show that this is still an open research problem.

Keywords: low-resolution · face recognition · blind face restoration

1 Introduction

Recent developments in deep neural network architectures have allowed to achieve impressive performance improvements on several computer vision tasks, including face recognition [24]. However, the accuracy of current face recognition methods remains a significant challenge on unconstrained and native low-resolution (LR) images such as those acquired in surveillance scenarios or from a wide field of view at distance [5]. Existing methods to deal with LR image constraints can be grouped into two main categories: (1) resolution-invariant learning and (2) image face restoration. Resolution-invariant learning methods try to develop a single feature space for both LR and high-resolution (HR) face images. These methods require a large number of LR and HR image pairs from the same subject for training, which are usually not available. As an alternative approach, image face restoration uses super-resolution and deblurring techniques to recovery a high-quality face image from its degraded low-quality counterpart. An additional advantage of these kind of methods is that they can be used for face detection, face recognition and many other vision tasks [25].

Y. HernÃąndez Heredia et al. (Eds.): IWAIPR 2023, LNCS 14335, pp. 455–467, 2024.
https://doi.org/10.1007/978-3-031-49552-6_39

Among existing algorithms for face image restoration, traditional methods predefine the degradation type before training, leading to poor generalization ability. Thus, in the last years, researchers pay more attention to the so-called blind face restoration (BFR) problem [32] taking into account that, mostly we cannot know the degradation type when a real-world image is captured. In this paper, we aim at studying the effectiveness of BFR to enhance the face recognition performance at LR face images. Specifically, we selected three state-of-the-art blind face restoration methods that have demonstrated excellent and remarkable abilities to generate realistic and faithful HR images. In addition, we choose three accurate face recognition methods to evaluate the impact of using the generated HR images on their performance. Both, synthesized and native low-resolution benchmarks are used for the experimental evaluation.

The main contributions of this work are as follows:

- We investigate the effectiveness of three state-of-the-art blind face restoration methods to improve the performance of three face recognition models at low-resolution images.
- We provide an extensive experimental evaluation by testing different combining methods of BFR and face recognition models on synthetic and native LR face datasets.

The remainder of this paper is organized as follows. Section 2 takes an overview of low-resolution face recognition and deep face restoration methods. In Sect. 3, we present the experimental setup used for evaluating blind face restoration methods on low-resolution face recognition scenarios. Section 4 presents the experimental evaluation carried out and exposes some discussion regarding the results obtained on this study. Finally, Sect. 5 summarizes the conclusions of this work.

2 Related Work

There is not a unique accepted criterion for classifying a face image as low-resolution. Most of the authors consider that a face image with bounding box smaller than 32×32 pixels, represents a great challenge for both humans and systems, but others accept a minimal face resolution of 16×16 pixels [14]. In any case, the minimum resolution required should ensure the performance of the face recognition method and thus, depends on the algorithm at hand.

Several methods have been proposed to deal with LR face images. They can be divided into two categories: (1) resolution-invariant learning [18,31] and (2) image face restoration [25,32]. The first category aims at extracting resolution-invariant features and learning a common space from both LR probe images and HR gallery images. The second category consist of enhancing the quality of the LR face images as an input of the face recognition system. This is the most intuitive way to deal with LR and quality degradation of the face images and is the focus of this paper.

2.1 Deep Face Restoration

According to degradation types, the face restoration can be divided into different tasks such as face deblurring, face super-resolution, face artifact removal and face denoising. Due to its great advances, deep learning-based methods have been adopted for face restoration tasks, including the development of basic Convolution Neural Networks (CNN) or Generative Adversarial Networks (GAN).

Face deblurring aims to recover a latent sharp face image from a blurred face image caused by various factors such as camera shake or object motion. Most of existing face deblurring methods take advantage of various facial priors including face landmarks [6], 3D facial model [20], semantic clues [29] and deep features that contains both the geometric and texture information [13]. Face super-resolution, also known as face hallucination, focuses on enhancing quality and resolution of low-resolution facial images. Current deep learning approaches [12,28] have investigated the use of GANs, wavelet coefficients prediction into deep networks and facial prior knowledge to super-resolve low-resolution face images. Face artifact removal bases on recovering high-quality face images from the low-quality face images that contain artifacts caused by lossy compression in the process of image storage and transmission. For example, in real-world applications, lossy compression techniques (e.g., JPEG, Webp, and HEVC-MSP) are widely adopted for saving storage space and bandwidth. Which lead to information loss and introduces undesired artifacts for recorded face images. Most of existing methods [16] aim at alleviating these undesirable artifacts such as blockiness, ringing, and banding caused by quantization and approximation in the compression process. Face denoising refers to removing the noise contained in the face image. Some CNN models [1,30] have improved denoising performance, due to their modeling capacity, network training, and design. However, the performance of current learning models is limited and tailored for a specific level of noise.

The main problem of these face restoration methods designed for one specific and known degradation is that they perform with limited generalization in real-world LR scenarios, where face images are often degraded owing to more than one factor such as compression, blur, and noise. That's why, in recent years, blind face restoration (BFR) [32], which recovers high-quality (HQ) face images from low-quality (LQ) inputs with unknown degradations, has become more practical and attracted increasing attention. Existing works typically exploit face-specific priors, including geometric priors [2], reference priors [15], and generative priors [26,27,33]. In recent years, those methods based on generative priors in face restoration have shown superior performance.

On the other hand, although the existing face restoration methods have demonstrated excellent and remarkable abilities to generate realistic and faithful images, their effectiveness for increasing the face recognition rates is still challenge. Many face restoration methods generate visually pleasant face images, but face recognition accuracy is lower than expected with their generated images because they produce new details and the original structure of the face images are not well preserved. In this sense, some works have proposed specific approaches to deal with this issue. For example, a super-resolution-based approach was presented in [23] to overcome the LR image constraints and improve the accuracy of a face recognition system based on pioneering descriptor-based techniques (Eigenface and BRISK). Evaluations on synthesized images from ORL, Caltech, and Chockepoints datasets showed an increase in recognition rates, where face images did not contain pose expressions and scale variations. A GAN was used in [22] to increase the image resolution at the feature level and empower face recognition in low-resolution images. The introduced network considers image edges and reconstructs high-frequency details to preserve the face structure. Experiments with recent face recognition methods on FERET dataset indicate that, by using super-resolving facial images generated with the proposed method improve the accuracy of these face recognition methods. Most of these works have evaluated the effectiveness of their proposals on non-native low-resolution datasets. Usually, artificially down-sampled images from HR images are used for testing. It is still unclear how effective recent BFR methods are for enhancing the face recognition performance on native low-resolution face images.

3 Experimental Setup

In this section, we introduce the blind face restoration and face recognition methods used for the benchmark evaluations. In addition, we describe the datasets employed for testing as well as some implementation details of selected methods.

3.1 Blind Face Restoration

For obtaining HQ face images from LQ inputs, we selected three state-of-the-art BFR methods including GPEN [27], GFP-GAN [26] and CodeFormer [33].

GPEN [27]: is a GAN prior embedded network learned to generate high quality face images from severely degraded ones. First, a GAN is pretrained for high-quality face image generation and embedded it into a U-shaped DNN as a prior decoder. Then, the GAN prior embedded DNN is fine-tuned on synthesized LQ-HQ face image pairs. The GAN blocks are designed to ensure that the latent code and noise input to the GAN can be respectively generated from the deep and shallow features of the DNN, controlling the global face structure, local face details and background of the reconstructed image.

GFP-GAN [26]: is framework that leverages rich and diverse priors encapsulated in a pretrained face GAN for blind face restoration. Specifically, GFP-GAN consists of a degradation removal module (U-Net) and a pre-trained face GAN as facial prior, which are connected by a direct latent code mapping and several Channel-Split Spatial Feature Transform (CS-SFT) layers in a coarse-to-fine manner. During training, intermediate restoration losses to remove complex degradation, a facial component loss with discriminators to enhance facial details, and a identity preserving loss to retain face identity, are introduced.

CodeFormer [33]: is a Transformer-based prediction network that casts blind face restoration as a code prediction task, showing superior robustness to degradation as well as rich expressiveness. Specifically, The codebook is learned by self-reconstruction of HQ faces using a vector-quantized autoencoder, which along with decoder stores the rich HQ details for face restoration. Taking the LQ features as input, the Transformer module predicts the code token sequence which is treated as the discrete representation of the face images in the codebook space. In addition, a controllable feature transformation module is introduced to enhance the adaptiveness for different degradations, that allows a flexible trade-off between restoration quality and fidelity.

3.2 Face Recognition

To assess the accuracy of face recognition on the HQ generated by the selected BFR methods, we choose three recent face recognition models such as MobileFaceNet [3], ShuffleFaceNet [19] and R100-ArcFace [7].

MobileFaceNet [3]: is an extremely efficient CNN model tailored for high-accuracy real-time face verification on mobile and embedded devices. It uses the residual bottlenecks proposed in MobileNetV2 [21] as their main building blocks, but with expansion factors much smaller. Moreover, the authors replace the Global Average Pooling layer for a Global Depth-wise Convolution (GDC) layer to obtain a more discriminative face representation, and use the Parametric Rectified Linear Unit (PReLU) as non-linear activation function due to its accuracy improvement over the Rectified Linear Unit (ReLU) function for face recognition.

ShuffleFaceNet [19]: is an efficient and lightweight architecture built upon ShuffleNetv2 [17] for the face recognition domain. It introduces several modifications for improving accuracy demonstrating its feasibility in real-time applications or computationally limited platforms. Similar to MobileFaceNet, ShuffleFaceNet adopts PReLU activation function as non-linearity and uses a linear 1×1 convolution layer following a GDC layer as the feature output.

R100-ArcFace [7]: is a face recognition model that employs the widely used ResNet100 CNN architecture [10] as embedding network. In order to enhance the discriminative power of this model and to stabilize the training process, an Additive Angular Margin Loss (ArcFace) function was proposed by the authors.

3.3 Databases

For the experimental evaluation, we use four LR face databases. Although our main goal is to assess the performance on native LR datasets, we include experiments on artificially synthesized LR images from the LFW database.

Synthesized LFW: Labeled Face in the Wild (LFW) [11] is a HR face verification benchmark that contains 13,233 web-collected images from 5,749 different identities, with large variations in pose, expression and illuminations. Given

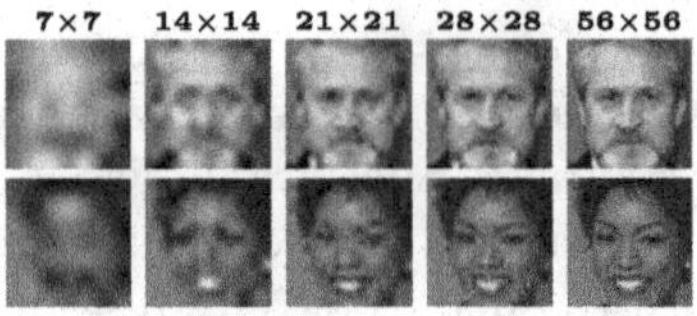

Fig. 1. Examples of synthetic LR face images from LFW database.

LFW images, we synthesize the corresponding low-resolution images employing down-sampling operation to artificially simulate the degradation process. Specifically, we use bicubic interpolation to generate LR images at five different resolutions: 7×7, 14×14, 21×21, 28×28 and 56×56, as is illustrated in Fig. 1. The evaluation protocol provides 6,000 face pairs, divided into ten subsets, each having 300 positive pairs and 300 negative pairs. For benchmarking, we implement two experimental settings. The first one, LR-to-HR pairs matching, is composed of pairs of low-resolution and high-resolution facial images. The second one, LR-to-LR pairs matching, consists of low-resolution pair images.

SCface [8]: is designed for testing face recognition algorithms in real-world surveillance scenarios. In order to achieve a realistic setup, 4,160 images of 130 subjects were acquired in uncontrolled indoor environment using commercially available surveillance cameras of varying quality. For each subject, there are 15 images in the visible spectrum taken at three different distances (d): d1 (4.2m), d2 (2.6m) and d3 (1.0m), by five surveillance cameras (5 images at each distance), and one high quality frontal mugshot image taken in controlled indoor illumination conditions environment by a digital camera. Figure 2 shows the LR images corresponding to one subject from the SCface database. For experimental settings, HR frontal mugshot images are employed as gallery, while images taken by surveillance cameras at distance 1, 2 and 3 are used as probes.

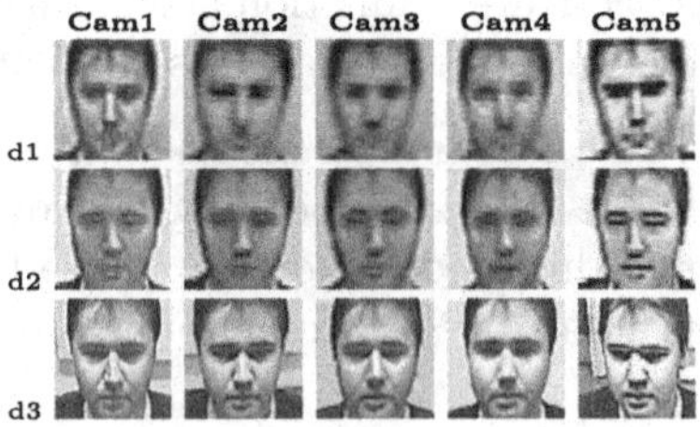

Fig. 2. LR images from one subject of SCface database.

TinyFace [4]: is a large-scale face recognition benchmark containing native unconstrained low-resolution face images. It consists of 169,403 native LR face images (average 20×16 pixels) from 5,139 labelled facial identities designed for 1:N recognition test. All the images are collected from public web data across a large variety of imaging scenarios, captured under uncontrolled viewing conditions in pose, illumination, occlusion and background. Figure 3(a) shows some examples of LR face images of the TinyFace dataset.

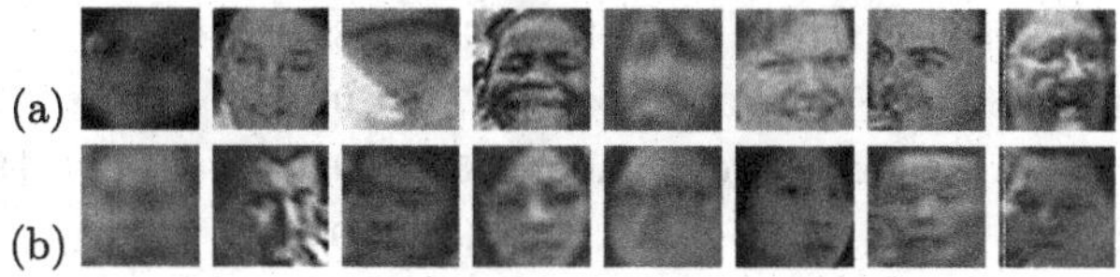

Fig. 3. Examples of LR face images from a) TinyFace database and b) QMUL-Surv Face database.

QMUL-SurvFace [5]: is a very challenging dataset, that contains 463,507 real-world native surveillance face images of 15,573 unique subjects. Moreover, the LR face images present uncontrolled appearance variations in pose, illumination, motion blur, occlusion and background clutter (See Fig. 3(b)). The face spatial resolution ranges from 6/5 to 124/106 pixels in height/width, and the average is 24/20 pixels. For the benchmark evaluation, we follow the verification protocol of QMUL-SurvFace.

3.4 Implementation Details

For blind face restoration, we used the released codes and models by the authors for GPEN[1], GFP-GAN[2] and CodeFormer[3] methods. All models were trained on synthesized LR databases. In the case of face recognition models, we use pretrained models on the cleaned MS1M dataset [9] that includes 5.1 million photos from 93K face identities. The faces are cropped and resized to 112 $\times$ 112, and each pixel (ranged between [0; 255]) in RGB images is normalised by subtracting 127:5 then divided by 128. All experiments in this paper are implemented on PyTorch.

4 Experiments and Discussion

In this section, we present and discuss the performance achieved by the selected face recognition methods: ShuffleFaceNet, MobileFaceNet and R100-ArcFace on both synthetic and native LQ face images. To examine the impact of blind face restoration, we compare the performance of face recognition models on the generated HQ images with those obtained on the original LQ images.

---

[1] https://github.com/yangxy/GPEN.
[2] https://github.com/TencentARC/GFPGAN/.
[3] https://shangchenzhou.com/projects/CodeFormer/.

Table 1. Verification accuracy (%) on synthesized LFW database for LR-to-HR pairs matching at different resolution sizes.

Method	7 × 7	14 × 14	21 × 21	28 × 28	56 × 56
ShuffleFaceNet	56.7	**82.1**	**98.5**	**99.4**	**99.4**
GPEN + ShuffleFaceNet	56.1	74.3	89.8	96.5	99.3
GFP-GAN + ShuffleFaceNet	59.4	78.7	91.2	97.0	99.3
CodeFormer + ShuffleFaceNet	**59.6**	81.5	92.9	97.6	99.3
MobileFaceNet	**62.1**	**85.3**	**94.8**	**98.5**	99.6
GPEN + MobileFaceNet	55.0	74.1	88.7	96.5	99.5
GFP-GAN + MobileFaceNet	57.6	75.7	89.9	96.2	99.2
CodeFormer + MobileFaceNet	61.0	81.6	92.9	97.9	99.5
R100-ArcFace	**58.2**	**87.5**	**97.6**	**99.4**	**99.6**
GPEN + R100-ArcFace	54.3	71.4	89.3	96.6	99.5
GFP-GAN + R100-ArcFace	55.4	71.4	88.1	96.5	99.4
CodeFormer + R100-ArcFace	57.2	80.3	92.9	97.7	99.5

Table 2. Verification accuracy (%) on synthesized LFW database for LR-to-LR pairs matching at different resolution sizes.

Method	7 × 7	14 × 14	21 × 21	28 × 28	56 × 56
ShuffleFaceNet	**63.1**	**77.8**	**89.9**	**96.7**	**99.4**
GPEN + ShuffleFaceNet	62.3	73.6	85.9	95.1	99.2
GFP-GAN + ShuffleFaceNet	63.0	73.5	86.3	94.7	99.2
CodeFormer + ShuffleFaceNet	61.6	76.6	88.9	96.3	99.2
MobileFaceNet	**67.3**	**79.8**	**91.5**	**97.2**	**99.6**
GPEN + MobileFaceNet	64.5	74.1	85.8	95.1	**99.6**
GFP-GAN + MobileFaceNet	65.7	74.2	85.8	94.6	99.5
CodeFormer + MobileFaceNet	62.9	78.3	89.1	96.2	99.5
R100-ArcFace	**65.8**	**82.5**	**94.8**	**98.6**	**99.7**
GPEN + R100-ArcFace	63.0	73.6	87.1	96.0	**99.7**
GFP-GAN + R100-ArcFace	62.3	73.1	85.1	94.6	99.6
CodeFormer + R100-ArcFace	58.3	77.2	89.7	96.7	99.6

4.1 Results on Synthesized LR Images

Following the standard protocol of unrestricted with labeled outside data, Table 1 and Table 2 show the verification accuracy on the synthesized LFW database for LR-to-HR and LR-to-LR pairs matching at different resolutions, respectively. As it can be seen, using blind face restoration degrades the performance of face recognition models. The best results are achieved by MobileFaceNet without employing any BFR method previously. In general, the verification accuracy for matching LR-to-HR pairs are lower than those obtained by matching LR-to-LR pairs, especially for very low-resolution sizes like 7 × 7. Although the usage of blind face restoration methods do not improve the performance of face recognition models, among the them, CodeFormer obtains higher accuracy values in the case of LR-to-HR pairs matching and, GFP-GAN for LR-to-LR pairs matching.

4.2 Results on Native LR Images

Tables 3, 4 and 5 present the performance on native low-resolution images from the SCface, TinyFace and QMUL-SurvFace databases, respectively. Similar to the results obtained on the synthesized LFW database, using BFR methods also decrease the performance of deep face recognition models on native surveillance LR images. We can observe that, in this scenario, the accuracy drops are greater, which reflect that BFR methods trained on artificially synthesized low-resolution images do not generalize well in front the true challenges of native surveillance images. These methods suffer the lack of native surveillance pairs of low-quality and high-quality facial images which are necessary for model training. Thus, when the training and test data distributions are very different, BFR becomes extremely challenging due to an extra need for domain adaptation. Moreover, in the surveillance scenarios, the captured images have additional variations such as occlusions, pose and illumination changes, that add complexity to the generation process. As result, several artifacts and noise are introduced in the generated images (see Fig. 4), which impact negatively in the performance of face recognition models.

From the quantitative results presented on Tables 3, 4 and 5, and the qualitative results shown in Fig. 4, we find that GPEN performs better that GFP-GAN

Table 3. Recognition Rates (%) at Rank-1 on SCface database.

Method	d1 (4.2 m)	d2 (2.6 m)	d3 (1.0 m)
ShuffleFaceNet	**48.8**	**94.0**	**99.5**
GPEN + ShuffleFaceNet	32.8	87.2	99.4
GFP-GAN + ShuffleFaceNet	28.0	86.9	98.8
CodeFormer + ShuffleFaceNet	32.6	87.8	98.8
MobileFaceNet	**60.9**	**97.1**	99.7
GPEN + MobileFaceNet	35.1	89.5	**99.8**
GFP-GAN + MobileFaceNet	26.3	86.8	99.2
CodeFormer + MobileFaceNet	32.5	88.2	99.2
R100-ArcFace	**67.7**	**99.2**	**99.8**
GPEN + R100-ArcFace	31.5	87.2	99.5
GFP-GAN + R100-ArcFace	24.5	81.5	99.2
CodeFormer + R100-ArcFace	30.2	84.2	99.1

Table 4. Face identification (%) results on TinyFace database.

Method	Rank-1	Rank-10	Rank-20	Rank-50	mAP
ShuffleFaceNet	**22.3**	**35.6**	**40.9**	**49.5**	**16.1**
GPEN + ShuffleFaceNet	15.4	26.1	31.1	39.3	11.1
GFP-GAN + ShuffleFaceNet	10.9	20.0	23.9	31.1	8.2
CodeFormer + ShuffleFaceNet	12.1	23.0	28.4	36.3	8.9
MobileFaceNet	**26.2**	**39.2**	**44.0**	**51.7**	**18.9**
GPEN + MobileFaceNet	16.9	27.4	31.9	40.4	12.1
GFP-GAN + MobileFaceNet	10.9	20.6	24.8	32.8	8.1
CodeFormer + MobileFaceNet	14.3	25.6	30.4	10.4	10.4
R100-ArcFace	**25.9**	**37.5**	**42.2**	**50.5**	**18.8**
GPEN + R100-ArcFace	14.7	25.8	30.5	37.7	10.6
GFP-GAN + R100-ArcFace	8.6	15.8	20.1	26.9	6.7
CodeFormer + R100-ArcFace	10.7	20.3	24.9	32.4	7.7

Table 5. Face verification (%) results on QMUL-SurvFace.

Method	TAR@FAR				AUC	Mean Accuracy
	30%	10%	1%	0.1%		
ShuffleFaceNet	**57.0**	**33.1**	**10.6**	**4.6**	**68.7**	**63.6**
GPEN + ShuffleFaceNet	51.1	26.3	6.2	1.8	64.3	60.6
GFP-GAN + ShuffleFaceNet	47.9	23.1	5.2	1.1	62.2	58.7
CodeFormer + ShuffleFaceNet	51.1	24.7	6.2	1.4	64.6	60.3
MobileFaceNet	**58.8**	**34.3**	**12.1**	**4.3**	**70.2**	**64.8**
GPEN + MobileFaceNet	51.3	25.9	6.5	1.3	64.5	60.4
GFP-GAN + MobileFaceNet	47.5	24.6	5.3	0.8	62.2	58.9
CodeFormer + MobileFaceNet	52.1	26.5	7.0	3.1	65.0	60.9
R100-ArcFace	**54.5**	**29.0**	**8.7**	**2.4**	**66.7**	**61.9**
GPEN + R100-ArcFace	49.1	25.1	6.7	1.5	63.3	59.2
GFP-GAN + R100-ArcFace	45.5	20.1	4.8	1.1	60.8	57.7
CodeFormer + R100-ArcFace	44.9	20.1	3.7	0.9	60.9	57.3

and CoderFormer, as well as the images recovered by GPEN are more satisfying to human visual perception. Nonetheless, the best performance is achieved by MobileFaceNet model without using any blind face restoration method.

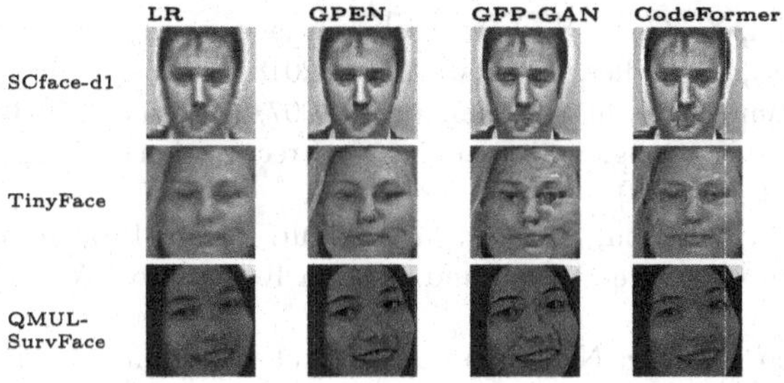

Fig. 4. Visual results of BFR methods: GPEN, GFP-GAN and CodeFormer on the SCface, TinyFace and QMUL-SurvFace datasets.

5 Conclusion

In this paper, we have presented a comprehensive evaluation of the impact of blind face restoration on the face recognition performance at LR imagery. Specifically, we use three state-of-the-art blind face restoration methods: GPEN, GFP-GAN and CodeFormer, to generate high-quality face images from synthesized and native low-resolution images. Then, we assess the performance of three well-established deep face recognition models: MobileFaceNet, ShuffleFaceNet and ResNet100-ArcFace on the generated high-quality images. Experimental results, on both synthetic and native LR images, show that state-of-the-art BFR algorithms are not effective to improve the accuracy of face recognition methods in low-resolution face images. This is because most of existing BFR methods have no access to native surveillance pairs of low-quality and high-quality images required in the training process. Mostly, face recognition and blind face restoration researches advance independently, which does not offer any benefit. For future research on the use of blind face restoration for low-resolution face recognition, it will be important to address these limitations and explore ways to improve the accuracy performance of models by correctly preserving the structure of the face image and its high-frequency details.

References

1. Anwar, S., Barnes, N.: Real image denoising with feature attention. In: Proceedings of the IEEE/CVF International Conference on Computer Vision, pp. 3155–3164 (2019)
2. Chen, C., Li, X., Yang, L., Lin, X., Zhang, L., Wong, K.Y.K.: Progressive semantic-aware style transformation for blind face restoration. In: Proceedings of the IEEE/CVF Conference on Computer Vision and Pattern Recognition, pp. 11896–11905 (2021)
3. Chen, S., Liu, Y., Gao, X., Han, Z.: MobileFaceNets: efficient CNNs for accurate real-time face verification on mobile devices. In: Zhou, J., et al. (eds.) CCBR 2018. LNCS, vol. 10996, pp. 428–438. Springer, Cham (2018). https://doi.org/10.1007/978-3-319-97909-0_46

4. Cheng, Z., Zhu, X., Gong, S.: Low-resolution face recognition. In: Jawahar, C.V., Li, H., Mori, G., Schindler, K. (eds.) ACCV 2018. LNCS, vol. 11363, pp. 605–621. Springer, Cham (2019). https://doi.org/10.1007/978-3-030-20893-6_38
5. Cheng, Z., Zhu, X., Gong, S.: Surveillance face recognition challenge. arXiv preprint arXiv:1804.09691 (2018)
6. Chrysos, G.G., Zafeiriou, S.: Deep face deblurring. In: Proceedings of the IEEE Conference on Computer Vision and Pattern Recognition Workshops, pp. 69–78 (2017)
7. Deng, J., Guo, J., Xue, N., Zafeiriou, S.: ArcFace: additive angular margin loss for deep face recognition. In: IEEE Conference on Computer Vision and Pattern Recognition (CVPR), pp. 4690–4699 (2019)
8. Grgic, M., Delac, K., Grgic, S.: SCface-surveillance cameras face database. Multimed. Tools Appl. **51**(3), 863–879 (2011)
9. Guo, Y., Zhang, L., Hu, Y., He, X., Gao, J.: MS-Celeb-1M: a dataset and benchmark for large-scale face recognition. In: Leibe, B., Matas, J., Sebe, N., Welling, M. (eds.) ECCV 2016. LNCS, vol. 9907, pp. 87–102. Springer, Cham (2016). https://doi.org/10.1007/978-3-319-46487-9_6
10. He, K., Zhang, X., Ren, S., Sun, J.: Deep residual learning for image recognition. In: IEEE Conference on Computer Vision and Pattern Recognition (CVPR), pp. 770–778 (2016)
11. Huang, G.B., Ramesh, M., Berg, T., Learned-miller, E.: Labeled faces in the wild: a database for studying face recognition in unconstrained environments (2007)
12. Jiang, J., Wang, C., Liu, X., Ma, J.: Deep learning-based face super-resolution: a survey. ACM Comput. Surv. (CSUR) **55**(1), 1–36 (2021)
13. Jung, S.H., Lee, T.B., Heo, Y.S.: Deep feature prior guided face deblurring. In: Proceedings of the IEEE/CVF Winter Conference on Applications of Computer Vision, pp. 3531–3540 (2022)
14. Li, P., Prieto, L., Mery, D., Flynn, P.: Face recognition in low quality images: a survey. arXiv preprint arXiv:1805.11519 (2018)
15. Li, X., Chen, C., Zhou, S., Lin, X., Zuo, W., Zhang, L.: Blind face restoration via deep multi-scale component dictionaries. In: Vedaldi, A., Bischof, H., Brox, T., Frahm, J.-M. (eds.) ECCV 2020. LNCS, vol. 12354, pp. 399–415. Springer, Cham (2020). https://doi.org/10.1007/978-3-030-58545-7_23
16. Liu, J., Liu, D., Yang, W., Xia, S., Zhang, X., Dai, Y.: A comprehensive benchmark for single image compression artifact reduction. IEEE Trans. Image Process. **29**, 7845–7860 (2020)
17. Ma, N., Zhang, X., Zheng, H.T., Sun, J.: ShuffleNet v2: practical guidelines for efficient CNN architecture design. In: Proceedings of the European Conference on Computer Vision (ECCV), pp. 116–131 (2018)
18. Makwana, P., Kumar Singh, S., Ram Dubey, S.: Resolution invariant face recognition. In: Tistarelli, M., Dubey, S.R., Singh, S.K., Jiang, X. (eds.) Computer Vision and Machine Intelligence. LNNS, vol. 586, pp. 733–745. Springer, Singapore (2023). https://doi.org/10.1007/978-981-19-7867-8_58
19. Martinez-Diaz, Y., Luevano, L.S., Mendez-Vazquez, H., Nicolas-Diaz, M., Chang, L., Gonzalez-Mendoza, M.: ShuffleFaceNet: a lightweight face architecture for efficient and highly-accurate face recognition. In: IEEE International Conference on Computer Vision Workshops (2019)
20. Ren, W., Yang, J., Deng, S., Wipf, D., Cao, X., Tong, X.: Face video deblurring using 3D facial priors. In: Proceedings of the IEEE/CVF International Conference on Computer Vision, pp. 9388–9397 (2019)

21. Sandler, M., Howard, A., Zhu, M., Zhmoginov, A., Chen, L.C.: MobileNetv2: inverted residuals and linear bottlenecks. In: IEEE Conference on Computer Vision and Pattern Recognition, pp. 4510–4520 (2018)
22. Shahbakhsh, M.B., Hassanpour, H.: Empowering face recognition methods using a GAN-based single image super-resolution network. Int. J. Eng. **35**(10), 1858–1866 (2022)
23. Singh, N., Rathore, S.S., Kumar, S.: Towards a super-resolution based approach for improved face recognition in low resolution environment. Multimed. Tools Appl. **81**(27), 38887–38919 (2022)
24. Wang, M., Deng, W.: Deep face recognition: a survey. Neurocomputing **429**, 215–244 (2021)
25. Wang, T., et al.: A survey of deep face restoration: denoise, super-resolution, deblur, artifact removal. arXiv preprint arXiv:2211.02831 (2022)
26. Wang, X., Li, Y., Zhang, H., Shan, Y.: Towards real-world blind face restoration with generative facial prior. In: Proceedings of the IEEE/CVF Conference on Computer Vision and Pattern Recognition, pp. 9168–9178 (2021)
27. Yang, T., Ren, P., Xie, X., Zhang, L.: GAN prior embedded network for blind face restoration in the wild. In: Proceedings of the IEEE/CVF Conference on Computer Vision and Pattern Recognition, pp. 672–681 (2021)
28. Yang, W., Zhang, X., Tian, Y., Wang, W., Xue, J.H., Liao, Q.: Deep learning for single image super-resolution: a brief review. IEEE Trans. Multimed. **21**(12), 3106–3121 (2019)
29. Yasarla, R., Perazzi, F., Patel, V.M.: Deblurring face images using uncertainty guided multi-stream semantic networks. IEEE Trans. Image Process. **29**, 6251–6263 (2020)
30. Yue, Z., Yong, H., Zhao, Q., Meng, D., Zhang, L.: Variational denoising network: toward blind noise modeling and removal. In: Advances in Neural Information Processing Systems, vol. 32 (2019)
31. Zeng, D., Chen, H., Zhao, Q.: Towards resolution invariant face recognition in uncontrolled scenarios. In: 2016 International Conference on Biometrics (ICB), pp. 1–8. IEEE (2016)
32. Zhang, P., Zhang, K., Luo, W., Li, C., Wang, G.: Blind face restoration: benchmark datasets and a baseline model. arXiv preprint arXiv:2206.03697 (2022)
33. Zhou, S., Chan, K., Li, C., Loy, C.C.: Towards robust blind face restoration with codebook lookup transformer. In: Advances in Neural Information Processing Systems, vol. 35, pp. 30599–30611 (2022)

Author Index

Y. Hernández Heredia et al. (Eds.): IWAIPR 2023, LNCS 14335, pp. 469–471, 2024.
https://doi.org/10.1007/978-3-031-49552-6

Printed in the United States
by Baker & Taylor Publisher Services